Music Research and Information Guides
Vol. 19

THE RECORDER

Garland Reference Library
of the Humanities
Vol. 1026

Music Research and Information Guides

OPERA
*A Research
and Information Guide*
by Guy Marco

LATIN AMERICAN MUSIC
A Reference Guide
by Malena Kuss

DANCE
An Annotated Bibliography
by Fred Forbes

FOLK MUSIC IN AMERICA
A Reference Guide
by Terry Miller

THE ART SONG
*A Research
and Information Guide*
by Douglass Seaton

THE BLUES
A Bibliographic Guide
by Mary L. Hart, Brenda M. Eagles, and Lisa N. Howorth

CHAMBER MUSIC
*A Research
and Information Guide*
by John H. Baron

PERFORMANCE PRACTICE, MEDIEVAL TO CONTEMPORARY
A Bibliographic Guide
by Roland Jackson

TUDOR MUSIC
*A Research
and Information Guide*
by Richard Turbet

PIANO INFORMATION GUIDE
An Aid to Research
by Robert Palmieri

THE TRADITIONAL MUSIC OF BRITAIN AND IRELAND
*A Research
and Information Guide*
by James Porter

POLISH MUSIC
*A Research
and Information Guide*
by William Smialek

EARLY AMERICAN MUSIC
*A Research
and Information Guide*
by James R. Heintze

THE SYMPHONY
*A Research
and Information Guide, Vol. I:
The Eighteenth Century*
by Preston Stedman

BAROQUE MUSIC
*A Research
and Information Guide*
by John H. Baron

MUSIC AND WAR
*A Research
and Information Guide*
by Ben Arnold

THE RECORDER
*A Guide to Writings about
the Instrument for Players
and Researchers*
by Richard Griscom and David Lasocki

THE RECORDER

*A Guide
to Writings about
the Instrument for
Players and
Researchers*

Richard Griscom
David Lasocki

GARLAND PUBLISHING, INC.
New York & London / 1994

Copyright © 1994 Richard Griscom and David Lasocki
All rights reserved

Library of Congress Cataloging-in-Publication Data

Griscom, Richard.
    The recorder : a guide to writings about the instrument for players and researchers / by Richard Griscom and David Lasocki.
      p.   cm. — (Music research and information guides ; vol. 19) (Garland reference library of the humanities ; vol. 1026)
    Includes index.
    ISBN 0-8240-2945-3
    1. Recorder (Musical instrument)—Bibliography.
I. Lasocki, David. II. Series. III. Series: Garland reference library of the humanities ; vol. 1026.
ML128.R31G75   1994
016.7883'6—dc20   94-28796
                                                    CIP
                                                     MN

Printed on acid-free, 250-year-life paper
Manufactured in the United States of America

To Frans Brüggen,

without whose existence we would never have bothered

Contents

Preface xi

Acknowledgments xvii

Advice on Obtaining Sources xxi

1 Bibliographies of Writings on the Recorder (and Bibliographic Essays) 3

2 General Surveys and Writings Covering Several Topics 6

3 Etymology, Symbolism, and Literary References 18

4 Periods: Historical 22

5 Periods: Modern 33

6 Studies of Particular Sizes of Recorder 47

7 Art and Iconography 54

8 Humor, Fantasy, and Fiction 58

9 Instrument Makers and Instruments: Historical 61

10 Collections of Historical Instruments 84

11 Instrument Makers: Modern 94

12 Construction and Design 108

13 Acoustics and Other Scientific Studies 130

14 Instrument Making and Manufacture 147

15 Choice of Instrument 158

16 Maintenance, Improvement, and Restoration 164

17 Historical Methods (Tutors) and Treatises 177

18 Performance Practices (Historical) 222

19 Technique and Performance (Modern) 245

20 New Techniques in Twentieth-Century Recorder Music 260

21 Ensembles 268

22 Pedagogy and Study 273

23 Biographies: Historical 278

24 Biographies and Interviews: Modern 285

25 Bibliographies and Discographies of Recorder Music 335

26 Repertory: General 342

27 Repertory: Medieval and Renaissance 348

28 Repertory: Baroque and Classical 352

29 Repertory: Modern 401

30 Miscellaneous Fipple Flutes 419

31 Recorder, Early Music, and Musical Instrument Periodicals 427

32 Societies 437

33 The Future of Research on the Recorder 440

Appendixes

1 Theses, Dissertations, and Similar Works Not Consulted 446

2 Articles in *FoMRHI Quarterly* 450

3 Articles in *Bouwbrief* 456

4 Conservatory Master's Theses 462

Index 465

Preface

SCOPE

This book is intended as a guide to writings about the recorder for players and researchers. We have tried to bear in mind the interests of both groups, who are by no means mutually exclusive. The players will be those, whether amateur or professional, who wish to find out more about the history, repertory, design, and technique of their instrument. The researchers will be those interested in learning what research has been done on the instrument and what directions research might take in the future.

Our emphasis has been on what is relevant, what is significant, and what is readily available in the United States. We have therefore narrowed the scope of the work as follows:

We have looked at those articles, books, dissertations, and theses devoted solely to the recorder as well as selected other writings that include significant sections on the recorder or are particularly relevant for other reasons. We have included historical methods (or tutors) but excluded modern methods and exercise books, knowing full well that these sometimes contain the same kind of material found in articles and books. For the most part, we have also excluded articles on the recorder and recorder players in mass-market magazines (among them, record-review magazines).

Because of the obvious importance and ready accessibility of certain periodicals—*The American Recorder, The Recorder and Music Magazine, Early Music, The Galpin Society Journal,* and *Tibia*—we have included all relevant articles from them. Coverage of other journals is as complete as possible, but not necessarily inclusive. The contents of newsletters such as *The Recorder News* and *The ARS Newsletter* were not examined or indexed.

We have omitted writings on the use of the recorder in primary or secondary education ("music education").

We have included a short chapter on other fipple flutes beside the recorder but made no attempt to be comprehensive on that subject, especially concerning their use in folk music.

We have tried to be comprehensive in our coverage of English-language materials from the United States, the United Kingdom, and Australia. As for other languages, we have completely indexed the recent major early music and recorder periodicals of France (*Flûte à bec [et instruments anciens]* and its short-lived successor, *Crescendo*), Germany (*Tibia*, *Concerto*), and Italy (*Il flauto dolce*). We have also indexed all the German books and dissertations we could discover—which, because of the German passion for research, is a goodly number. (Earlier articles in specialized German magazines have been omitted because they are unfortunately almost impossible to obtain in the United States.) Books and dissertations in French and Italian are covered much more spottily. Because few native English speakers know Dutch, we have generally excluded materials in that language, although we have indexed the early music magazine *Tijdschrift voor oude muziek*; articles from *Bouwbrief* have been relegated to an appendix. Because of their relative inaccessibility in the United States, not to mention the general language barrier, we have excluded virtually all materials in other languages.

To learn about relevant materials, we have systematically searched the relevant periodicals as well as standard bibliographic tools such as OCLC, RLIN, *RILM Abstracts* on CD-ROM, *The Music Index*, and *Dissertation Abstracts International* on CD-ROM.

We have included articles on the topic of transcription and arrangement, but not writings on specific transcriptions and arrangements. Similarly, articles on music originally written for instruments other than the recorder have been omitted.

Ephemeral articles—such as reviews of concerts, workshops, conferences, festivals, auctions, and exhibitions—have been excluded. We have also omitted citations to reviews of printed music and sound recordings. In our annotations, we have generally included brief citations to book reviews (at least from the standard recorder periodicals) in the hope that readers will

Preface

turn to them for further information—or perhaps an alternative point of view.

We have been able to include all articles published in the major periodicals through 1993, as well as all other items that had reached us by the end of that year. For two reasons, we have tried to examine all the items included. First, because we believe that accurate bibliographies can be compiled in no other way. Second, because we reasoned that if we had trouble gaining access to an item, readers would, too. In a few cases we considered it necessary to include a relatively inaccessible item because of its significance (notably the theses and dissertations listed in appendix 1).

The authors' initial division of labor was that Richard Griscom generally annotated the articles from *American Recorder* and *The Recorder and Music Magazine*, and David Lasocki all foreign-language materials, and we shared other English-language materials depending on their accessibility. The subject organization is largely David's and the indexing Richard's. Needless to say, we have both subsequently gone over the entire material.

We would be extremely grateful if readers could let us know (c/o the publishers) of any errors or omissions, however small. All such communications will be scrupulously acknowledged in the next edition.

ORGANIZATION OF THE BOOK

The book is divided into thirty-three chapters, arranged by broad subject. It begins with eight chapters on **general matters**: existing bibliographies of writings; general surveys; studies of etymology, symbolism, and literary references; material on historical periods, then modern; studies of particular sizes of recorder; art and iconography; and finally humor, fantasy, and fiction.

Next come eight chapters on **the instrument as a physical object**: historical makers and instruments (including biographical material on the makers); collections of historical instruments; modern makers (again including biographical material); construction and design; acoustics and other scientific studies;

instrument making and manufacture; the choice of instrument; and finally maintenance, improvement, and restoration.

Performance matters are treated in the next six chapters: historical methods and treatises; historical performance practices; modern technique and performance; new techniques in twentieth-century music; ensembles; and pedagogy and study.

After two **biographical** chapters, on performers, writers, and a few composers, historical and modern, come five chapters on recorder **music**, starting with bibliographies, then moving through the general repertory to the repertory of three broad periods (medieval and Renaissance, Baroque and Classical, and modern).

The body of the book concludes with four **miscellaneous** chapters: other fipple flutes; relevant periodicals; recorder societies; and an essay on the future of recorder research. Following that are four **appendixes**, on theses, dissertations, and similar works not consulted, as well as articles in *FoMHRHI Quarterly* and *Bouwbrief*.

The **index** is a comprehensive one that includes authors, book and dissertation titles, and subjects.

Each chapter begins with general studies or those that cover a number of topics. Citations in these sections are not repeated later in the chapter under the various specific headings, so the reader should beware that the entries under specific topics do not necessarily represent everything written on the topic. When in doubt, consult the index, which provides more detailed subject coverage.

Within each section of a chapter, the arrangement of entries is alphabetical by author, with the exception of chapter 17, "Historical Methods (Tutors) and Treatises," and sections of chapters 23–24 and 28–29, where the treatment is chronological.

In headings involving people's names, we have added birth and death dates wherever they could be ascertained, from the Library of Congress authority file and library catalogs, except where more recent information was contained in the sources cited.

Preface

FORMAT OF ENTRIES

We have conformed to the *Chicago Manual of Style* (14th ed.) in our citations, with the exception of the treatment of series titles, which are set off by parentheses. For ease of reference use, we have not abbreviated the titles of periodicals.

To make it easier for the reader to obtain books and dissertations, we have sought to include the ISBN and OCLC number (when there is no ISBN) for the former, and the UMI order number and OCLC number for the latter. ISBNs have been standardized in format, without hyphens.

All foreign titles are followed by our English translations in square brackets.

Whenever practical, we have combined citations for the original version of an item and its translations. The English versions are always listed first, regardless of whether English is the original language.

We have used the standard of pitch notation recommended in D. Kern Holoman, *Writing about Music* (Berkeley: University of California Press, 1988), which assigns c^1 to middle C. The series of octaves extending from two octaves below middle C to three octaves above middle C are: C, c, c^1, c^2, c^3, and c^4.

The book was composed using successive versions of WordPerfect and printed using version 5.2 with a Hewlett Packard LaserJet III. The typeface is CG Palacio.

Richard Griscom
Louisville, Kentucky

David Lasocki
Bloomington, Indiana

Acknowledgments

The authors would like to thank the following people for their invaluable help in preparing this volume:

Richard Griscom thanks his wife, Peggy Steele, for inspiring him to take up the recorder twelve years ago and for encouraging him to commence a study of recorder literature that led to his work on this book. He also thanks his entire family for sleeping in past six o'clock each morning during the past several years so that he could work alone and uninterrupted (except for the cats).

David Lasocki thanks his wife, Catherine, for continually urging him to find meaningful ways to use his bibliographic and writing skills; to make his work practical as well as scholarly; to see the big picture; and to temper his natural captiousness, carping, and cavilling with humanity and compassion. He also thanks his entire family for allowing him to hog the computer.

The American Recorder Society (in the form of its present and former editors and staff members: the late Sigrid Nagle, Waddy Thompson, Benjamin Dunham, and Allan Moore) exchanged subscriptions to various foreign early music and recorder journals in David Lasocki's name. Moreover, it was Waddy who put the authors in touch with each other when he discovered they were working concurrently but independently on bibliographies of writings about the recorder. *American Recorder* has also encouraged this book by publishing David Lasocki's bibliographical essays on recent publications about the recorder.

Jack Ashworth lent several issues of *The American Recorder* and, as director of the University of Louisville Collegium Musicum, offered Richard Griscom support and encouragement.

Timothy Cherubini loaned a book from the collection of Duke University.

Jan Epstein and Malcolm Tattersall, former editors of the Australian recorder magazine *The Recorder*, between them sent all the back issues and kept us in touch with developments in publication.

The Finnish Music Information Centre sent complimentary copies of the books by Herman Rechberger.

Ruth van Baak Griffioen sent a copy of her dissertation.

Karl-Werner Gümpel assisted in the translation of certain German and Spanish titles.

Dale Higbee sent photocopies of journals in his collection.

LeAnn House sent a copy of her dissertation.

Edgar Hunt answered questions about his anonymous contributions to *The Recorder and Music Mazazine*.

David Hunter offered advice on a few matters of style.

At Indiana University, David Lasocki's colleagues in the Music Library (especially David Fenske) provided computer and research support, and the Interlibrary Loan staff obtained numerous books and photocopies of articles.

Elenore Jacot helped with some tricky points in the French translations.

Gesa Kordes and Andreas Giger helped with some tricky points in the German translations.

Michelle Koth reported on a book in the collection of Yale University.

Without the multitude of good ideas contained in Donald W. Krummel's magisterial book *Bibliographies: Their Aims and Methods* (London & New York: Mansell, 1984), this volume would be far poorer. Don has also taken an interest in our work.

Eva Legêne checked the Dutch translations. Her students gave us many opportunities to learn that this book would be useful to recorder players.

Lia Levin sent a copy of her dissertation.

Alec Loretto showed us that not all important writings on the recorder have been published.

Alfred Mann provided us with a copy of his master's thesis.

Michael Marissen sent a copy of his dissertation. Thanks to Michael for taking recorder research seriously.

Acknowledgments   xix

John Martin lent us his considerable expertise on the acoustics of the recorder by taking responsibility for that section of the book.

Hermann Moeck and Reinhold Quandt answered queries about various Moeck publications. *Tibia*, published by Hermann Moeck Verlag, has also encouraged this book by making available German-language versions of David Lasocki's bibliographic essays on recent publications about the recorder.

We have benefitted from the work of the Bibliographic Standards for Reference Works Subcommittee, Reference and Public Service Committee, Music Library Association, particularly the contributions of Ann Basart, Harold Diamond, Jane Gottlieb, David Hunter, and Judy Tsou. David Hunter's Bibliography Roundtable at the annual meeting of the Music Library Association in 1989 also gave us both the opportunity to put together some preliminary thoughts on research and information guides.

Eve O'Kelly sent a copy of her master's thesis.

Ralph Papakhian assisted us in our early experiments with the transfer of WordPerfect files via the BITNET network—a technique that we found successful in exchanging citations and eventually revisions of chapters.

Luca Pellegrini helped with some tricky points in the Italian translations.

Laurence Pottier sent a copy of her dissertation.

Patricia Ranum sent copies of her articles.

Elisabeth Richter obtained copies of Swiss journals.

Arnold Riesthuis of LOAM lent David Lasocki his office and computer to make the list of articles from *Bouwbrief*, then proofread that list.

Benito Rivera helped with Latin translations.

C. Martin Rosen, Maryann Pazen, Laura Gayle Green, and Leslie Troutman supplied photocopies of various articles from *The Recorder and Music Magazine*.

Anthony Rowland-Jones sent copies of British articles and journals.

Adrienne Simpson sent copies of *Early Music New Zealand*.

STIMU (in the person of Guido van Oorschot and Jan Nuchelmans) sponsored the symposium on the Recorder in the 17th century that afforded David Lasocki the opportunity to write a preliminary version of the material on gaps in our knowledge and how we could fill them. Special thanks to Guido for taking recorder research seriously.

J.M. (John Mansfield) Thomson answered queries about his contributions to *The Recorder and Music Magazine*. We would like to acknowledge his attempts to raise the level of that magazine.

At the University of Louisville, the Interlibrary Loan staff supplied several books and photocopies of periodical articles. Richard Griscom also thanks the staff of the Dwight Anderson Music Library for their assistance and support.

Margie Wood supplied a copy of an article published in *The Canon*.

Angelo Zaniol sent copies of his articles.

Advice on Obtaining Sources

Books that are still in print may be ordered from any good bookstore. For out-of-print books, approach a reputable used bookstore, who can initiate a search (admittedly slow and uncertain) by means of lists, advertisements, and databases. Most of the books, theses, dissertations, and articles listed in this bibliography may be obtained on interlibrary loan from your university or college library (if you are affiliated with such an institution) or your local public library. Show the appropriate librarian this bibliography as verification of the item. The OCLC numbers or ISBNs will aid in obtaining the books, theses, and dissertations; the ISSNs of periodicals, the articles they contain. Libraries will often order foreign dissertations through the Center for Research Libraries in Chicago.

Most of the American dissertations can be purchased from University Microfilms International, 300 N. Zeeb Road, Ann Arbor, MI 48106 (phone [800] 521-3042); customers with academic addresses receive a considerable discount. The master's theses and the remainder of the dissertations can generally be purchased from the university where they were submitted.

If you cannot obtain a particular article on interlibrary loan, write to the periodical in question to purchase a back issue or offprint. The addresses of periodicals are found in chapter 31. In some cases, back issues are obtainable from University Microfilms International.

If in doubt, ask a reference librarian. Believe it or not, he or she is actually paid to help you with your research.

The Recorder

1

Bibliographies of Writings on the Recorder (and Bibliographic Essays)

The only previous specialized bibliographies of literature on the recorder are the work of Hugo Alker:

1. Alker, Hugo. *Blockflöten-Bibliographie* [Recorder bibliography]. (Biblos-Schriften, Bd. 27–28) Vienna: Universitätsbibliothek, 1960–61. OCLC #1216841.

    Although primarily a bibliography of recorder music, lists sources and general publications about the recorder and its repertory, as well as methods and instructional works. Coverage is unfortunately restricted to German, Austrian, and selected British publications. Negative review by Erich Katz in *The American Recorder* 4, no. 2 (May 1963): 20–21.

2. Alker, Hugo. *Blockflöten-Bibliographie* [Recorder bibliography]. 3 vols. Wilhelmshaven: Heinrichshofen, 1966–75. [Bd. 1]: *Blockflöten-Bibliographie* (1966). Bd. 2: *Nachtrag und Gesamtregister* [Supplement and complete index] (1969). Bd. 3: *Nachtrag 1970–1974* (1975; ISBN 3795901456).

    The bibliographies of sources and publications ("Quellen und Veröffentlichungen") take up relatively little space in this set (vol. 1, pp. 9–39; vol. 2, pp. 7–9; vol. 3, pp. 7–12). Entries are arranged in a single alphabetic sequence, and the alphabetic indexes ("Registern") included in volumes 2 and 3 offer no access by subject, making it difficult to locate books and articles on a particular topic. Typographical errors abound.

    Volume 1 reviewed by: Erich Katz in *The American Recorder* 8, no. 2 (Spring 1967): 60 and Walter Bergmann in *Recorder & Music Magazine* 2, no. 6 (August 1967): 194. Volume 2 reviewed by Dale Higbee in *The American Recorder* 11, no. 2 (Spring 1970): 67. Volume 3 reviewed by Higbee in *The American Recorder* 19, no. 1 (May 1978): 41–42 and by [Edgar Hunt] in *Recorder & Music* 5, no. 6 (June 1976): 199–200.

3. Alker, Hugo. *Blockflöten-Bibliographie* [Recorder bibliography]. Neuausgabe. 2 vols. Wilhelmshaven: Heinrichshofen, 1984. Bd. 1: *Systematischer Teil* [Systematic part]. ISBN 3795904218. Bd. 2: *Alphabetischer Teil* [Alphabetical part]. ISBN 3795904226.

The first part of volume 1 ("Instrumentenkunde, Aufführungspraxis" [Information on instruments, performance practice], pp. 11–51) is the most extensive bibliography compiled to (that) date of writings about the recorder as well as historical recorder methods. It also includes a selection of general writings on performance practice and the history of musical instruments, not to mention some puzzles (e.g., Otto Beneke's *Von unehrlichen Leuten* [On dishonest people] of 1863). Volume 2 is a curiously conceived alphabetical listing (by author or composer) of all the writings and music contained in volume 1. The citations for articles exclude page numbers; those for books, publishers' names. The English-language citations contain many typographical errors.

This bibliography is now most valuable for its citations of articles in pre-World War II German periodicals, difficult or impossible to obtain in the United States, and now largely of historical interest (e.g., *Der Blockflötenspiegel*, *Der Celler Spielmann*, *Hausmusik*, and *Zeitschrift für Hausmusik*).

Negative review by Edgar Hunt in *The Recorder and Music Magazine* 8, no. 9 (March 1986): 276, to which Alker puts up a weak defense (in German) in 8, no. 11 (September 1986): 335.

Since 1987, David Lasocki has been publishing essays on writings about the recorder for *The American Recorder*, with overlapping German translations in *Tibia*. These essays, which are arranged by topic (depiction in works of art, instruments, makers, making and design, performance practice and technique, players and teachers, and repertory), summarize and critically discuss recent research on the instrument.

4. Lasocki, David. "A Review of Research on the Recorder, 1985–1986." *The American Recorder* 28, no. 4 (November 1987): 145–56.

For a summary of the debate generated by the review of item 460 in this article, see chapter 14, "Instrument Making," under the subheading "The 'Ganassi Recorder' Controversy" (p. 153).

5. Lasocki, David. "The Recorder in Print: 1987–88." *American Recorder* 31, no. 1 (March 1990): 11–13, 35–42.

6. Lasocki, David. "The Recorder in Print: 1989-90." *American Recorder* 33, no. 1 (March 1992): 15-19, 38-44.

7. Lasocki, David. "The Recorder in Print: 1991-92." *American Recorder* 35, no. 2 (March 1994): 5-11, 30-35.

8. Lasocki, David. "Ein Überblick über die Blockflötenforschung, 1985-1987." *Tibia* 13, no. 4 (1988): 237-58.

9. Lasocki, David. "Ein Überblick über die Blockflötenforschung, 1988-1989." *Tibia* 16, no. 4 (1991): 585-99.

10. Lasocki, David. "Überblick über die Blockflötenforschung 1990." *Tibia* 18, no. 1 (1993): 355-64.

11. Lasocki, David. "Ein Überblick über die Blockflötenforschung, 1991." *Tibia* 19, no. 1 (1994): 1-13.

2

General Surveys and Writings Covering Several Topics

This chapter deals with books and articles providing a basic introduction to the recorder as well as sources that cover a variety of specific topics, too numerous to make classification under the individual topics practical.

SIGNIFICANT BOOK-LENGTH INTRODUCTIONS

These books represent the best general surveys of the instrument and its history. A new survey, taking into account the latest research in all countries, is urgently needed.

12. Hunt, Edgar. *The Recorder and Its Music.* Rev. and enl. ed. London: Eulenburg Books, 1977. xvi, 184 p. ISBN 0903873311. In French as: *La flûte à bec et son histoire* [The recorder and its history]. Paris: Editions Zurfluh, 1979. 186 p. Earlier editions: London: Herbert Jenkins, 1962. 176 p. OCLC #906928. New York: W.W. Norton, 1963. 176 p. OCLC #918692. In Dutch as: *De blokfluit en zijn muziek.* Wageningen: Zomer & Keuning, 1966.

A general introduction with an emphasis on history and repertory. Nearly half the book is devoted to a three-part history of the recorder, covering repertory and treatises from the Middle Ages through the decline of the recorder in the 18th century.

An introductory chapter on the origin of the recorder discusses the etymology of "recorder," reviews literary references to the instrument, and offers a table of the various sizes of recorders and the historical terms used to refer to them. Chapter 5 provides a good short survey of historical makers. The treatment of recorder technique in chapter 6 offers a balance of theory and practice, makes frequent references to historical treatises, and takes the unusual approach of introducing fingering by relating it to acoustical principles. The chapter on the 20th-century revival has been criticized for its autobiographical content, but Hunt's story, coming from one who experienced the revival first hand, is nonetheless interesting. The concluding chapter, "The Recorder Today," is a country-by-country survey providing information on the role of the recorder in schools, the names of prominent professional players and teachers, recorder societies, publishers, and makers. An appendix advises composers interested in writing for the recorder. The nine-page bibliography concentrates on pre-1960 writings. (Despite the scholarly underpinnings of the book, citations in the text are often brief and incomplete, leaving the inquisitive reader to consult the bibliography for more precise information.)

Hunt brought the last three chapters up to date for the 1977 edition but unfortunately failed to make more than a handful of necessary corrections to the earlier chapters. Reviewed by Dale Higbee in *The American Recorder* 20, no. 4 (February 1980): 170, Walter Bergmann in *Recorder & Music* 5, no. 12 (December 1977): 391, and Anthony Baines in *The Galpin Society Journal* 31 (May 1978): 168–69. 1962 ed. reviewed by Richard D.C. Noble in *The Consort* 19 (July 1962): 136–38.

13. Linde, Hans-Martin. *The Recorder Player's Handbook*. 2nd ed. (rev. and enl.). Trans. from the German by Richard Deveson. London: Schott, 1991. 149 p. Schott ED 12322. ISBN 0946535175. In German as: *Handbuch des Blockflötenspiels*. 2., brw. Ausg. Mainz: Schott, 1984. 131 p. ISBN 3795725313. Earlier edition: *The Recorder Player's Handbook*. Trans. by James C. Haden. London; New York: Schott, 1974. 107 p. OCLC #1689607. In German as: *Handbuch des Blockflötenspiels*. Mainz: Schott, 1962. 107 p. OCLC #2582721.

Revised and in an improved translation, Linde's book has much to offer intermediate and advanced players. Falls into three parts: "The Recorder," which concerns acoustics, sizes of instruments, and choosing and caring for the instrument; "Playing the Recorder," which covers fundamentals of technique; and "Recorder Music and its Performance," the largest section of the book, which concerns repertory and performance practice in music from the Middles Ages through the 20th century. (Linde's experience as a performer is in evidence in the advice he offers on performance practice, which is not covered by most other practical surveys of repertory.) Concludes with a rather Germanocentric bibliography.

1962 edition reviewed by Erich Katz in *The American Recorder* 7, no. 4 (Fall 1966): 14–15. 1974 edition reviewed by Edgar Hunt in *Recorder & Music* 5, no. 1 (March 1975). 1991 edition reviewed by Robert Ehrlich in *The Recorder Magazine* 12, no. 1 (March 1992): 21–22.

14. Wollitz, Kenneth. *The Recorder Book.* New York: Alfred A. Knopf; London: Gollancz, 1982. xxv, 259 p. ISBN 0394479734 (U.S. ed.); ISBN 0575031441 (U.K. ed.). In Italian as: *Manuale del flauto dolce.* (La vostra via, v. 176) Milan: Longanesi, 1982. 240 p. OCLC #14469872.
A fine handbook for beginning and intermediate performers. Nearly half the book is devoted to matters of technique: breathing, tonguing, fingering, practicing, ornamentation (both Renaissance and Baroque), alternate and trill fingerings, and compound articulations. The book is a practical one and includes many exercises. An appendix offers a "beginner's first lesson," a table of scales, and solutions to many of the problems encountered by novice players. The chapter on ensemble playing covers basic technical challenges, answers such practical questions as where to play and who should lead, explains the role of difference tones in tuning, and makes suggestions on how to go about preparing a program. The introduction briefly surveys the history of the recorder. In the chapter "Selecting and Caring for Your Recorder," Wollitz advocates plastic recorders for beginners and offers much sound advice on selecting and maintaining wooden instruments. Colin C. Sterne's narrative survey of recorder repertory is essentially a general history of music, and only in the section on the late Baroque is repertory discussed in any detail. Martha Bixler's and Joan Munkacsi's useful annotated bibliography of music for the recorder is categorized by difficulty and subarranged by instrumentation. Concludes with a glossary and a short, eclectic bibliography. The U.K. edition is slightly altered (some of the musical selections are different).
Reviewed in *Recorder & Music* 7, no. 5 (March 1982): 130 and by Edgar Hunt in *The American Recorder* 23, no. 2 (May 1982): 77. Portions of chapter 2 (How to Practice) and chapter 3 (Ornamentation) originally appeared in *The American Recorder* (see items 744 and 811).

OTHER IMPORTANT BOOKS

15. Peter, Hildemarie. *The Recorder: Its Traditions and Its Tasks.* English translation from the German edition by Stanley Godman. Berlin-Lichterfelde: Robert Lienau; New York: C.F. Peters, 1958. 76 p. OCLC #28740763. In German as: *Die Blockflöte und ihre Spielweise in Vergangenheit und Gegenwart.* Berlin-Lichterfelde: Robert Lienau, 1953. 79 p. OCLC #13921773.
One of the first monograph-length studies of recorder history and historical performance practice, now outdated but nonetheless of value for its fold-out charts covering both historical and modern fingering and ornamentation. The English translation is often clumsy and occasionally inaccurate.

Contents: The Structural and Acoustic Principles of the Recorder; Practical Problems of Recorder Playing (covering historical performance practice and ornamentation); The Recorder in the Music and Instrumentation of the late Middle Ages [i.e., the Renaissance] and the Baroque; The Recorder in the Present (including sections on modern methods, contemporary music, and "the tasks and opportunities of the recorder in the twentieth century"). Concludes with a four-page bibliography.
Reviewed by Suzanne Bloch in *The American Recorder* 1, no. 3 (Summer 1960): 14 and Anthony Baines in *The Galpin Society Journal* 12 (May 1959): 103.

16. Schmidt, Lloyd John. *A Practical and Historical Source-Book for the Recorder.* Ph.D. dissertation, Northwestern University, 1959. xv, 623 leaves. OCLC #16530374, #1920225. UMI order no. 59-04837.

One of the outstanding contributions to the literature about the recorder, still surprisingly little known. "At once a reference work and a history, it is an attempt to supply a single source for significant information about the recorder" (p. v). Although much of the study has been superseded by later research, it is jam-packed with information that could still be used (critically) to write recorder history. Its main faults are that Schmidt is uncritical about what modern authors have said, that he relies too heavily on secondary sources, and that he allows far too many typographical errors.

Contents: technical features of the instrument, fingerings, practical considerations (selection, basic technique, ensemble, care and maintenance), nomenclature, the recorder by period (primitive and ancient society, the Middle Ages to the 15th century; 15th century; 16th century; 17th century; 18th century; Bach, Handel, and Telemann; 19th century; 20th-century revival), the recorder in education, methods, the recorder in music literature, the recorder in literature, the recorder in art works. Appendixes cover: Pepys, Henry VIII's 1547 inventory, surviving historical specimens, collections and exhibitions, makers, the Chester recorders, unusual specimens, the sound hole, hand positions in depictions from 1386 through the 18th century, the American Recorder Society, the Society of Recorder Players, the Dolmetsch Foundation, glossary.

17. Thomson, J.M., ed. *The Cambridge Companion to the Recorder.* Cambridge: Cambridge University Press, forthcoming in 1995.

Contents to include: an introduction by Thomson; Howard Mayer Brown on the recorder in the Renaissance, with a repertory commentary by Anthony Rowland-Jones; Rowland-Jones on Baroque sonatas, chamber music, and cantatas; Adrienne Simpson on the "orchestral" use of the recorder; David Lasocki and Rowland-Jones on the early 18th-century recorder concerto; Lasocki on instruction books and methods, largely historical; Thomson on the revival of the recorder in the 20th century; Eve O'Kelly on later 20th-century recorder music; Lasocki on professional players before the 20th century; O'Kelly on modern professionals; O'Kelly on the recorder in education; Clifford Bartlett on facsimiles and editing; and a bibliographic essay by Rowland-Jones stressing writings on the general repertory, technique, and performance practice.

18. Welch, Christopher. *Six Lectures on the Recorder and Other Flutes in Relation to Literature.* London: Henry Frowde [for the] Oxford University Press, 1911. xvi, 457 p. OCLC #1867864. First three lectures reprinted as: *Lectures on the Recorder in Relation to Literature.* With a New Introduction by Edgar Hunt. London: Oxford University Press, 1961. ix, 191 p. OCLC #551595.

Pioneering essays that were highly influential in the 20th-century revival of the recorder.

Contents: Literary Errors on the Subject of the Recorder (item 39 updated); Tone and Effect of the Recorder; Hamlet and the Recorder (item 52 updated); Shakespeare's Allusions to Flutes and Pipes; Milton on Flutes and Flute-Players; and The Temple-Flute-Player and the Tomb-Piper. "Tone and Effect of the Recorder" discusses the qualities of the recorder as found in 17th-century sources (Mersenne, Milton, plays by Massinger and others, Pepys) as well as Handel's use of the instrument (a survey based on the Chrysander edition with special sections on the *flauto piccolo* and *Acis and Galatea*). Although Welch's numerous digressions and discursive footnotes make for slow reading, his scholarship and perceptiveness hold up well.

The 1961 reprint is reviewed by Eric Halfpenny in in *The Galpin Society Journal* 19 (1966): 163 and Alexander Silbiger in *The American Recorder* 3, no. 2 (May 1962): 20.

OTHER BOOKS

19. Alker, Hugo. *Die Blockflöte: Instrumentenkunde, Geschichte, Musizierpraxis* [The recorder: organology, history, musical practice]. (Wiener Abhandlungen zur Musikwissenschaft und Instrumentenkunde, Bd. 1) Vienna: H. Geyer, 1962. 76 p. OCLC #5780969. The chapter "Alte und neue Blockflöten" also appeared separately in *Das Musikinstrument* 10 (1961): 445–46.

Designed as an overview of the recorder for the "beginner and practicing musician." Divided into: (1) the instrument (terminology, material, recorder revival, modern makers), (2) advice for the buyer (types and models, quality, sizes, pitch, breath pressure, fingering), (3) recorder manufacturers (a survey, with types and materials), (4) recorder

General Surveys and Writings Covering Several Topics 11

maintenance, (5) playing suggestions (pitch, intonation, trouble-shooting), (6) recorder history (the highpoints of the Renaissance and Baroque), (7) performance practice (Renaissance as well as Baroque), (8) old and new recorders (including data on historical and modern instruments in Vienna), and (9) short bibliography. According to Erich Katz (review in *The American Recorder* 4, no. 2 [May 1963]: 21), the work is a reprint of item **1** omitting the (full) bibliography but adding the chapter on old and new recorders. Useful at the time of publication but now rather dated.

20. Dantimo, Stanley A., ed. *All About the Recorder*. Cleveland: Trophy Music Company, 1969.

    A series of brief essays "not intended for the connoisseur, but, rather, for anyone interested in Recorders [sic]," written by various experts whose biographies loom large on the page. The essays cover the history of the instrument, the recorder in education (at all levels) and music therapy, selection and standards, transposition, Baroque vs. German fingering, intonation, the solo sonata, and the American Recorder Society. Now seems very dated.

21. Degen, Dietz. *Zur Geschichte der Blockflöte in den germanischen Ländern* [On the history of the recorder in Germanic countries]. Kassel: Bärenreiter, [1936]. 206 p. OCLC #16476451; reprint, 1972. OCLC #580993.

    Long the most important book written about the recorder and still a mine of useful information almost sixty years on. Part I, on the instrument, covers names in various languages; sizes; range, fingering, and notation; design and material; and changes in external appearance. Part II, on recorder history, presents an overview through the 19th century, then looks at appearances of the recorder at the same time as the flute; then follow sections on the individual countries (Germany, the Low Countries, England [largely based on Welch, item **18**], Sweden, and Denmark). Concludes with a table of historical makers and surviving instruments, as well as an extensive bibliography. Highly recommended.

22. Hunt, Edgar. *The Recorder: A Handbook of Useful Information*. London: Schott, 1957. [14] p. OCLC #1542672.

    A survey of the instrument in pamphlet form, briefly covering: a definition of "recorder," ease of playing, ensemble playing, history, modern revival, sizes, choice of instrument, care, teaching, starting a recorder class, and repertory.

23. Manifold, John. *The Amorous Flute: An Unprofessional Handbook for Recorder Players and All Amateurs of Music*.

London: Workers' Music Association, 1948. xiv, 48 p. OCLC #5292613.

Promotes amateur music-making and the recorder as an advantageous instrument for it. Consists largely of historical information about the recorder, by now somewhat inaccurate but engagingly written. Includes a section on playing in a recorder consort. Glossary.

24. Thomson, John M. *Your Book of the Recorder.* 2nd. ed. London: Faber & Faber, 1974. 75 p. ISBN 0571048730. Earlier edition: London: Faber & Faber, 1968. 75 p. ISBN 0571082270.

Part of a series of Your Books intended for young adults which includes books on history, the arts, hobbies, crafts, sports, science, etc. Written in a simple, straightforward style. Fulfills its promise of being "a concise introduction to the recorder world, now in the midst of another golden age." Draws largely on Hunt (item 12) and articles in *The Recorder and Music Magazine,* especially by Bergmann. Chapters on sizes of recorders, first steps in learning, history (earliest days, Elizabethan music, Baroque, Handel/Bach/Telemann, 20th century), how recorders are made, and famous players and ensembles of today. Fingering chart and brief bibliography.

The second edition is virtually identical to the first, only a few sentences having been added at the ends of some of the chapters to bring them up to date.

ARTICLES

GENERAL SURVEYS

25. Barthel, Rudolf. "Die Blockflöte" [The recorder]. In *Handbuch der Musikerziehung* [Handbook of music education], edited by Hans Fischer, 474-84. Berlin: Rembrandt-Verlag, Konrad Lemmer, 1954.

An unusually interesting choice of subject matter for an overview: alternative fingerings and their intonation, warming up and tuning up, breathing and articulation, the repertory (very briefly), and the recorder orchestra and its repertory.

26. Dolmetsch, Carl F. "The Recorder or English Flute." *Music & Letters* 22, no. 1 (January 1941): 67-74.

Writing at a time when the recorder was not yet widely known and appreciated, Dolmetsch leaps to the defense of the instrument, drawing heavily on his own experience. Focuses on the current state of recorder playing and manufacturing. Discusses a few of the compositions he commissioned. Describes Arnold Dolmetsch's role in the revival of the recorder and the founding of the Society of Recorder Players. Concludes with the jingoistic statement (it was World War II, after all): "It should be a source of inspiration to enthusiasts that the rising generation of composers and players take a serious view of the recorder's place in the world of music and are setting out to re-establish and maintain the traditional supremacy in both instruments and players which England always [sic] enjoyed."

27. Donington, Robert. "The Recorders." *The Consort* 2 (December 1931): 7-11.

A brief introduction to the instrument, its qualities, technique, and repertory from a Dolmetsch family perspective. Mentions a few pieces by Bach, Handel, Purcell, and Woodcock, adding, with prescient understatement: "Specific music for recorders probably exists and only awaits discovery."

28. Fitzgibbon, H. Macaulay. "'Of Flutes and Soft Recorders.'" *The Musical Quarterly* 20, no. 2 (April 1934): 219-29.

A history of flutes and flute music that contains several errors and is generally founded on unreliable scholarship. The recorder is discussed only briefly on the first page. (One of the errors in this section: "[I]t was difficult to play in any but the major diatonic scale.") Briefly mentions the use of the recorder by Bach and Handel (pp. 224-25). The title of the article is taken from Milton's *Paradise Lost*.

29. Higbee, Dale. "The Recorder and Its Literature." *Music Journal* 23 (April 1965): 56-57.

An excellent brief introduction to the recorder, its history, and its revival. Includes a bibliography, discography, and list of addresses, all of which, because of their age, are now of little value.

30. Hunt, Edgar. "The Recorder and Its Music." *Proceedings of the Royal Musical Association* 75 (1949): 39-51.

A good short survey, which served as a starting point for Hunt's book *The Recorder and Its Music* (item 12). Falls into three sections: up to about 1650; from about 1650 to the end of the 18th century; and the 20th-century revival of the recorder. The first two sections cover, for each period, manuals and treatises on the recorder, the construction of the instrument and its common sizes and pitches, and repertory. The treatment of the 20th-century is anglocentric and thus incomplete.

31. Köhler, Wolfgang. "Die Blütezeit der Blockflöte: Anmerkungen zur historischen Stellung eines Instrumentes"

[The heyday of the recorder: remarks on the historical position of an instrument]. *Tibia* 12, no. 2 (1987): 421–26.

According to Köhler, it is the Baroque that is usually described as the high point in the development of the recorder. Thinks this view may have come about because of the early music movement's rediscovery of the Baroque era first, the discovery and editing of the Baroque solo literature, the ready available of modern copies of Baroque instruments. Curiously, he then switches to an entirely different question, setting up a straw man: "But was the recorder . . . really *the* solo instrument of the Baroque?" It was of course the most popular wind instrument for amateurs (until the flute took over that role), although it played a modest role in professional music. Then switches back to the original topic and seeks to place the heyday in the Renaissance, or perhaps even in the present day. Concludes with comments on the roles of the recorder in the 20th century. A curious article. Letter from Martin Heidecker in 12, no. 3 (1987): 547, and reply by Köhler, 548–49.

32. Manifold, J.S. "The Recorder." *The Canon* 3 (1950): 448–53; 508–18; 568–73; 624–31; 687–92.

Part 1: Definition, Nomenclature and Notation. Part 2: The Recorder in England, A Brief History. Part 3: Choosing an Instrument. Part 4: The Recorder Class and Repertoire. Part 5: Household Music.

A monograph-length series of articles, written to introduce readers to the recorder and to promote amateur music making. The introduction to the instrument, its history, and its repertory in the opening two parts is detailed and well written, but the reader should keep in mind that some facts have changed during the intervening forty years. Part 2, a history of the recorder in England, remains the most valuable part of the series and offers a good survey of 17th- and 18th-century repertory, including songbooks and methods as well as published chamber music. The information in the concluding three sections on selecting instruments, organizing recorder classes, and using modern instruments alongside recorders is dated and of little use.

33. Moeck, Hermann. "Il flauto dolce: Passato e presente" [The recorder: past and present]. *Il flauto dolce* 2 (January-June 1972): 1–2.

A brief overview of the recorder's history, its 20th-century revival, the technical problems of modern recorders, and thoughts on the future (avant garde).

34. Morgan, Fred. "A Player's Guide to the Recorder." *The Recorder: Journal of the Victorian Recorder Guild* 6 (June 1987): 1–4; 7 (December 1987): 10–16.

An excellent overview of the physical instrument. Part 1 covers "The recorder family" (names, pitch-designations, and sizes, with comments on the uses of the more unusual sizes) and "Pitch" (the pitches of early instruments and modern copies). Part 2 covers "Anatomy of the recorder" (a description of the parts of the instrument, with historical asides), "Making recorders" (materials, and factory-made vs. hand-made), and "Choosing a recorder" (based, in order of importance, on speech, intonation, beautiful sound, and fine appearance).

35. *New Grove Dictionary of Music and Musicians*. Edited by Stanley Sadie. London: Macmillan; Washington, DC: Grove's Dictionaries of Music, 1980. S.v. "Recorder," by Edgar Hunt (vol. 15, pp. 648-58). Updated version in *The New Grove Dictionary of Musical Instruments*. Edited by Stanley Sadie. London: Macmillan; New York: Grove's Dictionaries of Music, 1984. S.v. "Recorder," by Edgar Hunt (vol. 3, pp. 205-15).

The most accessible short overview of the recorder, divided into a brief first part and a disproportionately long second part. "The Instrument" describes the physical instrument, comments on etymology, and discusses sizes and names (in several languages). "History" concentrates on the Baroque period, with shorter discussions of the Renaissance and 20th century; it covers surviving instruments, makers, methods, repertory, teachers, and performers. The first version of the article seems to have been written around 1970; the second version simply adds twelve items from the 1970s and early 1980s to the bibliography, the text failing to take advantage of the research published in the meantime.

36. Salb, Michael. *Musikinstrumente: Die Blockflöte* [Musical instruments: the recorder]. Frankfurt: Zimmermann, 1990.

Not seen. Cited in *Basler Jahrbuch für historische Musikpraxis* 15 (1991): 280.

37. Scheck, Gustav. "Der Weg zu den Holzblasinstrumenten" [The path to woodwind instruments]. In *Hohe Schule der Musik: Handbuch der gesamten Musikpraxis*, 4: 1-100. Potsdam: Akademische Verlagsgesellschaft Athenaion, 1935.

This chapter, written by one of the most important flute/recorder players of this century, has been widely cited, partly because of the status of its author and partly because it treated the recorder (here dubbed "Längsflöte") on a par with the flute, clarinet, saxophone, oboe, and bassoon. The recorder section (pp. 3-23) covers name and history, breathing and fingering techniques, and a few words on the choice of instruments for Bach's Second Brandenburg Concerto and Cantata 106.

38. Veilhan, Jean-Claude, and Hugo Reyne. "La flûte à bec, instrument de l'amour" [The recorder, instrument of love]. *Diapason-Harmonie* 335 (February 1988): 52–54.
Briefly surveys the recorder, its history and symbolism.

39. Welch, Christopher. "Literature Relating to the Recorder." *Proceedings of the Musical Association* 24 (1897–98): 145–224. Updated version in item 18.
A landmark study in the modern revival of the recorder, this long, sometimes rambling, article covers a far broader range of topics than its title suggests.
Contents: Uncertainties of Lexicographers and Commentators; Misprints in *Hamlet*; Classification of Flutes; Quotations from old Writers; The Flute in Chaucer; Description of the Recorder; Henry VIII and the Recorder; The Recorder in Agricola, Praetorius, and Mersenne; The Flageolet; Puritan Attack on the Flute; Books of Instruction for the Flageolet and the Recorder; The Recorder changes its Name; Decay and Extinction of the Recorder; Errors of Sir John Hawkins, Dr. Burney, Mr. William Chappell, and Carl Engel.

40. Zaniol, Angelo. "Il flauto dolce" [The recorder]. *Strumenti e musica* 21, no. 8 (August 1978): 90, 92; no. 10 (October 1978): 106, 108; no. 11 (November 1978): 127–28, 130; no. 12 (December 1978): 114, 116; 22, no. 1 (January 1979): 104, 106; no. 2 (February 1979): 212, 214, 216; no. 3 (March 1979): 126, 128; no. 4 (April 1979): 114; no. 5 (May 1979): 150, 152; no. 7 (July 1979): 98, 100; no. 8 (August 1979): 248, 250; no. 9 (September 1979): 186, 188; no. 10 (October 1979): 153–54; no. 11 (November 1979): 164, 166; no. 12 (December 1979): 156, 158; 23, no. 1 (January 1980): 122, 124; no. 2 (February 1980): 220, 222; no. 4 (April 1980): 150, 152; no. 5 (May 1980): 144, 146; no. 6 (June 1980): 166, 168; no. 7 (July 1980): 122, 124; no. 8 (August 1980): 212, 214; no. 10 (October 1980): 188, 190; no. 11 (November 1980): 162, 164; no. 12 (December 1980): 144, 146; 24, no. 1 (January 1981): 182, 184, 186; no. 2 (February 1981): 136, 138, 140; no. 3 (March 1981): 130, 132; no. 4 (April 1981): 162, 164; no. 6 (June 1981): 138, 140, 142.

General Surveys and Writings Covering Several Topics

A survey of the early history of the recorder (Middle Ages, Renaissance, 17th century, late Baroque) almost the length of a small book. Preceded by an introduction, a bibliographic essay on the instrument, and a discussion of methods and studies. Zaniol displays a wide knowledge of the literature about the recorder. Useful evaluations.

MISCELLANEOUS TOPICS

41. "Q & A." *American Recorder* 31, no. 1 (March 1990): 34; 31, no. 2 (June 1990): 40–42; 31, no. 3 (September 1990): 34–36; 32, no. 1 (March 1991): 43; 33, no. 1 (March 1992): 45; 34, no. 4 (November 1993): 24–26.

A series of questions and answers covering a variety of topics. March 1990: breaking in a new recorder (adapted from a brouchure; see also a letter by Neil Seely in 31, no. 2 [June 1990]: 33), finding practice time (answered by James Tanguay). June 1990: trill markings (answered by Steve Rosenberg and Benjamin S. Dunham), meantone temperament (answered by Bob Marvin and Steve Silverstein), selecting a recorder (answered by Judith Linsenberg; see also letters by Martin Davidson and Nikolaus von Huene in 31, no. 4 [December 1990]: 25–26 and by Stephen T. Whitney in 32, no. 1 [March 1991]: 35 on the relationship between type of wood and sound quality). September 1990: the bass recorder in the Baroque (answered by David Lasocki), plastic crumhorns (answered by Benjamin S. Dunham). March 1991: deposits in the windway (answered by Philip Levin), alternate fingerings (answered by James Tanguay), music and war. March 1992: circular breathing (answered by Pete Rose), condensation (answered by James Tanguay). November 1993: voice flute (answered by Carolyn Peskin), recorking joints (answered by "Dear Georg"), cleaning the block and windway of the recorder (answered by Frances Blaker), agogic accents (answered by Benjamin Dunham).

3

Etymology, Symbolism, and Literary References

The origin of the word "recorder" has inspired a number of theories, ranging from "to sing like a bird" to "rememberance." Whatever the meaning of its name, the instrument has a rich history of symbolic use in music, literature, and the visual arts, most frequently representing birdsong, love, death, the supernatural, and the pastoral. This chapter covers sources on etymology, symbolism, and literary references. For the role of the recorder in the visual arts, see chapter 7.

* Bridge, J.C. "The Chester 'Recorders.'" Cited below as item 53.

    Bridge cites references made to the recorder by John Hawkins, Shakespeare, Samuel Pepys, John Evelyn, Charles Burney, and various Elizabethan poets. He also addresses the question of the etymology of "recorder," arguing in favor of "to record" as "to sing, chant, or warble like birds."

42. Manifold, J.S. *The Music in English Drama: From Shakespeare to Purcell.* London: Rockliff, 1956. 208 p. OCLC #404918.

    Several pages on the recorder appear in the first two parts, titled "Music in Shakespeare's Theatre" and "Music in Purcell's Theater." Includes a selection of direct references to the recorder in plays of the late-16th and 17th centuries. In Shakespeare's time, Manifold sees associations of the recorder with death and mourning, hearses and coffins, temples or churches, prayers, the appearance of gods or goddesses, resurrections, portents, and miracles. The primary association is not death but rather the idea of "*another world;* the supernatural; benevolent deities, whether Christian or pagan." Supports the origin of "recorder" in the verb "to record," which was used by Elizabethan authors in connection with birdsong. In the theater of Purcell's time, Manifold sees the recorder "shed

Etymology, Symbolism, and Literary References 19

fewer of its traditional associations" than some of the other instruments of the orchestra, while picking up an additional association with the pastoral, which possibly had its origin in the false belief that the *flûte douce* (as the recorder had come to be called) was a French instrument.

* Welch, Christopher. "Literature Relating to the Recorder." Cited above as item 39.
   Discusses the etymology of "recorder" on pp. 21-22 (1961 reprint). Literary references are cited in the sections "Quotations from Old Writers" and "The Flute in Chaucer."

ETYMOLOGY

43. Trowell, Brian. "King Henry IV, Recorder-Player." *The Galpin Society Journal* 10 (1957): 83-84.
    Suggests that the word "recorder" might have been derived from the Italian *ricordo* ("rememberance" or "souvenir"). Trowell conjectures that a recorder might have been given as a "memento" to the young Henry by an "Italian noble, merchant, or ecclesiastic," and hence the association was made. Unfortunately, *ricordo* does not seem to have been Italian either.

44. Higbee, Dale. "The Etymology of 'Recorder.'" *The Galpin Society Journal* 18 (1965): 128.
    Supports Trowell's theory (item 43) that "recorder" derived from a form of the Latin word *recordari* ("to remember").

45. Bergmann, Walter. "When a Treble Really WAS a Treble." *The Recorder and Music Magazine* 1, no. 10 (August 1965): 313.
    Summarizes the discussion of the etymology of "recorder" in items 43 and 44. Also cites a ca. 1700 print containing airs by Finger for "two and three treble flutes." Bergmann had assumed that the term "treble" was of 20th-century origin. Laurence Wright, in 1, no. 11 (November 1965): 341, suggests an origin from the English *to record*, meaning "*to memorise, to recall, to practise,* and to *recite, sing,* or *play.*"

SYMBOLISM

* Lasocki, David. "The Recorder in the Elizabethan, Jacobean and Caroline Theater." Cited below as item 75.

46. Libin, Laurence. "Sex and the Flute." *The American Recorder* 13, no. 3 (August 1972): 77-85.

The attention-grabbing title is slightly misleading, since the article is a broad study of the role of the generic flute in the history of civilization, both as a musical instrument and as a symbol associated primarily with the male gender. Much of the article is a survey of the flute's connotations—spiritual and magical, as well as sexual—in various prehistoric, ancient, and modern cultures. Unfortunately, Libin documents none of his sources. A letter by Isabel Kimble in 14, no. 1 (February 1973): 35–36, makes an unsupported argument that the flute is a female symbol. In the same issue, Libin replies and then goes on to correct several factual errors in his article.

47. Martin, Anne. "The Recorder and 'Bird Music.'" *Recorder & Music* 6, no. 9 (March 1980): 261–63.

    A survey of repertory in which the recorder imitates birdsong. There are no surprises here: *The Bird Fancyer's Delight*, arias by Handel, Arne, and Purcell; van Eyck's "Engels Nachtegaeltje"; Vivaldi's *Il Cardellino;* William Williams's *Sonata in Imitation of Birds;* and a few 20th-century compositions. Includes a bibliography and discography.

48. Pinson, Jean-Pierre. "A propos d'un si bémol" [About a b-flat]. *Le Tic-Toc-Choc* 4, no. 4 (May 1983): 6–9.

    An expressionistic essay on the character of the recorder (ethos with a touch of pathos).

49. Skins, Ron. "The Recorder as Image-Maker." *The Recorder and Music Magazine* 8, no. 8 (December 1985): 234–36.

    Surveys the recorder's extramusical associations—death, Eros, the pastoral, birdsong, the supernatural, etc.—supported by quotations from literature, all well known except for *Ralph Roister Doister* (a 16th-century play), Friedrich Dürrenmatt's *Die Physiker* [The Physicists], and Kingsley Amis's *Lucky Jim* (the recorder as a decidedly amateur instrument).

50. Turner, John. "Writing for the Recorder." (Performer's Platform) *Composer* 92 (Winter 1987): 17–21.

    As a recorder player giving advice to composers on writing for the instrument, Turner posits that in the Baroque repertory the two main uses of the recorder were for virtuoso decoration and ornamentation on the one hand and programmatic connections (rusticity, love, the supernatural, birds, and death) on the other hand. Recommends that composers ponder these historical uses, since they "can to some extent . . . [compensate] for the lack of strength and flexibility in the tone" of the recorder. Briefly discusses recent works by British composers that in his opinion successfully use variation and decoration or programmatic associations. Concludes with "some wholly practical notes on what to do and what not to do when writing for the instrument."

* Veilhan, Jean-Claude, and Hugo Reyne. "La flûte à bec, instrument de l'amour." Cited above as item 38.

51. White, Beverly. "The Human Lineage of the Fipple Flute." *The American Recorder* 19, no. 4 (February 1979): 151–53.

    A brief sociological history of the fipple flute from prehistoric times to the present. An emphasis is placed on the recorder and its extramusical associations. No footnotes, only a bibliography of secondary sources.

LITERARY REFERENCES

For other references, see under "Literary references," "Milton, John," and "Shakespeare, William" in the index.

52. Welch, Christopher. "Hamlet and the Recorder." *Proceedings of the Musical Association* 28 (1901–2): 105–37. Updated version in item 18.

    An exegesis of the well known scene from *Hamlet* (Act III, Scene ii) in which Hamlet calls for "the recorders." Welch believes Shakespeare intended a consort of no fewer than four players on stage. Covers other questions of staging. Concludes with an explication of some frequently misunderstood and misinterpreted phrases from the scene: "to withdraw with you," "I know no touch of it," "govern these ventages," "Give it breath with your mouth," "it will discourse most eloquent music," "look you, these are the stops," and "though you can fret me."

4

Periods: Historical

This chapter is concerned with surveys of the recorder in particular countries and historical periods as well as sources covering specific aspects of the recorder in the past that do not fit readily into the other chapters.

53. Bridge, J.C. "The Chester 'Recorders.'" *Proceedings of the Musical Association* 27 (1900–1901): 109–20.

    On 12 February 1901, Bridge brought the Chester recorders to a meeting of the Royal Music Association and read this paper, which is not so much a history of the Chester instruments as a summary of the little that was known at that time about the history of the recorder. The instruments were then played—apparently somewhat incompetently, judging from the Chairman's comments. Discussion followed.

    The information on the Chester recorders is confined to the first two pages of the paper and the "Discussion" section. In his paper, Bridge reports that the set of recorders comprise four instruments (pitched in f^1, d^1, c^1, and f) by Bressan that were discovered in a wooden box in 1886 when the Chester Archaeological Society moved into the Grosvenor Museum. During the course of the discussion, Christopher Welch asks about the pitch and wood type of the instruments. He also describes the role of the various sizes of recorder in the music of Handel. (See item 1122 for more information on Welch's participation.)

    Bridge cites references made to the recorder by Sir John Hawkins, Shakespeare, Samuel Pepys, John Evelyn, Charles Burney, and various Elizabethan poets. He addresses the question of the etymology of "recorder," arguing in favor of "to record" as "to sing, chant, or warble like birds." He also puzzles over suggestions that a membrane was traditionally placed over a special hole near the windway, but concludes that an experiment suggested by Mersenne in *Harmonie Universelle* is the basis for this "gigantic fiction."

54. Dolmetsch, Carl. "The Recorder and Flute." *The Consort* 14 (July 1957): 18–23.

A brief history of the recorder in the 16th-18th centuries with incidental comments on the flute. Contains much opinion presented as fact and many errors of fact.

55. Moeck, Hermann. *Typen europäischer Blockflöten in Vorzeit, Geschichte und Volksüberlieferung* [Types of European recorders in antiquity, history and folk tradition]. (Ausführlicher Bericht zum Referat auf der 2. Internationalen Arbeitstagung für die Erforschung der Volksmusikinstrumente Europas in Brünn) Celle: Moeck, 1967. 56 p. OCLC #24411722.

An excellent survey of the fipple flute. Curiously, the title, in using "Blockflöte" (recorder) as a synonym for "Kernspaltflöte" (fipple flute), is an example of a practice the author rightly condemns himself. In the short section on the recorder (pp. 34–35), reports that what seems to be the earliest surviving recorder (between 1200 and 1300) was found in Würzburg. Claims that the origin of the recorder should be sought in Italian folk instruments. Reviewed by Dale Higbee in *The American Recorder* 9, no. 3 (Summer 1970): 105.

56. Nosek, Margaret A. "The Recorder in the Sixteenth and Early Seventeenth Centuries." (Notizbuch für Studenten) *Bach* 5, no. 3 (July 1974): 29–34; 5, no. 4 (October 1974): 18–24; 6, no. 1 (January 1975): 17–23; 6, no. 2 (April 1975): 15–25.

Apparently an undergraduate paper revised for publication. Relies almost exclusively on secondary sources of varying authority (including notes from recorder-workshop discussions) and is rife with errors. Although certain sections are accurate, the scholarship on the whole is unreliable. Falls into several parts. Part I: Characteristics of the Renaissance Recorder; Renaissance Playing Techniques. Part II: Renaissance Ornamentation. Part III: Ornamentation of Chansons and Madrigals; Renaissance Use of the Recorder; the Popularity of the Recorder. Part IV: The Recorder in Seventeenth-Century England (covering the role of the recorder and its construction, composers, repertory, and tutors). Concludes with a bibliography.

RENAISSANCE

57. Bornstein, Andrea. *Gli strumenti musicali del Rinascimento* [Musical instruments of the Renaissance]. (Gli strumenti della musica, 17) Padova: Franco Muzzio, 1987. 315 p. ISBN 8870213870.

Includes a general chapter on woodwind instruments (pp. 29–38) and a short chapter on articulation (pp. 39–42). A long chapter on the flute family (pp. 43–73) contains a sizeable section on the recorder (pp. 44–56), largely derived from Virdung and the usual well-known sources with a smattering of references from inventories. Dismisses Hunt's suggestion (in item 12) that the term "ricordo" used in the future Henry IV's inventory (1388) was of Italian origin.

58. Hunter, Hilda. "Recorders Rampant." *Recorder and Music Magazine* 2, no. 1 (March 1966): 18.

   Explains the significance of the recorders that appear in the coat of arms of Margaret Vernon (*née* Pype), wife of Sir William Vernon (d. 1467). The shield appears in various buildings associated with the Vernon family.

59. Kaye, Martin. "The Cornett in Context, II: Employment." *Continuo* 11, no. 1 (January 1987): 2–6.

   Begins a stimulating article on the use of the cornett by pointing out that recorders seem to have had a much smaller role in Renaissance music than the pre-eminent one claimed for them by pioneering modern writers. Kaye identifies an effective, and apparently authentic, combination of soft instruments for four-part music as cornett, alto recorder, tenor recorder, and bass viol.

60. Wright, Laurence. "The Recorder Consort in the Renaissance." *The Recorder and Music Magazine* 1, no. 6 (August 1964): 179–80.

   A compilation of 15th- and 16th-century references to recorder consorts. Also discusses the composition of a typical consort (alto in G, two tenors, and a bass).

BAROQUE

61. Alizon, Jean-François. "Amateurs et professionels au XVIIIème siècle" [Amateurs and professionals in the 18th century]. *Flûte à bec* 5 (December 1982): 28–29. In English as: "Amateurs and Professionals in the 18th Century." *NEMA Journal* 2 (January 1985): [16–18].

   Written to refute the commonly heard modern statement that "the recorder was an instrument only for amateurs in the 18th century." Concludes that in fact perhaps one of the greatest advantages of the instrument was that it belonged "to different strata of society and culture."

62. Dolmetsch, Carl. "Recorder and German Flute during the 17th and 18th Centuries." *Proceedings of the Royal Musical Association* 83 (1957): 49–63.

Traces the parallel development of the recorder and flute in the 16th-18th centuries, citing many contemporary sources (mostly about the recorder). Concludes with evidence that the recorder was played through the end of the 18th century. The Discussion following the paper includes a description by Dolmetsch of six ways of "varying the volume as well as the colour of the recorder."

* Newman, Joel. "Eighteenth-Century Promenades." See items **NEWM/Comm**, **NEWM/Easy**, and **NEWM/Wals**.

63. *The Recorder in the 17th Century: Proceedings of the International Recorder Symposium Utrecht, 27-30 August 1993.* Edited by David Lasocki. Utrecht: STIMU, forthcoming in 1994-95.

Contents will include: David Lasocki, "The Recorder in England in the 17th Century"; Patricia Ranum, "*Tu-ru-tu* and *tu-ru-tu-tu*: Towards an Understanding of Hotteterre's Tonguing Syllables"; Ton Moonen, "Bore Measurements of Early Woodwind Instruments"; Beryl Kenyon de Pascual, "The Recorder 'Revival' in Late 17th-Century Spain"; Peter van Heyghen, "The Recorder in the Early 17th-Century Canzona and Sonata"; Philippe Bolton, "Problems in Building 17th-Century Recorders"; Laurence Pottier, "Iconography of the Recorder in Late 17th-Century France"; Martin Kirnbauer, "Fire Without Smoke? An Approach to Recorder Making in Nuremberg in the 17th Century"; Stefaan Ottenbourgs, "Sound Characteristics of Rottenburgh Recorders"; Ruth van Baak Griffioen, "A Field Guide to the Flowers of the *Fluyten Lust-hof*: Notes on the Familiarity of the Tunes Van Eyck Chose"; Thiemo Wind, "Jacob van Eyck's *Der Fluyten Lust-hof*: Composition, Improvisation, or . . . ?"; Jan Bouterse, "Dutch Recorders of the 17th Century in Relation to van Eyck"; Eva Legêne, "The Recorder in the Paintings of Edwaert Collier"; Barthold Kuijken, "Lack of 17th-Century Repertoire: Consequences for the Practical Musician"; and David Lasocki, "Gaps in Our Knowledge of the Recorder in the 17th Century and How They Could be Filled."

64. Waitzman, Daniel. "The Decline of the Recorder in the 18th Century." *The American Recorder* 8, no. 2 (Spring 1967): 47–51. Reprinted in *Recorder & Music Magazine* 2, no. 7 (November 1967): 222-25.

Proposes six reasons for the decline: (1) the instrument lacked a significant class of professional players, (2) the recorder's true nature was not appreciated, (3) the high tessitura of the instrument discouraged composers from writing idiomatically for the instrument, (4) the exploitation of the highest registers posed special problems for makers and players (Waitzman claims the addition of the bell key "might well have enabled the recorder to hold its own throughout the eighteenth century . . . "), (5) interest in clarino instruments was waning, and (6) the combination of the first five factors gave the recorder a bad reputation, which discouraged serious students from studying the instrument. Concludes with an essay on why the recorder has maintained its bad reputation in the 20th century and has thus failed to win the consideration it deserves as a professional instrument equal to the flute or oboe. Letters by William Metcalfe and Daniel A. Driscoll in *The American Recorder* 8, no. 3 (Summer 1967): 101-2. Waitzman replies to Metcalfe in 8, no. 4 (Fall 1967): 134; on the same page is a letter from Marcel Clark. Letter from Bruce Haynes in 9, no. 1 (Winter 1968): 33-34, to which Waitzman replies in 9, no. 3 (Summer 1968): 94-95. (See also Haynes's lengthy refutation published as item 354.) Letters by Fabienne Smith, Brian Crispin, and A.A. Savage in *Recorder & Music Magazine* 2, no. 8 (February 1968): 243. Carl Dolmetsch rises to Waitzman's (and his own) defense in item 355.

CLASSICAL

65. MacMillan, Douglas. "The Recorder in the Late Eighteenth and Early Nineteenth Centuries." *The Consort* 39 (1983): 489-97.

    Summarizes a Fellow of Trinity College London thesis on this subject. Lists fifty surviving recorders, seventeen pieces of music, twelve methods, and several pictures and references to the instrument in literature from the period in question. A useful compilation of information, although some is inadequately evaluated, and the author leaves to someone else the task of placing it in context and writing a real history. A letter from Dale Higbee in 40 (1984): 45-46 points out the need to distinguish recorders from czakans, vertical flutes, and flageolets.

66. Newman, Joel. "The 'Easy Recorder' Myth." (Eighteenth-Century Promenades, 2) *The American Recorder* 4, no. 3 (August 1963): 6.

    Cites the earliest source encountered by Newman that presents the recorder as an instrument anyone can play: *Essai sur la musique ancienne et modern* (1780) by Jean Benjamin de Laborde.

Geographical Focus

Austria

67. Seifert, Herbert. "Die Bläser der kaiserlichen Hofkapelle zur Zeit von J.J. Fux" [The winds of the imperial court Kapelle at the time of J.J. Fux]. In *Johann Joseph Fux und die barocke Bläsertradition: Kongressbericht Graz 1985*, edited by Bernhard Habla, 9–23. (Alta Musica, 9) Tutzing: Hans Schneider, 1987. ISBN 3795204941.

    Identifies those oboists of the court who are known to have also played the recorder: the Glätz brothers (Franz, Roman, and Xaver), Gottfried Muffat, and Ludwig Schön. In addition the organist and theorbist Georg Reutter was said to play the recorder "to perfection."

France

68. Bowers, Jane M. "'Flaüste traverseinne' and 'Flûte d'Allemagne': The Flute in France from the Late Middle Ages up through 1702." *"Recherches" sur la musique française classique* 19 (1979): 7–49.

    Although this article is mainly concerned with the transverse flute, it does mention some instances of the use (or possible use) of the recorder in France, and in its comprehensiveness and imaginative research methods it points the way for similar research on the recorder.

69. Ranum, Patricia. "A Sweet Servitude: A Musician's Life at the Court of Mlle de Guise." *Early Music* 15, no. 3 (August 1987): 347–60.

    Discusses the music making at the residence of one of the most important patrons in France in the late 17th century, Marie de Lorraine, also known as Mademoiselle de Guise. Both she and the director of her musical ensemble "clearly preferred the instruments in vogue during their youth: viols, recorders and theorbo." One of her composers-in-residence was Marc-Antoine Charpentier. Among her musicians was the recorder player Étienne Loulié. He may also have composed music for her and for another important patron, Elizabeth d'Orléans, known as Madame de Guise, the widow of Marie's nephew.

Germany

70. Polk, Keith. *German Instrumental Music of the Late Middle Ages: Players, Patrons and Performance Practice.* Cambridge: Cambridge University Press, 1992. xvi, 272 p. ISBN 0521385210.

    Who played instrumental music before the 16th century, who did they play for, and what do we know about their music? The surviving evidence published so far has given us scattered, tantalizing glimpses at a lost improvisatory tradition. Polk has now consolidated his work of a lifetime into a book that sheds more light on the subject that we might have expected. Begins with an overview of the instruments, including of course the recorder, which was generally an alternative instrument for professional musicians as well as a key instrument for amateurs. Discusses the courts and the cities, drawing on extensive archival research. All this, occupying more than half the book, introduces chapters on the music itself: "Sources and Written Repertory of Instrumental Polyphony" and "Approaches to Instrumental Performance Practice: Models of Extemporaneous Techniques." An essential book for all players of early wind instruments. Joan Rimmer in a review essay in *Music & Letters* 75, no. 1 (February 1994): 47–57 finds it "an extraordinarily inconsistent book, whose components sit uneasily together in a single volume."

Great Britain

71. Boxall, Maria. "Elizabeth Henthorn's Recorder Books." *Recorder & Music* 6, no. 9 (March 1980): 263–64.

    Written as an addendum to item 540. Describes two small "blank" books that a young amateur named Elizabeth Henthorn used in the late 17th century to record exercises, simple tunes, rudiments of music theory, and directions for fingering the recorder.

71.1. Galpin, Francis W. *Old English Instruments of Music: Their History and Character.* 4th ed., rev. with supplementary notes by Thurston Dart. New York: Barnes & Noble; London: Methuen, 1965. xxviii, 254 p. OCLC #744403 (U.S. ed.), #896676 (U.K. ed.). Earlier editions: London: Methuen & Co., 1910. xxv, 327 p. (Reprint: Clair Shores, Mich.: Scholarly Press, 1978. OCLC #4365687). Chicago: A.C. McClurg, 1911. xxv, 327 p. OCLC #6675999. 3d ed., rev.: London, Methuen, 1932. xxvii, 327 p. OCLC #1855001.

A history of instruments in England written at an early stage in the revival of the recorder. See chapter 7, "Recorder and Flute," which covers the recorder, flageolet, and tabor pipe, with an emphasis on folk and popular instruments.

72. Lasocki, David Ronald Graham. *Professional Recorder Players in England, 1540–1740.* 2 vols. Ph.D. dissertation, The University of Iowa, 1983. xxii, 985 leaves. OCLC #11878003, #15183439. UMI order no. 83-27401.

A comprehensive study of recorder playing in England by professional musicians between 1540 (from which date onwards significant numbers of relevant documents have survived) and 1740 (when the recorder virtually died out). It makes use of a wide variety of archival and musical sources, many unpublished.

Volume 1 discusses the settings and performing groups in which professionals played recorders. It also presents general conclusions about the recorder players themselves: their identity, training, musicianship, careers, rewards, and status.

The first part demonstrated for the first time the existence of a recorder consort at Court from 1540 to 1630 and considers its personnel, standard of performance, repertory, instruments, duties, rewards, and privileges (revised version published as item 74). A further chapter describes the reorganized single group of Court wind musicians, 1630–1685.

The second part treats the Renaissance recorder outside the Court. The recorder consort was employed by musicians of noblemen, theatre musicians (revised version published as item 75), and civic musicians (waits). The instrument also played a small role in the mixed consort.

The third part is devoted to the Baroque recorder, and its employment singly or in pairs in the music of the Court, noble households, the new public concerts, the theaters (especially their popular intermission entertainments), and the opera house.

Demonstrates that the study of music history from the perspective of the musicians who played the music yields insights into: the size and nature of the repertory; the dependence of the publishers on music written by and for professionals; the changes in musical style, instrumentation, and performance practices that came with the many foreign performer-composers; and the recorder itself—its attractions and limitations, and the reasons for its decline and fall. (Volume 2 is biographical: see chapter 23 under the subheading "Bassano family" [p. 279].)

This dissertation won the 1984 Distinguished Dissertation Award of the Council of Graduate Schools in America/University Microfilms International. A preliminary version was published as item 73. Further tidbits on recorder players in England may be found in passing in Peter Holman's masterly study *Four and Twenty Fiddlers: The Violin at the English Court 1540–1690* (Oxford: Clarendon Press, 1993).

73. Lasocki, David. "Professional Recorder Playing in England, 1500-1740." *Early Music* 10, no. 1 (January 1982): 23-29; 10, no. 2 (April 1982): 183-91. Part 1: 1500-1640; part 2: 1640-1740.

A preliminary version of the findings presented in item 72. Letter from Eleanor Selfridge-Field in *Early Music* 10, no. 3 (July 1982): 417, with a reply by Lasocki.

74. Lasocki, David. "The Recorder Consort at the English Court 1540-1673." *The American Recorder* 25, no. 3 (August 1984): 91-100; 25, no. 4 (November 1984): 131-35.

An abridged version of Part B from item 72. The Court recorder consort was established in 1540 by Henry VIII. Its members were five brothers of the Bassano family, four of whom had been previously employed at the Court as sackbut players around 1531. The Bassanos introduced "the highest standards of woodwind instrument making and probably a similar standard of recorder playing." Recruitment to the consort later came partly from second- and third-generation members of the Bassanos in England, partly from other foreign musicians or their descendents, and eventually from native musicians. Part One of the article traces the personnel changes in the recorder consort over the course of more than a century, speculates on the standard of performance, and reviews the repertory of the consort (which included compositions by consort members). Part Two describes the instruments and duties of the consort, as well as the reorganization of the wind musicians at the Court around 1630.

75. Lasocki, David. "The Recorder in the Elizabethan, Jacobean and Caroline Theater." *The American Recorder* 25, no. 1 (February 1984): 3-10.

Based on two chapters in item 72. Divided into two sections: "The Elizabethan Theater, 1574-1610," and "The Recorder in the Jacobean and Caroline Theater, 1610-1642." The Elizabethan period "saw the increasing use of instrumental music in the theater, both within the drama and during the intermissions between the acts, and the hiring of professional musicians by the companies." Recorders were called for by name only rarely during this period, the most famous appearance occuring in "Hamlet." In the Jacobean and Caroline theater, instrumental music played a significant role. Musicians played during intermission, covered entrances and exits of characters, and accompanied songs and dances. Also, music was used to reinforce particular moods and emotions in the plays. Lasocki sees recorders used in three contexts: "1) apparently representing 'the music of the spheres,' they are associated with the supernatural, death, and appearances of or portents from the gods; 2) they express love, whether supernatural or mortal; and 3) they announce entrances of royalty or nobility." Quotes numerous passages calling for recorders.

* Manifold, J.S. *The Music in English Drama: From Shakespeare to Purcell.* Cited above as item 42.

76. Omitted.

77. Merryweather, James. *"York Music": The Story of a City's Music from 1304 to 1896.* York: Sessions Book Trust, The Ebor Press, 1988. 181 p. ISBN 1850720347.
A detailed history of the York Waits, based on archival material, by a member of the modern group of the same name. Charmingly illustrated with photographs of that modern group masquerading as members of the historical Waits. Two inventories-after-death mention recorders; otherwise they are not mentioned in references to instruments owned or played by the Waits.

SPAIN

78. Kenyon de Pascual, Beryl. "Instrumentos e instrumentistas españoles y extranjeros en la Real Capilla desde 1701 hasta 1749" [Spanish and foreign instruments and instrumentalists in the Royal Chapel between 1701 and 1749]. In *España en la música de occidente: Actas del Congreso Internacional celebrado en Salamanca, 29 de octubre–5 de noviembre de 1985: Año de la Música,* edited by Emilio Casares Rodicio, Ismael Fernández de la Cuesta, and José López-Calo, 93–97. Madrid: Instituto Nacional de la Artes Escénicas y de la Música, Inisterio de Cultura, 1987. OCLC #17755060.
A brief overview. Mentions the arrival at the Court of the two Hauteloche brothers, woodwind players from Flanders, in 1690. (See also her chapter in item 63.) Throughout the first half of the 18th century, flutes and recorders were used in the Royal Chapel in only two contexts: (1) requiem masses, misereres, and lamentations; (2) villancicos and cantadas.

79. Martín, Mariano. "La flauta de pico y la flauta travesera en el siglo XVIII en españa" [The recorder and flute in Spain in the 18th century]. *Revista de musicología* 8 (1985): 115–18.

Asserts that the use of the recorder and flute in 18th-century Spanish music has been difficult to trace because the repertory has scarcely been cataloged, but that a few references are now beginning to turn up. Lists (without source) a *Cantada al Santísimo con dos flautas de pico* by one Iribarren.

UNITED STATES

80. Music, David W. "The Recorder in Early America." *The American Recorder* 24, no. 3 (August 1983): 102-5.

    Compendium of references to the recorder in 17th- and 18th-century American books and newspapers. Many of the citations are taken from advertisements. Speculates on what music might have been played and why the recorder apparently did not appear on concert programs. Includes an arrangement for recorder in F and piano of "The Nightingale," an anonymous piece published in New York ca. 1799-1803.

5

Periods: Modern

This chapter looks at general sources on the recorder in the 20th century (including its revival) as well as those focusing on aspects of recorder life in particular countries.

81. Boeke, Kees. "Recorder Now." *Early Music* 10, no. 1 (January 1982): 7-9.

Boeke touches upon a number of topics in this brief essay, offering some interesting and occasionally provocative insights. Attributes the ability of the recorder to either repel or entice listeners to its unusual, pure tone quality, which has strong extramusical associations for most listeners. Attempts to account for recorder players' persistent desire to obtain better instruments by noting that many players work under the delusion that, because sounding the recorder requires no special embouchure, the tone produced depends solely on the quality of the instrument. Asserts that the recorder became a protagonist in the revival of early music because it "lacked any successor after 1750," which "ensured its survival as the archetypal 'old instrument.'" Closes with reflections on the place of early music in musical life today and the ability of early and new music to revolutionize musical life and the way we think about music.

82. Braun, Gerhard. "Das sterbende Pan: Aspekte des Blockflötenspiels am Ende des 20. Jahrhunderts" [The dying Pan: aspects of recorder playing at the end of the 20th century]. *Tibia* 7, no. 3 (1982): 188-91.

Headed by a quotation from Theodor W. Adorno (1956): "Der Blockflöte ist der schmählichste Tod des erneut stets sterbenden großen Pan" [The recorder is the most ignominious death of the constantly dying Great Pan]. Begins with a resume of the recorder's role in Germany in the early 20th century, from Waldemar Woehl's view of the instrument as a kind of organ pipe that cannot really be affected by the player (1930), up to Adorno's attack, seconded by his student Heinz Klaus Metzger, on all attempts to play early music with its historical sound quality. These "naive beginnings" of course soon gave way to the "Baroque boom, still flourishing today" and a vastly changed attitude towards the recorder. Recorder making has taken similar giant steps. And the avant garde has made a great deal of the recorder's tone color(s), so that "from the historical model has come an instrument of our time. Here Pan lives or raises himself up constantly new, like a phoenix from the ashes."

83. Ehrlich, Robert. "Our Recorder Culture: A Pyramid Built on Sand?" *American Recorder* 34, no. 3 (September 1993): 7–11.

    "Adapted from a talk given at the International Recorder Symposium, Karlsruhe, 1992." An interesting and insightful essay on the sociology of recorder-playing "cultures." The pyramid referred to in the title has "star" professional performers at its apex, professional player-teachers at its center, and school-age students at its base. (Ehrlich argues that adult amateurs play no significant part in a recorder culture.) The health and the stability of the pyramid is dependent on its base; those countries with flourishing recorder cultures are also seen to support recorder instruction in the schools. Since most recorder players cannot support themselves solely by performing (unlike violinists and other mainstream instrumentalists), teaching is an essential source of income for recorder professionals, and support for the recorder at the school level provides these necessary teaching opportunities. Ehrlich compares the recorder cultures of Germany, the Netherlands, and Great Britain to show how his theory plays out in reality.

84. Ehrlich, Robert. "Prejudice, Practice and Pride: How to be a Happy Recorder Player." *The Recorder: Journal of the Victorian Recorder Guild* 12 (December 1990): 1–5; 13 (July 1991): 5–13.

    In light of Frans Brüggen's confessions (see items 959 and 965), it seems ironic that Robert Ehrlich names him, and the "Dutch recorder school" which followed in his wake, for establishing that almost uniquely twentieth-century musician the professional recorder player—defined as "someone who earns all or most of his or her living from playing and teaching the recorder." Ehrlich's persuasive and engagingly written tour de force, based on his Cambridge University master's thesis (item 1458), argues that "the emergence of a substantial number of professional recorder players in the last thirty years, concentrated in Northern Europe and particularly in Holland" is "a phenomenon very much the consequence of modern marketing techniques and the educational and welfare policies of the Dutch government." These new players "have succeeded in emancipating their instrument from its traditional, subservient role as the doubling instrument of the professional flautist or oboist. For the first time since the 16th century . . . we have a really detailed knowledge of how to play the recorder as a first instrument." Ehrlich examines in detail the role of the recorder in the Baroque era as well as the three branches of recorder playing in the 20th century: amateur, school, and professional. He concludes with a personal credo about why he calls himself a professional, how he freely adopts and adapts his repertory, and why he wants to learn to play the instrument even better. Highly recommended.

85. Felder, Denise. "Zur Entwicklung der Blockflöte im 20. Jahrhundert" [On the development of the recorder in the 20th century]. *Zeitschrift SAJM* 21, no. 1 (January 1993): 19–36; 21, no. 2 (March 1993): 3–17; 21, no. 3 (May 1993): 3–17; 21, no. 4 (July 1993): 3–17; 21, no. 6 (November 1993): 3–19.

A German translation of apparently her entire master's thesis (originally in French under the title "Contribution à l'étude de la renaissance de la flûte à bec au XXe siècle" [Contribution to the study of the renaissance of the recorder in the 20th century]). Each part includes French summaries.

Covers: what happened to the recorder in the late 18th and 19th centuries (diminishing number of recorder pieces; the development of English and French flageolets and czakans); the renaissance of the recorder in the 20th century in England (Dolmetsch) and Germany (Gurlitt, Danckert, Harlan); an "excursion" about the development of recorder design in the Middle Ages, Renaissance, and Baroque; alterations in design in the 20th century; recorder manufacture; recorder woods used by different makers, including the question about whether the material matters; the construction of a recorder; different fingering systems; tips on recorder performance (playing in, warming up, cooling down, care); copying early instruments; some "exotic" new instruments (by Paetzold, Twaalfhoven, Gosselink, MIDI by Suzuki, Grabbe); chart of sizes and names. An informed and useful overview, well illustrated.

86. Hauwe, Walter van. "Plädoyer für eine Akzentverschiebung im Blockflötenunterricht" [Plea for a shift in emphasis in recorder instruction]. *Tibia* 15, no. 2 (1990): 128–31.

Wide-ranging ruminations on the future of the recorder. The great change in the status of the recorder over the last twenty-five years has come about more from concertizing than from teaching. Although recorder players have written their own compositions, the significant new contributions to the literature have come largely from composers who do not play the instrument. Despite their enormous technical improvements, recorder players are frustrated with the quality of their literature from all periods. The recorder is accepted in many pop and folk music circles. Contemporary art music is on the periphery in our society, a place where the recorder is used to operating and is most at home. Too many recorder players aspire to being soloists, although only a handful really have the talent. The recorder should therefore: (1) return to the periphery, (2) get away from purely soloistic thinking, (3) return to the ensemble, where the instrument has its roots and in which the literature of various periods is concentrated. Unadulterated soloists should still be encouraged to be soloists, unadulterated teachers to teach, and unadulterated ensemble players to play in ensembles.

87. Letteron, Claude. "L'amateur de flûte à bec" [The recorder amateur]. *Flûte à bec & instruments anciens* 18 (June 1986): 26–28; 19 (September 1986): 23–24; 20 (1986): 27–28.

    Begins with the statistic that although many people buy recorders with the intention of learning to play them, most people abandon the effort within three years. Suggests that they do so because they are isolated musically. Proposes to remedy the situation with a kind of amateur recorder club where they can talk over their problems. Continues with further thoughts on recorder playing for amateurs: choice of method; problems of the individual; sight-reading; patience, fortitude, and fun. The second part of the article covers useful terms in several languages, and major publishers.

88. Noble, Richard D.C. "The Recorder in Twentieth Century Music: A Personal View." *The Recorder and Music Magazine* 1, no. 8 (February 1965): 243–44.

    Laments the failure of modern composers up to that date to produce recorder works that can stand on their own as significant compositions. Noble believes that composers have not taken the instrument seriously, and, as a result, the instrument has failed to assume its "place as a valid instrument to vie for public favour with other string and wind instruments in concert performance." He embarks on a survey of the 20th-century repertory, pointing out along the way why each piece falls short of greatness. But, "[w]ithout this pioneer work and without the virtuoso performers of the present day, ideas for greater advancement would not have arisen." Letter from John Turner in 1, no. 9 (May 1965): 277.

89. Moeck, Hermann. "Narziß macht den Musen Konkurrenz: Gespräch aus der Ferne zu einem immer wieder neuen Thema" [Narcissus gives the muses competition: a discourse from afar on a theme again and again new]. *Tibia* 14, no. 3 (1989): 490–95.

    Musings on narcissism, old and new, taking its inspiration from Christopher Lasch's *The Culture of Narcissism: American Life in an Age of Diminishing Expectation* (1979; German translation, 1982). Includes thoughts on Adorno's famous 1956 quotation about the recorder (see item 82), which Moeck finds "a harsh but not completely incorrect criticism measured against the dilletantish conditions of that time." He finds the quotation

Periods: Modern 37

perhaps relevant today from another side: the recorder runs the risk of becoming an instrument for "alternative types" [Aussteiger], as demonstrated by the "hypertrophy" of solo playing, done less for music and its interpretation than for "self-expression." He also cites recorder players who are interested only in modern recorder music and not the rest of musical life.

* O'Kelly, Eve Elizabeth. *The Recorder Today*. Cited below as item 820.

90. Pehrsson, Clas. "Is the Recorder a Legitimate Instrument in the 20th Century?" *American Recorder* 31, no. 4 (December 1990): 7-9. Another translation as "The Recorder—An Instrument in its Own Right in the Twentieth Century?" *E.R.T.A. Newsletter* 2 (November 1993): 1-3. In German as: "Die Blockflöte—ein vollwertiges Instrument im 20. Jahrhundert?" *Zeitschrift SAJM* 20, no. 2 (March 1992): 23-26.

    From a lecture delivered at the 1990 International Recorder Symposium in Karlsruhe, Germany. Begins by tracing the rise of the recorder from its relative obscurity before 1960 to its generally perceived status of legitimacy today. Questions whether the instrument has truly attained this status, since it lacks a body of significant compositions from established composers, performers are dissatisfied and move on to other musical pastures, the audience is specialized, and in music schools the recorder is not standing up against established instruments. Complains about the low standard of recorder teaching in music schools caused by shortcomings in pedagogy and method. Proposes to remedy that by an integration of technique and interpretation, to produce an "interpretation technique," which he hopes can lead to "closeness of style" and more relevant modern music making.

91. Vetter, Michael. "Leistungsmöglichkeiten der Blockflöte und ihre Tauglichkeit für die neue Musik" [Performance possibilities of the recorder and its suitability for new music]. *Kontakte* /5 (1966): 191-92.

    Argues that Jürg Baur's "recorder revolution" is not a revolution in the sense that the new will replace the old. The role of the recorder as an amateur, children's, and early music instrument will be supplemented by its avant-garde capabilities, as considerable as they may be.

92. Weilenmann, Matthias. "Aspecte—Anmerkungen zur Rolle der Blockflöte heute" [Aspects of/remarks on the role of the recorder today]. *Tibia* 13, no. 3 (1988): 193–95.

Like Braun (see item 82), Weilenmann begins with Adorno's attitude to the recorder (1956), an instrument "with a tone at once insipid and flaccid," contrasting that with Ganassi's view that the recorder was capable of imitating all aspects of the human voice. It was not until a few years after Adorno that Frans Brüggen and others began to take the recorder out of its "unreal existence" to establish it as a "regular" musical instrument. Insists that we should remember the basics for the recorder: (1) its true musical province was and is chamber music in its most diverse forms; (2) it plays a critical role in music education; (3) its professionals have their opportunities outside the normal concert circuit.

Comments on the importance of alternative and shade fingerings to achieve good intonation. Puts forward the theory that the recorder disappeared in the 18th century because it lacked players who would have treated it as a first instrument and therefore developed its potential (see also item 64). Believes that it is vital for us to study the sociological, political, and cultural environment of the instrument.

93. Weilenmann, Matthias. "Die Blockflöte—ein historisches Instrument in progressiver Rolle" [The recorder: an historical instrument in a progressive role]. *Quartalszeitschrift SAJM* 15, no. 2 (June 1987). Not seen.

94. "Why Don't Recorder Players Take Their Instrument Seriously?" *The American Recorder* 29, no. 2 (May 1988): 57–58.

Includes contributions by Richard McChesney, and Kenneth Wollitz and Nina Stern (adapted from "Some Thoughts on Workshops," *Historical Performance* 1, no. 1 [1988]: 42–44). Both essays support a fundamental belief: the better one plays, the more one enjoys playing. McChesney wonders why the level of playing remains so low among amateurs and why so few make any attempt to improve their playing. Stern and Wollitz raise the same questions and observe that many amateurs are strongly resistent to technical exercises and practice. Responses from readers appear in: 29, no. 4 (November 1988): 167–69; 30, no. 1 (February 1989): 38–39; and 30, no. 3 (August 1989): 122.

TWENTIETH-CENTURY REVIVAL

95. Katz, Erich. "In the Beginning." *The American Recorder* 2, no. 1 (Winter 1961): 3–4.

Katz's reminiscences of the early 20th-century revival of early music. Focuses on the necessary rejection of 19th-century "attitudes and prejudices" toward early music.

96. Kinsell, David. "J.C. Bridge and the Recorder." *Recorder & Music* 5, no. 5 (March 1976): 157-60.

A review of Bridge's role in the revival of the recorder, based on a study of material in the archives of the city of Chester. Covers the history of the Chester recorders. Includes the score of Bridge's Quartet for Recorders, first performed in 1901 and considered by Kinsell to be "almost certainly the first piece of 'modern' recorder music." Letter from Carl Dolmetsch in 5, no. 6 (June 1976): 216.

97. Kirnbauer, Martin. "'Das war Pionierarbeit.'—Die Bogenhauser Künstlerkapelle, ein frühes Ensemble alter Musik" ["That was pioneering work"—The Bogenhausen Künstkapelle, an early ensemble for early music]. In *Alte Musik: Konzert und Rezeption. Sonderband der Reihe "Basler Jahrbuch für historische Musikpraxis" zum 50. Jubiläum des Vereins der "Freunde alter Musik in Basel,"* edited by Veronika Gutmann, 37-67. Winterthur, Switzerland: Amadeus, 1992. OCLC #27882462.

Fills out the astonishing history of the Bogenhausen Künstlerkapelle (first sketched in item 99), which performed early music on recorders and other instruments from 1899 to 1939. The concert programs, the music collection, and the instruments used by the Kapelle have all survived (in an unnamed private collection) and are described by Kirnbauer. The instruments include recorders by J.C. Denner (including an ivory alto with double 6th and 7th fingerholes) and Jacob Denner (see also item 209), Bressan (two altos in an original case), Schuechbaur, Walch, J.W. Oberlender I, Schell, and anon., as well as a copy of a Denner alto made by the Munich maker Gottlieb Gerlach by 1909 (photograph), "probably the earliest [modern] copy of a Baroque recorder." The Germanische Nationalmuseum will be publishing a catalog of the instruments and a summary of the music holdings. An appendix to the article lists the main events in the life of the Kapelle and its woodwind instruments.

98. Linde, Hans-Martin. "Wie Pans Mysterium die Welt bewegt: Anmerkungen zu einem 'geschichtsträchtigen' Instrument: Blockflöte und Traverso" [How the mystery of Pan's moves the world: remarks on an instrument 'pregnant with history'—recorder and traverso]. *Neue Musikzeitung*, February/March 1984, 49-50.

After a long introduction on the meaning of flutes in the world, posits three phases in the rediscovery of the recorder in the 20th century: (1) an appreciation for the alleged "simplicity and plainness" of its tone, (2) a growing feeling for the wider musical and technical possibilities of the recorder as a "real" instrument, and (3) the dream of "authentic" playing based on historical sources.

99. Moeck, Hermann. "Zur 'Nachgeschichte' und Renaissance der Blockflöte" [On the "post-history" and renaissance of the recorder]. *Tibia* 3, no. 1 (1978): 13–20; 3, no. 2 (1978): 79–88. English translation, mostly of part 2, as "The Twentieth-Century Renaissance of the Recorder in Germany." Edited by Jean Seiler and William Hettrick. *The American Recorder* 23, no. 2 (May 1982): 61–68.

Part 1 takes us to the early 1920s. "As an orchestra and chamber music instrument, the recorder did not survive the Baroque period." But some recorder-like instruments were popular among amateurs in the second half of the 18th century and the whole of the 19th: the French flageolet, the English flageolet, and the czakan. Nevertheless, Carl Maria von Weber seems to have scored for the recorder twice (*Peter Schmoll und seine Nachbarn*, 1801; *Kleiner Tusch*, 1806) and Hector Berlioz once (*La fuite en Egypte*, 1853); Donizetti owned three recorders. The revival of the recorder came in the late 19th century (date not specified) when Professor Dumon of Brussels and his students played a march for eight recorders and drum in London. Around 1890 was founded the Bogenhausen Künstlerkapelle under Josef Wagener, an amateur group that lasted for fifty or sixty years (a detailed letter on the subject from Wagener is quoted). Beginning around 1924 Gustav Scheck became "perhaps the father of 'artistic' recorder playing." But the main instigator of the recorder revival was of course Arnold Dolmetsch. Independently, Wilibald Gurlitt, a musicologist in Freiburg, began using recorders in his Collegium Musicum in 1921 (letter from him quoted). Similarly, in 1922 the Nuremberg woodwind maker Georg Grässel made copies of the Kinsecker recorders in the Nuremberg museum; around 1924 Max Hüller followed suit and also made copies of various late Baroque recorders. In 1923 Werner Danckerts began using such copies in his early music performances in Jena, Dessau, and Erfurt (letter from Danckerts cites performances by others).

Part 2 covers in detail the recorder movement in Germany from the early 1920s through the 1930s (skirting around its association with the Hitler Youth Movement). Peter Harlan's search for a simple folk instrument playable by anyone (children in particular) was the impetus behind the movement. Discusses historical fingerings and the true origin of Harlan's "German" fingering (surprisingly, Ganassi's fingering chart). Explains that the confusion over fingering systems and the availability of

recorders in as many as seven pitches led many amateurs in Germany to give up the instrument.
An important article, based on much new research.

100. Pringle, Rosa. "Revival of the Ancient Recorder: An Interview with Irmgard Lehrer." *Etude* 59 (November 1941): 732, 782.
"During the past ten years there has been a very definite movement in Europe and in America to revive the ancient recorder so frequently mentioned in history and literature. The instrument has a peculiar appeal to children.—EDITOR'S NOTE." An interesting—and occasionally amusing—early account of the revival of the recorder written for the musical layman. Lehrer was "director of old instruments" at the Greenwich House Music School in New York City and founder and director of "The Center for Old Music." Describes the history of the recorder and quotes references to the instrument by Shakespeare and Pepys. Some of the quainter passages include Lehrer's account of the recorder's "temporary retreat before more aggressive instruments in our modern categories" and the caption "Recorders with a primitive stringed instrument" beneath a photograph of two recorder players and a harpsichordist.

POPULAR MUSIC

101. Noble, Richard D.C. "The New Recorder Sound." *The Recorder and Music Magazine* 1, no. 9 (May 1965): 275–76.
A profile of the Falling Leaves, an Oxford-based rhythm-and-blues band that employed the recorder.

102. Noble, Richard. "The Recorder in Pop: A Progress Report." *Recorder and Music Magazine* 2, no. 5 (May 1967): 135–36.
Discusses the use of the recorder by the Rolling Stones ("Ruby Tuesday") and Manfred Mann ("Trouble and Tea").

GEOGRAPHICAL FOCUS

AUSTRALIA

103. Hughes, Geoff. "Victorian Recorders Before the Guild." *The Recorder: Journal of the Victorian Recorder Guild* 14 (December 1991): 18–20.
Memoirs of the author's part in the recorder movement in Victoria from 1949 until the founding of the VRG in 1971. Among other things,

chronicles Fred Morgan's beginnings as the soprano recorder player in a church youth recorder group at the age of 16. Plenty of Aussie humor.

104. Tattersall, Malcolm. "The Recorder in the Twenty-First Century." *The Recorder* 17 (September 1993): 2–8.

Tattersall's valedictory article as editor of *The Recorder: Journal of the Victorian Recorder Guild*. He goes out with a bang not a whimper, attempting "to project emerging trends in the recorder world, particularly in Australia, into the medium-term future—the next five to fifteen years." The standard of instrument making has risen. Professional performance standards have increased dramatically too, but are levelling off. Recorder recitalists still have a relatively limited repertoire and play in one of two ghettos, early music or avant garde. "There is really not much work for a professional who plays only recorder." In schools, "the recorder is being treated less as a teaching aid and more as an instrument." The amateur playing community is shrinking and "greying." Still, the recorder's amateur repertory is better than that of many other instruments. Professionals and amateurs are tending to live in two different worlds. The future of the recorder will be less eventful than the recent past.

105. Waterman, Rodney. "Recorders . . . and All That Jazz." *The Recorder: Journal of the Victorian Recorder Guild* 6 (June 1987): 26–28.

Enthuses about Lazy Ade Monsbourgh, the "father" of Australian jazz, who has been playing the recorder in jazz and ragtime since the early 1950s. Also reveals that recorders were first manufactured in Australia by Monsbourgh and another jazz player, Don "Pixie" Roberts, "not directly as a result of the European Dolmetsch-led early music revival."

For more on Monsbourgh and Roberts, see Bruce Johnson, *The Oxford Companion to Australian Jazz* (Melbourne: Oxford University Press, 1987), 213–14, 246, passim.

BELGIUM

106. Boullet, Jean-Pierre. "La situation de la flûte à bec en Belgique" [The state of the recorder in Belgium]. *Flûte à bec* 3 (June 1982): 23–24.

Reports that, although the recorder is doing well in Flanders (the Dutch-speaking part of Belgium), in the French-speaking part of the country the instrument is little known and appreciated.

Periods: Modern

GERMANY

107. Rose, Pete. "Gerhard Braun on the Recorder and Education in Germany." *American Recorder* 34, no. 3 (September 1993): 12.

Interview conducted at the 1992 International Recorder Symposium in Karlsruhe, Germany. Covers: the position of the recorder in German musical life and how it is changing; prospects for professional study and employment in Germany; his promotion of new music; how avant-garde techniques and Johannes Fischer's work (see item 778) have broadened the dynamic range of the recorder; the future of the recorder.

108. Sayers, Keith. "Recorders on the Elbe." *Recorder & Music Magazine* 3, no. 10 (June 1971): 365–66.

Sayer makes observations on recorder playing in Germany, after having taught three years in Hamburg. Covers: the German educational system; the prevalence of German fingering and the problems it causes; popular instrument makers; the tendency toward overblowing and a "swooping" style of playing. The remarks on German fingering elicit a letter from Hermann Moeck in 3, no. 11 (September 1971): 411, with a reply from Sayers and a comment by Edgar Hunt.

ISRAEL

109. Tidhar, Shlomo. "Blockflötenspiel in Israel" [Recorder playing in Israel]. *Tibia* 3, no. 1 (1978): 38–39.

The recorder ("halilith") plays an important role in music education in modern Israel. Tidhar was the first Israeli recorder player to study abroad (with Linde in Basel). He now teaches in Tel Aviv, plays in a recorder consort and a Baroque ensemble that concertizes and broadcasts widely, and has written a recorder method. Israeli composers have begun to write for the instrument and a recorder factory has been set up in Gewim Kibbuz.

ITALY

110. Alton, Edwin. "The Recorder in Italy." *Recorder & Music* 5, no. 1 (March 1975): 6–7.

Alton, a frequent visitor to Italy as a recorder teacher, describes the activities and events of summer 1974. Covers: the musicianship of the children of Amico Dolci; the Sixth Summer Course organized by the Societa Italiana del Flauto Dolce (the Italian Recorder Society); the Society itself, its Bulletin, and its *Armonia Strumentale* music series; the First Competition for the Recorder (a composition contest sponsored by the

Society); Italian music shops. The article is followed by a report of recent activities of the Accademia del Flauto Dolce, based in Turin.

JAPAN

111. Tada, Ichiro. "The Recorder in Japan." *Early Music* 10, no. 1 (January 1982): 38–40.
A sketchy, incomplete history of recorder playing and making in Japan.

POLAND

112. Hunt, Rosemary. "The Polish Scene: Recorders and Early Music in Warsaw." *Recorder & Music Magazine* 3, no. 10 (June 1971): 367.
Describes the work of two Warsaw musicians: Jozef Klukowski, a recorder teacher at the music school, and a Professor Piwkowski, bassoonist and director of the school, who founded the early music group Fistulatores et Tubicinatores Varsovienses.

SOUTH AFRICA

113. Devroop, Chatradari. "Blockflöte und Apartheid? Aspekte der Musikerziehung in Südafrika" [Recorder and apartheid? Aspects of music education in South Africa]. *Tibia* 15, no. 3 (1990): 208–9.
Begins with a summary of the political and educational situation in South Africa, which of course has heavily favored the whites over the coloreds, Indians, and blacks. The small group of Indians, to whom the author belongs, has had more musical opportunities than the other non-whites, being able to study the recorder (although no other instrument) as well as music theory through high school. Almost all private music schools have been white. Each racial group has had its own universities, a few of which teach music (more theory than practice). Recorder teaching is generally poor, so that serious recorder players have to pick up what they can from recordings. The international boycott has severely restricted concert life and the flow of musical information.

SWITZERLAND

114. "Dokumentation: Die Konzertprogramme und die aufgeführten Werke." [Documentation: the concert programs and the works performed]. In *Alte Musik:*

Konzert und Rezeption. Sonderband der Reihe "Basler Jahrbuch für historische Musikpraxis" zum 50. Jubiläum des Vereins der "Freunde alter Musik in Basel," edited by Veronika Gutmann, 179-390. Winterthur, Switzerland: Amadeus, 1992. OCLC #27882462.

Concerns the concert programs of the "Freunde alter Musik in Basel" (Friends of Early Music in Basel). Peter Reidemeister presents a "little chronicle" of the FAMB board of directors. The second section consists of excerpts from the introductory texts of the yearly programs. The third section transcribes the programs (from 1942 to 1992); the fourth indexes them by composer and title. No fewer than forty-two recorder players are represented, most of them known primarily as players of other instruments. The changing fortunes of the recorder and its personnel in the FAMB concerts make fascinating reading.

For an earlier overview of the FAMB, see Kurt Deggeller, "Aus der Geschichte der 'Freunde alter Musik in Basel': Beobachtungen zur Konzerttätigkeit der Schola Cantorum Basiliensis in Basel," in *Alte Musik, Praxis und Reflection: Sonderband der Reihe "Basler Jahrbuch für historische Musikpraxis" zum 50. Jubiläum der Schola Cantorum Basiliensis,* edited by Peter Reidemeister and Veronika Gutmann, 77-90 (Winterthur: Amadeus, 1983).

UNITED STATES

115. Bergmann, Walter. "Recorder Playing in the States." *Recorder & Music Magazine* 3, no. 9 (March 1971): 344.

    A wry account of his trip to the [United] States in August 1970, teaching and visiting people in the recorder world. Assesses the state of the recorder movement in comparison with that in England.

116. Comstock, George W. "An Early American Recorder Consort." *American Recorder* 33, no. 4 (December 1992): 5.

    The story of the Niagara Falls High School Recorder Quartet, which played on recorders purchased in 1930 or 1931 from the Dolmetsch family by a man named Lidbury, the chief executive officer of the Oldbury Chemical Company. The quartet provided background music for various social functions throughout Niagara County, New York, for a couple of years and disbanded when the members graduated in 1932.

*   Dallin, Lynn. "'And Sweetly Trilled the Fipple Flute.'" Cited below as item 1119.

U.S.S.R. (FORMER)

117. Jürisalu, Heino. "Blockflötenmusik in der Sowjetunion" [Recorder music in the Soviet Union]. *Tibia* 12, no. 1 (1987): 364–66.

    Describes the growth of interest in the recorder in the Soviet Union during the 1970s, listing the most important teachers, groups, methods, and compositions.

118. Omitted.

6

Studies of Particular Sizes of Recorder

"The" recorder is of course a family of instruments of various sizes. This chapter discusses sources devoted to individual sizes in the past and present.

119. Benedikt, Erich. "Die Stimmlagen der Blockflöte und die Grossbass-Blockflöte" [The ranges of the recorder and contrabass recorder]. *Musikerziehung* 21, no. 1 (September 1967): 28–30.

After a long introduction on the various higher sizes of recorder and their names, discusses the bass and contrabass, their ranges, modern makers, and repertory.

120. Benedikt, Erich. "Recorders of Unusual Sizes." *Recorder & Music* 5, no. 2 (June 1975): 42–44.

An abridged English translation of item 121. A table of the various sizes (from garklein down to bass) lists the terms used to refer to the instruments in the 17th and 18th centuries.

121. Benedikt, Erich. "Ungewohnte Stimmlagen der Blockflöte und ihre Bedeutung" [Recorders with unusual ranges and their significance]. *Musikerziehung* 25, no. 4 (March 1972): 156–59; 25, no. 5 (May 1972): 210–12.

Discusses at some length the Baroque repertory (original and arrangeable) of recorders higher than the tenor (excluding the alto). An abridged English translation appeared as item 120.

122. Ganty, Henry [sic]. "Petit plaidoyer pour les grandes flûtes" [Small speech in defense of the large recorders]. *Flûte à bec & instruments anciens* 11 (June 1984): 35.

Largely on playing a voice flute or tenor recorder with continuo, the necessity for a fine instrument, choosing suitable repertory, and realizing the continuo in an appropriate manner.

123. Hunt, Edgar. "Fitting the Instrument to the Music." *Recorder & Music* 7, no. 9 (March 1983): 227-28.

A short survey of various sizes of recorders and their repertory. Covers the voice flute (d^1), fourth flute ($b\flat^1$), fifth flute (the modern soprano), sixth flute (d^2), octave flute (the modern sopranino), and Telemann's "flûte pastorelle," which Hunt believes to have been panpipes.

124. Meierott, Lenz. *Die geschichtliche Entwicklung der kleinen Flötentypen und ihre Verwendung in der Musik des 17. und 18. Jahrhunderts* [The historical development of the small members of the flute family and their use in the music of the 17th and 18th centuries]. (Wurzburger Musikhistorische Beiträge, 4) Tutzing: Hans Schneider, 1974. 279, 33 p. ISBN 3795201527.

A thorough and carefully reasoned study of the flageolet, small recorders, small fipple flutes with fewer fingerholes, the one-handed pipe, the fife, and the piccolo in the 17th-18th centuries. Recorders are dealt with in three sections: (1) a brief survey of nomenclature and surviving instruments [pp. 71-80]; (2) the "flautino" and "flauto piccolo" in Monteverdi, Praetorius, Schütz, and Schein [pp. 143-50]; and (3) France in the late 17th and early 18th centuries, drawing partly on the work of Eppelsheim (item **1278**) [pp. 155-75]. Essential reading.

GARKLEIN (c^3)

125. Thalheimer, Peter. "Aspekte zur Geschichte der Blockflöte in c''''" [Aspects of the history of the recorder in c^3]. *Tibia* 15, no. 3 (1990): 202-5.

After a survey of high recorder-like instruments in the Renaissance and early Baroque periods, describes a true recorder in c^3 that came to light during the restoration of the woodwind collection in the Musei Civici, Modena. This ivory one-piece instrument was made by the Nuremberg maker with the mark M (probably from the Mazel family) and dates from around 1670. Thalheimer goes on to describe an interesting set of high recorder-like instruments made by Carl Kruspe of Erfurt around 1930, as well as true c^3 recorders made by Rainer Weber since 1947 not to mention a few other modern makers. Letter from Erich Benedikt in 16, no. 1 (1991): 417-18.

Studies of Particular Sizes of Recorder

SOPRANINO (F^2)

126. Clark, Paul. "A Guide to the Sopranino." (For Younger Players) *Recorder and Music Magazine* 3, no. 12 (December 1971): 472-74.

    A cursory and incomplete survey of the solo and ensemble repertory for sopranino. Explains how the repertory can be extended by assigning the sopranino to soprano lines or by doubling a lower part at the octave. Begins by arguing that the sopranino is not suitable for young beginners because of the precise breath control it requires, nor is it negotiable by many adults because of its size. Clark believes that the ideal player of the instrument, therefore, is an experienced youth.

SIXTH FLUTE (D^2)

127. Higbee, Dale. "On Playing Recorders in D: Being a Short History of the Odd-Sized Recorders and Concerning the Revival of the Voice Flute & Sixth Flute." *The American Recorder* 26, no. 1 (February 1985): 16-21.

    Covers what the rather 18th-century subtitle says. Also suggests ways to adapt music for other instruments (alto recorder, flute, oboe) to the voice flute. Lists some modern makers of voice flutes and sixth flutes. Brief additions in 26, no. 3 (August 1985): 139. Letter from Alec V. Loretto in 27, no. 1 (February 1986): 38.

SOPRANO (C^2)

128. Lasocki, David. "The C Recorder in the 18th Century." *The American Recorder* 11, no. 1 (Winter 1970): 20-21.

    Although the alto in F was the most common recorder size in the late Baroque, many other sizes were in use. Lasocki isolates the popular subset of C instruments and aims "to collect all known written information about recorders in the key of C and to discuss some problems associated with them and their music." The instruments fall into three categories: the soprano as a fifth flute; the tenor as a fourth flute; and the soprano as a fourth flute. For each, Lasocki gives a summary of citations to the instrument in treatises of the time and a brief discussion of the repertory, when appropriate. Modern editions are cited in footnotes.

129. MacMillan, Douglas. "The Descant Recorder in the Early Eighteenth Century." *Recorder & Music* 7, no. 1 (March 1981): 12-13.

A brief discussion of the history and repertory of the fourth (b♭¹), fifth (c²), and sixth (d²) flutes. Letter from Ralph Leavis in 7, no. 3 (September 1981): 71.

VOICE FLUTE (D¹)

* Higbee, Dale. "On Playing Recorders in D: Being a Short History of the Odd-Sized Recorders and Concerning the Revival of the Voice Flute & Sixth Flute." Cited above as item 127.

130. Hunt, Edgar. "The Voice Flute." *The Galpin Society Journal* 10 (1957): 86–87.
   Briefly surveys the origins and repertory of the instrument.

131. Macmillan, Douglas. "The Voice Flute: An Historical Survey." *The Consort* 47 (1991): 5–7.
   Seeks to present "a distillation of the information available" on the voice flute and its music. Only a little of the information seems to be new (on the late 18th and early 19th centuries). Unfortunately, he does not distill but makes an emulsion—using only part of the available information, and committing several errors besides (the first names of Bressan and Dieupart; the dates of Schickhardt, the Talbot treatise, and Dieupart's suites). Moreover, the prose style is execrable. For a far better survey of the voice flute, see item 127.

TENOR (C¹)

132. Alker, Hugo. "The Tenor Recorder: Its Development, Special Characteristics & Repertoire." With additions and amendments by Edgar Hunt. *The Consort* 20 (July 1963): 166–73.
   Includes measurements of tenor recorders in the collection of the Vienna Kunsthistorisches Museum. Little of value on the repertory; rather, gives the standard recommendation that "the lack of original solo music for the tenor can be made up by the selection of suitable violin, oboe and viola da gamba [and viola, cello and soprano recorder] music."

* Lasocki, David. "The C Recorder in the 18th Century." Cited above as item 128.

133. White, Beverly. "Discovering the Tenor Recorder." *The American Recorder* 16, no. 2 (May 1975): 43–45.
    Defends the much-maligned instrument and suggests ways of expanding its limited repertory.

134. Wyatt, Theo. "Playing the Tenor and Bass." (Where Do I Start? [4]) *The Recorder and Music Magazine* 1, no. 7 (November 1964): 206–7.
    Opens with a few caveats to consider before taking up the tenor or bass (particularly the demands on fingers, breath, and pocketbook). Offers advice on selecting an instrument and adjusting to the changes necessary in breath support and articulation. Suggests that the best way to learn tenor or bass is through experience in a consort.

BASS (F)

135. Hersom, Herbert. "Bass Recorders in School." *Recorder and Music Magazine* 4, no. 1 (March 1972): 15–16.
    Although written with school children in mind, the article contains information of use to anyone learning the bass recorder. Includes a description of method books, advice on learning bass clef, and a discussion of possible solo repertory.

136. Hunt, Edgar. "The Baroque Bass." (The Bass Recorder) *The Recorder and Music Magazine* 1, no. 3 (November 1963): 74–75.
    A description of the instrument and its history. Although this was the era of the solo alto recorder, the bass was still played. Several period instruments have survived, as well as music for the instrument (Johann Friedrich Fasch's *Parties sur les fleut dous à 3* [ATB] and C.P.E. Bach's Trio for Viola, Bass Recorder, and Harpsichord, Helm 588). The Baroque bass was in use from about 1650 to 1750 and incorporated many of the design changes introduced to other woodwinds by the Hotteterres (jointed construction, tapered bore, a more refined tone quality, etc.). The bass in F (the "bassett") was generally direct blown, while the larger sizes employed the bocal. Some bassetts also included a simple RH4 key and an end post.

137. Hunt, Edgar. "The Modern Bass." (The Bass Recorder) *The Recorder and Music Magazine* 1, no. 4 (February 1964): 109–10.
    Concerns the history and design of the 20th-century bass. According to Hunt, the bass made its modern debut at the Haslemere Festival in 1926. Modern English basses followed Baroque models, while German basses

were patterned after Renaissance instruments. Makers modernized the instrument by extending its range to two octaves and a note and by adding keywork (in addition to the traditional RH4 key). Describes the various ways in which breath is directed to the windway in modern basses. Because of its weight, some means of support is necessary; Hunt recommends an end-pin rather than a sling. Letter from Donald Grimmer in 1, no. 6 (August 1964): 185-86.

138. Hunt, Edgar. "Playing the Bass Recorder." *Recorder & Music* 4, no. 8 (December 1973): 283-84.

    Much of the article concerns "the mechanics of the bass and finding a comfortable playing position." Describes the two basic types of instrument (direct blown and bocal) and available options, such as the addition of a sling and end-pin. Emphasizes the need for breath support and agility.

139. Hunt, Edgar. "The Renaissance Bass." (The Bass Recorder) *The Recorder and Music Magazine* 1, no. 1 (May 1963): 10-12.

    Reviews historical references to the instrument in Virdung, Ganassi, Praetorius, and the inventory of Henry VIII's instruments. Includes a photograph of a basset/bass/great-bass consort that was formerly a part of the Obizzi collection at Catajo, near Padua. Also discusses an extended great bass in the Vleeshuis at Antwerp. Hunt speculates that the makers of these larger instruments did not add keywork—except on the lowest hole—because it would have removed the flexibility of adjusting pitch by shading. Movable head joints did not appear until the time of Praetorius, since most instruments were made and voiced to be played as a part of individual consorts and there was little need for adjustment. Because most basses were blown direct, it was necessary to support the instrument between the legs; the fontanelle was added to protect the key and to avoid its accidental closing.

140. Oestreicher, Klaus. "Zur Geschichte der Baßblockflöte" [On the history of the bass recorder]. *Musik international* 12 (1981): 794-96.

    Goes over familiar territory: Virdung, Agricola, Henry VIII's inventory, Praetorius, Mersenne, Weigel, C.P.E. Bach, as well as a claimed recorder quartet by John Eccles (London, 1704) and a brief discussion of the problems of designing an instrument comfortable for the hands.

141. Primus, Constance M. "Beginning the Bass." *The American Recorder* 25, no. 2 (May 1984): 54-56.

    Covers basic technique: choosing between direct blown and bocal; finding a comfortable playing position; practicing breath control, intonation, and articulation; tips on reading bass clef. Includes an eight-item bibliography, "Practice Materials for Bass Recorders."

142. Primus, Constance M. "The Bass Recorder in Consort." *The American Recorder* 25, no. 3 (August 1984): 101–4.

    Reviews references to the bass recorder in Virdung and Praetorius, then offers several examples of bass parts from various types of consort music (including publications by Attaingnant, Holborne, and Praetorius). The bibliography lists modern editions of duets and trios with parts for bass recorders.

*   Wyatt, Theo. "Playing the Tenor and Bass." Cited above as item 134.

7

Art and Iconography

According to Mary Rasmussen and Friedrich von Huene (item 152), "Recorders began to appear frequently in western European art in the early 15th century, especially in Spanish paintings and in French/Franco-Flemish manuscript illuminations. . . . Because of its clear literary, rustic and allegorical associations, the late medieval and Renaissance recorder had perhaps a more varied sacred and secular iconography than any other musical instrument of the time except the bagpipe." The present chapter deals with the few studies that have been published on the recorder in works of art. The recorder is also dealt with in passing in Emanuel Winternitz's classic book *Musical Instruments and Their Symbolism in Western Art* (London: Faber & Faber, 1967; 2nd ed., New Haven: Yale University Press, 1979), especially chapter 2.

143. Ballester i Gibert, Jordi. "Retablos marianos tardomedievales con ángeles músicos procedentes del antiguo reino de Aragón. Catálogo" [Late medieval Marian altarpieces with musician angels from the ancient kingdom of Aragón: catalog]. *Revista de musicología* 13, no. 1 (1990): 123–201.

This catalog of 141 Aragonese altarpieces dating between 1350 and 1525 shows vertical flutes ("flauta recta") in eighteen of them and double pipes ("flauta doble") in five. As in Brown's catalog (item 144), the black and white reproductions are unfortunately too small to enable us to see any of these instruments clearly.

144. Brown, Howard Mayer. "Catalogus: A Corpus of Trecento Pictures with Musical Subject Matter." *Imago*

Musicae 1 (1984): 189-243; 2 (1985): 179-281; 3 (1986): 103-187; 5 (1988): 167-241.

An invaluable catalog of the surviving 14th-century Italian works of art with musical subject matter. The first two installments cover panel paintings, frescoes, and mosaics signed by or attributed to particular artists or their followers. The catalog, arranged alphabetically by artist, includes 2½-inch square black-and-white photographs of each work for identification purposes. Entries refer the reader to other sources where the pictures are reproduced—large enough, we hope, to be studied. His index reports recorders in fourteeen of the paintings and double recorders in no fewer than seventy-five. Unfortunately, some of the references are equivocal, and we wonder whether the whistle or fipple flutes that Brown detects in these pictures are true recorders.

145. Fischer, Pieter. "Music Paintings of the Low Countries in the 16th and 17th Centuries." *Sonorum Speculum* 50/51 (1972): 1-128.

Includes a reproduction and brief discussion (pp. 96-97) of a Vanitas by Evert Collier (1684), which depicts a recorder and a copy of Jacob van Eyck's *Der fluyten lust-hof* I (1646).

146. Frings, Gabriele. "'Flauti dolci' und 'pifferari': Bemerkungen zur Ikonographie der Blockflöte in der Renaissance" ['Flauti dolci' and 'pifferari': remarks on the iconography of the recorder in the Renaissance]. *Tibia* 17, no. 2 (1992): 117-24. [The author's last name, given as Limberg at the head of the article and in the table of contents, is corrected in an errata slip, in which Limburg (sic) is said to be her maiden name.]

Written to correct the notion in present-day art history writings that the recorder in 16th-century painting "is often *a priori* negatively classified and considered an indicator of low social degree" [eine sozial niedere Sinngebung]. Two recent publications are typical: Augusto Gentili, "Savoldo, das Bildnis und die Musikallegorie," in *Ausstellungskatalog "Savoldo und die Renaissance zwischen Lombardei und Venetien. Von Foppa und Giorgione bis Caravaggio,"* 71-77 (Milan, 1990); and Elhanan Motzkin, "The Meaning of Titian's 'Concert champêtre,' *Gazette des Beaux-Arts* 116 (1990): 53-65. Uses these two sources as the starting point for a consideration of paintings by Savoldo, Giorgione/Titian, Costa, Moroni, del Piomba, Frangipane, Raimondi, and others, showing that in both iconography and music practice the recorder possessed an elevated rank, far different from that of the "piffari" (shawms, trumpets, crumhorns, and cornetts).

* Griffioen, Ruth van Baak. *Jacob van Eyck's* Der Fluyten Lust-Hof *(1644–c1655)*. Cited below as item **1243**.
  Reports on the depiction of recorders in one hundred selected 17th-century Dutch paintings (far more than seem to have been used for item 152).

147. [Hersom, Herbert]. "Duet for Recorder and Harp." *Recorder & Music Magazine* 9, no. 6 (June 1988): 173–74.
  Concerns the depiction of a recorder player and harpist in a carved misericord (dating presumably from the 14th century) in Chichester Cathedral.

148. Hersom, Herbert. "The National Portrait Gallery in Yorkshire." *The Recorder and Music Magazine* 8, no. 1 (March 1984): 4–5.
  Includes a ca. 1763 portrait from the studio of Zoffany of David Garrick holding a recorder.

149. Hunt, Edgar. "Titian and the Recorder." *The Recorder Magazine* 10, no. 4 (December 1990): 94–95.
  Discusses a few paintings by Titian (ca. 1487–1576) that depict recorders, noting that "[i]n Renaissance times the recorder took over from the [ancient Greek] *aulos* as a symbol of love." Focuses in particular on *Venus and Cupid with a Lute Player* (Fitzwilliam, Cambridge), in which Venus holds a recorder. In *Three Ages of Man* (National Gallery of Scotland, Edinburgh), a young girl presents two recorders to a young man, who is already holding a recorder. *The Bacchanal* (Padro, Madrid) depicts two recorders in the hands of two women, with a third recorder by the foot of a woman. Titian's paintings were analyzed at far greater length by Winternitz (see the introduction to this chapter).

150. Koldeweij, Jos. "'The Best Flutes Come from a Donkey's Bone': The Recorder in 17th-Century Dutch Art = 'Van eens esels been de beste fleuyten comen': De blokfluit in de Nederlandse kunst van de 17e eeuw." In *Programma: Holland Festival Oude Muziek, 27 Augustus–5 September 1993*, 53–62. Utrecht: STIMU, 1993. In Dutch with parallel English translation.
  The recorder is one of the most frequently represented instruments in 17th-century art. It was popular among both sexes in all social classes, yet curiously almost all the players are "amateurs": beggars, drunkards, street musicians, artists, ladies, and gentlemen. In contrast to the instruments that have survived, the most commonly represented sizes of recorder are the soprano and alto; they were presumably played until they fell to

Art and Iconography 57

pieces, then thrown away. The recorder was played alone and in ensembles, indoors and outdoors, rarely however with an audience. The recorder was one of the instruments used to symbolize the sense of hearing and the transience of life (Vanitas). The recorder is also an obvious phallic symbol, a fact which did not escape the painters of the time. (The author's opinion that the recorder was also a phallic symbol in certain Vanitas paintings is debatable.) It could also symbolize lightheartedness and gaiety, as in a print depicting a recorder being made from a donkey's bone—hard work turning into pleasure for silly youth.

151. Montagu, Jeremy. "The Restored Chapter House Wall Paintings in Westminster Abbey." *Early Music* 16, no. 2 (May 1988): 239-49.

    Draws attention to a possible recorder among these wall paintings, painted between 1390 and 1404.

152. Rasmussen, Mary, and Friedrich von Huene. "Some Recorders in 17th-Century Dutch Paintings." *Early Music* 10, no. 1 (January 1982): 30-35.

    Opens with a short history of the recorder in art. The instrument often appeared in pastoral scenes, in Venus paintings, and in a variety of settings as a sexual symbol. Paintings of this period often reveal reliable details of construction, which can be helpful in designing modern copies of old instruments. In sum, "this genre is a fertile source of reliably delineated instruments and a reminder of the subtle symbolism which has always attended the relationship of musical instruments and western European art." Includes twelve black-and-white reproductions. See also Ian F. Finlay, "Musical Instruments in 17th-Century Dutch Paintings," *The Galpin Society Journal* 6 (1953): 52-69.

153. Slim, H. Colin. "Giovanni Girolamo Savoldo's *Portrait of a Man with a Recorder.*" *Early Music* 13, no. 3 (August 1985): 398-406.

    Concerns the painting by Savoldo (fl. 1508-1548), now in a private collection in New York. Identifies the music depicted (a sonnet-in-dialogue by Francesco Patavino) and discusses its significance. Confirms that 16th-century recorder players in Northern Italy played vocal music. See also Volker Scherliess's article, "Alles war hell in hell gemalt: Musikalische Bildthemen in der venezianischen Malerei" [Everything was painted in bright colors: musical depictions in Venetian painting], *Concerto* 2, no. 3 (April-May 1985): 16-29, which suggests that the painting may have been a gift for the man's bride, inviting her to musical (symbolically, sexual) union.

8

Humor, Fantasy, and Fiction

Because, we would guess, of its shape, its use in school music, and its largely amateur clientele, the recorder is often the butt of humor. This chapter is restricted to items in which members of the recorder world make fun of themselves and their instrument. We could not resist throwing in a fantasy as well as a short story we came across by a well-known American writer, knowing that it must be the tip of the iceberg.

154. Bergmann, Walter. ["Golden Rules for Ensemble Playing."] *The Recorder News,* June 1957. Reprinted in *The Recorder and Music Magazine* 9, no. 7 (September 1988): 188.

    ———. "Golden Rules for Ensemble Playing." *Recorder & Music* 5, no. 6 (June 1976): 191. Reprinted in *The Recorder and Music Magazine* 9, no. 7 (September 1988): 188.

    ———. "26 Golden Rules for Ensemble Playing." *The American Recorder* 13, no. 3 (August 1972): 76-77. Reprinted in *The American Recorder* 29, no. 3 (August 1988): 109-10.

    Humor with a pedagogical purpose. The 1988 version in *The American Recorder* includes an introduction offering the following history: At least three versions exist. A set of fourteen rules appeared in the June 1957 issue of *The Recorder News*. The original twenty-six rules appeared in *Recorder & Music* in 1976. The American edition of the twenty-six, published four years before the British, is an expanded version with the rules in a slightly different order.

155. Gemmach, Hans. "Die 'grüne Blockflöte'" [The "green recorder"]. *Tibia* 11, no. 3 (1986): 439-40.

An alleged portrait of 76-year-old recorder maker Joseph Bergner, who makes green recorders from Uzbekhian oak (*acer sogdos*).

156. Grasshoff, Fritz, and Hermann Moeck. *Den singende Knochen: Kurzgelochte Parahistorie zur echten Flötenforschung unter Benutzung des Tibilarium Moeckii d. i. Hermann Moecks wissenschaftliche Beschreibung wie man auf Bein und Holz geblasen hat und bläst* [Of the singing bones: brief parahistory of the true recorder research, making use of the *Tibilarium Moeckii*, i.e., Hermann Moeck's scholarly description of how one plays and has played on bone and wood]. Celle: Edition Moeck, 1971. 40 p.

    Humorous history of the recorder, based on facts gleaned from Moeck's dissertation (item **1472**). Review in *Recorder and Music Magazine* 4, no. 5 (March 1973): 174.

157. Halfpenny, Eric. "Fingering." *The American Recorder* 5, no. 4 (November 1964): 22. Reprinted from the *Recorder News* and the *ARS Newsletter* 18.

    A facetious description of four types of fingering (English, old English, German, and buttress).

158. Halfpenny, Eric. "Serpent in the Midst." *The American Recorder* 24, no. 2 (May 1983): 65.

    Five excerpts from a humor column of the same name that appeared in the *Recorder News* during the 1950s.

159. King, Ronald. *Recorder Humour*. London: Schott, 1976. ISBN 0901938572. 37 p.

    Thirty-one cartoons originally published in *The Recorder and Music Magazine*. Some seem dated and others are perhaps too British to register with Americans, but most are still amusing.

160. Thiem, Jon. "A Note on the Recorder in the Year 2440." *The American Recorder* 16, no. 2 (May 1975): 49–50.

    Broadly overinterprets a brief account of amateur music making in Louis Sébastien Mercier's 17th-century fantasy about Parisian life in the year 2440 (*L'an 2440*).

161. Updike, John. "The Man Who Became a Soprano." *The New Yorker*, 26 December 1988, 28–35.

A short story that considers the formation of an amateur recorder consort and the havoc it wreaks on the lives of its members. We will not give away any more of the plot, merely note the Adorno-like attitude of one of the members: "Fritz told him, 'The recorder is the easiest instrument in the world, next to the triangle and the tambourine. And I suppose the maracas.' There was a German pedantry to Fritz."

9

Instrument Makers and Instruments: Historical

This chapter covers both biographical material on historical recorder makers and surveys of their instruments. As far as it is possible to make the distinction from "surveys," the design and properties of historical instruments are treated separately in chapter 12.

INDEXES

162. Langwill, Lyndesay G. *An Index of Musical Wind Instrument Makers.* 6th ed. Edinburgh: Author, 1980. xix, 331 p. OCLC #6926848. Earlier editions: 1st ed., 1960. viii, 139 p. OCLC #1248341; 2nd ed., 1962. x, 202 p. OCLC #857756; 3rd ed., 1972. xii, 232 p. OCLC #515021; 4th ed., 1974. xv, 272 p. OCLC #3090256; 5th ed., 1977. xvi, 308 p. OCLC #3930370.

Written and published by an enthusiastic amateur bassoon player and organologist, "Langwill" rapidly became an indispensable tool for the wind researcher. The body of the book is an alphabetic index of makers, giving place of work, dates, brief biographical details, and surviving instruments. This is followed by an index by place of work and a bibliography. The main listing remained unaltered after the 4th edition, "Addenda and Corrigenda" being added in separate listings for the 5th and 6th editions, which also reproduce Friedrich von Huene's charts of makers' marks (from item 164). Item 163 is a complete revision.

First edition reviewed by Philip Bate in *The Galpin Society Journal* 13 (July 1960): 106. Second edition reviewed by C. K[enworthy] in *The Recorder and Music Magazine* 1, no. 1 (May 1963): 31. Third edition reviewed by Dale Higbee in *The American Recorder* 13, no. 4 (November 1972): 129, J.M. Thomson in *Recorder and Music Magazine* 4, no. 5 (March 1973): 173, and Philip Bate in *The Galpin Society Journal* 25 (July 1972): 134. Fourth edition reviewed by Edgar Hunt in *Recorder & Music* 5, no. 4 (December

1975): 125 and Jeremy Montagu in *The Galpin Society Journal* 29 (May 1976): 130. Review of the fifth edition by Dale Higbee in *The American Recorder* 20, no. 3 (November 1979): 134-35.

163. Waterhouse, William. *The New Langwill Index: A Dictionary of Musical Wind-Instrument Makers and Inventors.* London: Tony Bingham, 1993. 518 p. ISBN 0946113041.

Not yet seen. Not based on Langwill's *Index of Musical Wind Instrument Makers*, 6th ed. (item 162) but a completely new work intended to supersede it. See also Waterhouse's article, "Langwill and His Index," *The Galpin Society Journal* 39 (1986): 58-67.

MAKERS' MARKS

* Kirnbauer, Martin. "Überlegungen zu den Meisterzeichen Nürnberger 'Holzblasinstrumentenmacher' im 17. und 18. Jahrhundert" [Reflections on the makers' marks of the Nuremberg woodwind instrument makers in the 17th and 18th centuries]. Cited below as item 173.

164. von Huene, Friedrich. "Makers' Marks from Renaissance and Baroque Woodwinds." *The Galpin Society Journal* 27 (1974): 31-47.

Includes over 100 illustrations of makers' marks from recorders, flutes, cornetts, shawms, oboes, etc.

GEOGRAPHICAL FOCUS

165. Lerch, Tom. "Die Entwicklung des barocken Blockflötenbaus in Europa: Ein geschichtlicher Abriss" [The development of Baroque recorder construction in Europe: a historical outline]. *Das Musikinstrument* 37, no. 7 (July 1988): 16-20.

A brief survey with biographies of the principal makers based on previous research.

DENMARK

166. Duhot, Jean-Joël. "Une énigme musicale résolue? La flûte de van Eyck. Jean-Joël Duhot a rencontré Irmgard et Aksel Mathiesen" [A musical enigma solved? The van

Eyck recorder. Jean-Joël Duhot has met Irmgard and Aksel Mathiesen] *Flûte à bec & instruments anciens* 27 (March 1989): 9-11.

Concerns their discovery of a so-called "van Eyck recorder" in a Danish castle in 1985. The instrument seems to date from 1630-50 and is of a type that was used during Jacob van Eyck's lifetime. Although the Mathiesens claim this instrument as "totally unique," a few apparently similar ones have survived (notably the "Rosenborg recorders"—see item 219, etc.).

ENGLAND

167. Halfpenny, Eric. "Biographical Notices of the Early English Woodwind-making School, c. 1650-1750." *The Galpin Society Journal* 12 (May 1959): 44-51.

Brief biographies of five makers who produced French-style, jointed instruments in England: John Ashbury, Joseph Bradbury, Peter Bressan, Samuel Drumbleby, and the Stanesbys. Halfpenny argues that there was no connection between Peter Bressan and Pierre Jaillard Bressan, a position later refuted by Maurice Byrne in item **194**.

FRANCE

168. Giannini, Tula. *Great Flute Makers of France: The Lot and Godfroy Families, 1650-1900.* London: Tony Bingham, 1993. xxvi, 245 p. ISBN 094611305X.

Although Giannini's book is focused on the transverse flute and its prominent French makers in the 18th and 19th centuries, the flute makers of the early 18th century also made recorders. The recorder is mentioned several times in inventories-after-death. A recorder by Lot is shown in one of the plates. Giannini has also discovered that Jacques Christophe Naudot, the composer of some pieces that could be played on the recorder, was a "seller of flutes and of music" rather than a professional performer (his inventory-after-death, 1762).

We look forward enormously to the second installment of Giannini's researches: a book on the Hotteterre family.

169. Guidecoq, P. "Les buis de La Couture: Aux tourneurs qui créèrent la flûte à bec" [The boxtrees of La Couture: on the turners who created the recorder]. *Flûte à bec* 5 (December 1982): 14-18.

Fascinating historical information on turners and the cultivation of boxwood in the neighborhood of the Normandy town of La Couture Boussey (Eure moyenne), home of the Hotteterre family in the 17th century and later of many other important instrument makers such as Godfroy, Noblet, Buffet, and Thibouville-Martin. Coupled with some brief notes on the Hotteterres, marred by the contestable statement that "[i]t is not contested that the final form [of the recorder], called Baroque, is the work of the Hotteterres."

170. Lesure, François. "La facture instrumentale à Paris au seizième siècle" [Instrument making in Paris in the 16th century]. *The Galpin Society Journal* 7 (April 1954): 11–52.

A short overview introduces a series of archival documents, including inventories-after-death of the makers Mathurin de La Noue (d. 1544) and Philippe de La Canessière (d. 1551), and the musician Etienne Loré (d. 1553), which mention recorders. Note that this article is in French, despite being published in the English-language *GSJ*.

171. Thomé, Gilles. "Promenade baroque: Un dimanche à La Couture Boussey" [Baroque promenade: a Sunday in La Couture Boussey]. *Crescendo* 32 (March–April 1990): 25–29.

On Thomé's "Sunday walk" around La Couture Boussey he introduces us to the mayor of the town, its history, the local boxwood ("Boussey" is derived from "buxum," the Latin word for the wood), and finally its instrument museum.

GERMANY

172. Bruckner, Hans. "Die Pfeifenmacherei in Berchtesgaden" [Pipe making in Berchtesgaden]. *Tibia* 4, no. 2 (1979): 289–96.

Wood turning was associated with the Berchtesgaden monastery almost from its founding in 1100, although the first extant regulations date from the early 16th century. In the late 18th century the Berchtesgaden makers developed a special type of double recorder ("Paar Flauten") with narrow bore and small fingerholes. There survive recorders and double recorders by Albrecht or Jakob Plaikner (fl. 1696–1708), Johann (b. 1716) or Joseph (b. 1722) Eggl, and the following members of the Walch family: Augustin Walch (b. 1668) or his brother Andreas (b. 1672); their brother Georg (b. 1690); Georg's sons Johann Georg (b. 1764) and Lorenz (1735–1809); his grandson Lorenz II (1786–1862); and his greatgrandson Paul (1810–1873). Lorenz II's brother Andreas (b. 1777) was also a "Flautenmachermeister" as were several members of the Fischer family. An appetite-whetting article based on archival sources. Josef Zimmermann, *Die Pfeifenmacherfamilie Walch in Berchtesgaden* (Breslau, 1937) is cited in the bibliography. Letter from John Henry van der Meer in 4, no. 3 (1979): 441.

* Haynes, Bruce. "Johann Sebastian Bach's Pitch Standards: The Woodwind Perspective." Cited below as item 374.

173. Kirnbauer, Martin. "Überlegungen zu den Meisterzeichen Nürnberger 'Holzblasinstrumentenmacher' im 17. und 18. Jahrhundert" [Reflections on the makers' marks of the Nuremberg woodwind instrument makers in the 17th and 18th centuries]. *Tibia* 17, no. 1 (1992): 9–20.

"Despite the groundbreaking work of Ekkehard Nickel on Nuremberg woodwind making [see item 176], many kinds of questions on this complex theme are still open. . . . To these open questions belong, for example, those about the possibly surviving instruments of the Nuremberg 'pre-Denner era.' Bound up with this also is the question about the maker's marks of the craftsmen, which would make an attribution of these instruments possible." So begins this long, important article, which tries to answer those questions.

In Nuremberg wind making was a "free art" and the makers could belong to one of two guilds: first, the wood, bone, and brass turners; second, the "animal call" and horn makers (who also used ivory and bone). Makers' marks were obligatory. Individual marks had to be clearly differentiated, yet marks could be taken over by other makers. The only surviving guild book of marks contains largely sets of initials, only occasionally a name or symbol. Hieronymus Franciskus Kinsecker signed himself HF on all instruments; only the larger ones also included his name and city. A large number of small recorders and flageolets survive that have various attributes in common, including the "wave profile" that appears on Kinsecker's instruments. Therefore the makers can probably be associated with Nuremberg, and the waves correspond to the principal material of the horn call and horn makers—rippled animal horn. Many of these instruments have marks, particularly the initials D, H, M, O, and S, some of them later associated with "recorder makers" such as Schell, Denner, and Oberlender. The conclusion is that these initials belonged to the horn call and horn makers, being favored because of the small space available for a mark on the small instruments they made.

In 1697, Schell and J.C. Denner, horn call and horn makers who began to make exclusively woodwind instruments, used both the old initials (obligatory) and their signatures inside a banner (voluntary); before then their instruments had been sold by other makers under their own marks. The plain initial D has been attributed without cause to J.C. Denner; it is more likely to have belonged to the "forgotten" brother Johann Carl, who made "nothing but recorders and flageolets." The banner became an important attribute of a Nuremberg woodwind instrument, later copied by makers from Berchtesgaden and other cities. The I.C.DENNER mark was clearly used by other makers after Denner's death in 1707, through the mid

18th century. A similar sitution is likely with J.W. Oberlender I and his successors.

174. Kirnbauer, Martin, and Dieter Krickeberg. "Untersuchungen an Nürnberger Blockflöten der Zeit zwischen 1650 und 1750" [Investigations into Nuremberg recorders of the period 1650–1750]. In *Anzeiger des Germanischen Nationalmuseums 1987*, 245–81. Nürnberg: Germanische Nationalmuseum, 1987.

Detailed description of the authors' measurements of the historical recorders in the Nuremberg collection as well as "comparison instruments" of non-Nuremberg provenance. Reports (for the alto recorders, then the basses) on such measurements as the conicity of the bores, the position and size of the fingerholes, and the relative lengths of the pieces of the instrument. A unique study.

175. Meer, J.H. van der. "Nuremberg Instrument Makers of the 17th and 18th Centuries." *The American Recorder* 18, no. 2 (August 1977): 33–37; 18, no. 3 (November 1977): 65–69.

Covers makers of both string and woodwind instruments. The recorder makers mentioned are Hieronymus Franciskus Kinsecker and the Denner family. Includes photographs of a Kinsecker consort as well as tenor and bass instruments by J.C. Denner and altos by Jacob Denner.

176. Nickel, Ekkehart. *Der Holzblasinstrumentenbau in der Freien Reichsstadt Nürnberg* [Woodwind instrument making in the German free town Nuremberg]. (Schriften zur Musik, Bd. 8) Munich: Musikverlag Emil Katzbichler, 1971. ISBN 3873970082.

A doctoral dissertation (Friedrich-Alexander-Universität Erlangen-Nürnberg, 1969) of great importance. See especially part C, chapter 4, "Die Flötenbauer des 17. und 18. Jahrhunderts" [The recorder and flute makers of the 17th and 18th centuries], which covers the following recorder makers: the Herbst family, Hieronymus Franciskus Kinsecker, the Denner family, Johann Schell, Nikolaus Staub, Johann Benedikt Gahn, the Zick family, the Oberlender family, the Löhner (Lehner) family, and Georg Franz Carl. Detailed biographies based on archival research and descriptions of surviving instruments. Part B, chapter 5 includes a similar study of the 16th-century Schnitzer family. Also includes transcriptions and a discussion of the Nürnberg instrument inventories of 1575, 1598, and 1609.

ITALY

* Bernardini, Alfredo. "Woodwind Makers in Venice, 1790–1900." Cited below as item 211.

177. De Gregorio, Vincenzo. "Flauto a becco sopranino del secolo XVII" [Sopranino recorder of the 17th century]. *Il flauto dolce* 9 (June 1983): 36–37.

    Describes the discovery of a 17th-century sopranino recorder in an old house in Foligno in 1982. Includes a rough drawing.

178. Li Virghi, Francesco. "Il flauto diritto basso della collezione di Assisi" [The bass recorder in the collection at Assisi]. *Il flauto dolce* 10/11 (January–June 1984): 51–52.

    Briefly describes an anonymous Baroque bass recorder in the collection of the Biblioteca Comunale in Assisi, inside the Franciscan monastery. Includes a table of the deviations of the notes from equal temperament at a^1 = 415 Hz. The second page is a drawing with measurements.

179. Ongaro, Giulio. "16th-Century Venetian Wind Instrument Makers and Their Clients." *Early Music* 13, no. 3 (August 1985): 391–97.

    Brings to light and discusses a significant 16th-century contract between three of the wind players of the Doge of Venice and two Venetian wind makers (Jacomo Bassano and Santo Griti). The terms of the contract concern a promise to supply instruments (including recorders), and the players acting as agents for and lending money to the makers. Ongaro also furnishes the first documentary evidence of a link between the Venetian and Anglo-Venetian branches of the Bassano family.

180. Toffolo, Stefano. *Antichi strumenti Veneziani 1500–1800: Quattro secoli di liuteria e cembalaria* [Early Venetian instruments, 1500s–1800s: four centuries of instrument making]. Venice: Arsenale Editrice, 1987. 231 p. ISBN 8877430079.

    An enormous expansion of item 181. The chapter on wind instruments includes a disappointingly short section on the recorder (pp. 174–75). The following chapter on wind instrument making consists of brief studies of six makers, among them Santo Bassano and Andrea Fornari (documents about whom are presented in an appendix). Reviewed by John Henry van der Meer in *Galpin Society Journal* 41 (1988): 147–50.

181. Toffolo, Stefano. "La costruzione degli strumenti musicali a Venezia dal XVI al XIX secolo" [The construction of musical instruments in Venice in the 16th-19th centuries]. *Il flauto dolce* 14/15 (April/October 1986): 24-30.

A series of four short essays on various aspects of Venetian instrument making. The first essay quotes Francesco Griselini (1768) to the effect that under the rubric "il flautajo" [flute maker] one understands a craftsman who makes all wind instruments, "such as flutes, recorders, oboes, bagpipes, trumpets, horns, etc." The third essay is on the 16th-century maker Santo Bassano. The fourth essay, on Andrea Fornari, includes a transcription of a petition by him (1791) in which he lists the woodwind instruments he makes, among them alto recorder, third flute, and octave flute.

182. Vio, Gastone, and Stefano Toffolo. "La diffusione degli strumenti musicali nelle case dei nobili, cittadini e popolani nel XVI secolo a Venezia" [The distribution of musical instruments in the houses of nobles, citizens, and commoners in 16th-century Venice]. *Il flauto dolce* 17-18 (October 1987-April 1988): 33-40 (English abstract, 92-93).

Lists and analyzes the musical instruments mentioned in the inventories-after-death of 16th-century Venetians. Twenty-one of the more than twenty-six recorders (plus "a case") in these inventories can be assigned to members of the three social classes: nobles (nine), citizens (ten), and commoners (two). The recorder is the fourth most frequently mentioned instrument (after the lute, harpsichord, and clavichord).

THE NETHERLANDS

* Acht, Rob van, Vincent van den Ende, and Hans Schimmel. *Dutch Recorders of the 18th Century [in the Collection of The Hague Gemeente Museum]* = *Niederländischen Blockflöten des 18. Jahrhunderts in der Sammlung von Haags Gemeentemuseum.* Cited below as item 261.

183. Acht, Rob van. "Dutch Wind-Instruments, 1670-1820." *Tijdschrift van de Vereniging voor Nederlandse Muziekgeschiedenis* 38 (1988): 99-122. In Dutch as: "De bouw van houten blaasinstrumenten in Nederland in de periode 1670 tot 1820." *Bouwbrief* 49 (May 1988): 3-13; 50 (August 1988): 3-10. In German as: "Niederländische Blasinstru-

mente, 1670–1820." *Tibia* 15, no. 3 (1990): 169–85. An English version without the survey of extant instruments as: "Dutch Wind-Instrument Makers from 1670 to 1820." *Galpin Society Journal* 41 (1988): 83–101.

Draws together what is known about the school of woodwind makers that flourished in the Netherlands in the late 17th and 18th centuries. The school is more extensive than had previously been realized: no fewer than sixty-six recorders from nineteen makers survive, and inventories or advertisements show that a further ten makers made recorders. Gives biographical sketches of all the makers, lists the instruments now in The Hague as well as the whereabouts of other surviving instruments, and reproduces some of the makers' marks. Caution: van Acht sometimes uses "flutes" in the sense of transverse flutes, sometimes to mean both flutes and recorders. Letter from Günter Angerhöfer in *Tibia* 16, no. 1 (1991): 418.

For a previous short essay on this subject, see S.A.C. Dudok van Heel and Marieke Teutscher, "Amsterdam als centrum van 'fluytenmakers' in de 17e en 18e eeuw," in *Historische blaasinstrumenten: De ontwikkeling van de blaasinstrumenten vanaf 1600, Kasteel Ehrenstein te Kerkrade, 6–28 Juli 1974*, 53–56 ([The Hague]: Haags Gemeentemuseum, Gemeente Kerkrade, Wereldmuziekconcours Kerkrade, 1974); in English (trans. Peter Bree) as: "Amsterdam: From Flute Makers to Factories of Musical Instruments," in Phillip T. Young, *Loan Exhibition of Historic Double Reed Instruments*, iv–vii (Victoria, B.C.: University of Victoria, 1988).

184. Bouterse, Jan. "Historical Dutch Recorders in American Collections." *American Recorder* 33, no. 3 (September 1992): 14–18.

Describes the eight pre-1760 Dutch recorders extant in the United States: an alto by Abraham van Aardenberg, a soprano by Richard Haka, and an alto by "I-V-H" in the Shrine to Music Museum (Vermillion, SD); a sixth flute by Willem Beukers and an alto by Engelbert Terton in the Library of Congress; a soprano by Thomas Boekhout in the Metropolitan Museum of Art (New York, NY); and a bass recorder by Boekhout and an alto by Terton in private collections. For most of the recorders, the description offers physical specifications (including stamps and other markings), an evaluation of pitch and intonation, and an assessment of present playing condition. Includes several detailed drawings with measurements.

Dordrecht recorder

* Fitzpatrick, Horace. "The Medieval Recorder." Cited below as item **440**.

185. Weber, Rainer. "Recorder Finds from the Middle Ages, and Results of their Reconstruction." *The Galpin Society Journal* 29 (1976): 35–41.

Describes and discusses two medieval recorders discovered during excavations in Dordrecht and Würzburg (fragment). Includes a report on the Dordrecht excavation by Clemens von Gleich.

INDIVIDUAL MAKERS

BASSANO FAMILY

186. Kenyon de Pascual, Beryl. "Bassano Instruments in Spain?" *Galpin Society Journal* 40 (December 1987): 74–75.

Cites archival evidence from Spain to show that the cathedral of Rodrigo ordered recorders from England in 1567, and that in 1626 the cathedral of Huesca owned a case of eight recorders together with a very large recorder that had been bought in England at an unknown date. Suggests that these instruments were all made by the Bassanos in England.

187. Lasocki, David. "The Anglo-Venetian Bassano Family as Instrument Makers and Repairers." *The Galpin Society Journal* 38 (1985): 112–32.

Based on item 72, especially pp. 555–71. Summarizes the lives and careers of the family, then discusses in detail their making and repairing of recorders, other wind instruments, viols, and lutes. Suggests that the Bassanos made the large recorders depicted by Mersenne (1636). Speculates that the "rabbit's foot" mark found on many surviving 16th-century woodwind instruments belonged to the family (see also items 188 and 191).

188. Lasocki, David. "The Bassanos: Anglo-Venetian and Venetian." *Early Music* 14, no. 4 (November 1986): 558–60.

Drawing on recent evidence unearthed by Ongaro (item 179), demonstrates the relationship between the Bassanos who emigrated to England in the 1530s and those who remained in Venice. Speculates on the meaning of that relationship for instrument making in the 16th century, particularly that the rabbit's paw mark was used by both branches of the family. (But see item 191.)

189. Lasocki, David. "The Bassanos' Maker's Mark Revisited." *The Galpin Society Journal* 46 (March 1993): 114–19.

Summarizes the recent research on the Bassanos' maker's mark. Then presents a new theory: that the so-called "rabbit's foot" mark does in fact represent a silkworm moth, which appears on the Bassano family coat of arms (now thought to have been brought from Venice by the original five brothers).

190. Lasocki, David, with Roger Prior. *The Bassanos: Venetian Musicians and Instrument Makers in England, 1531-1665.* Aldershot, Hampshire: Scolar Press, forthcoming in 1994.

The most detailed account published to date of the Anglo-Venetian Bassano family. Covers: biographies; economic affairs, privileges and social standing; Jewish identity; performing; composing; instrument making and repairing; and the question: Was Emilia Bassano the Dark Lady of Shakespeare's Sonnets? Extensive bibliography. Appendixes include Music and the English Bassanos after 1665, and notes on Jacomo and the Venetian Bassanos. Intended to supersede the earlier study by Eleanor Selfridge-Field, "Venetian Instrumentalists in England: A Bassano Chronicle (1538-1660)," *Studi musicali* 8 (1979): 173-221.

191. Lyndon-Jones, Maggie. "The Bassano/HIE(RO).S/!!/ Venice Discussion." *FOMRHI Quarterly* 47 (April 1987): 55-61 (Communication No. 802).

Begins by summarizing what is now known about the Anglo-Venetian Bassano family as instrument makers (see **187-88,** and 179). Then adds important information and theories about surviving instruments and makers' marks that could be linked with the family. An appendix aims to list all surviving instruments with the marks HIE(RO).S. (or variants) and !! (or variants). Further suggestions about the !! maker's mark are in Douglas Kirk, "Cornetti and Renaissance Pitch Standards in Italy and Germany," *Journal de musique ancienne* 10, no. 4 (Summer 1989): 16-22.

192. Marvin, Bob. "A Bassano *flauto.*" *FoMRHI Quarterly* 41 (October 1985): 22-23 (Communication No. 651).

Gives suggested measurements for the type of recorder that might have played 16th-century "diminutions and ricercare, the best known perhaps being those of G[iovanni] Bassano (1585)."

* Ongaro, Giulio. "16th-Century Venetian Wind Instrument Makers and Their Clients." Cited above as item **179.**

BRESSAN, PETER (1663–1731)

193. Boydell, Barra. "Another Bass Recorder by Bressan." *The Galpin Society Journal* 32 (1979): 131–33.

    Description and measurements of an instrument housed in a private home near Dublin.

194. Byrne, Maurice Anthony. "Pierre Jaillard, Peter Bressan." *Galpin Society Journal* 36 (March 1983): 2-28.

    Previously, little was known of the life of Bressan, one of the great recorder makers of the Baroque era. In a tour de force of archival work, Byrne establishes Bressan's life in detail: his birth in Bourg-en-Bresse in 1663 as Pierre Jaillard, training (still a hazy area), appearance in London around 1691, marriage and family, residence, publishing ventures, association with Schuchart, denization, exhibitions of anatomical bodies and other objects, death while in Tournai, and will, as well as the difficulties over his estate and some vignettes from his business in the 1720s. He lived at Duchy House, formerly the town residence of the chancellor of the Duchy of Lancaster, so his maker's mark is presumably a representation of the red rose of Lancaster. Appendixes include the apprenticeship agreement, the will, and a partial inventory of Bressan's estate, recorded in November 1731. Unfortunately, marred by some awkwardnesses in prose and organization, but still well worth plowing through.

195. Byrne, Maurice. "More on Bressan." *Galpin Society Journal* 37 (March 1984): 102-11.

    Discusses in detail some legal cases involving Bressan and his estate. Brings to light some important new information, including the exact date of his arrival in England (1688), the fortune he had made by the time of his marriage in 1703, the falling off of his trade by 1715 (Byrne states this was because of the decline in popularity of the recorder), the financial extravagance of his temperamental wife, his eventual financial difficulties, and his leaving for Tournai to live alone in 1730.

196. Byrne, Maurice. "Peter Bressan." *Recorder & Music* 7, no. 10 (June 1983): 250.

    A summary of the biographical material in item **194**.

197. Chilton, Charles. "Recording for the BBC Sound Archives." *The Recorder and Music Magazine* 1, no. 10 (August 1965): 298.

    Describes a BBC project to record music played on original instruments—in particular, a group of Bressan recorders (including the instruments from the Chester Museum) played by Frans Brüggen, Edgar Hunt, Walter Bergmann, and Beverly Smith in March 1965.

198. Dart, Thurston. "Bressan and Schickhardt." *The Galpin Society Journal* 10 (1957): 85-86.
Written in response to 199 and 327. Discusses the forms and origins of Bressan's name and incorrectly identifies the maker named Schuchart as Johann-Jakob Schickhardt. Superseded by the work of Byrne (item 194).

199. Halfpenny, Eric. "The Bass Recorders of Bressan." *The Galpin Society Journal* 8 (1955): 27-31.
A detailed description, with measurements, of three Bressan basses housed in the following collections: Grosvenor Museum, Chester; St. Peter Hungate, Norwich; and Victoria and Albert Museum, London.

200. Hunt, Edgar. "Left-handed Recorders by Bressan." *The Galpin Society Journal* 37 (1984): 121.
A brief note on Hunt's examination of left-handed recorders in the Grosvenor Museum, Chester. Dale Higbee comments on his own left-handed Bressan voice flute in 38 (1985): 143.

201. Hunt, Edgar. "Life of a Bressan." *Recorder and Music Magazine* 2, no. 5 (May 1967): 157.
The story of the acquisition of Hunt's Bressan alto recorder ("my most valued possession"), his early performances on the instrument, its survival of an air-raid bombing, its appearance in several exhibitions, the performances on the instrument by Hunt and Frans Brüggen, Coolsma's plans to copy the instrument (see item 277), and the qualities that make it an excellent recorder.

202. "Woodwind Instruments by P-I Bressan." *The Galpin Society Journal* 17 (1964): 106-7.
Lists thirty-two recorders, their owners, and their sizes. See also the occasional "Current Register of Historic Instruments" scattered throughout *The Galpin Society Journal*.

Chester recorders

203. Bergmann, Walter. "The Chester Recorders." *The Recorder and Music Magazine* 1, no. 5 (May 1964): 141.
The Chester recorders were discovered in 1886, when a collection of antiquities belonging to the Chester Archaeological Society was moved to new quarters. The collection consists of six Bressan instruments: the traditional set of four "Chester" recorders (f^1, d^1, c^1, f), and two others (f^1,

e♭¹) that are locked away. Bergmann describes the instruments and offers a bibliography of literature.

* Bridge, J.C. "The Chester 'Recorders.'" Cited above as item 53.

204. Dolmetsch, Carl. "Cataclysms and the Chester Recorders." *Recorder & Music* 5, no. 6 (June 1976): 192-93.

    Dolmetsch's account of his work on the voicing and refurbishing of the Chester recorders. Paul Jacobs, in 5, no. 7 (September 1976): 239, questions whether Dolmetsch should have tampered with the Chester recorders, asserting that Dolmetsch rendered them useless as models for copies. Dolmetsch replies in 5, no. 8 (December 1976): 263 that he did only what was necessary to make them playable. Alan Davis rises to Dolmetsch's defense in 5, no. 9 (March 1977): 299.

* Kinsell, David. "J.C. Bridge and the Recorder." Cited above as item 96.

DENNER FAMILY

205. Kirnbauer, Martin, and Peter Thalheimer. "Jacob Denner (1681-1735)—New Aspects of his Biography and his Significance for the History of the Flute in Germany." *Early Music* (in preparation).
    Announced in item 173.

206. Nickel, Ekkehart. "Johann Christoph und Jacob Denner: Zwei Lebensbilder" [Johann Christoph and Jacob Denner: two biographical sketches]. *Tibia* 4, no. 3 (1979): 393-95.

    Sketches the lives of Johann Christopher Denner and his son Jacob, two of the most important woodwind makers of the late Baroque, based on material in item 176.

207. Warner, Robert Austin, and Friedrich von Huene. "A Jacob Denner Recorder in the United States of America." *The Galpin Society Journal* 21 (1968): 88-96.

    Discusses a recorder in the Stearns Collection as well as Denner recorders at the Royal College of Music, London, and the Musikhistorisk Museum, Copenhagen.

208. Young, Phillip T. "Woodwind Instruments by the Denners of Nürnberg." *The Galpin Society Journal* 20 (1967): 9-16.

   Lists twenty-seven recorders by Johann Christoph Denner and six by plain "Denner." Includes information on physical characteristics and ownership. J.H. van der Meer makes additions and corrections in 21 (March 1968): 208.

209. Young, Phillip T. "Some Further Instruments by the Denners." *The Galpin Society Journal* 35 (1982): 78-85.

   An update of 208. Includes five plates illustrating Denner recorders. John Henry van der Meer comments on one of the bass recorders in 36 (1983): 127-28.

FIRTH, POND & CO.

210. Thompson, Richard. "The Anachronistic Recorder." Illustration by Russell Gerhardt. *The American Recorder* 2, no. 4 (Fall 1961): 3.

   Discusses a mid-19th-century capped fipple flute made in New York by Firth, Pond & Co. Includes comments by Russell Gerhardt. Letter from Alfred H. Sinks in 3, no. 1 (February 1962): 22.

FORNARI, ANDREA (1753-1841)

211. Bernardini, Alfredo. "Woodwind Makers in Venice, 1790-1900." *Journal of the American Musical Instrument Society* 15 (1989): 52-73. An expanded English translation of: "Andrea Fornari (1753-1841) 'fabricator di strumenti' a Venezia" [Andrea Fornari (1753-1841), instrument maker in Venice]. *Il flauto dolce* 14/15 (April/October 1986): 31-36.

   Includes a study of the life and work of Andrea Fornari, who was primarily a maker of oboes and English horns but also of recorders (see also item 181).

HEITZ, JOHANN (CA. 1672-1737)

212. Hart, Günter. "Johann Heitz (1673-1737)." *Tibia* 2, no. 1 (1977): 207-8.

A short biography. Includes photographs of two of his alto recorders (Carse Collection, London; Dayton Miller Collection, Library of Congress, Washington, D.C.).

213. Kirnbauer, Martin, and Dieter Krickeberg. "Musikinstrumentenbau im Umkreis von Sophie Charlotte" [Musical instrument making in the circle of Sophie Charlotte]. In *Sophie Charlotte und die Musik in Lietzenburg*, herausgegeben anlässlich der Ausstellung vom 9. Juli bis zum 20. September 1987 als Beitrag zur 750 Jahr-Feier Berlins, 47–60. Berlin: Staatliches Institut für Musikforschung Preussischer Kulturbesitz, 1987.

Surveys the life and work of Heitz, fourteen of whose signed recorders survive (thirteen altos and one bass). Most of these have the unusual construction of a boxwood body with a tortoiseshell coating and ivory ornamentation. Suggests that Bressan, the only other maker known to have used tortoiseshell technique, could have been Heitz's teacher.

Hotteterre Family

214. Bowers, Jane. "The Hotteterre Family of Woodwind Instrument Makers." In *Concerning the Flute: Ten Articles Dedicated to Frans Vester* . . . , 33–54. Amsterdam: Broekmans en Van Poppel, 1984. OCLC #12363269.

Presents biographies of the seven principal known makers of the family: Jean (d. 1690/92?), Nicolas (*l'aîné*) (ca. 1637–1694), Louis (d. 1716), Nicolas (*le jeune* or Colin) (1653–1727), Jean (ca. 1648–1732), Martin (d. 1712), and Jacques (*le Romain*) (1674–1763). Includes an elaborate family tree on a folded insert. Concludes with a section on the eighteen extant Hotteterre instruments (three flutes, two oboes, five alto recorders, five tenor recorders, and three bass recorders). Describes the makers' marks and speculates on which of the Hotteterres might have used particular marks and made specific instruments. A table of the eighteen instruments offers details on the mark, materials, and present location for each. See also Bowers's article on Hotteterre in *The New Grove Dictionary of Musical Instruments* (New York: Grove's Dictionaries of Music; London: Macmillan, 1984).

215. Giannini, Tula. "Jacques Hotteterre le Romain and his Father, Martin: A Re-Examination Based on Recently Found Documents." *Early Music* 21, no. 3 (August 1993): 377–95.

Uses new archival documents to extend our picture of the Hotteterre family in several ways. Jean I had a previously unknown son called Jean, who was in the woodwind making business with his father and brother, Martin. Distinguishes two other Hotteterre workshops: those descending from Louis I and Nicolas I. Suggests that the makers' marks of these three workshops were "Hotteterre" with an anchor below; "N/Hotteterre" with a six-pointed star above; and "L/Hotteterre" with a fleur-de-lis above, respectively. Another previously unknown Hotteterre, Jacques, son of Louis I, was working for the British court as a musician in 1675; he is likely to have been an instrument maker too, and the man who introduced the French woodwinds to England. An inventory made of Martin's workshop a year before his death shows that he specialized in recorders and flutes; several sizes of recorder are mentioned—"petites," quintes, tailles, and basses. Jacques Hotteterre le Romain seems to have ceased making instruments in 1720 and had essentially retired by 1728. This article is presumably a foretaste of Giannini's promised book on the family (see item 168).

216. Hunt, Edgar. "A Hotteterre Tenor?" *Recorder & Music* 4, no. 9 (March 1974): 327.

Concerns a tenor in the Donaldson Collection at the Royal College of Music. Includes a description and measurement of the instrument. Concludes that the tenor "certainly looks like an Hotteterre and has the characteristic rounding of the upper part of the mouthpiece; but I should hesitate to pontificate and say that it *is* one, without studying more examples."

PALANCA, CARLO (D. 1783)

217. Bernardini, Alfredo. "Carlo Palanca e la costruzione di strumenti a fiato a Torino nel settecento" [Carlo Palanca and wind-instrument making in Turin in the 18th century]. *Il flauto dolce* 13 (October 1985): 22-26.

Principally an archival study of the life and work of bassoonist and woodwind maker Palanca (fl. 1719-d. 1783) from whom survive the greatest number and greatest variety of any 18th-century Italian woodwind maker. Criticizes the quality of his workmanship. Although one would expect his instrument making to have been influenced by the French (several French oboists were among his colleagues), he seems to have developed in isolation.

RIPPERT, JEAN-JACQUES

218. Puglisi, Filadelfio. "A Firenze un flauto diritto francese" [A French recorder in Florence]. *Il flauto dolce* 9 (June 1983): 37.

    A brief description of an alto recorder by Rippert in the Museo Stibbert, Florence (catalog no. 14289). Includes a photograph, a close-up of the maker's mark, and a drawing (without measurements).

ROSENBORG RECORDERS

219. Legêne, Eva. "The Rosenborg Recorders." *The American Recorder* 25, no. 2 (May 1984): 50–52.

    A companion to item 333. The two recorders were made before 1673 and transferred from the Royal Castle in Copenhagen to Rosenborg Castle sometime between 1673 and 1696. Speculates that one of the recorders was perhaps made by a member of the royal family—possibly the king—under the guidance of a professional maker, who made the second recorder as a model. Includes a facsimile of a handwritten copy, attributed to Jonas Plamqvist, of the preface to *Der fluyten lust-hof*, which includes an illustration of a recorder with an ornamented bell similar to that of the Rosenborg recorders. At the time the recorders were made, narwhal ivory was a precious material associated in the popular imagination with the unicorn. Reviews the allegorical associations of the unicorn and the recorder and offers an example from the visual arts that includes both images.

220. Mathiesen, Penelope. "Nature, Art and Music: The Rosenborg Recorders." *Continuo* 13, no. 4 (August 1989): 22–24.

    Brings us up to date on the Rosenborg recorders, describing Eva Legêne's receipt of a narwhal tusk and Fred Morgan's new copies made from that tusk (see items 333 and 219). Also discusses a painting by Gijsbrecht (1672) that includes recorders and other instruments apparently from the Danish royal collection.

*   Morgan, Fred. "A Recorder for the Music of J.J. van Eyck." Cited above as item 333.

ROTTENBURGH FAMILY

221. Ottenbourgs, Stefaan. "De familie Rottenburgh: Een van de talrijke muzikale dynastieen uit het barokke Brussel.

Deel 1: Genealogie. 2: De instrumenten" [The Rottenburgh family: one of the numerous musical dynasties of Brussels in the Baroque: 1: genealogy; 2. the instruments]. *Musica Antiqua* 5, no. 4 (November 1988): 152-58; 6, no. 1 (February 1989): 9-16. In German as: "Die Familie Rottenburgh: eine der zahlreichen musikalischen Dynastien aus dem barocken Brüssel." *Tibia* 14, no. 3 (1989): 477-89; 14, no. 4 (1989): 557-67.

Part 1 presents detailed biographies of all the musical members of the Rottenburgh family (four generations), based on archival records. Includes facsimiles of numerous documents. Part 2 discusses the various makers, their marks and addresses, then lists extant instruments (recorders, flutes, oboes, clarinets, bassoons, strings) made by the family with basic measurements of each instrument. Short sections on materials and pitch. Based on his Licentiaatsverhandeling, *De familie Rottenburgh: een muzikale dynastie te Brussel in de achttiende eeuw* (Katholieke Universiteit Leuven, 1986). Copies are obtainable from the author at Zepperenweg 214, B-3800 Sint-Truiden, Belgium.

SCHERER FAMILY

222. Young, Phillip T. "The Scherers of Butzbach." *The Galpin Society Journal* 39 (1986): 112-24.

The Scherers' country of residence was previously unknown. Young shows that they almost certainly lived in Butzbach, near Frankfurt. He reasons that two family members undoubtedly made wind instruments: Johannes Jr. and Georg Heinrich; evidence relating to the others is lacking. The Scherer stamps contain a confusing variety of letters and numbers, only a few of the difficulties of which Young has solved. A sole recorder survives (as compared with some sixty other woodwinds).

SCHLEGEL FAMILY

223. Küng, Andreas. "'SCHLEGEL A BALE': Die erhaltenen Instrumente und ihre Erbauer" ["SCHLEGEL A BALE": the surviving instruments and their makers]. *Basler Jahrbuch für historische Musikpraxis* 11 (1987): 63-88.

Reports his researches into the life and work of the Basel woodwind makers Christian Schlegel (ca. 1667-1746) and his son Jeremias (1730-92). Four recorders by Christian survive (including a double recorder). According to a document from 1759, Jeremias was still making recorders in that year, leading Küng to speculate that the case of four ivory recorders of his (two sopraninos and two altos) that are housed in the Paris Conservatoire date from around 1750 or later. Based on the author's Diplomarbeit, Schola Cantorum Basiliensis, Basel, 1976.

SCHUCHART, JOHANN JUST (CA. 1695–1758)

* Dart, Thurston. "Bressan and Schickhardt." Cited above as item **198**.

224. Libin, Laurence. "A Unique Soprano Recorder." (Reports) *The American Recorder* 29, no. 3 (August 1988): 113–14.

    Reports on the only extant Schuchart soprano, a ca. 1750 instrument now housed in the Cincinnati Art Museum.

SELMA, BARTOLOMÉ DE (D. 1616)

225. Pascual, B. Kenyon de. "The Wind-Instrument Maker, Bartolomé de Selma (†1616), His Family and Workshop." *The Galpin Society Journal* 39 (1986): 21–34.

    Identifies the maker firmly for the first time, describes his life, and discusses his will and inventory-after-death (which mentions tools and parts for recorders).

SETTALA, MANFREDO (1600–1680)

226. Puglisi, Filadelfio. "Signor Settala's 'armonia di flauti.'" *Early Music* 9, no. 3 (July 1981): 320–24.

    Describes a "multiple recorder" with five speaking pipes that was a part of a large collection of instruments made by Manfredo Settala (1600–1680), a Milanese physician.

227. Weber, Rainer. "Der Flauto Harmonico—Ein seltenes Instrument und sein Erbauer" [The *flauto harmonico*—a rare instrument and its inventor]. *Tibia* 17, no. 1 (1992): 20–26.

    Describes a curious instrument in the possession of the Museo Civico, Bologna, with a recorder pipe and four drone pipes attached to a crosspiece and mouth tube. It is identical to one depicted by Athanius Kircher in his *Musurgia universalis* (Rome, 1650) and said to have been invented by his friend Manfredo Settala. Gives a few biographical details of Settala and reproduces a miniature still life by Evaristo Baschenis that includes both a *flauto harmonico* (similar but not identical to the instrument in Bologna) and a clown-like portrait apparently of Settala himself (perhaps in a state of sickness); the other items in the picture show it to be in the Vanitas tradition of the Dutch 17th-century painters. The bulk of the article describes the Bologna instrument in detail. The melody pipe is in g^1; the drone pipes, in $b\flat^1$, d^2, g^2, and a^2 (with three fingerholes for $b\flat^2$, $c\sharp^2$, and d^3) (apparently at modern pitch). The drones overblow as the melody rises. The instrument plays in B♭, presumably A or even G at one of the higher Italian pitches. As the original is in poor condition, Weber made a copy. Speculates on the significance of the instrument.

STANESBY FAMILY

228. Byrne, Maurice. "Some More on Stanesby Junior." *The Galpin Society Journal* 45 (March 1992): 115–21.

    Written as a sequel to Halfpenny's articles on the Stanesbys (items 167 and 229). Mostly concerns the shenanigins over Stanesby Jr.'s will. A few new details of the family's earlier history. In light of Manfred Brach's recent researches (see item 351), the most significant item is an advertisement of Caleb Gedney that mentions his master Stanesby Jr.'s "mathematical calculation."

229. Halfpenny, Eric. "Further Light on the Stanesby Family." *The Galpin Society Journal* 13 (1960): 59–69.

    Contains additional biographical material to item 167. Appendix of surviving instruments by the Stanesbys and by Stanesby Jr.'s apprentice, Caleb Gedney, includes eight recorders by Stanesby Sr. and eleven by Stanesby Jr.

230. Halfpenny, Eric. "Technology of a Bass Recorder." *The Galpin Society Journal* 15 (1962): 49–54.

    Description of an instrument attributed to Stanesby Sr. dating from the late 17th century.

231. Hunt, Edgar. "Bressan and the Stanesby's [sic]." *Recorder & Music* 6, no. 7 (September 1979): 202.

    A brief article on the Stanesbys, Bressan being mentioned only once in passing. Summarizes the biographical information found in articles by Eric Halfpenny (items 167 and 229) and reprints the fingering chart from Stanesby Jr.'s *New System* (item 662).

STEENBERGEN, JAN

232. "Jan Steenbergen, Recorder Maker." *The Recorder and Music Magazine* 8, no. 3 (September 1984): 75–76.

Unsigned article based on information given in a booklet from Moeck Verlag. Brief background on Steenbergen, followed by information on the Moeck copies of his instruments. Letter from A. Dolf in 8, no. 6 (June 1983): 185.

TOWNSEND, JOHN (FL. CA. 1816–69)

233. Blanchfield, David. "A Nineteenth-Century English Recorder." *The Recorder Magazine* 10, no. 2 (June 1990): 34–35.

Reports on a sixth flute from the workshop of John Townsend (active ca. 1816–69). "As an historical artifact, this little 'English Flute' demonstrates that the recorder was still known and treasured well into the 19th century, a time when the flageolet was at the height of its short-lived popularity."

WIJNE, ROBERT (1698–1774)

234. Feldhaus, Hanne. "Robert Wijne (1698–1774), Holzblasinstrumentenmacher in Nijmegen: Biographisches und Bemerkungen über eine Sopranblockflöte von ihm" [Robert Wijne (1698–1774), woodwind instrument maker in Nijmegen: biography and observations on a soprano recorder of his]. *Tibia* 5, no. 3 (1980): 161–64.

Reports on newly unearthed biographical information about Wijne, based on material in the Nijmegen archives. Comments on his maker's mark (based on the Nijmegen coat of arms). Describes in detail a soprano recorder of Wijne's discovered at an antique dealer in The Hague in 1968. The instrument was restored by Friedrich von Huene (whose drawing of it and fingering chart are appended) and is now in Frans Brüggen's collection. Concludes with a list of Wijne woodwinds in other collections. M.C.J. Bouterse, "The Flutes of Robert and Willem Wijne," *FoMRHI Quarterly* 55 (April 1989), 29–36, includes the revelation that joints of some of the Wijnes' oboes and recorders were bored with the same reamers used for their flutes. He writes that they "(and perhaps other makers) did not always design a new instrument with new reamers, but tried to save time and money using existing reamers. I think that this trial-and-error method resulted sometimes in bad or 'difficult' instruments."

ZIEGLER, JOHANN (1820–1847)

235. Glassgold, A.C. "Another Anachronism?" *The American Recorder* 3, no. 3 (August 1962): 15–16.

Sequel to item 210. Discusses a keyed recorder made by Ziegler in Vienna. Glassgold describes a six-keyed soprano recorder made by Louis Lot in 4, no. 2 (May 1963): 27.

MISCELLANEOUS MAKERS AND INSTRUMENTS

236. Reyne, Hugo. "Quelques notes sur les facteurs de flûtes à bec du XVIème siècle" [Notes on the makers of recorders in the 16th century]. *Flûte à bec* 3 (June 1982): 33.

    Brief speculations on the identity of the three recorder makers whose marks were given by Ganassi (1535).

237. Rice, Albert R. "The Musical Instrument Collection of Michiel van Bolhuis (1764)." *Journal of the American Musical Instrument Society* 18 (1992): 5–21.

    The Groningen collector Michiel van Bolhuis left a great many books, scores, and musical instruments on his death in 1764. The auction catalog listed fifty-one instruments, including four recorders (among them a *flûte d'accord*, or double recorder, made by Michiel Parent, tuned in thirds) and a transverse flute by Johann Wilhelm Oberlender "with a mouthpiece similar to a recorder." Briefly discusses all the instruments.

238. Wenner, Martin. "Ein 'Flauto Curvo'" [A curved recorder]. *Tibia* 15, no. 1 (1990): 44–45.

    Describes a unique recorder, apparently from the 19th century, in which the top half is angled at about 145 degrees to the bottom half, like a bassethorn, and the end has a bell like that of an oboe d'amore. Considers it really "an English flageolet of tenor range" and dismisses the idea that it might be a joke. Unfortunately, gives no information about its provenance or whereabouts.

239. Omitted.

10

Collections of Historical Instruments

This chapter is concerned only with those articles and books about collections of historical instruments that discuss their recorders as well as a few items of related interest. To save space, catalogs and checklists of individual collections have not been included. (For a listing of the most important of those sources, see Vincent H. Duckles & Michael A. Keller, *Music Reference and Research Materials: An Annotated Bibliography*, 4th ed., rev. [New York: Schirmer Books, 1994], 477–92.)

240. Acht, Rob van. *Checklist of Technical Drawings of Musical Instruments in Public Collections of the World.* Celle: Moeck, 1992. 185 p. ISBN 3875490541.

    Based on the microfiche collection of technical drawings housed in the Documentation Centre for Musical Instruments at the Gemeentemuseum, The Hague. The original drawings are available from the original collections. Lists recorders from the collections in Berlin, Edinburgh, London, New York, Nuremberg, Oxford, Paris, The Hague; arranged by maker. Reproduces Jean-François Beaudin's drawing of an alto recorder by Carandet (Paris Conservatoire).

241. Lehman, Robert A. "Preparation and Management of a Descriptive Inventory for a Collection of Flutes." *Journal of the American Musical Instrument Society* 12 (1986): 137–48.

    Describes a computerized data-management program for making an inventory of a flute collection, using simple-system and Boehm-system transverse flutes as examples. Suggests that a similar format could easily be adapted for duct flutes (recorders and flageolets).

242. Marvin, Bob. "Recorders & English Flutes in European Collections." *The Galpin Society Journal* 25 (1972): 30–57.

A highly influential article, reporting the fruits of his tour of western European museums in 1970. Lists more than 200 instruments he saw, giving location, approximate pitch, quality of tone and intonation, material, markings, museum number, and comments. Then gives measurements of fifteen of those instruments and comments on their construction methods, voicing practices, etc. An appendix presents his preliminary comments on making copies of Renaissance instruments from the Vienna collection. Note that Marvin uses the term "English flutes" to mean recorders from the time of Hotteterre onwards.

243. Young, Phillip T. *4900 Historical Woodwind Instruments: An Inventory of 200 Makers in International Collections*. London: Tony Bingham, 1993. ISBN 0946113033. Earlier edition: *Twenty-five Hundred Historical Woodwind Instruments: An Inventory of the Major Collections*. New York: Pendragon Press, 1982. xii, 155 p. ISBN 0918728177.

New edition not yet seen. First edition is an inventory arranged alphabetically by makers' last names. Includes information on pitch, length, type of wood, ownership, etc. The book represents a vast revision and expansion of the inventories published in *The Galpin Society Journal*. Of the 122 makers covered, forty-two made recorders. An essential book. Reviewed by Jeremy Montagu, in *Early Music* 11, no. 2 (April 1983): 239–41, Dale Higbee in *The American Recorder* 24, no. 2 (May 1983): 75, and William Waterhouse in *The Galpin Society Journal* 38 (April 1985): 158–59.

AUSTRIA

SCHLÄGL

244. [Hunt, Edgar]. "Ivory Recorders at the Monastery at Schlägl, Austria." *The Recorder and Music Magazine* 8, no. 5 (March 1985): 138–39.
A summary of item **245**.

245. Pichler, Isfried H., and Richard Hinteregger. "Die Elfenbein-Blockflöten des Stiftes Schlägl" [The ivory recorders of the Schlägl monastery]. In *Schlägler Orgelkonzerte: Jubiläumsschrift zu den 10. Schlägler Orgelkonzerte*, edited by Rupert Gottfried Frieberger, 74–82 and figs. 33–34. (Musikwissenschaftliche Beiträge der Schlägler Musikseminare, Bd. 1) Rum bei Innsbruck: Helbling, 1979. OCLC #5941306.

In two sections. Pichler gives a history of how the instruments came into the collection; a biography of their maker, Johann Benedikt Gahn; a description of each of the three recorders (sopranino and two altos). Then Hinteregger describes his pitch measurements on the instruments. Several photographs show off the unique carvings.

SIGMARINGEN

246. Bär, Frank P. "Musikinstrumente auf Schloß Sigmaringen" [Musical instruments in Sigmaringen castle]. *Tibia* 17, no. 2 (1992): 124–31.

Lists and briefly discusses the wind instruments in the collection of the Fürstlich-Hohenzollernsche Schloß zu Sigmaringen an der Donau. It includes recorders by Gahn, Jacob Denner/Rijkel/Haka, Weis, A. Hochschwarzer (mid-19th century), and anonymous. For full details, see the author's *Die Sammlung der Musikinstrumente im Fürstlich-Hohenzollernschen Schloß zu Sigmaringen an der Donau*, Tübinger Beiträge zur Musikwissenschaft, Neue Folge, 1 (Tutzing: Hans Schneider, 1992).

VIENNA

247. Stradner, Gerhard. "Das Blasinstrumente in einem Inventar der Wiener Hofkapelle von 1706" [The wind instruments in an inventory of the Vienna court Kapelle of 1706]. *Studien zur Musikwissenschaft* 38 (1987): 53–63.

Discusses an inventory of the instruments that belonged to the music ensemble of the Viennese court in 1706. It included sixty recorders, among them such unusual ones as "altar posts that can be used as recorders" and "two great keys of St. Peter, [which can] also [be used] as recorders." A few 16th-century columnar recorders have survived; recorders in the shape of a key do not seem to have survived. The inventory was first published in Susanne and Theophil Antonicek, "Drei Dokumente zu Musik und Theater unter Kaiser Josph I," in *Festschrift Othmar Wessley zum 60. Geburtstag*, 11–37 (Tutzing: Hans Schneider, 1982).

CZECH REPUBLIC

PRAGUE

248. Puklický, Milan. "Die Holzblasinstrumente des Nationalmuseums Prag" [The woodwind instruments of the Nationalmuseum, Prague]. In *Bericht über das VI. Symposium zu Fragen des Instrumentenbaus—Holzblasinstru-*

mente des 17. und 18. Jahrhunderts, Michaelstein 28./29. November 1985, 39–42. Michaelstein/Blankenburg: Kultur- und Forschungsstätte Michaelstein, 1986. OCLC #17323787.
Briefly mentions their holdings of two alto recorders (Bressan, Denner) and five bass recorders (anonymous, Bressan, Gheier, Fridrich).

FRANCE

PARIS

249. Beaudin, Jean-François. "De nouveaux plans de flûtes anciennes du Musée du Conservatoire de Paris" [On new drawings of the early recorders in the Paris Conservatoire Museum]. *Flûte à bec & instruments anciens* 23 (1987): 26–27. In English as: "New Plans of Old Flutes." *The Recorder: Journal of the Victorian Recorder Guild* 8 (July 1988): 22–25.
Discusses the drawing of twenty-seven instruments in the Paris Conservatoire (eleven recorders, fourteen flutes, and two oboes) with brief descriptions of the most interesting instruments. Also lists instruments in Berlin and Edinburgh of which Beaudin has made drawings.

250. Bran-Ricci, Josiane. "Holzblasinstrumente im Museum des Conservatoire National Supérieur de Musique, Paris" [Woodwind instruments in the museum of the Paris Conservatoire]. *Tibia* 7, no. 2 (1982): 128–31.
The Paris collection was founded in 1864 on the acquisition of the important private collection of Louis Clapisson, son of an instrument maker in Lyon, and a composition and harmony teacher at the Conservatoire. The collection was strengthened by the more than 400 instruments from the private collection of the former director, Geneviève Thibault de Chamboure. Mentions recorders by Hans Rauch von Schratt, van Heerde, Hotteterre, Haka, Rippert, Bressan, Johann Christoph Denner, Heytz, Stanesby Sr., Jeremias Schlegel, Gahn, and Oberlender, as well as several double recorders (including an ivory one signed Anciuti, Milan, 1719). An appetite-whetter.

251. Garden, Greer. "Models of Perfection: Woodwind Instruments from the Museum of the Paris Conservatoire." *Recorder and Music Magazine* 4, no. 4 (December 1972): 116–17.

Briefly describes selected instruments, including several recorders from the 16th–18th centuries. Includes photographs of some of the recorders and flutes.

252. Tellier, Michelle. "Musée Instrumental du Conservatoire de Paris: Les flûtes à bec renaissances" [Instrumental museum of the Paris Conservatoire: The Renaissance recorders]. *Flûte à bec* 3 (June 1982): 31–33.
    Notes on nine Renaissance instruments in the collection.

253. Tellier, Michelle. "Musée Instrumental du Conservatoire de Paris: Les flûtes à bec baroques" [Instrumental museum of the Paris Conservatoire: The Baroque style recorders]. *Flûte à bec* 2 (February 1982): 36–41.
    A brief descriptive overview, divided into instruments "for the eye" ("remarkable for their visual qualities") and those "for the ear" ("which deserve to be heard").

GERMANY

MUNICH

254. Schmid, Manfred Hermann. "Die Blockflöten des Musikinstrumentenmuseums München" [The recorders of the musical instrument museum in Munich]. In *Bericht über das VI. Symposium zu Fragen des Instrumentenbaus— Holzblasinstrumente des 17. und 18. Jahrhunderts, Michaelstein 28./29. November 1985*, 18–39. Michaelstein/Blankenburg: Kultur- und Forschungsstätte Michaelstein, 1986. OCLC #17323787.
    The Munich recorders consist of two 16th-century great basses by Hans Rauch von Schratt; two sopraninos by Rippert; two anonymous mid-17th-century sopranos; altos by Rippert, Heitz, Oberlender I, and anonymous; a tenor by Rippert; and basses by J.C. Denner (fourteen in all). Discusses the provenance of the collection (the recorders were largely taken over from the old Bavarian Nationalmuseum). Describes each recorder (no detailed measurements) and its maker. Claims that one of the von Schratt recorders may be represented in a miniature by the Munich court painter Hans Mielich (*ca.* 1570). Suggests that the Rippert instruments, made in ivory, were originally part of a seven-member consort (similar to the Nuremberg Kinseckers). The costliness of the materials and other evidence points to the recorders having belonged to the Bavarian court, where

several members of the ducal family were enthusiastic recorder players (and Jacques Loeillet was hired in 1715).

NUREMBERG

255. Kirnbauer, Martin and Dieter Krickeberg. "Untersuchungen an Nürnberger Blockflöten der Zeit zwischen 1650 und 1750." In *Anzeiger des Germanischen Nationalmuseums 1987*. Nürnberg, 1987. ISSN 0341-8383.
Reviewed in *Tibia* 14, no. 4 (1989): 609.

256. Kirnbauer, Martin. "Historische Holzblasinstrumente in der Sammlung des Germanischen Nationalmuseums in Nürnberg" [Historical woodwind instruments in the collection of the German National Museum in Nuremberg]. *Tibia* 14, no. 2 (1989): 424–29.
A "brief overview" of the approximately 500 woodwind instruments in the Nuremberg collection, which is divided into various parts. The part designated "old" (inventory numbers with the prefix MI), which has survived since the founding of the museum in 1853, came partly from older collections, such as those of Nuremberg churches or town musicians. The recorders mentioned in the overview are by Rauch von Schrattenbach, Kinsecker, J.C. Denner, Gahn, Staub, Oberlender, Schell, Zick, Jacob Denner, and Eichentopf.

ITALY

BOLOGNA

257. Puglisi, Filadelfio. "The 17th-Century Recorders of the Accademia Filarmonica of Bologna." *The Galpin Society Journal* 34 (1981): 33–43.
Description of eleven of the thirteen surviving recorders that were in use by the Accademia between its founding in 1666 and the death of its founder in 1675. Nine are marked "P. GRE/C/E" and two "C. RAFI." Selected bore measurements and drawings. These recorders were evidently intended to be played as a homogeneous group.

VERONA

258. Pasquale, Marco di. "Gli strumenti musicali dell'Accademia filarmonica di Verona: un approccio documentario"

[The musical instruments of the Accademia Filarmonica of Verona: a documentary approach]. *Il flauto dolce* 17-18 (October 1987-April 1988): 3-17.

An exhaustive study of references to musical instruments in the archives of the Accademia. Looking at the many listings of recorders in the Accademia's inventories made between 1562 and 1716, skillfully distinguishes five different groups of instruments and identifies the provenance of the first two groups.

259. Weber, Rainer. "Die Instrumentensammlung der Accademia Filarmonica in Verona und Probleme ihrer Restaurierung" [The instrument collection of the Accademia Filarmonica of Verona and problems of its restoration]. *Tibia* 6, no. 2 (1981): 313-19.

At least a part of the famous instrument collection of the Accademia has survived (under the inventory numbers 13247-13307). The large recorders consist of two basses in C (by Hans Rauch von Schratt) and bassets in F, a basset in F with extension to D, three basses in B♭, and two great basses in F (all with the double "rabbit's foot" mark [see items 187-189]). Presents a little biographical information on the Rauch family. After surveying the flutes, cornetts, crumhorns, and dulcian-like instruments in the collection, discusses his restoration of the entire collection in 1971-73.

* Weber, Rainer. "Some Researches into Pitch in the 16th Century with Particular Reference to the Instruments in the Accademia Filarmonica of Verona." Cited below as item 375.

THE NETHERLANDS

260. *The Recorder Collection of Frans Brüggen*. Drawings by Frederick Morgan. Tokyo: Zen-On, 1981. 36 p. + 18 technical drawings. OCLC #8820565.

Booklet with photographs of seventeen late-17th-century and 18th-century recorders with captions (including some errors), the name of the previous owner, and recordings of Brüggen's on which the instrument is featured. Also includes eighteen sheets of drawings with detailed measurements. All contained in a portfolio. Reviewed in *Recorder & Music* 7, no. 5 (March 1982): 129 and by Dale Higbee in *The American Recorder* 23, no. 3 (August 1982): 122.

The Hague

261. Acht, Rob van, Vincent van den Ende, and Hans Schimmel. *Niederländische Blockflöten des 18. Jahrhunderts = Dutch Recorders of the 18th Century: Sammlung = Collection Haags Gemeentemuseum*. Text in English and German. Descriptions of instruments by Jan Bouterse; measurements of instruments made with the assistance of Ella Siekman. Celle: Moeck, 1991. 163 p. ISBN 387549038X.

    A coffee-table sized book devoted to fifteen 18th-century recorders in the collection of the Gemeentemuseum in The Hague. van Acht's introduction summarizes his material on Dutch recorder makers of the period (from item **183**). The makers represented are Abraham van Aardenberg, Willem Beukers, Thomas Boekhout, one of the van Heerdes, Frederik de Jeger, I. Roosen, Engelbert Terton, and Robert Wijne. For each recorder the body of the book presents a description, an X-radiograph, a color photograph, a line drawing, measurements, and the pitches of the notes. An appendix lists all surviving Dutch recorders of this period with their locations.

    Jeremy Montagu in *Early Music* 19, no. 4 (November 1991): 636-41 criticizes the lack of information on who took the measurements (of dimensions and pitch) and how. Also reviewed by Eve O'Kelly in *The Recorder Magazine* 11, no. 4 (December 1991): 121-22, David Ohannesian in *American Recorder* 33, no. 1 (March 1992): 29-30, and Friedrich von Huene in *The Galpin Society Journal* 46 (March 1993): 195-97.

Sweden

Stockholm

262. Karp, Cary. "Baroque Woodwind in the Musikhistoriska Museet, Stockholm." *The Galpin Society Journal* 25 (July 1972): 80-86.

    Lists the woodwinds in the Stockholm collection made before ca. 1750 but discusses only the Eichentopf oboe da caccia. The collection includes recorders by Bressan, J.C. Denner, Eichentopf, van Heerde, I.W. Oberlender, Pfegl, Rykel, Sattler, Staub, and Steenbergen.

United States

* Bouterse, Jan. "Historical Dutch Recorders in American Collections." Cited above as item **184**.

263. Oler, Wesley M. "My Collection of Modern Replicas." *The Recorder and Music Magazine* 1, no. 7 (November 1964): 197–99.
   Describes his collection of instruments, addresses questions frequently asked of him, and explains why he chose to collect replicas rather than original instruments. Letter from Virginia C. Oler in 1, no. 8 (February 1965): 249.

264. Powers, Wendy. "Checklist of Historic Recorders in American Private and Public Collections." *The American Recorder* 30, no. 2 (May 1989): 56–66.
   A catalog of eighty recorders held in fourteen collections. Each entry includes information on size, key, maker, date, markings, construction, number of sections and fingerholes, length, citations for illustrations, and general bibliographic citations. Includes photographs of ten instruments.

265. Powers, Wendy. "Historic Recorders in American Private and Public Collections: An Update." *American Recorder* 32, no. 1 (March 1991): 17–20.
   Sequel to item 264, providing details on new acquisitions and changes in ownership for seven collections. Includes photographs of six instruments in the Shrine to Music Museum, Vermillion, South Dakota.

ANN ARBOR, MICHIGAN

266. Warner, Robert Austin, and Friedrich von Huene. "The Baroque Recorders in the Stearns Collection of Musical Instruments." *The Galpin Society Journal* 23 (1970): 69–81.
   Description of four recorders that were restored and studied: a bass by Souvé and altos by Fische, Sattler, and Denner. Fingering charts are included for the altos. Lyndesay G. Langwill suggests that "Souvé" should be "Jouve" in 24 (1971): 124, which Warner then disputes in 25 (1972): 146.

NEW YORK CITY

267. Libin, Laurence. "Holzblasinstrumente im Metropolitan Museum of Art in New York" [Woodwind instruments in the Metropolitan Museum of Art, New York]. *Tibia* 5, no. 1 (1980): 28–31.
   The musical instruments of the "Met" are in the André Mertens Gallery, given by the widow of the famous impresario in his memory. Visitors can listen to recordings (occasionally also live performances) of the instruments with musicians such as Frans Brüggen and Michel Piguet. The

catalog of 1904 is no longer current and is now being updated. The group of recorders is not large compared with those of other collections but still contains representative instruments. Mentions in particular an anonymous Renaissance alto recorder at high pitch in maple; a 17th-century ivory flageolet in G stamped "De Haze"; an experimental double flageolet by Collin (by 1830); an ebony soprano recorder by Boekhout (ca. 1700); alto recorders by I.W. Oberlender, Gahn, and Bradbury; a set of soprano, alto, and tenor recorders, probably by Kinsecker; and a boxwood *flûte d'accord* by Ammann.

268. Nagle, Sigrid. "Musical Instruments at the Metropolitan Museum of Art." *The American Recorder* 15, no. 4 (November 1974): 111–17.

Concerns the collection in general. Includes photographs of the case of recorders and flutes as well as a few individual recorders.

VERMILLION, SOUTH DAKOTA

269. Larson, André P. "Original Bass Recorders in the United States." *The American Recorder* 26, no. 4 (November 1985): 171–72.

Reports on two early bass recorders recently acquired by The Shrine to Music Museum at the University of South Dakota in Vermillion: one in G (ca. 1552–1590), formerly in the Galpin collection, and one in D by Johann Christoph Denner.

RUSSIA

ST. PETERSBURG (FORMERLY LENINGRAD)

270. Jürisalu, Heino. "Die Leningrader Sammlung und ihre Flöteninstrumente" [The St. Petersburg collection and its flutes and recorders]. *Tibia* 5, no. 2 (1980): 105–7.

Gives a brief history of the collection, which was based on 360 instruments from the Belgian collector Snoeck, then absorbed various other collections. Now contains about 200 flutes and recorders, half of which are folk instruments. The thirty recorders, half of them anonymous, chiefly stemmed from the Snoeck collection. They include alto recorders by Bressan, Lot, and Parent, tenor recorders by Hotteterre and Bizey, and an anonymous Italian great-bass recorder from the 16th century.

11

Instrument Makers: Modern

This chapter looks at writings about the life and work of modern recorder makers. We have also included one directory of makers that appeared in a series of articles. For more recent directories see *Register of Early Music in America* (New York: Early Music America, 1989) and *Supplement to the Register of Early Music in America* (New York: Early Music America, 1991) as well as the *1994 NEMA Early Music Yearbook* (London: National Early Music Association, 1994).

DIRECTORIES

271. "Les facteurs et fabriquants de flûtes à bec" [Makers and manufacturers of recorders]. *Flûte à bec* 1 (June 1981): 12; 2 (February 1982): 21.

    Reyne, Hugo. "Les facteurs et fabricants de flûtes à bec dans le monde entier: Liste durement établie" [Makers and manufacturers of recorders worldwide: list compiled with difficulty]. *Flûte à bec* 6 (March 1983): 34–36.

    Reyne, Hugo. "Les facteurs et fabricants de flûtes à bec dans le monde entier: Liste durement et fraîchement établie" [The makers and manufacturers of recorders worldwide: list compiled anew and with difficulty]. *Flûte à bec & instruments anciens* 8 (September 1983): 16–18.
    A directory of modern makers' names, addresses, and phone numbers, arranged by country. Reyne's updates, despite the efforts mentioned in the titles, are full of amusing misprints.

Individual Makers and Manufacturers

Bariaux, Daniel

272. Ritchie, Jacqueline. "Entretien avec Annie Sturbois et Daniel Bariaux" [Interview with Annie Sturbois and Daniel Bariaux]. *Flûte à bec* 3 (June 1982): 18–20.

    Covers: their early recorder making, what they like about the profession, their training, the "harmonization" of a recorder, the meaninglessness of the term "copy," their contacts with recorder players, woods, the aesthetic of the Baroque recorder, and the types of recorders they make.

Beaudin, Jean François

273. Epstein, Jan. "Jean François Beaudin." *The Recorder: Journal of the Victorian Recorder Guild* 5 (November 1986): 1–6.

    Interview. Covers: background, the recorder scene in Canada, his model of tenor recorder as an equivalent of the flute and oboe, copying the Quantz flute, "working in the style of the old makers," what makes a good instrument.

Bigio, Robert

274. "Robert Bigio: Flute and Recorder Maker." *Recorder & Music* 7, no. 7 (September 1982): 173–74.

    Covers: his career as a flutist; his work as a maker of headjoints for modern flutes; his subsequent interest in wood turning and his work on baroque flutes and recorders; his tools and workshop; the historical instruments he has chosen as models.

Boudreau, Jean-Luc

275. Gagnon, Robert, and François Filiatrault. "Interview avec Jean-Luc Boudreau, facteur de flûtes à bec" [Interview with Jean-Luc Boudreau, recorder maker]. *Le Tic-Toc-Choc* 4, no. 4 (May 1983): 10–11.

    Covers: his background, making and playing, Ganassi recorders, copying early instruments, Renaissance vs. Baroque recorders, temperament, woods, and his projects.

276. Kirk, Douglas. "An Interview with Jean-Luc Boudreau." *Continuo* 15, no. 2 (April 1990): 2–5.

Boudreau declares that he no longer even tries to produce "authentic copies" of original instruments, but rather recorders that will suit the demands of modern players for register balance, reliability, and "a certain resistance" in the blowing.

COOLSMA, HANS

277. Kliphuis, Harry. "First 'Coolsma Bressan.'" *Recorder & Music Magazine* 2, no. 10 (September 1968): 334.

An account of Hans Coolsma's formal presentation of his first Bressan copy to Edgar Hunt, owner of the original instrument. Describes Coolsma's deviations from the original, assesses the quality of the copy, and summarizes Coolsma's comments on the production of replicas.

CRANMORE, TIM

278. [Hunt, Edgar?]. "Tim Cranmore: An Interview." *Recorder & Music* 7, no. 11 (September 1983): 282.

Interview conducted at the Boston Early Music Festival and Exhibition. Covers: his start as a biochemist; his training; the instruments he uses as models; the various pitch standards he uses for his copies.

DOLMETSCH FAMILY

See also under the subheadings "Dolmetsch, Arnold" and "Dolmetsch, Carl" in chapter 29, "Biographies and Interviews: Modern."

279. Farleigh, John. "Carl Dolmetsch and Leslie Ward: Musical Instrument Makers, Haslemere." In his *The Creative Craftsman*, 168–86. London: G. Bell & Sons, 1950.

Begins by seeing Arnold Dolmetsch's instrument making (and playing) as part of "a movement that to-day is recognised as the rebirth of the crafts." Then interviews Dolmetsch and Ward (head of the Dolmetsch keyboard department) about: makers being able to play the instruments they make, Arnold Dolmetsch's work, taking up his mantle, making "improvements" to early instruments, producing "better" instruments than the early ones, craftsmanship, materials, instrument decoration, the condition of surviving early instruments, plastic recorders, Carl's training, and the satisfaction of active music-making.

280. Hunt, Edgar. "Arnold Dolmetsch, die Dolmetsch-Sammlung und das Familienunternehmen" [Arnold Dolmetsch, the Dolmetsch collection, and the family enterprise]. *Tibia* 7, no. 3 (1982): 198–200.

Summarizes the life of Dolmetsch, emphasizing his unantiquarian interest in old instruments and his attempts to "improve" them. Dolmetsch's collection, formerly kept in his house at Haslemere, has now mostly gone to the Horniman Museum, London. It includes the famous "lost" Bressan (later found, of course) and another recorder by Stanesby. The family firm went backrupt and has now been replaced by the new firm of J. & M. Dolmetsch.

281. Stuart, Charles. "'Dolmetscherie' Today." *The Musical Times* no. 1301 = 92, no. 7 (July 1951): 297–303.

Covers the activities of the post-war Dolmetsch workshops, particularly the making and manufacture of recorders, lutes, viols, and keyboard instruments. Describes the work of Carl Dolmetsch on the voicing and tuning of recorders. During this period, Carl worked with each recorder—approximately ten—each day before it left the shop. Briefly mentions the "superplastic" soprano recorder "which is selling at just over a guinea in tens of thousands." Also mentions Carl Dolmetsch's activity in the commission of new recorder music.

GEIGER, GEORG

282. Epstein, Jan. "Profile: Georg Geiger." *The Recorder: Journal of the Victorian Recorder Guild* 9 (February 1989): 20–23.

Covers: his taking up the recorder late in life; his training in recorder making; his partnership with Clas Pehrsson; the problems of making recorders in Australia; his philosophy of recorder making (making instruments to suit individual needs).

HAYNES, BRUCE (B. 1942)

283. McRae, Lee. "Bruce Haynes: Performer, Instrument Maker, and Teacher." *The American Recorder* 14, no. 2 (May 1973): 46–49.

Profile written while Haynes was preparing to fill in temporarily for Frans Brüggen at the Hague Conservatory. Haynes started his career as an oboe player and took up the recorder only after becoming disillusioned with the professional opportunities of an oboist. He received a fellowship to study with Brüggen. After passing his exams, he still believed he could not support himself by playing, so he began work in Boston with von

Huene, who needed an experienced player to help voice and tune instruments. His increased interest in low-pitch Baroque oboes and recorders led him to open a workshop of his own on the west coast, where he continued to perform. Discusses why Brüggen selected Haynes as his replacement and reports the differences Haynes sees between American and European players.

HUBER, GERHARD

284. Ettlin, Alex. "Gerhard Huber, Blockflötenbau Horgen: ein Firmenporträt" [Gerhard Huber Recorder Factory in Horgen: a portrait of the company]. *Zeitschrift SAJM* 21, no. 6 (November 1993): 35–42.

    A brief overview of the development and work of the Huber factory (which took over the Nägeli company in 1967). Lots of photographs of the production.

HULSENS, GUIDO (B. 1954)

285. Ritchie, Jacqueline. "Entretien avec Guido Hulsens, Fluthier" [Interview with Guido Hulsens, recorder maker]. *Flûte à bec* 2 (February 1982): 19–20.

    Hulsens is both recorder maker and recorder player. Covers: the advantages of being both, the qualities of different Baroque recorders, Baroque composers writing for an instrument, the differences between Renaissance and Baroque instruments, modern recorder making, recorders for the music of van Eyck, and copying early recorders.

JAMES, CLARENCE

286. Bitters, David L. "Hand Crafting Recorders: A Visit to the Workshop of Clarence James." *The American Recorder* 20, no. 1 (May 1979): 10–13.

    Opens with a discourse by Bitters on the continued interest in hand-crafted instruments despite the wide availability and affordability of mass-produced instruments. James, a professional tool and die maker living in Columbus, Ohio, began making recorders part-time in 1974. Describes some of the machines and tools used in his workshop and relates his early experiences making recorders. Lists the types of recorders he has produced and assesses their tone quality.

287. "Clarence James: Recorder Maker." *Recorder & Music* 7, no. 3 (September 1981): 72–73.

Brief profile. Includes photographs of several machines and finished recorders.

KELISCHEK, GEORGE

288. Oler, Wesley M. "A Visit to the Kelischek Workshop." *The American Recorder* 8, no. 2 (Spring 1967): 54–57.

Written following a visit to George Kelischek's workshop in suburban Atlanta. Begins by describing the various rooms and their contents. The biography of Kelischek covers: his musical education; his apprenticeship as a cabinet maker; his early work (by the age of seventeen) making stringed instruments; his subsequent apprenticeship with the Moeck workshops and eventual appointment as foreman of the shop's stringed instrument section; his decision 4½ years later to open his own shop; his immigration to Canada and his move to Atlanta. Concludes with a description of the design of his krummhorns and "Kelhorns."

KLEMISCH, GUIDO

289. "Guido Klemisch." *Recorder & Music* 7, no. 1 (March 1981): 23.

Brief profile of the performer and instrument maker. Includes a photograph of seven of his recorders.

KOCH, WILLIAM (1892–1970)

290. Koch, John. "William Koch: 1892–1970." *The American Recorder* 12, no. 1 (February 1971): 5–9.

Covers: his move from New York City to Haverhill, New Hampshire; his early years in the country-inn and antique businesses; his start in recorder making; his experiments with the shrinkage of various woods; his keyless bass recorder; a description of the steps he takes in making a recorder.

KÜNG, FRANZ (1906–1983)

291. "Franz Küng†." *Tibia* 8, no. 2 (1983): 356.

Short obituary. Küng was originally a piano maker. He began making recorders in Switzerland in 1938 and set up a factory during World War II. In 1974 he appointed his sons Andrea and Thomas as his successors.

292. "Obituary: Franz Küng." *Recorder & Music* 7, no. 11 (September 1983): 303.

LEVIN, PHILIP

293. Sacksteder, Richard. "Profile: Philip Levin." *The American Recorder* 20, no. 2 (August 1979): 58–62.

Covers: his musical training and early introduction to the recorder; his move from Miami to New York City to study the bassoon; his growing interest in early music and the recorder; Music for a While; his experiments with voicing, which led to his first work repairing recorders in a spare room of his apartment; his expansion into instrument making; the problems one confronts when copying museum instruments; the instruments he currently makes and plans to make; ethical issues in the business of instrument making; his wish that the scope of the American Recorder Society were broadened; the early music scene in New York and the growth of early music in general.

294. Valleau, Douglas. "Of Woods and Reeds and Sealing Wax and Fagotti and Things: Philip Levin in Conversation." *Continuo* 7, no. 1 (October 1983): 6–13.

Covers: woods, Baroque bassoons, and testing copies.

LORETTO, ALEC V.

295. "Establishing Historic Instruments: A Conversation in Auckland with Alec Loretto." *Early Music New Zealand* 3, no. 2 (June 1987): 22–27.

Covers: the beginnings of the early music movement in New Zealand, his influences as a maker of recorders and harpsichords, his visits to Europe, his commissions, the current recorder scene in New Zealand, the future of the recorder, his plans.

296. [Hunt, Edgar]. "Alec Loretto: An Interview." *Recorder & Music* 6, no. 4 (December 1978): 101–2.

Covers: changes he has observed in recorder playing since his last visit to Europe in 1972; the idea of "schools" of recorder makers; the different approaches makers take to their work; his exhibit of instruments in Bruges; his plans; his provocative articles in *Early Music* (item 502) and *The Recorder and Music Magazine* (item 501).

297. [Hunt, Edgar]. "An Interview with Alec Loretto." *The Recorder and Music Magazine* 8, no. 1 (March 1984): 6–9.

Covers: his impressions of the exhibition compared to others he has attended; why exhibitors exhibit; how a regional or national "school of playing" helps makers define a market; block-making courses at the Royal

Conservatorium in The Hague; his controversial series of articles in *Early Music* (item 502); the rising standard of quality in recorder making; the future of the recorder; his plans.

298. [Hunt, Edgar]. "European Impressions: Dutch Playing, Modern and Historic Instruments." *Recorder and Music Magazine* 4, no. 4 (December 1972): 122-23.

    An interview with Alec Loretto, presumably conducted by Edgar Hunt. At the time, Loretto was in the midst of a year of study in Europe and had just returned from Holland. Covers: the perceived change in Brüggen's style after he abandoned modern instruments in favor of historical copies; the difference between modern and historical recorders, which he likens to the difference between a piano and a harpsichord; the Brüggen "bulge" and other characteristics of Dutch playing; his experience attending the Northumbrian Recorder and Viol School in Durham; his plans.

299. "Recorders Made by Alec Loretto." *Recorder & Music* 5, no. 12 (December 1977): 388-90.

    A profile of Loretto, accompanied by photographs of twenty of his instruments.

300. Simpson, Adrienne. "Making Recorders of Gidgee, Tawa and Black Maire: Two New Zealanders Discuss the Recorders that Come from Down-under." *Continuo* 10, no. 2 (November 1986): 2-5. Reprinted in *NEMA Journal* 8 (January 1988): 14-19.

    Interview with Alec Loretto. Covers: living in New Zealand, teaching in Europe, the proliferation of makers of recorders based on historical models worldwide, his making of unusual types of recorders, the woods he uses (including ones from Australia and New Zealand), the desirability of amateurs learning to improve and maintain their own instruments, and his wish for more recorder makers to share the "tricks of the trade." Letter from Lee Collins in 11, no. 6 (June 1987): 10; reply by Loretto in 11, no. 11-12 (December 1987): 16.

MARVIN, BOB

301. Marvin, Bob. "Letters from Bob Marvin." *Continuo* 3, no. 4 (January 1980): 3-9.

    Covers: autobiographical material, his philosophy of recorder making, the qualities of recorders of different periods, and the recorder as an imitator of early voice techniques, including criticism on these grounds of the style of recordings made on his instruments. See also the letter from Norman Stansfield, 3, no. 7 (April 1980): 6-10. Picking up on Marvin's advocacy of "Zen instrument making," Stansfield suggests we may gain insights into recorders and their playing by studying the shakuhachi.

MOECK, HERMANN (1896–1982)

302. "Hermann Moeck senior†." *Tibia* 8, no. 1 (1983): 273.

Obituary. As well as founding the firm that still bears his name, Moeck was an important instrument collector; his collection now belongs to the University of Göttingen. See also Hermann Moeck Jr.'s "50 Jahre Moeck Verlag und Musikinstrumentenwerk: Festrede beim Jubiläum am 5. September 1980," *Tibia* 5, no. 3 (1980): 199–202.

MOECK, HERMANN, JR. (B. 1922)

303. Pratt, Bill. "Dr. Hermann Moeck Talks about His Firm." *The American Recorder* 14, no. 1 (February 1973): 3–8.

An interview with Dr. Hermann Moeck Jr. Covers: Moeck's beginnings as a publisher (*Der Blockflötenspiegel* and *Zeitschrift für Spielmusik*); the role of the Youth Music Movement in the revival of the recorder; Peter Harlan and the invention of German fingering; Moeck's entry into recorder production in 1949; work with von Huene on the Rottenburgh series of recorders; mass-production vs. hand-crafting; the demise of the Meister recorders as a result of changing tastes in tone quality; the shift in emphasis from playability to historical accuracy in the design of Moeck's historical instruments.

304. Quandt, Reinhold. "Dr. Hermann Moeck wird 70" [Dr. Hermann Moeck turns 70]. (Das Porträt) *Tibia* 17, no. 3 (1992): 194–97. Also a short tribute by Ulrich Thieme for the editors of *Tibia*, "Ein Hermannsdenkmal," 215.

An overview of Moeck's important work as an instrument manufacturer and publisher since he took over from his father in 1960.

MOECK VERLAG

305. "Moeck: Music Publishers & Instrument Makers." *Recorder & Music Magazine* 2, no. 8 (February 1968): 270.

A brief description of the company's publishing and manufacturing activities.

Monin, Claude

306. Hunt, Edgar. "A Recorder for France." *Recorder and Music Magazine* 4, no. 5 (March 1973): 161.

    Brief profile of Claude Monin, a French telecommunications engineer who makes recorders modelled after Hotteterre instruments.

307. Ritchie, Jacquelin. "Rencontre avec Claude Monin" [Meeting with Claude Monin]. *Flûte à bec* 3 (June 1982): 21–22.

    Monin was the first modern recorder maker in France (1968). Briefly covers: his early experiments, the uniqueness of the recorder, voicing, the essentials of a good recorder, and modifying a bad recorder.

Paetzold, Joachim

308. Schmidt, Susanne. "'Primitives Instrument voller Rätsel'—Ein Gespräch mit den Tübinger Flötenbaumeister Joachim Paetzold" ["Primitive instrument full of puzzles"—a conversation with the Tübingen recorder maker Joachim Paetzold]. *Tibia* 12, no. 3 (1987): 518–19.

    Covers: his background, including his introduction to the recorder; his production; his development of a new round foot for the recorder; his lack of "overperfection." A humorous report on "the roguish recorder maker."

Prescott, Thomas

309. Brodie, Gary. "Recorder Makers at Home." *The Recorder Magazine* 13, no. 1 (March 1993): 17–18.

    A chatty account of visits to the workshops of Tom Prescott in New Hampshire and Friedrich von Huene in Boston, Massachusetts.

* Prescott, Thomas M. "Making Recorders." Cited below as item 455.

310. Redsell, Matthew James. "The Life and Times of a Recorder Maker." *Continuo* 11, no. 5 (May 1987): 2–6.

    Covers: how Prescott works with his partner, Rob Gilliam-Turner; how he apportions his time; how many instruments they make; his background (detailed); makers he admires; hand-turning vs. template-turning; the state of the business; how orders are generated; what he would look for in an apprentice (including "previous experience not required").

ROESSLER, HEINZ

311. Sayers, K.J. "The Roessler Recorder." *Early Music* 3, no. 1 (January 1975): 19–20.
    Observes that players and makers have become increasingly interested in improving the recorder's flexibility and expressivity, but the demand for inexpensive instruments has led to manufacturing techniques that suppress these qualities (see items 501 and 502 for more on the topic). Sayers advocates the recorders made by Heinz Roessler as instruments that are carefully made and embody many sought-after characteristics.

SAUNDERS, JOANNE

312. Saunders, Joanne. "Reflections of a Recorder Maker." *The Recorder: Journal of the Victorian Recorder Guild* 9 (February 1989): 29–30.
    Brief comments on her training with Fred Morgan and the difficulties of recorder making.

SILVERSTEIN, STEVEN

313. Valleau, Douglas. "A Conversation with Steve Silverstein in Boston." *Continuo* 6, no. 11 (September 1983): 11–15.
    Covers: background, the qualities of an instrument maker, copying and testing early instruments, tools, finishing, and materials.

SOUBEYRAN, CLAIRE

314. Duhot, Jean-Joël. "Facture restauration recherche: Claire Soubeyran" [Instrument-making restoration research: Claire Soubeyran]. *Flûte à bec & instruments anciens* 17 (December 1985/February 1986): 18–21.
    Interview. Covers: her study (undertaken at the Dayton Miller Collection and the Smithsonian Institution, Washington, D.C.) of the deforming influence that the wrappings (of cork or waxed thread) of the joints exert on the bore of the flutes, her philosophy of restoration of early flutes, and combining restoration and making in her life. Soubeyran is primarily a maker of early flutes; she has made only one copy of an early recorder.

STIEBER, ERNST

315. Cawley, Margaret E. "Ernst Stieber, Tuebingen: 50 Years an Instrument Maker." *The American Recorder* 12, no. 4 (November 1971): 113–22.

    An idyllic portrait illustrated by many photographs. Topics related to recorder-making include: his apprenticeship with Max Schuster and Paul Seckendorf; his acquisition of an E.G. Kirst one-keyed flute, which subsequently served as a model for several copies; his great-bass recorders; his daily routine; why he remained in Europe.

316. Hunt, Edgar. "Ernst Stieber: Recorder Maker." *Recorder & Music Magazine* 3, no. 4 (December 1969): 130.
    A brief profile.

STURBOIS, ANNIE

* Ritchie, Jacqueline. "Entretien avec Annie Sturbois et Daniel Bariaux" [Interview with Annie Sturbois and Daniel Bariaux]. Cited above as item **272**.

TOYAMA, NOBUO

317. Burakoff, Gerald. "An Interview with Nobuo Toyama." (The Recorder in Education) *American Recorder* 31, no. 2 (June 1990): 15–17.

    Covers: the history of the Toyama Musical Instrument Company; his decision in the early 1950s to experiment with the manufacture of plastic recorders for schools; the appearance of his plastic instruments under the name Aulos in the mid 1950s and the role they have played in elementary music education in Japan; quality control in the production of Aulos recorders; improvements to instruments through research and development; the Aulos alto based on an instrument by Richard Haka; the lack of a market for plastic Renaissance-style recorders; current trends in plastics; differences in buying habits among the United States, Japan, and Europe; sales of English fingering (70%) vs. German (30%); recorder instruction in Japan. Letter from Tada Ichiro in 30, no. 3 (September 1990): 37.

VON HUENE, FRIEDRICH (B. 1929)

* Brodie, Gary. "Recorder Makers at Home." Cited above as item **309**.

* Lewis, Mildred. "How Recorders Are Made at the Workshop of Friedrich von Huene." Cited below as item **443**.

318. Merger, Carl E. "Friedrich von Huene: The Man, His Work, and His Family." *The American Recorder* 11, no. 1 (Winter 1970): 3–7. Reprinted in *Recorder & Music* 5, no. 2 (June 1975): 59–60.

    Covers: his apprenticeship with Verne Q. Powell; why recorders are difficult to make; his measurement and study of historical instruments; the establishment of his workshop; a general description of the layout and workflow of the shop; his Guggenheim fellowship; his plans.

319. Moeck, Hermann. "Friedrich der Grosse fünfzig (20.2.1979)" [Frederick the Great, 50 (20 February 1979)]. *Tibia* 4, no. 2 (1979): 327.

    An appreciation of Friedrich von Huene.

320. Post, Nora. "An Interview with Friedrich von Huene." *The American Recorder* 23, no. 4 (November 1982): 147–49.

    Covers: his experience playing recorder, flute, and squeezebox as a youth; how, at the age of sixteen, lathing cannons for model ships led to an interest in flutemaking; the need to make instruments that are pleasing to both the ear and eye; how he selects instruments to copy; why he does not copy anonymous recorders, no matter how excellent they might be; the fine distinction between handcrafting and mass-producing instruments; his views on plastic recorders; differences between American and European makers in their attitude toward their work.

321. Redsell, Matthew James. "Ingeborg von Huene." *Continuo* 13, no. 1 (February 1989): 2–5.

    Ingeborg, the wife of Friedrich von Huene, discusses their life and work, including the role that she and her children have played in the family business.

322. Ritchie, Jacqueline. "Un grand facteur américain: Friedrich von Huene" [A great American maker: Friedrich von Huene]. *Flûte à bec & instruments anciens* 24 (1988): 3–5.

    Covers: his background, the beginnings of the early music revival, his instrument making, the decoration of instruments, and making copies of old instruments.

WILLMAN, JOHN

323. [Hunt, Edgar?]. "John Willman: An Interview." *Recorder & Music* 7, no. 5 (March 1982): 118-19.

    Covers: his apprenticeship in machine engineering; his musical study; his decision to make recorders; the voicing and bore design of Bressan recorders and the difficult task of copying them; the importance of using low pitch for modern copies.

MISCELLANEOUS

324. Geissmann, Annemarie. "Der Blockflötenbau in der Schweiz" [Recorder making in Switzerland]. *Tibia* 15, no. 1 (1990): 43-44.

    Only two Swiss recorder makers from the Baroque period are known: Christian Schlegel and his son Jeremias. Briefly sketches their lives, then moves on to modern makers: the recorder firms (Küng, Huber, Fehr, which collectively produce 20-30,000 instruments per year) and the private makers (Santi Occorso, Olivier Delessert, Andreas Schwob, Ernst Meyer, Andreas Schöni, and Dieter Graf). Ends with the curious statement that "One must not forget that no literature about recorder making exists!"

12

Construction and Design

This chapter deals with sources that discuss the construction and design of recorders, historical and modern—that is, the properties of the instruments themselves. It includes such special topics as English vs. German fingering, electronic recorders, modernizing the recorder, the bell key, one-handed recorders, and woods. For information on the making and manufacture of recorders, see chapter 14.

325. Bolton, Philippe. "La flûte à bec" [The recorder]. *Flûte à bec & instruments anciens* 13/14 (December 1984/March 1985): 2–3. Copies obtainable from the author at Le Grand Portail, F-84570 Villes-sur-Auzon, France.

    Defines recorder (fixed embouchure consisting of windway plus lip; thumb-hole for octaving) and describes its basic acoustics and tone production. Summarizes the differences among Renaissance, Ganassi, and Baroque recorders. Looks forward to collaboration between musicians and makers to produce suitable instruments for our own time.

326. Dessy, Raymond, and Lee Dessy. "The Principles of Recorder Design Explained." *The American Recorder* 33, no. 2 (June 1992): 7–14.

    Clearly explains much of our understanding of the acoustics of the recorder bore. Relates many aspects of the recorder's tone, pitch, and sound radiation to the way the open and closed finger holes affect the internal standing waves. Explains the role of the speaker hole and the relationship of blowing pressure to sounding frequency. Mentions some aspects of the tone-production process and the contribution of the various voicing factors to the tone and stability of notes. A few curious statements cannot be followed up because of the journal's customary policy of avoiding footnotes. Dessy answers readers' questions in 33, no. 3 (September 1992): 33–35. Alec V. Loretto discusses the effect of bore shape on intonation in 33, no. 4 (December 1992): 25.

* Felder, Denise. "Zur Entwicklung der Blockflöte im 20. Jahrhundert" [On the development of the recorder in the 20th century]. Cited above as item 85.

327. Halfpenny, Eric. "The English Baroque Treble Recorder." *The Galpin Society Journal* 9 (1956): 82–90.

    Detailed description of the physical characteristics of the 18th-century alto recorder based on an examination of thirteen instruments. Includes measurements of eight instruments and photographs of four.

328. Haynes, Bruce. "The Baroque Recorder: A Comparison with Its Modern Counterpart." Drawings by Friedrich von Huene. *Recorder & Music Magazine* 2, no. 11 (December 1968): 364–68. Reprinted in *The American Recorder* 10, no. 1 (Winter 1969): 3–8.

    Calls for a return to standards of the past. In his explanation of the differences between a typical modern recorder and its Baroque prototype, Haynes makes compelling arguments in favor of retaining many of the characteristics that had been considered flaws in older instruments, such as their soft, nasal tone quality. Also covers voicing, construction of the windway, undercut holes, and low pitch. Includes drawings of altos by Bressan, J.C. Denner, and Küng, as well as cut-away drawings of the head of a Baroque alto. Correction by Haynes in *Recorder & Music Magazine* 3, no. 1 (March 1969): 20.

329. Hunt, Edgar. "The Renaissance Recorder." *The Consort* 19 (July 1962): 116–21.

    An introduction to the characteristics of the Renaissance recorder, including a chart comparing the basic measurements of Renaissance, Baroque, and modern instruments.

330. Omitted.

* Lerch, Tom. "Die Entwicklung des barocken Blockflötenbaus in Europa: Ein geschichtlicher Abriss" [The development of Baroque recorder making: an historical outline]. Cited above as item 165.

331. Loretto, Alec V. "A New Angle on Finger Holes." *The Recorder Magazine* 10, no. 3 (September 1990): 64–66.

    Presents three reasons why makers use angled fingerholes: to place the holes in more convenient positions for the hands; to avoid drilling into a socket; and to adjust the tuning of the instrument.

332. Marvin, Bob. "A Serviceable Early Baroque Flauto." *FoMRHI Quarterly* 16 (July 1979): 50–51 (Communication No. 226).

Taking his cue from the dimensions of three surviving instruments (two in Vienna, one in The Hague), discusses the slightly tapering bore that might be appropriate for a recorder to play early 17th-century music.

333. Morgan, Fred. "A Recorder for the Music of J.J. van Eyck." *The American Recorder* 25, no. 2 (May 1984): 47–49. In Spanish as: "Una flauta dulce para la musica de J.J. van Eyck." *Musica Antiqua* 1 (June 1986): 44–49.

Because of its positioning in the Vellekoop edition of Jacob van Eyck's *Der fluyten lust-hof*, many modern scholars—Morgan among them—have assumed that that collection included the drawing of a recorder that actually belonged to the instructions by Paulus Matthysz (see item 592). Nevertheless, the collection does require a recorder with a range of two octaves and one note. Because of its extraordinary range, such an instrument has been considered a missing link between "the small-range Renaissance recorders and the Hotteterre type." The idea of building such a recorder has intrigued many makers, including Morgan, who decided to use Matthysz's drawing as a model. After several attempts, he concluded that the instrument must employ a "choke bore" in order to utilize the high harmonics of the instrument. His theory seemed to be confirmed in 1982, when he and Ture Bergstrøm measured two narwhal ivory recorders that Eva Legêne had seen in the Rosenborg Castle in Copenhagen (see item 219), which had such a bore and range. He concludes: "At this time, I think the Rosenborg recorders provide us with the models we need." (A different view of the Matthysz drawing is taken by Legêne in her contribution to item 63.)

334. Morgan, Fred. "Old Recorders and New Ones." *The Recorder: Journal of the Victorian Recorder Guild* 1 (1984): 12–16.

"A sort of 'recorder maker's speculative history of recorder design,' supported by reference to some examples of the maker's craft from earlier centuries." Discusses cylindrical-bore recorders, choke-bore recorders, [Jean] Hotteterre's instrument-making ("solidly based on the work of his predecessors"), modern changes, recent interest in playing recorders to suit the music, and the position of the recorder today.

335. Myers, Herbert W. *The Practical Acoustics of Early Woodwinds*. D.M.A. thesis, Stanford University, 1981. vi, 134 leaves. OCLC #7648851. UMI order no. 81-09026.

A comprehensive account of the acoustics of many early woodwinds, based on practical rather than theoretical knowledge of their behavior. Covers tone holes, bore shapes, materials and keywork—which are applicable to recorders as well as other instruments. A chapter on tone generators includes several pages on recorder voicing. Most of the information in the thesis is summarized in table form in a useful appendix, which gives the result of each specific change to a general aspect of each type of instrument. For the recorder, summarizes the effects of altering the size, undercutting, and position of finger holes; changing the basic bore shape; introducing local expansions or contractions in the bore; changing the wall material; and changing the dimensions of the window and windway.

336. Read, Robin. "Recorder Tone." *Recorder and Music Magazine* 2, no. 1 (March 1966): 7–9.

    Focuses on the effects of design, construction, selection of wood, and voicing on a recorder's tone. Also describes the importance of a comfortable playing position, an appropriate vibrato, and proper breath control.

337. Sandner, Erich. "Irrtum bei Blockflöten?? Steht die Sopran- und Tenorblockflöte in B?" [An error in recorders?? Are the soprano and tenor recorder pitched in B♭?]. *Das Musikinstrument* 29, no. 6 (June 1980): 906, 908.

    As the title suggests, argues that the C recorders are really pitched in B♭. As Hermann Moeck pointed out immediately, however, "The error of Erich Sandner is quickly cleared up" (*Tibia* 5, no. 3 [1980]: 210). His argument is based on his not having distinguished between instruments with seven upper fingerholes (like the recorder) and those with six (like the fife). Sandner's suggestion that all recorders should be treated as transposing instruments relative to C fingerings goes against long-standing practice.

338. Tuschner, Wolfram. "Die frühen Holzblasinstrumente im Lichte der mittelalterlichen Tonlehren" [Early woodwind instruments in the light of the medieval modes]. *Tibia* 8, no. 3 (1983): 401–6.

    An imaginative discussion of the transition from woodwind instruments with six upper fingerholes into those with seven (including of course the recorder) in the light of the tetrachord system of the *Musica enchiriadis* and the later Guidonian hexachord system.

339. Zaniol, Angelo. "A chaque musique sa flûte à bec" [To each type of music its recorder]. *Flûte à bec* 5 (December 1982): 32–35; 6 (March 1983): 3–14. In English as: "The

Recorders of the Middle Ages and Renaissance." *Continuo* 8, no. 1 (November 1984): 2–7; 8, no. 2 (December 1984): 12–15; 8, no. 3 (January 1985): 6–9. In German, with updates, as: "Jeder Musik ihre Blockflöte: Blockflöten des 14./15.–17. Jahrhunderts." *Tibia* 13, no. 2 (1988): 73–83.

A helpful survey of our state of knowledge of medieval and Renaissance recorders, based on pictures, treatises, surviving examples, and modern attempts to make similar instruments. Classifies such recorders into five main types: Medieval, Renaissance I, Renaissance II, Renaissance III, and "van Eyck."

BASS AND GREAT-BASS RECORDERS

340. Bloodworth, Denis. "A New Design of Bass Recorder." *The Recorder Magazine* 12, no. 1 (March 1992): 3–5.

    Describes a bass recorder made by Albert Lockwood, interesting for its novel keywork, bore design, and close positioning of tone holes.

341. Haynes, J.L. "The Production Recorder." *Recorder & Music* 6, no. 1 (March 1978): 12–13.

    Describes the construction of a bass recorder with a square bore.

342. Waechter, Wolfram. "Klingendes Sperrholz: Testbericht über die neuentwickelte Paetzold-Kontrabaßblockflöte" [Plywood resounding: test report on the newly developed Paetzold contrabass recorder]. *Tibia* 2, no. 2 (1977): 302–3, 305–6.

    "At first sight, it appears to be some piece of modern technical equipment, designed less by an instrument maker than by an architect. And people who in buying a recorder put visual appearance above sound are certainly in for a bit of a shock. . . . " Waechter reports at length (small print) on the "facts and figures," "development history," and "details" of the new conical instrument made of thick plywood, close in shape to an organ pipe. Followed by some critical remarks and an enthusiastic note on its "sound and response possibilities" for avant-garde recorder music. A helpful report on an important development in modern recorder making.

CARVED RECORDERS

343. Hess, Stanley. "An Apology for the Carved Recorder." *The American Recorder* 9, no. 2 (Spring 1968): 43–47.

Begins by exploring briefly the relationship between functionality and aesthetic design. Notes that the end rings, beading, and swells of the Baroque recorder were not necessary to the instrument's structure and were added solely to improve appearance. "'Useless' ornamentation is part of a craftsman's art." Hess's own interests lie in scrimshawing in relief. He includes drawings of eight plans for carved recorders taken from his notebooks. He doubts, however, that carved instruments will ever become common because of "the 'functional' taste of our time." See also item **344**, a sequel.

344. Hess, Stanley. "Tone Building, Figuratively Speaking, with the Baroque Recorder." *The American Recorder* 21, no. 2 (August 1980): 55–59.

    Reports that von Huene was reluctant to pursue the kind of high-relief carving proposed by Hess in item **343** for fear that the carving—particularly the depth of the window—would affect the tonal properties and voicing of the instrument. A number of years later, Hess took up instrument making (he is a professor of art) and was able to realize many of the planned carvings, although several were musical failures. He concludes that the deep windows produced by high-relief carving can be accommodated by proper venting. The article includes photographs and illustrations of the recorders. Letter from Friedrich von Huene in 21, no. 4 (February 1981): 191 offers photographs of six carved recorders dating from the eighteenth-century. Letter from Hess (with more photographs) in 23, no. 4 (November 1982): 175.

ENGLISH VS. GERMAN FINGERING

345. Clark, Paul. "Eurobore." *The Recorder Magazine* 11, no. 4 (December 1991): 115–17.

    Compares the pitches that require different fingerings in the German and English systems and determines which system provides easier fingering combinations involving these pitches. (English comes out on top.) Concludes with an account of Edgar Hunt's role in promoting mass-produced English-fingered recorders in the 1930s. Responses from Hermann Moeck and Carl Dolmetsch appear in 12, no. 1 (March 1992): 15–18.

346. "English or German Fingering." (What's Wrong with My Recorder?) *The Recorder and Music Magazine* 1, no. 8 (February 1965): 247.

    Explains the differences between the two fingering schemes and shows how one can determine which scheme to use on a particular recorder by examining its tone holes.

347. "A New 'Fingering' from France." (What's Wrong with My Recorder?) *The Recorder and Music Magazine* 1, no. 9 (May 1965): 278.

Brief discussion of an advertisement announcing a *flûte à bec française*, which supposedly combines the advantages of both English and German fingering.

ELECTRONIC RECORDERS

348. Marvuglio, Matt, and Tony Marvuglio. "Wired for Sound." *American Recorder* 32, no. 2 (June 1991): 11-13.

Begins with a description of Musical Instrument Digital Interface (MIDI) technology and MIDI wind controllers, which first appeared in 1987. Early wind controllers emulated the flute, clarinet, and saxophone, but not until 1991 did the first electronic recorders appear: the Suzuki MIDI recorder SRW-100 and the Yamaha WindJamm'r-EW20. The remainder of the article reviews these two instruments and offers advice to traditional recorder players who are planning to take up a MIDI wind controller. Letter from William T. Conklin in 32, no. 3 (September 1991): 35-36.

KEYWORK

See also below under "Modernizing the recorder."

349. Halbig, Hermann. "Geschichte der Klappen an Flöten und Rohrblattinstrumenten bis zum Beginn des 18. Jahrhunderts" [The history of keys on woodwind instruments to the beginning of the 18th century]. *Archiv für Musikwissenschaft* 6 (1924): 1-53.

A detailed study, based on treatises and surviving instruments, of the number, positioning, and construction of early woodwind keys. Still valuable.

MEASURING AND MEASURMENTS

350. Bolton, Philippe. "Mesurer une flûte ancienne" [Measuring an early recorder]. *Flûte à bec & instruments anciens* 17 (December 1985/February 1986): 12-16. Copies obtainable from the author at Le Grand Portail, F-84570 Villes-sur-Auzon, France.

Useful detailed instructions with photographs and diagrams.

351. Brach, Manfred. "On Three Well-Proportioned Alto Recorders." *FoMRHI Quarterly* 60 (July 1990): 35–40 (Communication No. 987). "How to Design a Recorder." *FoMRHI Quarterly* 61 (October 1990): 40–47 (Communication No. 1007). Slightly abridged German version of the combined articles as "Von der alten Kunst, 'auff allerhand Arth' Blockflöten zu entwerfen" [On the ancient art of designing recorders 'of sundry kinds']. *Tibia* 18, no. 4 (1993): 610–16.

In these articles, Brach opens up new territory for our understanding of early recorders and flutes by studying the proportions of the instruments and the mathematical thinking behind them. Such proportions are difficult to see if the measurements are made in millimeters, as is customary nowadays. Using the contemporaneous linear measures, Brach first looks at recorders from Frans Brüggen's collection made by Thomas Stanesby Sr. (English foot), Peter Bressan (Burgundian foot), and Johann Heitz (Saxon foot), showing how the lengths of the various parts of the instruments follow strict ratios. In each case the foot is divided into inches, then lines (1/12ths of an inch). For example, the sounding length of Stanesby's recorder is exactly 18 inches, or 216 lines; he "made his instrument . . . with stupendous accuracy: there are no tolerances at all!" The lengths of the head joint, middle joint, and foot joint are in the ratio 16:13:25. "The position of the central point of the six finger holes is exactly 8 inches (i.e., 4/9 sounding length); the position of the first finger hole is exactly 5/8 sounding length." Did Stanesby intend to use two squares ($16 = 4^2$; $25 = 5^2$) and a cube ($216 = 6^3$)? Brach goes on to show that Bressan and Heitz based their sounding lengths on different numbers with equally interesting properties.

Then Brach looks at the measurements of two further recorders by Bressan, which have significant properties when measured in other ancient French units (aune and toise), and a recorder by Thomas Stanesby, Junior (old Amsterdam foot [voet]). Is this stretching the argument too far? In any case, if Brach is correct, his findings lead to a great many questions, which he is the first to ask. We look forward to reactions and questions from modern makers and scholars. See also his "Alte Traversflöten maßanalytisch untersucht" [The measurements of Baroque flutes investigated], *Tibia* 14, no. 1 (1989): 331–340; and "How to Design a Traverso," *FoMRHI Quarterly* 69 (October 1992): 21–26 (Communication No. 1121).

351.1. Karp, Cary. "Woodwind Instrument Bore Measurement." *Galpin Society Journal* 31 (May 1978): 9–28.

A mathematically based article discussing the problems of bore measurement and encouraging the development of uniform procedures for obtaining and recording such measurements.

352. Mathiesen, Irmgard Knopf, and Aksel H. Mathiesen. "Ein Messungsprojekt: Datamatische Behandlung von Messungen an historischen Holzblasinstrumenten" [A measurement project: computerized treatment of measurements of historical woodwind instruments] *Tibia* 11, no. 3 (1986): 175–87.

Discusses the computerized collection of measurements of historical recorders and two computerized methods of scaling such measurements to produce instruments at a different pitch (e.g., a^1 = 440 Hz instead of 430 Hz). Letters by Tom Lerch and Klaus Bickhardt and reply to Lerch by the Mathiesens in 12, no. 1 (1987): 394–96.

353. Weber, Rainer. "Zur Vermessung von historischen Holzblasinstrumenten" [On the measuring of historical woodwind instruments]. *Tibia* 13, no. 2 (1988): 114–19.

Traditional methods of measuring historical woodwind instruments have literally left their mark on the instruments in the form of scratches. Fortunately, electronic methods are taking their place. In any case, the measuring is in the hand of the measurer. Moreover, wood shrinks over the years, and researchers have introduced the idea of shrinking factors. But these are only reliable when the instrument has metal rings for comparison (ivory or horn rings can shrink more than wood). Quantz discussed reboring instruments to compensate for their shrinking with use, and reboring grooves are sometimes visible on the insides of fingerholes. The amount of shrinkage varies with the type and origin of the wood as well as the part of the trunk from which it is taken. Now, wood can also expand again with moisture. Reports an experiment with the remoisturizing of a 30-year-old piece of oak of known initial dimensions; within 3 days it was roughly back to the original dimensions, although some ovality remained. Another problem in measuring can be grooves in the wall of the bore. Still, the measurements of historical instruments can teach us a great deal.

MODERNIZING THE RECORDER

Daniel Waitzman's 1967 article on the decline of the recorder in the 18th century (item **64**) concluded with a call for recorder makers to modernize the instrument. This essay touched off a debate conducted in the pages of *Recorder & Music Magazine* for the following two years. The articles are presented below in chronological order:

* Waitzman, Daniel. "The Decline of the Recorder in the 18th Century." Cited above as item **64**.
  Concludes with an essay on how the 20th-century recorder has retained the qualities that led to the demise of the 18th-century instrument, and for this reason the recorder has failed to win the consideration it deserves as a professional instrument equal to the flute or oboe. For letters in reply to Waitzman, see the entry in chapter 4.

354. Haynes, Bruce. "The Decline: A Further Scrutiny." *Recorder & Music Magazine* 2, no. 8 (February 1968): 240–42.
  An article-length refutation of item **64**. Argues that the only real improvements to the modern recorder will come from the study and imitation of historical instruments. One should not equate evolution with progress. It is quite possible that many of the qualities Waitzman considers faults were looked upon favorably in the 18th century (for example, the absence of keywork, the distinction between "good" and "bad" notes in a key, and the soft sound of the instrument). Haynes does not see the point of creating Waitzman's "truly modern recorder": "Shall we make the recorder into a romantic instrument in order to better play the music of the Baroque?" Haynes also believes that a bell-key is "unnecessary for Baroque, and even many modern, pieces." In contemporary music, "bell-keys, trill-keys, and whisper-keys will have no more (or less) musical significance than door keys." Letters by Alan D. Jackson and Michael Rice in 2, no. 9 (May 1968): 285. See also Carl Dolmetsch's response (item **355**).

355. Dolmetsch, Carl. "Which Way to Turn the Clock?" *Recorder & Music Magazine* 2, no. 9 (May 1968): 283–84.
  Written in response to item **354**. Takes issue with Haynes's criticism of the voicing of Dolmetsch recorders, citing the success of his own work on the Chester recorders: "Who but a bigoted antiquarian could prefer the wheezy, ill-voiced and out-of-tune performance of most early recorders?" Believes the recorder must be adapted to suit large concert halls, and sees the addition of bell and lip keys and the modification of the bore as appropriate improvements. Challenges Haynes "to produce the ideal Baroque-cum-thoroughly-modern recorder." Responses by Steven Silverstein and Bruce Haynes in 2, no. 10 (September 1968): 330.

356. Ashton, Don. "In Defence of Keywork." *Recorder & Music Magazine* 2, no. 10 (September 1968): 313.

Agrees with Waitzman (item 64) and Dolmetsch (item 355) that the recorder merits continued development, but takes issue with Dolmetsch's characterization of keywork as "complicated, cumbersome, clicking, sticking and often leaking encrustations." Argues that well-crafted keywork is free of these deficiencies. Dolmetsch's own bell-key, however, is a "medievally engineered appendage." Defends extensive keywork as a means of fitting instruments to smaller hands.

357. Hunt, Edgar. "Recorder Making Today." *Recorder & Music Magazine* 3, no. 1 (March 1969): 7–10.

Discusses various trends in recorder-making in the late 1960s, a time when several makers—such as Coolsma and von Huene—were returning to 18th-century ideals (curved windways, wider bores, a reedier tone, low pitch, etc.). Compares nine modern altos (made by Arnold Dolmetsch, Dolmetsch Ltd., Fehr, Küng, Coolsma, Mollenhauer, and von Huene) with his own Bressan alto, the instrument that embodies his ideals. During the course of the article, Hunt makes several points in response to the "modernized recorder" controversy. He opposes extending the range of the instrument and adding keywork. In general, his views agree with those of Bruce Haynes (see items 354 and 328). Letter from Don Ashton in 3, no. 2 (June 1969): 66 concerns the bell key.

358. Munrow, David. "Is It Authentic?" *Recorder & Music Magazine* 3, no. 1 (March 1969): 12–14.

Asked to write about the instruments he uses in performance, Munrow takes the opportunity to offer his thoughts on authenticity in instrument-making and the debate over modernization. "A few practical improvements to old instruments seem to me all to the good if they make life easier." For example, he favors the practicality of plastic reeds and added keys on crumhorns, but some departures—such as all-plastic crumhorns—are less successful.

359. Ashton, Don. "The Value of Keywork." *Recorder & Music Magazine* 3, no. 5 (March 1970): 159–60.

Written in reaction to articles on the modernized recorder and the bell key (see items 364 and 365). Explains the traditional functions of keywork (to bring holes within reach, to increase an instrument's range, to allow one finger to shut more than one hole, to provide alternate fingerings) and proposes an unusual argument in favor of keywork on the recorder—one that "has not yet been propounded": " . . . the 'feel' of the instrument beneath one's fingers. Modern methods . . . have made what originally arose largely out of necessity into the science of producing equality of balance and control throughout the instrument. . . . Unless the recorder player plays other instruments it will be rather difficult for him to understand what he is missing in this respect, but the day will come!"

360. Waitzman, Daniel. "A Plan to Promote the Development of a Modernized Recorder." *The American Recorder* 12, no. 3 (August 1971): 71–72. Reprinted in *Recorder and Music Magazine* 4, no. 1 (March 1972): 10–11 under the title "A Plan to Promote a Modernized Recorder."

A quixotic call for the application of modern woodwind technology to the recorder. Does not explain exactly what modernization of the recorder would entail, but goes on at great length in describing its benefits. "If the recorder could be improved as much as the flute has been in the past two-and-a-half centuries, an instrument as technically superior to the modern Boehm flute as the bell-keyed recorder is to the one-keyed flute might result." Concludes with a proposal that the American Recorder Society fund an honorarium for the development of this modern instrument—a proposal the ARS apparently adopted, since the announcement of a $1,000 honorarium appears in 14, no. 3 (August 1973): 107. Letter from R.W. Church in *Recorder and Music Magazine* 4, no. 3 (September 1972): 90 questions Waitzman's assumption that a modernized recorder would represent an improvement over the traditional one.

361. Reinhard, Bruno. "La flûte à bec: Des clés pour le futur!" [The recorder: keys for the future!]. *Flûte à bec & instruments anciens* 15 (June 1985): 2–3.

Compares the qualities of the flute and the recorder in the Renaissance and Baroque eras. Then discusses why the flute superseded the recorder around 1750. Quotes Cavaillé-Coll (1840) to the effect that the recorder could have been improved by a sliding bevel operated by a system of keywork. Although this would still present problems, Reinhard believes that modern musicians and makers could create a 20th-century recorder that preserves the instrument's timbre, articulation, and attack.

362. Marvin, Bob. "A Flexible Recorder." *FoMRHI Quarterly* 41 (October 1985): 21 (Communication No. 649).

What would a truly modern recorder be like? Marvin proposes several modifications: a windway short enough to allow players to shade it with their upper lips; a springy plug; a springy junction between the windway and the labium; a deformable windway roof; and a deformable body. He concludes: "The result might be a large wet noodle, not much like a recorder, but it would be quite flexible to play."

363. Moeck, Hermann. "Zum 100. Mal die völlig beklappte Blockflöte erfunden . . . " [For the 100th time, the fully keyed recorder invented . . .]. *Tibia* 13, no. 4 (1988): 293.

A patent for a fully keyed recorder was taken out in 1988 by Arnfred Rudolf Strathman of Melsdorf. Moeck writes: "Why make it simple when it can be made complicated?!" Describes why the notes outside the basic scale of the recorder can be made with forked fingerings, which also produce a less uniform (and less boring) tone. Does not understand what is patentable about the new "invention." For diagrams and a description of the new instrument, see C.R., "Flöte (Blockflöte mit Klappensystem)," *Instrumentenbau Zeitschrift* 43 (December 1988–January 1989): 138–39.

The Bell Key

364. Waitzman, Daniel. "The Bell Key." *Recorder & Music Magazine* 2, no. 10 (September 1968): 324–27. Reprinted in *The American Recorder* 9 (Winter 1968): 3–6.

Although the technique of closing the bell of a fipple flute was mentioned as early as 1528 by Agricola, it was not until the early 1950s that someone devised a key to stop the bell. The bell key offers the player a variety of fingerings (including a managable one for $f\#^3$) and increases the range of the instrument. Waitzman claims that "the instrument becomes louder, more brilliant, and more assertive. Its emotional scope is widened beyond that of a flauto dolce." Includes a table of fingerings for two full octaves above $b\flat^2$. Steven Silverstein argues against the bell key, and William F. Koch Sr. corrects a factual error in *The American Recorder* 9, no. 3 (Summer 1968): 94. Corrections by Waitzman in *Recorder & Music Magazine* 2, no. 11 (December 1968): 363 (with a letter from Fabienne Smith) and 3, no. 1 (March 1969): 20. Edgar L. Eichhorn describes his experiments with bell keys in *The American Recorder* 10, no. 1 (Winter 1969): 31.

365. Waitzman, Daniel. "Bell-key Probe." *Recorder & Music Magazine* 3, no. 3 (September 1969): 86.

Written in response to item 357. Describes the requirements of a bell-keyed recorder. (See also item 366, which is based on this article.)

366. Waitzman, Daniel. "The Requirements of a Good Bell-Keyed Recorder." *The American Recorder* 12, no. 2 (May 1971): 39–40.

Describes the qualities that should be present in a specially designed bell-keyed recorder that are not found in a conventional recorder with a bell key added (what Waitzman calls the "compromise recorder"). The instrument should be constructed in a way that the high register is in tune

Construction and Design

with the key closed. Certain bell-keyed fingerings should work with acceptable intonation and tone. The middle and high registers should be favored in voicing. Both a right- and a left-hand bell key should be mounted to eliminate completely the need for using the knee to close the bell and to offer a wider variety of fingering combinations. Above all, the key must be airtight. Item 365 is an earlier version of this article.

367. Tsukamoto, Takashi. "Another Bell Key." *Recorder & Music* 5, no. 2 (June 1975): 45–47.

    Claims that lengthening the foot joint of a recorder an inch or so produces the same effect as closing the bell. By placing a keyed hole in the lengthened foot at the position of the original bell hole, a player may simulate the opening and closing of a bell key without having to block the end of the instrument. The editor (Edgar Hunt) appends a note saying that the idea seems to be a good one, but he would first want to verify that common alternate trill fingerings are not affected.

ONE-HANDED RECORDERS

368. Tsukamoto, Takashi. "A One-handed Recorder." *Recorder & Music* 6, no. 9 (March 1980): 258–60, 265.

    Describes a system of closed keys that allows a person with one hand to play the recorder. Includes a fingering chart. Mentions other possible key systems, including one using open keys, but concludes that the particular closed-key system described in detail is the most practical. Edgar Hunt, in a postscript, states his preference for open-keyed systems, which allow the thumb to assume its traditional role and do not require heavy key springs. Letter from A.J. Davey in 7, no. 3 (September 1981): 71.

369. Hunt, Edgar. "Another One-handed Recorder." *Recorder & Music* 7, no. 3 (September 1981): 66–67.

    Sequel to item **368**. Describes two open-keyed recorders made by Bernhard Mollenhauer. Both instruments have a normal thumb hole without keywork.

370. Hunt, Edgar. "The One-handed Recorder." *Recorder & Music* 7, no. 6 (June 1982): 145.

    Summarizes items **368** and **369** and includes a photograph of the Tsukamoto keywork applied to a Zen-On Bressan alto and Stanesby Jr. soprano.

PITCH AND TUNING

See also chapter 18, "Performance Practices (Historical)," under the subheading "Pitch and tuning" (p. 241).

371. Allain-Dupré, Philippe. "Letter ouverte sur la justesse de la flûte à bec en 1983" [Open letter on the justness of the recorder in 1983]. *Flûte à bec & instruments anciens* 9 (December 1983): 9-12.

    A rather disorganized series of philosophical thoughts on the nature of justness of pitch on recorders in general, and copies of historical instruments in particular. Includes analyses of four temperaments (meantone, Pythagorean, Werkmeister III, and Zarlino).

372. Bergmann, Walter. "Authenticity or Snobbery?" *Recorder & Music* 5, no. 8 (December 1976): 260.

    Argues in support of modern pitch and equal temperament. Writing some time before the authenticity movement had reached larger ensembles, Bergmann believes that adopting historical standards would make it impossible to play with "professional orchestras or players of modern instruments" and thus "[t]he recorder player will be pushed back into his little corner of thirty years ago." Letter from Ross Winters in 5, no. 9 (March 1977): 299.

373. Davenport, Mark. "Recorder Pitch: Always Throwing Us a Curve." *American Recorder* 34, no. 1 (March 1993): 7-10.

    Argues that true authenticity in instrument making is unattainable, "perhaps even undesirable." Shows, through an excellent survey of articles by Bruce Haynes, Bob Marvin, Angelo Zaniol, and others, that extant historical instruments vary considerably in their levels of pitch, making it impossible to draw reliable conclusions about historical pitch standards. Then proceeds to demonstrate why effective copies could not be created even if exact pitch standards were known. Suggests that "we can begin to search for that 'perfect' instrument using another set of standards—not based obsessively on strict scientific data but rather with a combination of solid research, practicality, and contemporary aesthetic judgments." Letter from Alec V. Loretto in 34, no. 2 (June 1993): 39.

374. Haynes, Bruce. "Johann Sebastian Bach's Pitch Standards: The Woodwind Perspective." *Journal of the American Musical Instrument Society* 11 (1985): 55-114. In French as: "Les diapasons à l'époque de Jean-Sebastien Bach: L'apport des instruments à vent." *Flûte à bec &*

instruments anciens 22 (1987): 11-19; 23 (1987): 4-8; 24 (1988): 11-18; 26 (November 1988): 11-17.

A long, minutely argued evaluation of the pitches that J.S. Bach's woodwind players would have used. Haynes introduces a wide variety of evidence—theoretical writings, surviving instruments, notation, and contemporaneous tuning measurements and devices—to support his argument that four absolute standard pitches were in use during the late Baroque era: two types of choir pitch and two types of chamber pitch. In numerous asides and appendixes he supplies much other useful information about Baroque pitch in other places, the transmission of Baroque woodwind instruments, the use of surviving instruments to determine pitch, modern players' experience with historical pitches, surviving French woodwind instruments, and Leipzig woodwind makers contemporary with Bach. A tour de force.

375. Weber, Rainer. "Some Researches into Pitch in the 16th Century with Particular Reference to the Instruments in the Accademia Filarmonica of Verona." *The Galpin Society Journal* 28 (April 1975): 7-10.

Reports the results of a study of thirteen low-pitched recorders in the Verona collection: five bassetts in f, three basses in B♭, two great basses in F, and a bassett in f with an extension down to d (all with the double "rabbit's foot" mark), as well as two basses in c (with the double trefoil mark). Although he notes minor variations among the instruments, Weber concludes that eleven instruments are pitched at a^1 = 450 Hz and two are at a^1 = 465. Also looks at flutes and cornetts in the collection.

376. Zaniol, Angelo. "The NF Treble Recorder at the Museum der Stadt Meran." *FoMRHI Quarterly* 33 (October 1983): 14-16 (Communication No. 485).

Makes the point that most Italian music of the late Baroque was performed at around modern pitch (it could also be higher—see item **374**). Hence the need for "recorderists seriously concerned with authenticity" to find suitable instruments from the period to be models for modern makers. One such may be an alto recorder stamped "NF" in the Museum der Stadt Meran, described by Zaniol, which he believes is either a Tyrolean alto in F at a^1=440 Hz or a French alto in G at a^1=390 Hz.

VON HUENE'S CALL FOR STANDARD PITCH

377. von Huene, Friedrich. "A Plea for Standard Pitch." *The American Recorder* 12, no. 3 (August 1971): 77-78. An abridged version appears in *Recorder & Music* as item **378**.

The tendency toward ever-rising pitch standards can be traced back to the 18th century and has continued in the 20th century despite modern means of keeping matters under control. By loosely observing modern standards, many makers produce incompatible instruments. Von Huene recommends that all makers strictly adhere to the same pitch standards (For his own instruments, he uses a^1 = 440 for modern pitch, a^1 = 415 for old pitch, and a^1 = 394 for old French pitch and tunes instruments at 70° F.) He argues that there is no need for a^1 ever to exceed 440. Carl Dolmetsch, in 13, no. 1 (February 1972): 32, offers excuses for the sharpness of one of the Dolmetsch plastic recorders von Huene tested. Other responses: Theodore Mix in 13, no. 3 (August 1972): 100-101 and Hermann Moeck in 13, no. 4 (November 1972): 138.

378. Hunt, Edgar. [Fidelio, pseud.] "A Question of Pitch." *Recorder & Music* 5, no. 10 (June 1977): 324-25.

An abridgement of item 377. (Hunt used the pseudonym "Fidelio" because the overture begins with the pitches E-B♮-B♮, which, using German pitchnames, is "EHH.")

379. Hunt, Edgar. "Questions of Pitch." *Recorder & Music* 6, no. 10 (June 1980): 292-93.

A sequel to item 378. Explains that variations in pitch between different makes of instruments are often the result of some makers tuning instruments cold and others tuning them warmed up. Also offers a brief history of pitch standards from the late 17th century to the present, with an emphasis on the various British standards.

380. Hunt, Edgar, and Friedrich von Huene. "A Question of Pitch Again." *Recorder & Music* 7, no. 5 (March 1982): 119-20.

Sequel to item 379. An 1884 petition submitted to Bismarck by the editors of the *Zeitschrift für Instrumentenbau* shows that attempts to establish an international pitch standard date back to at least the late 19th century. Includes a translation.

381. Freeman, Willa Fowler. "'Once More, With Feeling': A Plea for Standard Pitch." *Continuo* 6, no. 7 (April 1983): 5-7.

Discusses item 377 and the state of thought on the issue in 1983. See also comments by Susan Prior, "The Difference a Pitch Makes," p. 14; and a letter from von Huene and a reply by Prior, 6, no. 9 (June 1983): 27.

VOICING

* Joof, Laura Beha. "Recorder Voicing and Tuning, and Use of the Tuning Machine." Cited below as item 526.

* Levin, Philip. "Voicing and Tuning." Cited below as item 527.

382. Willoughby, Andrew A. "Das Intonieren von Blockflöten: Antworten auf einen Fragebogen" [The voicing of recorders: replies to a questionnaire]. *Tibia* 10, no. 1 (1985): 245-52.

    Summarizes the replies (by forty-one recorder makers and players worldwide) to Willoughby's questionnaire on the results of specified changes in aspects of recorder voicing (the length of the wind canal, raising or lowering the roof or floor of the wind canal, etc.). See also his "Recorder Voicing—Answers to my Questions," *FoMRHI Quarterly* 34 (January 1984): 57-69 (Communication No. 514); untitled reply by Angelo Zaniol in 35 (April 1984): 41-43 (Communication No. 529) with a response by Willoughby in 36 (July 1984): 30 (Communication No. 541).

383. Woods, Timothy. "Recorder Voicing Structures." *FoMRHI Quarterly* 41 (October 1985): 32-33 (Communication No. 654). Revised version in *The Recorder and Music Magazine* 8, no. 8 (December 1985): 239-41.

    Describes three different types of formation of the "inner ramp," labelled "early," "late," and "bad" (most modern recorders). Also comments on the height of the block. Studies four recorders in the Royal College of Music collection, concluding that "knowledge of adjusting the basic quality of the instrument and . . . of the correct setting up procedure was lost in the 19th century." (The revised version is better written but omits significant ideas.)

WOODS

384. Bolton, Philippe. "Les bois dont on fait les flûtes" [The woods of which recorders are made]. *Flûte à bec* 3 (June 1982): 13-15. Copies obtainable from the author at Le Grand Portail, F-84570 Villes-sur-Auzon, France.

    Begins with the statement: "If in theory the wood has no influence on the character of the instrument, it is otherwise in practice." Discusses the effect of the wood on both the timbre of the instrument and the windway.

Then briefly summarizes the types of wood used in different eras. Finally, describes some general properties of wood as a material.

385. Davidson, Martin. "Observations on the Relation between Wood and Tone Quality in Recorders." *The American Recorder* 16, no. 3 (August/September 1975): 88–90.

    Argues, sarcastically at times, that a correlation between wood type and tone quality does not exist; therefore, one should select a recorder based on perceived tone quality and the stability and weight of the wood. Contradicted by David R. Brooks in 16, no. 4 (February 1976): 156–58; see also item 391.

386. Dolmetsch, Carl. "Is There Magic in Wood?" *Recorder & Music Magazine* 3, no. 6 (June 1970): 217.

    Argues that choice of wood has little bearing on a recorder's tone. The key factors are voicing and the player's ability.

387. Kuhweide, Peter. "Cedernholz für den Flötenblock" [Cedar for the recorder block]. *Das Musikinstrument* 39, no. 11 (November 1990): 22–23.

    Discusses the properties of cedar, nowadays used extensively for recorder blocks.

388. Kuhweide, Peter. "Une précision accrue: le buis et les 'bois de buis'" [An increased precision: the boxwood tree and boxwood]. *Das Musikinstrument* 39, no. 11 (November 1990): 89–90.

    Discusses the properties of boxwood, the classic wood for recorders in the Baroque era.

389. Levin, Philip. "Which Wood Should I Choose?" *The American Recorder* 27, no. 2 (May 1986): 60–63.

    Begins by listing eight factors involved in choosing wood (hygroscopic quality; ability to disperse moisture; surface texture; density; acoustical reflectivity; acoustical "liveness"; visual appeal; and the size, weight, and style of instrument in question). Then discusses the qualities of nine specific types (and subtypes) of wood. Concludes that the choice of wood generally has less effect on loudness or tone than the design of the voicing and the bore, although a wood that is dimensionally unstable can defeat efforts to produce a precise voicing. Moreover, since the greatest cost in mass producing recorders is the few minutes of personal attention they receive, they are likely to receive more attention and thus be better instruments if they are made from an expensive wood.

390. Loretto, Alec. "This Way, or That?: Some Comments on the Direction of Grain in Woodwind Instruments." *Recorder & Music* 5, no. 1 (March 1975): 2-4.

As its wood dries out, a recorder may bend, lose its roundness, and split or crack. The direction of the grain determines which areas are most susceptible to damage. When the annual rings run vertically (looking at the recorder in cross section), there is a tendency to split on the sides; horizontal rings encourage splitting along the top or bottom. Because damage to the windway and labium can be disastrous, splits and cracks along the side are preferable. Despite this fact, "nearly all modern makers build their recorders with the annual rings horizontal, whereas nearly all the surviving museum instruments have their annual rings running vertically."

391. Moeck, Hermann. "Auf Holz geblasen: Wissenswertes über ein Baumaterial für Musikinstrumente" [Blowing on wood: things worth knowing about a building material for musical instruments]. *Tibia* 1, no. 2 (1976): 81-87.

Takes issue with Davidson's contention that the wood has nothing to do with the tone of an instrument (item **385**; see also Moeck's review of Davidson's article in the same issue, pp. 105-6). Asserts that "the differences in color between two particular materials certainly depend not only on their resonance properties . . . but among other things also on the surface conditions, e.g., with recorders, on the frictional resistance in the wind canal and the condition of the bore." The amount of vibration also depends on the thickness of the material. Finds Davidson's "psychological" method of allowing listeners to differentiate materials acoustically to be useless. Notes the trend towards using harder woods over the last 500 years, as consort playing gave way to solo playing.

Goes on to discuss the general effect of moisture on wood, the use of ivory and metal on woodwind instruments, the repairing of cracks, and the effect of individual players on instruments. Ends with useful descriptions of the most common woods (maple, pear, plum, bubinga, box, cocobolo, grenadilla, ebony, and "polymer wood" or "atom wood" [maple, pear, etc. impregnated with varnish and hardened with gamma rays]), their properties and uses.

392. Reviers, Bruno de. "De nouveaux bois pour la facture des flûtes à bec: 1. Sélection d'essences exotiques & réalisation d'une flûte en kuredhi" [On new woods for recorder making: 1. Selection of exotic species and realization of a recorder in kuredhi]. *Flûte à bec & instruments anciens* 23 (March 1987): 9-13.

Discusses the testing of twenty-six different woods from the Maldive islands with a view to finding some that were suitable for the making of recorders. Gives the botanical and local names of the woods, their native uses, and their densities. Concludes that maru, wakaru, ran'doo, and kuredhi were the most suitable. Then describes Claude Monin's making of an alto recorder in G at 415 Hz based on an instrument by Dupuis at 398 Hz (Paris, ca. 1680; Paris Conservatoire E.368/C.388). Concludes that kuredhi is "a wood remarkably adapted to the making of recorders for soloists, because of its durability, its density, the polish of its surfaces, and its aesthetics." Errata included in item 393.

393. Reviers, Bruno de. "De nouveaux bois pour la facture des flûtes à bec: 2. Réalisation d'une flûte en randoo" [On new woods for recorder making: 2. Realization of a recorder in randoo]. *Flûte à bec & instruments anciens* 24 (1988): 23–25.

Takes as its point of departure the idea that "[t]he use of exotic woods for making recorders was a current practice in the Baroque era." Describes Monin's making of a soprano recorder at 415 Hz based on an instrument by Rippert at 398 Hz (Paris Conservatoire E.1515) from a Maldivian wood called ran'doo (found also in India, southeast Asia, and Australia). Finds that wood "perfectly adapted for the making of recorders."

394. Reviers, Bruno de. "De nouveaux bois pour la facture des flûtes à bec. 3: Réalisation d'une flûte en wakaru (cocotier)" [On new woods for recorder making: 3. Realization of a recorder in wakaru (coconut)]. *Flûte à bec et instruments anciens* 26 (November 1988): 7–10.

Begins with comments on coconut wood, which proved hard to work with. Then describes Monin's making of a second alto recorder based on the instrument by Dupuis—this time in F, in the belief that Bach's *fiauti d'echo* consisted of altos in G and F—and discusses the properties of the instrument. Followed by a comparative review of the three instruments and conclusions about their woods and the art of copying early instruments.

395. Zadro, Michael G. "Woods Used for Woodwind Instruments Since the 16th Century." *Early Music* 3, no. 2 (April 1975): 134–36; 3, no. 3 (July 1975): 249–51.

Part 1, a general historical survey, may be of passing interest, but it is the dictionary of woods in part 2 that make this article most valuable to recorder players. Provides the Latin names, geographic sources, and densities of specific woods within seventeen broad wood types. A descriptive paragraph offers information on texture, grain, and color. Brian Woods makes a minor correction, adds to Zadro's warning about skin irritation by certain woods, and includes an eight-title bibliography for the study of woods in 4, no. 2 (April 1976): 233. Zadro responds briefly in 4, no. 4 (October 1976): 497.

13

Acoustics and Other Scientific Studies

by

John Martin with Richard Griscom and David Lasocki

ACOUSTICS AND THE RECORDER by John Martin

Most aspects of our lives at the sharp end of the 20th century are affected by science and technology, so much so that we rarely consider what the two words mean and how they differ. We may consider science as being the methods we use to try to understand nature, and technology as being the strategies we use to solve problems associated with human needs. So, very loosely science takes things apart, while technology puts things together. We are used to thinking of science and technology in that order: science increases our knowledge, which technology then applies. It is easy to forget that, during much of history, technology has come first.

Musical instruments are good examples of this. Most traditional instruments have their roots in pre-history. The many ways in which various materials can be shaped and acted upon to produce sounds must have been known from very early times, and put to use to produce instruments that could imitate human or natural sounds. Instruments would have developed through processes of trial and error, not through the application of an understanding of how sound behaves.

By the time scientific enquiry (in any modern sense) was beginning, the recorder was already well established. In this case, technology preceded science. The design and manufacture of recorders came far in advance of attempts to investigate them and understand how they work.

In studying the acoustics of the recorder, we are concerned with measuring the sound it produces and relating the measurements to factors determined by the recorder maker or player. Among the important factors in the sound which can be measured are its loudness (amplitude), pitch (frequency), quality (timbre), directional pattern, and the way which it builds up and dies away. The maker determines the recorder's shape, the measurable factors here including details of the windway, window, and lip (collectively known as the "voicing"); the length and shape of the bore; and the position and size of the fingerholes. The player has control over the speed with which air enters the windway (through the blowing pressure), the way in which the airflow starts and stops (by articulation), and the stopping of the fingerholes (open, closed, or partially vented).

Acoustically, the recorder is closely related to the flute and organ flue pipe, with which it shares certain features. All three instruments have a common sound production mechanism. But whereas the flutist can exercise wide control over the tone and dynamics by altering the relative position of the mouth and instrument, in the recorder and organ pipe that position is fixed by the maker. Whereas each organ pipe is designed to play only one note at a fixed level, the recorder shares with the flute the ability to play a wide range of notes by opening holes along the length of the instrument, and to alter the qualities of each note by varying the breath pressure. This close relationship means that, in addition to the research that has been done specifically on the recorder, much research on the other two instruments is also relevant.

As an example, let us look at how the recorder produces a sound. The writings we have annotated begin with Sir Francis Bacon in the early 17th century (item 396) who, on this question, speculated that a sound is produced because the air blown into the recorder is constricted by the block in the headpiece. Bacon did not mention the lip as being important in sound production.

Mersenne, a few years later, realized the importance of the lip, since an organ pipe with a badly made or misplaced lip will not speak. He thought that the airstream is divided by the lip, and that the body of the pipe contributes to the heaviness and other qualities of the sound, although he was unable to be more specific.

Euler (item 397) realized that the vibration of air in the bore is accompanied by compressions and expansions, and that the airstream from the windway starts this vibration. To Euler, the lip was just the junction of the inside surface of the tube, along which the air from the windway can creep, as well as an opening through which the vibrating air in the bore can communicate with the atmosphere.

In 1738, Vaucanson wrote that air from the windway collides violently with the lip, thereby setting all the parts of the wood of the recorder in vibration, which in turn sets the surrounding air into vibration, causing sound. (Jacques de Vaucanson, *Le mécanisme du fluteur automate* [Paris: Jacques Guerin, 1738]; English translation, *An Account of the Mechanism of an Automaton, or Image Playing on the German-Flute*, trans. J.T. Desaguliers [London: T. Parker, 1742]; facsimile of both versions with preface by David Lasocki [Buren, The Netherlands: Frits Knuf, 1979].)

An explanation that approaches our modern understanding was printed in 1830 by Sir John Herschel. He was apparently the first to realize that the oscillatory flow of air through the mouth of an organ pipe carries the jet with it, causing the jet to switch in and out of the pipe. "Thus the current passing over the aperture is kept in a constant state of fluttering agitation, alternatively grazing and passing free of its edge, at regular intervals." (Sir John F.W. Herschel, *Sound* [Encyclopaedia metropolitana, 4; n.p., 1830].)

Each of the explanations mentioned above suffered from the limited observations that were available. (Nowadays we can photograph a smoke-laden jet illuminated by a stroboscopic light, thus getting a series of instantaneous pictures of the jet.) The usefulness of scientific theories is judged by their ability to predict. As our ability to observe and measure improves, through better technologies, our theories need to be modified or replaced so that they produce more precise predictions. This generally means adopting more specialized mathematical tools.

Our present understanding of the above-mentioned question is as follows. The player blows air into the windway at the top of the instrument. This forms a jet of air that emerges and travels across the window to the lip. If we consider a note to be already sounding, then the standing wave in the bore causes a flow of air in and out of the window. This tends to carry the jet with it as it emerges from the windway, producing a wave on the jet that travels along it at about half the central jet speed and growing in magnitude. The jet tip then sweeps back and forth across the lip, so that the jet itself blows alternately into and out of the bore. Providing that the correct phase relationship exists between the driving force so produced and the standing wave in the bore, the sound continues. This relationship depends on the speed of the jet.

In order to describe this model mathematically, we need to construct differential equations. That is, they contain not just quantities such as position and amplitude, but also the rates at which these quantities change. The equations also need to reflect the non-linear behavior of the jet. (If the jet behavior were linear, then doubling the sideways movement of the jet tip would double the jet flow into the bore. This does not happen because the jet does not have a uniform cross-section—it is slower at the edges than in the middle—and because it has a finite width.) Equations such as these cannot generally be solved algebraically but can be solved using step-by-step numerical methods. Computers have made these mathematical models more practical to use.

In the present century we have a range of powerful tools for studying the sounds of musical instruments: oscilloscopes to display how the sound varies with time; spectrum analyzers to display how the sound varies with frequency; and computers with which we can process our measurement data and make predictions from increasingly sophisticated mathematical models. Since von Lüpke published the first modern investigation of the recorder in 1940, measurement and calculation techniques have improved, and our understanding has increased—as documented in the entries that follow. Since the 1960s our knowledge of the acoustics of wind instruments in general, and flute-like instruments in particular, has increased considerably through the work of researchers including Arthur

Benade, John Coltman, Samuel Elder, and Neville Fletcher. A good account of much of this recent work is given by Fletcher and Rossing (item 399), while Martin (item 411) reports on a substantial investigation of the recorder based on these modern developments.

HISTORICAL STUDIES

396. Bacon, Francis. *Sylva sylvarum, or, A Natural History in Ten Centuries*. London: William Lee, 1627.

    Bacon's work appears to be the first in which a scientific study of the recorder is reported. In "centuries" 2 and 3, Bacon investigates sounds produced by a variety of things, including recorders, and reports his results, suggestions for further experiments, and speculations. A few examples: he suggests that when a recorder is blown, it is the sudden expansion of the air as it leaves the windway that causes the sound (116); he tries playing the recorder with the end near different materials, such as sand, water, snow, a silver basin, a woolen carpet, ashes, etc., and reports on whether the sound remained or was "quite deaded" (159); and he suggests the experiment of making a recorder with two mouthpieces, one at each end, and playing a tune in unison to see "whether the sound be confounded, or amplified, or dulled" (161).

397. Euler, Leonhard. *Dissertatio physica de sono.* . . . Basel, 1727. English translation included in: R. Bruce Lindsay, ed. *Acoustics: Historical and Philosophical Development*. Stroudsburg: Dowden, Hutchinson & Ross, 1973. OCLC #632083.

    Euler, a famous name in the history of mathematics, presented this dissertation to the University of Basel at the age of 20. His interest in acoustics lasted for many more years. In 1759 he wrote a long memoir about the theory of sound that was later published by the Berlin Academy.

    Euler devotes several paragraphs to "flutes" and their sounds, noting that "the explanation of the nature of these sounds has bothered investigators in a wonderful way in every age." He comments that when a recorder is played, "air blown in through the mouthpiece can force its way through the slit along the length of the tube by creeping over the inside surface. . . . It is clear that when the air enters the tube, the air already contained in it will be compressed along its length. When this air expands again, it goes too far and in turn is compressed again by the surrounding atmosphere, so that vibratory motion is thus produced in the tube. This vibration is the cause of the sound. And so the true cause of the sound in flutes is found."

He gives a method for calculating the frequency of sound produced by an open cylindrical pipe, knowing its length and the air pressure, commenting: "I leave to my honorable competitors the examination of the sounds of pipes which do not have the same width at all points, i.e., are either convergent or divergent."

INTRODUCTORY STUDIES

398. Bixler, Martha, and Richard Sacksteder. "On the Application and Misapplication of Acoustical Theory to Wind Instruments." *The American Recorder* 17, no. 4 (February 1977): 136–42.

    Uses two well-known acoustical theories to explain wind instrument operation. The classical theory looks at standing wave patterns in conical and cylindrical pipes, which may be open or closed at either end. Various instruments are classified as F[lute] type (fundamental wavelength = twice tube length; all harmonics present) or C[larinet] type (fundamental wavelength = four times tube length; only odd harmonics present). The recorder is F type, and some aspects of its fingering and tuning can therefore be explained. The Helmholtz theory adds some analysis of the sounding mechanism but predicts that instruments will be less stable than they actually are. Bixler and Sacksteder note that more recent theories include the non-linear affects of the sounding-producing mechanism although more work needs to be done on the initial "transient" of a note. (Item 411 includes a mathematical model for analyzing transients.)

399. Fletcher, Neville H., and Thomas D. Rossing. *The Physics of Musical Instruments*. New York: Springer-Verlag, 1991. xvii, 620 p. ISBN 0387969470.

    Aimed at the reader "with a reasonable grasp of physics and who is not frightened by a little mathematics." Covers the general principles governing the acoustics of most traditional instruments as well as aspects of particular instruments. Six pages on the recorder in the chapter on flutes and flue organ pipes. Discusses some of the consequences of the recorder's conical shape and some acoustical relationships with performance technique.

400. Martin, John. "Acoustics for Beginners: Some Sound Advice for Recorder Players." *The Recorder: Journal of the Victorian Recorder Guild* 2 (March 1985): 26–29.

    Adapted from the author's lecture at the Recorder '84 festival in Melbourne. Applies some basic properties of sound and standing waves to aspects of recorder fingering, bore shapes, and sound production. Many of the demonstrations that illustrated the lecture are described for the reader to try.

401. Medley, Daphne, "Tuning and Acoustics." *The Recorder Magazine* 12, no. 4 (December 1992): 99–101.

A fine introduction to Pythagorean tuning, equal temperament, and mean-tone tuning. Tables show the relative difference between intervals under the various systems. Corrections to the tables appear in 13, no. 1 (March 1993): 21.

GENERAL STUDIES

402. Castellengo, Michèle. *Contribution à l'étude éxperimentale des tuyaux à bouche.* Doctoral thesis, Université de Pierre et Marie Curie, Paris, 1976.

Describes an extensive experimental study of blown pipes, including flutes, recorders, organ pipes, and various folk instruments. Reports and displays graphically a wide range of measurements, the usefulness of which is limited by the absence of any theoretical framework for the data to test (or to put the date in perspective).

403. Castellengo, Michèle. "La flûte à bec" [The recorder]. *Flûte à bec* 2 (February 1982): 9–15. Reprinted from *L'Audiophile* 5 (June 1978).

Based on the principle that the recorder "is the ideal instrument of study for the acoustician, because most of its parameters have been determined through its construction." Then briefly discusses the function of the beak, the breath, articulation, sound characteristics (including sonograms of an alto recorder and a Boehm flute), the positioning of the fingerholes, the material, intonation, and the choice of modern instrument or historical copy.

* Dessy, Raymond, and Lee Dessy. "The Principles of Recorder Design Explained." Cited above as item 326.

404. Driscoll, Daniel A. "Acoustical Characteristics of the Alto Recorder." *The American Recorder* 8, no. 4 (Fall 1967): 109–13.

A readable treatment, for an audience that has little or no background in musical acoustics, of the way in which the shape of the bore affects the harmonic structure of the recorder's sound. The descriptions of the source of the sound and the production of a tone are not entirely correct in the light of later research. Letter from Driscoll in 9, no. 3 (Summer 1968): 94 refers the reader to item 416.

405. Elder, Samuel A. "Physical Basis of Woodwind-Recorder Voicing (Abstract)." *Journal of the Acoustical Society of America* 35, no. 11 (November 1963): 1901.

The abstract of a paper presented at a meeting of the Society in November 1963 at the University of Michigan. Asserts that certain aspects of recorder voicing can be related to the relationship between edgetone modes and pipe resonance modes. (Subsequent researchers have clarified the distinction between edgetones and the sounding mechanisms of flutes, recorders, and organ pipes. See, for example, Elder's own discussion in "Edgetones Versus Pipetones," *Journal of the Acoustical Society of America* 64 [December 1978]: 1721-23.)

406. Fletcher, Neville H., and Lorna M. Douglas. "Harmonic Generation in Organ Pipes, Recorders and Flutes." *Journal of the Acoustical Society of America* 68, no. 3 (September 1980): 767-71.

The sound produced by instruments driven by air jets (flutes, recorders, and organ pipes) depends in a complicated way on the interaction between the jet and the resonance modes of the pipe resonator. Fletcher and Douglas present a simplified model that concentrates on details of the interaction between the jet and the lip. They studied and checked experimentally the effects of certain parameters on the harmonic structure of the sound produced. Found that, as blowing pressure is varied, the odd and even harmonics behave in two nearly independent groups. Also that the overall level of even harmonics depends strongly on the position of the lip in the jet, being least when the lip is in a symmetrical position.

407. Herman, Robert. "Observations on the Acoustical Characteristics of the English Flute." *American Journal of Physics* 27 (January 1959): 22-29.

A discursive presentation of the recorder and some aspects of its acoustics. Herman reports on von Lüpke's investigation and quotes the conclusions while noting that in his experience recorders are generally somewhat richer in harmonics than reported there. (von Lüpke's experimental method may explain this.) He reports on a study of the theory of recorder fingering, unfortunately not providing the mathematical background. Also reports the results of investigations into intonation and blowing pressure, commenting that various notes have different sensitivity to blowing pressure, which makes control of intonation quite difficult for the novice. On the basis of his discussion, puts forward some criteria for a "good" recorder.

408. Lottermoser, Werner. "Von der Akustik der Blockflöte" [On the acoustics of the recorder]. *Instrumentenbau-Zeitschrift* 31 (1977): 757–59.
   Not seen. According to *RILM Abstracts*, concerns the factors affecting the resonance frequencies of the recorder.

409. Lüpke, Arndt von. "Untersuchungen an Blockflöten" [Investigations into recorders]. *Akustische Zeitschrift* 5 (1940): 39–46. English summary: Leo Beranek. "Investigation of Block Flutes." *Journal of the Acoustical Society of America* 12, [no. 2] (October 1940): 307–8.
   The first modern study of recorder acoustics. Describes measuring the harmonic content of the sound of a number of alto and soprano recorders mechanically blown in an acoustically damped (anechoic) room. The sound pressure and blowing pressure of the recorders were measured for each note over two octaves, and their transient response was studied. He concludes: (1) In comparison to almost all other instruments the tone is lacking in harmonics. (2) The third harmonic is in general stronger than the second, owing to the conical bore. (3) The number and strength of the overtones decrease as one progresses up the scale to a certain limit at which the recorder becomes overblown; at that point the harmonics suddenly become strong and remain so for the rest of the scale. (4) The sound pressure rises steadily through the lower octave and then falls at the beginning of the second octave. (5) The measured strength of the second harmonic relative to the fundamental depends strongly on whether the note is cross-fingered. (6) The maximum range of wind pressures needed for playing a scale in tune is about 1:6, the higher pressures being needed for the higher notes.
   Martin (item **411**) shows that von Lüpke's conclusions about relative harmonic strengths depend strongly on the microphone position he used in the anechoic room and, therefore, are highly suspect.
   The author of the English summary immediately confesses his unfamiliarity with the instrument: "The block flute is a sort of fife and is unknown to me. Those who manufacture musical instruments will undoubtedly recognize it and call it by its proper name." The only confusing effect, however, is the mistranslation of "Altflöte" as "old flute" rather than "alto recorder."

410. Lyons, Donald H. "Resonance Frequencies of the Recorder (English Flute)." *Journal of the Acoustical Society of America* 70, no. 5 (November 1981): 1239–47.
   Compares measured and calculated resonant frequencies of an alto recorder. In the calculations, assumes a constant temperature and an "ideal" recorder with cylindrical head and conical body and foot. Then applies perturbations to this to approximate a real recorder. Determines the

effect of the window experimentally, finding it to act like an open extension of the tube about 35 mm long. Finds good agreement between measured and calculated frequencies.

411. Martin, John Stuart. *A Study of Acoustical Aspects of the Recorder in Relation to its Historical Development and Technique.* Ph.D. thesis (Physics), University of New England, Armidale, NSW, Australia, 1987.

A theoretical and experimental study of the acoustics of the recorder. Begins with a brief history of the instrument, followed by a review of previous modern acoustical studies and a few acoustical speculations from earlier times. Then outlines the basic acoustics of the recorder, with special emphasis on sound radiation, the formation of the jet by blowing through the windway, the resonance patterns of the bore and finger holes, and the interaction of the jet with the pipe. Applies these results to various aspects of recorder sound production, such as voicing, tone, attack, overblowing, multiphonics, and pitch. Followed by a discussion of how the acoustical results relate to aspects of recorder design, historical development, and performance practice. A revised version will be published as *The Acoustics of the Recorder* (Celle: Moeck, 1994).

412. Martin, John. "The Acoustics of the Recorder." *Acoustics Australia* 14, no. 2 (August 1986): 43–46.

Summarizes much of the author's thesis on recorder acoustics (item 411) in a non-technical fashion. Includes a discussion of how the jet formed at the windway exit interacts with the lip to produce a sound. Followed by a discussion of the role of the bore shape and finger holes.

413. Martin, John. "The Acoustics of the Recorder." *The Recorder: Journal of the Victorian Recorder Guild* 7 (December 1987): 22–27. Reprinted in *Recorder News (The Society of Recorder Players [New Zealand] Incorporated)* (January 1988): 2–11.

Based on item 412, but adapted for audiences knowing more about the recorder and less about acoustics. Includes a discussion of Francis Bacon's writings about the recorder.

* Mathiesen, Irmgard Knopf, and Aksel H. Mathiesen. "Ein Messingsprojekt Datamatische Behandlung von Messungen an historischen Holzblasinstrumenten." Cited above as item 352.

414. Mühle, Christoph. *Untersuchungen über die Resonanzeigenschaften der Blockflöte* [Investigations into the resonance modes of the recorder]. (Schriftenreihe Das Musikinstrument, Bd. 16) Frankfurt/Main: Verlag Das Musikinstrument, 1979. ISBN 3920112733.

A Braunschweig dissertation (1966). Relates the results of measurements on an artificially blown recorder to mathematical ways of calculating its resonance frequencies. Among other things, concludes that there is an increase in the amplitude of harmonics that lie near the resonant frequency of the player's mouth cavity; and moisture in the breath may narrow the windway, causing an increase in frequency and in the amplitude of the even harmonics.

* Myers, Herbert W. *The Practical Acoustics of Early Woodwinds.* Cited above as item 335.

415. Steinkopf, Otto. *Zur Akustik der Blasinstrumente: Ein Wegweiser für den Instrumentenbauer* [On the acoustics of wind instruments: a guide for the instrument maker]. Celle: Moeck, 1983. 84 p. ISBN 3875490207.

Studies a range of wind instrument types, including cylindrical and conical bores, open and closed at one end. Illustrates these types by a range of instruments including serpent, brass instruments, various transverse flutes, cornett, and recorder. Demonstrates ways of calculating the corrections to the effective sounding length caused by various components, such as the recorder mouth and open holes. Includes a table of tone hole calculations for the Moeck Rottenburgh alto recorder.

416. Turicchi, Thomas Edwin. *A Study of the Acoustical Properties of a Renaissance, Baroque, and Contemporary Fipple Flute (Recorder).* Ph.D. dissertation, Catholic University, 1966. 86 leaves. OCLC #9227924. UMI order no. 66-12715.

Investigates two recorders from the Library of Congress (a Renaissance and a Baroque) and a modern recorder. Measures pitch, sound power, and harmonic content vs. blowing pressure. Relates the results to edgetone theory (not now thought to be an important factor). Correctly notes the effect that the lip offset has on harmonic content, particularly the second harmonic. Suggests a method for discovering the original temperament of a recorder based on the pitches at which its ratio of sound power out to blowing power in is greatest. (Turicchi's measurements of this ratio often approach 100%, although item 411 quotes other measurements that never exceed 1%. The sound production mechanism in flute-like instruments is known to be inherently inefficient, which casts some doubt on Turicchi's conclusions.)

Acoustics and Other Scientific Studies

SPECIFIC TOPICS

BEATS AND DIFFERENCE TONES

417. Martin, John. "It's the Extra Beating that Makes the Difference (More Kitchen Physics for Recorder Players)." *The Recorder: Journal of the Victorian Recorder Guild* 11 (June 1990): 1-4.

    A simple explanation of beats and difference tones (Martin loves puns) and their implications for intonation, temperament, and recorder ensemble performance. Suggests simple experiments so that the reader can illustrate points in the text.

418. Middleton, James. "Those 'Buzzing Ears.'" *Recorder & Music* 5, no. 2 (June 1975): 51.

    Briefly describes "beats" and difference tones in reply to a query that had appeared in a previous issue: "Recorders make your ears buzz, and I shall be glad to learn if anybody has any ideas for camouflaging this." Beats are caused by two instruments playing the same note slightly out of tune and can be eliminated by more closely matching the pitch. Difference tones are faint pitches created when two notes are sounded together. They cannot be avoided and are in fact more prominent when tuning is accurate.

BREATH PRESSURE

419. Bak, N. "Pitch, Temperature and Blowing-Pressure in Recorder-Playing: Study of Treble Recorders." *Acustica* 22 (1969/70): 295-99.

    Of interest for attempting to find whether the player's mouth size and shape affect the frequency of the note played. By introducing a resonator volume into the airstream before it reaches a recorder, attempts to find a relationship between volume and sounding frequency, although the measured effects were too small to allow this. (Item 411 includes a study of mouth effects, concluding that mouth volume may affect a note's timbre and readiness to overblow.) Bak also finds that the effect on sounding frequency of increasing temperature could be explained by the expected increase in sound velocity. Also studies the dependence of the frequency of a note on the blowing pressure, finding that the experimental data produced points close to a straight line when plotted on log-log graph paper.

420. Bak, Niels. "A Physical and Physiological Study of Blowing Technique in Recorder Playing." *Annual Report*

of the *Institute of Phonetics, University of Copenhagen* 10 (1976): 223-72. In abridged German translation as: "Eine physikalische und physiologische Untersuchung der Blastechnik des Blockflötenspielers." *Das Musikinstrument* 27, no. 5 (May 1978): 812-14.

Notes the difference between the "German" and "English" recorder schools regarding the role of the player's mouth. The "German" school holds that forming different vowel shapes with the mouth affects the recorder's tone, whereas the "English" school denies the mouth any role other than to provide an unimpeded flow of air into the windway. Bak finds no experimental evidence that mouth volume can affect recorder tone. By making continuous x-ray recordings of players' mouths, however, he finds that professional players at least sometimes alter the flow of air into the windway with their lips. He makes interesting comments on the difficulties of measuring the blowing pressure used by players because of lip movement, and notes that measurements of pressure in the recorder windway can be used to monitor blowing pressure.

421. Bak, Niels. "Investigating the Influence of Blowing Technique on Pitch and Tone in Recorder Playing." *Annual Report of the Institute of Phonetics, University of Copenhagen* 6 (1971): 307-13.

A short account of preliminary experiments for the investigation described more fully in item **420**. Concludes that the resonance conditions of the player's mouth cavity have no effect on the pitch or tone of the recorder, and that variations in blowing pressure are of paramount importance for playing quality.

422. Davidson, Martin. "Variation of Pitch of a Tenor Recorder with Blowing Pressure." *The American Recorder* 3, no. 3 (August 1962): 17-19.

Describes measurements of pitch being made while blowing each note of an unidentified tenor recorder at three pressures: "soft, medium, and hard." Finds variations of up to 89 cents; a few notes were consistently sharp or flat. Makes no attempt to measure the blowing pressure quantitatively.

423. Dunn, John. "'The Middle of the Note.'" *Recorder & Music* 5, no. 9 (March 1977): 291-92. In Italian as: "Il centro della nota." *Il flauto dolce* 9 (June 1983): 28-29.

Written in response to items **424** and **429**. Reports the results of a computer program designed to determine "the resonant frequencies of the tube for any given fingering pattern" on a plastic alto. As with Wyatt's recorder (see item **429**), the lowest notes are sharp and must be underblown, while the highest notes (f^3 and g^3) are flat and must be overblown—exactly the opposite of what is desired. The octave from c^2-c^3 is more balanced, requiring slight overblowing low in the range, then a switch to underblowing at mid-octave.

424. Osmond, D.W.J. "The Optimum Breath Pressure for the Recorder." *Recorder & Music* 5, no. 7 (September 1976): 227–30; 5, no. 8 (December 1976): 258–60. In Italian as: "La pressione ottimale del fiato nel flauto dolce." *Il flauto dolce* 9 (June 1983): 24–28.

    Written in response to Theo Wyatt's statement in item 429 that an ideal recorder would play in tune with equal breath pressure across its range. Studies experimentally and theoretically the breath pressure required to play in tune across the compass of the recorder. Concludes that playing pressure "should be directly proportional to frequency, and so double over each octave," and that the absolute values of the pressure required are dominated by details of the geometry of the windway. Assumes that in the windway viscous effects are predominant, and that after leaving the windway the transverse vibration of the air jet is due to the drag of the stationary air on either side of it.

    Martin (item 411) calls into question some of Osmond's assumptions and conclusions. It appears that the air does not remain long enough in the windway for viscous effects to predominate, and that the relationship between playing pressure and jet velocity is governed instead by Bernoulli's law. Also, a result that Osmond uses to discuss tapering windways omits an important factor that leads to results opposite to those expected.

425. Raudonikas, F. "Blown Resonance of Baroque Flute-Traverso IV: The Tone and the Blowing Pressure." *FoMRHI Quarterly* 28 (July 1982), 26–33. (Communication No. 419).

    Explains the blowing mechanism of the Baroque flute with the aid of measurements of blowing pressure and sounding frequency for two alto recorders from the Leningrad Museum. At low blowing pressures, a quiet "ghost" sound can be produced. For this note, the jet has time to oscillate once more than usual before it reaches the lip. At higher breath pressures, the graph of frequency vs. pressure can be plotted on log-log paper and divided into three zones: the transitional zone (where the frequency rises rapidly), the working zone (in which the player usually operates and in which the graph is nearly straight), and the overexcitation zone (prior to the note overblowing). Gives explanations in terms of the change of phase of the jet oscillation as it crosses the recorder mouth. Raudonikas's unfamiliarity with English and the physical layout of the page both make this a difficult article to read.

426. Wogram, Klaus, and Jürgen Meyer. "Über den spieltechnischen Ausgleich von Intonationsfehlern bei Blockflöten" [On the adjustment through playing technique of intonation errors on recorders]. *Tibia* 10, no. 2 (1985): 322–35. "Prolog" by Hermann Moeck, p. 321.

On the graphical measurement of loudness, breath pressure, and pitch deviation to test the performance of several recorders and recorder players. Letter from Andreas Schnur in 10, no. 3 (1985): 478; reply by Wogram in 11, no. 1 (1986): 77–78.

427. Wogram, Klaus, and Jürgen Meyer. "Zur Intonation bei Blockflöten" [On the intonation of recorders]. *Acustica* 60, no. 3 (June 1984): 137–46.

Reports on a study of the dependence of intonation on blowing pressure for a number of artificially blown recorders, the results being displayed effectively on three-dimensional graphs. Wogram and Meyer chose five recorders with different blowing characteristics and tested them with a group of players of various levels of musical training. They found that the players adjusted their playing technique very little to suit the different characteristics of the instruments. Based on this observation, they propose criteria for determining the quality of a recorder.

428. Wyatt, Theo. "Measuring Breath Pressure." *The American Recorder* 28, no. 2 (May 1987): 57–59.

Remarks that "[m]easuring pressure along with pitch takes almost all the guesswork out of retuning and is much easier [to do] than most people think." Describes using a water U-tube (manometer) to measure blowing pressure. Inclining the manometer at 30 degrees to the horizontal doubles its sensitivity and allows the manometer scale to directly display the blowing pressure. Wyatt supplies logarithmic graph paper, noting that graphs of blowing pressure vs. pitch should be close to a straight line when drawn on it. Comments that notes that lie off this line may need retuning; gives a few practical hints. Letter from Gary Greenhut in 28, no. 3 (August 1987): 127.

429. Wyatt, Theo. "My Complimentary Recorder." *Recorder & Music* 5, no. 4 (December 1975): 120–22. In Italian as: "Osservazioni su un flauto dolce campione ricevuto in omaggio," *Il flauto dolce* 9 (June 1983): 22–24.

After receiving a complimentary soprano recorder, Wyatt experimented with the measurement of breath pressure across the range of several recorders he often used in order to refute the maker's claim that it is normal for c^2 on the descant to be blown twice as hard as c^1 and half as hard as c^3. Wyatt's belief before taking the measurements was that an ideal instrument would require equal breath pressure across its range. To his surprise, he discovered that a significant increase in pressure was indeed required on all of his instruments, although not as great as the maker of his complimentary recorder had claimed. Wyatt calls for a published standard to specify a relationship between pitch and breath pressure. See also item 424.

Fingerings

430. Brindley, Giles. "A Method for Analyzing Woodwind Cross-Fingerings." *Galpin Society Journal* 22 (March 1969): 44–46.

Describes the experimental study of the positions of the antinodes in a tenor recorder, made by sliding a thin hollow brass tube connected to a stethoscope in and out of the bore. Finds the end correction to vary smoothly from 61 mm (for e^1) to 43 mm (for e^2), attributing this to the greater pressure needed for blowing high notes. (Since, however, a similar variation is found when passive resonances are measures, this explanation is probably incorrect.) Uses basic acoustical principles to analyze fingering patterns, quoting some approximate theoretical expressions for determining the effect on sounding frequency of an open or closed finger hole.

Tone Quality

431. Ando, Yoshinori, and Tatsuro Shima. "Physical Properties of Sustained Part of the Treble Recorder Tone and its Subjective Excellence of Quality." *Ongaku Gaku = Journal of the Japanese Musicological Society*, 23, no. 2 (1977): 81–101. Abstracted as "Physical Properties of Treble Recorder Tones Suitable for Baroque Music." *Journal of the Acoustical Society of America* 64, suppl. no. 1 (fall 1978): S151.

Investigates how the quality of alto recorder tones depends on various physical properties of the tones. The quality was judged by professional recorder players, experienced recorder players, and amateurs using paired comparison of real and synthesized tones. The best tones showed a decay rate of harmonic amplitude of 4dB/harmonic, a level difference between odd and even harmonics of 10db, with small frequency fluctuation in the second and third harmonics. Frequency fluctuation in higher harmonics was judged harmful for quality.

432. Driscoll, Daniel A. *Synthetics of a Recorder Tone-color.* Master's thesis, Renssellaer Polytechnic Institute, 1964. Not seen.

433. Omitted.

14

Instrument Making and Manufacture

This chapter deals with writings about modern recorder making and manufacture. (For an apparently unique source on making from the 18th century, see items 684–86.) Items on the properties of the instruments themselves are dealt with in chapter 12.

434. Benedikt, Erich. "Zum Selbstbau verschiedener Flöten" [Making various types of flutes yourself]. *Musikerziehung* 29, no. 1 (September 1975): 13–16.

    Begins by describing the various types, including of course recorders, defines some terms, then draws attention to differences in the numbers of fingerholes. A curious article that does not live up to its title.

435. Benn, Nicholas, John Cousen, and Henry Woledge. "A Great Consort: Made and Described by Nicholas Benn, John Cousen, and Henry Woledge." *The Recorder and Music Magazine* 1, no. 3 (November 1963): 93.

    The authors set out in fall 1962 to make a great consort (tenor in c′, basset in f, quart-bass in c, and great bass in F) after 16th-century models. Describes the process they used and the qualities of the resulting instruments.

436. "Birth of a Recorder." *The Recorder and Music Magazine* 1, no. 2 (August 1963): 40–41; 1, no. 3 (November 1963): 86–87.

    A series of twelve captioned photographs showing the steps taken in manufacturing Schott's Concert recorders.

437. Bolton, Philippe. "La naissance d'une flûte à bec" [The birth of a recorder]. *Flûte à bec & instruments anciens* 10

(March 1984): 12–15. Copies obtainable from the author at Le Grand Portail, F-84570 Villes-sur-Auzon, France.
A brief description with photographs of the steps in making a recorder.

438. Duggan, Peter T. "A Practice Baroque Recorder." *The Recorder and Music Magazine* 9, no. 5 (March 1988): 118–20.
Offers details on how to make a practice recorder with Baroque fingering by filling and redrilling the bottom four holes of a Bressan Zen-On alto. Corrections in 9, no. 6 (June 1988): 157.

439. Dullat, Günter. *Holzblasinstrumentenbau: Entwicklungsstufen und Technologien* [Woodwind instrument making: stages of development and technology]. Celle: Moeck, 1990. 330 p. ISBN 3875490320.
According to the preface, the book was finished in 1984 but publication was delayed. Divided into three parts: (1) stages of development and technology, (2) the instruments, and (3) materials and tools. The section on the recorder (pp. 74–80) briefly discusses sizes and consorts, design (including the influences of the tone holes), and stages in recorder making; includes some drawings and measurements. Reviewed by Karl Ventzke in *Tibia* 15, no. 4 (1990): 312–14.

440. Fitzpatrick, Horace. "The Medieval Recorder." *Early Music* 3, no. 4 (October 1975): 361–64.
Reports a recorder maker's research, experimentation, and "blunders" in the course of reconstructing a consort of medieval recorders. Of particular interest is the account of the "Dordrecht" recorder (ca. 1250) in the Gemeentemuseum at the Hague, which Fitzpatrick was able to replicate and use as a model for the other instruments in the consort.

* Fussenegger, Gernot. "Holzflöten und ihr Bau am Beispiel einer Blockflöte." Cited below as item **1461**.

441. Gohin, Henri. "Les étapes de la facture d'une flûte à bec" [The stages in the manufacture of a recorder]. Edited by Laurent Hay. *Flûte à bec* 3 (June 1982): 16–17.
A brief attempt to "set forth the major stages in the manufacture."

* Hunt, Edgar. "Recorder Making Today." Cited above as item **357**.

442. Hunt, Edgar. "Recorders Based on Eighteenth-Century Models." *Recorder & Music* 5, no. 10 (June 1977): 338–39.

Sequel to item 357. Reports on two instruments: Rössler's Oberlender model alto and the Zen-On Bressan model alto. Hunt's own Bressan instrument served as the model for the latter, and he draws favorable comparisons between the original and the plastic copy.

443. Lewis, Mildred. "How Recorders Are Made at the Workshop of Friedrich von Huene." *The American Recorder* 1, no. 4 (Fall 1960): 4–6.

Begins with a biographical sketch and a description of von Huene's measurement and study of historical instruments. Then takes the reader through the process of making a recorder, from the selection of the wood to the application of the varnish. Since the description is not overdetailed, much of what is said would apply to recorder-making in most workshops.

444. Loretto, Alec V. "Furniture and Recorders: The Problems with Making Copies." *The American Recorder* 30, no. 4 (November 1989): 143–44.

Explains why makers choose not to make exact copies of instruments. They deviate from historical models in order to accommodate modern tastes for double holes, modern fingering, and tuning at $a^1 = 415$ Hz. Because such adjustments can be made in a number of ways, no two historical copies are alike. Makers are guided by their own experience, and inevitably the results vary considerably.

445. Loretto, Alec V. "Plastic Recorders." *The Recorder Magazine* 13, no. 1 (March 1993): 3–4.

Concerns the process of producing handmade plastic recorders. Although blocks of plastic can be tooled similarly to wood, plastic's tendency to shatter or melt presents special problems, which Loretto describes. Makers of handmade plastic instruments often use a wooden block to help absorb condensation. (A few even line the windway with wood.) Although many makers have produced handmade plastic instruments, Loretto knows none who have "tooled up for larger production runs."

446. Loretto, Alec V. "So You'd Like to Become a Recorder Maker, or, Come on in—the Water's Fine!" *The American Recorder* 28, no. 3 (August 1987): 101–3.

Gives advice to would-be makers of historical recorders on how to go about learning their craft: study original instruments, read, "have a go" at making, seek feedback, join the staff of a factory or become an apprentice, take lessons, and attend courses. Letter from Ingeborg von Huene in 28, no. 4 (November 1987): 177 emphasizes the importance of good business skills.

447. Loretto, Alec. "Improvements or Modifications—Which?" *The Recorder and Music Magazine* 8, no. 8 (December 1985): 236–38.

Response to a letter from A. Dolf in 8, no. 6 (June 1985): 185. Loretto and Moeck exchange views over why Moeck changed his mind about the feasibility of mass-producing recorders with high, narrow windways. Moeck says that only advances in knowledge and technology have made such mass-production possible. Loretto cites, in addition, competition from other factories; the influence of teachers, smaller workshops, and performances on original instruments; pressure from players; and writings on the subject. Reply to Loretto by Hermann Moeck in 8, no. 9 (March 1986): 275; response by Loretto in 8, no. 11 (September 1986): 334–35.

448. Marvin, Bob. "Making Renaissance Recorders." *Continuo* 9, no. 4 (January 1986): 2–7. In French as: "Faire des flûtes à bec renaissance." *Flûte à bec & instruments anciens* 21 (1987): 3–8.

Personal musings on: what constitutes a "copy," his experiments with different types of Renaissance recorders and their suitability for the music of different parts of that period, double recorders, woods, his attitude to making, an instrument's "resistance," his equipment, his wishes.

449. Marvin, Bob. "A Recorder Odyssey: Searching for a Renaissance Consort." *Recorder and Music Magazine* 4, no. 4 (December 1972): 118–21. Reprinted as a letter in *The American Recorder* 13, no. 3 (August 1972): 102–3.

Describes Marvin's work on a set of nine historical copies (at pitches F, c, c, f, g, c^1, c^1, g^1, and c^2) to play 16th- and early 17th-century music at both 8' and 4' pitches. Most of the models were found in Viennese collections and copied during summer 1970. Offers details on the problems of balance and intonation he encountered and how he resolved them. Includes an account of his return to Europe with the instruments in winter 1971–72 "to try music on them and to search for a location with enough good players to further develop the instruments in a musical context."

450. Moeck, Hermann. "Recorders: Hand-made and Machine-made." *Early Music* 10, no. 1 (January 1982): 10–13. In German as: "Blockflöten—'handgemacht' und in Serie und einige andere Bemerkungen" [Recorders—"hand-

made" and mass-produced, and several other observations]. *Tibia* 7, no. 3 (1982): 184–87.

Begins with a brief history of recorder making and manufacturing from Dolmetsch to the 1960s. Points out that the important difference between the two types of instruments is the fact that hand-made recorders aim at being completely individual, with all the peculiarities in fingering and intonation of the original being copied, whereas mass-produced recorders strive to produce even intonation with normal fingerings. No high-quality recorders can be made by machine alone; voicing and tuning must still be done by hand. Concludes with some predictions, including that "wooden recorders, because of the quality of their sound, will maintain their position" in competition with plastic instruments.

451. Moonen, Toon. "Das Umrechnen von Holzblasinstrumenten" [The scaling of woodwind instruments]. *Tibia* 14, no. 1 (1989): 347–49. Translation of: "Het omrekenen van houtblaasinstrumenten." *Bouwbrief* 51 (November 1988): 19–20.

Moonen reminds us that surviving examples of early woodwind instruments are not always made to a convenient standard pitch, so that copies of them must be scaled up or down, although makers "do not publicize" the fact. Discusses scaling factors in organ building. Gives a practical example of the scaling up to a^1 = 415 Hz of the Bressan alto recorder formerly in the collection of Edgar Hunt.

452. Morgan, Fred. "Making Recorders Based on Historical Models." *Early Music*, 10, no. 1 (January 1982): 14–21.

Outlines the reasons for using old instruments as models and then explains, step by step, the process that should be used in copying historical instruments. When selecting an instrument to be copied, the maker should play as many old instruments as possible. Once selected, the instrument must be measured carefully. Much can be learned from an examination of the woodworking techniques used by the original craftsmen, but sometimes there can be good reasons for making adjustments to the design of an instrument. Covers tools for reaming the bore, cutting the windway, making blocks, and undercutting tone-holes. Concludes by noting that "we still have some way to go before our instruments are as good as those of the earlier times." An important, influential article.

453. Morgan, Fred. "Old Recorders: Our Design Heritage." *The Recorder: Journal of the Victorian Recorder Guild* 2 (March 1985): 8–11.

Gives "some idea of what must take place before a maker can offer a player an instrument which, while genuinely based on an old recorder, can be played at one of today's standard pitches, and in tune in one of today's accepted temperaments." Points out that "a true and exact copy" is impossible; rather, "the detail of its design and execution represents a good deal of experience, thought, work, and even originality on the part of the maker."

454. Ohannesian, David. "I Couldn't Make an Exact Copy If I Tried!" *American Recorder* 32, no. 2 (June 1991): 8–10, 36–37.

Concerns the challenges facing modern recorder makers and the choices confronting players when selecting an instrument. Explains why it is impossible to make a perfect instrument and often undesirable to make an exact copy. Modern makers tend to incorporate the attributes of historical models that meet their own particular needs and disregard others as insignificant, so copies become the product of a maker's individual taste. The practices and trends of modern performance also influence the design of modern copies. Today's players are not the players of centuries ago, so there are good reasons for historical copies to vary from the models. "The 'perfect' recorder doesn't exist, because there will always be players with divergent styles, a variety of halls to cope with, different tunings with which to experiment, changing combinations of tonal color, and a wealth of literature."

455. Prescott, Thomas M. "Making Recorders." *The American Recorder* 24, no. 3 (August 1983): 95–98.

Describes in detail the process of making a batch of his Boekhout sopranos. Includes a short bibliography on recorder making.

456. Robinson, Trevor. *The Amateur Wind Instrument Maker.* Rev. ed. [Amherst]: University of Massachusetts Press, 1980; London: Murray, 1981. 116 p. ISBN 0870233122. Earlier edition: [Amherst]: University of Massachusetts Press, 1973. 115 p. OCLC #671988. In German as: *Historische Blasinstrumente—selbst gebaut.* Neu-Ulm: Ekkehart Stegmiller, 1983.

Written by a biochemist who truly is an "amateur wind instrument maker." Introductory chapters cover: equipping the shop, sources of designs, pitch and tuning, making measurements, materials and methods for making wooden instruments, choice of wood, boring and reaming, joints, decorations, keys, placement of finger holes, and finish. Then a chapter is devoted to each type of wind instrument, including the recorder. Appendixes cover some museum collections, sources of materials, making shell augers, useful addresses, and inch/metrical equivalents. Bibliography.

According to the preface, the revised edition contains "many improvements." These consist of a few additions (notably a section on making a Renaissance alto recorder) and updated appendixes. First edition reviewed by Edgar Hunt in *The Galpin Society Journal* 27 (April 1974): 149-50.

457. Snelling, Virginia. "Flûte à bec médiévale" [Medieval recorder]. *Flûte à bec & instruments anciens* 17 (December 1985/February 1986): 11.
   Based on an interview with recorder maker John Hanchet. Describes his attempts to make a medieval recorder based not only on the Dordrecht instrument (damaged and incomplete) but on modern folk instruments and a painting (1425) in which a recorder has a windcap-like mouthpiece.

458. Zaniol, Angelo. "Copying Old Recorders." *The American Recorder* 27, no. 3 (August 1986): 103-7.
   Courageously attempts to "tell the truth" about modern recorder makers who claim to be copying early recorders. Divides such makers into three categories: (1) intransigent purists (who, impossibly, set out to measure and reproduce their models as exactly as possible), (2) compromisers (who are willing to make necessary reasonable adjustments but are careful not to distort an instrument's character), and (3) free-and-easy copiers (whose instruments bear little resemblance to the originals). Provides much food for thought for both makers and potential buyers of "copies."

THE "GANASSI RECORDER" CONTROVERSY: A CAUTIONARY TALE

In 1987, in the course of his review of recent research on the recorder (item 4), David Lasocki discussed Angelo Zaniol's important survey article on medieval and Renaissance recorders (item 339). Zaniol had, among other things, looked at the attempts of modern makers to find a type of recorder that would play with the fingerings in Ganassi's *Opera intitulata Fontegara* of 1535 (item 562) and have the same range. Zaniol had remarked that, "If the mystery has at last been solved, it is thanks to the research of Fred Morgan," and he had gone on to note Morgan's discovery that a slightly modified copy of a damaged Renaissance recorder in g^1 in the Kunsthistorisches Museum, Vienna (catalog number C 8522) would fit the bill. Zaniol had concluded that "After Fred Morgan, other makers including the author [i.e., Zaniol] have tried to make 'Ganassi' recorders, each looking to rediscover the ideal form and proportions; for the instrument remains very much a hypothetical reconstruction." Although Zaniol's article had by then been published twice (and was about to be published again), no one has ever written to the journals in question to dispute his statement concerning Morgan's precedence.

In the same review of research (item 4), Lasocki reviewed an article by Alec V. Loretto (item 460) that described four possible approaches to making a "Ganassi" recorder. Loretto had cited no actual recorder makers in conjunction with any of these approaches, couching them in terms of "hypothetical" makers who might use them. But, knowing of Morgan's work through his celebrated article of 1982 (item 452) and Zaniol's comments, Lasocki summed up: "Alec Loretto has recently considered four possible approaches to the 'Ganassi,' coming out strongly in favor of that taken by Morgan."

This conclusion initiated a lengthy and heated debate by Lasocki, Loretto, and Morgan in the pages of *The American Recorder* and *The Recorder Magazine* (and behind the scenes by mail, fax, and phone). Benjamin S. Dunham, who had recently become editor of *The American Recorder*, rather than publishing the protagonists' latest letters, closed the correspondence by summarizing the debate and the content of those letters (31, no. 1 [March 1990]: 29–30). Edgar Hunt, then editor of *The Recorder Magazine* also declared the correspondence closed (10, no. 2 [June 1990]: 38-40). Loretto, believing himself vindicated, privately circulated a spiral-bound, photocopied booklet presenting his view of the debate under the title: *"The Ganassi Affair": An Overlong Melodramatic Comedy.*

The main point at issue in the debate was the question of who had been the first to make a Ganassi recorder based on Vienna C 8522—Loretto or Morgan. Lasocki argued in favor of Morgan, for the reasons mentioned above. Morgan supplied information that he first measured C 8522 in 1970 and gave drawings of it to several makers, began his first copies in 1975, sent the first one to Frans Brüggen in 1976, made commercial copies in 1978, and gave drawings to his class on recorder making in The Hague in 1979-80, from which drawings students all over the world began to make commercial copies. Asked by Lasocki to support his own claim, Loretto produced evidence that was suggestive rather than conclusive and had some puzzling aspects. Let us then say that Loretto supplied information that he sketched the Vienna instrument in 1972, made a copy in 1973, and sold his first copy in 1974. A significant fact has emerged since the closing of the public debate: Klaus Scheele, one of the makers to whom Morgan gave measurements of the Vienna instrument in 1970, has reported that he showed them to Loretto when he visited "some years later . . . and I think he made an instrument based on them in my workshop" (letter to David Lasocki, 10 November 1990).

What can we conclude from all this? First, we may deduce the apparent chronology. Fred Morgan was the first to measure Vienna C 8522, and a number of makers, including Alec Loretto, made use of those measurements. Loretto was the first to realize that a copy of the Vienna instrument could be made to function as a Ganassi recorder. Morgan came to that conclusion independently a couple of years later, and his copies became famous through the recordings and concerts of Frans Brüggen. Incidentally, a third maker, Bob Marvin, made a Ganassi recorder using a different approach around the same time (see item 459). Morgan was the first to publish an article about the approach to a Ganassi recorder through the Vienna instrument.

Second, in the interests of the historical record, it would be wise for makers who wish to claim they were first (or before someone else) in any area of research or construction to document that claim accurately. A good way to establish such a claim would be to write up the work and submit it for publication in a journal of sufficiently wide distribution among the interested public of players, makers, and scholars. (Loretto's chosen method of "publication"—preparing a booklet to accompany two lectures in New Zealand—condemned his work with the Ganassi recorder to remain outside the mainstream of recorder making and its public record.) Another way would be to have a recorder player make a recording on the instrument and have the relevant details of the instrument mentioned in the program notes accompanying that recording. Without such documentation, in retrospect a claim is difficult to prove.

Let us add that neither the editors of *The American Recorder* and *The Recorder Magazine* nor many readers of the debate could understand why Loretto and Morgan were arguing so vehemently, yet clearly both makers felt their reputations were on the line. What seems to matter more to the public than who did something first is who does it best. To a player, the quality of a recorder is what counts.

459. Marvin, Bob. "A Ganassi flauto." *FoMRHI Quarterly* 11 (April 1978): 40–46 (Communication No. 118).

    Reports the experiments and thinking behind his making of a Ganassi recorder [in 1975] based on the frontispiece of Ganassi's *Fontegara* (1535). Also mentions Morgan's approach without naming the Vienna instrument.

460. Loretto, Alec. "When Is a Ganassi Recorder Not a Ganassi Recorder?" *The American Recorder* 27, no. 2 (May 1986): 64–66. Simultaneously published in *Early Music New Zealand* 2, no. 2 (June 1986): 3–8. Reprinted with additional sentence in *The Recorder and Music Magazine* 9, no. 10 (June 1989): 288–91.

    Describes four different (allegedly hypothetical) approaches to making a Ganassi recorder, working from: (1) the known range of the instrument, (2) Ganassi's fingering chart, (3) the chart and the frontispiece picture in Ganassi's treatise, (4) a suitable surviving instrument of the time. Although certain phrases suggest that Loretto was making a logical progression from worst to best method, he has denied that, claiming that his article only "attempted to discuss the problems facing a maker" (letter to the editor, *The American Recorder* 29, no. 3 [August 1988]: 128).

    The sentence added to the article in 1989 was: "He made his first Ganassi copy in 1973 and published his first Ganassi article in 1974." The latter claim seems to relate to item **462**, which was first distributed as a mimeographed booklet accompanying a lecture (only "publication" in the broadest sense of the term—a communication to a public, in this case the people who attended his lecture).

461. Lasocki, David. [Letters to the Editor]. *The Recorder Magazine* 10, no. 1 (March 1990): 17; 10, no. 2 (June 1990): 39-40.

    In the first letter, Lasocki summarizes the debate to date and offers a bibliography of the relevant sources. In the second, he discusses Loretto's evidence.

462. Loretto, Alec V. "A Ganassi Model Recorder in Vienna?" *The Recorder Magazine* 10, no. 2 (June 1990): 35–38.

    Published in response to the controversy generated by item **4**. Reprints the contents of a booklet accompanying a lecture at the Auckland Teachers'

College, New Zealand, in 1974, and expanded in 1978. The 1974 installment begins by comparing the bores of medieval, Renaissance, and Baroque recorders and describing how the recorder depicted in Ganassi's *Fontegara* matches none of the traditional models. Vienna C 8522 is said to embody many of the features of the Ganassi instrument; Loretto describes it and speculates on its provenance. The 1978 supplement responds to Bob Marvin's article (item **459**) by discussing the Ganassi frontispiece, how Vienna C 8522 differs from the recorders in the illustration, and how Marvin approached the design of his own Ganassi model.

15

Choice of Instrument

This chapter covers articles that give advice about choosing instruments. A special section is devoted to plastic instruments.

463. Akar, Etienne. "Ça y est, je me suis payé une belle flûte" [There we are: I've bought a beautiful recorder]. *Flûte à bec & instruments anciens* 18 (June 1986): 19; 19 (September 1986): 37–38; 20 (December 1986): 25–26.

    Whimsical reminiscences on the author's "pitiful" collection of recorders ("a plastic and a Rottenburgh"), his decision to buy a new Baroque copy, and his delight in its properties.

464. Ball, Christopher. "Renaissance and Baroque Recorders: Choosing an Instrument." *Early Music* 3, no. 1 (January 1975): 11–19.

    A survey of commercially available wooden recorders, with advice for the potential buyer. Tone quality and intonation should be the principal factors in choosing a recorder; the former is purely personal preference, but the latter can be measured, and Ball suggests some problematic notes and octave leaps to test. Describes the differences between the bore, range, and tone quality of Renaissance and Baroque recorders and how these are important considerations if a player can afford only one recorder. Renaissance and Baroque instruments are considered separately, and the surveys proceed maker by maker. Those included are: Bärenreiter, Coolsma, John Cousen, Dolmetsch, Fehr, Heinrich, Hopf, von Huene, Küng, Moeck, Mollenhauer, and Richard Palm. The evaluations are generally based on tone quality, intonation, price, and breath requirements. An appendix lists the instruments and their 1975 prices.

* Davidson, Martin. "Observations on the Relation between Wood and Tone Quality in Recorders." Cited above as item 385.

Choice of Instrument

465. Davidson, Martin. "Of Bleeps, Slurps, and Presbycusis." *The American Recorder* 9, no. 4 (Fall 1968): 113–14.

    Older players should take hearing loss into account when selecting an instrument. High-frequency loss often masks harmonics and the high-pitched "bleeps" of improperly tongued notes. Lower-pitched instruments (tenor and bass) work best. If a soprano or alto is required, it should be one that does not easily overblow. Despite these caveats, the sound of the recorder is less rich in harmonics than most other instruments, making it one of the best choices for older beginning musicians.

466. Delahousse, D., Alain Sobczak, and B. Reinhardt, eds. "Conseils pour le choix et l'entretien des flûtes à bec" [Advice on the choice and maintenance of recorders]. *Flûte à bec* 1 (June 1981): 5–10.

    Basic information on types and sizes of recorders, terminology relating to parts of the instrument, types of wood, and short- and long-term maintenance.

467. LaBarre, Kenneth. "On Selecting a Recorder." *The American Recorder* 13, no. 3 (August 1972): 74–76.

    Describes what one should consider when evaluating a recorder. The broad areas are general appearance, quality of craftsmanship, tone quality, response, range, and intonation. Letter from Daniel Waitzman in 14, no. 1 (February 1973): 35–36.

468. Loretto, Alec V. "Which?: Some Comments on the Ways in Which Recorders are Described by Their Makers, Players and Others." *Recorder & Music* 5, no. 6 (June 1976): 190–91.

    Examines the following phrases, often found in advertising for historical copies, and explains what qualities should be present in instruments thus described: "modelled on Bressan" (or some other well known maker), "incorporating Bressan principles," "copy of Bressan," "Bressan copy," "Bressan model," "exact copy of Bressan."

469. Newman, Joel. "Recorders Recommended and Otherwise: A Survey of A.R.S. Examiners' Views." *The American Recorder* 8, no. 2 (Spring 1967): 52–53.

    Of historical interest only, because of its age. Reports the results of a survey completed by the eighteen members of the ARS Examiners' Board, who were asked to assign ratings of "recommended," "satisfactory," or "unsatisfactory" to "nine widely available brands of recorders."

* Ohannesian, David. "I Couldn't Make an Exact Copy If I Tried!" Cited above as item 454.

470. Saunders, Gordon. "Choosing a Recorder." *Continuo* 3, no. 10 (Summer 1980): 16–18.

    Discusses choice of woods, Renaissance vs. Baroque models, and testing the headjoint alone.

471. Schnoll, David. "Choosing Recorders for a Balanced Ensemble." *Continuo* 2, no. 5 (February 1979): 7–8.

    Describes the disastrous results of mixing makes and models of recorders in an ensemble. Promotes the idea of using Renaissance recorders by a single maker; failing that, (1) mixing and matching one make, or (2) using any Renaissance recorders, or (3) using Baroque recorders that speak badly in the low register.

472. von Huene, Friedrich. "Recorder Clinic." *The American Recorder* 4, no. 1 (February 1963): 5–6.

    Describes the factors one should consider when selecting an instrument.

473. Wyatt, Theo. "Choosing an Instrument." *The American Recorder* 18, no. 2 (August 1977): 44–46.

    Strongly advocates the purchase of a plastic instrument "unless you are quite sure that a plastic one is not good enough for you." Offers the following advice for purchasing wooden instruments: there is little correlation between price and musical quality; test the instrument yourself; check intonation of octaves; and pay close attention to tone quality, responsiveness, and flexibility.

474. Wyatt, Theo. "The Perfect Instrument: Does It Exist?" *Recorder and Music Magazine* 2, no. 4 (February 1967): 105.

    Postscript to item 533. In response to a number of readers who wrote him asking why it is not possible to purchase a recorder free of intonation problems, Wyatt explains why there is no perfect instrument.

475. Wyatt, Theo. "Treble Chance." *The Recorder and Music Magazine* 8, no. 4 (December 1984): 108–9.

    Reports the results of an informal test of five instruments, which were played behind a screen and rated by assembled students at Theobalds Park. Concludes that there is a "tenuous and shaky correlation between price and musical quality" when choosing an instrument. (The title of the article, incidentally, is a pun. The expression refers to that section of the British football pools [a weekly competition based on predicting the results of professional soccer matches] on which one can win the most money—sometimes millions of pounds. A treble recorder is the British name for an alto.) See also Wyatt's postscript in 8, no. 5 (March 1985): 148, which offers mathematical support for his conclusions.

476. "Why I Own and Use More than One Alto Recorder." *The American Recorder* 13, no. 1 (February 1972): 14–15; 13, no. 2 (May 1972): 54–57; 13, no. 3 (August 1972): 93–95.
    Responses to a letter sent by Arthur Nitka to the ARS Board and ARS certified teachers.

PLASTIC INSTRUMENTS

477. Catrice, Jean-Noël. "Flûtes à bec alto en plastique" [Plastic alto recorders]. *Flûte à bec* 2 (February 1982): 22–24.
    A comparative review of the plastic alto recorders on the market in November 1981. Covers: physical characteristics, timbre, intonation, pitch, condensation, and response to double tonguing.

478. "How Do They Stand Up?: Three Recorder Professionals Test Three Plastic Recorders." *American Recorder* 32, no. 3 (September 1991): 14–17.
    Transcription of a conversation between Marilyn Boenau, Frances Blaker, and Judith Linsenberg as they evaluate four Yamaha Rottenburgh altos, two Zen-On Bressan altos, and two Aulos Hakas.

479. "Panorama des flûtes à bec en plastique" [Panorama of plastic recorders], ed. Jean-Noël Catrice. *Flûte à bec* 1 (June 1981): 15.
    Brief table of information on 11 types of plastic soprano recorders, including yes-or-no answers to that essential question: "Is this recorder a musical instrument?"

480. Reyne, Hugo. "Une rétrospective des flûtes à bec en plastique disponibles sur le marché français" [A retrospective on plastic recorders available on the French market]. *Flûte à bec & instruments anciens* 9 (December 1983): 19–22.

Lists plastic recorders with Baroque fingering available in France (make, price, tested pitch). Instruments with German fingering are excluded.

481. Wyatt, Theo. "Which Recorder?: A Consumer's Guide to Plastic Instruments." *The American Recorder* 23, no. 4 (November 1982): 151–57. Reprinted, with revisions, in *Recorder & Music* 7, no. 10 (June 1983): 253–63. In French as: "Quelle flûte choisir? Guide du consommateur pour l'achat d'un instrument en plastique." Edited by Hugo Reyne. *Flûte à bec & instruments anciens* 9 (December 1983): 23–32.

    An evaluation of most plastic instruments sold in the United States during the early 1980s—a total of twenty-nine instruments (two sopraninos, fourteen sopranos, ten altos, and three tenors). The version in *Recorder & Music* "excludes those instruments not available in the United Kingdom and includes a number of models not sold in the USA when the survey was started." Using scientific equipment, Wyatt measured the breath pressure needed for a person to play each note on each instrument exactly in tune. He then averaged the pressures for each note and smoothed out the curve over the range of pitches to arrive at an "average acceptable profile." A panel of listeners evaluated the tone quality of each pitch (whether it sounded over- or underblown, more suitable for solo or ensemble use, or generally acceptable).

    The results of the study are summarized in bargraphs showing each instrument's deviation from the standard profile. A summary table lists model names, prices, technical specifications, and features. Wyatt concludes that there is a wide choice of passable instruments at reasonable prices, but standards of intonation are poor.

482. Wyatt, Theo. "Which Recorder?: A Supplement." *The American Recorder* 24, no. 3 (August 1983): 110–12.

    Supplement to the *American Recorder* version of item **481**. "It covers three recorders that have appeared on the U.S. market since that article was written . . . ; it includes some afterthoughts on pulling out . . . ; it updates information on the Dolmetsch soprano; it offers a revised assessment of those instruments with solo pretensions; and it repairs a couple of inadvertent omissions from the original article."

483. Wyatt, Theo. "Which Recorder?: A Consumer's Guide to Recent Plastic Instruments." *The Recorder and Music Magazine* 9, no. 12 (December 1989): 342–46.

    A sequel to the RMM version of item **481**, covering sixteen models that had appeared on the market since the publication of the original article.

484. Wyatt, Theo. "Which Recorder?: A Supplement." *The Recorder Magazine* 10, no. 2 (June 1990): 32–34.

A second sequel to the *Recorder & Music* version of item **481**, covering three new instruments available in the United Kingdom (Aulos Tenor 311, Aulos Descant 103, and Moeck Flauto 1).

16

Maintenance, Improvement, and Restoration

This chapter is concerned with writings on the maintenance and improvement of modern recorders and the restoration of historical ones. General sources are followed by ones on the specific topics of carrying cases, condensation, joints, keys, oiling, tone quality, and voicing and tuning.

MAINTENANCE AND REPAIR

485. Bouterse, Jan. *Die Blockflöte: Tips für Anschaffung und Pflege, Stimmkorrekturen, Reparaturen* [The Recorder: tips on buying and care, tuning correction, and repairs]. Celle: Moeck, 1992. 80 p. ISBN 3875490401. Originally in Dutch as *De blokfluit, handleiding voor aanschaf, onderhoud, bijstemmen en kleine reparaties* (author, Alphen aan de Rijn, Netherlands, 1990). For English summary, see item **1483.3**.
Not seen. Source: Moeck catalog.

486. Brown, Adrian. *The Recorder: A Basic Workshop Manual.* Brighton: Dolce Edition, 1989. 45 p. DOL 112. OCLC #26822283.
The slightly misleading title hides a useful book for the non-specialist on playing-in a new instrument, daily care and maintenance, special problems of different sizes and types of recorder, correcting the tuning and pitch, voicing, what makes a good recorder, and woods. Short list of suppliers of tools and materials. A slightly abbreviated translation of the first two chapters appears as item **487**. Reviewed by Jeremy Montagu in *FoMRHI Quarterly* 57 (October 1989): 8 and Benjamin Dunham in *American Recorder* 32, no. 4 (December 1991): 36.

487. Brown, Adrian. "Pflege der Blockflöte und kleinere Reparaturen" [Care of the recorder and small repairs]. *Tibia* 15, no. 2 (1990): 106–11.

A slightly abbreviated translation of the first two chapters of item 486. Covers: playing-in a new instrument; daily management and maintenance (warming up, storage, oiling, types of oil, clogging, removing the block, cleaning the block and wind canal, problems with mold, replacing the block, tenons, greases, and wrapping thread).

* Delahousse, D., Alain Sobczak, and B. Reinhardt, eds. "Conseils pour le choix et l'entretien des flûtes à bec" [Advice on the choice and maintenance of recorders]. Cited above as item 1419.

488. Duhot, Jean-Joël. "Entretenir une flûte: Jean-Joël Duhot a rencontré Claire Soubeyran" [Recorder maintenance: Jean-Joël Duhot has met Claire Soubeyran]. *Flûte à bec & instruments anciens* 20 (1986): 3–7.

Interview covering in detail: humidity and its effect on recorders, oiling, cracks, precautions, repairs (some by the player), accidents, aging and deformation, the properties of different woods (including a chart of ten woods and their vulnerability to several risks), joints, and dealing with an early instrument.

489. Duhot, Jean-Joël. "S.O.S. flûte à bec: Jean-Joël Duhot a rencontré Irène Oki" [SOS recorder: Jean-Joël Duhot has met Irène Oki]. *Flûte à bec & instruments anciens* 22 (1987): 2–5.

Oki is in charge of regulating and tuning recorders for the firm of Adège, who, according to their advertising slogan in the same issue, "make woods sing." She discusses the care and maintenance of the block, the edge, and the windway, as well as the qualities of different modern woods.

490. Geiger, Georg. "The Compleat Recorder Para-Medic; or, How to Put a Recorder in Trim While Keeping Your Sanity, Part 1." *The Recorder: Australia's Journal of Recorder and Early Music* 15 (June 1992): 19–23.

Begins with terminology and information on the ideal condition for a recorder as well as advice on how to check it. Continues with instructions for cleaning and oiling. Part 2 is scheduled to cover revoicing and tuning procedures.

491. Hunt, Edgar. "Looking after Your Recorder." *Recorder & Music* 7, no. 6 (June 1982): 144–45; 7, no. 7 (September 1982): 168; 7, no. 8 (December 1982): 196–97.

The first part concerns wood recorders and their maintenance, specifically: the types of wood used for recorders, oiling the bore, condensation and its attendant problems, breaking in a new instrument, and joints (both cork and thread). The second part covers the adjustment of a tightly fitting block and the protection of wood recorders from adverse environmental conditions. The series ends with a description of Hunt's homemade carrying case. For more on the care of wood recorders, see Hunt's reply to a letter from John Rowe in 8, no. 12 (December 1986): 362.

492. Jacobs, Guido. "Enkele tips voor het onderhoud van historische houtblazers" [A few tips on the maintenance of historical woodwinds]. *Musica Antiqua* 3, no. 1 (February 1986): 13–14, 19–20.

Concentrates on recorders. Good photographs.

493. Saunders, Gordon. "Recorder Care and Playing-in." *Continuo* 3, no. 3 (December 1979): 4–9.

Practical advice on how to maintain recorders.

494. Stern, Claudio. "A Brief Workshop Manual for Recorders." *Early Music* 7, no. 3 (July 1979): 359–65.

A guide to minor repairs and maintenance that players may perform on their own instruments. Covers: correcting the tuning of octaves by enlarging or reducing the size of finger holes, raising or lowering the overall pitch of the instrument, improving the voicing by removing and replacing the block or by oiling, and adjusting resistance to breath pressure by moving the block. Describes the proper technique for cleaning and oiling the instrument. Concludes with a prudent warning against tampering with historical instruments.

495. von Huene, Friedrich. "Recorder Clinic." *The American Recorder* 4, no. 1 (February 1963): 5–6; 4, no. 3 (August 1963): 10–11.

A series of articles answering readers' questions. The first installment advises a reader who wonders whether a small hair dryer could be used to dry out an instrument during performance breaks (fine, so long as the instrument does not become too hot). The second installment answers the question "How do I care for my recorder?"

496. Wyatt, Theo. "Recorder Surgery." *Recorder and Music Magazine* 4, no. 3 (September 1972): 86–87.

"[An] essential part of every teacher's professional skill must be the ability to diagnose faults in instruments, particularly of intonation, and to put them right." Mostly concerned with the diagnosis rather than the "putting right," for which Wyatt refers the reader to his 1966 article, item 533. Covers problems with both wooden and plastic instruments.

IMPROVEMENT

497. Fajardo, Raoul J. "How to Improve Your Recorder." *The American Recorder* 11, no. 3 (Summer 1970): 91–92. Reprinted in *Recorder and Music Magazine* 3, no. 12 (December 1971): 443–45.

Proposes solutions to three problems: clogged windways (suggests applying a wetting agent); inefficient response caused by an improperly positioned lip (suggests either sanding down the windway or adding a veneer of maple, depending on whether the edge is low or high); and response difficulties of problem high notes (suggests inserting an adjustable inner sleeve of rolled paper or plastic into the headpiece at the position of a node for the troublesome note).

Daniel A. Driscoll, in 11, no. 4 (Fall 1970): 150, recommends a small lump of modeling clay as a satisfactory substitute for the plastic ring and recommends that amateurs not attempt adjustments to the windway. Friedrich von Huene, in 12, no. 2 (May 1971): 66, notes a "marked increase" in the number of instruments sent to his workshop for correction of amateur repairs after the appearance of this article. He advises caution and amends a few of Fajardo's suggestions based on his own experience. A brief article in *Recorder and Music Magazine* 4, no. 6 (June 1973): 195 reports that several manufacturers of plastic recorders have adopted the concept of the "acoustic ring" to narrow the bore of the headjoint and improve response. A similar report appears in Fajardo's letter in *The American Recorder* 14, no. 2 (May 1973): 73.

498. Fajardo, Raoul J. "Thumb Hole Reinforcement for the Recorder." *The American Recorder* 10, no. 2 (Spring 1969): 61.

Advocates attaching a thin brass plate to the recorder to reinforce the thumb hole.

499. Glassgold, Cook. "Thoughts on Thumb-rests." *The American Recorder* 3, no. 2 (May 1962): 21.

Outlines the controversy over the use of thumbrests. Offers instructions for making a rubber thumbrest. Letter from David Emerson in 3, no. 4

(November 1962): 27 describes a thumbrest for a tenor recorder that requires no drilling.

500. Loretto, Alec V. "Adjustable Lip on the Recorder." *Recorder & Music Magazine* 3, no. 8 (December 1970): 278–79.

Describes Loretto's experiments with adjustable lips (edges) on a great bass in F. By changing the position and angle of the lip, he was able to improve the response of the recorder in individual registers, albeit at the expense of the other registers.

501. Loretto, Alec. "Experiments at Celle." *Recorder and Music Magazine* 4, no. 5 (March 1973): 156–57.

Describes Loretto's attempts to improve the tone and flexibility of Moeck Rottenburgh recorders by adjusting the size and shape of the windway. "The result was what I hoped for—a much richer sound combined with a very real ability to play loudly and softly, particularly in the upper register." Letter from Theodore Mix in 4, no. 7 (September 1973): 243 emphasizes that the modifications were neither authorized nor requested by Moeck. Letters by Loretto and Hermann Moeck in 4, no. 8 (December 1973): 285–86. Loretto's letter points out that his experiments were carried out only to satisfy his curiosity. He also includes a bibliography of writings on experiments with and modifications of instruments. Moeck emphasizes that the changes constitute "modifications" that are not necessarily "improvements" and that Moeck has no intention of altering the production of the instruments. In a reply that follows, Loretto admits to using the term "improvements" in his *Early Music* articles.

502. Loretto, Alec. "Recorder Modifications: In Search of the Expressive Recorder." *Early Music* 1, no. 2 (April 1973): 107–9; 1, no. 3 (July 1973): 147–51; 1, no. 4 (October 1973): 229–31.

This series of articles might better have been titled "How to Construct a New Block," since, except for a brief discussion of modifying the windway ceiling, the only modification covered is the replacement of a recorder's block to improve flexibility. Loretto emphasizes that at the conclusion of his twenty-step process the recorder can be "fully restored to its original condition" by replacing the new block with the old. Includes a list of tools required, with photographs of each. In 2, no. 1 (January 1974): 49, Friedrich von Huene cautions the amateur against tampering with the voicing of his instruments, because "too many recorders are made unplayable." In the same issue (p. 53), Gordon Wood offers instructions for constructing a two-part block with a lathe and a routing or milling machine. Frank Hubbard, in 2, no. 3 (July 1974): 201–3, finds it discouraging to think that professionally crafted recorders "should be considered capable of almost casual improvement by amateurs instructed by a magazine article." Loretto responds to the latter in 3, no. 1 (January 1975): 77.

RESTORATION

For a useful classified, annotated bibliography on this subject, see Cary Karp, ed., *The Conservation and Technology of Musical Instruments: A Bibliographical Supplement to Art and Archaeology Technical Abstracts, Volume 28* (Marina del Rey, California: The Getty Conservation Institute, 1992).

503. Weber, Rainer. "Dokumentation von Schäden an Holzblasinstrumenten: Auszug aus einem Referat der Tagung der Arbeitsgemeinschaft der Restauratoren (AdR) in Bochum 1989" [Documentation of damage to woodwind instruments: summary of a lecture given at the conference of the study group of restorers (AdR) in Bochum, 1989]. *Tibia* 16, no. 1 (1991): 383–85.

A fine brief overview of woodwind instrument restoration. Describes three kinds of damage: through use (e.g., breath moisture), dependent upon the construction (mechanical weak points), and dependent upon the material (shrinkage, corrosion). Joints and keys are especially vulnerable. Woodwind instruments are complex creations that need to be constantly under surveillance by museums.

504. Zadro, Michael G. "Aspects on [sic] the Restoration of Woodwind Instruments." *The American Recorder* 15, no. 1 (February 1974): 7–11, 28.

The best article-length treatment of the topic. Although Zadro considers it a "fundamental guide to restoration practices," he goes into quite a bit of detail on certain topics, such as repairing loose or broken ferrules, selecting an appropriate glue, repairing split joints, and rewrapping tenons.

505. Zadro, Michael. "Guide to the Restoration of Woodwind Instruments." *Early Music* 2, no. 3 (July 1974): 169–73.

Outlines basic steps that can be taken to preserve historical woodwind instruments. Of particular interest to recorder players are the sections on repairing split joints, the use of glues, and preservation treatment for wood. Includes a list of suppliers for ivory, glues, and a wood preservative. Jeremy Montagu, in 3, no. 1 (January 1975): 75, cautions against the application of some of Zadro's techniques. Zadro defends his suggestions in 3, no. 3 (July 1975): 289-91, followed by a response from Montagu, which Zadro addresses in 4, no. 1 (January 1976): 83-84.

Specific Topics

Carrying Cases

506. Glassgold, Cook. "The Glassgold Gatherall." *The American Recorder* 2, no. 4 (Fall 1961): 4-5.
    Step-by-step illustrated instructions on how to customize a briefcase so that it may serve as a recorder case.

507. Godwin, Joscelyn. "A Design for a Recorder Case." *The American Recorder* 13, no. 1 (February 1972): 10-11.
    Instructions on making a case for SpSATB recorders using a briefcase, foam rubber, lining, and miscellaneous supplies. Letter from B.W. Loughry in 13, no. 4 (November 1972): 140.

Condensation

508. Burford, Freda. "Coping with Condensation." *The Recorder and Music Magazine* 9, no. 9 (March 1989): 249.
    Describes the problems that condensation can cause during performance and raises several questions about the conditions that cause blockage, but unfortunately does not suggest solutions. Letter from Maria Boxall in 9, no. 12 (December 1989): 357 concerns the distinction between saliva and condensation. Burford offers suggestions on controlling saliva in 10, no. 2 (June 1990): 39, but Roy Brewer advises against them in 10, no. 3 (September 1990): 71.

509. "Condensation." (What's Wrong with My Recorder?) *The Recorder and Music Magazine* 1, no. 4 (February 1964): 105.
    Explains the causes and treatment of clogging due to condensation. Clogging of the windway—a problem particularly in the winter—can be reduced by warming up the instrument before playing. Once clogged, the windway can be cleared by blowing sharply through it. Since the wood of a new recorder is especially sensitive to moisture, the instrument must be broken in slowly to avoid excessive swelling and damage to the windway. Letter from Theo Wyatt in 1, no. 5 (May 1964): 154.

510. "Controlling Salvation [sic]." *The American Recorder* 25, no. 4 (November 1984): 158.

Reprints a letter from *The New England Journal of Medicine* in which Carl E. Dettman recommends the placement of a patch of scopolamine in the mouth in order to suppress salivation and presumably prevent clogged windways. Emil Kmetec and Harold Kohn argue against this practice, noting that the scopolamine might control salivation but would have little or no effect on condensation in the windway.

511. Loretto, Alec V. "Self Inflicted Injuries and the Average Recorder Player." *The Recorder and Music Magazine* 9, no. 2 (June 1987): 34–35.

Describes the serious damage that can be inflicted on the labium by pressing against it while attempting to clear condensation from the windway. Suggests several alternatives to protect the delicate edge.

512. Muskett, Michael. "On Wetting One's Whistle." *Recorder and Music Magazine* 4, no. 2 (June 1972): 46, 54.

While visiting a few villages in Spain, the author encountered among folk musicians the practice of running water through fipple flutes before playing them—people who actually "wet their whistles." The author discovered that the technique "helps to eliminate clogging trouble during the warming up period. A little water, cider, or wine should be run through the windway, or the top of the recorder dipped in water; the instrument can then be dried and the excess water blown out." The author, however, confines himself to the use of water, "my duty-free allowance having been kept for more appreciative 'whistles.'" Edgar Hunt, in item 30 (p. 42), notes that Francis Bacon "recommends us to wet our whistles to get a more solemn sound" in his *Natural Philosophy*.

JOINTS

513. Fader, Bruce. "Cork Joints Affect Your Playing." *The American Recorder* 11, no. 2 (Spring 1970): 51–53.

Describes the adverse effects of leaky or wobbly joints on a recorder's performance. Recommends wrapping corks with a non-adhesive Teflon tape and explains the acoustical reasons for the success of this method: air vibration losses in the bore affect the initial transient of the sound.

514. Levin, Philip. "Joints." (Instrument Care) *The American Recorder* 23, no. 3 (August 1982): 117.

A guide to the maintenance and repair of joints. Although the emphasis is on cork, Levin recognizes that historical makers used thread or string and that many makers of replicas continue to prefer string to cork. Both types of joints should be separated and wiped after use. Cork is kept supple by applying tallow-based cork grease. (Vaseline should be avoided.) Describes the steps taken to replace a cork joint.

515. "Looking after the Joints." (What's Wrong with My Recorder?) *The Recorder and Music Magazine* 1, no. 5 (May 1964): 138.

Joints are made airtight in one of three ways: (1) wrapping the tenon with waxed thread, (2) wrapping the tenon with cork, or (3) lining the socket with cork. Describes how to wrap a tenon with thread and how to maintain (but not replace) cork.

516. "What's Wrong with My Recorder?" *The Recorder and Music Magazine* 1, no. 7 (November 1964): 212.

How to fix the loose joints and plugs that may result from extended periods of idleness.

Keys

517. Blood, Brian. "Dear Doctor." *The Recorder Magazine* 13, no. 3 (December 1993): 89.

Discusses the causes of key noise and suggests improvements to minimize the problem.

Oiling

518. Joof, Laura Beha. "Dear Recorder Doctor . . . " *The Recorder: Journal of the Victorian Recorder Guild* 8 (July 1988): 32–33. Reprinted from *Boston Early Music News*, September 1985.

Detailed advice on oiling recorders.

519. Levin, Philip. "Oiling Recorders." *The American Recorder* 23, no. 1 (February 1982): 27.

Describes why oiling is important: oil makes the surface resistant to moisture penetration—thus preventing cracks—and enhances the acoustical reflectivity of the instrument. (Some woods are treated by the recorder maker to make oiling unnecessary.) Gives instructions for oiling a recorder, warning of the damage that can be caused by careless oiling.

520. Moeck, Hermann. "Ist die 'pflegeleichte' Blockflöte noch 'in'?" [Is the "easy care" recorder still "in"?]. *Tibia* 4, no. 3 (1979): 384–87.

Discusses ways of ameliorating the consequences of wood being a live material that "works" according to the temperature and humidity. For a light wood, such as maple or pear, paraffin can be used, allowing the wood to breathe without letting moisture be absorbed. But this does not mean that the player should not take care of the instrument by letting it dry; the advantage is that it does not have to be oiled. Unfortunately, this process cannot be applied to hard woods, such as palisander, grenadilla, or ebony, the only protection for which is to oil them regularly. Discusses the technique of oiling and the choice of oils (paraffinum subliquidum, silicone oil, linseed oil, tung oil, hemp-seed or soy oil, and polyethylene glycol [cites item 505 for others]).

521. Simmons, Terry. "The Good Oil . . . What *Really* Happens When You Oil Your Recorder?" *The Recorder: Australia's Journal of Recorder and Early Music* 17 (September 1993): 15-22. Reprinted in *FoMRHI Quarterly* 74 (January 1994): 59-63.

After summarizing the views of the "plenty" and "sparing" schools of thought on oiling recorders, gives a short chemistry lesson on the properties of oils. Then discusses how oiling changes the instrument and how the two schools are both right (for two different types of oil). We should just not mix the two approaches. Finally gives advice on how and where to oil. An essential article.

Tone quality

522. Fader, Bruce, and Raoul J. Fajardo. "Improving the Tone of Plastic Recorders." *The American Recorder* 12, no. 2 (May 1971): 41-43.

A soft material (fiberglass, foam, felt, balsa wood) positioned over or under the windway of a plastic recorder will effectively suppress harsh overtones. Describes how to construct several devices based on this principle that help improve the shrill, strident tone produced by many plastic recorders.

523. Fajardo, Raoul J. "Enhancing the Recorder Sound." *Recorder & Music Magazine* 3, no. 5 (March 1970): 172-74.

Describes Fajardo's unusual experiments with the application of electronic reverberation and amplification to recorders. "Although an echo may seem like a small matter, it can make the difference between an ordinary recorder sound and a sound that neighbours will call 'beautiful.'"

524. Kottick, Edward L. *Tone and Intonation on the Recorder.* New York: McGinnis & Marx, 1974. ii, 27 p. OCLC #12963416.

Begins with the premise that "the aim of every performer should be to play his instrument in tune, with the best possible tone and the widest dynamic range." Seeks to show the recorder player how to achieve this aim, in three stages. First, by maintaining the instrument properly (smoothing the bore, cleaning the fingerholes and windway, keeping tight cork joints, oiling). Second, by achieving the optimum tone (fingers relaxed but not leaking air, responsive thumb, embouchure, breath-pressure, vibrato, dynamics). Third, by tuning the instrument (bringing a whole instrument down or up to pitch, principles and techniques of tuning, tuning individual notes). Packs an amazing amount of useful information into a short space. Highly recommended. Reviewed by Edgar Hunt in *Recorder & Music* 5, no. 1 (March 1975).

VOICING AND TUNING

525. Bolton, Philippe. "Remplacer le bouchon de sa flûte à bec pour lui donner une nouvelle voix" [Replacing the block of your recorder in order to revoice it]. *Flûte à bec* 4 (September 1982): 9–12; 5 (December 1982): 19–21; 6 (March 1983): 15–19.

    Detailed instructions, with line drawings, on how to go about this delicate task.

526. Joof, Laura Beha. "Recorder Voicing and Tuning, and Use of the Tuning Machine." *The American Recorder* 26, no. 4 (November 1985): 155–59.

    Presents a clear description, with drawings of parts of a recorder's voicing. Describes fifteen principles of voicing. Specifies tone holes that influence the tuning of each note (f^1-g^3 on alto). Offers advice on using tuning machines to measure pitch and lists five tuners on the market.

*   Kottick, Edward L. *Tone and Intonation on the Recorder.* Cited above as item **524**.

527. Levin, Philip. "Voicing and Tuning." (Instrument Care) *The American Recorder* 25, no. 3 (August 1984): 105–7.

    A thorough discussion of the topic by an experienced maker. Introduces the concept of voicing and why adjustments are occasionally necessary. Describes the components of the mouthpiece and how certain modifications to the windway, window, and labium alter voicing. Recommends trying a commercial anti-condensation product on a clogging recorder before resorting to revoicing. Discusses the different types of voicings used on the four main categories of recorders (simple and crudely finished, simple and well finished, more sophisticated but not quite "historical," and historical). Describes modifications that can be made to correct overall pitch and the relative intonation of individual notes. Adjustments are made either by changing the size of the toneholes, by pulling out the head, or by adding material to or removing material from the bore. Levin emphasizes that adjustments to voicing and tuning should not be undertaken by amateurs.

* Loretto, Alec V. "A New Angle on Finger Holes." Cited above as item 331.

528. Loretto, Alec V. "Yet More on Tuning Recorders." *The Recorder Magazine* 10, no. 1 (March 1990): 2-4; 10, no. 2 (June 1990): 30-31.

   Describes the techniques used by makers to adjust the tuning of recorders. Loretto believes that most problems found in today's instruments can be corrected by either filling or undercutting individual holes, and he places particular emphasis on the description of those two techniques. Part Two presents a table of standard English fingerings and the open holes that govern the tuning of each. Loretto shows how the filling or undercutting of a particular hole can affect notes other than the one needing adjustment. "The surprising thing is that in spite of these conflicts and contradications, those who tune recorders can actually produce results which make life easier for the players."

529. Martin, John. "Flattening Your Recorder." *The Recorder: Journal of the Victorian Recorder Guild* 15 (June 1992): 8.

   This alarming title hides a discussion of two ways to uniformly lower the pitch of a recorder, both of which effectively involve increasing the thickness of the window.

530. Massy, James. "The Flattening Effect of 'Pulling Out' the Recorder." *Recorder & Music* 6, no. 2 (June 1978): 34-35.

   Through controlled tests, Massy determines that extending the length of an instrument results in an increasing degree of flattening in the lowest octave, but in the second octave the instrument quickly becomes less flat. Concludes that recorders should be pulled out no more than necessary, and, when playing on a pulled-out instrument, one should be gentle with the high notes, which will have a tendency toward sharpness.

531. "Some Notes on Intonation." (What's Wrong with My Recorder?) *The Recorder and Music Magazine* 1, no. 6 (August 1964): 187.

   Briefly discusses a few reasons why a recorder might go out of tune (accumulation of dirt in fingerholes, excessive oiling, disintegration of the cork).

* Willoughby, Andrew A. "Das Intonieren von Blockflöten: Antworten auf einen Fragebogen" [The voicing of recorders: replies to a questionnaire]. Cited above as item 382.

532. Wyatt, Theo. "A Note on Intonation." *Recorder and Music Magazine* 4, no. 1 (March 1972): 9.

    Intonation problems can occur when the socket of the head joint is longer than the tenon of the middle joint. Offers several possible repairs for both plastic and wooden instruments.

533. Wyatt, Theo. "Tuning Your Own Recorder." *Recorder and Music Magazine* 2, no. 1 (March 1966): 11-12; 2, no. 2 (July 1966): 37-39.

    Explains how to correct the faults of an out-of-tune recorder. Part One describes the principles governing pitch and tuning, the most important being the "ease of escape" principle ("the ease with which the pressure waves can escape from the tube to be equalized with the outside air"). Includes a table of pitches and the tone holes that govern their tuning. Part Two describes methods that Wyatt has used to correct his own instruments. Explains how to adjust for overall flatness or sharpness and how to undercut or fill individual holes.

17

Historical Methods (Tutors) and Treatises

Three classes of musicians have always played the recorder: professionals, adult amateurs, and children. With the possible exception of Ganassi's *Fontegara*, no extant early instructions could have provided adequate instruction for professionals. This is hardly surprising, because those musicians have always been taught orally. In the Renaissance and Baroque periods they served as apprentices, receiving their training from masters with little or no written assistance. In the 20th century, would-be professionals generally begin with private teachers then go on to music schools or conservatories, instruction books serving primarily as a source of exercises, studies, and progressive repertory.

By the 16th century there were enough amateurs in France and Germany to warrant the publication of general instruction books that included material on the recorder. The rise of the middle class in the 17th and 18th centuries and the concomitant interest in self-instruction brought with it a spate of recorder "tutors" (or methods, to use a more modern term), particularly in England. Yet, despite the extravagant claims of some publishers, none of these instructions was ever intended to bring amateurs to anything like a professional standard of performance.

In all periods, whether the pupils have been professional or amateur, the finer points of performance, such as breath control, intonation, ornamentation, and musical interpretation, have been learned with the aid of a teacher; they can hardly be imparted by a book. All instruction books are written for people who can hear contemporaneous music-making and absorb its style by ear. In the absence of the sound, even the most comprehensive instructions fail, the reader seeking in vain to develop that "bon goût," or good taste, which early writers considered so essential. Recorder instructions of the past can therefore give us only a small idea of what recorder playing was like in a few scattered places at arbitrary times. (This introduction and some annotations are based on David Lasocki's chapter "Instruction Books and Methods for the Recorder to the Present Day" in item 17.)

A note on terminology: Mary Vinquist defines "tutors" as "those sources of a didactic or pedagogical nature which treat three or more aspects of recorder playing" (item 534, p. 21). We have preferred the term "methods." She also discusses (as we do) supplementary sources containing information on one or two aspects of recorder playing as well those "universal" music methods that contain a small amount of information on a number of instruments including the recorder.

534. Vinquist, Mary. *Recorder Tutors of the Seventeenth and Eighteenth Centuries: Technique and Performance Practice.* Ph.D. dissertation, University of North Carolina, 1974. viii, 328 leaves. OCLC #3083623. UMI order no. 75-15714.

A detailed look—always conscientious and sometimes inspired—at the Baroque recorder methods known in 1974 ("Tutto il bisognevole" [item 584], Bismantova [item 598], and Loulié [item 610] were rediscovered afterwards). Classifies the contents of the methods as general characteristics (such as musical examples and pirating of material), technique (posture, wrist position, hand placement, finger and thumb position, mouth and lips, tone production, tonguing syllables, and fingerings) and performance practice (application of tonguing syllables, meter, tempo, rhythm, and ornaments). It is a pity the dissertation was never published.

The appendixes are at least as useful as the body of the dissertation. Appendix A is an updating of Warner's bibliographic information (see item 536), adding biographical material on the authors and publishers. Includes bibliographic information on methods that are not extant (including some not in Warner: *The Compleat Instructor to the Flute. The Third Book* [London: John Young, ca. 1700]; *The Gentlemen's Diversion; or, the Flute Made Easie* [London: J. Young, ca. 1702]; *The New Flute Master, the 7th Edit.* [London: J. Walsh and J. Hare, 1711]; *The New Flute Master for the Year 1725* [London: J. Walsh and J. Hare, 1725]; *The New Flute Master for the Year 1728* [London: J. Walsh and J. Hare, 1727]; and *The New Flute Master for the Year 1733* [London: J. Walsh?, 1732]). Appendix B is an updating of Lasocki's composite fingering charts (see item 728) with extra material on fingerings for trills, *battements*, and *flattements*. Appendix C contains the sections on "graces" (ornaments) from eight English methods. Appendix D reproduces the sections on meter, tempo, and rhythm from Freillon-Poncein (item 644) and Hotteterre (item 650).

535. Warner, Thomas Everett. *An Annotated Bibliography of Woodwind Instruction Books, 1600–1830*. (Detroit Studies in Music Bibliography, 11) Detroit: Information Coordinators, 1967. xvi, 138 p. OCLC #187969.

    Cites fifty-five books with instructions for the recorder. Still constitutes the most complete published bibliography of such books. Each entry includes: name of author and date; full title transcription (with original spelling, punctuation, and layout); pagination; notes (reason for dating, later editions, relation to other works, etc.); and library holdings. Partially updated by Vinquist (item 534). Reviewed by David Lasocki in *Recorder & Music Magazine* 3, no. 2 (June 1969): 71.

536. Warner, Thomas E. *Indications of Performance Practice in Woodwind Instruction Books of the 17th and 18th Centuries*. Ph.D. dissertation, New York University, 1964. vi, 459 leaves. OCLC #2405434. UMI order no. 65-01678.

    An overview of woodwind performance practice that would have been influential if it had been published in the 1960s. Consists of chapters on: (1) general aspects; (2) articulation (including brief looks at Ganassi and Mersenne as well as detailed discussions of Freillon-Poncein and Hotteterre); (3) tempo (including the views of Freillon-Poncein and Hotteterre); (4) dynamics; (5) "alteration" (melodic ornamentation and rhythmic alteration, the latter including Hotteterre on inequality); (6) improvisation (improvisation of ornaments, including *The 5th Book of the New Flute Master*; cadenzas, including summaries of Hotteterre's *L'art de preluder*; and extempore variations); and (7) miscellaneous considerations (including Blankenburg's differentiation of enharmonic pairs). The first draft of Warner's important bibliography of woodwind methods (item 535) is found on leaves 244–426.

EARLIER LISTINGS AND SURVEYS

537. Rawski, Conrad. *Flute, Recorder, and Oboe Before 1800: A Selected Bibliography*. M.S. thesis, Library Science, Western Reserve University, 1957. 52 leaves.

    The earliest serious attempt to list recorder instruction books and other writings. Intended as "a fairly accurate checklist which may serve as a basis for more extensive and detailed bibliographic investigation" (Preface). Based largely on the catalog of the Dayton C. Miller Collection, Library of

Congress, and William C. Smith's catalog of the publications of John Walsh, as well as Degen (item 21) and Welch (item 18). Its main weakness was the lack of explanation of exactly what about the flute, recorder, and oboe is contained in the non-methods.

538. Riley, Maurice W. "A Tentative Bibliography of Early Wind Tutors." *Journal of Research in Music Education* 6 (Spring 1958): 3–24.
"Early" here means through mid 19th century, except in the case of the flute. Arranged by instrument, where recorder methods are lumped in with "Flute Tutors." Brief annotations. Completely superseded by items 535 and 534.

539. Simpson, Adrienne. "A Short-Title List of Printed English Instrumental Tutors up to 1800, Held in British Libraries." *R.M.A. Research Chronicle* 6 (1966): 24–50.
Published just after the appearance of Warner's bibliography (item 535). Simpson acknowledges that in Warner "the bibliographic material is fuller than was possible in a short-title list, and the listings from American libraries supplement and provide many duplicates for the material held in British libraries. I decided to allow my list to stand unchanged so that readers might have an overall picture of British sources." Includes cross-references to Warner. Has allowed "one or two discrepancies to stand . . . mainly in matters of approximate dating."

540. Hunt, Edgar. "Early Recorder Methods." *Recorder & Music* 6, no. 6 (June 1979): 166–70.
A short chronological survey from the early 16th to mid 18th centuries, with an admitted emphasis on English methods. Includes rules for gracing, examples of preludes, and facsimiles of frontispieces, all excerpted from the methods.

THE RENAISSANCE AND EARLY BAROQUE RECORDER

"INTRODUCTIO GSCHRIBEN UF PFIFEN"

541. Staehlein, Walter. "Neue Quellen zur mehrstimmigen Musik des 15. und 16. Jahrhunderts in der Schweiz" [New sources of polyphonic music of the 15th and 16th centuries in Switzerland]. *Schweizer Beiträge zur Musikwissenschaft*, Ser. III, Band 3. Bern & Stuttgart: Paul Haupt, 1978, 57-83 at 62-64 and Figs. 4-5.

Describes a five-leaf manuscript book, headed only "Discant" (Basel, Universitätsbibliothek, Ms. F. X. 38), and reproduces three facsimile pages. It was probably written out for the 15-year-old Bonifacius Amerbach around 1510. (The appelation "Introductio gschriben uf pfifen" comes from the Amerbach estate catalog of 1578.) The instructions depict a discant recorder in G, giving fingerings, an explanation of mensural notation, and a series of exercises.

VIRDUNG, SEBASTIAN (B. 1465?)

542. Virdung, Sebastian. *Musica getutscht und auszgezogen durch Sebastianum Virdung, Priesters von Amberg, und alles Gesang ausz den Noten in die Tabulaturen diser benanten dryer Instrumenten der Orgeln, der Lauten und der Flöten transferieren zu lernen Kurtzlich gemacht zu eren den hochwirdigen hochgebornen Fürsten unnd Herren: Herr Wilhalmen, Bischove zü Straszburg, seynem gnedigen Herren* [Music translated into German and excerpted by Sebastian Virdung, priest of Amberg. Everything there is to know about transcribing songs from notes into the tablatures of these three given instruments: the organ, the lute, and the recorder—made simple. In honor of his gracious lord, the most reverend, high-born prince and lord, Wilhelm, Bishop of Strassburg (trans. from item 553)]. Basel: [M. Furter], 1511. RISM BVI, p. 865.

The first published instructions for the recorder appeared in two similar German publications of the early 16th century. The author of the first, Sebastian Virdung, served as a chaplain and singer in Heidelberg and other cities, including Basel, where his *Musica getutscht und auszgezogen* was published. In writing for the first time in the vernacular and seeking to present "everything . . . made simple," Virdung was clearly aiming at the amateur musician. His instructions for the recorder consist largely of descriptions of how to finger the instrument. He gives two systems of notation: one in effect a fingering chart, the other a type of tablature containing one symbol for each note which could be used to notate music. Contrary to later practice, the holes are numbered from lowest (1) to highest (8). His only other technical information is that you must blow into the instrument as well as "learn how to coordinate the articulations . . . with the fingers."

Virdung reports that the recorder, which nominally had eight fingerholes, in practice had nine: the lowest hole was doubled to allow for both left-handed and right-handed playing, the unused hole being stopped with wax. He discusses (and depicts in woodcuts) recorders of three sizes: discant in g^1, tenor in c^1, and Baßcontra or Bassus in f, all of which were notated an octave lower than they sounded. The discant and tenor had a range of an octave and a minor seventh; the bass, an octave and a sixth. Four to six recorders were generally put together in a case called a *coppel*: two discants, two tenors, and two basses. In four-part music, the range of the *contra* part determined whether one used two discants, tenor, and bass or else discant, two tenors, and bass.

543. *Livre plaisant et tres utile pour apprendre a faire ordonnez toutes tablatures hors le discant dont par lesquelles lon peult facilement et legierement aprendre a jouer sur les manicordion, luc, et flutes* [Entertaining and very useful book to learn to have at your command all tablatures except the discant, by means of which one can easily and swiftly learn to play on the organ, lute, and recorder]. Antwerp: G. Vorsterman, 1529.

A loose, partial contemporaneous French translation of Virdung's *Musica getutscht*.

544. *Dit is een seer schoon boecxken om te leeren maken alderhande tabulatueren wten discante. Daer duer men lichtelijck mach leeren spelen opt, clavecordium, luyte, fluyte* [This is a nice little book for learning all kinds of tablatures except the discant, by means of which one can easily learn to play the organ, lute, and recorder]. Antwerp: Jan van Ghelen, 1568.

A literal Flemish translation of the French (item 543). The two versions have been published in a joint facsimile (Amsterdam: Frits Knuf, 1973).

545. Luscinius, Othmar. *Musurgia, seu praxis musicae: illius primo quae instrumentis agitur certa ratio* [Musurgia, or The practice of music: a sure method of music which deals first with instruments]. Strasbourg: Johann Schott, 1536.
Loosely based on Virdung's *Musica getutscht*.

546. Virdung, Sebastian. *Musica getutscht, Basel 1511*. Originalgetreuer Nachdruck nach dem Exemplar der Preussischen Staatsbibliothek Berlin. Mit einem Nachwort neu herausgegeben von Leo Schrade. Kassel: Bärenreiter, 1931. [111, 12] p. OCLC #26107205.
Facsimile.

547. Virdung, Sebastian. *Musica getutscht, 1511*. (Publikationen älterer praktischer und theoretischer Musikwerke, Bd. 11) New York: Broude Brothers, 1966. [111] p. OCLC #29049019.
Facsimile.

548. Virdung, Sebastian. *Musica getutscht, 1511*. Faksimile-Nachdruck, herausgegeben von Klaus Wolfgang Niemöller. (Documenta musicologica, Erste Reihe: Druckschriften-Faksimiles, 31) Kassel: Bärenreiter, 1970. [118] p. ISBN 3761800045.
Facsimile. Includes a selected bibliography of previous editions and studies of Virdung's treatise.

549. Bullard, Beth Alice Baehr. *Musical Instruments in the Early Sixteenth Century: A Translation and Historical Study of Sebastian Virdung's* Musica getutscht *(Basel, 1511)*. Ph.D. dissertation, University of Pennsylvania, 1987. xi, 433 leaves. OCLC #19899794. UMI order no. 87-25143.

550. Bullard, Beth, trans. and ed. *Musica getutscht: A Treatise on Musical Instruments (1511) by Sebastian Virdung*. (Cambridge Musical Texts and Monographs) Cambridge: Cambridge University Press, 1993. xii, 275 p. ISBN 0521308305.
An English translation with an introduction (nearly as long as the treatise itself) covering the following topics: why one should study *Musica getutscht*, a biography of Sebastian Virdung, the publication history of the treatise, the "offspring" of the treatise. An appendix includes transcriptions of documents pertaining to Virdung and the treatise. The book is based on item 549.

551. Mayer, Christian. *Sebastian Virdung* Musica getutscht: *les instruments et la pratique musicale en Allemagne au début du XVIe siècle* [Sebastian Virdung's *Musica getutscht*: instruments and musical practice in Germany at the beginning of the 16th century]. Paris: Éditions du Centre National de la Recherche Scientifique, 1980. ISBN 2222026954.
A detailed study. Includes a complete French translation.

552. Wright, Laurence. "Sebastian Virdung: Musica getutscht und aussgezogen (Basel 1511)." *The Recorder and Music Magazine* 1, no. 10 (August 1965): 301-3.

Brief description of the treatise followed by a translation of the significant passages relating to the recorder. Includes facsimiles of the relevant illustrations, fingering chart, and tablature symbols.

553. Hettrick, William E. "Sebastian Virdung's Method for Recorders of 1511: A Translation with Commentary." *The American Recorder* 20, no. 3 (November 1979): 99-105.

An excellent summary of the treatise followed by a complete translation of the section on the recorder.

* Hettrick, William E. "Identifying and Defining the *Ruszpfeif*: Some Observations and Etymological Theories." Cited below as item 1411.

554. Stradner, Gerhard. *Spielpraxis und Instrumentarium um 1500: dargestellt an Sebastian Virdung's Musica getutscht (Basel 1511)* [Performing practice and instruments around 1500, described in Sebastian Virdung's *Musica getutscht* (Basel, 1511)]. 2 vols. (Forschungen zur älteren Musikgeschichte, Veröffentlichungen des Institutes für Musikwissenschaft der Universität Wien, Band 4/I-II) Vienna: Verband der Wissenschaftlichen Gesellschaften Österreichs, 1983. ISBN 3853695159.

A detailed study. See especially the section "Flöten" (Vol. 1, pp. 281-89).

555. Scharenberg, Sointu. "Sebastian Virdungs 'Musica getutscht'—ein Sachbuch? Der Traktat von 1511 neu gelesen" [Sebastian Virdung's *Musica getutscht*—a practical book? The treatise of 1511 read anew]. *Tibia* 18, no. 2 (1993): 421-30.

Evaluates Virdung's achievement: removing *musica instrumentalis* from Latin treatises and describing its practice in the vernacular; systematically classifying the instruments; giving [almost] the earliest advice on recorder education; and inventing methods of intabulation for the organ, lute, and recorder. Virdung straddles the Middle Ages and Renaissance in his thinking.

AGRICOLA, MARTIN (1486–1556)

556. Agricola, Martin. *Musica instrumentalis deudsch, ynn welcher begriffen ist, wie man nach dem Gesange auff mancherley Pfeiffen lernen sol, auch wie auff die Orgel, Harffen, Lauten, Geigen und allerley Instrument und Seytenspiel nach der rechtgegründten Tabelthur sey abzusetzen* [A German instrumental music, in which is contained: how to learn to play many kinds of wind instruments from vocal notation, and also how to set music into the appropriate tablature for the organ, harp, lute, fiddle, and all kinds of keyboard and string instruments (trans. from item 561)]. Wittenberg: Georg Rhau, 1529. Cited in RISM BVI, p. 70.

Martin Agricola was the Cantor of the Protestant Latin school in Magdeburg. His *Musica instrumentalis deudsch* was written in "German rhythm and meter for a special reason, so that youth and others who want to study this art might all the more easily understand it and retain it longer." The information on the recorder is similar to Virdung's. The middle size is called both tenor and altus, the latter mistakenly being depicted a little smaller in the woodcut. Rather than describing each fingering Agricola refers readers to his fingering charts—one for each size of instrument—which contain some differences, giving the impression, as William E. Hettrick remarks, "that he had experimented with three individual instruments, rather than using just one size and duplicating its fingerings for the other two." Agricola says that graces (*Mordanten*), which make the melody *subtil*, must be learned from a professional (*Pfeiffer*).

557. Agricola, Martin. *Musica instrumentalis deudsch, darin das Fundament und Application der Finger und Zungen, auff mancherley Pfeiffen als Flöten, Kromphörner, Zincken, Bomhard, Schalmeyen, Sackpfeiffen und Schweitzerpfeiffen etc. Darzu von dreierley Geigen, als welschen, polisschen und kleinen Handgeiglein und wie die Griffe drauff auch auff Lauten künstlich abgemessen werden, item vom Monochordo, auch von künstlicher Stimmung der Orgelpfeiffen und Zimbeln, etc. Kürtzlich begriffen, und für unsere Schulkinder und andere gmeine Senger aufs verstendlichst und einfeltigst jtzund newlich zugericht* [A German instrumental music, containing the basic rules and application of the fingers and tongue on many kinds of wind instruments, such as recorders, krummhorns, cornetts, pommer, shawms,

bagpipes, and Swiss flutes, etc. In addition, concerning three kinds of fiddles, the Italian, the Polish, and the little hand-fiddle, and how the finger positions may be skillfully gauged on them, and also on the lute. Also concerning the monochord and the skillful tuning of organ pipes and small bells, etc. Briefly summarized and now newly arranged for our school children and other beginning singers in the most understandable and simple way (trans. from item 561)]. Wittenberg: Georg Rhau, 1545. RISM BVI, p. 71.

The substantially rewritten text of Agricola's second edition of 1545—aimed at "our schoolchildren and other beginning singers"—includes some significant differences and additions. He mentions, approvingly, the use of vibrato (*zitterndem Wind*) for woodwind instruments, and he includes the earliest account of woodwind articulation. Maxima, longs, breves, semibreves, minims, and semi-minims take the syllable *de*; semi-minims can also take *di ri*, the articulation for the shorter note-values (fusas and semi-fusas). Finally, he remarks that in the very small note-values of *passaggi* (*Colorirn*), some musicians use the articulation *tell ell ell ell ell el le*, which he calls the "flutter-tongue" (*flitter zunge*).

558. Agricola, Martin. *Musica instrumentalis deudsch, erste und vierte Ausgabe, Wittemberg 1528 und 1545.* In neuer diplomatisch Genauer, zum Teil facsimilierter Ausgabe. (Publikation älterer praktischer und theoretischer Musik-Werke, Bd. 20) Leipzig: Breitkopf & Härtel, 1896. 295 p. OCLC #19005535. Reprinted: New York: Broude, 1966. OCLC #29049010.
Diplomatic "facsimile" of both eds.

559. Agricola, Martin. *Musica figuralis deudsch (1532). Im Anhang: Musica instrumentalis deudsch (1529); Musica choralis deudsch (1533); Rudimenta musices (1539).* Hildesheim; New York: G. Olms, 1969. OCLC #223955.
Facsimile of 1st ed.

560. Hettrick, William E., trans. & ed. *Musica instrumentalis deudsch: A Treatise on Musical Instruments (1529 and 1545) by Martin Agricola.* Cambridge: Cambridge University Press, in process of publication.

561. Hettrick, William E. "Martin Agricola's Poetic Discussion of the Recorder and Other Woodwind Instruments." *The American Recorder* 21, no. 3 (November 1980): 103-13; 23, no. 4 (November 1982): 139-46; and 24, no. 2 (May 1983): 51-60. Reprinted in *The Recorder and Music Magazine* 8, no. 4 (December 1984): 127-29, 116; 8, no. 5 (March 1985): 139-48; 8, no. 6 (June 1985): 171-79; and 8, no. 7 (September 1985): 202-12.

A translation with commentary of the woodwind sections in the 1529 and 1545 editions. The translation is accompanied by a complete facsimile. Hettrick's skillful rhymed couplets evoke the spirit and character of the original. Includes transcriptions of fingering charts.

GANASSI, SILVESTRO, (B. 1492)

562. Ganassi, Sylvestro. *Opera intitulata Fontegara. La quale i[n]segna a sonare di flauto cho[n] tutta l'arte opportuna a esso i[n]strumento massime il diminuire il quale sarà utile ad ogni i[n]strumento di fiato et chorde: et a[n]chora a chi si dileta di canto* [Work entitled "Fontegara," which instructs in playing the recorder with all the proper art of this instrument especially the creation of diminutions that will be useful for all wind and string instruments as well as those who practice singing]. Venice: author, 1535.

Sylvestro Ganassi, the author of the first book devoted entirely to recorder playing, was a notable player employed by the Doge of Venice and the Basilica of San Marco. Ganassi's is at once the most revealing and the most frustrating of all recorder methods. He declares that "the aim of the recorder player is to imitate as closely as possible all the capabilities of the human voice," and that the instrument was indeed capable of doing so. He then describes an astonishingly well-developed, expressive style of playing, achieved by good breath control, alternative fingerings, a wide variety of articulations, and extensive use of graces and divisions. Yet he fails to specify the musical contexts in which these techniques were used, and we cannot hear the "practised and experienced" 16th-century singer he holds up as a model.

Ganassi gives the interval of a thirteenth as the basic range of the three sizes of recorder (sopran, tenore, and basso). In addition, he describes his discovery of a further interval of a seventh, including the accidentals of ♯1, ♭3, ♯4, and ♯5 in the third octave, making a total compass of two octaves and a sixth.

According to Ganassi, imitation of the voice has three interdependent "indispensable peculiarities." The first is "a certain artistic proficiency," part of which seems to be the ability to perceive the nature of the music.

The second is *prontezza* (dexterity or fluency), achieved "by varying the pressure of the breath and shading the tone by means of suitable fingering." The third is *galanteria* (elegance or grace), achieved by articulation, for which Ganassi uses three basic kinds of syllables—*te che, te re*, and *le re*—and by the use of ornaments, the "simplest ingredient" of them being the trill, which varies according to the expression. The majority of Ganassi's treatise is taken up with a series of tables of the divisions or *passaggi* that may be applied to a melodic line. As Howard Mayer Brown has suggested (in his illuminating article on the composer in *The New Grove* 7:143–44), the complex rhythms of some of Ganassi's *passaggi* seem to be an "attempt to capture in print the essentially free rhythmic style of some improvisations."

563. Ganassi, Silvestro. *Opera intitulata Fontegara, Venezia 1535*. Milano: La Musica Moderna, 1934. [158] p. OCLC #3975474.
Facsimile.

564. Ganassi, Silvestro. *Opera intitulata Fontegara*. (Bibliotheca musica bononiensis, sezione 2, no. 18) Bologna: Forni, 1969. [161] p. OCLC #3826293.
Facsimile.

565. Ganassi, Silvestro. *Opera intitulata Fontegara*. (Prattica di musica, Ser. A, 3) Rome: Società italiana del flauto dolce, 1991. 108 p. OCLC #29845298.
Facsimile with introduction in Italian by Luca de Paolis.

566. Ganassi, Silvestro. *Opera Intitulata Fontegara, Venice 1535: A Treatise on the Art of Playing the Recorder and of Free Ornamentation*. Edited by Hildemarie Peter. Berlin-Lichterfelde: Robert Lienau, 1959. 108 p. OCLC #1135554.
English translation by Dorothy Swainson from the German translation (item 567). Brown warns that it is "not wholly satisfactory." Reviewed by Thomas Binkley in *The American Recorder* 1, no. 2 (Spring 1960): 19.

567. Ganassi, Silvestro. *La Fontegara: Schule des kunstvollen Flötenspiels und Lehrbuch des Diminuierens, Venedig, 1535*. Herausgegeben von Hildemarie Peter. Deutsche Übersetzung von Emilia Dahnk-Baroffio und Hildemarie Peter. Berlin-Lichterfelde: Robert Lienau, 1956. 108 p. OCLC #2116299.

German translation (again, Brown warns that it is "not wholly satisfactory").

568. Peter, Hildemarie. "An Introduction to Ganassi's Treatise on the Recorder (1535)." *The Consort* 12 (July 1955): 18–23.
A summary of the contents of Ganassi's *Fontegara* with a little commentary.

CARDANO, GIROLAMO (1501–1576)

569. Cardan, Jerome. *De Musica* [On music]. Written ca. 1546. First published in *Hieronymi Cardani Mediolensis opera omnia*. Lyons: Sponius, 1663. *De Musica*. 1568, rev. 1574. Vatican Ms 5850.

Jerome Cardan, the great Italian Renaissance philosopher, mathematician, and physician, was a keen amateur player, who learned the instrument from a professional teacher, Leo Oglonus, as a child in Milan. Cardan's first treatise both confirms Ganassi's account and gives glimpses into aspects of recorder playing otherwise undocumented before the 20th century.

He is the first to mention an unnamed higher size of recorder (in d^2). He is interested in the partial closing of the bell hole to produce a tone or semitone below the natural lowest note. After stressing the importance of breath control to follow the expression of the music, he makes the important distinction between the amount and the force of the breath. One of his ways of controlling intonation is by closing the bell hole, by means of which "all tones can be turned into semitones and dieses" (a diesis is half a small semitone).

Cardan articulates the recorder by means of Ganassi's three basic forms of syllables, like him unfortunately giving no examples of their use in pieces of music. He adds that the tongue can be used either extended or turned up towards the palate, improving, varying, and coloring the notes. He describes a trill or vibrato called a *vox tremula* in which "a tremulous quality in the breath" is combined with a trilling of the fingers to vary the interval from anything between a major third and a diesis. He is especially enthusiastic about the use of the interval of a diesis—"a sound than which nothing finer, nothing sweeter, nothing more pleasant can be imagined"—which can also be produced by repercussively bending back the tongue. Finally, Cardan confirms the importance of diminution technique in recorder playing.

In his second treatise of the same title, Cardan discusses the use of the recorder and other woodwinds in ensemble, stressing the need to keep together to match intonation, tone, and mood.

570. Cardanus, Hieronymus. *Writings on Music.* Trans. and ed. with an Introduction by Clement A. Miller. (Musicological Studies & Documents, 32) [Rome]: American Institute of Musicology, 1973. 227 p. OCLC #1081538.

A translation of Cardan's two treatises on music and selected miscellaneous writings.

571. Miller, Clement A. "Jerome Cardan on the Recorder." *The American Recorder* 12, no. 4 (November 1971): 123–25.

Summarizes the discussion of the recorder in Cardan's two treatises.

JAMBE DE FER, PHILIBERT (CA. 1515–CA. 1566)

572. Jambe de Fer, Philibert. *Epitome musical des tons, sons et accordz, es voix humaines, fleustes d'Alleman, fleustes à neuf trous, violes, & violons* . Lyons: Michel du Bois, 1556.

The only French author of the 16th century to write about the recorder was Philibert Jambe de Fer, a composer and singer. He comments at length on the French name of the instrument, *fleutte à neuf trouz* (flute with nine holes), which he finds inappropriate since one of the two lowest holes must be stopped; he would prefer *fleute d'Italien* (Italian flute) or the Italian name *flauto*. He also mentions the curious practice of "some Frenchmen" of stopping the thumbhole, making the fingering like that of a cornett.

His fingering chart has been taken as the earliest evidence of buttress- or supporting-finger technique—the keeping down of the third finger of the lower hand whenever possible—although it is used for only three notes (the tenor's $b\flat^1$, c^2, and d^2). For the rest of recorder playing he refers readers to "good teachers."

573. Lesure, François. "*L'épitome musical* de Philibert Jambe de Fer (1556)." *Annales musicologiques* 6 (1963): 341–46, [i-xl]. Also published separately, Neuilly-sur-Seine: Société de Musique d'Autrefois, 1964.

Introductory essay and facsimile of treatise.

574. Hunt, Edgar. "L'epitome musical de Philibert Jambe de Fer (1556)." *The Recorder and Music Magazine* 1, no. 8 (February 1965): 250.

A brief biography of Jambe de Fer gleaned from François Lesure's preface to the facsimile edition (item 573) and a description of the treatise's place among other 16th-century publications on musical instruments.

ZACCONI, LODOVICO, 1555–1627

575. Zacconi, Lodovico. *Prattica de musica utile et necessaria si al compositore per comporre i canti suoi regolatamente, si anco al cantore per assicurarsi in tutte le cose cantabili* [Musical practice, useful and necessary to the composer to compose songs in a regular manner as well as to singers to be sure about everything to do with singing]. Venice: B. Carampello, 1596.

Ganassi's three sizes of recorder are still mentioned by Zacconi. He gives their ranges as g^1 to f^2 (canto), c^1 to a^2 (tenore), and f to $b\flat^1$ (basso), all notated an octave lower than sounding.

576. Zacconi, Lodovico. *Prattica de musica*. Hildesheim; New York: Georg Olms, 1982. ISBN 3487071843.

Facsimile of 1596 and 1622 editions.

VIRGILIANO, AURELIO

577. "Il dolcimelo d'Aurelio Virgiliano dove si contengono variati passaggi, e diminutioni cosi per voci, come per tutte sorte d'instrumenti musicale; con loro accordi, e modi di sonare [Aurelio Virgiliano's *Il dolcimelo*, in which are found *passaggi* and diminutions either for voices or for all kinds of musical instruments; with their charts and methods of playing]." Bologna, Civico Museo Bibliografico Musicale, Ms. C. 33 (ca. 1600).

As well as ricercars intended for or playable on the recorder, *Il dolcimelo* includes a fingering chart for a discant recorder in G.

578. Virgiliano, Aurelio. *Il dolcimelo*. Ed. Marcello Castellani. (Archivum musicum, Collana di testi rari, 11) Florence: Studio per edizioni scelte, 1979.

Facsimile.

579. Gutman, Veronika. "Il Dolcimelo von Aurelio Virgiliano: Eine handschriftliche Quelle zur musikalischen Praxis um 1600" [Aurelio Virgiliano's *Il dolcimelo*: a manuscript source on performance practice ca. 1600]. In *Basler Studien zur Interpretation der alten Musik*, 107–39. (Forum

Musicologicum: Basler Beiträge zur Musikgeschichte, 2) Winterthur: Amadeus, 1980.
A detailed listing and commentary.

PRAETORIUS, MICHAEL (1571–1621)

580. Praetorius, Michael. *Syntagma musicum ex veterum & recentiorum ecclesiasticorum autorum lectione, polyhistorum consignatione, variarum linguarum notatione, hodierni seculi usurpatione, ipsius denique musicæ artis observatione: in cantorum, organistarum, organopœorum, cæterorumque; musicam scientiam amantium & tractantium gratiam collectum; et secundum hunc generalem indicem toti operi præfixum, in quatuor tomos distributum, à Michaele Praetorio Creutzbergensi . . . Tomus secundus: De Organographia* [A musical treatise gathered from a reading of old and new ecclesiastical authors, from the teachings of learned men, from writings in various languages, from modern usage, and finally from observation of the art of music itself: for the benefit of singers, instrumentalists, instrument makers, and others who love and deal with the science of music; arranged in four volumes according to this general index prefixed to the whole work, by Michael Praetorius of Kreuzburg . . . Volume two: On musical instruments]. Wolfenbüttel: Elias Holwein, 1619.

The relatively modest amount of material on the recorder that the German composer Michael Praetorius included in his encyclopaedic *Syntagma musicum* has received a large amount of attention because of his scale drawings of no fewer than eight sizes (klein Flötlein or exilent in g^2, discant in c^2 or d^2, alt in g^1, tenor in c^1, basset in f, bass in B♭, and grossbass in F) as well as the four-holed *gar kleine Plockflötlein*. He gives the range of the instrument as a thirteenth (largest sizes) or fourteenth (smaller sizes), although a skilled player could sometimes ascend four or even seven degrees higher.

Praetorius seems to have been the first to explain that recorders can confuse the ear into believing that they sound an octave lower than pitch—which is presumably why they were commonly notated an octave lower. His charts show that recorders could be used in at least three ranges of consort: 2' (discant, alt, and tenor), 4' (alt, tenor, and basset), and 8' (tenor, basset, and bass). Finally, he proposed cutting the recorder "in two at a point on the upper half, between the beak and the first fingerhole" and making a kind of tuning slide, to raise or lower the pitch of the

Historical Methods (Tutors) and Treatises

instrument. This is of course similar to the Baroque practice of "pulling out" the top joint to lower the pitch only.

581. Praetorius, Michael. *Syntagma musicum. Band II: De Organographia, Wolfenbüttel 1619.* Faksimile-Nachdruck herausgegeben von Wilibald Gurlitt. (Documenta Musicologica. Erste Reihe: Druckschriften-Faksimiles, 14) Kassel: Bärenreiter, 1958. 235 p. OCLC #22197679, #398783.
Facsimile.

582. Praetorius, Michael. *The Syntagma musicum of Michael Praetorius. Volume Two: De Organographia, First and Second Parts.* In an English trans. by Harold Blumenfeld. New York: Bärenreiter, 1949. vi, a-x, 80, 3 p. OCLC #5790696. 2d. ed. New York: Bärenreiter, 1962. vii, a-x, 80, 3 p. OCLC #253074. Reprinted: New York: Da Capo Press, 1980. 158 p. ISBN 030670563X.
Includes a translation of the *Theatrum Instrumentorum* appendix.

583. Praetorius, Michael. *Syntagma Musicum, II: De Organographia, Parts I and II.* Trans. & ed. David Z. Crookes. (Early Music Series, 7) Oxford: Clarendon Press, 1986. xx, 104 p., 42 plates. ISBN 019316406X.
Reviewed by Edgar Hunt in *The Galpin Society Journal* 41 (October 1988): 142–44.

THE TRANSITION RECORDER

"TUTTO IL BISOGNEVOLE"

584. "Tutto il bisognevole per sonar il flauto da 8 fori con pratica et orecchia" [Everything necessary for playing the recorder with skill and taste]. Manuscript, 1630. Biblioteca Marciana, Venice, Mss. Ital. Cl. IV. No. 486.
The earliest instructions for the transition recorder (between the Renaissance and late Baroque styles) are ostensibly in this anonymous Venetian manuscript method, which its scribe dated 1630. It seems to be addressed to the amateur who knew something of singing, or at least the well-known tunes of the day. The author depicts a recorder in three joints with Baroque turnery at each tenon, although the bore still appears to be cylindrical. For the first time the fingering chart is for a recorder in f^1,

showing fingerings up to g^3 (including $f\#^3$, although curiously not f^3) with supporting-fingering technique. If this method really was written in 1630, we need to revise our notions of the development of the recorder in the 17th century; it may turn out with further research, however, that the method dates from the third quarter of the century.

585. Delius, Nikolaus. "Die erste Flötenschule des Barock?" [The first recorder method of the Baroque?] *Tibia* 1, no. 1 (1976): 5–12.
A study of "Tutto il bisognevole."

MERSENNE, MARIN (1588–1648)

586. Mersenne, Marin. *Harmonie universelle, contenant la théorie et la pratique de la musique, où il est traité de la nature des sons, et des mouvemens, des consonances, des dissonances, des genres, des modes, de la composition, de la voix, des chants, et de toutes sortes d'instrumens harmoniques* [Universal harmony, containing the theory and practice of music, in which is treated the nature of sounds as well as tempos, consonances, dissonances, genres, modes, composition, the voice, songs, and all kinds of musical instruments]. Paris: Sébastien Cramoisy, 1636.

In his great encyclopaedic *Harmonie universelle*, Father Marin Mersenne devotes a section to recorders, which he calls "Flustes d'Angleterre, que l'on appelle douces, & à neuf trous" [English flutes, which are called sweet and nine-holed]. Mersenne's engraving shows a dessus recorder still made in one piece with a slight inverse conical bore. His fingering chart uses lines to depict closed holes, in a similar manner to the recorder tablature used later in the century in England (see below), apart from the fingering - -2- ----, which for some reason is shown by means of one closed and seven open circles. The range of the tenor as shown in this chart is two octaves, c^1 to c^3 ("although some give it only the range of a thirteenth"), with completely Baroque fingering including the supporting-finger technique. The dessus, taille or haute-contre, and basse "make the small register (*petit jeu*), as those that follow make the large register; but they can be tuned together, like the large and small registers of organs." The large register consists of the basse in f together with two lower sizes which are never specified, although the lowest is said to be from seven to eight feet in length.

Mersenne says nothing about the articulation of the recorder, but his instructions for the cornett give us some idea of current practice. It may be sounded in four ways: (1) with wind alone, like organ pipes (slurring); (2) with tongue and lip, pronouncing *ta ta ra ra ra ra ra ra* descending or ascending in diminutions (his examples also show *ta ta ra ta ra ta ra ta ra ta ra* for dotted notes); (3) with the tongue alone, for all lengths of note except sixteenth-notes, for which one uses the second method; and (4) with the lip, giving a lip-stroke every second note (he shows pairs of sixteenth-notes tongued *taa*). He shows two methods of articulating a cadential trill: the first with *tara tara tara ta*; the second with the wind alone (slurred), "which imitates the voice and the most excellent method of singing well."

587. Mersenne, Marin. *Harmonie universelle, contenant la théorie et la pratique de la musique*. Paris, 1636. Édition facsimilé de l'exemplaire conservé à la Bibliothèque des arts et métiers et annoté par l'auteur. Introd. par François Lesure. Paris: Centre National de la Recherche Scientifique, 1963. 3 vols. OCLC #6333609.

Facsimile of the copy with the author's annotations.

588. Mersenne, Marin. *Harmonie Universelle: The Books on Instruments*. Trans. Roger E. Chapman. The Hague: Martinus Nijhoff, 1957. xii, 596 p. OCLC #394914.

589. Köhler, Wolfgang. *Die Blasinstrumente aus der "Harmonie Universelle" des Marin Mersenne: Übersetzung und Kommentar des "Livre cinquiesme des instrumens à vent" aus dem "Traité des instruments"* [The wind instruments from Marin Mersenne's *Harmonie universelle*: translation of and commentary on the "Livre cinquiesme des instrumens à vent" from the "Traité des instruments"]. Celle: Moeck, 1987. Edition Moeck Nr. 4038. vi, 400 p. ISBN 387549290.

Reviewed by Edgar H. Hunt in *The Galpin Society Journal* 44 (March 1991): 180.

590. Köhler, Wolfgang. "Die Blasinstrumente aus der 'Harmonie Universelle' des Marin Mersenne und ihre Bedeutung für die Aufführungspraxis heute" [The wind instruments from Marin Mersenne's *Harmonie universelle* and their significance for performance practice today]. *Tibia* 13, no. 1 (1988): 1–14.

Adapted from item **589**. Only a little material specifically about recorders.

TRICHET, PIERRE (1586 OR 87-1644?)

591. Lesure, François. "Le Traité des instruments de musique de Pierre Trichet, Les instruments à vent" [The treatise on musical instruments by Pierre Trichet: the wind instruments]. *Annales musicologiques* 3 (1955): 283-387.

The same three names for the recorder as Mersenne's are given by Pierre Trichet in his *Traité d'instruments* (ca. 1640). Unfortunately Trichet has nothing else of value to say about recorders.

MATTHYSZ, PAUL (1613 OR 14-1684)

592. M[atthysz], P[aulus]. *Vertoninge en onderwyzinge op de hand-fluit* [(Fingering) depictions and instructions for the recorder]. Amsterdam: Paulus Matthysz, 1649?

Found with two of the extant copies of Jacob van Eyck's *Der fluyten lust-hof I* (1649; 2nd ed., 1655) and generally associated with him nowadays, but signed "P.M." and apparently designed for Matthysz's collection *'t Uitnement kabinet II* (1649), the title page of which refers to "een korte onderwyzinge op de hand-fluit" (a short instruction for the recorder). Strictly speaking, it is therefore incorrect to speak of "van Eyck fingerings" for the recorder. (See item 1244, p. 377.) Fingering instructions only (in prose) for C instrument.

BLANKENBURG, GERBRANT QUIRIJNSZOON VAN (CA. 1620-1707)

593. Blanckenburgh, Gerbrandt. *Onderwyzinge hoemen alle de toonen en halve toonen, die meest gebruyckelyck zyn, op de handt-fluyt zal konnen t'eenemael zuyver blaezen, en hoe men op yeder 't gemackelyckst een trammelant zal konnen maken, heel dienstigh voor de lief-hebbers* [Instructions for how one can learn to play all the most usual tones and semitones on the recorder in tune, and how one can make a trill in the easiest way on each one—very useful for music lovers]. Amsterdam: Paulus Matthysz, 1654. Also found with one of the extant copies of Jacob van Eyck's *Der fluyten lust-hof I* (2nd ed., ca. 1655). [Warner No. 1; Vinquist, 151-52]

Blankenburg was an organist and carillonneur in the Netherlands. *Onderwyzinge* is said to have been written at the request of Matthysz, the publisher. Fingering instructions (in prose) for C instrument, plus two bits of advice: stop the holes neatly; if you blow too hard or too softly, your intonation will suffer. Blankenburg's idiosyncratic fingering chart is noteworthy for giving separate fingerings for enharmonically equivalent notes (although the difference usually consists of slightly more or less shading of one fingerhole) and one or more trill fingerings for every pitch (again involving only one fingerhole).

594. Blanckenburgh, Gerbrandt. *Onderwyzinge hoemen alle de toonen en halve toonen, die meest gebruyckelyck zyn, op de handt-fluyt zal konnen t'eenemael zuyver blaezen*. . . . Münich: Oscar, 1871. OCLC #4197739, #24862149.
Reprint.

595. Blanckenburgh, Gerbrandt. *Onderwyzinge hoemen alle de toonen en halve toonen, die meest gebruyckelyck zyn, op de handt-fluyt zal konnen t'eenemael zuyver blaezen*. . . . Münster: Mieroprint Musikverlag, 1989. 10, 12 p.
Reprint of 1871 ed. with German trans. and afterword.

596. Dart, Thurston. "Four Dutch Recorder Books." *Galpin Society Journal* 5 (March 1952): 57–60.
Briefly describes Blankenburg's *Onderwyzinge* (including a transcription of the fingering chart), *Der gooden fluyt-hemel* (1644), and Jacob van Eyck's *Der fluyten lust-hof*.

THE BAROQUE RECORDER

BISMANTOVA, BARTOLOMEO

597. Bismantova, Bartolomeo. "Compendio musicale. In cui s'insegna à Principianti il vero modo, per imperare con facilità, le Regole del Canto Figurato, e Canto Fermo; come anche per Comporre, e suonare il Basso Continouo, il Flauto, Cornetto, e Violino; come anche per Acordare Organi, e Cembali" [Musical compendium, in which is taught to beginners the true method to command with ease the rules of figured song and plainsong, as well as to compose and play the basso continuo, recorder, cornett, and violin, and also the organ and harpsichord]. Manuscript, Ferrara, 1677. Biblioteca Municipale di Reggio Emilia, Ms. Reggiani E. 41.

The manuscript *Compendio musicale* by Father Bartolomeo Bismantova, a wind player in Reggio Emilia and Ferrara, is dated 1677, although the version that has come down to us seems to be that prepared for the printer in 1694. A note by the author informs us that it was not published because of the death of his patron, the abbott Ferrante Bentivoglio, that year. The treatise has an extensive section, "Regola per suonare il Flauto Italiano" [rule for playing the recorder] about a recorder in g^1 "of three joints such as those used today" (he also gives a scale beginning on d^1).

Bismantova's instructions are full of the wisdom of an experienced professional. To lower the pitch, pull out the head joint "then also lengthen [the recorder] just a bit at the foot joint, so that all the pitches will be in tune." If the recorder is more than a semitone away from the right pitch and cannot be adjusted by elongating the tube, carefully place a little bit of wax on one part of the windway (*linguetta*) to adjust it. When playing the recorder in dry weather or in summer, use a feather to oil the inside of the pipe with high-class olive, sweet almond, or jasmine oil, to soften the recorder and make the high notes come in tune.

In his repetitive style, Bismantova insists that all wind instruments should be played "in a singing manner and not otherwise, and also in imitation of one who sings." His tonguing syllables are mostly similar to the Renaissance ones. The direct tongue (*de*) is used for all note values from a breve to an eighth-note; the reverse tongue (*de re le re*), for eighth-, sixteenth-, and thirty-second-notes; two other types of syllables (*de che* and *der ler*) are little used, except (curiously for the first one) in accompanying in cantabile style. What is new is the importance now given to the smooth tongue (*lingua legata*), or slurred pairs of notes: *de a de a de a*; this presumably reflects the influence of violin technique. Bismantova gives a practical method for learning a piece of music: speak the various articulations first in rhythm; only after mastering that, practice the fingerings on the instrument. His fingering chart is marked with the sign "t" to indicate the appropriate finger to shake for trills.

598. Bismantova, Bartolomeo. *Compendio musicale (Ferrara 1677)*. (Archivum musicum, Collana di testi rari, 1) Firenze: Studio per edizioni scelte, 1978. 123 p. OCLC #12666729.

Facsimile. Reviewed by Edgar Hunt in *Recorder & Music* 6, no. 4 (December 1978): 122.

599. Cavicchi, Adriano. "Prassi strumentale in Emilia nell'ultimo quarto del seicento: Flauto italiano, cornetto, archi" [Instrumental practice in Emilia in the last quarter of the 17th century: recorder, cornett, strings]. *Studi musicali* 2, no. 1 (1973): 111–43.

A transcription of Bismantova's treatise together with the small amount of biographical information we have about the author.

600. Dickey, Bruce, Petra Leonards, and Edward H. Tarr. "The Discussion of Wind Instruments in Bartolomeo Bismantova's *Compendio Musicale* (1677): Translation and Commentary = Die Abhandlung über die Blasinstrumente in Bartolomeo Bismantovas *Compendio Musicale* (1677): Übersetzung und Kommentar." *Basler Jahrbuch für historische Musikpraxis* 2 (1978): 143–87.

English and German translations of Bismantova's sections on wind instruments together with extensive helpful commentary. The original text is given in an appendix.

601. Castellani, Marcello. "The *Regola per suonare il flauto italiano* by Bartolomeo Bismantova (1677)." *The Galpin Society Journal* 30 (1977): 76–85.

A useful discussion of Bismantova's section on the recorder.

ENGLAND, 1679-1695

Although the French approach to the new type of recorder is not documented until later in the 17th century, we can gain some idea of it from the methods of England, where the taste for French music and instruments brought first the flageolet, then the recorder into vogue among amateurs. Thomas Greeting, a royal violinist who supplemented his income by teaching amateurs such as the wife of the famous diarist Samuel Pepys, wrote a method for the flageolet, *The Pleasant Companion* (2nd ed., London: John Playford, 1673; 1st ed. not traced but claimed to be as early as 1661 or 1667 and definitely published by 1668). This served as a model for such books for over a century: a few rudiments of music are followed by a fingering chart and a selection of "lessons," or popular tunes of the day. Those who had already learned the flageolet by "dot-way," as its tablature was known, were presented the recorder by the same procedure. (As the title of a method that has not survived proclaims: *The Recorder or Flute made easie; by exact and true directions, shewing the manner and way of playing on that fashionable Instrument by the Notes of the Flagelet; whereby the meanest capacity may, with a little spare time, attain his desire* [London: J. Clarke, 1683].)

A few methods were aimed at children: J[ohn] B[anister II]'s *The Most Pleasant Companion* announces "plain and easy rules and instructions for young beginners"; *The Compleat Instructor to the Flute*, similar "directions." Robert Carr's *The Delightful Companion* has "plain and easy instructions for beginners," to be used in conjunction with a teacher. Banister is the only significant professional author represented among these methods; the remainder are anonymous or else put together by unknowns (Carr) or music sellers (John Hudgebut's *A Vade Mecum*, Humphrey Salter's *The Genteel Companion*).

The four earliest methods—Hudgebut, Banister, Carr, and Salter—are the most revealing because of their use of the flageolet tablature, which indicates slurs and fingerings for ornaments. Generally enharmonic sharps and flats are distinguished. The ornaments discussed are elementary ones derived from the French style: the trill, beginning on the upper auxiliary or main note (at first called the "beat," later the "shake" or "close shake"); the mordent, beginning on the main note or with a rising appoggiatura ("shake," then "beat" or "open shake"); the slur; the slur and mordent; and the "double shake," a warbling trill across the registers on g^2. The intervals involved in these ornaments are not always a plain tone or semitone. Carr also has a chart for trill fingerings, some of which are ingeniously conceived.

602. Hudgebut, John. *A Vade Mecum for the Lovers of Musick, Shewing the Excellency of the Rechorder: With some Rules and Directions for the Same. Also, some New Ayres Never Before Published.* London: N. Thompson for John Hudgbut, 1679. [Warner No. 7; Vinquist, 153-54]

603. B[anister], J[ohn II]. *The Most Pleasant Companion, or Choice New Lessons for the Recorder or Flute, Being a New Collection of New Lessons, Set Forth by Dots and Notes. To Which is Added, Plain and Easie Rules and Instructions for Young Beginners.* London: Printed for John Hudgebutt, 1681. [Warner No. 9; Vinquist, 156-57]

604. [Carr, Robert]. *The Delightful Companion: or, Choice New Lessons for the Recorder or Flute, to Which is Added, Several Lessons for Two and Three Flutes to Play Together. Also Plain and Easie Instructions for Beginners, and the Several Graces Proper to This Instrument.* 2nd ed. London: John Playford and John Carr, 1686. 1st ed. announced 1682. [Warner No. 15; Vinquist, 163-65]

605. Salter, Humphry. *The Genteel Companion; Being Exact Directions for the Recorder: With a Collection of the Best and Newest Tunes and Grounds Extant.* London: Printed for Richard Hunt and Humphry Salter, 1683. [Warner No. 13; Vinquist, 160-61]

606. Myers, Herbert W. "Three Seventeenth-Century English Recorder Tutors." *The American Recorder* 7, no. 2 (Spring 1966): 3-6.

    A thoughtful discussion of John Hudgebut, *A Vade Mecum*, John Banister II, *The Most Pleasant Companion*, and Humphrey Salter, *The Genteel Companion* (items 602, 603, and 605). Because of their resemblance to one another, Myers treats them as a single source and does not distinguish among them in the article.

607. Dart, Thurston. "Recorder 'Gracings' in 1700." *The Galpin Society Journal* 12 (1959): 93-94.

    A transcription with commentary of "Rules for Gracing on the Flute," taken from British Library Add. MS 35043 (f. 125), a volume of miscellaneous instrumental music from the late 17th century. (Reprinted in item 534, p. 293.)

608. Davies, Malcolm. "The Marks and Rules for Gracing— Easy Baroque Ornamentation from English Sources." *The Recorder Magazine* 13, no. 2 (September 1993): 39-41; 13, no. 3 (December 1993): 69-71.

    Part 2 includes the "Rules for Gracing on the Flute."

HUYGENS, CONSTANTIJN (1596-1687)

609. Huygens, Christiaan. "Tons de ma flute" [Notes of my recorder]. Manuscript, 1686. Universiteitsbibliotheek Leiden, Codex Hugenianus 1, p. 231. Transcribed in

Christiaan Huygens, *Œuvres complètes*, Vol. 20: *Musique et mathématique; Musique; Mathématiques de 1666 à 1695*, 104. The Hague: Martinus Nijhoff, 1940. OCLC #25280555.
Fingering chart. Transcribed in item **1244**, p. 380.

LOULIÉ, ÉTIENNE (1654–1702)

610. Loulié, Étienne. "Méthode pour apprendre à jouer de la flûte douce" [Method for learning to play the recorder]. Manuscript. Paris, Bibliothèque Nationale, fonds fr. n. a. 6355, XIX-XX.

The first French method for the Baroque recorder was written by Étienne Loulié, a musician and music director in the celebrated ensemble attached to the household of Marie de Lorraine (better known as Mademoiselle de Guise), later music teacher to the Duke of Chartres (who was to become regent of France). According to Patricia Ranum's researches (see item **613**), in the 1680s Loulié wrote the first draft of this recorder method and several other methods and treatises, perhaps for Mademoiselle de Guise's academy for children of the nobility, later presumably putting all these methods to good use in his instruction of Chartres. The tablature and some of the wording in Loulié's recorder method seem to derive from the earliest English methods. As his method was intended for adolescents, it is fairly elementary—failing, for example, to discuss ornaments, which depend on taste and can be formed only under a good teacher. Yet we learn that he taught the tonguing syllables *tu* and *ru*. Loulié revised and simplified the method in 1701 or 1702, after seeing Freillon-Poncein's (item **644**).

Attention was first drawn to Loulié's manuscript treatises by Albert Cohen in his article "Étienne Loulié as a Music Theorist," *Journal of the American Musicological Society* 18, no. 1 (Spring 1965): 70-72.

611. Semmens, Richard. "A Translation of Etienne Loulié's Method for Learning How to Play the Recorder." *The American Recorder* 24, no. 4 (November 1983): 135–45.

A complete translation based on the first version of the method. Significant variants found in the second version are recorded in footnotes. Musical examples are transcribed in a clear hand. Semmens places the method in its historical context, explains Loulié's tablature, and summarizes his discussion of ornaments. Claims that, because of its excellent organization and presentation of material, the method is a historical document that "is also of demonstrable practical value." Patricia M. Ranum, in 25, no. 3 (August 1984): 119-21, discusses the problems one encounters when editing Loulié's manuscripts and corrects several errors in Semmens's translation. She also speculates on the dating of the revised manuscript based on a death date of 1702 rather than 1707 as found in Brossard.

612. Semmens, Richard. "Étienne Loulié's 'Method for Learning How to Play the Recorder.'" *Studies in Music from the University of Western Ontario* 6 (1981): 7–23.

A summary of the method supported by lengthy excerpts of the original French with English translation. A large part of the article is devoted to the sections on ornamentation and articulation. Semmens again places the method in its historical context and compares Loulie's technique of tablature with that of his contemporaries.

613. Ranum, Patricia M. "Étienne Loulié (1654–1702): Musicien de Mademoiselle de Guise, pédagogue et théoricien" [Étienne Loulié (1654-1702): musician to Mademoiselle de Guise, pedagogue, and theorist]. *"Recherches" sur la musique française classique* 25 (1987): 27–76; 26 (1988–90): 5–49.

A lengthy scholarly article, putting forward a number of plausible hypotheses about Loulié's life, based on the surviving archival evidence. Speculates on the dating and circumstances of his manuscript recorder method. His inventory-after-death lists eight "fluttes" (recorders [and flutes?]).

614. Ranum, Patricia M. "Étienne Loulié: Recorder Player, Teacher, Musicologist." *American Recorder* 32, no. 1 (March 1991): 7–11, 34.

A popularized biography focusing on his years of service under Mademoiselle de Guise, his later work with Henri Foucault as an arranger and copyist, and his work on acoustics with mathematician Joseph Sauveur. References to his career as a recorder player are scattered throughout, and particular mention is made of the content and sources of the recorder method.

TALBOT, JAMES (1664–1708)

615. Baines, Anthony. "James Talbot's Manuscript (Christ Church Library Music Ms 1187)." *The Galpin Society Journal* 1 (1948): 9–26.

The article that first told the world about Talbot's celebrated manuscript on musical instruments (c.1692-95), discovered by Robert Donington. A short general introduction to the manuscript, followed by a transcription of Talbot's remarks on wind instruments and a commentary by Baines. Talbot included measurements for tenor and bass recorders by Bressan (the section for alto recorder is left blank), as well as listing the pitches of the sizes of recorder known to him (sopranino, soprano, voice flute, tenor, bass, great bass).

England: *The Compleat Flute-Master* and Successors, 1695-1780

When John Walsh and Joseph Hare entered the music publishing business in 1695, they immediately issued a recorder method, *The Compleat Flute-Master*, with the most extravagant claim of all. Their amusing preface includes a shrewd commentary on the work of their predecessors and a fond hope for their own: "Many of our employ have been very industrious to oblige the public in this manner; though they were not very full in their instructions, yet they found their endeavors very successful. Since therefore their imperfect rules have proved thus fortunate, we have reason to hope that this attempt of ours (being more correct than any yet extant, having all the rules that can possibly be expressed by way of printing) will have an effect answerable to its design, the main end we aim at being only the public advantage. . . ." Walsh and Hare were successful beyond their wildest dreams. They could certainly never have predicted that their fingering chart and ornament instructions were to be pirated and incorporated into most English methods (as well as *The Bird Fancyer's Delight*) until as late as 1780, when the ornaments must surely have greatly puzzled the performers of Classical songs and dances.

This series of methods is treated as a group here. None of them has anything significant to add besides selections of the latest tunes. (The other English methods are treated separately below.)

616. *The Compleat Flute-Master, or, The Whole Art of Playing on ye Rechorder, Layd Open in Such Easy & Plain Instructions, that by them ye Meanest Capacity May Arrive to a Perfection on that Instrument, with a Collection of ye Newest & Best Tunes, Composed by the Most Able Masters, to Which is Added an Admirable Solo.* London: J. Hare and J. Walsh, 1695. [Warner No. 18; Vinquist, 166-68]

    In addition to the ornaments found in the earlier English methods, the instructions in *The Compleat Flute-Master* mention the "sigh" (equivalent to the French *accent*) and the "double relish" (trill with turn), and give directions for adding graces on ascending, descending, and repeated notes when they are not marked.

617. Lasocki, David. "The Compleat Flute-Master Reincarnated." *The American Recorder* 11, no. 3 (Summer 1970): 83–85.

A discussion of *The Compleat Flute-Master*, particularly the fingering chart and ornament instructions. Identifies many of the tunes appearing in the twenty-three pages of music that follow the text. Reprints two tunes by Henry Purcell that are of interest for their ornaments.

618. *The Compleat Instructor to the Flute The Second Book. Containing Very Plain & Easie Directions for Young Beginners, With Variety of ye Newest & Best Tunes.* . . . London: J. Young, 1700. [Warner No. 33; Vinquist, 173-74]

619. *The Flute-Master Compleat Improu'd, or, The Gentlemens Diversion Made More Easie Than Any Yet Extant. Book the First. Containing Plain & Easier Directions for Young Beginners, with Variety of the Newest & Best Tunes, Compos'd & Contrived for that Instrument by the Most Eminent Masters.* . . . London: John Young, 1706. [Warner No. 38; Vinquist, 181]

620. *The Fifth Book of the New Flute Master Containing The Most Perfect Rules and Easiest Directions for Learners on the Flute Yet Extant. Together wth an Extraordinary Collection of Aires Both Italian and English.* . . . London: J. Walsh and J. Hare, 1706. [Warner No. 39; Vinquist, 182]

621. B., T. *The Compleat Musick-Master: Being Plain, Easie, and Familiar Rules for Singing, and Playing on the Most Useful Instruments Now in Vogue, According to the Rudiments of Musick. Viz, Violin, Bass Viol, Flute, Treble-Viol, Haut-boy, Tenor-Viol.* . . . *The Third Edition, with Additions.* London: William Pearson, 1722. [Warner No. 56; Vinquist, 198-99]

622. *The New Flute Master for the Year 1729 Containing the Most Compleat Rules & Directions for Learners on ye Flute.* London: J. Walsh and Joseph Hare, 1728. [Warner No. 57; Vinquist, 202-03]

623. *The Second Book of the Flute Master Improv'd Containing the Plainest Instructions for Learners, with Variety of Easy Lessons by the Best Masters*. London: D. Wright Jr., ca. 1730. [Warner No. 60; Vinquist, 207]

624. [Prelleur, Peter]. *The Modern Musick-Master, or, The Universal Musician.* . . . London: Printing Office in Bow Church Yard, 1730. Part II is entitled: *Directions for Playing on the Flute with a Scale for Transposing Any Piece of Musick to ye Properest Keys for that Instrument.* . . . [Warner No. 59; Vinquist, 204-6]

   A series of seven anonymous methods. The method for the flute (*The Newest Method for Learners on the German Flute*) is of interest as being a (partial) translation of Hotteterre's instructions.

625. Prelleur, Peter. *Instructions & Tunes for the Treble Recorder, from "The Modern Musick-Master," c. 1731*. Edited by Edgar Hunt. London: Schott, 1960. OCLC #7220777.

   A facsimile of *Directions for Playing on the Flute* (from item 624).

626. Prelleur, Peter. *The Modern Musick-Master, or, The Universal Musician, 1731*. Edited by Alexander Hyatt King. (Documenta Musicologica. Erste Reihe: Druckschriften-Faksimiles, 27) Kassel: Bärenreiter, 1965. 48 p. OCLC #27138322. The recorder method is also published separately as *Directions for Playing on the Flute*.

   Facsimiles. Reviewed by Erich Katz in *The American Recorder* 7, no. 2 (Spring 1966): 20.

627. Newman, Joel. "A Commentary on the *Directions for Playing on the Flute* (c. 1731)." (Eighteenth-Century Promenades, 1) *The American Recorder* 4, no. 1 (February 1963): 3–4; 4, no. 2 (May 1963): 3–4.

   Newman describes the contents of the method: the title page (reproduced in facsimile) and the familiar engraving on the title-page verso depicting a gentleman playing a recorder by a lake; the instructions on playing the recorder; elementary music theory; ornamentation; and how to transpose violin and vocal works so that they fit on the recorder. Newman identifies the twenty-one opera airs (nearly all by Handel) in the anthology of thirty pieces at the end of the method. Summarizes the "marks and rules for gracing," which, although Newman did not know it, were lifted ultimately from *The Compleat Flute-Master*.

*   Davies, Malcolm. "The Marks and Rules for Gracing—Easy Baroque Ornamentation from English Sources." Cited above as item 608.
    Part 1 includes the ornament instructions from item 624.

628. *Directions for Playing on the Flute with a Scale for Transposing any Piece of Musick to ye Properest Keys for that Instrument.* . . . London: Benjamin Cooke, ca. 1735. [Warner No. 67; Vinquist, 211-12]

629. Wright, Daniel. *The Compleat Tutor for ye Flute Containing the Newest Instructions for that Instrument.* London: Author, ca. 1734. [Warner No. 69; Vinquist, 213-14]

630. *The Compleat Tutor for the Flute. Containing the Best and Easiest Instructions for Learners to Obtain a Proficiency.* . . . London: John Johnson, ca. 1745. [Warner No. 72; Vinquist, 217-18]

631. *The Compleat Tutor for the Flute Containing the Best and Easiest Instructions for Learners to Obtain a Proficiency.* . . . London: John Simpson, ca. 1746. [Warner No. 75; Vinquist, 219-20]

632. *The Complete Flute Master Containing the Best & Easiest Rules to Learn that Favorite Instrument.* . . . London: John Tyther, ca. 1750. [Warner No. 82; Vinquist, 224-25]

633. *The Muses Delight. An Accurate Collection of English and Italian Songs, Cantatas and Duetts, set to Music for the Harpsichord, Violin, German-Flute, &c. With Instructions for the Voice, Violin, Harpsichord or Spinnet, German-Flute, Common-Flute, Hautboy, French-Horn, Bassoon and Bass-Violin.* . . . Liverpool: John Sadler, 1754. Eds. of 1756, 1757, and 1758 entitled *Apollo's Cabinet: or the Muses Delight.* . . . [Warner No. 88; Vinquist, 228-29]

634. *The Compleat Tutor for the Flute Containing the Best and Easiest Instruction for Learners to Obtain a Proficiency.* . . .

London: Peter Thompson, 1754. [Warner No. 89; Vinquist, 230-31]

635. *The Compleat Tutor for the Flute Containing the Best and Easiest Instructions for Learners to Obtain a Proficiency.* . . . London: Thompson & Son, ca. 1760. [Warner No. 95; Vinquist, 232]

636. *The Complete Flute Master Containing the Best & Easiest Rules to Learn that Favorite Instrument.* . . . London: Thomas Bennett, ca. 1760. [Warner No. 98; Vinquist, 233-34]

637. Rutherford, David. *The Compleat Tutor for ye Flute Containing the Newest Instructions for that Instrument.* London: Dad. Rutherford, ca. 1760. [Warner No. 99; Vinquist, 235]

638. *The Compleat Tutor, for the Common Flute, Containing the Best and Easiest Instructions for Learners to Obtain a Proficiency.* . . . London: Chas. & Saml. Thompson, ca. 1765. [Warner No. 103; Vinquist, 236]

639. *The Compleat Tutor for the Flute Containing the Best and Easiest Instructions for Learners to Obtain a Proficiency.* . . . London: R. Bremner, ca. 1765. [Warner No. 103a; Vinquist, 237-38]

640. *Compleat Instructions, for the Common Flute, Containing the Easiest and Most Modern Methods for Learners to Play, Carefully Corrected by Eminent Masters.* . . . London: Longman and Broderip, ca. 1780. [Warner No. 135; Vinquist, 241-42]

SPEER, DANIEL (1636–1707)

641. Speer, Daniel. *Grund-richtiger kurtz-leicht-und nöthiger jetz wol-vermehrter Unterricht der musicalischen Kunst* [Basic, short, easy, and necessary, instruction in the art of

music, now augmented]. 2nd ed. Ulm: Georg Wilhelm Kühnen, 1697. [Warner no. 25]

Includes a fingering chart for *Quart-Flöten* (soprano recorder) with a range of two octaves.

DOUWES, CLAAS (CA. 1650–CA. 1725)

642. Douwes, Claas. *Grondig ondersoek van de toonen der musijk* [A thorough examination of music]. Franeker: Adriaan Heins, 1699. [Warner No. 27]

Douwes, an organist and schoolmaster in Tzum, Friesland, wrote this instruction book, apparently directed at provincial musicians and comprising mostly information on music theory and contemporaneous keyboard practice. His short section on the recorder describes in words the fingerings for a tenor recorder with the range c^1 to d^3.

643. Douwes, Claas. *Grondig ondersoek van de toonen der musijk*. Franeker: Adriaan Heins, 1699. Edited by Peter Williams. (Early Music Theory in the Low Countries, 2) Amsterdam: Frits Knuf, 1970.

Facsimile.

FREILLON-PONCEIN, JEAN-PIERRE

644. Freillon-Poncein, Jean-Pierre. *La veritable maniere d'apprendre a jouer en perfection du haut-bois, de la flute et du flageolet, avec les principes de la musique pour la voix et pour toutes sortes d'instrumens* [The true way to learn to play with perfection the oboe, recorder, and flageolet, with the principles of music for the voice and all kinds of instruments]. Paris: Jacques Collombat, 1700. [Warner No. 35; Vinquist, 176-77]

La veritable maniere by Freillon-Poncein, who is said to have been the Prévost of the Grande Écurie at the Versailles court, was the first published French method for the Baroque recorder. It was intended primarily for the oboe, however, and adds little to our knowledge of recorder technique. The fingering chart, shown by means of schematic figures of a recorder, introduces fully chromatic fingering for the first time, apparently with equal half-steps. Trill fingerings are described for the first octave only. Of considerable interest are the extensive instructions for ornaments and for articulation (like Loulié, using the tonguing syllables *tu* and *ru*).

645. Freillon-Poncein, Jean-Pierre. *La veritable maniere d'apprendre a jouer en perfection du haut-bois, de la flute et du flageolet, avec les principes de la musique pour la voix et pour toutes sortes d'instrumens*. Geneva: Minkoff Reprint, 1972. 72 p. OCLC #669818. Published with Amand van der Hagen, *Méthode nouvelle et raisonnée pour le hautbois* (Paris, ca. 1792).
Facsimile.

646. Freillon-Poncein, Jean-Pierre. *The True Way to Learn to Play Perfectly the Oboe, the Recorder, and the Flageolet Along with the Principles of Music for Voice and All Kinds of Instruments*. Translated with introduction by Catherine P. Smith. Brooklyn: The Translations Center, Brooklyn College, City University of New York, 1969. 115 leaves. OCLC #10424976.

647. Freillon-Poncein, J.P. *On Playing Oboe, Recorder, & Flageolet*. Translated with an introduction by Catherine Parsons Smith. Bloomington: Indiana University Press, 1992. ISBN 0253288819.
According to the introduction, the translation was "extensively revised" for this edition. Brief introduction, footnotes, and selected bibliography. Examples given in facsimile.

648. Freillon-Poncein, Jean-Pierre. "The True Way to Learn to Play the Oboe, Recorder, and Flageolet Perfectly." Translated and edited by Catherine P. Smith. *The American Recorder* 23, no. 1 (February 1982): 3–10.
The introduction offers a brief biography followed by a summary of the treatise. The translation includes chapters 5 (tonguing) and 12 (characteristics of dance forms) and excerpts from chapters 6 (meter), 7 (preluding), and 8 (trilling).

649. Lasocki, David. "Freillon-Poncein, Hotteterre, and the Recorder." *The American Recorder* 10, no. 2 (Spring 1969): 40–43.
A general introduction to Freillon-Poncein's *La veritable maniere*. Includes the text of the part devoted exclusively to the recorder, with a parallel English translation. Compares it in detail with Hotteterre's method (item 650, published seven years later). Judging from the preludes composed by

both authors, the standard of recorder playing in France was much higher than had been believed.

HOTTETERRE, JACQUES (1674–1763)

650. Hotteterre, Jacques. *Principes de la flute traversiere, ou flute d'allemagne, de la flute a bec, ou flute douce, et du haut-bois, divisez par traitez* [Principles of the flute, recorder, and oboe, divided into treatises]. Paris: Christophe Ballard, 1707. [Warner No. 42; Vinquist, 185-88]

As the order of instruments named on the title page suggests, Jacques Hotteterre le Romain's *Principes de la flûte* was conceived primarily as a method for the transverse flute, which had recently become "one of the most fashionable instruments" in France. Although, as Hotteterre says, the recorder had "its merits and its partisans, just like the flute," he gives the recorder a secondary role by placing its section after that of the flute and referring recorder players to the flute section for information on articulation and ornaments. Hotteterre had recently assumed the duties of *Flûte de la chambre du roy* (Flute of the king's chamber), concentrating on playing the flute and the musette. Although the engraving in his tutor of two hands playing a recorder has become strongly identified with the Baroque recorder in modern writings, his familiarity with the instrument has been questioned (e.g., in item 654.1).

In his fingering charts, Hotteterre seems to have been the first author to use the now familiar symbols—black circles for closed fingerholes, white circles for open fingerholes, and half-blackened circles for half-closed or "pinched" fingerholes—systematically and divorced from a picture of the instrument. Although his method of showing trill fingerings is equivalent to Carr's, Hotteterre's adoption of these symbols makes them much easier to comprehend. He devotes a chapter to explaining the fingerings for the *battement* (mordent) and *flattement* (a fingered vibrato). The other ornaments—*port-de-voix* (ascending appoggiatura), *coulement* (descending appoggiatura), *accent*, and *double cadence* (trill with turn)—are described in a manner that leaves their rhythm and accentuation open to interpretation. (Hotteterre adds to his instructions on ornaments in the preface to his *Pièces pour la flûte traversière et autres instruments, avec la basse continue*, op. 2 [Paris, 1708; 2nd ed., 1715].)

Hotteterre's instructions on articulation once again use the syllables *tu* and *ru*. *Tu* serves for all long notes. *Tu* and *ru* are used for *notes inégales*, dotted figures, repeated and leaping sixteenth-notes, and two (occasionally four) quick notes that fall between two longer notes. (For the most recent research on the background to these syllables, see item 713.) In addition, two, three, or more notes can be slurred together; Hotteterre freely notates slurs—including long ones—in his improvisatory preludes and *traits*.

651. Hotteterre, Jacques. *Principes de la flûte traversière, ou flûte d'Allemagne, de la flûte à bec, ou flûte douce, et du haut-bois, divisez par traitez*. Amsterdam, Aux d'epens d'E. Roger (1728) [sic]. Kassel: Bärenreiter, [1942]. 46, 48 p. OCLC #22040172. Reprinted, 1973. Reissued on new plates in 1982 as part of the series Documenta musicologica (1. Reihe, Druckschriften-Faksimiles, 34). 46, 53 p. ISBN 3761800746.

Facsimile of the ca. 1710—*not* 1728—edition (Amsterdam: Estienne Roger) with outdated German translation and afterword by Hans Joachim Hellwig.

652. Hotteterre, Jacques. *Principes de la flûte traversière*. Geneva: Minkoff Reprint, 1973. 53 p. ISBN 2826601067. Published with [Charles] De Lusse, *L'art de la flûte traversière* (Paris, 1760).

Facsimile of the 1720 ed. (Paris: Ballard).

653. Hotteterre, Jacques. *Principles of the Flute, Recorder & Oboe (Principes de la flûte)*. Translated with Introduction and Notes by Paul Marshall Douglas. New York: Dover, 1983. xv, 73 p. ISBN 048624606X. First published in 1968 under the title *Rudiments of the Flute, Recorder and Oboe*.

English translation based on the 1707 ed. Includes facsimile reproductions of selected musical examples and figures. Comparative review by Dale Higbee of this and item 654 in *The American Recorder* 11, no. 2 (Spring 1970): 63–65.

654. Hotteterre, Jacques. *Principles of the Flute, Recorder & Oboe*. Translated and edited by David Lasocki. London: Barrie & Rockliff; New York: Praeger, 1968. 88 p. OCLC #11390983 (U.K. ed.), OCLC #448622 (U.S. ed.).

English translation also based on the 1707 ed. Extensive introduction and footnotes. Comparative review by Dale Higbee of this and item 653 in *The American Recorder* 11, no. 2 (Spring 1970): 63–65.

654.1. Hunt, Edgar. "Thoughts on Hotteterre's Recorder Fingerings." *The American Recorder* 27, no. 4 (November 1986): 151.

Hotteterre "seems to be writing from the point of view of a flute player, not as someone who has made an intimate study of the recorder." Criticizes four of Hotteterre's trill fingerings for the recorder as being unnecessarily out of tune and/or ugly and suggests that recorder players follow flutists in finding fingerings that are as in tune as possible.

655. Hotteterre, Jacques. *L'art de preluder sur la flûte traversière, sur la flûte-a-bec, sur le haubois, et autres instruments de deβus* . . . Op. 7 [The art of preluding on the flute, recorder, oboe, and other soprano instruments . . .]. Paris: composer & Boivin (also composer & Foucault), 1719. [Warner No. 52]

A method to learn how to improvise preludes. Includes an extensive set of preludes for the flute, many of which are indicated as playable on the recorder, as well as a set intended for the recorder. Also includes two sets of *traits*, or exercises, "in the style of caprices, which one makes when one so to speak plays about [*badiner*] on an instrument." Followed by lessons on modulation, cadences, keys, transposition, and meter (including *notes inégales*). Concluded by two preludes with continuo. A curious compilation of valuable material, both textual and musical.

656. Hotteterre, Jacques. *L'art de préluder sur la flûte traversière, sur la flûte-a-bec, sur le haubois et autres instruments de deβus.* . . . Geneva: Minkoff Reprint, 1978. 65 p. ISBN 2826606727.

Facsimile.

657. Hotteterre, Jacques. *L'art de preluder sur la flûte traversière, sur la flûte-a-bec, sur le haubois et autres instruments de deβus.* . . . Modern edition by Michel Sanvoisin. Paris: Éditions Aug. Zurfluh, 1966. 76 p. OCLC #11608294.

Transcription, typographically having somewhat the appearance of a facsimile. The musical examples have been transposed from French violin clef to treble clef and the little strokes denoting the measure changed to barlines. It served its purpose in its day, but the facsimile is far preferable.

658. Boyer, Margareth Anne. *Jacques Hotteterre's* L'art de préluder: *A Translation and Commentary.* M.M. thesis, Conservatory of Music, University of Missouri-Kansas City, 1979. vi, 290 leaves. OCLC #4875945.

Not seen.

Schickhardt, Johann Christian (ca. 1680-1762)

659. Schickhardt, Johann Christian. *Principes de la flûte contenant la maniere d'en joüer & la connoissance de musique necessaire pour cela / Avec quarante deux airs à 2 flutes*, Op. 12 [Principles of the recorder, containing the way of playing it and the knowledge of music necessary for that / with 42 airs for two recorders]. Amsterdam: Estienne Roger, ca. 1710-15. [Warner No. 55/63; Vinquist, 196-97]

 The recorder method of the prolific German woodwind composer Johann Christian Schickhardt is disappointing, consisting of little more than the duets, which could admittedly have been used for teaching purposes. He borrows Hotteterre's fingering and trill fingering charts with minor alterations. The main interest of the tutor is a couple of musical examples that show the articulation syllables *ti* and *ri* in dotted figures, a modification of the French vowel sound for Dutch and German speakers.

660. Schickhardt, Johann Christian. *Principes de la flûte.* . . . (Essercizi di musica, 3) Roma: La Stravaganza, [1987]. Facsimile with a preface by Marco di Pasquale. OCLC #18983374.

 The introduction includes a useful note on the differences—intentional and perhaps otherwise—between the fingering charts of Hotteterre and Schickhardt.

661. Lasocki, David. "A Newly Rediscovered Recorder Tutor." *The American Recorder* 9, no. 1 (Winter 1968): 18–19.

 A study of Schickhardt's *Principes de la flûte*. (See also item **899**.)

Stanesby, Thomas (ca. 1668-1734)

662. Stanesby, Thomas, Jr. *A New System of the Flute a'bec, or Common English-Flute.* London, 1732? [Warner No. 66]

 This most unusual 18th-century instructional document about the recorder is by the celebrated maker Thomas Stanesby Jr., "humbly dedicated to all those gentlemen who like the instrument." Stanesby proposed to make the tenor, rather than the alto, the standard size of recorder, and included a comprehensive fingering chart containing several notes above the customary Baroque upper limit of d^3 (the equivalent of the alto's g^2).

663. Higbee, Dale. "A Plea for the Tenor Recorder by Thomas Stanesby Jr." *The Galpin Society Journal* 15 (1962): 55–59.
A facsimile, with introduction, of Stanesby's *A New System*.

MAJER, JOSEPH FRIEDRICH BERNHARD CASPAR (1689–1768)

664. Majer, Joseph Friedrich Bernhard Caspar. *Museum musicum theoretico practicum, das ist, Neueroeffneter theoretisch- und practischer Music-Saal* . . . [Theoretical and practical musical museum; that is, Newly disclosed theoretical and practical music room]. n.p.: Georg Michael Majer, 1732. 2nd ed., Nuremberg: Johann Jacob Cremer, 1741. [Warner No. 65; Vinquist, 208-09]

665. Majer, Joseph Friedrich Bernhard Caspar. *Museum musicum theoretico practicum, das ist, Neueroeffneter theoretisch- und practischer Music-Saal.* . . . Ed. Heinz Becker. Kassel: Bärenreiter, 1954.
Facsimile of 1st ed.

666. *Joseph Friedrich Bernhard Caspar Majers Neu-eroeffneter theoretisch- und praktischer Music-Saal (Nuremberg, 1741).* Ed. Eitelfriedrich Thom. Blankenburg/Michaelstein: Kultur- und Forschungstätte Michaelstein, n.d.
Facsimile of 2nd ed.

667. Newman, Joel. "The Recorder in Majer's *Museum Musicum 1732.*" *The American Recorder* 3, no. 1 (February 1962): 6–8.
Describes the treatise in general and offers a translation (with commentary) of the section on the recorder. Includes facsimiles of fingering charts. Letter from Wesley M. Oler in 3, no. 2 (May 1962): 23 takes issue with Newman's comments on the insignificance of buttress fingering in the history of the instrument. Newman admits his mistake in 3, no. 3 (August 1962): 22 and provides a list of eleven historical methods, four of which call for buttress fingering. See also the letter from John R. Kelsey in 4, no. 2 (May 1963): 27.

EISEL, JOHANN PHILIPP

668. Eisel, Johann Philipp. *Musicus αυτοδιδακτος, oder Der sich selbst informirende Musicus, bestehend sowohl in Vocal-als üblicher Instrumental-musique* [Musicus autodidaktos; or, The self-taught musician, for both vocal and common instrumental music]. Erfurt: Johann Michael Funcken, 1738. [Warner No. 71; Vinquist, 215-16]

    Includes fingering charts for alto recorder and *Quart-fleute* (fourth flute = soprano recorder!). Also refers to a *Tenor-Fleute* (tenor recorder).

669. Eisel, Johann Philipp. *Musicus αυτοδιδακτος, oder Der sich selbst informirende Musicus, bestehend sowohl in Vocal- als ubl. Instrumental-musique.* Leipzig: Zentralantiquariat der Deutschen Demokratischen Republik, 1976. 108 p., [16] leaves. OCLC #4744754.

    Facsimile.

BERLIN, JOHANN DANIEL (1714-1787)

670. Mosand, John. "Ein wenig bekanntes Buch über Musik und Instrumentenspiel: Johann Daniel Berlin, Musicaliske Elementer, 1744" [A little-known book about music and instrumental playing: Johann Daniel Berlin's *Musicaliske Elementer* (The elements of music), 1744]. *Tibia* 8, no. 1 (1983): 276-79.

    Briefly describes Berlin's book, which was published in Trondheim, Norway. According to Mosand, "Besides the customary alto recorder are also mentioned an octave- or *kleine Blockflöte* in f^2 (sopranino), a *Quint-Blockflöte* [fifth flute!] in d^2, a *Quart-Blockflöte* [fourth flute!] in c^2 (soprano), and an *Alt-Blockflöte* in c^1 (tenor). . . . The range of the [alto] recorder in Berlin's fingering chart goes to $c^{4\prime\prime}$ [including a fingering for $f\sharp^3$].

TANS'UR, WILLIAM (1699?-1783)

671. Tans'ur, William. *A New Musical Grammar, or, The Harmonical Spectator.* . . . London: Author, 1746. 2nd ed., 1753. 3rd ed., 1756. [Warner No. 79; Vinquist, 221-23]

    Elementary instructions: hand placement, fingering charts, and the need to transpose pieces outside the range of the instrument. The most interesting part is the statement "Of Flutes there are many Sizes, as a Concert Flute; a Third Flute; a Fifth, and a Sixth, and an Octave Flute."

672. Tans'ur, William. *The Elements of Musick Display'd*. . . . London: Stanley Crowder, 1767. Book III entitled *The Elements of Musick Made Easy: or, an Universal Introduction to the Whole Art of Musick. Book III. Containing, the Structure of Musical Instruments: with the Scale of Musick Applicable to Each; and Directions Thereunto. viz. the Pitch-Pipe, and its Use: the Organ, or Harpsichord: the Bassoon and Haut-boy: the Bass Viol, Violin, and Guittar: the German and Common Flutes*. . . . [Warner No. 113; Vinquist, 239-40]
Section on the recorder derived from 3rd ed. of item **671**.

QUANTZ, JOHANN JOACHIM (1697-1773)

673. Quantz, Johann Joachim. *Versuch einer Anweisung die Flöte traversiere zu spielen* [Essay of a method for playing the flute]. Berlin: Voss, 1752. [Warner No. 85]
Quantz's celebrated flute method is of course far more than that: it constitutes the most comprehensive compendium of information about performance practice of the entire 18th century. Although Quantz does not treat the recorder directly, he did write for the instrument and his advice is extremely valuable for recorder players (see item **1284**).

674. Quantz, Johann Joachim. *Versuch einer Anweisung die Flöte traversiere zu spielen*. Introduction in German by Barthold Kuijken. Wiesbaden: Breitkopf & Härtel, 1988. xxi, iii, 334, [20] p. OCLC #20163689.
Facsimile of 1st ed.

675. Quantz, Johann Joachim. *Versuch einer Anweisung die Flöte traversiere zu spielen*. Munich: Deutscher Taschenbuch Verlag; Kassel: Bärenreiter, 1992. x, 424 p. OCLC #29935835.
Facsimile of 1st ed.

676. Quantz, Johann Joachim. *Versuch einer Anweisung die Flöte traversiere zu spielen*. Edited by Hans-Peter Schmitz. (Documenta musicologica. 1. Reihe: Druckschriften-

Faksimiles, 2) Kassel: Bärenreiter, 1953. OCLC #6562628, #15387304, #19366657, #21770619.
Facsimile of 3rd (1789) ed.

677. Quantz, Johann Joachim. *On Playing the Flute*. Translated and edited by Edward R. Reilly. 2nd ed. London: Faber & Faber; New York: Schirmer Books, 1985. OCLC #12836076 (U.K. ed.), #11971764 (U.S. ed.). 1st ed. London: Faber & Faber; New York: Schirmer Books, 1966. OCLC #255669, #16364312 (U.K. ed.), #1634136 (U.S. ed).

An excellent English translation with extensive introduction and footnotes. Based on Reilly's *Quantz's* Versuch einer Anweisung die Flöte traversiere zu spielen: *A Translation and Study*, 2 vols. (Ph.D. dissertation, University of Michigan, 1958). See also his *Quantz and his* Versuch: *Three Studies* (New York: Galaxy Music Corporation for the American Musicological Society, 1971).

678. Quantz, Johann Joachim. *Essai d'une méthode pour apprendre à jouer de la flute traversiere*. Berlin: Chrétien Frédéric Voss, 1752.

French version, prepared by the author and published by the same publisher.

679. Quantz, Johann Joachim. *Essai-méthode de flûte traversière*. 2nd ed. Paris: Éditions Aug. Zurfluh, 1990. 1st ed., 1975. 21, xv, 6, 336 p. OCLC #7446619, #17202638.
Facsimile of French version.

* Reilly, Edward R. "Quantz and the Recorder." Cited below as item **1284**.

* Sterne, Colin C. "Quavering, Quivering, and J.J. Quantz." Cited above as item **754**.

680. Lasocki, David. "Quantz and the Passions: Theory and Practice." *Early Music* 6, no. 4 (October 1978): 556–67. In Italian as "Quantz e la teoria delle passioni: Gli effetti del clima estetico sulla prassi esecutiva nei secoli XVII e XVIII." *Syrinx: Bollettino ufficiale Accademia Italiana del Flauto* 17 (July–September 1993): 30–34.

Pulls together what Quantz has to say about the passions or affections in several parts of his *Versuch*. Then uses the information to gain insight into the interpretation of the composer's Trio Sonata for Recorder, Flute, and Continuo in C Major (QV 2:2). See also Christian Albrecht, "Quantz und die Affekte" [Quantz and the passions], *Quartalszeitschrift SAJM* 16, no. 3 (September 1988); 16, no. 4 (December 1988); and 17, no. 3 (September 1989).

MINGUET É IROL, PABLO (D. 1801?)

681. Minguet y Irol, Pablo. *Reglas, y advertencias generales que enseñan el modo de tañer todos los instrumentos mejores, y mas usuales* . . . [Rules and general advice that teaches the method of playing all the best and most common instruments]. Madrid: Joachin Ibarra, 1752-74. Part VI is entitled: *Reglas, y advertencias generales para tañer la flauta traversera, la flauto dulce, y la flautilla, con varios tañidas, demonstradas, y figuradas en diferentes laminas finas, por musica, y cifra, para que qualquier aficionado las pueda comprehender con mucha facilidas, y sin maestro* . . . [Rules and general advice for playing the flute, recorder, and pipe, with various descriptions, fingering charts, and fine illustrations, for music and its notation, so that any amateur can understand it easily and without a teacher]. 1754. [Warner No. 87; Vinquist, 226-27]

Minguet's section on the recorder has a fingering chart and some elementary guidance on holding the instrument. The chart includes alto fingerings for f♯³ and for g♯³ through c⁴. Of special interest is the use of "pinching" on holes other than the thumbhole.

682. Minguet é Irol, Pablo. *Reglas, y advertencias generales que enseñan el modo de tañer todos los instrumentos mejores.* . . . Geneva: Minkoff Reprint, 1981. 120 p. ISBN 2826607030.
Facsimile.

683. Lasocki, David. "A Spanish Recorder Tutor." *The American Recorder* 9, no. 2 (Spring 1968): 49-50.
Translates the section on the recorder and gives a facsimile of the fingering chart. The method is also mentioned by Dale Higbee in item 727.

DIDEROT, DENIS (1713-1784)

684. Diderot, Denis, and Jean Le Rond d'Alembert. *Encyclopédie, ou dictionnaire raisonné des sciences, des arts et des métiers* . . . [Encyclopedia or analytical dictionary of the sciences, arts, and trades]. 17 vols. Vols. 1-7, Paris: Briasson, 1751-65; vols. 8-17, Neufchâtel: Faulche, 1765-72. Also *Recueil de planches, sur les sciences, les arts libéraux, et les arts méchaniques, avec leur explication* [Collection of plates on the sciences, liberal arts, and mechanical arts, with their explanations]. 11 vols. Paris: Briasson, 1762-72.

In a volume published in 1756 there appear articles on the flute and recorder and related instruments by Diderot himself, partially borrowed from Hotteterre's *Principes*. The article on the recorder ("flûte douce ou à-bec") summarizes Hotteterre's descriptions of how to hold the instrument and place the fingers, how to "pinch" the high notes, etc., and his fingering and trill charts are reproduced in their entirety. The novel part of the article is its unique description of the recorder and how it was made. The article on the flute borrows Hotteterre's ornaments and articulation syllables (although according to other sources the latter had been abandoned by the wind players of the day). The plates of *lutherie* depict tools used in woodwind making. The *Encyclopédie* also contains short entries on the *dessus de flûte à bec* (sopranino; vol. 4, 1754), *haute contre de flûte à bec* (soprano—range of a fourteenth; vol. 8, 1765), *quinte de flûte à bec* (tenor—range of a sixteenth; vol. 13, 1765), and *basse de flûte à bec* (bass—range of a thirteenth; vol. 2, 1751)

685. *Art du faiseur d'instruments de musique et lutherie. Extrait de l'Encyclopédie méthodique "Arts et métiers mécaniques,"* Paris 1785. Geneva: Minkoff Reprint, 1972.

Facsimile of sections on instruments and making from the 1785 reworking of item **684**. Includes the article on the recorder as well as those on the *dessus, quinte,* and *basse* (although curiously not the *haute contre*) *de flûte à bec;* also includes the plates.

686. Lasocki, David. "Diderot and the Recorder." *Recorder & Music Magazine* 2, no. 6 (August 1967): 190.

Summarizes the 1756 *Encyclopédie* article on the recorder. Translates Diderot's description of the instrument and how it was made.

REYNVAAN, JOOS VERSCHUERE (1739–1809)

687. Reynvaan, Joos Verschuere. *Muzijkaal kunst-woordenboek* . . . [Dictionary of the art of music]. Amsterdam: Wouter Braue, 1795. Covers A–M only.

The article "Flauta Bocca (Italiaansch)" includes a fingering chart for the alto recorder going up to $c\flat^4$ with alternative fingerings for many notes. Reynvaan considered that in order to facilitate the playing of music written for violin or flute, one should learn C fingering as well as F, although "this would really work only for a *Quart-fluit* [fourth flute]."

SWAINE, N.

688. Swaine, N. *The Young Musician, or the Science of Music, Familiarly Explained; with a Glossary of Musical Terms, and Phrases.* Stourport: G. Nicholson, ca. 1818. [Warner No. 361]

Considers the *English flute* the "properest" wind instrument for children and "an excellent introduction" to the transverse flute. Believes it necessary "nearly to plug up the thumb or under hole" then slide the thumb across the small opening, rather than using "pinching" for the high notes. Fingering charts for an instrument in d^1 with a range of two octaves.

18

Performance Practices (Historical)

All recorder players who play music of earlier times sooner or later have to deal with performance practice. The study of historical treatises and other sources of information about notation and performance techniques of the past has been an important part of recorder research for decades. This chapter looks at sources that treat performance practice specifically for the recorder. For general sources on performance practice see Roland Jackson, *Performance Practice, Medieval to Contemporary: A Bibliographic Guide* (New York: Garland, 1988) and Mary Vinquist & Neal Zaslaw, *Performance Practice: A Bibliography* (New York: W.W. Norton, 1971) as well as the regular bibliographies in *Basler Jahrbuch für historische Musikpraxis*, *Performance Practice Review*, and *Tijdschrift voor oude muziek* (for details, see chapter 31).

For many years, the Early Music Movement has taken it for granted that the "best" way—sometimes, the only way—to perform early music is by reconstructing the historical manner of performance as closely as possible—or in other words, "authentically." But during the last ten years or so, a debate about "authenticity" has been raging in musicological circles. Or rather, Richard Taruskin and a few hardy souls have been battling the Early Music world with a view to demonstrating that some of its assumptions have been unfounded (see item 695). Taruskin has pointed out two essential truths: (1) We can know only a limited amount about the performance styles of the past. (2) Early Music performers, even when they know something about historical styles, consciously or unconsciously adopt aspects of modern performance style and blend them with the historical. Yet, in Taruskin's latest views, all modern performers cannot help but be "authentically" of our own times.

The main thing is to be honest about what we are doing and to endeavor to create performances that communicate with modern audiences. Furthermore, we can all take a leaf out of the book of popular music, where this evening's performance is everything and the work only a vehicle for the performance.

This new view of early music performance has not made performance practice invalid or historical research useless. We should just be cautious about the prescriptions of the "Three D's" (Dolmetsch, Dart, and Donington) and authors of that ilk. Performance-practice research produces valuable information that modern performers can use as they see fit. Such information can be inspiring, puzzling, frustrating, or maddening. But to ignore it is to be, in a word, uneducated.

For the performance practice of individual composers, see chapter 28.

689. "Due giorni con Frans Brüggen" [Two days with Frans Brüggen]. *Il flauto dolce* 5 (January/June 1974): 3–18, 23–27; 6 (January/June 1976): 3–22.

Transcript of a recorder master class held in Rome, 16–17 June 1973; edited and translated from the English by Franco Salvatorelli. Brüggen discusses student performances of: Handel's recorder sonatas in A minor, C major (i, ii), D minor (i, ii), and F major (ii); Jacques Hotteterre's Suite in E (originally C) Minor, op. 5, no. 2 (Prélude, Allemande); and van Eyck's *Pavane Lachrymae* and *Onder de linde groene*.

690. Coomber, David. "Rhetoric and Affect in Baroque Music." *The Recorder: Journal of the Victorian Recorder Guild* 3 (November 1985): 23–27.

In the belief that "a knowledge of the rhetorical language employed in the Baroque period is needed in order to play [music of that period] well," explains some basic rhetorical terms, then uses them to discuss the structure of the first movement of Telemann's Sonata for Alto Recorder and Continuo in D Minor (TWV 41:d4).

691. Dinn, Freda. *Early Music for Recorders: An Introduction and Guide to Its Interpretation, and History, for Amateurs.* London: Schott, 1974. 58 p. ISBN 0901938076.

Intended as an introduction to performance practice. Part I analyzes and discusses the interpretation of three fantasias by Byrd and five pieces by Holborne. Part II discusses Handel's G-Minor Sonata, Henry Thornowitz's Sonata da Camera in F Major, and a Suite in G Major by Louis de

Caix d'Hervelois, offering written-out realizations of the ornaments. Recommends for further reading the "3 D's," Emery on Bach's ornaments, and Quantz. A curious book, which must have seemed old-fashioned even at the time of publication. Reviewed by MMCA [Michael Arno?] in *Recorder & Music* 5, no. 1 (March 1975): 21.

692. Hund-Davies, Malcolm. "A Review of Historical Styles of Recorder Playing." *Recorder & Music* 6, no. 3 (September 1978): 66–68; 6, no. 4 (December 1978): 98–100; 6, no. 5 (March 1979): 133–35.

    Covers the 20th century (Part One), the Baroque (Part Two), and the Renaissance (Part Three). Part One is short and sketchy; the discussion of modern recorder technique focuses on phrase markings and dynamics, and little is offered on the avant garde beyond a description of the techniques employed in Hans-Martin Linde's *Music for a Bird*. Part Two concerns tonguing, rhythm, *Affekt*, and ornamentation in the music of the French and Italian Baroque. Also briefly covered are vibrato, trills, the "shape" of notes, and the structure of the Baroque recorder. Part Three covers articulation and ornamentation in Renaissance and early Baroque music and describes the characteristics of the Renaissance recorder. Offers examples of diminution and ornamentation.

693. Jolibert, Bernard. "Les suites des XVIIe et XVIIIe siècles pour flûte à bec et leur interpretation musicale" [17th- and 18th-century suites for recorder and their musical interpretation]. *Flûte à bec & instruments anciens* 16 (October 1985): 22–26.

    Briefly discusses the character and performance of seventeen types of Baroque dance movement.

* Köhler, Wolfgang. "Die Blasinstrumente aus der 'Harmonie Universelle' des Marin Mersenne und ihre Bedeutung für die Aufführungspraxis heute" [The wind instruments from Marin Mersenne's *Harmonie Universelle* and their significance for performance practice today]. Cited above as item 590.

694. Lasocki, David, and Betty Bang Mather. *The Classical Woodwind Cadenza: A Workbook*. New York: McGinnis & Marx, 1978. ix, 60 p. OCLC #7628502.

    Aims to teach the reader to improvise cadenzas for pieces from the Classical period (made over a tonic six-four chord towards the end of a concerto or sonata movement). Based on eighteenth-century theory and practice (as reflected in the surviving written-out cadenzas), discussed in Lasocki's *The Eighteenth-Century Woodwind Cadenza* (M.A. thesis, The University of Iowa, 1972). Also briefly deals with the cadenza-like ornamentations at a final half cadence, as a lead-in to a new section, at the end of the first ritornello, and on the dominant chord at a full cadence—all situations found in Baroque recorder music, some examples from which are cited.

* Lasocki, David. "Quantz and the Passions: Theory and Practice." Cited above as item 680.

695. Lasocki, David. "The Great Authenticity Debate." *The Recorder: Journal of the Victorian Recorder Guild* 14 (December 1991): 1–8.

Presents a new view of "authentic" performance of early music that has developed during the last decade, thanks largely to the American musicologist Richard Taruskin. Covers: the impossibility of a philosophical definition of an authentic performance; the limits to our knowledge of the past; the modernity of "authentic" performances; the politics of authenticity; and some conclusions about research, creativity, and adventure, drawing on some jazz and recorder performances. For Lasocki's pre-Taruskin ideas, see his "'Authenticity' in Performances of Early Music," *Recorder & Music* 5, no. 12 (December 1977): 384–87. For Richard Taruskin's latest ideas, see his "Tradition and Authority," *Early Music* 20, no. 2 (May 1992): 311–25.

696. Montagu, Jeremy. "The Sound of Music." *The Consort* 36 (1980): 355–60.

An eloquent plea to perform early music on the instruments for which it was written. Points out the differences among the sound and tuning of recorders of the Middle Ages, early Renaissance, and late Renaissance.

697. Rowland-Jones, Anthony. *Playing Recorder Sonatas: Interpretation and Technique.* Oxford: Clarendon Press, 1992. xiv, 221 p. ISBN 0198790023.

Presents a great deal of information on performance practice and technique, historical and modern, through the study of movements from sonatas (by Handel, Telemann, Delavigne, Herbert Murrill, and Fontana, with passing references to Riccio, Corelli, Paisible, Schickhardt, Anne Danican-Philidor, J.B. Loeillet, Pugnani, Walter Leigh, Lennox Berkeley, and Robert Schollum). Deals with sound and expression, dynamics, rhythmic inequality, articulation, ornamentation and improvisation, tempo, repeats, expressive fingering, and even a section on "authenticity" making concessions to the latest views. Highly readable, even in the footnotes (readers should just not be lulled into believing that the prescriptions for performance are the only possible approach). Good illustrations of the visual aspect of the Baroque era. A unique and important book. Review by Robert Ehrlich in *The Recorder Magazine* 12, no. 3 (September 1992): 83-84.

698. Thorn, Benjamin. "Will the Real Recorder Please Stand Up?" *The Recorder: Journal of the Victorian Recorder Guild* 13 (July 1991): 1-2.

   In fact a short essay on authenticity in both early and modern musical performance, particularly by the recorder.

*   Warner, Thomas E. *Indications of Performance Practice in Woodwind Instruction Books of the 17th and 18th Centuries.* Cited above as item 536.

699. Winters, Ross. "Historical Source Material." *The Recorder Magazine* 12, no. 3 (September 1992): 77-81.

   Written not "to provide an exhaustive account . . . but rather to try to raise the reader's awareness of what is involved in a stylistic performance." Topics receive only cursory treatment, but the reader is referred to books, treatises, and music for further explanations. Part One covers music of the 16th and early 17th centuries, with an emphasis on issues related to articulation and ornamentation. Part Two, on the Baroque, begins by describing the importance of classical rhetoric to music of the period, the concepts of *affect* and *loci topici,* and the affective nature of dance movements and keys. The discussion of articulation emphasizes tonguing syllables. Explains the relationship between *messa di voce,* vibrato, and appoggiaturas and concludes with a discussion of Baroque ornamentation.

GEOGRAPHICAL FOCUS

FRANCE

700. Davis, Alan. "Jacques Hotteterre and the French Style." *Recorder & Music* 4, no. 9 (March 1974): 319-22.

   Begins by contrasting Italian Baroque and French Baroque styles. Gives a brief overview of Hotteterre's life and works. Offers a cursory introduction to the *agréments* and *notes inégales.*

701. Marvin, Robert. "Playing French Late Baroque Music on the Recorder." *The American Recorder* 9, no. 2 (Spring 1968): 39-41.

   Gives a performer's own practical advice on the interpretation of French Baroque style, based on treatises by Hotteterre and Freillon-Poncein.

Covers articulation (tonguing of *notes inégales*, Hotteterre's "reverse tonguing," when to use *pointée*) and ornamentation (trills, *flattement, battement, port de voix, coulement,* and *accent*). David Lasocki, in 9, no. 3 (Summer 1968): 96, contributes additional information on the trill, breath vibrato, and *flattement,* and mentions the preface to Hotteterre's *Pièces pour la flûte traversière* (1708) as an important source on French Baroque performance practice.

702. Mather, Betty Bang. *Interpretation of French Music from 1675 to 1775 for Woodwind and Other Performers; Additional Comments on German and Italian Music.* New York: McGinnis & Marx, 1973. 104 p. OCLC #890838.

    A comprehensive survey of French late Baroque and early Classical woodwind performance practice, based on contemporaneous evidence. Divided into "rhythmic inequality" (including meter and tempo), articulation, and ornaments. Widely cited. Generally holds up well after twenty years (for more recent research, see especially item 713). Reviewed by Anthony Baines in *The Galpin Society Journal* 28 (April 1975): 143–44.

703. Rowland-Jones, Anthony. "First Steps in Applying French Polish." *American Recorder* 33, no. 3 (September 1992): 9–13.

    Uses the first movement of the Sonata op. 2, no. 5 ("La Persan") by Philibert Delavigne to illustrate the fundamentals of performance practice for music of the French Baroque. Based in part on chapter 4 of item 697. Begins by offering some background to the sonata. Explains the differences between the French and Italian Baroque styles. Presents a set of guidelines for determining whether a piece should be played with or without inequality. Briefly addresses the complicated issue of articulation, then shows how an informed performer might approach the Delavigne movement. His suggestions are summarized in an accompanying annotated solo part, which specifies articulation, phrasing, inequality, dynamics, and ornamentation.

GERMANY

* Polk, Keith. *German Instrumental Music of the Late Middle Ages: Players, Patrons and Performance Practice.* Cited above as item 70.

ITALY

704. Garrido, Gabriel. "La flûte à bec dans la musique italienne: Propositions d'interprétations" [The recorder in Italian music: propositions for interpretation]. *Flûte à bec* 3 (June 1982): 34–35.

Briefly discusses treatises, sizes of instrument, pitch, and temperament in 16th- and 17th-century Italy. Reprinted from the liner notes to his album *Musique italienne pour la flûte à bec* (Lausanne, Switzerland, VDE-GALLO 30-324).

SPECIFIC TOPICS

ARTICULATION

704.1. Arthur, Bradford. "The Articulation of Hotteterre's *Tu-Ru*." *The American Recorder* 14, no. 3 (August 1973): 79–82.

Like Lasocki (see item 710), Arthur speculates on how Hotteterre's *tu-ru* articulation syllables might have been pronounced in 18th-century France. "The puzzle of musical reconstruction is also necessarily a puzzle of linguistic reconstruction." He supports Lasocki's interpretation of the *r* (pronounced by brushing or tapping the tongue against the alveolar ridge), but disagrees with Lasocki's suggestion that the *t* be pronounced "sharply against the teeth." The French *t* should be unvoiced and unaspirated. Suggests trying *thu* rather than *tu* or *du*. The proper pronunciation of the syllables produces, at slow tempos, a natural *notes inégales*, which gradually smooths out as the tempo increases. Proper pronunciation also affects articulation; the *tu* may be preceded by a distinct articulation, whereas very little more than a soft elision with the preceding note is possible with the *ru*.

705. Castellani, Marcello, and Elio Durante. *Del portar della lingua negli instrumenti di fiato. Per una corretta interpretazione delle sillabe articolatorie nella trattatistica dei secc. XVI-XVIII.* (Archivum Musicum, Collana di studi, B) Firenze: Studio per Edizioni Scelte, 1979. 177 p. OCLC #7855993.

The longest study of early woodwind articulations made to date. Begins with the foundations of articulation: tongue and mouth positions for various vowels and consonants. Then summarizes the effects of the tonguing syllables used by authors from Ganassi to Drouet (1827), and briefly considers "Onomatopea and instrumental articulation." The extensive appendix (pp. 77–172) includes excerpts in the original languages of the articulation instructions from Ganassi, Agricola, Dalla Casa, Rogniono, Artusi, Brunelli, Rognoni, Mersenne, Bismantova, Freillon-Poncein, Hotteterre, and several other 18th-century authors.

706. Goetz, Freddy. "Les articulations sur la flûte" [Articulations on the recorder]. *Flûte à bec* 5 (December 1982): 22–24.

    A brief summary of the articulation instructions of Ganassi, Agricola, Hotteterre, and Quantz.

707. Greenberg, Abraham. "Articulation in Recorder Playing: A Phonetic Study." *The American Recorder* 24, no. 3 (August 1983): 99–101.

    Greenburg, a specialist in speech and hearing sciences, uses modern English phonetics, rather than historical sources, as the starting point for a review of articulation syllables. Emphasizes the need to adjust vowel sounds in order to achieve maximum resonance over the range of the instrument. Although many of the articulation syllables found in historical and modern tutors are mentioned in the Introduction, Greenburg does not compare his recommendations with these earlier sources, so the reader is left to decide how Greenburg's suggestions fit into the context of historical performance practice.

708. Houle, George. "Tongueing and Rhythmic Patterns in Early Music." *The American Recorder* 6, no. 2 (Spring 1965): 4–13.

    Claims that most modern players strive to make all tonguing—single and double—sound alike, although there are strong indications that players before 1750 used a variety of attacks with the intention of producing different sounds: "Instruments with limited possibilities of dynamic range and tone color need the variety of sound afforded by these tonguings far more than our 'perfected' modern instruments, but the benefits are not only greater interests in the sounds, but greater liveliness of rhythmic design." Moving from simple to complex, Houle covers the articulations presented in a dozen early method books. Double-tonguing patterns are summarized in a one-page table. Also demonstrates how knowledge of dance steps can aid players in the analysis of articulation patterns in dance music, using the *galliard* and *courante française* as examples. Letter from E. Neal Bozarth Jr. in *The American Recorder* 7, no. 2 (Spring 1966): 23 corrects an error in the bibliography.

709. Hübner-Hinderling, Renate. "Artikulation oder Der Versuch, die Musik mit der Sprache zu versöhnen—nicht nur für Blockflötisten" [Articulation, or the attempt to

reconcile music and speech—not only for recorder players]. *Tibia* 16, no. 2 (1991): 421–24.

Headed by a quotation from Monterverdi: "... che l'oratione sia padrona dell'armonia e non serva" [that language be the master of harmony and not the servant]. Extends this concept to articulation syllables, which the author believes are usually too abstract. Suggests instead using a vast array of real words and nonsense fragments (sample: DOdeka, DAEdalo, DEdito, DOrothee, DOridi, DEttero) of two–five syllables, varying in length and accentuation.

710. Lasocki, David. "The Tongueing Syllables of the French Baroque." *The American Recorder* 8, no. 3 (Summer 1967): 81–82.

Aims to "clear up some misunderstandings which have arisen in the English-speaking world over the pronunciation of the tonguing syllables of the French school." Cites Hotteterre, Freillon-Poncein, and Quantz. Concludes that "the syllable *tu* was pronounced sharply against the teeth; the syllable *ru* was pronounced with the tongue against the teeth ridge. Thus, any sequence of *turuturu* etc., was an alternation of sharp and soft articulations."

711. Leonards, Petra G. "Artikulation auf Blasinstrumenten im 16. und 17. Jahrhundert: Ein Beitrag zur Spieltechnik der Blasinstrumente vor dem geistesgeschichtlichen Hintergrund dieser Zeit" [Articulation on wind instruments in the 16th and 17th centuries: a contribution to the playing technique of wind instruments against the background of the history of ideas of this period]. *Tibia* 5, no. 1 (1980): 1–9.

Begins with the background: "The music aesthetics of the 16th–17th centuries (especially in Italy and German-speaking countries) demands that everything, from the design of the composition to the detailed treatment of the text, has the goal of imitating nature or else speech by musical means and should serve the performance of the affective contents of the underlying text. It is the duty of the singer to bring out the affects of the text in performance. For instrumentalists something similar holds true . . . they should . . . 'bring the music toward speech.'" The means for doing so are the articulation syllables of the day. Goes on to summarize the various syllables and their uses. A useful summary—and a salutary warning about the background. Letter from Elli Edler-Busch in 5, no. 2 (1980): 155.

712. Linde, Hans-Martin. "Vom 'cantablen' Spiel auf der Blockflöte" [On 'cantabile' playing on the recorder]. *Zeitschrift SAJM* 20, no. 2 (March 1992): 17–21.

A thought-provoking article. "Cantabile" means "in a singing style," although such a style varies from era to era. The Baroque did not yet know the "endless melody" of the 19th century. "Cantabile style" also means a "speaking" performance, and in this the recorder has a rich reserve of means of articulation. Yet the earlier articulation syllables must have changed under the influence of the violin style in the 18th century. Does vibrato belong to a singing tone? In the Baroque the word implied a variety of ornaments of different speeds. Our best teacher of the "cantabile" is to play early vocal pieces and ponder the meaning of the text, perhaps even try to set text to instrumental pieces.

713. Ranum, Patricia M. "A Fresh Look at French Wind Articulations." *American Recorder* 33, no. 4 (December 1992): 9-16, 39.

Supports the hypothesis that French Baroque wind articulations should mimic the phrasing of contemporary French song lyrics. Ranum present four lessons (covering the pronunciation of *tu* and *ru*, phrasing, "harshness" vs. "sweetness," and *note inégales*) intended to provide an introduction to the practice of articulation based on word-music relationships. Among her theories is one that the tonguing syllables *tu* and *ru* convey contrasting emotional messages (*tu*, bright and assertive; *ru*, tender and gentle) and that a contemporary French player, keeping this contrast in mind, would have "scrutinized the notation, the harmony, and the melody for clues to the passions being expressed and adapted his tonguing to mimic vocal rhetoric." Ranum maintains that no two players would necessarily have articulated a passage exactly the same way, but each would have phrased the music according to individual perceptions of vocal conventions of the time. Letters by Bob Marvin (in 34, no. 1 [March 1993]: 30-34) and George Goebel (in 34, no. 2 [June 1993]: 34-39), each with a lengthy reply by Ranum.

714. Reiss, Scott. "Articulation: The Key to Expressive Playing." *The American Recorder* 27, no. 4 (November 1986): 144-49.

An excellent summary of the types of articulation syllables found in Renaissance and Baroque wind treatises. Classifies the syllables into single tonguing, gutteral double tonguing, and lateral double tonguing. Also goes beyond those treatises both to recommend the use of historical syllables in places not sanctioned by them (for performing the music of times and places they do not cover) and to invent variations on those syllables ("logical extensions of historic techniques"). Finally, stresses the importance of using articulations to make *music*. Responses from Bernard Krainis, Benjamin S. Dunham, and Bob Marvin, and a reply by Reiss in 28, no. 2 (May 1987): 83-85. Dunham continues the debate in 28, no. 3 (August 1987): 126. More letters, from Frederic Palmer and Eduardo Vargas, in 28, no. 4 (November 1987): 177-78, with a reply by Reiss. Krainis responds to

Palmer and Vargas in 29, no. 2 (May 1988): 74–76. Palmer responds in 29, no. 3 (August 1988): 128.

715. Rowland-Jones, Anthony. "Recorder Slurring." *American Recorder* 34, no. 2 (June 1993): 9–15; 34, no. 4 (November 1993): 6–11; 35, no. 1 (January 1994): 7–12.

Part I: Renaissance and Early Baroque. A survey of articulation practices during the Renaissance and early Baroque as described in historical treatises. Begins by distinguishing between "non-slur slur signs" and true slurs, which Rowland-Jones sees as falling into four categories: real slur, articulated (or pulsed) slur, simulated (or faked) slur, and portamento slur. Although Rowland-Jones cites examples from relevant repertory, the focus of the article is more on the theoretical than on the practical. The general reader might be overwhelmed by the numerous references to historical methods and treatises and tend to overlook the author's practice of presenting issues in black and white that are better suited to shades of gray. David Lasocki, in 34, no. 3 (September 1993): 27–29, questions whether methods and treatises can tell us much about how music was performed in its day and asserts that we should exercise the freedom to play early music "any way we please" because historical authenticity is an impossible goal (see item 695 for more on this topic).

Part II: The Later Baroque. Reviews the scanty treatment of slurring in Baroque tutors and attempts to fill in the gaps by drawing conclusions on slurring practices from the markings in English methods. Then briefly discusses the slurring practices of French and English Baroque composers as well as Handel, Bach, and a few miscellaneous composers. Although a handful of composers (Couperin, Bach, Telemann) are fairly specific in their marking of slurs, most composers—including such major ones as Handel and Purcell—marked few slurs. Rowland-Jones best summarizes the situation in the section on Handel: "Handel, like nearly all other Baroque composers, leaves slurring, along with ornamentation, to the good taste and imagination of the performer. . . . Ultimately, each player should strive to reach the stage of understanding where he can confidently make up his own mind, as Handel would have expected."

Part III: The Technique of Slurring. Discusses the "three main impediments to perfection of legato slurring . . . 1) register breaks, 2) complex finger movements, and 3) 'fingering noise.'" Explains how players can overcome these slurring challenges, using the aria "Sheep May Safely Graze" from Bach's Cantata 208 and Martinu's Divertimento for Two Recorders as examples. Techniques include alternate fingerings, variations in tonguing, and adjustments to breath pressure. Concludes with exercises and a suggestion of suitable practice repertory.

* Rowland-Jones, Anthony. "A Slur on Slurring? A Problem in Recorder Playing." *NEMA Journal* 9 (July 1988): 1-6. Cited below as item 772.

716. Omitted.

CONTINUO REALIZATION AND ACCOMPANYING

717. Blaker, Frances. "Continuo Viewed from Above." *American Recorder* 34, no. 2 (June 1993): 19-20.

    Observes that continuo accompaniment is often overlooked by both soloists and audiences. Encourages recorder players to learn as much as they can about continuo and to listen carefully to what is going on beneath them. Emphasizes that continuo realization follows certain rules but also allows ample room for creativity and expression. Concludes with remarks on what Blaker likes to hear in continuo playing, including her opinion that continuo instruments should be heard more prominently than they are in most modern performances. "[N]ot every single note of a top line needs to be heard as clearly as possible. Some notes are best masked."

718. Boxall, Maria. "Realizing the Realization." *Recorder and Music Magazine* 4, no. 2 (June 1972): 53-54.

    Advice to keyboardists on the realization of continuo accompaniments for recorder works.

719. Goebels, Franzpeter. "Mit-Teilungen: Erfahrungen und Anregungen eines Klavierspielers" [Communications: experiences and suggestions of a keyboard player]. *Tibia* 13, no. 1 (1988): 14-18.

    For recorder players good accompanists—real musical partners—are hard to find, as C.P.E. Bach already remarked 250 years ago. Suggests it would be a helpful exercise to make transcriptions of keyboard pieces for recorder and keyboard, and gives a number of examples (the Fitzwilliam Virginal Book, Rameau, Bartók's *Mikrokosmos*, Couperin, Domenico Scarlatti, J.S. Bach, Mozart, Yoram Paporisz's *Begegnungen am Klavier*, Schumann, Chopin).

DIVISIONS

720. Erig, Richard, with Veronika Gutmann, ed. *Italienische Diminutionen: Die zwischen 1553 und 1638 mehrmals bearbeiteten Sätze = Italian Diminutions: The Pieces With*

More Than One Diminution from 1553 to 1638. (Prattica musicale, 1) Zürich: Amadeus Verlag, Bernhard Päuler, 1979. OCLC #13793256.

The introduction to this extremely useful edition includes an excellent overview of contemporaneous articulation for wind instruments (pp. 30–44). The editors recognize that when those conventions are followed, "the diminutions seem no longer as uniform or as just expressions of great virtuosity, as they may appear at first glance."

721. Habert, Andreas. "Wege durch die *Division Flute*: Zur Variationspraxis in der englischen Kunst- und Volksmusik des 17. Jahrhunderts" [Ways through the *Division Flute*: on variation practice in English art and folk music of the 17th century]. *Basler Jahrbuch für historische Musikpraxis* 11 (1987): 89–138.

Uses *The Division Flute*, the well-known set of divisions for the recorder published by John Walsh in 1706-8, as the starting point for a wide-ranging look at the role of divisions in the English music of the 17th century. Noteworthy for Habert's classification schemes. Divides the divisions in *The Division Flute* into four stylistic types: (1) similar to those found in Christopher Simpson's *The Division Viol* (1659), or in other words, old-fashioned; (2) similar to those of the violin virtuosos represented in *The Division Violin* (1684, etc.); (3) influenced by French music; and (4) influenced by folk music. Further classifies the variation technique employed in the divisions as (a) harmonically oriented, (b) melodically oriented, and (c) a mixture of the two. Finally, distinguishes among three compositional plans for a set of divisions. Habert also argues that the divisions based on folk music are as primitive as the work of the country fiddlers of the day and should therefore not be interpreted as figured basses: an appropriate performance of these divisions would be with no realization of the bass—perhaps even without bass—and alternating or combining the melody instruments of a folk ensemble (violin, shawm, recorder).

722. Hullfish, William R. "The Division Flute: An Introduction to Playing Upon a Ground." *NACWPI Journal* 27, no. 2 (Winter 1978–79): 4–23.

Consists of: table of contents of *The Division Flute*, brief biographies of its composers, the origins of some of the basses, quotations from Christopher Simpson's *Division-Violist* (1659) on improvising divisions to a ground, all the basses, and a six-step method for improvising such divisions based on Simpson's and the author's own ideas.

723. Hullfish, William. "Improvising Divisions upon a Ground." *The American Recorder* 21, no. 2 (August 1980): 73-78.

Summarizes the instructions for division found in Christopher Simpson's *Division Violist* (1659) and demonstrates how the technique is employed in "Faronell's Ground" in *The Division Flute*. Offers his own eight-step guide to improvising divisions and includes a transcription from lute tablature of "Divisions on Browning" (pp. 76-78). Portions of the article first appeared in his "Divisions: The Art of Improvising Your Own," *Divisions* 1 (September 1978): 4-13.

FINGERING AND FINGERINGS

724. Bloodworth, Denis. "The Baroque-fingered Recorder." *The Recorder and Music Magazine* 8, no. 5 (March 1985): 151-53.

Briefly examines the differences between Baroque fingering and modern English fingering.

725. Carse, Adam. "Fingering the Recorder." *The Music Review* 1, no. 2 (1940): 96-104.

An important early article on historical fingerings. Opens with a chronological listing of twenty-five historical methods. Among them are most of the known sources on fingering the recorder. Describes the various ways that fingering charts are presented in the methods. Discusses the heavy plagiarism among them and the high frequency of error, particularly in the charts. Then proceeds with an analysis of the fingerings suggested for each note on the alto, from f^1 to g^3. Identifies German and English-French systems of fingering in the charts and distinguishes between the two.

726. Davis, Alan. "Playing Baroque Recorders with Original Fingering." *The Recorder Magazine* 12, no. 2 (June 1992): 47-50.

Explains the history of modern "English" fingering, how it differs from authentic Baroque fingering, and the advantages that authentic fingering holds for the Baroque repertory. The main sources for authentic fingerings are historical fingering charts and the instruments themselves. One of the most authoritative charts is the one included in Hotteterre's *Principes* (1707). The subtle distinctions between enharmonics are easier to accomplish with authentic fingering. The two "problem" notes on historical recorders are b^2 and $c\sharp^3$, but "[t]hese two notes apart, Hotteterre's fingerings used on an appropriate recorder produce excellent results, and make it much easier to work with a keyboard tuned in some form of unequal temperament." Anthony Rowland-Jones, in a letter in 12, no. 3 (September 1992): 87, proposes solutions to the tuning problems associated with c♯³. In the letter that follows, Edgar Gordon offers similar advice for b♭² and b¹.

727. Higbee, Dale. "Third-Octave Fingerings in Eighteenth-Century Recorder Charts." *The Galpin Society Journal* 15 (1962): 97–99.

Written to dispute the claim in item 725 that a fingering for f♯³ is not given in early charts. Higbee presents examples from Thomas Stanesby Jr., Pablo Minguet é Irol, Joos Verschuere Reynvaan, and Majer.

728. Lasocki, David. "17th and 18th Century Fingering Charts for the Recorder." *The American Recorder* 11, no. 4 (Fall 1970): 128–37.

A concordance of thirty-three historical charts for F recorders, keyed to Warner's bibliography of instruction books (item 535). Five charts for recorders in C are listed separately.

729. Newman, Joel [Flauto Piccolo, pseud.]. "Stützfingering Un-buttressed." *The American Recorder* 4, no. 2 (May 1963): 14–15.

The impetus of the article was a series of letters written to refute Newman's claim (in item 667) that buttress fingering had played an insignificant role in the history of the recorder. Newman admits his mistake and reports on historical references to the fingering. Begins by citing the passage from the *Method for the Recorder in F* (Edition Schott 4469) by F.J. Giesbert that resurrected the technique in the 20th century. Reports Edgar Hunt's observation that the earliest evidence of buttress fingering might be the reference in Jambe de Fer's *Epitome musicale* (1556; see items 573 and 574). Hunt also notes that "[i]t is also in Hudgebut and others *before* Hotteterre." Newman reports the results of a poll of fourteen performers, most of whom oppose the use and teaching of the technique.

ORNAMENTATION

Renaissance

730. Baratz, Lewis Reece. "Improvising on the Spagna Tune." *The American Recorder* 29, no. 4 (November 1988): 141–46.

The first of two important articles by Baratz on extemporization in 15th-century music. Shows how to analyze a tenor and make two parts against it, drawing on the writings of Tinctoris and Gaffurius.

731. Baratz, Lewis Reece. "Fifteenth-Century Improvisation, Take Two: Building a Vocabulary of Embellishments." *American Recorder* 31, no. 2 (June 1990): 7–11.

Works backwards from the method described in item 730, reducing the superius part of two 15th-century works to a skeletal outline, and observing the underlying counterpoint. Then analyzes the intervals involved, identifies the embellishments used in those intervals, and organizes them into tables for practical use. Finally, uses the tables to create an improvisation on a popular song. Recommended.

732. Bixler, Martha. "An Introduction to Renaissance Ornamentation." *The American Recorder* 8, no. 4 (Fall 1967): 107–9; 9, no. 4 (Fall 1968): 108–12.

Begins by explaining the differences between Renaissance and Baroque melodic embellishment. Summarizes the rules of Renaissance ornamentation, citing treatises by Silvestro Ganassi, Diego Ortiz, Hermann Finck, and Ludovico Zacconi. In the second part of the article, Bixler applies ornamental formulas recommended by Ganassi and Ortiz to a villançico by Juan del Enciña. Includes a bibliography of primary and secondary sources.

733. Seibert, Peter. "Ornamentation for Consort Players: First Steps." *The American Recorder* 25, no. 4 (November 1984): 136–38.

Offers basic formulas for simple Renaissance ornamentation. Includes a bibliography of sources for further study.

734. Waldo, Andrew. "So You Want to Blow the Audience Away? Sixteenth-Century Ornamentation: A Perspective on Goals and Techniques." *The American Recorder* 27, no. 2 (May 1986): 48–59.

Some of the best advice in print on learning to ornament in 16th-century style using historical sources and modern practice techniques. Includes a selected bibliography of sources for madrigal diminutions, ornamentation manuals without diminution pieces, and modern books and articles on the subject. A valuable appendix indexes by title virtually all the diminution pieces in ornamentation sources, 1535–1638.

Baroque

735. Betz, Marianne. "Verzierungspraxis im italienischen Stil am Beispiel der Sonate op. 5/9 von A. Corelli" [Ornamentation in the Italian style as exemplified in Arcangelo

Corelli's Sonata, op. 5, no. 9]. *Tibia* 8, no. 2 (1983): 343–50.

Corelli's sonatas for violin and continuo, op. 5 (first published in 1700), were performed by recorder players in the 18th century and still are today. Betz looks in detail at one of the sonatas in *sonata da camera* style as ornamented by Corelli's student Francesco Geminiani, Geminiani's Irish student Matthew Dubourg, and the modern recorder players Frans Brüggen and Hans-Martin Linde. "In contrast to the luxuriant, virtuoso, performer-centered ornamentation style of Geminiani, and even more of Dubourg, the present-day style of ornamentation, here represented by Brüggen and Linde, shows a stronger inclusion of rational aspects which are combined to a greater or lesser extent with virtuoso elements." A revealing analysis.

736. Conrad, Ferdinand. "Embellishments in Baroque Music: An Approach to a Practical Method." *Recorder & Music Magazine* 3, no. 2 (June 1969): 51–57. Reprinted from *The Recorder News* 26 (October 1959) and 27 (December 1959). In German as: "Die Verzierung in der Barockmusik: Versuch einer methodisch-praktischen Anleitung für Melodieinstrumente." *Hausmusik* 20 (1956): 157-69.

Describes the execution of the *agréments*, placing an emphasis on sensitivity to the *Affekt* of the music. Also covers ornamentation "in the Italian style" (i.e., divisions). Well done for its time, but by today's standards Conrad places too great an emphasis on "rules."

737. Hunt, Edgar. "An Introduction to Baroque Ornamentation." *The Recorder and Music Magazine* 9, no. 9 (March 1989): 246–49; 9, no. 10 (June 1989): 281–82.

Part One describes the execution of the appoggiatura, trill, mordent, slide, and *port de voix*. Hunt shows how they might be applied to the slow movement of Handel's C-Major Recorder Sonata. Part Two offers guidelines, based on musical taste and sensibility, for introducing ornamentation into performances of Baroque music and shows how the practice may be applied to the minuet from Barsanti's F-Major Recorder Sonata. Begins with a warning against adopting long legato phrasing for the music of the Baroque. Argues that in the Renaissance all notes—even ornaments—were articulated, and "[b]y the time of Purcell the ornamentation which came in with the French and Italian styles was slurred even though the music generally was clearly articulated."

738. Lasocki, David. "Late Baroque Ornamentation: Philosophy and Guidelines." *The American Recorder* 29, no. 1 (February 1988): 7–10.

Practical advice, following up on item 740. "[E]xplores the philosophy of late Baroque ornamentation and offers guidelines to performers on learning to improvise stylishly." Compares the purposes of ornamentation in the late Baroque and its purposes today, and draws parallels between Baroque ornamentation and jazz improvisation. Encourages players to become familiar with music of the period (particularly vocal music) and the style of the composer being studied. Urges players to adopt whatever views of the past suit their own modern purposes. Supports Quantz's advice that ornamentation should be introduced only when necessary. Finally, suggests that performances should be "fresh, vivacious, spontaneous, and adventurous." Letter from Scott Reiss in 29, no. 3 (August 1988): 128.

739. Mather, Betty Bang, and David Lasocki. *Free Ornamentation for Woodwind Instruments, 1700–1775: An Anthology with Introduction.* New York: McGinnis & Marx, 1976. 158 p. OCLC #2530444.

Consists mainly of an anthology of examples of written-out ornamentation, from Corelli, Babell, Vivaldi, Bach, Telemann, Quantz, Nardini, Carlo Besozzi, La Barre, Hotteterre, Jean-Baptiste Loeillet, Montéclair, Mr. R[ippert], Boismortier, and Blavet. Shows both simple and ornamented melody lines (in some cases, by *de*-ornamenting complex melodies, such as Bach's). A good many of the examples are written or suitable for the recorder. The introduction discusses the sources, the differences between French- and Italian-style ornamentation, the notation of ornamentation, "rules" for Bach and Telemann (extracted by Putnam Aldrich and William Pepper), rules by Quantz and Lorenzoni, the performance of the ornamentations, trio-sonata ornamentation, contemporaneous reports of "excesses," and ways for the modern performer to learn how to ornament. One of the appendixes lists other 18th-century woodwind ornamentations in modern publications. Reviewed by M.B. [Maria Boxall?] in *Recorder & Music* 5, no. 9 (March 1977): 307 and Anthony Baines in *The Galpin Society Journal* 31 (May 1978): 176.

740. Mather, Betty Bang. "Developing Baroque Ornamentation Skills." *The American Recorder* 29, no. 1 (February 1988): 4–6.

Adapted from *The Flutist Quarterly* 12, no. 1 (Winter 1987): 22–26. Recommends that students of ornamentation "begin by practicing one ornament at a time—passing tone, trill, turn, etc.—wherever possible within a phrase." Demonstrates the application of this method by taking the first three phrases of the Larghetto from Handel's C-Major Sonata and ornamenting it thirteen ways using thirteen categories of ornamentation. Also shows how Phrygian cadences might be ornamented, citing examples from Telemann and Quantz. Letter from Scott Reiss in 29, no. 3 (August 1988): 128.

741. Mather, Betty Bang. "Making Up Your Own Baroque Ornamentation." *The American Recorder* 22, no. 3 (August 1981): 55–59. Reprinted from *Woodwind World—Brass & Percussion* 19 (March/April 1980): 12–16.

For the player who already has a basic understanding of ornamentation. Mather offers simple, practical advice firmly grounded in scholarship. Rather than pointing readers in the direction of historical treatises and tutors, she encourages study of the music of the period. Since many composers occasionally wrote out explicit melodic embellishments and ornaments, by analyzing and memorizing these patterns players can improve their own ornamentation. "An excellent way to learn authentic ornamentation practices is to play through ornamented music." Describes the differences between set and free ornamentation. Offers guidelines on when and how to ornament and lists seven precautions taken from Quantz. Makes valuable suggestions on how to practice ornamentation techniques.

742. McGrady, Richard. "Corelli's Violin Sonatas and the Ornamentation of Handel's Recorder Sonatas." *Recorder & Music Magazine* 3, no. 10 (June 1971): 357–59.

Shows how ornamentation used in the slow movements of Corelli's sonatas for violin and continuo, op. 5, can be applied to the Handel sonatas. Based on an early edition of the Corelli that includes elaborate, written-out ornamentation supposedly by the composer. Specific techniques include filling in melodic gaps with a series of turns and embellishing final Phrygian cadential figures.

743. Stansfield, Norman. "Ornamentation in 18th Century French and Japanese Flute Music." *Continuo* 7, no. 3 (December 1983): 8–11.

Expands ideas introduced in a letter to the journal (see item 301). Finds parallels between the two styles of ornaments.

744. Wollitz, Kenneth. "An Introduction to Baroque Ornamentation." *The American Recorder* 7, no. 1 (Winter 1966): 4–10.

History of the *agréments* and instructions for their execution. Much of the material is reprinted in chapter 3 of item 14.

PITCH AND TUNING

See also chapter 12, "Construction and Design," under the subheading "Pitch and tuning" (pp. 122–24).

745. Craven, John. "Harpsichord Tuning, Pure and Simple: A Guide to Playing with Recorders." *Recorder and Music Magazine* 4, no. 5 (March 1973): 169–71.

Concerns a description of modified meantone tuning. One paragraph address the topic of playing with recorders.

746. Haynes, Bruce. "Beyond Temperament: Non-Keyboard Intonation in the 17th and 18th Centuries." *Early Music* 19, no. 3 (August 1991): 357–81.

Modern recorder players sometimes assume that historical recorders were built in some kind of temperament, such as mean-tone. Haynes makes it clear that for such instruments "temperament" is not even possible. He writes that "[w]ithout a fixed tuning, intonation is influenced by technical situations, subjective perceptions, even differences in dynamics." He discusses just intonation as well as various historical temperaments that were used for keyboard instruments. Woodwind fingering charts sometimes distinguish between enharmonic pairs, such as D♯ and E♭, the latter being higher by a comma. The concept of major and minor semitones "logically leads to intonation models that resemble various [mean-tone] temperaments." Eighteenth-century sources suggest different solutions to the problem of how melody instruments and keyboard instruments should play together.

747. Wyatt, Theo. "A Question of Temperament." *Recorder and Music Magazine* 4, no. 6 (June 1973): 192–93.

Describes just intonation, mean-tone tuning, and equal temperament. Wyatt's purpose is to explain "why E♯ is not the same as F" and why this difference requires a player "to add or subtract fingers at a moment's notice to trim his chords to the demands of intonation."

PRELUDING

748. Lasocki, David. "Preluding on the Recorder in England in the Early 18th Century." *Recorder & Music* 6, no. 7 (September 1979): 194–97.

During the 18th and early 19th centuries, instrumentalists engaged in a practice known as "preluding" or "flourishing," the improvisation of a passage to introduce a composed piece of music. Lasocki reviews the history of the practice as documented in historical sources and describes surviving examples of composed preludes. "They consist mainly of chord notes and basically stepwise passagework without time signature or regular metre, and of course they stay within the home key." Contemporary writers mentioned the value of preludes in preparing the ear of the audience for the key of the piece to follow, but Lasocki speculates that preludes must have also served the purpose of preparing the performer by providing an opportunity "to warm and tune the instrument, to exercise the fingers, to test the acoustics of the room, and again, to accustom themselves to the key and its particular difficulties on their instrument."

749. Mather, Betty Bang, and David Lasocki. *The Art of Preluding, 1700–1830, for Flutists, Oboists, Clarinettists and Other Performers.* New York: McGinnis & Marx, 1984. 78 p. ISBN 0941084086.

Begins with an introduction defining the prelude and setting it in its historical context (based on item **748**). Briefly defines musical style in both formal music and preludes between the late 17th century and the early 19th century. Then surveys the published collections of preludes for that period, beginning with Freillon-Poncein and Hotteterre, quoting a few examples from each and giving performance advice. A final section sets out a method for learning to improvise preludes, based partly on Hotteterre's *L'Art de préluder* (1719) and citing a few recorder preludes from a recorder method, *The New Flute Master* (1729), as examples. Indexes of preludes by composer, instrument, and key.

Rhythm

750. Babitz, Sol. "On the Need for Restoring Baroque Inequality." *The American Recorder* 9, no. 1 (Winter 1968): 7–8.

Supports the use of inequality as a means of playing "quantitative accents" on instruments incapable of producing an accent by means of dynamics (e.g., the recorder).

* Houle, George. "Tongueing and Rhythmic Patterns in Early Music." Cited above as item **708**.

Vibrato

751. Carter, Stewart. "The String Tremolo in the 17th Century." *Early Music* 19, no. 1 (February 1991): 43–59.

Citing a wide array of evidence, shows that the 17th-century string tremolo has been frequently misinterpreted. Originally intended as an imitation of the organ tremulant, it was performed by repeating several (usually four) notes of the same pitch in the same bow stroke, lightly articulated with a gentle pressure of the finger on the bow or bow hair, perhaps accompanied by left-hand vibrato. He suggests that wind players might emulate the organ tremulant by means of finger vibrato or breath vibrato, or even by shaking the instrument. To our knowledge, the term "tremolo" occurs only once in the published recorder literature: in the "Canzona con il tremolo 'La Grimaneta'" for "flautin & fagotto" from Giovanni Battista Riccio's *Il terzo libro delle divine lodi musicali* (Venice, 1620).

752. Dickey, Bruce. "Untersuchungen zur historischen Auffassung des Vibratos auf Blasinstrumenten" [Investigations into the historical use of vibrato on wind instruments]. *Basler Jahrbuch für historische Musikpraxis* 2 (1978): 77-142.

An overview of the subject, shorter than one would expect from the number of pages because of the inclusion of many musical examples and tables. Divided into: questions of terminology, finger vibrato (including Ganassi, Cardan, Blankenburg, Hotteterre, *The Modern Musick-Master*), and breath vibrato (including Agricola). The ornament instructions in Salter and Carr are also discussed, because of the variability of the intervals they encompass (similar to Ganassi's *tremoli*) and because the tablature sometimes seems to indicate a vibrato rather than a trill or mordent. Of particular interest is the analysis of the use of the *flattement* in a duo suite by Pierre Philidor (1718), which is reproduced in facsimile. Includes fingering charts from Ganassi, Blankenburg, Hotteterre, and *The Modern Musick-Master*.

753. Moens-Haenen, Greta. *Das Vibrato in der Musik des Barock* [Vibrato in the music of the Baroque]. Graz: Akademische Druck- u. Verlagsanstalt, 1988.

Chapter 5 ("Das Vibrato auf Holzblasinstrumenten" [Vibrato on woodwind instruments], pp. 83-101) includes a long discussion on the finger vibrato for the recorder as described by authors of the 17th and 18th centuries, based partly on the work of Dickey (item 752.). Deals with Blankenburg, Hudgebut, Salter, Carr, *The Compleat Flute-Master*, Bismantova, Loulié, and Hotteterre.

754. Sterne, Colin C. "Quavering, Quivering, and J.J. Quantz." *The American Recorder* 18, no. 3 (November 1977): 71-72.

Presents historical evidence in support of the diaphragm vibrato.

Miscellaneous

755. Rowland-Jones, Anthony. "Putting the Clock Back." *The Recorder: Australia's Journal of Recorder and Early Music* 17 (September 1993): 12.

    Points out and translates a short passage in Marin Mersenne's *Harmonie universelle* (Paris, 1636) to the effect that "it is possible to sound a tune or a song on the recorder and at the same time to sing the bass line . . . in such a way that a person can play a duet on his own."

19

Technique and Performance (Modern)

This chapter discusses books and articles about recorder technique and modern performance practice. To save space, modern recorder methods and exercise books have been excluded (although it is not always possible to draw the line, item 756 being an obvious borderline case). General sources are followed by those on specific topics: articulation, breathing, dynamics, fingering and fingerings, intonation and tone, practicing, sight-reading, and vibrato. Note that "extended" or avant-garde techniques are treated separately in chapter 20, and matters connected with recorder ensembles are found in chapter 21.

Books

756. Hauwe, Walter van. *The Modern Recorder Player*. 3 vols. London: Schott, 1984–1992. ISBN 0901938963 (vol. 1; Schott ED 12150); ISBN 0946535043 (vol. 2; Schott ED 12270); ISBN 0946535191 (vol. 3; Schott ED 12361). German translation of vol. 1 by Matthias Weilenmann as *Moderne Blockflötentechnik*. Mainz: Schott, 1987.

A work of enormous importance: a detailed account of recorder technique in the 20th century written by a player and teacher of international standing. For the first time in history we can feel that professional secrets are being given away to the layperson. If only Ganassi and Hotteterre had told us as much as this. . . . Contents: Vol. 1: How to hold the recorder; How to move the fingers; About breathing; About articulation. Vol. 2: About scales and arpeggios; About trills; About vibrato; More about articulation. Vol. 3: The fingers; More about breathing; Humming; Articulation; Appendixes (Wind noise, Some more dynamics, Some tricks and gimmicks).

Vol. 1 reviewed by John Tyson and Louise Austin in *The American Recorder* 27, no. 2 (May 1986): 78–79 and by Ross Winters in *The Recorder and Music Magazine* 8, no. 3 (September 1984): 89–90. Vol. 2 reviewed by John Tyson in *The American Recorder* 29, no. 3 (August 1988): 123 and by P[aul] C[lark] in *The Recorder and Music Magazine* 9, no. 5 (March 1988): 134. Vol. 3 reviewed by Robert Ehrlich in *The Recorder Magazine* 12, no. 2 (June 1992): 51–52.

757. Rowland-Jones, Anthony. *Recorder Technique: Intermediate to Advanced.* 2nd ed. Oxford and New York: Oxford University Press, 1986. 170 p. ISBN 0193223422. Earlier edition, with title *Recorder Technique:* London: Oxford University Press, 1959. 151 p. OCLC #2087490.

The first edition was based on a series of articles that first appeared in *The Recorder News* and were later reprinted in *The American Recorder Society Newsletter* and *The American Recorder* (see items 768 and 769). The advice on technical matters was intelligent and the capsule descriptions of the repertory stimulating. The second edition, the subtitle of which makes manifest what was only implicit before, was thoroughly revised in the light of technical improvements to instruments and by players as well as research into recorder history and performance practice. Covers: knowing your instrument, breathing, tonguing, intonation, alternative fingerings, high notes, dynamics, tone, ornamentation, practice, and performance. Appendix 1 presents "a personal selection of music which an amateur player approaching the advanced stage will wish to explore (now more listings than commentary), and appendix 2 is a selected annotated bibliography. An essential book for amateurs. Reviewed by Martha Bixler in *The American Recorder* 29, no. 2 (May 1988): 65. Also reviewed [by Edgar Hunt] in *The Recorder and Music Magazine* 9, no. 1 (March 1987): 15. First edition reviewed by Walter Bergmann in *The Galpin Society Journal* 13 (July 1960): 106.

758. Waitzman, Daniel. *The Art of Playing the Recorder.* New York: AMS Press, 1978. xviii, 106 p. ISBN 0404160107.

As the author observes in his preface, this book is "not a 'method,' in the conventional sense." Like item 757, the book consists primarily of text, contains few musical examples, and describes the physical details of holding and playing the instrument without the assistance of photographs or illustrations. As supplementary reading for the serious recorder student, the book has much to offer, and Waitzman's approach is thought provoking if not sometimes controversial. His spirited advocacy of the bell-keyed recorder (see item 364 and others above) is continued here, but it does not dominate the book. The table at the end of chapter 7 includes alto fingerings up to $b\flat^4$, although Waitzman notes that those above f^4 "are of theoretical interest only."

Contents: Chapter 1: The Qualities Required of a Good Concert Recorder [including coverage and advocacy of the bell-keyed recorder]. Chapter 2: Holding the Recorder (Supporting the Instrument; The Position of the Hands). Chapter 3: Tonguing. Chapter 4: Tone (Embouchure; Breathing and Breath Control; Some Precautions for Public Performance; Vibrato; Some Remarks on Intonation). Chapter 5: The Operation of the Speaker-Vents and the Control of Intonation (Pinching and Half-holing; The Use of Additional Holes, and of Duplicate Fingerings, for Intonational Control). Chapter 6: Summary of Factors Governing Register Selection and Tone Quality; Some Additional Remarks on Tone. Chapter 7: Fingering.

Reviewed by Edgar Hunt in *The Galpin Society Journal* 33 (1980): 143 and *Recorder & Music* 6, no. 4 (December 1978): 122, and by John Turner in *Early Music* 7, no. 1 (January 1979): 123-25. In the *Recorder & Music* review, Hunt chides Waitzman for his preoccupation with the bell key. Waitzman defends himself in 6, no. 6 (June 1979): 183. "Indeed, the failure of the recorder community to adopt and develop the bell-keyed recorder suggests that the recorder lacks a viable class of true professionals—which is, in fact, exactly the case."

ARTICLES

759. Clark, Paul. "Not for You?" *Recorder & Music Magazine* 2, no. 11 (December 1968): 370-72.

    Advice for the intermediate player. Suggests learning trills, practicing scales and simple tunes in all keys, playing by ear, improvising, and learning new clefs and transpositions.

760. Clark, Paul. "Recorder Player's ABC." *Recorder & Music Magazine* 3, no. 2 (June 1969): 61-62.

    Covers, under alphabetic rubrics, topics relating to tonguing and articulation: the disputed value of adjusting mouth size and shape with shifts in register; tonguing syllables; standards of articulation; double tonguing; and vibrato.

761. Clark, Paul. "Yodelling for the Recorder Player." *Recorder & Music* 6, no. 9 (March 1980): 264-65.

    Exercises to develop proper breath support for the various registers of the instrument. Involves oscillating between notes in different registers—a technique Clark likens to yodelling.

762. Dolmetsch, Carl F. "On Playing the Recorder." *The Consort* 7 (July 1950): 18-21.

    An introduction to recorder technique.

763. Hauwe, Walter van. "Fundamental Recorder Techniques." *The Recorder: Journal of the Victorian Recorder Guild* 4 (May 1986): 18–23; 5 (November 1986): 7–11; 6 (June 1987): 20–25.
Adapted from item 756.

764. Hauwe, Walter van. "Towards a Modern Recorder Technique." *The Recorder: Journal of the Victorian Recorder Guild* 12 (December 1990): 20–22.

Van Hauwe describes having worked to get the recorder taken seriously in Holland, the salutary effect that learning Berio's *Gesti* had on Frans Brüggen's playing, the vastly increased virtuosity of recorder students in the last fifteen years, the new importance of ensemble work for professionals, the need for better recorder repertory, and what kinds of features we might reasonably expect in a truly modern recorder.

* Hunt, Edgar. "Playing the Bass Recorder." Cited above as item 138.

765. Kneihs, Hans Maria. "Musical Structure and Interpretation with Reference to Marcello's Sonata in D Minor." *The Recorder: Journal of the Victorian Recorder Guild* 3 (November 1985): 15–19.

Analyzes the first movement of Benedetto Marcello's sonata from a simple Schenkerian standpoint. Also discusses the importance of analysis to performers. Summarizes the three principal means of interpretation on the recorder: dynamics, rhythmical alteration, and articulation. Finally, discusses using these means to interpret the Marcello movement in the light of the analysis.

766. Michatz, Hans-Dieter. "You Must Have a Story To Tell." *The Recorder: Journal of the Victorian Recorder Guild* 7 (December 1987): 17–18.

A brief plea for recorder players to experiment with approaches to performance in order to appeal to a wider audience.

767. Mundhenke, Heike. "Blockflöte und Klavier—Möglichkeiten und Schwierigkeiten des Zusammenspiels" [Recorder and piano—possibilities and difficulties of playing together]. *Tibia* 16, no. 3 (1991): 501–8.

The repertory for recorder and piano includes both traditional and avant-garde works of the 20th century. The playing of these instruments together brings up problems of intonation as well as balance (because of

Technique and Performance (Modern)

their different sound quality and dynamic range). Recorder players should, in particular, do everything they can to increase, or imply the increase of, their dynamic range. Goes on to discuss the problems in two sample pieces from the repertory: Gordon Jacob's *Suite* and John Casken's *Thymehaze*.

768. Rowland-Jones, A. "Technique." *The American Recorder* 1, no. 1 (Winter 1960): 3-4, 6, 18.

    Concerns practice. Specific topics include breathing and tonguing, fingering, thumbing, and sightreading. "Eleventh in the series of articles by Mr. [Rowland-]Jones which have been reprinted, with permission from *The Recorder News* of England, in the *The American Recorder Society Newsletter*."

769. Rowland-Jones, A. "Technique." *The American Recorder* 1, no. 2 (Spring 1960): 3-6.

    Concerns preparation for performance. Specific topics include style, speed, phrasing, dynamics, ornamentation, and direction. Twelfth and final installment in the series.

770. Wyatt, Theo. "On Being Your Own Teacher." (The Recorder in School) *The Recorder and Music Magazine* 1, no. 5 (May 1964): 133-34.

    Brief article on recorder technique written for school teachers who are not professional musicians but who are required to teach recorder. The treatment of the topic is concise and to the point, and any beginning player would find Wyatt's advice helpful—particularly his discussion of fingering, the thumb, breathing, and articulation.

SPECIFIC TOPICS

ARTICULATION

771. Davis, Alan. "Articulation on the Recorder." *Recorder & Music* 5, no. 1 (March 1975): 5-6.

    Questions and answers. Covers: the meaning of "articulation"; the proper way to tongue; variety in tonguing (long/short and hard/soft); articulation as an expressive device; double and triple tonguing.

* Reiss, Scott. "Articulation: The Key to Expressive Playing." Cited above as item 714.

772. Rowland-Jones, Anthony. "A Slur on Slurring? A Problem in Recorder Playing." *NEMA Journal* 9 (July 1988): 1-6.

The problem in question is slurring across the recorder's register breaks (alto: g^2-a^2, d^3-e^3, f^3-g^3)—difficult to do without causing "at the least, a tiny articulation transient" (click). Prefers to use light tonguing (what he calls "y tonguing"). Rejects Scott Reiss's view (see item 714) that recorder players should *never* use true slurs, which he believes existed even in the Baroque era, although he concedes that lightly tongued slurs are "firmer, more distinct, and project better."

773. Tattersall, Malcolm. "When is a Slur not a Slur?" *The Recorder: Journal of the Victorian Recorder Guild* 11 (June 1990): 13–16.

    The basic answer to Tattersall's pertinent question is, of course, when it's a tie or a phrasing mark. He gives guidance on how to tell a true slur from a phrasing mark, as well as which slurs can be ignored.

BREATHING

774. Edler-Busch, Elli. "'Blasdruck' oder 'druckschwacher Ansatz'?" ['Breath-pressure' or 'weak-pressure blowing'?]. *Tibia* 6, no. 2 (1981): 319–27.

    A long article on what the author has dubbed the "weak-pressure blowing technique." Because it is thought to be "quite self-evident," this has never been thoroughly described. Applies the technique to the flute and recorder.

775. Fischer, Johannes. "Vom Traum der Unendlichkeit, oder Versuch einer Anleitung zur Zirkuläratmung für Blockflötisten" [Of the dream of endlessness; or, Essay of an introduction to circular breathing for recorder players]. *Tibia* 18, no. 1 (1993): 346–51.

    Describes how the author became familiar with circular breathing, discusses recorder pieces that require or are facilitated by this technique, then gives a detailed description of how to learn it. Concludes with a short bibliography. See also the companion article by Wladimir Katchmartchik, "Zur Entwicklungsgeschichte der Permanentatmung" [On the developmental history of breathing with permanent exhalation], *Tibia* 18, no. 1 (1993): 341–46.

776. Gray, Arlen. "Air for the Recorder." *The American Recorder* 6, no. 1 (Winter 1965): 6–8.

    Instructions and exercises for developing proper breathing techniques.

DYNAMICS

777. Bergmann, Walter. "Recorder Dynamics." *Recorder & Music* 4, no. 9 (March 1974): 316–17.

   Argues that dynamic contrast is possible on the recorder. The pitch of the lowest notes is affected only marginally by a change in breath pressure. High notes can be corrected by adjusting the size of the thumbhole aperture. For the middle octave, pitch can be corrected by using alternate fingerings. Mentions several mechanical devices for counteracting unwanted pitch changes. The perception of a shift in dynamics can also be enhanced by varying articulation.

778. Fischer, Johannes. *Die dynamische Blockflöte* [The dynamic recorder]. Celle: Moeck, 1990. 44 p. ISBN 387549041X. Edition Moeck Nr. 4048.

   A slim but still valuable book—a combination of textbook and method—on an important subject. Chapter 1 lists the basic dynamic properties of the recorder. Chapter 2 outlines the methods of achieving dynamics (decrescendo and crescendo; dynamic gradation of single notes or groups and within the course of a melody). Chapter 3 discusses and illustrates technical problems in breathing and fingering. Chapter 4, on application, outlines the criteria of a good instrument, then dynamic variation in solo, duet, and ensemble playing as well as in the music of various eras. Chapter 5, "practical realization," introduces (1) a system of symbols for fingerholes and fingerings, (2) a series of exercises for independence of fingers, breath pressure, and finger technique, (3) notes on fingering combinations, and (4) examples from the repertory. Chapter 6 consists of fingering tables at intervals of a quarter-tone. The final chapter is a short bibliography. Reviewed by Pete Rose in *American Recorder* 32, no. 2 (June 1991): 22–23.

779. Sokoll, Christa. "Dynamik des Blockflötenspiels" [Dynamics in recorder playing]. *Musica* 40, no. 1 (January–February 1986): 31–37.

   Describes the use of alternative fingerings to produce real dynamic contrasts on the recorder. Gives many examples from 20th-century works plus two of the Baroque echo effect. See also her letter in *Tibia* 18, no. 1 (1993): 417. The author brings the article up to date in a letter to the editor of *Tibia* 18, no. 1 (1993): 417.

FINGERING AND FINGERINGS

780. Clark, Paul. "Digitalism." *Recorder & Music* 6, no. 7 (September 1979): 197–98.

An essay emphasizing that there is more to recorder playing than simply putting the correct fingers in the correct places and blowing. We should "know first the sounds we want to make, then we should know the instrument we mean to use. Instruments and their fingerings are Means. The Ends are the sounds we strive for."

781. Clark, Paul. "Goldenfingers—1: A Guide to Recorder Technique." *Recorder & Music* 4, no. 7 (September 1973): 234–36.

    An excellent essay review of methods and exercise books that concern finger technique.

782. Clark, Paul. "Inflectious Cases." *The Recorder and Music Magazine* 8, no. 1 (March 1984): 17–18.

    Concerns the basic principles of adjusting recorder fingering: "covering holes below the 'speaking' hole will flatten the pitch; the further the added finger is from the speaking hole, the less effect it will have; the more fingers are added, the greater the flattening will be." These rules can be applied to adjust intonation and to increase the dynamic range of the instrument.

783. Davenport, LaNoue, and Erich Katz. "Controversy: I. Alternate Fingerings." *The American Recorder* 5, no. 4 (November 1964): 11–13. Reprinted from *ARS Newsletter* 20.

    Davenport argues that alternate fingerings should almost never be used. Followed by a reply from Erich Katz, who denounces a dogmatic opposition to their use.

784. Davis, Alan. "Fingering the Recorder." *Recorder & Music* 4, no. 12 (December 1974): 439–40.

    Questions and answers about fingering technique. Recommends practicing exercises and scales to improve technique rather than relying on traditional repertory. Explains how to dissect difficult passages. Describes proper finger and thumb positioning. Explains the purpose and use of alternate fingerings.

*   Halfpenny, Eric. "Fingering." Cited above as item 157.

785. Höffer-von Winterfeld, Linde. "Griffkombinationen und Klangfarben auf der Blockflöte" [Fingering combinations and tone color on the recorder]. *Tibia* 1, no. 2 (1976): 77–80.

Höffer-von Winterfeld has followed up on Michael Vetter's *Il flauto dolce ed acerbo* by developing his ideas about fingerings systematically in *Der neue Weg* (Hamburg: Hans Sikorski, ?) and practically in *21 Lektionen* (Hamburg: Sikorski, 1967) and *Diarium für Jeannette* (Zürich: Pelikan, ?). Stresses that the fingers must not hold the recorder tight but balance it among the lower lip, the right thumb, and one of three fingers of the left hand (first, second, or third). Then outlines her fingering system, emphasizing alternative fingerings that permit nuance and variety in timbre. Finally, mentions, but does not elaborate on, the problem of playing in tune with alternative fingerings.

786. Massy, Jim. "The Taped Recorder, or, 'How Low Can You Get.'" *Recorder & Music* 7, no. 6 (June 1982): 142.
    Instructions for using Scotch tape on the lowest fingerholes to demonstrate the effects of leaks caused by faulty finger placement.

787. Reichenthal, Eugene. "Effective Use of Exceptional Fingerings." *American Recorder* 32, no. 4 (December 1991): 16–17.
    A collection of miscellaneous alternate fingerings that address problems of dynamic contrast (particularly in the Affettuoso movement of Telemann's D-Minor Sonata (TWV 41:d4) and the production of certain high notes ($c\#^3$, e^3, c^4). Most of the alternate fingerings involve shading or leaking. Letter from Anthony Rowland-Jones in 33, no. 2 (June 1992): 35.

High notes (including $f\#^3$)

See also chapter 18, "Performance Practices (Historical)," under the subheading "Fingering and fingerings" (pp. 235–36).

788. Dolmetsch, Carl. "High F Sharp." *The Recorder & Music Magazine* 8, no. 9 (March 1986): 275.
    Claims discovery (1929) of the "knee technique" for playing $f\#^3$ on the alto recorder and of the method for slurring up to the note from the E or F below (published 1954, discovered earlier), as well as the invention and patenting of the bell key. Also gives a fingering for the note.

789. Hunt, Edgar. "Recorder Fingerings." *The Galpin Society Journal* 14 (1961): 75–76.
    Discusses the use of a key to produce $f\#^3$ on the alto recorder.

790. Hunt, Edgar. "Fingering the High Notes on the Recorder." *The Galpin Society Journal* 11 (1958): 90–91.
Fingerings for f♯³–c⁴.

791. Juritz, J.W.F. "Recorder Fingerings." *The Galpin Society Journal* 13 (1960): 91–92.
Mentions his discovery of a satisfactory fingering for f♯³ on the alto recorder by stopping the bore at the bottom of the foot joint, and his subsequent invention of a bell key. Gives alternative fingerings for some high notes that it facilitates. Also mentions several fingerings, of which – 1-3 -567 is typical, which sound at two close frequencies, depending on breath pressure. Claims that these "are of interest as showing how far current acoustical theory is from accounting for the behaviour of the recorder." (It is in fact possible to calculate the resonances associated with fingerings such as these. Martin [item 411] analyses a related fingering.)

Thumb technique

792. "Forum." *American Recorder* 31, no. 1 (March 1990): 33.
Bernard Krainis, Scott Reiss, and Philip Levin offer their thoughts on thumb technique—in particular, the advantages and disadvantages of using the thumbnail on the thumbhole.

793. Glassgold, Cook. "The Amateur's Wandering Thumb." *The American Recorder* 4, no. 2 (May 1963): 15.
Advises affixing a piece of wood or plastic above the thumb hole to prevent the thumb from "slipping away from home base."

Trills

794. Rowland-Jones, A. "Three Blind Mice and Baroque Trills." *The Recorder and Music Magazine* 8, no. 1 (March 1984): 14–16.
An exercise to develop trilling techniques, based on the well-known tune.

795. Rowland-Jones, A. "Some Trill Fingerings in the Three Blind Mice (TBM) Exercise." *The Recorder and Music Magazine* 8, no. 2 (June 1984): 47–48.
Sequel to item **794**, covering the application of the exercise to keys other than C major and the necessary alternate fingerings. Letter from Edgar Gordon in 8, no. 3 (September 1984): 79.

Technique and Performance (Modern)

INTONATION AND TONE

See also chapter 16, "Maintenance, Improvement, and Restoration," under the subheadings "Tone quality" and "Voicing and tuning" (pp. 173–76).

796. Bergmann, Walter. "Teaching Intonation." (The Recorder in School) *The Recorder and Music Magazine* 1, no. 10 (August 1965): 294–96.

    Advice on teaching children to hear and to correct intonation problems. Emphasizes the importance of training the ear to recognize and diagnose the problem; by comparison, adjusting the pitch is a simple matter.

797. Carlson, Marilyn, and Richard Jacoby. "Intonation." *The American Recorder* 13, no. 2 (May 1972): 43–45.

    Suggests several techniques and exercises to improve intonation. Emphasizes the importance of developing eartraining and sightsinging abilities. Describes how an instrument should be warmed up, tuned, and adjusted. Shows how alternate fingerings and shading can be used to correct problems with individual pitches. Gives instructions for adjusting the size of tone holes.

* Kottick, Edward Leon. *Tone and Intonation on the Recorder.* Cited above as item 524.

798. Praetorius, Martin. "Elektronische Stimmgeräte—für Blockflöten zu empfehlen?" [Electronic tuners—to be recommended for recorders?] *Tibia* 12, no. 2 (1987): 453–54.

    Gives advice on how to use the electronic tuners made by two manufacturers with recorders.

* Read, Robin. "Recorder Tone." Cited above as item 336.

799. "Recorder Tone." *Recorder & Music Magazine* 3, no. 4 (December 1969): 128–30.

    Reprinted from a pamphlet prepared by the House of Schreiber. Describes how a recorder generates sound and the effect that breath pressure has on tone, dynamics, and pitch. The quality that affects tone most significantly is the presence of upper partials, which contributes to the richness of the tone. Includes several charts.

800. Reichenthal, Eugene. "Partial Venting." *Recorder & Music* 5, no. 6 (June 1976): 193–95.

Describes several alternate fingerings that involve the partial venting of certain holes. Shows how the fingerings might be employed to improve tone, flexibility, and intonation.

801. Reiss, Scott. "Pitch Control: Shading and Leaking." *The American Recorder* 28, no. 4 (November 1987): 136–39.

Discusses the controlling of pitch on the recorder by means of shading ("the partial obstruction of an open hole, resulting in the lowering of the pitch") and leaking ("the partial uncovering of a closed hole, resulting in the raising of the pitch"). Letters from Gene Reichenthal and Anthony Rowland-Jones in 29, no. 2 (May 1988): 73–74. Reichenthal picks up on Rowland-Jones's discussion of the c^3 and d^3 in Telemann's D-Minor Sonata (TWV 41:d4) in 29, no. 3 (August 1988): 128.

802. Zimmermann, Manfredo. "Differenzierte, nicht temperierte Intonation, oder: Was klingt falscher als zwei (Block)Flöten?" [Differentiated, not tempered, intonation; or What sounds more out of tune than two flutes/recorders?]. *Tibia* 18, no. 4 (1993): XXXVII–XL.

In flute and recorder playing, difference tones are quite audible. (The phenomenon was even remarked upon by Georg Andreas Sorge as long ago as 1745.) Gives some examples, then describes how players can use difference tones to practice playing better in tune (seven sample exercises). Concludes with a short bibliography.

PRACTICING

803. Andresen, Ken. "Don't Waste Your Time Practicing!" *American Recorder* 32, no. 4 (December 1991): 7–10.

Suggestions for focusing practice time and making practice more efficient. Includes specific routines for warming up and preparing repertory.

804. Carduelis, Susan. "Use Your Head—Play from Your Heart." *American Recorder* 33, no. 2 (June 1992): 20–22.

Describes how practice techniques can be improved through an awareness of how the brain works. Repetitive actions are controlled by the lateral cerebellum, which processes small patterns of motion more effectively and reliably than large ones. Difficult passages should therefore be broken down into small parts, which can be isolated and repeated until each becomes automatic. Also reviews the functions of the left and right hemispheres of the brain and suggests that practice sessions progress from mechanical exercises (left hemisphere) to the most expressive (right hemisphere).

805. Cline, Gilbert D. *The Cornetto: A Guide Toward Performance, Within Historical Context, Indicating the Use of the Recorder as a Companion Instrument.* D.M.A. essay, University of Oregon, 1990. 295 p. OCLC #25142669 or #26078427.

    Largely a study of cornett playing based on historical practice (the meaning of the first part of the awkwardly expressed title). Advises would-be cornettists, especially those without woodwind experience, to play the recorder concurrently, in order to develop finger facility while resting the embouchure.

806. Dinn, Freda. "The Art of Practising." *Recorder & Music Magazine* 2, no. 11 (December 1968): 355-57.

    Covers: posture, technique, practicing, interpretation, keyboard accompaniment, and sight-reading.

807. Leber, Eric. "An Approach to Practicing." *The American Recorder* 3, no. 2 (May 1962): 3-6; 3, no. 3 (August 1962): 6-8.

    Covers: stance, breathing, tone, tonguing, dynamics, fingering, exercises, ear training, rhythm, "eye training," and "the practice regime."

808. Prior, Susan. "Enjoy Your Practicing and Improve Your Playing." *The American Recorder* 26, no. 3 (August 1985): 113-15.

    Advice on practicing the following: breath control, playing by ear, sight-reading, intonation, scales and arpeggios, and difficult passages.

809. Prior, Susan. "Warming Up on the Recorder." *The American Recorder* 25, no. 1 (February 1984): 12-13.

    Begins by describing the purpose of warming up. Emphasizes the importance of mental preparation. Recommends that one quarter of a practice session be devoted to warming up. Suggests specific exercises to improve breathing, tone production, finger control, and tonguing.

810. Roth, Ruth C. "Ten or More Ways to Improve One's Playing without Touching the Recorder." *The American Recorder* 12, no. 3 (August 1971): 82-86.

    Describes areas of development that one can work on away from the recorder: posture, diaphragmatic and abdominal breathing, long breaths, rhythm, finger exercises, tonguing, ear training, listening to professional performers, reading, and use of a tape recorder.

811. Wollitz, Kenneth. "Some Random Thoughts on Practicing." (Der Getreue Musikmeister) *The American Recorder* 15, no. 3 (August 1974): 81–85.

Well-written, sensible advice. Emphasizes the importance of self-awareness and the benefits of daily practice—regardless of how short the session might be. Describes exercises for improving tone control and gaining facility with high notes. Encourages productive use of the metronome. Suggests fragmentation and repetition for working out difficult passages. Chapter 2 of item 14 is a considerably expanded version of this article.

SIGHT-READING

812. Ferguson, Suzanne. "Sight-Reading." *The American Recorder* 26, no. 2 (May 1985): 66–68.

Advice for consort players. Since most sight-reading problems involve rhythm, the suggestions concern counting, keeping one's place, and working through difficult rhythmic passages.

813. Hunt, Edgar. "Some Thoughts on the Notation of Music for Recorders." *The Recorder Magazine* 13, no. 2 (September 1993): 37–38.

A brief historical survey of the various clefs that have been used to notate the pitch of recorders since the 16th century.

814. [Koch, John]. "Editor's Notes: On Reading Alto Clef, with Special Thanks to Kenneth Wollitz." *The American Recorder* 11, no. 1 (Winter 1970): 33.

A brief introduction, offering no particular advice other than to "do it and do it often." Wollitz suggests three Hortus Musicus editions (134, 136, and 137) as a suitable course of study.

815. Krainis, Bernard, and Erich Katz. "Controversy: II. The Bass Recorder's Clef." *The American Recorder* 5, no. 4 (November 1964): 13–14. Reprinted from the *ARS Newsletter* 24.

Krainis argues that experienced bass-recorder players expect parts to be notated in bass clef. Katz, in defense of an edition of his with the bass part notated in treble clef, explains that the treble clef should pose no difficulty, since most bass players first learned a higher pitched instrument. Krainis agrees, but maintains that the practice is confusing and should be used only when unavoidable. See also the exchange between Lionel H. James and Walter Bergmann in *Recorder and Music Magazine* 4, no. 1 (March 1972): 12.

816. [Newman, Joel]. "Score Versus Parts." (Flauto Piccolo's Corner) *The American Recorder* 1, no. 3 (Summer 1960): 5.
An argument in favor of performing from scores. Letter from Roy Miller in 2, no. 1 (Winter 1961): 26.

817. Wollitz, Kenneth. "Learning to Read the Staff in New Ways." *The American Recorder* 26, no. 1 (February 1985): 13–15.
Covers four skills that increase a player's versatility in an ensemble: learning both F and C fingering, reading up an octave on the alto, reading bass clef, and reading alto clef. Suggests methods, exercises, and repertory.

VIBRATO

818. Davis, Alan. "Vibrato on the Recorder." *Recorder & Music* 4, no. 10 (June 1974): 350–51.
A good, short introduction to the technique and application of vibrato.

20

New Techniques in Twentieth-Century Recorder Music

Several book-length studies deal with the topic of "extended" or avant-garde recorder techniques in the 20th century. These three are the most important:

819. O'Kelly, Eve Elizabeth. *The Recorder in Twentieth-Century Music*. M.Phil. thesis, Goldsmith's College, University of London, 1985. Vol. 1: *The Recorder, its Music and Technique in the Twentieth Century;* Vol. 2: *A Catalogue of Twentieth-Century Recorder Music*.

    The first volume considers the instrument, gives a history of its revival, surveys the modern recorder repertory (serious rather than educational; conservative and avant-garde), then discusses avant-garde techniques. The catalog is arranged by medium (pieces for one recorder, then those for two recorders, etc.). Each entry gives the (O'Kelly) catalog number of the work, composer's name and dates, the title and publication date, the publisher, commercial recordings (if any), and the exact instrumentation. There is a composer index and a list of publishers (address given as city and country only).

820. O'Kelly, Eve. *The Recorder Today*. Cambridge: Cambridge University Press, 1990. xiv, 179 p. ISBN 0521366607.

    In book form, O'Kelly's study of the recorder in the 20th century (item **819**) has been improved by making the order of some of the sections more logical, bringing the writing up to date in the light of new research and compositions, and borrowing Herman Rechberger's tables of non-standard fingerings for the alto recorder (see item **827**). Unfortunately, the catalog has also been cut down considerably, so that instead of "comprising as full a listing as possible of modern recorder compositions," it now "contains some 400 works out of about 800 known to me," the selection having been made on the basis of suitability for professional or semi-professional performance, current availability, and "sufficient musical merit." It still represents one of the best books ever written about the recorder. Reviewed by Pete Rose in *The American Recorder* 31, no. 4 (December 1990): 31–32. Reviewed by P[aul] C[lark] in *The Recorder Magazine* 10, no. 4 (December 1990): 113.

821. Vetter, Michael. *Il flauto dolce ed acerbo. I: Anweisungen und Übungen für Spieler neuer Blockflötenmusik = Instructions and Exercises for Players of New Recorder Music.* Celle: Moeck, 1969. Edition Moeck Nr. 4009. 87 p. OCLC #7684727. Parallel text in German and English.

The long-awaited *magnum opus* by one of the two main pioneers of avant-garde recorder music. (A note states laconically that the five-year delay in publishing was for "many reasons . . . for which neither the publisher not least the aut[h]or can be blamed." Whether the reader could really "be sure that Michael Vetter's method is today as actual [up to date] as at the time of its beginning" is another matter.) As these quotations suggest, the English translation is quaint enough to be humorous but still accurate enough to be understood. The title of Vetter's book celebrates the transformation of the recorder, by means of new techniques, into "a new instrument which combines and mixes the characteristics of the *flauto dolce* with that of a '*flauto acerbo*' in a natural way." Nearly half the book consists of fingering charts—for regular notes, flageolet tones, and multiphonics in the open, closed, and covered registers. The remainder consists of discussions of embouchure, articulation, breathing, vibrato, and dynamics, illustrated with musical examples from the literature of the avant garde (or, in some cases, Baroque or modern derrière garde). Fifteen pages of exercises at the end explore these special techniques. Daniel Waitzman, in his review (*The American Recorder* 11, no. 1 [Winter 1970]: 16–19), noted that no attempt is made to identify the relative importance of individual fingerings in the list. He also questioned the need for special "white noise" fingerings, since such sounds can be produced "with virtually every fingering, through variations in embouchure." Vetter does not mention covering or shading the window, or humming or whistling into the instrument. Another objection that might be made, incidentally, is that all recorder fingerings, and particularly the special ones, are very much dependent upon the individual instrument (Vetter used to play a Moeck); therefore, tables have limited value. Waitzman concluded—and we concur: "Despite its limitations, this is a book that must be studied by all serious students of the recorder, whether or not they are interested in playing twentieth-century music." Also reviewed by David Lasocki in *Recorder & Music Magazine* 3, no. 4 (December 1969): 146. Part II of the book has never appeared.

Other General Writings

822. Baur, Jürg. "Revolution der Blockflöte" [Recorder revolution]. *Instrumentenbau-Zeitschrift* 17, no. 2 (1963): 363–64.

Begins by noting the erstwhile place of the recorder as an instrument for children, "Hausmusik," and folk music, with restricted compass and means of expression. Goes on to relate how Baur met Michael Vetter and learned about his development of new techniques. Briefly describes Baur's *Mutazioni* and *Incontri*, which make use of some of these techniques. Finally, encourages other recorder players to take them up and looks forward to new developments in recorder making.

823. Braun, Gerhard. *Neue Klangwelt auf der Blockflöte* [New sound world on the recorder]. (Musikpädagogische Bibliothek, Band 16) Wilhelmshaven: Heinrichshofen, 1978. 100 p. ISBN 3795901766.

A short overview of avant-garde recorder technique and notation, profusely illustrated with musical examples. A short consideration of pedagogical aspects, including group improvisation with recorders, is followed by the heart of the book: discussions (including useful analyses) of works by Karkoschka (*mit/gegen sich selbst*), Lechner (*Varianti*), Heider (*Musik im Diskant*), Schönbach (*Canzona da sonar III*), Braun (*minimal music II, Monologe I, Nachtstücke*), and Berio (*Gesti*). Followed by the briefest of looks forward, and a short bibliography of writings and works. Chapter 2 also published separately (see item 1322); an expanded version of the discussion of *mit/gegen sich selbst* published as item 1365.

824. Clemencic, René. "Neue Klang- und Ausdrucksmöglichkeiten der Blockflöte" [New possibilities for sound and expression on the recorder]. *Oesterreichische Musikzeitschrift* 26, no. 4 (April 1971): 222–30.

An excellent overview of new recorder techniques, beginning with the little-asked question "Why?" (Clemencic sees the interest in new sound possibilities of traditional instruments as part of the reaction against serial composition and the exploration of electronic sounds.) Divides the techniques into "normal instrument" (blowing, singing, speaking and laughing, piping, hitting), "prepared instrument" (covered, closed, covering the labium, narrowing the windway; playing without footpiece, without mouthpiece, mouthpiece only), and combinations thereof. Illustrated with examples from the repertory. Concludes with a short list of pieces (including several of his own unpublished ones).

825. Gannon, Lee. "Studies for the Beginner in 20th Century Performance." *American Recorder* 31, no. 4 (December 1990): 20–22.

A description of Gannon's six concert etudes for alto recorder, which explore a number of modern performance techniques. Includes a reproduction of Etude No. 1, with accompanying notes for performance.

826. Rechberger, Herman. "Anwendung der Blockflöte in der zeitgenössischen Musik" [The use of the recorder in contemporary music]. Unpublished typescript, 1977, rev. 1982. 40, [xii] p. Formerly available through the Finnish Music Information Centre, Helsinki, Finland.

Consists largely of special fingerings for variations in tone color, trills, dynamics, microintervals, closed and covered registers, flageolet tones, multiphonics, multiphonic trills, and whistle tones. Notes on notation for manipulating parts of the instrument, producing vibrato and oscillations, singing into the instrument, etc., with examples from Berio, Braun, Busotti/Vetter, Dolci, Gümbel, Hashagen, Linde, Rechberger, Rihm, and Serocki. Estimates that the number of fingering combinations on the recorder is around 19,500.

827. Rechberger, Herman. *Die Blockflöte in der zeitgenössischen Musik* [The recorder in contemporary music]. 1987. 78 p. Can be ordered from the author, Laajavuorenkuja 5 B 11, 01620 Vantaa 62, Finland, or the Finnish Music Information Centre, Runeberginkatu 15 A 1, 00100 Helsinki, Finland.

A complete revision of item **826**, thanks to computer technology (Macintosh). Notes on articulation, vibrato, glissandi, and tremolos. Then fingering tables for basic notes; trills; alternate fingerings; closed, open, and half-closed notes; tone-color fingerings; dynamics; microintervals; closed and covered registers; flageolet tones and multiphonics in all registers; and whistle tones. Followed by notes on notation in works by Berio, Braun, Busotti/Vetter, Heider, Linde, Rechberger, Rihm, Serocki. Indexes of fingerings by basic note (alto recorder, soprano recorder) and a "statistical index" of single notes on the alto recorder (a total of 2,519 fingerings).

828. Thorn, Benjamin. "'New' Sounds from Old Pipes." *The Recorder: Journal of the Victorian Recorder Guild* 10 (December 1989): 5–9.

A thoughtful and intelligent discussion of some modern recorder techniques by a recorder-playing composer who makes use of them. Covers ways of creating the illusion of dynamic range (rhythmic shifting, tonguing, timbral alterations) and "brave new sounds" (flutter tonguing, glissandi and portamenti, burbles, percussion effects, multiphonics, and singing).

829. Troman, Robin. "Technique contemporaine de la flûte à bec" [Contemporary recorder technique]. *Flûte à bec & instruments anciens* 11 (June 1984): 12.

   The inaugural article in the series, announcing no fewer than twenty-four further articles covering the subjects: acoustics, lip (of the recorder), body alone, desynchronization, discography, fingerings, fingers, dynamics, flageolet tones, flutter tonguing, glissando, microintervals, multiphonics, repertory, circular breathing, breath, solfège, sputtato, ultra-high notes, head alone, trills, vibrato, voice, and whistle tones. Unfortunately, the series was never completed.

830. Troman, Robin. "Souffle" [Breath]. *Flûte à bec & instruments anciens* 13/14 (December 1984/March 1985): 15.

   Summarizes with musical examples (by DuBois, Berio, Botero, Hirose, and D. Tosi) several means of producing an "impure" tone on the recorder through the passage of air (flutter tonguing with air, sputato with air, double tonguing with air, white noise, and covering the window).

831. Troman, Robin. "Flûte à bec contemporaine" [Avant-garde recorder]. *Flûte à bec & instruments anciens* 15 (June 1985): 6–8; 16 (October 1985): 2; 19 (September 1986): 3–4.

   Part 1: discusses with musical examples the use of the body of the recorder alone; desynchronization of fingers, tongue, and voice; and voice plus instrumental sounds. Part 2: describes a method for learning circular breathing. Part 3: briefly discusses the fundamental produced by covering the end of the recorder and the result of manipulating it, notably a series of partials similar to the "whistle tones" of the flute.

832. Vetter, Michael. "Apropos Blockflöte." *Melos: Zeitschrift für neue Musik* 35, no. 12 (December 1968): 461–68.

   An overview of avant-garde techniques for the recorder, apparently aimed at composers. Briefly surveys: alternative fingerings, range, tone color, dynamics, vibrato, percussive effects, ring modulator effect, and multiphonics.

833. Vetter, Michael. "The Challenge of New Music." *Recorder and Music Magazine* 2, no. 5 (May 1967): 133. In German as: "Die Chance der Blockflöte in der neuen Musik" [The

prospect for the recorder in new music]. *Kontakte* /3 (1966): 107-8.

Introduces the recorder as an instrument for truly modern music, including a listing of its potential: quarter tones, alternative fingerings with different tone colors, extended range, glissandi, multiphonics, singing into the instrument, loose lips, wood or paper in the wind canal, moving the block, manipulation of the labium, as well as various kinds of vibrato and articulation. The English version is an abridgement of the German.

COMPOSERS' GUIDES

834. Enfield, Patrick. "Writing for the Recorder and Piano." *Recorder and Music Magazine* 4, no. 5 (March 1973): 169.

    Advice from a published composer. Letter from A.D. Jackson in 4, no. 6 (June 1973): 205 offers more suggestions. Reply by Enfield follows.

835. Glassgold, Cook. "Why Compose for the Recorder?" *The American Recorder* 3, no. 1 (February 1962): 3-4.

    The thoughts of composer Seymour Barab.

836. Margolis, Bob. "A Composer's Guide to the Recorder." *The American Recorder* 16, no. 4 (February 1976): 113-22.

    Includes charts of instrument registers, underblown harmonics, quarter tones, multiphonics, and closed-bell tones. The bibliography lists representative recorder music and books which may be of use to the composer who is unfamiliar with the instrument. Corrections and additions by Stephen A. Malinowski in 17, no. 1 (May 1976): 6.

837. Silbiger, Lex, and Alexander Breed. "Notes on Composing for the Recorder." *The American Recorder* 6, no. 4 (Fall 1965): 5-6.

    A cursory explanation of range, fingering, dynamics, articulation, vibrato, and notation—what one would expect to find in a good orchestration textbook. Daniel Waitzman, in 7, no. 1 (Winter 1966): 30, takes issue with some of the advice and questions why special effects were not mentioned in the article.

* Turner, John. "Writing for the Recorder." Cited above as item 50.

838. Ward, Stuart. "Composing for the Advanced Recorder Player." *Recorder & Music* 5, no. 4 (December 1975): 118-20.

Covers: the various sizes of recorders and effective ways of combining them with other instruments; range (with a chart showing fingerings for f#³-c⁴ on the alto); dynamics; style; avant-garde techniques. Letter from A. Scott in 5, no. 6 (June 1976): 216 concerns Ward's comments on the guitar as an accompanying instrument.

839. Worrall, David. "Composing for a Large Recorder Ensemble." *The Recorder: Journal of the Victorian Recorder Guild* 3 (November 1985): 8–12.

Discusses the characteristics of recorders in large ensembles, and particularly the problems of performances by amateurs. Also describes his *Silhouettes* for recorder ensemble and tape (1984), written to exploit these characteristics and overcome these problems.

MULTIPHONICS

840. Barata, Antonio. "Sources of Information on Woodwind Multiphonics: An Annotated Bibliography." *Perspectives of New Music* 26, no. 1 (Winter 1988): 246–56.

An excellent way of gaining perspective on the use of multiphonics in recorder playing. The only recorder sources discussed are Alan Davis's *Treble Recorder Technique* (London: Novello, 1983) and items **821, 832,** and **836**.

841. Kientzy, Martine. *Les sons multiples aux flûtes à bec* [Multiphonics on the recorder]. Paris: Editions Salabert, 1982.

Not seen. According to the review by Claude Letteron in *Flûte à bec* 5 (December 1982): 38 it "Reviews all the special fingerings that enable multiphonics to be obtained . . . as well as quarter tones above and below a given note on all sizes of recorder. Still, the work specifies that it includes only a 'selection of 1,191 fingerings from the 2,170 indexed during the course of preliminary research.'"

842. McCauley, Denis. "Playing 'Chords' on the Recorder." *Recorder & Music Magazine* 3, no. 4 (December 1969): 124–25.

A brief introduction to multiphonics on the recorder, accompanied by a chart showing eighteen fingerings and the resulting "chords." Item **843** is a response to this article.

843. Clark, Paul. "The Rechorder." *Recorder & Music Magazine* 3, no. 7 (September 1970): 235–36.

Written in reaction to item **842**. Raises the following questions: Why did McCauley choose to use the sopranino rather than the alto for his multiphonic experiments? Is sustained practice of multiphonics safe for the instrument? Are the chords "balanced," or are certain pitches stronger than others? Clark also challenges the accuracy of McCauley's notation and questions the aesthetic value of some of the multiphonic "chords."

NOTATION

844. Schmidt, Ursula. *Notation der neuen Blockflötenmusik: Ein Überblick* [Notation of new recorder music: an overview]. Celle: Moeck, 1981. 60 p. ISBN 3875490134.

Surveys the various forms of notation used by composers of avant-garde recorder music, under the following headings: exact notation, free notation, fingering indications, vibrato, blowing and articulation techniques, notation of actions, and graphic scores. No fewer than 271 short musical examples taken from only 35 sources. Composers would do well to take note of the inconsistencies in notation that Schmidt unearths. Includes a short bibliography and a list of the musical sources. Originated as an Examensarbeit, Staatliche Hochschule für Musik Köln, 1979.

21

Ensembles

This chapter covers matters of technique, practice, performance, and organization connected with recorder ensembles, large and small.

846. Bamforth, Dennis A. "The Recorder Orchestra." *The Recorder Magazine* 13, no. 2 (September 1993): 50–51.
    Part I: The History. Brief notes on the various recorder orchestras that have existed in England since the 1960s.

847. Barthel, Rudolf. "Consigli per un complesso di flauto dolce" [Advice for a recorder ensemble]. *Il flauto dolce* 1 (January/June 1971): 3–8.
    Said to be a revised translation of "Aus der Arbeit eines Blockflötenchores" [From the work of a recorder orchestra] (1956). Discusses large recorder ensembles. Practical advice on instrumentation, tuning, intonation, articulation, seating, rehearsing, orchestration (including instrumental characteristics), and dynamics.

* Bergmann, Walter. "Golden Rules for Ensemble Playing." Cited above as item 154.

848. Clark, Paul. "Consorting with Teenagers." *Recorder & Music Magazine* 3, no. 6 (June 1970): 199-200.
    This un-PC title by PC hides suggestions of three- to six-part compositions suitable for recorder ensembles.

849. Eastman, Richard. "The Neutral Tune." *American Recorder* 32, no. 4 (December 1991): 11–14.
    Describes an exercise developed by Eastman to help consorts recognize and reenforce the musical style of a piece of music.

Ensembles

850. Maarbjerg, Mary. "The Care and Feeding of a Recorder Consort." *American Recorder* 31, no. 3 (September 1990): 7–10.

    Describes the formation of her own amateur consort and offers ten rules to help insure successful collaboration among a diverse group of players.

851. Mett, Silke. "Intonation im Ensemblespiel—Theorie und Praxis" [Intonation in ensemble playing: theory and practice]. *Tibia* 14, no. 4 (1989): 573–80.

    A useful overview of the important but neglected subject of tuning and recorders. Covers: the problem of a recorder out of tune with itself; combination tones and their consequences for the intonation of a recorder ensemble; practical exercises on various intervals (two players); intonation problems in the course of a melody; exercises for three and four players.

852. Phillips, Michael H. "A Singular Consort." *Recorder & Music* 5, no. 5 (March 1976): 160.

    Describes the use of overdubs to create a one-player "consort" on recorded tape.

* Primus, Constance M. "The Bass Recorder in Consort." Cited above as item 142.

853. Rosenberg, Marvin. "The Efficient Consort Rehearsal." *The American Recorder* 24, no. 2 (May 1983): 66.

    Ten suggestions "that will make rehearsals more productive."

* Seibert, Peter. "Ornamentation for Consort Players: First Steps." Cited above as item 733.

854. Simpson, Adrienne. "Variety in Consort Playing." *Recorder and Music Magazine* 2, no. 5 (May 1967): 139–40.

    Describes two methods: by varying the recorder texture and by adding instruments (e.g., plucked and bowed string instruments, percussion).

855. Skins, H.R. "First Steps in Consort Playing." (Where Do I Start? 3) *The Recorder and Music Magazine* 1, no. 6 (August 1964): 181–83.

    An introduction to consort playing as a valuable learning experience for beginning players. Outlines the "problems and techniques" of consort playing, including how to select a leader, matching instruments, and improving intonation. The second half of the article discusses repertory for recorder duet and trio, with an emphasis placed on arrangements.

856. Weineck, Isolde Maria. "Blockflötenchöre und Kantoreipraxis" [Recorder choirs and choir practice]. *Tibia* 8, no. 3 (1983): 443–46.

    Discusses an interesting German phenomenon. In recent years, the "evangelische" (Lutheran) church has been adding recorder choirs to its traditional vocal choirs and trombone choirs. The structure and organization of such a recorder choir have been developed in particular by the Kirchenkreis Tecklenburg. The musical means available to the recorder choir, alone and in combination with other instruments, are quite varied.

857. White, Beverly. "Consensus Musicus and the Small Ensemble." *The American Recorder* 13, no. 4 (November 1972): 122–23.

    Essay in support of shared leadership and teamwork in small ensembles.

858. Winters, Leslie. "The Making of a Recorder Consort." *Recorder and Music Magazine* 4, no. 5 (March 1973): 165–67; 4, no. 6 (June 1973): 196–98.

    Good advice concerning matters of technique in ensemble playing. Covers: breathing and breath control; intonation; ensemble; how to approach a new piece; articulation and phrasing; dynamics and accents.

859. Wollitz, Kenneth. "Ensemble Playing." *The American Recorder* 22, no. 4 (November 1981): 103–11.

    Reprinted from chapter 6 of item 14. A thorough and insightful treatment of the special problems encountered when recorder players play together. Begins by describing the concept of teamwork in a musical group and the social dynamics of playing with other musicians, noting that compromises and adjustments tend to make group playing a civilizing experience. Wollitz then moves to specific problems: where to play (indoors in a relatively live room); how to pace the rehearsal; deciding who, if anyone, should lead; tuning (including an extensive discussion of beats and difference tones); playing in time; dynamics; instrumentation; and preparing a program (covers selection and order of the pieces, "potpourri" vs. "thematic" programs, and handling stage fright). Letter from Hazel Mosely in 24, no. 1 (February 1983): 43.

860. Wyatt, Theo. "Am I Too Loud?" *Recorder & Music* 5, no. 5 (March 1976): 161.

Ensembles

Wyatt (not Gerald Moore) explains why consort performers need to play more softly than solo performers.

861. Wyatt, Theo. "Chamber Music v Massed Playing." *Recorder & Music Magazine* 3, no. 8 (December 1970): 273-74.

Concerns the phenomenon of massed playing, in which chamber music is performed with multiple players—sometimes more than twenty—assigned to each part. Wyatt wonders why such performances are common among amateur recorder players and concludes that the reason is a "generally low standard of competence. We don't play one to a part because we can't." He argues that massed playing is fine if it provides a means for players to perform music they otherwise could not, but chamber performance should remain a goal for all players. Responses from Alan G. Bartlett, Brian Crispin, and Edgar Gordon in 3, no. 9 (March 1971): 323-25.

862. Wyatt, Theo. "On Tuning Up." *Recorder & Music* 7, no. 2 (June 1981): 34-35.

Emphasizes two points: consorts should not tune to A, since tuning by fifths and fourths on C (for F instruments) and G (for C instruments) with all players using the same fingering is more reliable; and consorts should not need to tune their instruments prior to performance, because physical adjustments made to the instruments during rehearsal should be matched precisely for the performance.

863. Wyatt, Theo. "The Techniques of Consort Playing." *Recorder & Music* 6, no. 10 (June 1980): 288-92. Reprinted in *The American Recorder* 24, no. 1 (February 1983): 3-6.

Wyatt sees chamber music as "primarily a social activity" in which each player's chief responsibility is not to spoil the music for the others. By listening and adjusting to the other members of the consort, individual players can improve both the music and the group experience. Specific advice includes: learn to read ahead; listen for barlines and cadences; learn to recognize when something is wrong; use visual contact and physical motion to ensure accuracy in ensemble; learn how to take a chord apart and tune it. Letter from Judith I. Whaley in 24, no. 3 (August 1983): 127 describes how a blind player can participate in a consort, contrary to Wyatt's comment that a "blind player is doomed, sadly but inevitably, to being a soloist."

864. Wyatt, Theo. "The Well-tempered Consort." *Recorder & Music* 4, no. 12 (December 1974): 431-32; 5, no. 2 (June 1975): 51-52.

Advice on organizing and managing an amateur consort. The first part suggests ways to identify appropriate players for the group. The second part covers leadership, assignment of parts, repertory, public performance, and the value of having an experienced mentor available to coach the group during the first few rehearsals.

22

Pedagogy and Study

This chapter is a mixed bag of sources, some on the education of both professional recorder players and amateurs, others on recorder methods and their assessment. Recorder methods themselves are excluded, as are sources about "music education" (i.e., primary and secondary school recorder teaching).

865. "The American Recorder Society Education Program." Levels IA and IB: *The American Recorder* 22, no. 1/2 (May 1981): 19-20; Levels II and III: 21, no. 3 (November 1980): 120-28. Also issued to ARS members as a separate publication; revised versions were published in 1984 and 1987.

    These publications define the ARS Education Program, set the goals for each level, and include helpful study guides, which "provide the player with a structured program in technique, theory, ear training, sight-reading, and performance practice. They also suggest a repertoire." Includes bibliographies of performing editions, books, and periodicals.

* Bergmann, Walter. "Teaching Intonation." Cited above as item **796**.

866. Braun, Gerhard. "Die Blockflöte als idealer Klangschnuller? Zehn Thesen zum Blockflötenunterricht und Blockflötenspiel" [The recorder as ideal sound-pacifier? Ten theses on recorder instruction and playing] *Zeitschrift SAJM* 17, no. 4 (December 1989): 3-10.

    Proposes and offers commentary on the following "theses": (1) the recorder is a real musical instrument, (2) it needs to be taught as a real wind instrument from the beginning, (3) it is a many-sided instrument because of the different historical and modern types, (4) students should be taught to "hear," (5) recorder music for children should not "short-change" them, (6) recorder instruction should be methodical, (7) although the recorder has a repertory stretching back over five centuries, there are few pieces of great artistic value, (8) the emphasis in recorder teaching should be on expression, (9) recorder teachers should introduce their students to the new sound world of modern recorder music, (10) recorder teaching should develop the student's musical perception.

867. Feldman, Anna. "The Adult Intermediate Recorder Student." *Continuo* 4, no. 10 (Summer 1981): 13–17; 5, no. 1 (October 1981): 15–20.

Advice on teaching such a student. Discusses breathing exercises, relaxation, finger exercises, articulation, rhythm, and pitch. Includes a list of nine recommended sets of etudes.

868. Heymann, Ulrike. "Blockflötenschulen—Kriterien für ihre Beurteilung" [Recorder methods—criteria for their evaluation]. *Tibia* 6, no. 1 (1981): 257–61.

Describes the evaluation of recorder methods of the previous ten years on their treatment of: the preface, elementary musicianship, posture and holding of the instrument, breathing, articulation, fingering technique, practice material, repertory, and appearance.

869. Thomas, Jean W., comp. "A Practical Guide to Recorder Method Books and Related Material: An Annotated Bibliography." *The American Recorder* 20, no. 3 (November 1979): 111–17.

"[A] guide to instruction books, methods, and handbooks that are now generally available." The bibliography is divided into three categories: beginning methods for C and F recorders (fifty-nine entries); methods for bass recorder (four entries); and recorder handbooks (six entries). Informative, evaluative annotations.

870. Thorn, Chris. "Getting the Most Out of the Red Book." *Recorder & Music* 7, no. 6 (June 1982): 143.

A guide to *The Recorder Book* by Steve Rosenberg (Schott 11380). Includes a few corrections.

871. Ventzke, Karl. "Blockflöten-Schulwerke der 30er Jahre" [Recorder methods of the 1930s]. *Tibia* 16, no. 1 (1991): 378.

A list of twenty-nine methods published in Germany between 1930 and 1940, giving only cities of publication, not publishers. Ventzke notes that neither Peter (item 15) nor Alker (item 1) gives the publication dates of these methods.

872. Waechter, Wolfram. "Kommerz, Kind oder Kunst? Motivationen und Zielsetzungen für Blockflötenunterricht heute" [Commerce, child or art? Motivations and objectives for recorder teaching today]. *Tibia* 2, no. 3 (1977): 355-59.

Astonishingly, 28.5% of students in German music schools study the recorder. Unfortunately, most of them learn the soprano recorder from unqualified teachers. Outlines some of the misconceptions behind such teaching. Goes on to list the necessary contents of the "artistic aspect" of recorder playing (general musicianship, musical style, practicing, breathing and vibrato, etc.), which could be taken for granted for any other serious instrument. Comes up with two obvious but neglected suggestions for improving teaching: (1) "The student must, after receiving instruction, be able to play the recorder better than before"; (2) an "[only] moderately good musician can scarcely be a good teacher." Concludes with a plea for a synthesis of musicianship and pedagogy.

873. Weilenmann, Matthias. "Voraussetzungen und Ziele des Blockflötenunterrichts" [Assumptions and goals of recorder instruction]. *Quartalszeitschrift SAJM* 16, no. 2 (June 1988): 3-8.

Proposes and discusses three theses: (1) The recorder is not a starting instrument; (2) the recorder is not an instrument for mass playing; (3) the recorder is basically not an instrument for the primary school. Ends with comments on the tone and repertory of the instrument.

874. "Where Do I Start?" *The Recorder and Music Magazine* 1, no. 4 (February 1964): 112-13.

Advice for the beginner. Advocates the recorder as a first instrument because it is inexpensive and easy to learn. Recommends starting on the soprano. The alto is second choice—seemingly because of its greater expense. Suggests a number of instruction books and emphasizes the importance of a good teacher.

UNIVERSITIES, COLLEGES, AND CONSERVATORIES

875. O'Sullivan, Patricia. "The Recorder in the Universities." *The Recorder Magazine* 11, no. 3 (September 1991): 88-89.

A table showing the extent of recorder studies at thirty-two universities in Great Britain. Includes information on: degrees offered, whether the recorder is taught, whether lessons are funded, and whether early music ensembles and early music coursework are available. Additions and corrections appear in 11, no. 4 (December 1991): 116. An expanded and updated table appears in 12, no. 3 (September 1992): 67-68.

876. "The Recorder Goes to College." (The Recorder in Education) *American Recorder* 31, no. 2 (June 1990): 18-19.

A directory of twenty colleges and universities that offer degree programs in recorder. Each entry includes the name of the recorder instructor and an address and telephone number for inquiries. Separate sidebars describe in greater detail the program at the Oberlin Conservatory and the pre-collegiate program at Indiana University. Letter from Susan G. Sandman regarding Wells College in 31, no. 4 (December 1990): 26.

877. Seiler, Jean W., comp. "Degree Programs in Early Music in the United States and Canada." *The American Recorder* 24, no. 1 (February 1983): 15-19.

Describes twenty-five "undergraduate and graduate degree programs in recorder, other early instruments, or early music, as well as programs accepting these instruments in fulfillment of the applied music requirement." Listings include degrees offered, ensembles and their performing opportunities, faculty, and application procedures.

EXAMINATIONS

878. Hunt, Edgar. "The Trinity College of Music Recorder Examinations." *Recorder & Music* 6, no. 12 (December 1980): 350-51; 7, no. 1 (March 1981): 8-9; 7, no. 2 (June 1981): 35-37.

Describes the examination process and expectations for: the lower grades (part 1), the higher grades (part 2), and the Licentiate and Fellowship diplomas (part 3).

879. O'Sullivan, Patricia. "The 1991-1994 Trinity College Examination Syllabus." *The Recorder Magazine* 10, no. 4 (December 1990): 115-16; 11, no. 1 (March 1991): 20-21; 11, no. 2 (June 1991): 52-53.

A survey of the repertory for soprano and alto recorder covered in Grades 1-5 of the program. Examines the selections with a critical eye and offers many suggestions for interpreting individual pieces.

880. Sherman, Elna. "Trinity College Recorder Examinations." *The American Recorder* 5, no. 3 (August 1964): 6-7.

General description of the examinations, accompanied by a few sample theory questions.

GEOGRAPHICAL FOCUS

FRANCE

881. "L'enseignement de la flûte à bec en France" [The teaching of the recorder in France]. *Flûte à bec* 1 (June 1981): 36–41.

    An attempt at a complete listing of French music schools and conservatories that teach the recorder, arranged by province.

882. Tellier, Michèle. "L'enseignement de la flûte à bec en France" [The teaching of the recorder in France]. *Flûte à bec* 6 (March 1983): 38-46.

    A list of the names, addresses, and phone numbers of French recorder teachers, arranged by province.

GERMANY

883. Martin, Anne. "The Recorder in Education in West Germany." *Recorder & Music* 7, no. 11 (September 1983): 299–301.

    Examines the role of the recorder in primary education in Germany, particularly in comparison with the role of the instrument in English schools. In West Germany, the recorder is used as a melodic instrument to reinforce singing activities and as a tool to develop the ear: "[T]he strength of the recorder is in its 'pop[u]lar' use, its pre-eminence in Orff work and in professional playing. Here in Britain it plays a much stronger 'instrumental' rôle both in school and among adult amateurs, as well as being played by professional players."

THE NETHERLANDS

884. Michon, Claire. "Petit guide pratique de 'L'école hollandaise'" [Brief practical guide to the "Dutch School"]. *Flûte à bec* 5 (December 1982): 25-27.

    A directory of Dutch conservatories with comments on their recorder teachers and teaching. For a long-outdated view by the player who caused the situation to change, see Frans Brüggen, "The Recorder in Holland," *The American Recorder* 2, no. 4 (Fall 1961): 6.

23

Biographies: Historical

This chapter is concerned with purely or largely biographical sources about historical recorder players and significant composers for the instrument as well as other related figures. For biographical material on recorder makers, see chapter 9. Further material on composers will be found in sources about their works (see chapter 28).

885. "Composers of Recorder Music, Recorder Players and Recorder Makers." *Recorder & Music* 7, no. 11 (September 1983): 291–92; 8, no. 1 (March 1984): 24–25; 8, no. 5 (March 1985): 155–56; 8, no. 9 (March 1986): 268–69.
    A biographical dictionary. Ends mysteriously, after completing the letter G.

886. Haynes, Bruce. "Telemann's *Kleine Cammer-Music* and the Four Oboists to Whom it was Dedicated." *Musick* 7, no. 4 (March 1986): 30–35. Reprinted in *Journal of the International Double Reed Society* 15 (1987): 27–32.
    A revised version of the preface to the facsimile edition of the Telemann collection published by Musica Musica, Basel, 1983. Discusses the collection, pointing out that although the composer said that it could be played by many instruments (including the recorder), it was primarily intended for the oboe. Biographical sketches of the dedicatees: François La Riche, Johann Christian Richter, Johann Michael Boehm, and Peter Glösch, all of whom were oboists and at least one of whom (Boehm) was also a recorder player.

* Lasocki, David Ronald Graham. *Professional Recorder Players in England, 1540–1740.* Cited above as item 72.

Biographies: Historical

BARSANTI, FRANCESCO (CA. 1690–1775)

887. Sharman, Ian G. "Francesco Barsanti: A Fuller Biography and a Discussion of his *Concerti Grossi* (Op 3)." *Brio* 26, no. 1 (Spring/Summer 1989): 4–10.
    Adds to the biographical account in item 1229.1 with new details of Barsanti's life in Scotland (ca. 1735–ca. 1743) and back in London, coming up with solid evidence for the first time of his likely death date (around 1 May 1775). Followed by comments on the form and style of the Concerti Grossi. Complemented by item 1231.

888. Lasocki, David. "More on the Life of Francesco Barsanti." *Brio* 27, no. 2 (Autumn/Winter 1990): 78–79.
    Comments on some statements in item 887 about Barsanti's arrival and early years in England as well as his visit to Dublin in 1740.

BASSANO FAMILY

* Lasocki, David, with Roger Prior. *The Bassanos: Venetian Musicians and Instrument Makers in England, 1531–1665.* Cited above as item 190.

* Lasocki, David Ronald Graham. *Professional Recorder Players in England, 1540–1740.* Cited above as item 72.
    Volume 2 consists of detailed biographies of all the professional musicians who played the recorder in England during the period in question, many of them being discussed for the first time. Especially long sections are devoted to the Bassano family, the founders and mainstays of the Court recorder consort (revised version published as part of item 190), and James Paisible, the most important player of the Baroque recorder in England.

BOBBIN, TIM (1708–1786)

889. Kenworthy, C. "Graver and Fluter." *The Recorder and Music Magazine* 1, no. 8 (February 1965): 250.
    A biography of Tim Bobbin, 18th-century author, teacher, artist, and amateur recorder player.

DEMOIVRE, DANIEL (FL. 1687–1731)

890. Lasocki, David. "The Life of Daniel De Moivre (fl. 1687–1731)." *The Consort* 45 (1989): 15–17.

   In response to Michael Stratford's remark about the lack of information on Demoivre's life (see item 1236), Lasocki compiles and expands on biographical information he gathered while conducting research for item 72.

HOTTETERRE, JACQUES (1674–1763)

891. House, Delpha LeAnn. *Jacques Hotteterre "le Romain": A Study of his Life and Compositional Style.* Ph.D. dissertation, The University of North Carolina at Chapel Hill, 1991. vii, 309 leaves. OCLC #25560593. UMI order no. 92-16727.

   Studies Hotteterre's compositions in depth, concluding that he made a satisfying synthesis of the French and Italian styles, thus justifying his nickname "le Romain," whether or not he ever made a trip to Rome. In addition, presents the most detailed biography of Hotteterre published to date, although because the family re-used first names a great deal, the genealogy of the family is confusing, and new information turns up all the time (see item 215). Reports the discovery of a fascinating letter from Hotteterre to Wilhelm von Uffenbach (1723) about books and scores he had been commissioned to buy for Uffenbach, as well as advice on adjusting musette reeds.

LOEILLET FAMILY

892. Priestman, Brian. "An Introduction to the Loeillets." *The Consort* 11 (July 1954): 18–26.

   An important early article, reporting his researches on the Loeillet family, distinguishing among John, Jean-Baptiste, and Jacques, and correcting errors of earlier researchers. Insightful stylistic analysis of the music of all three composers.

893. Thomson, J.M. "An Introduction to the Loeillets and Particularly John." (Musical Biography) *The Recorder and Music Magazine* 1, no. 6 (August 1964): 183.

   A brief biography of John Loeillet, with only passing mention of Jean Baptiste and Jacques. Edgar Hunt, in 1, no. 7 (November 1964): 215, gives information on John's London address, which John Thorne corrects in 1, no. 9 (May 1965): 277-78. Morag Deane makes further corrections in item **894**.

894. Deane, Morag. "John Loeillet of London." *Recorder & Music* 6, no. 8 (December 1979): 226-29.

A biography based for the most part on 18th-century documents (rate books, announcements, advertisements, etc.), unfortunately containing many errors of transcription and misunderstandings. Also addresses the question of Loeillet's place of residence in London, which had first been raised by Edgar Hunt and John Thorne (see item **893**). Includes a facsimile of the entry for Loeillet in Sir John Hawkins' *History* and a transcription of Loeillet's will. Superseded by item **897**.

895. Deane, Morag. "Jacob [i.e. Jacques] Loeillet and Jean Baptiste Loeillet de Gand." *Recorder & Music* 6, no. 10 (June 1980): 286-88.

Offers biographies of the two musicians (in the case of Loeillet de Gand, the information is necessarily scant). Includes a diagram of the Loeillet family tree (corrected in *Recorder & Music* 6, no. 11 [September 1980]: 323). Also introduces the notion that Loeillet de Gand died earlier than had been suspected; in the records of deaths in Lyon, Deane discovered an entry for one Luillet on 11 November 1715.

896. Janzen, Rose-Marie. "The Loeillet Enigma." *The Consort* 39 (1983): 502-6. In French as: "L'énigme des Loeillets" [The enigma of the Loeillets]. *Flûte à bec* 5 (December 1982): 6-9. In German as: "Die Identität von Jean-Baptiste Loeillet" [The identity of Jean-Baptiste Loeillet]. *Tibia* 7, no. 1 (1982): 1-6.

Reviews the known facts of the lives and publications of John, Jean-Baptiste, and Jacques Loeillet. Points out that, although there is enough evidence to distinguish Jean-Baptiste from John, we know nothing firm about Jean-Baptiste's life other than his birthdate. Janzen suggests sensibly that he could be researched in the archives of Lyons and other French noble houses.

897. Lasocki, David. "A New Look at the Life of John Loeillet (1680-1730)." *The Recorder and Music Magazine* 8, no. 2 (June 1984): 42-46. Also in *Concerning the Flute: Ten Articles Dedicated to Frans Vester . . .* , 65-73. Amsterdam: Broekmans en Van Poppel, 1984. OCLC #12363269.

An expanded version of a section of a chapter in item **72**. "[R]e-examines John Loeillet's life on the basis of all the available evidence, some of which has not previously been cited in the literature on the family."

Offers extensive information on Loeillet's activity as a theater musician. A slightly different version includes new findings on the extent of his estate.

RYDER, DUDLEY (1691-1756)

898. Lasocki, David. "Dudley Ryder, An Amateur Musician and Dancer in England (1715-16)." *The American Recorder* 28, no. 1 (February 1987): 4-13.

    Discusses the references to music and dance in the diary that Sir Dudley Ryder kept while he was a law student in London, 1715-16. "Ryder played the viola da gamba and recorder, sang a little, listened to singing more, attended the odd concert and church performance, and danced a great deal." He reports playing the recorder ten times, by himself and with his friends on recorder or gamba, and hearing the professional recorder player Daniel Demoivre. Since we know next to nothing about the recorder playing of individual amateurs at that time, Ryder's diary entries on the instrument are valuable, slim though they may be.

SCHICKHARDT, JOHANN CHRISTIAN (CA. 1682-1762)

899. Lasocki, David. "Johann Christian Schickhardt (ca. 1682-1762): Woodwind Composer, Performer and Teacher." *Recorder & Music* 5, no. 8 (December 1976): 254-57; 5, no. 9 (March 1977): 287-90.

    A popular biography based on item 901.

900. Lasocki, David. "Johann Christian Schickhardt." *Tibia* 2, no. 3 (1977): 337-43.

    A slightly expanded version of item 899. Includes facsimiles of a manuscript dedication (with signature) and of a page from the recorder method.

901. Lasocki, David. "Johann Christian Schickhardt (ca. 1682-1762): A Contribution to his Biography and a Catalogue of his Works." *Tijdschrift van de Vereniging voor Nederlandse Muziekgeschiedenis* 27, no. 1 (1977): 28-55.

    The most thorough biography and catalog of works available. Briefly assesses his contributions as a composer. Also presents evidence that the portrait reproduced on the cover of *Recorder and Music Magazine* 2, no. 2 (July 1966) is not of Schickhardt as once thought.

902. Lasocki, David. "Schickhardt in London." *Recorder & Music* 6, no. 7 (September 1979): 203-5.

Reports on two concert announcements found in *The London Stage 1600–1800* (Carbondale, Illinois: Southern Illinois Press, 1960-68) that place Schickhardt in London in 1732. Lasocki speculates on the circumstances surrounding the publication of the twenty-four sonatas in all keys (op. 30) in light of this new evidence. Also includes a bibliography of editions of Schickhardt's music that had appeared since the publication of item 899.

TALBOT, JAMES (1664–1708)

903. Unwin, Robert. "'An English Writer About Music': James Talbot 1664-1708." *Galpin Society Journal* 40 (1987): 53-72.

    Traces Talbot's life in detail. Suggests that his unfinished treatise on musical instruments represents his contribution to a broader treatise on music in collaboration with Henry Purcell. Cites an archival document which suggests that Talbot taught the recorder to the 11-year-old son of his patron, Charles Seymour, Duke of Somerset. Also quotes the text of an ode Talbot wrote on Purcell's death (1695), set to music by Gottfried Finger, that includes a section for recorder ("the melancholy flute") and theorbo.

VALENTINE FAMILY

904. Medforth, Martin. "The Valentines of Leicester: A Reappraisal of an 18th-Century Musical Family." *The Musical Times* 1666 = 122, no. 12 (December 1981): 812-18.

    A biographical overview of the Valentine family, who were musicians in Leicester from around 1670 into the 19th century. Because of the uniqueness of the name, it seems probable that the family included Robert Valentine (b. 1674?), who emigrated to Italy, where he worked as an oboist and published much recorder and other woodwind music. Summarizes what is known of his life and comments briefly on his compositional style.

WOODCOCK, ROBERT (FL. 1722–1730)

905. Lasocki, David, and Helen Neate. "The Life and Works of Robert Woodcock, 1690–1728." *The American Recorder* 29, no. 3 (August 1988): 92–104.

    "The purposes of our article are: first, to demonstrate that there was only one Robert Woodcock, a marine painter, amateur woodwind player, and composer; second, to present new biographical information about him; and finally, to discuss the concertos in the light of this information as well as musical evidence, concluding that the sole Robert Woodcock probably did compose the concertos published under his name." Quotes in full the biographical accounts written in the late 1720s by George Vertue, which are verified and supplemented through an examination of parish registers and wills. The remainder (and major part) of the article concerns the music, particularly the question of authorship. Summarizes past arguments and identifies their strengths and weaknesses. Through an extensive stylistic analysis, concludes that Woodcock wrote either most or all of the twelve concertos attributed to him. Ends with a bibliography of modern editions and a discography. Edgar Hunt, in *The Recorder and Music Magazine* 9, no. 8 (December 1988): 220-21, reviews the history of the Woodcock controversy in an announcement noting the publication of this article.

ZELLBELL, FERDINAND (1698-1765)

906. Holm, Anna Lena. "Ferdinand Zellbell d.ä.:s inkomster år 1722" [Ferdinand Zellbell Sr.'s Income for the Year 1722]. *Svensk Tidskrift för Musikforskning* 73 (1991): 85-96. Includes short English summary.

A fascinating datebook recently acquired by the Kungliga Musikaliska Akademiens Bibliotek in Sweden contains the financial accounts of the Stockholm organist and composer Ferdinand Zellbell Sr. (1698-1765) for the year 1722. It reveals that he played at various events; taught the harpsichord, recorder, lute, and violin; sold music (including recorder music) and instruments; made and repaired harpsichords and lutes; acted as a censor; and rented out rooms.

24

Biographies and Interviews: Modern

This chapter looks at 20th-century performers and other persons associated with the recorder (teachers, editors, writers, publishers, composers). For recorder makers, see chapter 11; for composers of recorder music, see also chapter 29.

* "Composers of Recorder Music, Recorder Players and Recorder Makers." Cited above as item 885.

907. Rose, Pete. "On the Cutting Edge." *American Recorder* 32, no. 4 (December 1991): 35; 33, no. 1 (March 1992): 31–33; 33, no. 2 (June 1992): 37; 33, no. 3 (September 1992): 26–27; 33, no. 4 (December 1992): 26–27; 34, no. 1 (March 1993): 27–29; 34, no. 2 (June 1993): 27–28; 34, no. 3 (September 1993): 30–35; 34, no. 4 (November 1993): 27–28.

    December 1991: profiles of Helen Rees (item **1089**) and Philadelphia-based jazz recorder player Joel Levine and an essay on special effects. March 1992: discusses several new compositions for solo recorder: *Atembogen* by Gerhard Braun, *Ofrenda* by Mario Lavista, *Largo* by Guus Janssen, and, briefly, *The Voice of the Crocodile* by Benjamin Thorn. June 1992: profiles of Andrew Waldo and Rodolfo Guzman. September 1992: a discussion of the evolution of Joel Levine's jazz style and a profile of John Tyson. December 1992: an account of recent performances by Eva Legêne of modern works (item **1050**) and a profile of Frances Blaker (item **936**). March 1993: profile of Aldo Abreu (item **911**) and a description of Johannes Fischer's *Blockflöten-Instalation* (a contraption connecting fourteen recorders to a single mouthpiece). June 1993: profile of Johnny Reinhard and updates on Tui St. George Tucker, Bob Margolis, and Michael Vetter. September 1993: discusses *Four Diversions* by John Turner, *Four Pieces* by Donald Bousted, and *Pipistrelli gialli* by Benjamin Thorn. November 1993: profile of Richard and Elaine Henzler (item **1021**) and reviews of new publications.

908. Thomson, John M. *Recorder Profiles*. London: Schott, 1972. 77 p. ISBN 0901938092.
Sketches of fourteen people associated with the recorder, based on a series of articles first published in *Recorder and Music Magazine* between 1963 and 1971: Walter Bergmann (item 931), Frans Brüggen (item 961), René Clemencic (item 972), Ferdinand Conrad (item 978), LaNoue Davenport (item 982), Carl Dolmetsch (item 998), Edgar Hunt (item 1031), Bernard Krainis (item 1043), Hans-Martin Linde (item 1056), David Munrow (item 1068), Kees Otten (item 1078), Gustav Scheck (based on item 1099), Christopher Taylor (item 1108), and Michael Vetter (item 1117). Reviewed by Theo Wyatt in *Recorder and Music Magazine* 4, no. 5 (March 1973): 173–74.

909. Veilhan, Jean-Claude, and Hugo Reyne. "Les flûtistes à bec au XXe siècle: pionniers et sillons" [The recorder players of the 20th century: pioneers and followers]. *Diapason-Harmonie* 335 (February 1988): 54–55.
Briefly surveys these players, dividing them into national schools of England, Germany, Switzerland, the Netherlands, Belgium, Austria, and of course France, but not the United States.

ABREU, ALDO

910. [Dunham, Benjamin S.?] "AR Interviews Aldo Abreu—A Conversation about Competitions." (Tidings) *American Recorder* 33, no. 4 (December 1992): 4–5.
Winner of the 1991 Concert Artists Guild Award. (Abreu was the first recorder player to win since 1971.) Covers: advice on preparing for a competition; how to cope with losing; his concert itinerary; his hope that contemporary recorder music will remain accessible to audiences.

911. Rose, Pete. "'The Kid.'" (On the Cutting Edge) *American Recorder* 34, no. 1 (March 1993): 27–28.
Profile of Aldo Abreu. Covers: his study with Ricardo Kanji and Michael Barker at the Royal Conservatory in The Hague; his interpretation of Andriessen's *Sweet*; his work promoting music from Latin America.

ADAMS, PIERS

912. Homfray, Tim. "Beyond the *Ash Grove*." *Music Teacher* 70, no. 7 (July 1991): 12–13.
Based on an interview with Piers Adams. Mostly concerned with his views on the recorder in schools but also contains biographical material.

ALTON, EDWIN (D. 1982)

913. Dolci, Danilo. "Edwin Alton." *Il flauto dolce* 4 (July/December 1973): 11–12.
    A charming portrait of Alton's success at teaching the recorder to children in Sicily after his retirement from school teaching in England. Excerpted from Dolci's *Chissà se i pesci piangono: Documentazione di un'esperienza educativa* [Do fish cry? Documentation of an educational experience] (Torino: Giulio Einaudi, 1973), 201–4 (in which the recorder is also mentioned).

914. Y[ates], T[homas]. "Obituary: Edwin Alton." *Recorder & Music* 7, no. 9 (March 1983): 243.

AMSTERDAM LOEKI STARDUST QUARTET

See also under the subheading "Brüggen, Daniel."

915. "Amsterdam Loeki Stardust Quartet in Milwaukee." *American Recorder* 34, no. 2 (June 1993): 6–7.
    Consists of captioned photographs.

916. Quandt, Reinhold. "Das Amsterdam Loeki Stardust Quartet." (Das Porträt) *Tibia* 14, no. 4 (1989): 587–91.
    Covers: the origin of the group and its name; their opting for ensemble rather than solo playing; their (generally negative) thoughts on the recorder as solo instrument; the division of labor for their repertory; their decision-making (each has a "veto"); how they practice; tips on ensemble playing; what repertory would not work on the recorder; their stage practice; their "gags"; national differences in recorder students; and the future of the recorder (new music, so that the instrument can continue to live).

ANDERSON, NATASHA

917. Clarke, Zana. "Natasha Anderson." (Profile) *The Recorder: Journal of the Victorian Recorder Guild* 13 (July 1991): 3–4.
    Anderson was the winner of the open solo section of the First Australian Recorder Competition (1990). Covers her training, especially her work at Melbourne University.

Arno, Michael (1937–1988)

918. Lambe, Joan. "Obituary: Michael Arno." *The Recorder and Music Magazine* 9, no. 9 (March 1989): 258.

    Brief obituary of the English recorder player, a former member of the Lydian Consort, a collaborator with Collegium Saggitarii and the Sheridan ensemble, and a frequent recitalist.

919. T[homson], J.M. "Michael Arno." (Profile) *Recorder & Music* 4, no. 9 (March 1974): 323–24.

    Covers: his musical education; his recording credits; the influence of Brüggen; the need to institute in England a school of recorder playing similar to that in Holland; his interest in Baroque music and conservative 20th-century works; his belief that ornamentation can easily be overdone; his preferred instruments; his contribution to the English early music scene.

Baghuis, Elly

920. Bergmann, Walter. "Elly Baghuis Talks to Walter Bergmann." *Recorder and Music Magazine* 2, no. 5 (May 1967): 142.

    Covers: her study with Brüggen; her teaching at the Hague Conservatory; the examinations administered at the conservatory; the standard of playing in Holland; her Wigmore Hall concert; her musical tastes.

Ball, Christopher (b. 1936)

921. T[homson], J.M. "Christopher Ball & the Praetorius Consort." *Recorder & Music* 4, no. 9 (March 1974): 339–40.

    Covers: the influence of Frans Brüggen and Sebastian Kelber on his self-taught style of playing; his use of vibrato and rubato as expressive devices; origins of the Praetorius Consort; performances and recording projects; his work as an orchestral conductor and photographer; his earlier career as a clarinetist.

Barab, Seymour (b. 1921)

* Glassgold, Cook. "Why Compose for the Recorder?" Cited above as item **835**.

BARTHEL, RUDOLF

922. Bergmann, Walter. "Rudolf Barthel." *Recorder & Music* 6, no. 6 (June 1979): 185.
Obituary.

BEIJER, ERIK

923. Helsloot, Loes. "*RECORDERS:* Een eigentijdse bewerking van middeleeuwse muziek" [RECORDERS: a modern arrangement of medieval music]. *Tijdschrift voor oude muziek* 1, no. 5 (1986): 126.
An interview with Erik Beijer and Saskia Coolen, two of the performers of RECORDERS, a piece of experimental music theater for tape, recorder, and lighting, premiered in Amsterdam on 16 November 1986.

BENSE, ROTRAUD

924. Bergmann, Walter. "Recorders in the D.D.R." *Recorder & Music Magazine* 2, no. 8 (February 1968): 239.
A review of performances heard in Magdeburg in June 1967 and profiles of two of the players: Thekla Waldbaur and Rotraud Bense.

BERGMANN, WALTER (1902–1988)

925. Hersom, Herbert. "Walter Bergmann." *The Recorder and Music Magazine* 9, no. 6 (June 1988): 169–71.
An obituary focusing on Bergmann's work with children.

926. Hunt, Edgar. "Walter Bergmann: An Eightieth Birthday Tribute." *Recorder & Music* 7, no. 7 (September 1982): 166–67.
A biography focusing on his early years in England following his emigration from Germany.

927. Hunt, Edgar. "Obituary: Walter G. Bergmann." *The Recorder and Music Magazine* 9, no. 5 (March 1988): 125.

928. Lasocki, David. "Walter Bergmann (1902–1988) as Editor, Author, and Mentor." *Continuo* 15, no. 5 (October 1991): 2–6.

Emphasizes Bergmann's contributions not mentioned in his obituaries (which covered his recorder classes and his involvement with amateur recorder players as teacher, conductor, arranger, and accompanist). Discusses his editing and his development of the recorder catalog for Schott's in London; his articles on Barsanti, Purcell, and Telemann; and his role as a mentor, enabling European professional recorder players to perform in England, and Lasocki to learn about editing and research. Select bibliography of Bergmann's own articles and editions as well as profiles and obituaries of him.

929. Moeck, Hermann. "Walter Bergmann 24.9.1902–13.1.1988." *Tibia* 13, no. 3 (1988): 203.
    Brief obituary.

930. Parkinson, Janice M. "Dr. Walter Bergmann: Musician, Hobby: Music." *The American Recorder* 13, no. 2 (May 1972): 40–41.
    Portrait consisting of quotations from Bergmann and others. Covers: his musical training; his emigration from Germany to England; his association with Schott's, London; his classes in recorder; his support of arrangements as a means of offering players "access to the complete world of music"; his current projects.

931. [Thomson, J.M.] "Walter Bergmann." (Profile) *The Recorder and Music Magazine* 1, no. 5 (May 1964): 156–58. Reprinted in item 908.
    Covers: his amateur music-making while studying and practicing law; his imprisonment by the Nazis and eventual immigration to England in March 1939; his association with Michael Tippett; his work as a teacher, adjudicator, editor, author, and composer.

932. "Walter Bergmann." *Early Music* 16, no. 2 (May 1988): 318–19.
    Brief obituaries by J.M. Thomson and Michael Tippett.

933. Wyatt, Theo. "Obituary: Walter Bergmann." *The American Recorder* 29, no. 2 (May 1988): 66.

BIXLER, MARTHA (B. 1927)

934. [Hunt, Edgar]. "Martha Bixler: An Interview." *Recorder & Music* 4, no. 12 (December 1974): 430–31.

Covers: her introduction to the recorder as a child and the beginning of her serious study several years later with LaNoue Davenport; the American Recorder Society's teachers' examination; her teaching; her study of articulation; her work with Trio Il Flauto Dolce and the New York Pro Musica Renaissance Band; her impressions of England.

935. Weber, Rhoda. "Martha Bixler: A Profile." *The American Recorder* 11, no. 3 (Summer 1970): 79-82.

Covers: her schooling at Smith and Yale; her move to New York; her introduction to the work of LaNoue Davenport while working as a secretary for Alfred Knopf Jr.; her teaching in New York City; the Manhattan Consort; Trio Il Flauto Dolce; producing a good recorder tone; contemporary recorder music; her plans.

BLAKER, FRANCES

936. Rose, Pete. "And Disciple." (On the Cutting Edge) *American Recorder* 33, no. 4 (December 1992): 26-27.

Covers: her study with Eva Legêne, Marion Verbruggen, and Michael Barker; her current modern repertory and the compositions she is planning to add to it; her move from Cleveland to Atlanta; her work on a recorder practice handbook.

BLOCH, SUZANNE (B. 1907)

937. Bixler, Martha, and Ken Wollitz. "An Interview with Suzanne Bloch." *The American Recorder* 29, no. 4 (November 1988): 136-40.

Covers: her trip to England in 1933 to study with Arnold Dolmetsch, her eventual purchase of a restored lute from Dolmetsch and her return to Haslemere, her introduction to the recorder through Carl Dolmetsch, concerts with Carl Dolmetsch in New York City, her role in the founding of the American Recorder Society, Margaret Bradford and Irmgard Lehrer, the early days of the Society. Letter from Frances Dwight in 30, no. 1 (February 1989): 37.

BOECKMAN, VICKI (B. 1955)

938. "A Recording in the Making." *American Recorder* 32, no. 2 (June 1991): 27-28.

Vicki Boeckman describes the process of recording her *Early Italian Baroque* compact disc (KontraPunkt 32059).

BOEKE, KEES (B. 1950)

939. Epstein, Jan, and Ursula Grawe. "Conversation with Kees Boeke and Walter van Hauwe." *The Recorder: Journal of the Victorian Recorder Guild* 3 (November 1985): 1-7.

   Covers: impressions of the recorder scene in Australia, early music audiences, the recorder scene in the Netherlands, their musical education, limitations of the recorder, and encouraging new music.

BONSOR, BRIAN (B. 1926)

940. Praetz, Barbara. "Conversation with Brian Bonsor." *The Recorder: Journal of the Victorian Recorder Guild* 2 (March 1985): 2-7.

   Covers: his background, his arrangements and compositions, teaching amateurs, the need for professionals to support SRP, the recorder scene in Britain, his experiences in Australia, and the need for non-avant-garde compositions.

BORNEFELD, HELMET (1906-1990)

941. Thalheimer, Peter. "Abschied von Helmut Bornefeld" [Farewell to Helmut Bornefeld]. *Tibia* 15, no. 2 (1990): 136.

   Brief obituary.

BRAUER, EMIL (1891-1976)

942. Hunt, Edgar. "Obituary: Emil Brauer, 1891-1976." *Recorder & Music* 5, no. 7 (September 1976): 239.

BRAUN, GERHARD (B. 1932)

943. Thieme, Ulrich. "Capriccio und Ständchen: Gerhard Braun zum Sechzigsten" [Capricco and serenade: Gerhard Braun on his 60th]. *Tibia* 17, no. 2 (1992): 133.

   Musings on Braun's career as "composing flutist/recorderist and fluting/recordering composer," teacher and initiator of flute/recorder festivals ("specialty: symposiums—unlike in ancient Greece, alcohol-free"), and editor. Illustrated tongue-in-cheek with the title page of the flute sonatas, Op. 1, by the 18th-century "Mr. Braun."

BROWN, HOWARD MAYER (1930–1993)

944. Grawe, Ursula, and Jan Epstein. "A Conversation with Howard Mayer Brown." *The Recorder: Journal of the Victorian Recorder Guild* 1 (1984): 2–7.

Covers: performance practice and performers (the "fundamental tension between scholarship and performance"), early music and recorder performance in the U.S.A. ("the recorder is to some extent passing out of fashion"), the future of the recorder, and advice for the Australians.

945. "Howard Mayer Brown: ARS Past President, 1930–1993." *American Recorder* 34, no. 2 (June 1993): 5.

Obituary. Letter from Richard Sacksteder in 34, no. 3 (September 1993): 29 clarifies the history of the University of Chicago's Collegium Musicum.

BRÜGGEN, DANIEL

See also under the subheading "Amsterdam Loeki Stardust Quartet."

946. O'Kelly, Eve. "Daniel Brüggen." *The Recorder Magazine* 11, no. 4 (December 1991): 107–11.

Covers: reflections on the Amsterdam Loeki Stardust Quartet and the interaction of its members; the difficulties of putting together good programs; the instruments owned by members of the group; the types of instruments used on tour; the effect of the acoustics of halls on performances and the need to select repertory on short notice to fit the characteristics of a particular hall; his views on authenticity in instrument making; tuning practices of makers; his dislike of plastic instruments because they, unlike wood instruments, fail to embody the vicissitudes of life; his thoughts on teaching; his plans; and the future of the quartet.

BRÜGGEN, FRANS (B. 1934)

947. Brelsford, Edmund, and Gerhart Niemeyer. "Conversation at Saratoga." *The American Recorder* 7, no. 2 (Spring 1966): 7–11; 7, no. 3 (Summer 1966): 9–11.

Conversation among Frans Brüggen, Hans-Martin Linde, and Hans Ulrich Staeps at the 1965 International Recorder School at Skidmore College, Saratoga Springs, NY. Covers: Part One: the ARS recorder school; the role of educators and professional players in the recorder movement; why the recorder often is not taken seriously; the effects of the fast pace of American life on musical development; what players need to know about the music they play; the need for standardization in music terminology; the importance of promoting the development of a modern repertory for recorder. Part Two: the scope of "technique"; how the recorder seems more generally suited for women than for men and for introverts rather than for extroverts; the historical appropriateness of playing soft; the need to resist making compromises for twentieth-century ears; how Brüggen plays in public only for the money and the applause; the limits of attempts at authenticity; the practical reasons that force professional players to play modern recorders rather than historical ones; how interest in the recorder wanes beyond childhood.

948. Cohen, Joel. *Reprise: The Extraordinary Revival of Early Music*. Boston: Little, Brown, 1985. xvi, 227 p. ISBN 0316150371.

Includes a characteristically opinionated, perhaps overcute, but always insightful chapter on Frans Brüggen.

949. Drillon, Jacques. "Frans Brüggen et la rhétorique" [Frans Brüggen and rhetoric]. *Flûte à bec* 3 (June 1982): 3–10.

Introductory note: "Here is the fourth chapter of a book which, according to the author, was 'realized'—not written—in 1977 by Jacques Drillon about Frans Brüggen. Constructed as a radio broadcast—i.e., 'montaged' and built from various interviews—it attempts to encircle the personality of the great Dutch recorder player, but also to define the phenomenon that has crystallized around his personality. It therefore makes appeal equally to completely involuntary witnesses. The remainder of the book is and will remain unpublished." Consists of short quotations by Brüggen himself (provocative, as always), other modern musicians from his circle, and such "witnesses" as Céline, Diderot, Jean-Luc Godard, Pascal, and Wittgenstein.

950. Ehrlich, Robert. "Frans Brüggen, oder: Die Vermarktung eines Star-Musikers" [Frans Brüggen, or: the marketing of a star musician]. *Tibia* 18, no. 2 (1993): 449–53.

Entertainingly discusses how Brüggen's natural talents as a performer and teacher were augmented in the 1960s, first, by Telefunken's marketing techniques, to make him into a "star" on a par with popular soloists on the violin, piano, or cello, and second, by the Dutch government's lavish provision for education and the arts, to make a "Dutch school" from his students and their students, etc. Another fine article based on one of his master's theses (item 1458). Concludes that the "product" was so successful that Brüggen was "not only successfully sold as a solo recorder player but also became a legend, a cult figure—a name that is unseparable from the idea of recorder, just like Xerox and photocopying, Ford and the car, or Hoover and the vacuum cleaner." Letter from Bruce Haynes and reply by

Robert Ehrlich (both in English) in 18, no. 4 (1993): 669. Letters to the editor from Bruce Haynes with reply by Ehrlich (18, no. 4 [1993]: 669) and Jeremias Schwarzer (19, no. 1 [1994]: 83).

951. Epstein, Jan. "An Interview with Frans Brüggen." *The Recorder: Journal of the Victorian Recorder Guild* 8 (July 1988): 8–10. Reprinted from *The Melbourne Report*, April 1988.

    Covers: his students; his training; the reasons for the strength of the recorder movement in the Netherlands; the importance of Fred Morgan's recorder making; and his Orchestra of the 18th Century.

952. Hedlund, H. Jean. "An Untenable Esthetic Posture." *The American Recorder* 14, no. 1 (February 1973): 12–14.

    Reports on Brüggen's contributions to the First International Recorder Festival in Bruges in summer 1972. Questions the intentions of the aural and physical mannerisms apparent in his playing. The first part of the argument criticizes the aesthetics of three compositions performed at the festival: Berio's *Gesti*, Kees Boeke's *Tombeau d'Hotteterre*, and the Netherlands Recorder Trio's *Sourcream, 1971*. The remainder attempts to discredit Brüggen's playing aesthetic on the grounds that he was unable to articulate his position convincingly to the audience at Bruges when challenged by his critics. Letter from J. Hill in 14, no. 3 (August 1973): 110.

953. Horner, Keith. "Frans Brueggen on the Baroque Recorder." *Early Music* 2, no. 2 (April 1974): 101–3.

    Edited version of an interview broadcast on BBC Radio 3 in October 1973. Brüggen discusses the following topics, among others: the advantages of playing authentic instruments, the difficulty of achieving a proper balance between the recorder and other instruments, historical recorder virtuosi, the use of vibrato in Baroque instrumental music, the modern ear's attachment to playing in tune, and *notes inégales*. Letter from James Middleton in *Recorder & Music* 4, no. 12 (December 1974): 442.

954. Kenyon, Nicholas. "An Interview with Frans Brüggen." *The American Recorder* 24, no. 4 (November 1983): 150–53.

    " . . . [A] condensation of an interview broadcast in 1982 over WNYC, New York." Covers: recorder playing in Holland during his youth, his introduction to the recorder by his older brother, his thoughts on the popularity of the recorder, his shift to historical instruments in the 1950s, the qualities he looks for in modern copies, using variation in pitch as an expressive device, the transverse flute, the early music movement, the Orchestra of the 18th Century.

955. Moeck, Hermann. "Frans Brüggen 50." *Tibia* 9, no. 3 (1984): 191–93.

A tribute. First a short biography, emphasizing his recent activities as conductor of the Orchestra of the 18th Century. ("Finally freed from the recorder! Coming to terms with true masterpieces!") Then an evaluation of his importance to the recorder, manner of playing and his mannerisms, preferences in repertory (not mediocre recorder literature), always making "contemporary" music, and dealings with avant-garde recorder music.

956. Moreno, Emilio. "Una pequeña conversacion con Frans Brüggen, director de orquesta" [A brief conversation with Frans Brüggen, orchestra conductor]. *Musica Antiqua* 7 (February 1987): 6–10.

Almost all on conducting. But, asked the capping question: "recorder or conducting?" Brüggen replies: "The recorder for me gives body to a physical, corporeal love, and the orchestra makes corporeal a spiritual love. And love is composed of these two aspects. I am in love with both."

957. Nastasi, Mirjam. "Frans Brüggen im Gespräch mit Mirjam Nastasi" [Frans Brüggen in conversation with Mirjam Nastasi]. (Das Porträt) *Tibia* 7, no. 3 (1982): 193–96.

Covers: his beginning the recorder to stop his being "bored to death" during World War II; his graduation (a program of Handel, Walter Leigh, and Franz Reizenstein, "a ludicrously simple [one] compared with today"); his musical influences (Fischer-Dieskau, Heifetz, Leonhardt, Bijlsma); his fascination for an "amateur instrument with a limited repertory"; the recorder's modest role in the early music movement; "authentic" performance vs. exorcism; his preference for 17th-century music over that of the 18th century; the recorder today in Holland; his relationship to the audience; Brüggen clones; the potential of the modern repertory, especially electronics; his orchestra; but his continuing playing of the recorder "with heart and soul."

958. Nuchelmans, Jan. "'Muziek blijft toch een soort schaakspel'" [Music is like a kind of chess game]. *Tijdschrift voor oude muziek* 1, no. 1 (15 February 1986): 5–7.

Interview with Frans Brüggen. Short answers to a variety of subjects, including: his recorder collection, authenticity, conducting, and the young generation of recorder players.

959. Péteri, Judit. "A Conversation with Frans Brüggen in Budapest." *Hungarian Music Quarterly* 1, no. 2 (1989): 13–18.

Brüggen begins by saying that "The literature of the Baroque recorder and even that of the transverse flute is so poor that after a while you start longing for a larger repertoire." But he confesses, "I still give 70 concerts a year on average as a recorder player. Perhaps it is just the programs that have changed a little. For example, I don't play Handel sonatas any more; before I used to play them very often."

960. [Shapiro, Daniel R.] "An Interview with Frans Brueggen." *The American Recorder* 15, no. 3 (August 1974): 71–76. Reprinted in *Recorder & Music* 5, no. 1 (March 1975): 7–11.

Covers: how modern performers of early music should try to assume the state of mind of musicians of the past, the need to study "formulas and instrumental ideas" rather than pieces, the importance of knowing the conventions of classical oratory, the influence of Gustav Leonhardt on his playing, his preference of original instruments to copies, how the "engines" of modern copies are too big and overpowering, how players should exploit the flexibility in pitch available on melody instruments.

961. [Thomson, J.M.] "Frans Brüggen." (Profile) *The Recorder and Music Magazine* 1, no. 6 (August 1964): 165. A slightly expanded version appears in item 908.

Covers: his musical education, his decision to pursue a career as a performer rather than as a scholar, the reasons he chose the recorder, his preference for sitting while playing, his acknowledged limitations as a flutist, his current projects, Berio's *Gesti* (in item 908 only), the importance of commissioning new works.

962. Thomson, J.M., and Theo Wyatt. "Frans Brueggen and the New Mannerism: A Symposium." Drawings by Linda Kitson. *Recorder & Music Magazine* 3, no. 11 (September 1971): 399–403.

When speaking to the Music Club of London on 25 May 1971, Brüggen provokes a spirited dialogue with audience members—Theo Wyatt in particular—by playing his recording of a Hotteterre Suite for two recorders, in which long notes are enveloped in a crescendo and diminuendo with a corresponding fluctuation in pitch. Thomson transcribes the exchange. Brüggen says that he sacrifices intonation in favor of flexibility, and Wyatt replies that the effect becomes monotonous. The transcription of the dialogue is followed by two short essays by Wyatt and Thomson. Wyatt stresses the importance of intonation and says that Brüggen is wrong to subordinate intonation to expressiveness. Thomson defends Brüggen, calling him "the pioneer of a new Mannerism that necessarily expresses the late 20th century feeling of disintegrating structures." Letter from M.B.

Robinson in 3, no. 12 (December 1971): 455–57, with a response from Thomson.

963. Vitz, Carol. "Frans Brueggen: A Personal Profile of the Dutch Recorder Virtuoso." *The American Recorder* 10, no. 1 (Winter 1969): 12–14.

A highly subjective and romanticized portrait of Brüggen, based on an interview with the author. Covers his childhood, education, musical training, lifestyle, and plans. The author was quite enamored of Brüggen, which might explain the fanzine character of the article.

964. White, Beverly. "Frans Brueggen's Visit to Oberlin, 1973: A Recollection." *The American Recorder* 14, no. 3 (August 1973): 87–89.

Report of a lecture by Brüggen on Jacob van Eyck. Discusses performance practice, drawing on Ganassi, Ortiz, Jambe de Fer, and Simpson, among others. (The article also includes a review of the Sour Cream concert that followed the lecture.)

965. Winters, Ross. "Frans Brüggen." *Music and Musicians* 37, no. 7 (March 1989): 29–32.

Covers: his early days as a student of Kees Otten, his collaboration with Gustav Leonhardt in the 1960s, his thoughts on the performances and compositions heard recently at an avant-garde recorder week in Amsterdam, the move by younger players away from solo playing, his decision to slow the pace of his solo career because "I do not have the energy any longer," his early experiences as a conductor of Telemann's *Tafelmusik* for a recording project late in the 1960s, his dissatisfaction with the literature for recorder, the genesis of the Orchestra of the Eighteenth Century, its focus on live performance, the evolution of the orchestral repertory, the differences between modern orchestras and orchestras of authentic instruments, why the modern orchestra's repertory lies between Brahms and Stravinsky, and his immediate plans for the orchestra.

BURGESS, CHRIS

966. Ferris, Jill, and Janet Norman. "Chris Burgess." (Profile) *The Recorder: Journal of the Victorian Recorder Guild* 1 (1984): 17–18.

Covers his background, emphasizing the difficulties an Australian has had in studying to be a professional recorder player.

BUTT, VALERIE

967. "Valerie Butt." (Recorder Personalities) *Recorder & Music* 4, no. 11 (September 1974): 428.
    Brief profile.

CASTELLANI, MARCELLO

968. Delius, Nikolaus. "A la gloire de ma flûte: Marcello Castellani" [To the glory of my flute: Marcello Castellani]. *Tibia* 14, no. 3 (1989): 512–18.
    Although Castellani teaches recorder as well as traverso at the Verona conservatory, this interview is exclusively concerned with his background, his attitude to early music as a Florentine, the Italian flute literature, early music in Italy, and his work for SPES (Studio per edizioni scelte).

CLARK, PAUL (B. 1927)

969. Loretto, Alec, and Adrienne Simpson. "'Progress Will be Made': Paul Clark on Amateur Recorder Playing." *Early Music New Zealand* 2, no. 4 (December 1986): 10–16.
    Interview. Covers: learning the recorder, attitudes towards the instrument, the standards of amateur performance, technique, the role of virtuosi, consort music, the soprano recorder as the modern standard, his playing, and the future of the recorder.

970. Loretto, Alec, and Adrienne Simpson. "Conversation with Paul Clark." *The Recorder: Journal of the Victorian Recorder Guild* 6 (June 1987): 15–18.
    An interview, almost completely different from item 969. Covers: how he became involved with the recorder; his and others' arrangements for the recorder, including his philosophy of arranging; the failure of English recorder music to travel abroad; the problems of the soprano recorder having become the modern standard; his plans; and his wishes for the future of recorder music.

CLEMENCIC, RENÉ (B. 1928)

971. Kubitschek, Ernst. "René Clemencic im Gespräch mit unserem Mitarbeiter Ernst Kubitschek" [René Clemencic in conversation with our collaborator Ernst Kubitschek]. (Das Porträt) *Tibia* 5, no. 2 (1980): 114–16.

Covers: his training on the recorder (Staeps, Collette, Höffer-von Winterfeld, Schmitz, Nitschke), the founding of his ensemble (Musica Antiqua, later the Clemencic Consort), his study of philosophy and its bearing on his music-making, his directorship of his ensemble, his recorder playing, his composing (not electronic!), his teaching (only summer courses), and his hobbies.

972. Thomson, J.M. "René Clemencic." *Recorder & Music Magazine* 2, no. 10 (September 1968): 320–21. Reprinted with slight revisions in item 908.

    Covers: his musical education, first playing the piano, then switching to recorder; his introduction to his first teacher, Hans Ulrich Staeps; his founding of the Musica Antiqua of Vienna; his plans to produce 17th-century opera; his work with contemporary music as a composer and performer; his plans.

CLINGAN, JUDITH (B. 1945)

973. Dixon, Kay. "Judith Clingan, Composer." *The Recorder: Journal of the Victorian Recorder Guild* 12 (December 1990): 23–25.

    Covers: her upbringing, her (largely self-) training as a composer, and her interest in the recorder.

CONRAD, FERDINAND (1912–1992)

974. "Ferdinand Conrad." (Recorder Personalities) *Recorder & Music* 7, no. 5 (March 1982): 133.
    Brief biography.

975. Köneke, Hans W. "Ferdinand Conrad zum 65. Geburtstag" [Ferdinand Conrad on his 65th birthday]. (Das Porträt) *Tibia* 2, no. 1 (1977): 223–26.

    Begins with a quote from Conrad about the importance of "soul" in music making. Then covers: his training, particularly with Gustav Scheck; his early performing career; his work with the early music group that he founded, Kammermusikkreis Ferdinand Conrad, which included a recorder quartet; his affinity for singers; his teaching in Hannover and on summer courses, including his aptitude for it. Ends with a select discography.

976. Lützen, Ludolf. "Ferdinand Conrad† (23.1.1912–24.2.1992)." *Tibia* 17, no. 2 (1992): 131–32.

Obituary, concentrating on his last years. Followed by a short tribute, "Für Ferdinand," by Ulrich Thieme (for the *Tibia* editorial staff).

977. Mascher, Ekkehardt. "Zum 75. Geburtstag von Ferdinand Conrad" [On Ferdinand Conrad's 75th birthday]. *Tibia* 12, no. 1 (1987): 354.

An outline of his life and a listing of the music performed at a celebration of his birthday in January 1987.

978. [Thomson, J.M.] "Ferdinand Conrad." (Profile) *The Recorder and Music Magazine* 1, no. 11 (November 1965): 343. Reprinted in item **908**.

Covers: his musical training—including study with Gustav Scheck, who introduced him to the recorder; his involvement with Kammermusikkreis Scheck-Wenzinger, and a 1936 performance of Brandenburg Concerto No. 4 with Scheck in Paris; his move to Hanover and the founding of Kammermusikkreis Ferdinand Conrad; the shortage of good instruments in Germany; his preference for the flute for modern music; his musical tastes; his plans.

COOLEN, SASKIA

* Helsloot, Loes. "*RECORDERS*: Een eigentijdse bewerking van middeleeuwse muziek" [RECORDERS: a contemporary adaptation of medieval music]. Cited above as item **923**.

COOMBER, DAVID

979. Simpson, Adrienne. "David Coomber in Conversation." *Early Music New Zealand* 1, no. 1 (March 1985): 3-7.

Interview. Covers: his background, living in New Zealand, the instruments he plays, his repertory, his recorder making, and his plans.

COTTE, ROGER

980. Reyne, Hugo. "Interview de Roger Cotte" [Interview with Roger Cotte]. *Flûte à bec & instruments anciens* 9 (December 1983): 3-5.

Covers: the beginnings of his career, the repertory of his students, his interest in the flageolet, his recordings and films, why he left France for Brazil, the early music scene in Brazil, and his current and future projects.

CRAMER-CHEMIN-PETIT, JEANNETTE

981. Höffer, Linde. "Abschied von Jeannette Cramer-Chemin-Petit" [Farewell to Jeannette Cramer-Chemin-Petit]. *Tibia* 13, no. 1 (1988): 29.

   Obituary. Covers: her training with Höffer and Aurèle Nicolet; her early performing; the works her father, Hans Chemin-Petit, wrote for her; her involvement with new playing techniques; and her teaching.

DAVENPORT, LANOUE (B. 1922)

982. [Thomson, J.M.] "LaNoue Davenport." (Profile) *The Recorder and Music Magazine* 1, no. 4 (February 1964): 111. Reprinted with slight revisions in item 908.

   Covers: his beginnings as a jazz trumpet player in Texas; his introduction to the recorder in a music history class in New York City; the Manhattan Consort; the New York Pro Musica; his fondness for the crumhorn; his extramusical interests; his observations on the early music movement.

983. Wollitz, Kenneth. "An Interview with LaNoue Davenport." *The American Recorder* 10, no. 4 (Fall 1969): 107–9, 130.

   Covers: his musical education; his introduction to the recorder; his work with the New York Pro Musica; instrumentation, authenticity, performance practice, and improvisation; the need to learn as many other instruments as possible; his family.

984. Wollitz, Ken, and Marcia Blue. "An Interview with LaNoue Davenport." *The American Recorder* 30, no. 1 (February 1989): 4–7.

   Covers: his origins as a jazz player in Texas, his composition study with Erich Katz in New York, his quick introduction to the recorder one month before his public debut, his role in the revival of the American Recorder Society (ARS) after World War II, the history and character of the early ARS, his teaching career, early workshops and regional chapters, the ARS editions, the role of the ARS in promoting early music in the United States, the importance of amateurs to the ARS. Letter from Margaret Duncan Greene in 30, no. 2 (May 1989): 81–82.

DEERENBERG, BALDRICK

985. [Hunt, Edgar]. "Baldrick Deerenberg." (Recorder Personality) *Recorder & Music* 5, no. 2 (June 1975): 73.

A brief profile of the Dutch player. Covers: his academic posts; his introduction to the recorder as a university student in Amsterdam; his study with Brüggen at the Royal Conservatory; his concertizing, broadcasting, and recording.

DELIUS, NIKOLAUS (B. 1926)

986. Gerhold, Hartmut. "Nikolaus Delius zum 65. Geburtstag: Brief eines Kollegen und ehemaligen Schülers" [Nikolaus Delius on his 65th birthday: letter from a colleague and former student]. *Tibia* 16, no. 3 (1991): 542-44.

Covers: his teaching; radio performances and recordings; editing of about 50 editions; articles; membership of the editorial team of *Tibia*; curiosity; his "romantic" playing; and a plea for him to write a flute method.

DINN, FREDA (1910-1990)

987. Hunt, Edgar. "Freda Dinn, GRCM, ARCM, ATCL." *The Recorder Magazine* 10, no. 3 (September 1990): 71-72.

Obituary. See also 10, no. 2 (June 1990): 57 and Herbert Hersom's letter in 10, no. 4 (December 1990): 112.

988. [Thomson, J.M.] "Freda Dinn." (Profile) *The Recorder and Music Magazine* 1, no. 7 (November 1964): 211-12.

Covers: her musical education, introduction to the recorder as a teacher at the Royal College, work with music pedagogy at the Froebel Institute at Roehampton, research and writing projects, interests.

DOLCI, AMICO (B. 1957)

989. "Amico Dolci." (Recorder Personality) *Recorder & Music* 5, no. 1 (March 1975): 40.

990. Bergmann, Walter. "Amico Dolci: An Interview." *Recorder & Music* 5, no. 12 (December 1977): 382-83.

Covers: his required two years of civil service in Italy, to begin in a few days on his 20th birthday; the work of his father on social reform in Sicily;

his introduction to the recorder and eventual study at the Conservatorium in Palermo; the composition of *Ricercari;* his favorite repertory and composers; his plans. Letter from Inga Kristina Fraccaro in 6, no. 1 (March 1978): 27.

DOLCI, DANILO (B. 1924)

991. Alton, Edwin H. "Danilo Dolci and il Flauto Dolce." *Recorder & Music Magazine* 3, no. 8 (December 1970): 294–95.

Describes Alton's work in Sicily with Danilo Dolci, the Italian social reformer. One of Dolci's goals was to introduce the recorder into Sicilian primary and secondary school curricula, and Alton was called in to encourage and instruct those interested in learning the instrument—particularly school teachers. All of Dolci's children played the recorder, and thirteen-year-old Amico Dolci was already "a most skillful and promising performer."

DOLMETSCH, ARNOLD (1858–1940)

992. Campbell, Margaret. *Dolmetsch: The Man and His Work.* London: Hamish Hamilton, 1975. xv, 318 p. ISBN 0241891760.

A well-balanced account of the life and work of Arnold Dolmetsch, the man who reintroduced the recorder to the world in the early 20th century. The famous events for the recorder are of course mentioned: Dolmetsch buying a Bressan recorder at Sotheby's in 1905, acquiring a copy of *The Compleat Flute-Master* soon afterwards, losing the Bressan at Waterloo Station in 1919, and succeeding in making a copy of it later that year. And the family's recorder playing is mentioned in passing thereafter. Yet the recorder was only a small part of Dolmetsch's work in performance, instrument making, and scholarship, as the book engagingly relates. Reviewed by Edgar Hunt in *The Galpin Society Journal* 29 (May 1976): 132–34.

DOLMETSCH, CARL (B. 1911)

993. Bennett, Rodney M. "Carl Dolmetsch and Joseph Saxby's Fifty-Year Partnership." *The American Recorder* 24, no. 1 (February 1983): 24–25.

Begins by describing Saxby's background and how the two first met in the early 1930s. Although Dolmetsch assumed responsibility for both the family firm and the Haslemere Festival after the death of his father in 1940, the duo continued to perform, and as of 1982 had completed forty-four tours. Includes a brief account of the demise of Arnold Dolmetsch Ltd. in the late 1970s and the incorporation of J. & M. Dolmetsch and Haslemere Musical Instruments in the early 1980s.

994. Dolmetsch, Carl. "In at the Start." *Recorder & Music* 4, no. 9 (March 1974): 325.
Reminiscences complementing those of Miles Tomalin in item 1113.

995. Hedrick, Peter. "An Interview with Carl Dolmetsch and Joseph Saxby." *The American Recorder* 15, no. 2 (May 1974): 43-47.
Covers: the story of Dolmetsch losing his father's Bressan recorder at Waterloo Station, the work of his father with performance practice, his distaste for charlatanism in performers, instrument making, the history of the Dolmetsch-Saxby collaboration, authenticity, the Dolmetsch Foundation.

996. "Mr. Recorder—Carl Dolmetsch zum 80. Geburtstag" [Mr. Recorder—Carl Dolmetsch on his 80th birthday]. *Tibia* 16, no. 4 (1991): 632-33.
A short biography and tribute.

997. O'Kelly, Eve. "Mr Recorder." *The Recorder Magazine* 11, no. 2 (June 1991): 48-51.
A profile of Carl Dolmetsch on the occasion of his 80th birthday. Covers: his early musical education; his assumption of responsibility for the family workshops after 1940; his career as a performer and his many commissions; his children and their musical activities; his views on modern technical virtuosity, the practice of transcription, and avant-garde composition; his study with his father.

998. [Thomson, J.M.] "Carl Dolmetsch." (Profile) *The Recorder and Music Magazine* 1, no. 1 (May 1963): 21-22. Revised and expanded version appears in item 908.
Covers: the move to Haslemere during World War I, his musical education, the early days of the Haslemere Festival, his assumption of responsibility for the Festival and for the Dolmetsch workshops in 1940, life during World War II, his ideas for new instruments, his dislike of the trend toward making modern instruments based on historical models, why the recorder has not been accepted as a serious instrument, his desire to modernize the recorder, his extramusical interests. (The version in item 908 includes an account of the loss of his father's Bressan alto at Waterloo Station.)

999. Valleau, Douglas. "An Interview with Carl Dolmetsch." *Continuo* 4, no. 5 (February 1981): 6–13; 4, no. 6 (May 1981): 6–12; 4, no. 7 (April 1981): 3–11.

Based on a tape recording made in 1974. Covers: his reminiscences, recorder tone, and playing early music.

EHRHARDT, SUSANNE

1000. Zetzmann, Liz. "An Interview with Susanne Ehrhardt." *The Recorder: Journal of the Victorian Recorder Guild* 14 (December 1991): 9–10.

Covers: her training on the clarinet and recorder in the former East Germany, then in Western Europe; attitudes towards the recorder in East Germany; what she enjoys playing; the character of Hirose's *Meditation*; her interest in modern music; her teaching; and her playing (100–120 concerts per year!).

EHRLICH, ROBERT (B. 1965)

1001. Lasocki, David. "The Art of Becoming a Recorder Player: Four European Professionals in Conversation with David Lasocki." *American Recorder* 32, no. 3 (September 1991): 9–13.

An interview with Walter van Hauwe, Conrad Steinmann, Robert Ehrlich, and Ulrike Volkhardt. Covers: their own training, how they teach, what attracts them about the recorder, what it means to be a "professional," the balance of technique and musicianship, extending the recorder's repertory, how the new generation of professionals is going to make a living.

ECCLES, LANCE

1002. Tattersall, Malcolm. "Profile: Lance Eccles." *The Recorder: Journal of the Victorian Recorder Guild* 8 (July 1988): 26–28.

Based on an interview. Covers: his training, his work with The Reluctant Consort, and his composing and arranging (with comments by Tattersall).

FERGUSON, SUZANNE

1003. Ritchie, Jacqueline. "Entretien avec Susan [sic] Ferguson: une fondation à la mémoire du Dr Erich Katz aux États

Enis [sic]" [Interview with Suzanne Ferguson: a foundation to the memory of Dr. Erich Katz in the United States]. *Flûte à bec et instruments anciens* 26 (November 1988): 24–25.

Covers: the Erich Katz Foundation, the Katz recorder composition prize, recorder playing in the United States, recorder works for children, and American recorder works.

FOR FOUR RECORDER QUARTET

1004. "Meeting up with the For Four Recorder Quartet." *American Recorder* 31, no. 3 (September 1990): 16.

A brief profile of the Boston-based group and its members: Roxanne Layton, Linda Lunbeck, James Ryder, and Roy Sansom.

GALPIN, FRANCIS W. (1858–1945)

1005. Higbee, Dale. "Francis W. Galpin: Recorder Player." *The American Recorder* 5, no. 4 (November 1964): 9–11. Revision of an article in *ARS Newsletter* 35.

Begins with a brief biography. Describes Galpin's activities as a member of a recorder consort during the first quarter of the 20th century and identifies the instruments used by the group. Lists seven recorders from Galpin's collection that are now in the Museum of Fine Arts, Boston.

GARRIDO, GABRIEL

1006. Lacornerie, Agnès, and Patricia Lavail. "Interview de Gabriel Garrido" [Interview with Gabriel Garrido]. *Flûte à bec & instruments anciens* 11 (June 1984): 7–8.

Covers: his studies at the Schola Cantorum Basiliensis, his liking for Ganassi and the music of the 16th century, the repertory of his recorder quartet (Pro Arte), and his teaching at the Conservatoire de Musique Ancienne in Geneva and in Italy.

GIESBERT, FRANZ JULIUS (1896–1972)

1007. H[unt], E[dgar]. "Obituary: Julius Giesbert." *Recorder and Music Magazine* 4, no. 3 (September 1972): 99.

1008. von Huene, Friedrich. "A Visit with Franz Julius Giesbert." *The American Recorder* 24, no. 3 (August 1983): 107-8.

In summer 1969, von Huene visited Neuwied, West Germany, to examine Giesbert's collection of historical recorders. He also took the opportunity to conduct a brief interview with Giesbert. Covers: his activity as one of the early proponents of the recorder in Germany, his work as an editor of recorder music, his encounters with Hans Conrad Fehr and Peter Harlan. Opens with a brief biography.

GLANVILLE-HICKS, PEGGY (1912-1990)

1009. Tattersall, Malcolm. "Peggy Glanville-Hicks." *The Recorder: Journal of the Victorian Recorder Guild* 12 (December 1990): 5.

Obituary.

GLASSGOLD, A.C. (COOK) (1899-1985)

1010. Taylor, Ralph. "Cook Glassgold, 1899-1985: A Reminiscence." *The American Recorder* 26, no. 3 (August 1985): 116-17.

Includes an account of Glassgold's role in the initial design of *The American Recorder*. See also the obituary in the *New York Times*, 15 February 1985. Letter from Frank Plachte in 26, no. 4 (November 1985): 183.

GOODYEAR, STEPHEN (1915-1983)

1011. "Obituary: Stephen Goodyear." *The Recorder & Music Magazine* 7, no. 12 (December 1983): 325.

GRAYSON, ARNOLD

1012. Wollitz, Kenneth. "An Interview with Arnold Grayson." *The American Recorder* 19, no. 3 (November 1978): 100-3.

Covers: his early musical training and introduction to the recorder, teaching, running his music shop, and plans to work with Richard Taruskin on editions of partbooks in original notation (Ogni Sorte Editions, published in Miami, then Coconut Grove, Florida).

GÜMBEL, MARTIN (1923–1986)

1013. Braun, Gerhard. "Abschied von Martin Gümbel" [Farewell to Martin Gümbel]. *Tibia* 12, no. 1 (1987): 353–54.

   A tribute by one of the students of the German flautist and composer, who wrote several avant-garde works for recorder.

HALFPENNY, ERIC (1906–1979)

1014. Byrne, Maurice. "Eric Halfpenny, 1906–79: An Obituary." *The Galpin Society Journal* 33 (March 1980): 1–7.

   Includes a list of his publications. A brief initial notice appears in 32 (May 1979): 130.

1015. "Eric Halfpenny." *Recorder & Music* 6, no. 6 (June 1979): 185.

   Brief obituary.

HARLAN, PETER (1898–1966)

1016. "Peter Harlan." (Tributes) *Recorder and Music Magazine* 2, no. 3 (November 1966): 94.

   Obituary.

HART, DAVID (D. 1988)

1017. "Tributes to David Hart." *The American Recorder* 29, no. 3 (August 1988): 111–12.

   Reminiscences by Jack Ashworth, Lucy Cross, R.J. Alcala, Mary Springfels, Wendy Gillespie, and Martha Bixler. Two additional tributes in 29, no. 4 (November 1988): 171.

HAUWE, WALTER VAN (B. 1948)

1018. Boragno, Pierre. "Une interview exclusive de Walter van Hauwe" [An exclusive interview with Walter van Hauwe]. *Flûte à bec & instruments anciens* 7 (June 1983): 9–10.

   Covers: the recent emergence of the recorder as "a true professional instrument," Frans Brüggen's teaching methods, developing a professional recorder technique, the "practicality" of the Dutch school, his book, not thinking too much when performing, and staying fresh.

* Epstein, Jan, and Ursula Grawe. "Conversation with Kees Boeke and Walter van Hauwe." Cited above as item 939.

* Lasocki, David. "The Art of Becoming a Recorder Player: Four European Professionals in Conversation with David Lasocki." Cited above as item 1001.

1019. Weilenmann, Matthias. "Walter van Hauwe." (Das Porträt) *Tibia* 11, no. 1 (1986): 33–37.
Begins with a short biography. Then covers: his attitude of "the new in the old," which affects his approach to historical sources; his love of the vast technical possibilities in new music; the basis of music as "'peep,' emphasis, and noise"; the increasing conservatism in early music performance over the last 20-30 years; his own need to push boundaries; the "crisis" of both the recorder and the arts in general today, partly a consequence of composers not playing their own works and players not composing their own works, and improvisation as a way forward; his approach to teaching (helping students to find their own path); his playing of the traverso and shakuhachi.

HAYNES, BRUCE (B. 1942)

* McRae, Lee. "Bruce Haynes: Performer, Instrument Maker, and Teacher." Cited above as item 283.

HENZLER, RICHARD AND ELAINE

1020. Reiter, Andrea. "The World According to Richie." *American Recorder* 34, no. 4 (November 1993): 12–14, 23.
Interview with Richard Henzler, proprietor of Courtly Music Unlimited in New York City. Covers: his wife's and his promotion of the recorder through Courtly Music Unlimited's "American Performers on Recorder" series, the conditions that restrict the acceptance of the recorder as a serious instrument in the United States, why he is in the business of early music, the buying habits of recorder players, recommendations for selecting a recorder, the broadening of musical interests among recorder players, his musical training, his practice habits.

1021. Rose, Pete. [Profile of Richard and Elaine Henzler]. (On the Cutting Edge) *American Recorder* 34, no. 4 (November 1993): 27-28.
   Covers: their performances, repertory, plans, and thoughts on the future of the recorder.

HÖFFER-VON WINTERFELD, LINDE (1919-1993)

1022. Höffer-von Winterfeld, Linde. "Aus dem Leben einer Blockflötenspielerin" [From the life of a recorder player]. *Tibia* 10, no. 1 (1985): 274-77.
   Autobiographical sketch, including the background to her various methods and studies. Asides on the importance for the recorder of Michael Vetter and Frans Brüggen.

HÖLLER, GÜNTHER (B. 1937)

1023. Stockmeier, Wolfgang. "Günther Höller." (Das Porträt) *Tibia* 9, no. 3 (1984): 189-90.
   Covers: the role of the recorder in new music, his partnerships with modern recorder composers, the need to avoid fanaticism in interpreting early music, playing with non-"historically informed" musicians, historical vs. modern instruments, his training; and his teaching. Unfortunately, Höller is laconic and the interviewer allows himself to speak as much as the interviewee.

HOLST, IMOGEN (1907-1984)

1024. "Obituary: Imogen Holst, CBE." *The Recorder and Music Magazine* 8, no. 2 (June 1984): 69.
   Brief account of her accomplishments as a composer and editor of recorder music.

HOLTSLAG, PETER (B. 1957)

1025. Nallen, Evelyn. "Peter Holtslag in Conversation with Evelyn Nallen." *The Recorder & Music Magazine* 9, no. 1 (March 1987): 6-7.
   Covers: the British recorder world, the future of the recorder, and his plans.

HOPKINS, BERNARD J. (1915–1986)

1026. "Bernard J. Hopkins, C.Ss.R., 1915–1986." *The American Recorder* 28, no. 1 (February 1987): 19–21.

   A collection of short remembrances with an introductory tribute by Suzanne Ferguson. Contributors: Dennis W. Hopkins, George Kriehn, Martha Bixler, Frances Dwight, Winifred Jaeger, Mary K. Whittington, Richard Conn, Ellen Alexander, and Lee McRae.

HÜNTELER, KONRAD

1027. Struck, Annette. "Konrad Hünteler." (Das Porträt) *Tibia* 12, no. 3 (1987): 499–504.

   Covers: his background; whether one player can play flute, Baroque flute, and recorder successfully; the potential of the Baroque flute in modern music; "every music its correct flute"; differences in tone between early flutes and modern copies; helping students play both stylishly and with individuality; his contribution to a new recorder method; male and female flutists; his ensemble experience; and his hobbies.

HUNT, EDGAR (B. 1909)

1028. Dolmetsch, Carl. "A Birthday Tribute to Our Chairman, Edgar Hunt." *Recorder & Music Magazine* 3, no. 2 (June 1969): 74–75.

   Dolmetsch's reminiscences on the occasion of Hunt's 60th birthday. Covers: Hunt's first performance at the Haslemere Festival in 1931, Hunt's support of English fingering, the founding of the Society of Recorder Players, Hunt's work as a teacher, Hunt's publications and editions, Anglo-French classes at Roehampton.

1029. Ehrlich, Robert. "Edgar Hunt." (Das Porträt) *Tibia* 18, no. 3 (1993): 532–36.

   Hunt's book *The Recorder and its Music* (item 12) has never been translated into German. For this reason, the aim of the interview is to present information generally familiar to English-speaking readers (not to mention French- and Japanese-) but not German-. Covers the octogenarian Hunt's involvement with the recorder from his student days to the present. Concludes with some new thoughts on modern recorder music, the recorder in jazz, and the recorder's place in the musical spectrum.

1030. Ferguson, Suzanne. "An Interview with Edgar Hunt." *The American Recorder* 23, no. 1 (February 1982): 11–16.

Covers: his introduction to early music, the compilation of his recorder method and its unfavorable reception by the Dolmetsches, a performance of Bach's *Peasant Cantata* at Haslemere in 1931, the school recorder movement, his favorite 20th-century recorder music, the bell key, recorder examinations in England, the Society of Recorder Players and its local chapters, the Galpin Society, his work with the viola da gamba, the *English Harpsichord Magazine*, recent developments in performance practice. Letter from Gene Reichenthal in 27, no. 1 (February 1986): 38 states that Hunt's first trip to the United States was in 1971 rather than 1981.

1031. [Thomson, J.M.] "Edgar Hunt." (Profile) *The Recorder and Music Magazine* 1, no. 2 (August 1963): 53. Reprinted with slight revisions in item 908.

Covers: his musical education as a flutist and his introduction to the recorder, his work in the 1930s importing recorders with English fingering, the founding of the Society of Recorder Players, his teaching at Trinity College.

1032. "A Tribute to Edgar Hunt." *The Recorder Magazine* 11, no. 1 (March 1991): 15-18.

On the occasion of Hunt's retirement from the editorship of *The Recorder Magazine*. Contributors: Enid Hunt, Philip Thorby, Paul Clark, Frans Brüggen, Mary Cavalier-Smith, Eileen Hadidian, Chris Eyre, Dorothy Kenyon, Brian Bonsor, Herbert Hersom, Carl Dolmetsch, Guido M. Klemisch, Maureen McAllister, Theo Wyatt, Roy Murray, Graham Danbury, and Kees Otten.

KANJI, RICARDO

1033. T[homson], J.M. "Ricardo Kanji—Recorder, Baroque Flute and Cornett." *Recorder and Music Magazine* 4, no. 5 (March 1973): 158-59.

Profile. Covers: his youth in Brazil, his study of flute at the Peabody Conservatory in Baltimore, his study of recorder and Baroque flute with Brüggen in the Hague, early music at the Hague Conservatory, the experience of winning one of the two third prizes in the 1972 Bruges International Competition, his work with the cornett, his thoughts on Brüggen as a teacher.

KATZ, ERICH (1900-1973)

1034. Atwater, Betty Ransom, ed. "Erich Katz: Teacher-Composer, 1900-1973." *The American Recorder* 14, no. 4 (November 1973): 115-35.

A collection of photographs, historical documents, and reminiscences of friends and colleagues. Includes a bibliography of Katz's books, articles, compositions, and arrangements for recorders (a more complete listing than the one found in 12, no. 3 [August 1971]: 106).

1035. Davenport, LaNoue. "Erich Katz: A Profile." *The American Recorder* 11, no. 2 (Spring 1970): 43-45.

Covers: his teaching style; his years in Germany, his emigration and establishment in New York City, his role in the revitalization of the ARS after World War II, his move to California.

* Katz, Erich. "In the Beginning." Cited above as item 95.

1036. Plachte, Frank. "Tribute to Erich Katz 1900-73." *Recorder & Music* 4, no. 9 (March 1974): 330.

Obituary. Includes a summary of his literary and musical publications.

1037. Primus, Constance. "Erich Katz: The Pied Piper Comes to America." *The American Music Research Center Journal* 1 (1991): 1-19.

An extensive profile, falling into several sections, each devoted to a particular facet of his career: Teacher; Director and Performer; Music Director of the American Recorder Society; Editor, Arranger, and Composer. Primus did her research in the Erich Katz archives in the American Music Center at the University of Colorado. As a biography, the article is sketchy and offers little beyond what is already available in other published sources.

1038. Seibert, Peter, and Martha Bixler. "Remembrances of Erich Katz: Interviews with Winifred Jaeger and Hannah Katz." *The American Recorder* 30, no. 2 (May 1989): 52-55.

Two separate interviews: Seibert with Jaeger, and Bixler and Marcia Blue with Katz. Jaeger interview covers: her introduction to Katz; Katz's youth; his immigration to England and his eventual move to the United States; his early teaching appointments; the early days of the American Recorder Society; the incorporation of the ARS; its annual concerts; the growth of the Society's membership. Katz interview covers: Erich Katz's studies in Germany; his work as a music copyist; their early days in New York City; his early involvement in the ARS. Includes excerpts from Hannah Katz's "Reminiscences of Erich Katz," written in 1983.

KELBER, SEBASTIAN (1934?–1977)

1039. Braun, Gerhard. "Sebastian Kelbert." *Tibia* 3, no. 1 (1978): 32–33.
   Obituary.

KLEMISCH, GUIDO

* "Guido Klemisch." Cited above as item 289.

KNEIHS, HANS MARIA (B. 1943)

1040. Epstein, Jan, and Ursula Grawe. "Hans Maria Kneihs." (Profile) *The Recorder: Journal of the Victorian Recorder Guild* 2 (March 1985): 12–15.
   Covers: his background, the beginnings of an Australian "school" of recorder playing, European "schools," the connection between professionals and school teaching, the challenge of the recorder.

1041. "From Cello to Recorder." *Recorder & Music Magazine* 3, no. 11 (September 1971): 408.
   Brief profile of Hans Maria Kneihs, written on the occasion of his first performance in London. Kneihs studied cello and piano at the Vienna Music Academy because the recorder was not offered as a major instrument. After becoming a cellist in the orchestra of the Austrian Broadcasting Association, he returned to the recorder in 1961 and became active as a soloist. In 1964, he was appointed professor of recorder at the Vienna Music Academy.

KRAINIS, BERNARD (B. 1924)

1042. Nagle, Sigrid, with Marcia Blue. "An Interview with Bernard Krainis." *The American Recorder* 30, no. 3 (August 1989): 97–101.
   Covers: his introduction to the recorder at the age of 21; his decision to abandon anthropology and economics to become a music major at New York University; his introduction to the American Recorder Society (ARS) through Erich Katz; his founding, with Noah Greenberg, of the New York Pro Musica; the lack of concern for historical performance practice in the Pro Musica; his exposure to the writings of Quantz in the mid-1960s; his thoughts on tonguing; Suzanne Bloch; Alfred Mann; his years with the ARS; the International Recorder School at Saratoga; his attempts to make the ARS a teaching organization; his plans; why most recorder players are

not more serious about their instrument. Letter from Gary Greenhut in 30, no. 4 (November 1989): 164.

1043. [Thomson, J.M.] "Bernard Krainis." (Profile) *The Recorder and Music Magazine* 1, no. 10 (August 1965): 304–5. Reprinted with slight revisions in item 908.

Covers: his introduction to the recorder at the age of twenty-one, his early recordings for Esoteric, his work with the New York Pro Musica, his performances with his trio, the American Recorder Society, the hazards of early music, ornamentation, his repertory, recent concert appearances in Great Britain.

LASOCKI, DAVID (B. 1947)

1044. Mathiesen, Penelope. "Woodwinds and Research: An Interview with David Lasocki." *Continuo* 15, no. 3 (June 1991): 8–12.

Covers: his training as a performer and development of interest in editing and research; the advantages for research of being employed as a music librarian; his writings, past and present; and new views on "authenticity" in early music performance (see also item 695).

1045. Lasocki, David. "Recorder Players and I." *Early Music New Zealand* 1, no. 4 (December 1985): 3–10.

A lighthearted account of the writing of his dissertation (item 72).

1046. Tattersall, Malcolm. "Profile: David Lasocki." *The Recorder: Journal of the Victorian Recorder Guild* 12 (December 1990): 7–12.

Covers his: training as a performer and researcher; editing of early woodwind music, especially the Handel sonatas; dissertation; work as a music librarian; and research plans.

LEENHOUTS, PAUL

1047. Wollitz, Kenneth, and Martha Bixler. "An Interview with Paul Leenhouts and Han Tol." *The American Recorder* 28, no. 2 (May 1987): 52–54.

Covers: their backgrounds, the Brüggen school of recorder playing, breathing techniques, being forever "new," the current lack of interest in the Baroque period, their ensembles, seven ways of producing dynamics on the recorder, their instruments, Renaissance vs. Baroque sounds, thumb rests, the impatience of American students, subsidies and recorder students in the Netherlands.

LEGÊNE, EVA (B. 1945)

1048. Bixler, Martha, and Kenneth Wollitz. "An Interview with Eva Legêne." *The American Recorder* 27, no. 3 (August 1986): 96–101.

Covers: her background, her experience teaching in America and Denmark, the problems of finding a career for recorder players, the instruments she plays, the (lack of) difficulty of modern recorder music, audiences, the expressive power of the recorder, playing in tune, the Rosenborg recorders.

1049. Epstein, Jan. "Conversation with Eva Legêne." *The Recorder: Journal of the Victorian Recorder Guild* 7 (December 1987): 1–4.

Covers: her background and training, her teaching, modern music for recorder, her attitude to early performance, the Rosenborg recorders, the recorder in works of art.

1050. Rose, Pete. "Mentor." (On the Cutting Edge) *American Recorder* 33, no. 4 (December 1992): 26.

Describes several modern compositions performed by Legêne at the 1992 Berkeley Festival and discusses her efforts to promote contemporary music.

LEHRER, IRMGARD

* Pringle, Rosa. "Revival of the Ancient Recorder: An Interview with Irmgard Lehrer." Cited above as item 100.

LINDE, HANS-MARTIN (B. 1930)

* Brelsford, Edmund, and Gerhart Niemeyer. "Conversation at Saratoga." Cited above as item 947.

1051. Braun, Gerhard. "Es ist wie mit einem Fernrohr. . . . Gespräch mit Hans-Martin Linde" [It's like with a telescope. . . . Conversation with Hans-Martin Linde]. (Das Porträt) *Tibia* 3, no. 2 (1978): 101–5.

Covers: his studies with Gustav Scheck, concentrating on the modern flute and the development of a "modern" musicianship; his dislike of historical specialization; the ease with which musicians can switch pitches and learn performance practice these days; tuning and temperament; his move away from the modern flute to the recorder and historical flutes, because of the difficulty of doing all three adequately; the need for modern flutists to know something of historical practice; his approach to composition ("I simply compose for my instrument"); the connection of present and past for him (like "an old-fashioned telescope, made in two pieces that slide inside one another"); and his performances today. List of his compositions.

1052. Katz, Helen. "Hans-Martin Linde, a Profile." *The American Recorder* 10, no. 2 (Spring 1969): 43–44.

Covers: his musical training; problems of playing both modern and early instruments; his teaching at the Schola Cantorum in Basel; other professional commitments.

1053. Lasocki, David. "Hans-Martin Linde Talks to David Lasocki." *Recorder and Music Magazine* 2, no. 5 (May 1967): 141–42.

Covers: his playing of the Baroque flute; modern vs. old pitch; his use of Fehr instruments; his favorite recorder works and composers; Basel; his experiences touring, recording, and conducting; his performances with Brüggen in 1965; the Vivaldi "flautino" controversy; his children.

1054. Thiede, Christiane, and Wolfgang Lempfrid. "Ich fühle mich als singender Mensch" [I consider myself a singing human]. *Concerto* 45 (July/August 1989): 9–13.

An interview with Hans-Martin Linde. Why has Linde transformed himself largely from a woodwind player into a conductor these days? "I was lucky, in the middle of my life, to be able to begin somewhat anew, instead of teaching Handel sonatas on the recorder or, in the best cases, Mozart concertos on the traverso, for the next 25 years."

1055. Thieme, Ulrich. "Hans-Martin Linde wird 60" [Hans-Martin Linde turns 60]. *Tibia* 15, no. 3 (1990): 199.

A short tribute, expressing astonishment that, on the one hand, the energetic and youthful Linde has already reached 60 and, on the other hand, the celebrated pioneer of the 1950s and 60s had not reached 60 sooner.

1056. Thomson, J.M. "Hans-Martin Linde." (Profile) *Recorder and Music Magazine* 2, no. 1 (March 1966): 10. Reprinted in item 908.

Covers: his introduction to early music through Gustav Scheck, his friendship with August Wenzinger and his association in 1957 with the Schola Cantorum at Basle, the appeal of the Baroque flute, his favorite Baroque compositions and composers, his own compositions and editions, the importance of articulation and vibrato, the instruments he plays, his work with Frans Brüggen, his interests.

LYNN, MICHAEL

1057. Mathiesen, Penelope. "An Interview with Michael Lynn." (Winds of Yore: What's New with Old Woodwinds?) *Continuo* 14, no. 3 (June 1990): 9–11.

Covers: his start on the recorder at the age of five; his childhood in Bloomington, Indiana; his studies at Oakland University in Rochester, Michigan; his self-instruction on Baroque flute; the types of flutes and recorders he plays; his teaching at Oberlin; makers of good Baroque flutes; the shift from Baroque to Classical repertory in many original-instrument orchestras; his work preparing modern editions and facsimiles; the Master of Music in Performance on Early Instruments degree at Oberlin.

MARX, KARL (1897–1985)

1058. Braun, Gerhard. "Abschied von Karl Marx" [Farewell to Karl Marx]. *Tibia* 10, no. 3 (1985): 427.

A tribute to the German composer, "one of the pioneers of contemporary recorder music."

1059. Braun, Gerhard. "Karl Marx." (Das Porträt) *Tibia* 3, no. 1 (1978): 29–30.

A tribute to Marx on his 80th birthday. Covers: his training, career as a teacher, and changing compositional style. Includes a facsimile of the holograph of the first of his *Drei Etüden für Blockflöte (allein)* (1958).

1060. Marx, Karl. "Begegnungen mit der Blockflöte" [Encounters with the recorder]. *Tibia* 3, no. 1 (1978): 30–32.

Describes his pre-World War II experiences in writing for the recorder, from his encounter with the Bogenhausen Kunstkapelle in the early 1920s, through learning the instrument with Konrad Lechner in the 1930s, to his first compositions (for the Berlin Recorder Quartet that included Manfred Ruëtz and Gustav Scheck), and several other works for Ruëtz. Ends with a complete list of his woodwind compositions as well as a recording of three of them.

MELLOR, ROBYN

1061. Tattersall, Malcolm. "Traveller's Tales." *The Recorder: Journal of the Victorian Recorder Guild* 10 (December 1989): 2-4.

    An interview with Robyn Mellor. Covers: her studies in The Hague with Michael Barker, her work back in Australia.

MELVILLE, ALISON

1062. "Alison Melville." (Recorder Personality) *Recorder & Music* 6, no. 10 (June 1980): 305.
    Brief biography.

MICHATZ, HANS-DIETER

1063. Grawe, Ursula. "Profile: Hans-Dieter Michatz." *The Recorder: Journal of the Victorian Recorder Guild* 3 (November 1985): 20-22.

    Covers: his background, reasons for settling in Australia, attitude to performing Baroque music, and career plans.

MIESSEN, MARIJKE

1064. Rivers, Lynton, and Jan Epstein. "Conversations with Marijke Miessen." *The Recorder: Journal of the Victorian Recorder Guild* 5 (November 1986): 16-20.

    Covers: her background, the obligation to teach, teaching, European "schools," repertory (ancient and modern), early music audiences, analysis, keeping performances fresh.

MILES, REBECCA

1065. "Rebecca Miles." (Recorder Personality) *The Recorder and Music Magazine* 9, no. 3 (September 1987): 74.
    Brief biography.

MIX, THEODORE

1066. Whitney, Maurice C. "The Magnamusic Story." *The American Recorder* 13, no. 3 (August 1972): 73–74.

    Profile of Theodore Mix and Magnamusic, the retail music shop he founded that specializes in early music.

MUNROW, DAVID (1942–1976)

1067. Hunt, Edgar. "David Munrow." *Recorder & Music* 5, no. 7 (September 1976): 222.

    Obituary.

1068. Thomson, J.M. "David Munrow." *Recorder & Music Magazine* 2, no. 9 (May 1968): 278–80. Reprinted with slight revisions in item 908.

    Covers: his study of the recorder and bassoon, his exposure to folk music while teaching in South America, his belief that early music performing traditions might be found in folk origins, his three years at Cambridge, his tenure with the Royal Shakespeare Theatre Wind Band, the origins of the Early Music Consort of London, the need for good modern recorder music, his favorite composers.

1069. Thomson, J.M. "Erudition and Entertainment: Three London Instrument Exhibitions." *The American Recorder* 28, no. 2 (May 1987): 65–67.

    The first report, about an exhibition of the late David Munrow's own instrument collection, includes biographical material on him.

1070. "Tributes to David Munrow." *Early Music* 4, no. 3 (July 1976): 376–80.

    Reminiscences by Anthony Lewis, Nigel Fortune, James Bowman, Oliver Brookes, John Turner, James Tyler, Andreas Holschneider, Arthur Johnson, Jasper Parrott, John Willan, John Currie, Christopher Monk, Meirion Bowen, Robert Donington, Jeremy Noble, and Anthony Mulgan.

MURRAY, DOM GREGORY (1905–1992)

1071. Dewey, Monica. "Obituary: The Rev. Dom Gregory Murray, O.S.B." *The Recorder Magazine* 12, no. 3 (September 1992): 92.

    Brief reminiscences.

NALLEN, EVELYN

1072. "Interview with Evelyn Nallen." *The Recorder and Music Magazine* 8, no. 9 (March 1986): 266–67.
    Briefly covers: her recorders, studies, Australian tour, marriage.

1073. Rodgers, Gwen. "Evelyn Nallen." *The Recorder: Journal of the Victorian Recorder Guild* 3 (November 1985): 28–30.
    Profile. Covers: living with a recorder player (husband Michael Copley), 1984 recorder festivals in England and Australia, her career plans.

NEWMAN, HAROLD

1074. Wollitz, Kenneth. "An Interview with Harold Newman, Music Publisher." *The American Recorder* 13, no. 1 (February 1972): 3–5.
    Interview with the founder of Hargail Music. Covers: his informal musical education, his introduction to the recorder through Shakespeare's *Hamlet*, his early work with the American Recorder Society, the founding of Hargail Music, his work as a sound-recording producer, the expansion of his business into instrument sales.

NITKA, ARTHUR

1075. "Tributes to Arthur Nitka." *The American Recorder* 23, no. 1 (February 1982): 20–21.
    The reminiscences of twelve friends and associates.

O'KELLY, EVE

1076. "Eve O'Kelly." (Recorder Personality) *The Recorder and Music Magazine* 9, no. 1 (March 1987): 29.
    A two-paragraph biography.

OTTEN, KEES

1077. "Kees Otten." (Recorder Personality) *Recorder & Music* 6, no. 4 (December 1978): 124.
    A brief profile of "the father of recorder playing in Holland."

1078. [Thomson, J.M.] "Kees Otten." (Profile) *The Recorder and Music Magazine* 1, no. 3 (November 1963): 71. Reprinted with slight revisions in item 908.

Covers: his musical education playing clarinet, saxophone, and recorder; his decision against a career in jazz in favor of one in conventional art music; his teaching at the Amsterdam Muzieklyceum; playing with the Amsterdam Recorder Ensemble, Muziekkring Obrecht, and Syntagma Musicum; audiences; his changing attitude toward virtuosity.

PEHRSSON, CLAS (B. 1942)

1079. Braun, Gerhard. "Clas Pehrsson." (Das Porträt) *Tibia* 9, no. 2 (1984): 115-18.

Covers: how he came to the recorder; the rarity of recorder makers in Scandinavia; the (relatively undeveloped) situation of the recorder in Scandinavia; Scandinavian recorder composers; the question of whether to specialize in early or modern music; the recorder in modern music and the lack of development of a true modern recorder; playing recorder music on the appropriate instruments; the isolation of the recorder in the world of music; what the recorder is good and bad at, and how to end the questions about its status.

1080. Epstein, Jan. "Conversation with Clas Pehrsson." *The Recorder: Journal of the Victorian Recorder Guild* 9 (February 1989): 4-8.

Covers: his background and training, Musica Dolce, his teaching and other recorder teaching in Sweden, on not trying to make the recorder equal to other instruments, the difficulty of achieving a high standard of performance on the recorder, playing from memory, and the future of the recorder.

PETRI, MICHALA (B. 1958)

1081. Bergmann, Walter. "Michala Petri." *Recorder & Music* 5, no. 7 (September 1976): 225.

Interview. Covers: her concert at the SRP Festival, amateur recorder playing in Denmark, her studies with Ferdinand Conrad at the Hochschule in Hanover, her practice routine, her concertizing and recording, her impressions of London, her favorite composers, her plans.

1082. "Michala Petri." (Recorder Personality) *Recorder & Music* 5, no. 3 (September 1975): 110.

Brief profile written when Petri was seventeen years old and just emerging as a prominent player.

1083. Quandt, Reinhold. "Michala Petri." (Das Porträt) *Tibia* 14, no. 1 (1989): 341–45.

Covers: her transformation from "Wunderkind" to "The Paganini of the recorder"; her feeling for recorder vs. flute; her studies with Ferdinand Conrad; her ensemble playing with Heinz Holliger, Pinchas Zukerman, and James Galway; the frontiers of expression on the recorder; the demise of the Petri family trio; virtuosity on the recorder; the suitability of music for the recorder; her attitude towards modern music; the German public for recorder concerts; the early 19th-century czakan repertory.

1084. Wollitz, Kenneth, and Martha Bixler. "An Interview with Michala Petri." *The American Recorder* 27, no. 1 (February 1986): 4–8.

Covers: her background, practicing, tonguing, playing from memory, sizes of recorder, finger technique, repertory, concertizing, and teaching.

PICKETT, PHILIP (B. 1952)

1085. "Philip Pickett." (Recorder Personality) *Recorder & Music* 5, no. 9 (March 1977): 295.

Covers: his study at the Guildhall School and his eventual appointment as a professor there in 1972, the New London Consort, his performances and recordings with other artists.

PRIOR, SUSAN

1086. Goodman, Jan. "An Hour with Susan Prior." *Continuo* 1, no. 8 (May 1978): 3–7; 1, no. 9 (June 1978): 4–9; 1, no. 10 (July/August 1978): 2–5.

Part 1 is largely on the Baroque flute. Part 2, on the recorder, features comments on what constitutes idiomatic repertory for the instrument, including transcriptions. Part 3 continues those comments as well as some on instrumental combinations and ensembles.

RECONDO, EZEQUIEL M.

1087. Thomson, J.M. "Il flauto dolce at Pamparato." *Recorder & Music* 4, no. 11 (September 1974): 415–16.

Concerns the 7th Festival dei Saraceni, its music courses, and particularly an Argentinian pupil of Frans Brüggen's, Ezequiel M. Recondo, who was responsible for the recorder teaching.

REES, HELEN

1088. Rees, Helen. "The China Syndrome." *The Recorder Magazine* 11, no. 1 (March 1991): 3-4.

    An autobiographical account of Rees's training on the recorder and her study of Chinese music in Shanghai and ethnomusicology in Pittsburgh. Also briefly discusses her current recorder repertory.

1089. Rose, Pete. [Profile of Helen Rees]. (On the Cutting Edge) *American Recorder* 32, no. 4 (December 1991): 33.

    Based on an interview conducted in Pittsburgh, where Rees was occupied with post-graduate studies in ethnomusicology during 1990-91. Describes her study of Chinese music and discusses specific 20th-century compositions in her recorder repertory.

REISS, SCOTT (B. 1951)

1090. Lasocki, David. "Scott Reiss and Baroque Recorder Concertos: The Making of a CD." *Continuo* 14, no. 4 (August 1990): 2-4.

    Covers: his start as a clarinetist; his study at Antioch College; his participation in the Antioch Consort, the Folger Consort, and the Hesperus Baroque Ensemble; his selection of concertos by English (Babell), French (Naudot), German (Telemann and Graupner), and Italian (Vivaldi) composers for his first commercial recording; the recording sessions in the Folger Shakespeare Library; problems encountered finding a commercial producer and distributor; his assessment of the results.

ROBBINS, SHIRLEY

1091. Plachte, Frank L. "Profile: Shirley Robbins." *The American Recorder* 20, no. 3 (November 1979): 107.

    Covers: her musical training; her work as a faculty member and director at Idyllwild, a campus of the University of Southern California; her recorded performances; her plans.

RODGERS, GWEN

1092. Norman, Janet. "I Just Wanted Someone to Play With." *The Recorder: Journal of the Victorian Recorder Guild* 14 (December 1991): 21–24.

    An interview with Gwen Rodgers, founding President of the Victorian Recorder Guild. The title of course is the reason she did the founding. An account of her involvement in the Guild, more personal than item **1451**.

ROSENBERG, STEVE

1093. Nagle, Sigrid. "An Interview with Steve Rosenberg." *The American Recorder* 21, no. 3 (November 1980): 116–18.

    Covers: his introduction to early music through performances of the New York Pro Musica; his studies and performances in France; Les Ménestriers; his move to New Zealand, where he taught and began performing solo recitals; instrument making in Australasia; thoughts on Bernard Krainis, Frans Brüggen, David Munrow, and others; his move to North Carolina to participate in an artist-in-residence program.

1094. Willet, William C. "An Interview with Steve Rosenberg." *The American Recorder* 26, no. 2 (May 1985): 75.

    Briefly covers: his recent tour of Australasia, the acoustics of concert halls.

SALKELD, ROBERT (B. 1920)

1095. [Thomson, J.M.] "Robert Salkeld." (Profile) *The Recorder and Music Magazine* 1, no. 9 (May 1965): 279–81.

    Covers: his musical education and introduction to the recorder, his teaching at Morley College and eventual professorship at the London College of Music, the Modern Music for Recorders series, his promotion of 20th-century music for recorder, his editorial work, the Morley College Recorder Consort.

SCHECK, GUSTAV (1901–1984)

1096. B[ergmann], W[alter]. "Gustav Scheck." *The Recorder and Music Magazine* 8, no. 4 (December 1984): 114.

    Brief obituary.

1097. Delius, Nikolaus. "Gustav Scheck." (Das Porträt) *Tibia* 1, no. 1 (1976): 27–30.

The first issue of *Tibia* began, appropriately, with a "portrait" of the 75-year-old Scheck, a major figure in the German flute world of the 20th century, and a pioneer on both the recorder and the traverso. Unlike most other such portraits, not an interview but a long biographical sketch by a distinguished former student.

1098. Gärtner, Jochen. "Abschied von Gustav Scheck" [Farewell to Gustav Scheck]. *Tibia* 9, no. 2 (1984): 118–19.

Long obituary, stressing his contributions to German flute playing. Includes a list of some of his most important students.

1099. Lasocki, David. "Gustav Scheck." *Recorder & Music Magazine* 2, no. 7 (November 1967): 215–17.

Covers: his musical education and his decision not to pursue medicine as a career, his introduction to the recorder in 1929, his partnership with August Wenzinger and the formation of Kammermusikkreis Scheck-Wenzinger, his opposition to the Nazis, the founding of the Staatliche Hochschule für Musik in Freiburg, his tours and recordings, his instruments, his decision to concentrate on the flute, his thoughts on historical ornamentation treatises, his extramusical interests.

1100. Scheck, Gustav. "A Flautist's Reminiscences." *Recorder & Music Magazine* 2, no. 9 (May 1968): 280.

Covers: his start on the modern flute at the the age of ten, his introduction to the recorder sometime after he had joined the Hamburg Philharmonic Orchestra as principal flutist, the program of his first recorder recital, his versatility on a variety of flutes.

SHAW, BERNARD (1856–1950)

1101. Thomson, J.M. [Edward Goetz, pseud.]. "Did Shaw Play the Recorder?" *The Recorder and Music Magazine* 1, no. 11 (November 1965): 326–27.

The author saw a wooden tenor recorder on display at Shaw's home, which raised the question posed in the title. During the 1890s, Shaw wrote several favorable reviews of concerts by Arnold Dolmetsch, and the two eventually became friends. Dolmetsch presented Shaw with a clavichord in the 1920s, and Carl Dolmetsch believes that "it's very likely he also made him a tenor recorder." Although there is no evidence that Shaw actually played the instrument, the custodian of Shaw's house thinks that he did, since "[h]e kept the instrument in the garden hut so he could play without disturbing them in the house." See also Joel Newman, "GBS—Enemy of the Recorder?" *The American Recorder* 2, no. 3 (Fall [i.e., Summer] 1961): 6, which concerns Shaw's review of an 1885 "historical concert" at Albert Hall. Shaw writes, "[t]he effect of the *flauti dolci* music was, on the whole, quaintly execrable," which is likely to have been an indictment of the performance and not necessarily of the instrument. (A. Rowland-Jones offers excerpts from other accounts of the concert in *The Recorder and Music Magazine* 1, no. 7 [November 1964]: 213.)

SHERMAN, ELNA

1102. Palme, Natalie. "Elna Sherman." *The American Recorder* 6, no. 1 (Winter 1965): 19.
Obituary.

SPARR, THEA VON (1915–1988)

1103. "Thea von Sparr." (Recorder Personality) *Recorder & Music* 4, no. 12 (December 1974): 459.

1104. Trantow, Rüdiger. "Thea von Sparr 12.5.1915–23.3.1988." *Tibia* 13, no. 3 (1988): 203–4.
A long obituary of Dorothea Gräfin (Countess) von Sparr, a student of Gustav Scheck who made some recordings in the 1950s. She was also active as a keyboard player. Quotes some thoughts of hers on the rewards of recorder playing and the qualities of a good teacher—which Trantow, a student of hers, believes she possessed herself.

STAEPS, HANS ULRICH (1909–1988)

* Brelsford, Edmund, and Gerhart Niemeyer. "Conversation at Saratoga." Cited above as item 947.

1105. H[unt], E[dgar] H. "Prof. Hans-Ulrich Staeps." *The Recorder and Music Magazine* 9, no. 8 (December 1988): 225.
Obituary, including a selected list of compositions.

1106. Primus, Constance M. "Memories of Hans Ulrich Staeps, 1909–1988." *The American Recorder* 29, no. 4 (November 1988): 147.
Reminiscences that recapitulate some of the biographical information presented in item 1107. Includes an excerpt from the soprano recorder part

of *East-West* (1988), which apparently was Staeps's last composition. See also William E. Hettrick's letter in 30, no. 2 (May 1989): 81.

1107. Reichenthal, Eugene. "A Profile of Hans Ulrich Staeps." *The American Recorder* 20, no. 4 (February 1980): 144-48.

Opens with a few recollections of Staeps's activity at workshops and in the classroom. In response to Reichenthal's request for information on his life and career, Staeps sent an autobiographical account, which constitutes the major part of the article. Covers: his early musical education, his introduction to the recorder as a type of physical therapy following an attack of pleurisy, the principles guiding his work as a composer, the importance of Hindemith to music of the 20th century, his trips to Taiwan to lecture and to organize a recorder teaching program, his plans. Includes an SAT setting by Staeps of Orlando Gibbons's "The Silver Swan."

STEINMANN, CONRAD (B. 1951)

* Lasocki, David. "The Art of Becoming a Recorder Player: Four European Professionals in Conversation with David Lasocki." Cited above as item 1001.

TAYLOR, CHRISTOPHER

1108. Thomson, J.M. [Francis Wood, pseud.]. "Christopher Taylor." *Recorder & Music Magazine* 2, no. 8 (February 1968): 250-51. Reprinted in item 908.

Covers: his introduction to the recorder at the age of thirteen, his stint with the Grenadier Guards, his work in a variety of pit orchestras and London-based professional orchestras, the difficulty of switching quickly from recorder to flute, Indo-Jazz Fusions, his extramusical interests, his playing on film soundtracks.

TAYLOR, STANLEY (1902-1972)

1109. Davies, Peter. "Tribute to Stanley Taylor." *Recorder and Music Magazine* 4, no. 4 (December 1972): 151.

Obituary.

TAYLOR CONSORT

1110. [Thomson, J.M.] "The Taylor Consort." (Profile) *The Recorder and Music Magazine* 1, no. 8 (February 1965): 246–47.
    The Taylor Consort was founded by Stanley Taylor and included his daughter Christine and sons Richard and Christopher. Covers: Taylor's musical education, his lessons with Walter Courvoiser, his conducting experience at the Royal College, his introduction of the recorder to his sons, Britten's *Noye's Fludde*, Richard's and Christopher's playing engagements outside the Consort.

THOMSON, JOHN MANSFIELD (B. 1926)

1111. Nagle, Sigrid. "An Interview with J.M. Thomson." *The American Recorder* 23, no. 2 (May 1982): 55–59.
    Covers: the reasons for his move from Australasia to England; his work with *Composer* magazine and his experience as a book editor, which led to his appointment as editor of *Recorder & Music Magazine*; the genesis of *Early Music* and the changes the journal has undergone; why he became interested in early music; the Early Music Network and the National Early Music Association; his work on a history of New Zealand music. Alec V. Loretto makes a few corrections concerning the recorder in New Zealand in 22, no. 1/2 (May 1981): 43.

THORBY, PHILIP

1112. "Philip Thorby." (Recorder Personality) *Recorder & Music* 5, no. 7 (September 1976): 237.
    Brief profile.

TOL, HAN

* Wollitz, Kenneth, and Martha Bixler. "An Interview with Paul Leenhouts and Han Tol." Cited above as item 1047.

TOMALIN, MILES

1113. Tomalin, Miles. "Early Days." *Recorder & Music* 4, no. 8 (December 1973): 271–74.
    Reminiscences. Covers: his start on a recorder purchased by his father from Arnold Dolmetsch, subsequent study with Dolmetsch, performances

Biographies and Interviews: Modern 331

at Haslemere, experiences as a teacher, loss of prized instruments at a picnic on the Sussex Downs, service in Spain in the Anglo-American International Brigade.

VEILHAN, JEAN-CLAUDE

1114. Reyne, Hugo. "Interview de Jean-Claude Veilhan: 'autour des Quatre Saisons de Vivaldi'" [Interview with Jean-Claude Veilhan: concerning Vivaldi's *Four Seasons*]. *Flûte à bec & instruments anciens* 8 (September 1983): 3–13.

    On recorder arrangements of *The Four Seasons*, principally Veilhan's own, including technical questions (dynamics, playing alto and soprano recorders at the same time); also covers recordings of recorder music ("most . . . bore me to death").

VERBRUGGEN, MARION (B. 1950)

1115. Bixler, Martha, and Kenneth Wollitz. "An Interview with Marion Verbruggen." *The American Recorder* 26, no. 4 (November 1985): 148–53.

    Covers: her background, modern recorder music, teaching, practicing, making music, repertory, trills, vibrato, breath, sight reading, and (lack of) finger tension.

1116. Paterson, Scott. "A Visit from Marion Verbruggen." *Continuo* 3, no. 10 (Summer 1980): 11–15.

    Covers: relaxed playing, articulation, other comments on technique and expression.

VETTER, MICHAEL

1117. Thomson, J.M. "Michael Vetter." *Recorder & Music Magazine* 3, no. 9 (March 1971): 317–19. Reprinted in item 908.

    Covers: his background; working with Cooke, Baur, du Bois, and Stockhausen; the suitability of the recorder for modern music—"Only the avant-garde have put life into this century's recorder music"; the importance of the voice for music making; his composing for the recorder, especially in *Aulodien*, and for the voice; his dislike of Baroque recorder music; and the big questions of his life: Why do human beings need theology, and What is music?

VOLKHARDT, ULRIKE

* Lasocki, David. "The Art of Becoming a Recorder Player: Four European Professionals in Conversation with David Lasocki." Cited above as item 1001.

WAITZMAN, DANIEL (B. 1943)

1118. Nagle, Sigrid. "Daniel Waitzman: A Profile." *The American Recorder* 15, no. 2 (May 1974): 48–50.

   Covers: his study with Bernard Krainis at the age of thirteen, and his subsequent work with the Krainis Consort; his study of musicology at Columbia University; his professional engagements with the Clarion Concerts Orchestra, the Bach Aria Group, and the D'Ariel Trio; his 1971 Carnegie Hall debut; his thoughts on the Baroque flute and the Baroque recorder; his campaign in support of the bell-keyed recorder; his preference for a 19th-century conical Boehm flute; the poor quality of modern recorders; inferior standards of workmanship and playing in the early music community; the wrong-headedness of attempts at authenticity.

WAKEFIELD, J. HOMER

1119. Dallin, Lynn. "'And Sweetly Trilled the Fipple Flute.'" *Etude* 72, no. 5 (May 1954): 12–13, 61.

   A profile of J. Homer Wakefield, a musicologist and member of the piano faculty at Brigham Young University. In 1939 Wakefield is said to have "organized the American Society of Recorder Players," which gave three annual festivals before disbanding. Also describes the collection of 100 early instruments he assembled at the university.

WATERMAN, RODNEY

1120. Waterman, Rodney. "With the Recorder in Italy—A Personal Journey." *The Recorder: Journal of the Victorian Recorder Guild* 4 (May 1986): 29–33.

   Describes his studies with Kees Boeke in Italy and the Netherlands, and some of his experiences, musical and non-musical, in both countries and later in Paris and elsewhere.

WEILENMANN, MATTHIAS (B. 1956)

1121. Keller-Löwy, Walter. "Ein Interview mit dem Blockflötisten Matthias Weilenmann" [An interview with recorder player Matthias Weilenmann]. (Das Portrait) *Pan Zeitung: Musik in Beruf, Freizeit, Erziehung und Therapie*, April 1992, 11, 13.

Covers: the place of the recorder today, why he was attracted to the recorder, his attitude to ornamentation, the public for the recorder, new recorder music, his hobbies, his training, his attitude to music, and his pet likes and dislikes.

WELCH, CHRISTOPHER (1832–1915)

1122. Higbee, Dale. "Christopher Welch, Flute and Recorder Historian." *The American Recorder* 20, no. 2 (August 1979): 64–66.

Traces Welch's activity as a scholar, moving chronologically through his career. Focuses on papers delivered to the Musical Association at the turn of the century ("Literature Relating to the Recorder" and "Hamlet and the Recorder," both published in item 18). Also includes an account of Joseph Bridge's presentation of a paper on the Chester recorders (item 53) and Welch's questions during the discussion that followed. The little biographical information available on Welch is supplemented by a letter written to Higbee by a resident of Lamyatt, Somerset, where Welch spent most of his life. In an "Addendum" to this article in 20, no. 4 (February 1980): 173 Higbee considers the etymology of the word "recorder" and Welch's theory (now discounted) that the word derived from the verb "to record" in the sense of "to sing like a bird."

WILKINSON, RUTH

1123. Barnes, Julie. "Ruth Wilkinson." (Profile) *The Recorder: Journal of the Victorian Recorder Guild* 4 (May 1986): 34–35.

Covers: her background, career, teaching, plans.

WINGERDEN, JEANETTE VAN

1124. "Jeanette van Wingerden." (Recorder Personality) *Recorder & Music* 5, no. 5 (March 1976): 188.

A one-paragraph biography.

1125. Thomson, J.M. "Jeannette [sic] van Wingerden." *The Recorder and Music Magazine* 1, no. 10 (August 1965): 311.
A brief profile.

WINTERS, ROSS

1126. "Ross Winters." (Recorder Personalities) *Recorder & Music* 7, no. 5 (March 1982): 133.
A brief profile.

25

Bibliographies and Discographies of Recorder Music

This chapter discusses bibliographies of recorder music, both general and about individual genres. Writings about the recorder music of one country (Australia) are also included and there is a lone discography. Sources about recorder music for schools are excluded.

* *   Alker, Hugo. *Blockflöten-Bibliographie* [Recorder bibliography]. 1960–61. Cited above as item **1**.

* *   Alker, Hugo. *Blockflöten-Bibliographie* [Recorder bibliography]. 1966–75. Cited above as item **2**.

* *   Alker, Hugo. *Blockflöten-Bibliographie* [Recorder bibliography]. 1984. Cited above as item **3**.
    Alker's bibliographies of recorder music are arranged by medium. Coverage is provincial, with an emphasis on German imprints and few listings outside Europe. Original works for recorder are listed alongside teaching pieces, arrangements, and music for various other instruments that is playable on recorder (particularly the tenor, the compiler's hobbyhorse). Errors, both typographical and bibliographical, are plentiful. The listing of editions in the order of the titles found on them does the reader the disservice of separating related editions (the *uniform titles* used in library cataloging are designed to overcome this problem).
    From the uniformly hostile reviews Edgar Hunt's reaction is worth repeating: "We long for a bibliography compiled by someone who knows the music from the inside, who can separate the real music from the arrangements and the 'school' music, and can somehow contrive to guide the inquirer. A card-index mind or a computer are not good enough; one would be better off with a handful of publishers' catalogues" (review, *Recorder & Music* 5, no. 6 [June 1976]: 199–200). In defending himself, Alker stated his belief that "in spite of many deficiencies, errors, and omissions,"

the publishers and many readers had found the volumes worth while (letter to the editor, *The Recorder and Music Magazine* 8, no. 11 [September 1986]: 335). *Caveat emptor.*

1127. Höffer-von Winterfeld, Linde, and Harald Kunz. *Handbuch der Blockflöten-Literatur* [Handbook of recorder literature]. Berlin: Bote & Bock, 1959. 139 p. OCLC #360681.

Bibliography primarily of music for the recorder, arranged systematically according to instrumental combinations and indexed by author and title. Includes publishers' numbers as well as prices in 1959 Deutsche Marks. One page of literature on the recorder. Brief section on methods.

Walter Bergmann, in *The Galpin Society Journal* 13 (1960): 107-8, strongly criticizes the compilers for omitting all American, Belgian, Dutch, French, and Hungarian publications; omitting important English publications and writings on the recorder; confusing arrangements and original works; confusing types of works; and giving erroneous information. Reviewed by Bernard Krainis ("inaccurate as well as incomplete") in *The American Recorder* 1, no. 4 (Fall 1960): 7.

1128. Hosoda, Tsutomu. *A Descriptive Catalogue of Recorder Music.* Tokyo: Academia Music, 1987. xxix, 263 p. ISBN 4870170361.

Not seen. The following is reproduced (accurately) from a publicity brochure: "This catalogue contain the whole collection of musics in recorder which the Library of Kunitachi College of Music has been acquired up to January, 1984. The catalogue describes each musics in detail, such as edition number, format, editor, range and all playable formation. At the end of the catalogue, there is index depending upon instrument and its formation. This catalogue is highly recommended not only to a player and love of recorder music, but also those who are fond of consort, such as Viola da gamba, and researcher on Renaissance-Baroque music."

1129. Letteron, Claude. *Catalogue général: musique pour flûte à bec 1989 = General Katalog: Musik für Blockflöte = General Catalogue: Music for Recorder = Catálogo general: música para flauta dulce.* Paris: Éditions Aug. Zurfluh, 1989. A–H, xxiv, 417 p. ISBN 287750056X.

The most comprehensive attempt yet made to compile a catalog of the recorder music (original compositions, arrangements, and editions) published in the 20th century. The preface, table of contents, headings, and list of abbreviations are in French, German, English, and Spanish. The entries are in the language of publication. Divided into three sections called "Volumes": (1) by instrumentation, (2) by historical period, and (3) by subject (easy pieces, Christmas music, film music, jazz and pop, and folk music). Index of composers and list of publishers (with abbreviations).

Seems to have been compiled from publishers' catalogs, with all their attendant inaccuracies, ambiguities, and lack of source information. A helpful first step in finding recorder music, but its information should always be verified. Note the provision for revision: "The first edition of the catalogue will be followed each year by a supplement indicating new sheet music published that year. Afterwards the catalogue will be periodically updated to include these supplements as well as to delete the titles of works no longer available" (Preface). Reviewed in *Recorder and Music Magazine* 9, no. 11 (September 1989): 319-20.

1130. Loonan, Martin A. *Guidebook to Published Recorder Music: 13th to 17th Centuries.* n.p.: author, 1962. 18 p. OCLC #21714147.
Not available for examination. Reviewed by Erich Katz in *The American Recorder* 4, no. 2 (May 1963): 19-21.

1131. Loonan, Martin A. *Guidebook to Published Recorder Music of the Late Baroque.* n.p.: author, 1962. 21 p. OCLC #17847441.
Not available for examination.

1132. Newman, Joel. "Apt for Recorders." (Flauto Piccolo's Corner) *The American Recorder* 4, no. 3 (August 1963): 19.
A checklist of Renaissance and early Baroque dance repertory that is suitable for recorders.

1133. Newman, Joel. "A Walsh Catalog of Recorder Music." (Eighteenth-Century Promenades, 3) *The American Recorder* 4, no. 3 (August 1963): 6-9; 4, no. 4 (November 1963): 3-4.
Reproduces the catalog of recorder music found in William C. Smith's bibliography of Walsh's publications (London: The Bibliographical Society, 1948, Plate 28). Analyzes the contents of the catalog and describes how the selections reflect the musical tastes and practices of the time. Offers separate comments on the publications in each category (music for unaccompanied recorder, for two recorders, for two recorders and continuo, and for one recorder and continuo).

1134. Newman, Morris. "Contemporary Music for Recorders." *The American Recorder* 3, no. 3 (August 1962): 9-10.
A bibliography of five duets, fifteen trios, seven quartets, and two works for larger ensembles.

* O'Kelly, Eve Elizabeth. *The Recorder in Twentieth-Century Music.* Cited above as item 819.

* O'Kelly, Eve Elizabeth. *The Recorder Today.* Cited above as item 820.

1135. Rasmussen, Mary, and Donald Mattran. *A Teacher's Guide to the Literature of Woodwind Instruments.* Durham, NH: Brass and Woodwind Quarterly, 1966. viii, 226 p. OCLC #318430.

    Aimed at high school and college teachers (and their students). Principally covers the flute, oboe, clarinet, bassoon, and saxophone. The recorder is the object of scathing humor (sample: "About the only really honest reasons we can think of for taking up the recorder are poverty and lack of time" [p. 181]). At least it shows the attitude of woodwind players to the instrument in the mid-1960s (before the Brüggen revolution). Chapters on "Recorder Solos" (pp. 99–107), "Recorder Ensembles" (pp. 147–55), "Recorder Methods and Studies" (pp. 181–83); also "Discography: Recorder" (pp. 219–20; five items!). Each chapter consists of discussions of the value and style of the repertory it covers, followed by a bibliography of the works (with editions and symbols for grade level). Very opinionated, but fun—if you are not a recorder enthusiast.

UNACCOMPANIED RECORDER

1136. Brock, John Earl. "A Checklist of Music for Unaccompanied Recorder." *The American Recorder* 23, no. 3 (August 1982): 103–6.

    A listing of Brock's collection. Each entry includes the following: composer, title, publisher and publisher's number, date of publication, difficulty (on a scale of 1 to 7), information on avant-garde techniques, number and size of pages, a subjective evaluation ("+" for good or "0" for bad), and citations to periodical reviews. Excludes "purely mechanical exercises and . . . music with electronic accompaniment."

1137. [Newman, Joel]. "The Lonesome Recorder." (Flauto Piccolo's Corner) *The American Recorder* 1, no. 4 (Fall 1960): 8.

    A brief bibliography of published collections of music for solo recorder.

RECORDER WITH GUITAR

1138. Clark, Paul. "Music for Recorders and Guitar: A Selection." *Recorder & Music* 7, no. 7 (September 1982): 179-81.

    An essay review of a handful of publications—for the most part collections of arrangements.

1139. Letteron, Claude. "Répertoire partitions: Flûte à bec et guitare" [Printed repertory: recorder and guitar]. *Flûte à bec* 2 (February 1982): 25-32.

    A listing of printed music for recorder and guitar, classified into anthologies, periods, and folk.

RECORDER WITH PIANO

1140. Skins, H.R. "Recorder and Piano: A First Choice of Music." (Where Do I Start? 2) *The Recorder and Music Magazine* 1, no. 5 (May 1964): 142-43.

    Recommends repertory for soprano and piano, alto and piano, and two altos and piano—mostly arrangements and anthologies, many now out of print.

RECORDER WITH STRINGS

1141. Dinn, Freda. "Exploring the Repertoire I: Recorders and Strings." *Recorder and Music Magazine* 4, no. 4 (December 1972): 127-28.

    Annotated bibliography of music—nearly all published by Schott—for young beginners. The series continues with item **1171**.

SOLO SONATAS

1142. Loonan, Martin A. "A Listing of Late Baroque Solo Sonatas for Alto Recorder." *The American Recorder* 12, no. 3 (August 1971): 86-90.

    Includes 195 works. Table lists key, numbering, and information on modern editions.

 *   McGowan, Richard A. *Italian Baroque Solo Sonatas for the Recorder and the Flute*. Cited below as item **1195**.

RECORDER CONCERTOS

1143. Gronefeld, Ingo. *Flötenkonzerte bis 1850: Ein thematisches Verzeichnis* [Flute concertos to 1850: a thematic catalog]. 2 vols. to date. Tutzing: Hans Schneider, 1992– ISBN 3795207118.

    The beginnings (from Abel to Quantz) of a comprehensive thematic catalog of concertos for "flute" (including recorder) up to 1850. Includes double concertos, group concertos, symphonies concertantes, overture-suites, early forms of concertos, variations, and single movements for both flute and recorder, although it is not clear whether it will include chamber concertos. As well as well-known concertos, the catalog draws our attention to a number of "lost" works listed in 18th-century catalogs but apparently not extant (Albinoni, anonymous, Brescianello, Dömming, Fasch, and Magini) and some works by Peter Johann Fick, Nicola Fiorenza, Graun, and Anton Heberle not yet published in modern editions. Also includes some (but by no means all) listings of modern editions.

GEOGRAPHICAL FOCUS

AUSTRALIA

1144. Tattersall, Malcolm. "Australian Music for Recorder." *The Recorder: Journal of the Victorian Recorder Guild* 1 (1984): 19–22.

    A bibliography of seventy-five works, arranged by composer. Partly annotated (duration, style, difficulty, recommendation). Excludes arrangements and those pieces written for any instrument or any woodwind instrument that can be played on the recorder.

1145. Tattersall, Malcolm. "Wider Horizons: More Australian Recorder Music." *The Recorder: Journal of the Victorian Recorder Guild* 6 (June 1987): 5–8.

    A supplement to **1144**. Discusses general trends in the writing, performing, and distributing of Australian recorder music in the 1980s. The "Not-so-small addendum" adds 48 works to the previous list.

DISCOGRAPHIES

1146. Paterson, Scott, and David Lasocki with Dawn Culbertson. *A Discography of the Recorder. Volume 1: Recordings Available in North America, 1989.* New York: The American Recorder Society, 1992.

    "*The American Recorder Society Discography Project* was initiated to observe the Society's fiftieth anniversary in 1989. The long-term goal of the project is to catalog and index all recordings involving the recorder, whether available or out of print, from all countries. The present volume is a first step toward that goal. It deals with those [269] recordings that were available in North America in 1989 . . . thereby providing an overview of the recorder on disc and tape at that point in the instrument's history" (Introduction). The main listing is alphabetical by recording company, then by catalog number within each company's listings. Indexes are provided of titles (of the recording), composers and works, recorder players, recorder makers (of instruments used on the recordings), performers other than recorder players, and annotators (writers of liner or program notes.)

26

Repertory: General

This chapter deals with writings about general recorder repertory or that of more than one period. It includes discussion of edition practice as well as transcriptions and arrangements. Sources about the music of individual periods are found in chapters 27 (medieval and Renaissance), 28 (Baroque and Classical), and 29 (Modern). Questions of performance practice are treated in chapters 18–20.

1147. Cook, S. Ronald, Jr. "The Copyright Law & the Recorder Player." *The American Recorder* 26, no. 1 (February 1985): 22–23.
   Answers frequently asked questions, covering the following topics among others: how to determine whether a piece of music is protected under copyright, making a copy of all or part of a publication, making multiple copies, receiving exemption from royalty payments. See also Gerald Burakoff's letter in 26, no. 2 (May 1985): 76.

1148. Ganty, Henri. "Le récital de flûte à bec sans basse" [The unaccompanied recorder recital]. *Flûte à bec & instruments anciens* 8 (September 1983): 14–15.
   An essay on the problems of playing such a recital, including choice of repertory and instruments, and knowing your audience and venue.

1149. Hunt, Edgar. "Playing from a Facsimile." *Recorder & Music* 7, no. 1 (March 1981): 6–7.
   A survey of selected early editions and treatises available in facsimile.

1150. Hunt, Edgar. "Some Recorder Trios." *Recorder & Music* 5, no. 5 (March 1976): 154–56.
   Brief descriptions of the following works, with a generous excerpt from the beginning of each (in most cases the entire first page): Johann

Christoph Faber, *Parties sur les fleut dous;* R. Müller-Hartmann, *Suite;* Michael Meech, *Puppet Show;* Timothy Moore, *Suite in G;* Alexandre Tansman, *Suite;* Paul Hindemith, recorder trio from *Plöner Musiktag.*

1151. Hunt, Edgar. "The Right Instrument." *The Recorder and Music Magazine* 9, no. 6 (June 1988): 150–51.

    Concerns music intended to be playable on a variety of instruments, including the following repertory: 16th-century dance and chanson collections; 17th-century French instrumental duets; and flute music and bassoon music that can be played on an alto recorder by substituting the French violin clef. Hunt also explains that composers usually have a particular instrument or instruments in mind when composing, and alternative instrumentations often prove to be impractical.

1152. Middleton, James. "The Concert Encore and the Recorder Player." *Recorder & Music* 4, no. 11 (September 1974): 399–400.

    Concerns the encore repertory for recorder consorts. Suggests that performers pursue arrangements, since the original repertory suitable for encore performance is limited.

1153. Taylor, Laurence. "Recorder Literature." (Flute Facts) *The Instrumentalist* 12, no. 1 (September 1957): 102–3, 110; 12, no. 2 (October 1957): 86–87, 90.

    Of historical interest only. Explains to flute players that recorder music is also playable on the modern flute. Written at a time when most flutists assumed that Handel wrote seven sonatas for flute, and Telemann's Suite for Recorder and Strings in A Minor could not "be purchased in a modern edition except for *flute* solo." Taylor informs his readers that much of what is considered to be standard Baroque flute literature is actually recorder music, and he encourages them to continue to explore the recorder repertory for suitable flute music.

1154. Thorn, Chris. "What is Right for the Recorder." *The Recorder and Music Magazine* 8, no. 1 (March 1984): 25–26.

    A response to an article by Gregory Lewin in 7, no. 12 (December 1983). Concerns the question of identifying an "authentic" repertory for the instrument. Letter from Lewin in 8, no. 2 (June 1984): 61.

1155. Tol, Han. "Letter from Holland." *The Recorder: Journal of the Victorian Recorder Guild* 6 (June 1987): 29–31.

    Includes instructions for recorder players on how to locate early printed music for the instrument in *Répertoire international des sources musicales*

[RISM] (unfortunately Tol confuses prints with manuscripts throughout) and order it from libraries that hold it.

CHRISTMAS REPERTORY

1156. Hopkins, Bernard J. "Celebrating Christmas with Recorders." *The American Recorder* 15, no. 3 (August 1974): 77-80.

    Suggests possibilities for both liturgical and non-liturgical use. Recommended music includes a few original compositions for recorders, but most are adaptations of choral music and published arrangments for recorders.

EDITIONS

1157. Hettrick, William E. "What to Look for in Editions of Early Music." *The American Recorder* 18, no. 4 (February 1978): 98-100.

    A general guide to what a performer may expect to find in a good performing edition, with a few caveats. Describes incipits and what they can tell the performer about the original staff, clef, key signature, time signature, pitch, and time values. Warns against editorial abuse of barlines and time signatures. States that editorial markings must be clearly marked, particularly the addition of accidentals. Suggests that the editor's choice of clefs—often not a concern for other performers—can be an important factor when considering an edition for a recorder consort.

1158. Lasocki, David. "What Kind of Editions of 18th-Century Woodwind Music Do We Want?" *Recorder & Music* 5, no. 7 (September 1976): 223-24. Reprinted from *Woodwind World—Brass & Percussion* 15, no. 1 (Winter 1976): 10-11, 49.

    Compares the categories of editions that support "authentic" style and "Romantic" style and the types of players who use them. "Authentic" editions are based on an Urtext, and additions are either clearly marked in the text or noted in an appendix. "Romantic" editions set forth the editor's own conception of performance without distinguishing this conception from the composer's text. Since American publishers during the mid-1970s were continuing to cater to the market for "Romantic" editions, and European "authentic" editions were expensive and difficult to obtain, American players interested in "authentic" style found themselves in the midst of an "edition crisis." Lasocki sees two solutions: American publishers could publish historically informed "Romantic" editions, or editions could be published with edited parts and an unedited score (or vice versa). "Ultimately, education is the answer."

1159. Michel, Winfried. "Editionskunde—ein Stückchen Verbraucheraufklärung: Zur Bearbeitungspraxis von Instrumentalmusik des 18. Jahrhunderts" [The theory of making editions—a little consumer explanation: on the practice of arranging 18th-century instrumental music]. *Tibia* 4, no. 2 (1979): 297-301.

Many musicians do not know, or do not want to know, about the role of the editor—the "middleman" between composer and performer. Seeks to arouse caution about the work of editors and set forth criteria to be used when buying music (citation of sources, fidelity to the text, good setting of the figured bass, readable notation). Uses as examples some modern editions/arrangements for recorder of Corelli violin sonatas that smooth out his characteristic leaps. Editors need to be good musicians. All good advice. Unfortunately, Michel has blotted his copybook by passing off his own compositions in 18th-century style as the work of "Simonetti" and Haydn, fooling many discerning musicians in the process.

1160. Murray, Dom Gregory. "Editions and Arrangements." *Recorder & Music Magazine* 3, no. 4 (December 1969): 123-24.

Distinguishes between editions (publications of music originally for recorders or for unspecified instruments) and arrangements (adaptations of music not originally for recorders).

TRANSCRIPTION AND ARRANGEMENT

1161. Bergmann, Walter. "An Editor Explains." *The American Recorder* 5, no. 4 (November 1964): 26-27.

Defends the transcription of music usually considered inappropriate for the instrument (cites pieces by Schumann and Schubert as examples). Bergmann believes they are necessary to stimulate interest and intellectual growth in less experienced players.

1162. Clark, Paul. "Raiding the Larder." *The Recorder and Music Magazine* 1, no. 8 (February 1965): 237

Gillett, Eric. "We've Been Raiding the Larder, too." *The Recorder and Music Magazine* 1, no. 9 (May 1965): 274.

Clark, Paul. "Second Foray." *The Recorder and Music Magazine* 1, no. 11 (November 1965): 327.

Describes Clark's success at adapting a number of early 20th-century compositions—mostly French flute and oboe music—for performance on the recorder. Gillett describes his adaptation of several pieces by Mozart, Bach, and Beethoven for a group of recorder, strings, and piano.

1163. Gillett, Eric. "Making Arrangements." *Recorder & Music* 5, no. 6 (June 1976): 197-98.

Discusses three qualities that an arranger should consider when determining whether a particular piece of music is suitable for transcription: technical feasibility, interest to players, and musical taste.

1164. Mann, Alfred, Bernard Krainis, and Erich Katz. "Controversy: III. The Question of Arrangements." *The American Recorder* 5, no. 4 (November 1964): 14-19. Reprinted from the *ARS Newsletter* 23 & 25.

A lengthy and lively exchange, initiated by Mann's review, "Music for Amateurs," *Notes* 12, no. 4 (September 1955): 652-55. Krainis disagrees with Mann's belief that Renaissance viol music should be left only to viol players. Katz explains why he chose to produce practical rather than scholarly editions and how his work constitutes "arrangement," since it involves much more than simple transcription. Mann explains his position in more detail in a letter that follows.

* Murray, Dom Gregory. "Editions and Arrangements." Cited above as item **1160**.

1165. Prior, Susan. "In Search of Recorder Music: Transcriptions." *The American Recorder* 24, no. 4 (November 1983): 146-49.

Suggests dozens of 15th-18th century pieces and collections that are suitable sources for borrowing. Since all of the examples can be read at sight (assuming a certain prowess with clefs), these "transcriptions" are informal ones. Prior describes techniques that enable players to extend themselves beyond the recorder repertory. Recommends borrowing from the Baroque literature for flute, violin, and—in particular—the bassoon ("the compass, response to articulation, and comfortable keys are similar to those of the alto recorder"). Includes a bibliography of sources mentioned in the text.

1166. Whitney, Maurice C. "Adapting Choral Music for Recorders." *The American Recorder* 13, no. 1 (February 1972): 9.

    Describes several types of choral settings that fit well on recorders. Recommends a list of five titles as a suitable starting point.

1167. Wyatt, Theo. "Arranging—a Practical Survey." *Recorder and Music Magazine* 4, no. 2 (June 1972): 55-58.

    Advice for the novice arranger. Recommends madrigals and Bach chorales as good beginning pieces and describes some basic techniques for arranging them (transposing, adjusting octaves, changing pitches when no other solution is available). Suggests general sources of music suitable for arrangement.

27

Repertory: Medieval and Renaissance

This chapter covers those few sources that deal with the medieval and Renaissance repertory of the recorder. Questions of performance practice for that repertory are dealt with in chapter 18.

1168. Dikmans, Greg. "Florid Italian Instrumental Music circa 1600: An Introduction." *The Recorder: Journal of the Victorian Recorder Guild* 4 (May 1986): 5–13.

   Analyzes the influence of diminution practice on the instrumental forms of the period, concentrating on the works of Girolamo dalla Casa, Giovanni Bassano, and Dario Castello (one of whose sonatas is reproduced in facsimile).

1169. Fox, Charles Warren. "An Early Duet for Recorder & Lute." *Guitar Review* 9 (1949): 84–85.

   Concerns an arrangement of Jacobus Barbireau's song "Een vrolic wesen" published in *Livre plaisant et tres utile pour apprendre a faire & ordonner toutes tabulatures* . . . (Antwerp, 1529). The last part of *Livre plaisant* is devoted to the recorder, and on the opposite page from a fingering chart for bass, tenor, and discant (g^1) recorders is a part to "Een vrolic wesen," which the author suspects is to be played with the two-part lute accompaniment found earlier in the volume. Fox surmises that this is the oldest known duet for two specified instruments. Includes a transcription of the duet.

1170. Hopkins, Bernard J. "Polychoralism, Anyone?" *The American Recorder* 18, no. 2 (August 1977): 40–43.

   Advocates adapting antiphonal music, both choral and instrumental, for recorder ensemble. The bibliography lists nine publications that include suitable music, mostly dating from the 16th century (composed by Handl, Gabrieli, and Palestrina, among others).

1171. Hunt, Edgar. "Exploring the Repertoire 2: Renaissance Music." *Recorder and Music Magazine* 4, no. 6 (June 1973): 194–95.

Continues item **1141**. Describes three collections of importance, "the staple diet for a renaissance group": the *Danserye* (1551) of Tielman Susato, the *Pariser Tanzbuch* (1530) of Pierre Attaingnant, and *Liber Fridolini Sichery* (ca. 1500). The second half of the article surveys individual works and miscellaneous collections in modern editions.

* Polk, Keith. *German Instrumental Music of the Late Middle Ages: Players, Patrons and Performance Practice.* Cited above as item **70**.

1172. Wright, Laurence. "The Music of the Renaissance." *The Recorder and Music Magazine* 1, no. 9 (May 1965): 264–66.

"[P]resents a few historically-attested cases of music that was played on recorder." Assembles, from a variety of secondary sources, citations documenting the use of the recorder in both sacred and secular music. Particular emphasis is placed on secular song collections of the 16th century. Since Wright wrote, music for the recorder consort at the English Court in the 16th–17th centuries has been discovered (see item **74**).

HOLBORNE, ANTONY (D. 1602)

1173. Mitchell, David. "Antony Holborne and his Five Part Dances." *Recorder & Music* 4, no. 9 (March 1974): 313–15; 4, no. 10 (June 1974): 375–79; 5, no. 1 (March 1975): 28–32; 5, no. 2 (June 1975): 53–55; 5, no. 5 (March 1976): 162–64.

Begins by offering what little biographical information is available on Holborne. Reprints the complete dedication of the *Pavans, Galliards, Almains* (1599) and lists surviving copies. Notes that forty-nine of the sixty-five pieces may be performed using SATTB recorders. For the remaining sixteen, the only problem is the range of the bass line. The majority of the article consists of a catalog of the sixty-five works, offering musical analyses, lists of modern editions (and corrections of errors found therein), suggested instrumentation, and caveats for performers. Figures 16–19, which were inadvertently omitted from Part 3, appear in an editorial in 5, no. 2 (June 1975): 41. Corrections reported in 4, no. 11 (September 1974): 395 and 5, no. 2 (June 1975): 41. See also Joel Newman, "The Whole of Holborne," *The American Recorder* 5, no. 3 (August 1964): 4–5, which includes a list of the sixty-five pieces with information on modern editions (available in 1964).

MORLEY, THOMAS (1557–1603?)

The following two items represent early views on the particular grouping of instruments known as the "mixed consort," as Warwick Edwards has dubbed it. (It was known in the late 16th and early 17th centuries as "English consort" [Praetorius] or just plain "consort"; the term "broken consort" applied to this grouping is modern.) For more recent research, see item 72, chapter 11, and Peter Holman, *Four and Twenty Fiddlers: The Violin at the English Court 1540-1690* (Oxford: Clarendon Press, 1993), 131-39. Both recorder and flute were used as the wind instrument in the consort, depending on the circumstances, along with various bowed and plucked string instruments.

1174. Dart, R. Thurston. "Morley's Consort Lessons of 1599." *Proceedings of the Royal Musical Association* 74 (1947–48): 1–9.

Presents the following argument regarding the role of the recorder in the *Consort Lessons:* "The 'flute' part was intended for a bass recorder (once, for a tenor recorder). Some of the flute parts are found in the Cambridge MSS. headed *for the recorder*. I am aware that in the contemporary painting of the Masque at Sir Henry Unton's wedding, a sextet of musicians is playing on instruments exactly corresponding to those of the *Consort Lessons,* except that a transverse flute is shown. But (i) the transverse flute was much less a chamber music instrument than the recorder, (ii) several contemporary inventories list 'a large recorder for the consort' quite separately from the chest of ensemble recorders, (iii) the ranges of Morley's and Rosseter's parts do not suit any of the then standard sizes of flute. Moreover, the solo recorder parts of Morley's contemporaries Schütz, Schein, Rossi and Riccio have the same C clefs as Morley's and are undoubtedly for bass recorder."

1175. Rowland-Jones, A. "Scottish Muses and the 'Consort Lessons.'" *Recorder and Music Magazine* 2, no. 2 (July 1966): 34–36. Reprinted in *The American Recorder* 7, no. 4 (Fall 1966): 12–13.

Although Dart claimed in 1947 (see item 1174) that the flute part of the *Consort Lessons* was intended for bass recorder, a decade later he changed his mind in favor of the tenor transverse flute in G, offering the following reasons: a painting of the masque at Sir Henry Unton's wedding in the National Portrait Gallery shows a transverse flute being played by a member of a group corresponding to Morley's consort; and the lessons were intended for performance by the City Waits, a musical group that frequently played out of doors, thus making performance on recorder improbable. Rowland-Jones offers further support for performance on the transverse flute. A ceiling painting in a Scottish castle depicts the nine muses performing on a group of instruments paralleling Morley's ensemble, and Euterpe is shown playing a low-pitched transverse flute. Rowland-Jones notes that "the Morley consort may deliberately have been or became associated with the instruments pertaining to the Muses." Based on the evidence of the painting, "recorder players should withdraw any residual claims to be authentic participants in Morley's consort."

SUSATO, TIELMAN (FL. 1529–1561)

1176. Sandford, Gordon. "Tielman Susato's Dances of 1551." (Basic Repertoire for Recorders) *American Recorder* 31, no. 3 (September 1990): 33.
Describes and evaluates available editions of *Danserye*.

1177. Thorn, Chris. "Susato's 'Danserye.'" *The Recorder and Music Magazine* 9, no. 1 (March 1987): 2–5.
Describes the contents of the collection as published in F.J. Giesbert's edition (Schott, 1936). Susato's title page indicates that the dances are suitable for "all instruments," and Thorn suggests some effective combinations. When played on recorders, the standard sixteenth-century quartet (g^1, c^1, c^1, f) is preferred over the modern SATB quartet. Briefly describes the various dance types and their character. Discusses Giesbert's edition and its errors, which are summarized and corrected in a two-page table with accompanying musical examples.

28

Repertory: Baroque and Classical

This chapter is concerned with sources on the Baroque and Classical repertory of the recorder. It begins with general sources, then deals with music for one particular combination of instruments (flute and recorder). Finally it looks at the music of individual composers, including questions of performance practice related specifically to their music. An especially large section is devoted to the recorder music of J.S. Bach, including items on the identity of the mysterious *fiauti d'echo* scored for in his Fourth Brandenburg Concerto.

1178. Hunt, Edgar. "Trio-Sonatas with Recorder." *Recorder & Music* 5, no. 9 (March 1977): 293–95; 5, no. 10 (June 1977): 325–27; 5, no. 11 (September 1977): 360–61.

> A survey of the repertory and available modern editions. Part One covers compositions for recorder, oboe, and continuo, including works by Telemann, John Loeillet, Finger, Vivaldi, Hotteterre, and others. Part Two similarly treats works for recorder, violin, and continuo by Handel, Telemann, and others. The last installment covers works for recorder with various other instruments and continuo: viola da gamba (by Antonio Lotti and Telemann), horn (by Telemann), harpsichord (by Telemann), and transverse flute (by Quantz).

1179. Hunt, Edgar. "Trio Sonatas with Two Recorders." *Recorder & Music* 6, no. 2 (June 1978): 35–38.

> A survey of the repertory for two recorders and continuo.

1180. Hunt, Edgar. "Quartet Sonatas." *Recorder & Music* 6, no. 9 (March 1980): 277.

> A brief discussion of the repertory for three melodic instruments (including at least one recorder) and continuo. Includes works by Alessandro Scarlatti and Purcell for three altos and continuo; a suite for two altos, one tenor, and continuo by Christian Friedrich Witt; and a

number of works for recorder, two other melody instruments, and continuo by Telemann and Johann Friedrich Fasch. A few 20th-century works are also mentioned.

1181. Jolibert, Bernard. "Les sonates de chambre baroques" [Baroque chamber sonatas]. *Flûte à bec et instruments anciens* 26 (November 1988): 20-22.

History and background on the sonata, with some typical and unusual examples of form in recorder sonatas.

1182. Lewis, Edgar Jay, Jr. *The Use of Wind Instruments in Seventeenth-Century Instrumental Music.* Ph.D. dissertation, University of Wisconsin, 1964. vii, 526 leaves. OCLC #2133278. UMI order no. 64-03928.

Divided by instrument: chapters on the cornett, trombone, bassoon, and trumpet are followed by one on "The Flute and the Oboe" (pp. 427-92). As one might expect, however, the transverse flute plays a miniscule role in the chapter, which mostly concerns the recorder (although the author's ignorance of the terminology of the day leads him to conclude that the music could have been performed on either instrument). Discusses and briefly analyzes recorder music by Johann Schmelzer (*Sonata a 7 flaut*, of which the first page—in tablature!—is reproduced), Nicolaus Adam Strungk, William Topham, William Williams, Godfrey Finger, Raphael Courteville, Daniel Purcell, James Paisible, J.V. Burckart, Alessandro Scarlatti, and Marc Antoine Charpentier, among others. Distinguished largely by the author's resourcefulness in obtaining music, some of which has still not been published in modern editions.

1183. Staeps, Hans Ulrich. *Problems and Readings of Historical Models: Concerning the Recorder Literature of the Late Baroque.* Vienna: Doblinger, 1966. 21 p. OCLC #3371829. In German as: *Probleme und Lesarten historischer Modelle zur Blockflötenliteratur des Spätbarock.* Vienna: Doblinger, 1966. 22 p. OCLC #16530338.

"Lecture held in the U.S.A. on the occasion of the 1st International Recorder School, Skidmore College, Saratoga Springs, N.Y., Summer 1965." Although the title might suggest the topic of historical performance practice, Staeps's subject is a more controversial one: "vitalizing" models for performance—in other words, altering musical texts when one encounters perceived errors, be they great or small. He demonstrates this practice with musical examples from Telemann, Handel, and Pepusch. Many of the changes constitute subjective aesthetic "improvements" in voice leading, functional harmony, rhythm, and the order of movements, not the correction of obvious errors. The justification for the alterations is often questionable: "It is idle to wonder what Pepusch may have intended with this curious bass part, whether he had our solution in mind and notated the entire line in the same octave simply because of indolence. No one can say with certainty, but we should be resolute enough to act in accordance with a plausible hypothesis." Or: "The result is a most unattractive progression, awkward and scarcely comprehensible at the moment it occurs. Had Telemann elected to interrupt the basis [sic] line by rests at the appropriate points, a solution worthy of Bach might have been forthcoming." Ends with this anti-historicist credo: we should seek out "the correct, the best possible solution: not *against* the composer of the past, but *for* him; *not against the older tradition, but with the accoutrements of a later tradition, and the guide of our scholarship.*" Reviewed by Walter Bergmann in *Recorder and Music Magazine* 2, no. 4 (February 1967): 117.

1184. Thieme, Ulrich. "Die Blockflöte in Kantate, Oratorium und Oper" [The recorder in cantata, oratorio, and opera]. *Tibia* 11, no. 2 (1986): 81–88; 11, no. 3 (1986): 161–67; 12, no. 4 (1987): 558–66.

Reminds us that the use of the recorder in Baroque vocal music is important but largely uncharted territory. Lists, and sometimes discusses, much of this repertory. Divided according to time and place: Italian and German vocal music, 1600–1665; France; German opera and cantatas after the Thirty Years' War. The third part, despite its title "The 17th Century," in fact covers only England during that century. The article is useful in showing the range of works involved. Unfortunately, Thieme's account is weakened by his unfamiliarity with several important modern English writings on this subject (including items 74, 1189, and 1283).

1185. Thieme, Ulrich. *Die Blockflöte in Kantate, Oratorium und Oper des 17. Jahrhunderts* [The recorder in cantata, oratorio, and opera in the 17th century]. Celle: Moeck, 1989. Ed. Moeck Nr. 4050. 24 p. ISBN 3875490436.

An off-print of item **1184**. Short favorable review by Hans-Martin Linde in *Tibia* 15, no. 2 (1990): 145.

RECORDER WITH FLUTE

1186. Hunt, Edgar. "Recorder and Flute." *Recorder & Music Magazine* 2, no. 8 (February 1968): 244–45.

Surveys the repertory for flute and recorder in combination. Begins by describing the use of the instruments in the 18th century. Although a wealth of literature exists for paired recorders and paired flutes, only rarely were the instruments combined. Hunt cites the following works: Johann Joachim Quantz, Trio Sonata for Recorder, Flute, and Continuo in C Major,

QV 2:2; Johann Friedrich Fasch, Sonata for Flute, Two Recorders, and Continuo in G Major; Georg Philipp Telemann, Quartet for Recorder, Two Flutes, and Continuo in D Minor (from *Musique de table*); Jacques Loeillet, Sonata for Two Flutes, Two Voice Flutes, and Continuo in B Minor; and Georg Philipp Telemann, Concerto for Recorder and Flute in E Minor. In the 20th century, there is Hans-Martin Linde's Trio for Recorder, Flute, and Harpsichord.

1187. Linde, Hans-Martin. "The Simultaneous Use of Recorder and Flute by Baroque Composers." *Recorder & Music Magazine* 2, no. 9 (May 1968): 281–82. In German as: "Die Gegenüberstellung von Block- und Querflöte in einigen Werken des Spätbarock." *Musica* 22, no. 5 (September/October 1968): 416–17.

Describes the qualities of the 18th-century flute and recorder and how their differences are exploited (or ignored) in the five works listed in item **1186**.

1188. Lasocki, David. "Flute and Recorder in Combination: Recent Additions to the Baroque Repertoire." *Recorder & Music* 4, no. 11 (September 1974): 391–95.

Sequel to item **1187**. Since the publication of Linde's article, additional works for flute and recorder have come to light and been published. Lasocki identifies the pieces, considers a number of problems associated with them, and discusses their treatment of recorder and flute. The works are: Johann Samuel Ender's *Pièces* in G major for two recorders, two flutes, strings, and continuo; Johann Christoph Pepusch's *Six Concerts*, op. 8, for two recorders, two flutes (or oboes or violins), and continuo; and Pierre Prowo's *Sonata a 3* in C minor for alto recorder, flute, and continuo. Also briefly mentions modern works for recorder, flute, and harpsichord: Hans-Martin Linde's Trio, Piet Ketting's Fantasia; and Jan van Dijk's *Musique à trois*.

GEOGRAPHICAL FOCUS

ENGLAND

1189. Bergmann, Walter. "Three Pieces of Music on Henry Purcell's Death." *The Consort* 17 (July 1960): 13–19.

Discusses John Blow's *An Ode on the Death of Mr. Henry Purcell*, Henry Hall's *A Peace of Musike upon the Death of Mr. H. Purcell*, and Jeremiah Clarke's *On Henry Purcell's Death*, all three of which include parts for recorders. Concludes that these composers "rose to the highest degree of their respective creative power, an indication of the deep emotional impression which Purcell's untimely death made on his contemporary fellow composers."

1190. Lasocki, David. "The Detroit Recorder Manuscript (England, c. 1700)." *The American Recorder* 23, no. 3 (August 1982): 95-102.

The Detroit Public Library holds a manuscript of English provenance that contains "some of the repertory that Paisible and other professional recorder players presented in the public concerts and theatre entertainments in London in the 1690s." Included are seventeen sonatas for alto recorder and continuo by Gottfried Finger, James Paisible, William Williams, and Edward Finch; two sets of divisions on a ground bass for alto and continuo by Finger; and an alto duet by Williams. All of the pieces have survived in other sources. Offers a complete listing of the contents (including concordances and modern editions), biographies of the four composers, and essays on the milieu and compositional style of the works.

FRANCE

1191. Fiedler, Jörg. "Brunettes ou petits airs tendres: Unterrichts- und Unterhaltungsmusik des französischen Barock" [*Brunettes* or *petits airs tendres*: instructional and entertainment music of the French Baroque]. *Basler Jahrbuch für historische Musikpraxis* 12 (1988): 65-79.

An overview of the "brunette" (a French song of the 17th and 18th centuries the text of which often mentioned brunettes) and some collections of transcriptions for flute (or recorder, etc.) made by Montéclair and Hotteterre, apparently with pedagogical intent. Includes a discussion of contemporaneous precedents for using a second melody instrument on the bass line.

1192. Lemaître, Edmond. "L'Orchestre dans le Théâtre Lyrique Français chez les continuateurs de Lully 1687-1715" [The orchestra of the Théâtre Lyrique Français under Lully's successors, 1687-1715]. *"Recherches" sur la musique française classique* 26 (1988-90): 83-131.

Briefly discusses the recorder in French opera after the death of Lully. The scores mostly use the vague term "flûte[s]" and have parts in the range g^1 to c^3, which fits both the alto recorder and the transverse flute. Sometimes the terms "flûte d'Allemagne," "flûte allemande," or "flûte traversière" distinguish the transverse flute; only rarely is the recorder indicated by the terms "flûte à bec" or "flûte douce." Lemaître goes on to discuss which sizes of recorder were intended. Like the violin family, recorders carried the vocal designations "dessus," "haute-contre," "taille," "quinte," and "basse." He argues that these should be equated with the sopranino, soprano, alto, tenor, and bass (or great bass) recorders, respectively. The sopranino was sometimes also called "petite dessus de flûte" or "petite flûte." Lemaître whets one's appetite to see the scores he mentions by Bourgeois, Campra, Charpentier, Colasse, and Destouches.

1193. Pottier, Laurence. "Le répertoire de la flûte à bec en France à l'époque baroque (musique profane)" [The repertory of the recorder in France during the Baroque period (secular music)]. Doctoral dissertation, Université de Lille, 1992. 4 vols. 536, 81, 70, 113 p.

An important comprehensive overview of a hitherto neglected subject. Vol. 1 consists of chapters on: the flute and recorder before the Baroque era; the recorder during the Baroque; Baroque recorder methods in France; Baroque recorder making in France; the iconography of the Baroque recorder in France; the suite; the *sonate*; the concerto; the cantata; other pieces (Hotteterre's preludes, Montéclair's brunettes); Lully's ballets and *comédies-ballets*; ballets by other composers; Lully's *tragédies en musique*; *tragédies en musique* by other composers; and the decline of the recorder in France. Vol. 2 contains source documents. Vol. 3 is a catalog of the art works considered. Vol. 4 is a bibliography of the music considered.

ITALY

1194. McGowan, Richard Allen. *Italian Baroque Solo Sonatas for the Recorder and the Flute*. Ph.D. dissertation, University of Michigan, 1974. 517 leaves. OCLC #4845655. UMI order no. 75-00756.

Has a much greater scope than the title suggests. Chapter 1 discusses recorder design and acoustics (Renaissance and Baroque models). Chapter 2 surveys the development of flute playing and literature, not only in Italy but in France, Germany, Austria, and England; it includes a good overview of publishing trends in Europe that could usefully have been included in item **1195**. Chapter 3 lists and describes first editions and primary manuscripts of the Italian Baroque recorder sonata repertory. McGowan limits himself, unhelpfully, to sonatas which, according to their titles, are primarily intended for the recorder or flute, excluding works designated principally for the violin and optionally other treble instruments. Chapter 4 analyzes selected sonatas: Marcello, Bellinzani (both extended discussions), Barsanti, Vivaldi, and Sammartini (based on the Parma manuscript only). Chapter 5, on performance practices and idiomatic treatment, includes such neglected topics as the connection of movements and when to repeat a section; some ideas on rhythm and ornaments have been superseded by recent research. Appendixes cover secondary musical sources, three composers whose flute sonatas are believed lost, and a list of modern editions. Overall, this dissertation is one of the high points of the literature about the recorder.

1195. McGowan, Richard A. *Italian Baroque Solo Sonatas for the Recorder and the Flute.* (Detroit Studies in Music Bibliography, 37) Detroit: Information Coordinators, 1978. 70 p. ISBN 0911772901.

Based on item 1194, conflating its chapter 3 with appendix 1, leaving appendixes 2 (lost flute sonatas) and 3 (modern editions) alone—an unhelpful organization that results in the separation of sources and editions based on them. As in his dissertation, McGowan limits himself to sonatas which, according to their titles, are primarily intended for the recorder or flute, excluding works designated principally for the violin and optionally other treble instruments. Nevertheless, this is still a useful list. (A few quibbles: Grano was not Italian but an Englishman of French descent, and beware typos, the most glorious of which is "duplicity" for "duplication.")

1196. Selfridge-Field, Eleanor. "Instrumentation and Genre in Italian Music, 1600–1670." *Early Music* 19, no. 1 (February 1991): 61–67.

Many recorder players have the impression that 17th-century Italian instrumental music was intended to be played on "all sorts of instruments." Eleanor Selfridge-Field shows that this impression is "largely illusory, at least with reference to canzonas, sonatas and ricercars. [Such a designation] is found in only a handful of prints after 1615." When instruments are named, the recorder is rarely one of them, being found only in collections by Riccio (Venice, 1620), Picchi (Venice, 1625), Marini (Bavaria, 1626), and Neri (Venice, 1651).

THE NETHERLANDS

* Dart, Thurston. "Four Dutch Recorder Books." Cited above as item 596.

1197. Rasch, Rudi A. "Some Mid-Seventeenth Century Dutch Collections of Instrumental Ensemble Music." *Tijdschrift van de Vereniging voor Nederlandse Muziekgeschiedenis* 22, no. 3 (1972): 160–200.

A study of *Der gooden fluyt-hemel* (1644) and *'t Uitnement kabinet* (1646–49), both of which contain pieces written for C recorder or that could be played on it. Discusses bibliographical information, concordances, the composers, musical form, and instrumental usage. Concludes with a detailed table of contents of both collections.

Individual Composers

Bach, Carl Philipp Emanuel (1714–1788)

1198. Hofmann, Klaus. "Gesucht: ein Graunsches Trio mit obligater Bassblockflöte. Ein Ermittlungsbericht—mit Seitenblicken auf ein Trio Carl Philipp Emanuel Bachs" [Sought: a trio by Graun with obbligato basso recorder—a research report, with side-glances at a trio by Carl Philipp Emanuel Bach]. *Tibia* 17, no. 4 (1992): 253–62.

   C.P.E. Bach's celebrated Trio Sonata for Bass Recorder, Viola, and Continuo in F Major (Helm 588) has long been thought to have a unique instrumentation. Hofmann reports that he has now reconstructed the original version of a sister work for the same combination and in the same key by one of the Graun brothers. At the same time, Hofmann shows that the compass of the recorder part in the Bach work, f-c^2, was originally intended to be f-d^2, the second version having been made partly by the composer and partly by a copyist. That Bach did intend a bass recorder is proved by his own comment on a piece of paper pasted in the manuscript: "The bass recorder goes from f to c^2; F major, C major, and G major are the most comfortable keys for it."

Bach, Johann Sebastian (1685–1750)

1199. Baron, Samuel. "J.S. Bach: The Flauto and Traverso." In *Johann Sebastian: A Tercentenary Celebration*, edited by Seymour L. Benstock, 11–18. (Contributions to the Study of Music and Dance, no. 19) Westport, Conn.: Greenwood Press, 1992. ISBN 031327441X.

   Contrasts the roles of the recorder and flute in Bach's cantatas. Bach used the recorder for sad and mournful states, the pastoral (and by extension, the Nativity), and funerals. Claims that "the slow movement of the *Brandenburg Concerto No. 4* is a Nativity piece, even though it is not designated as such." The flute, by contrast, "is an athlete, a virtuoso, with a penchant for vivid decoration . . . more cheerful and forthcoming . . . in the imperative mode," and it also depicts "an inspired yet unstable state of trembling ecstasy."

1200. Davis, Alan. "Bach's Recorder Parts: Some Problems of Transposition." *Recorder and Music Magazine* 4, no. 2 (June 1972): 47–50.

   Concerns a subset of Bach's works including recorder: those "which, although almost certainly intended for the recorder, do not seem to fit the compass of the standard alto in F." The instrumental work falling into this category is Brandenburg Concerto No. 4, which Davis believes was intended for an alto in G (Flauto I) and an alto in F (Flauto II). In his introduction to the vocal works, Davis reviews the problems presented by *Cornett-ton, Chorton,* and *Kammerton.* He then discusses in detail five problematic cantatas: Cantata 161 ("Komm, du süße Todesstunde"), Cantata 103 ("Ihr werdet weinen und heulen"), Cantata 182 ("Himmelskönig, sei willkommen"), Cantata 106 ("Gottes Zeit ist die allerbeste Zeit"), and Cantata 18 ("Gleich wie der Regen und Schnee vom Himmel fällt").

Letters from Barrie Helmer in 4, no. 4 (December 1972): 126 and James Middleton in 4, no. 6 (June 1973), both with replies by Davis. K.J. Sayers writes in response to the latter in 4, no. 7 (September 1973): 243. Middleton challenges Davis's view that the recorder parts of Cantata 161 were intended for two voice flutes fingered as altos. He suggests that, although the second part is indeed for voice flute, the first part is for an alto in F. Sawyer's letter addresses Davis's comment that he knows of no 18th-century source that mentions the "knee stopping" technique for producing f^3. Sawyer offers no such source, but rather supports the ϕ13457 fingering suggested by Majer (item 664).

1201. Dolmergue, Sylvie. "Jouer les partitas de Bach à la flûte à bec: Essai autour de l'allemande de la partita no. 2 en re mineur" [Play Bach's partitas on the recorder: essay about the allemande of Partita no. 2 in D minor]. *Crescendo* 33 [i.e., 34] (September–October 1990): 24–30.

Surprisingly few authors have attempted to discuss the interpretation of recorder compositions in the light of their musical structure. Dolmergue is therefore to be applauded for taking on such a task for a movement from one of J.S. Bach's solo violin partitas, the allemande from the Partita No. 2 in D Major (BWV 1004), edited by Frans Brüggen, especially as this movement presents the additional difficulty of how the recorder should deal with the transcription of a string original containing some polyphony and a wide melodic range. Briefly, but helpfully, she covers rubato, breathing, form, harmonic structure, how to give the impression of harmony, melodic line, and rhythm.

1202. Edridge, Tom. "Arranging Keyboard Bach for Recorders." *Recorder and Music Magazine* 4, no. 1 (March 1972): 4–5.

More helpful than the advice on arranging techniques (which is rather simplistic) are the recommendations of specific works suitable for transcription, including several fugues from *The Well-Tempered Clavier* and *The Art of Fugue,* two slow movements from the organ sonatas, and several variations from *The Goldberg Variations.* Letters by A. Gregory Murray and Theo Wyatt in 4, no. 2 (June 1972): 51–52, 71.

1203. Francis, John. "What Bach Wrote for the Flute, and Why." *Music & Letters* 31, no. 1 (January 1950): 46–52.

Of little more than historical interest. A superficial survey of Bach's use of the recorder and flute in his vocal and instrumental works. The reasons given for Bach's choice of one instrument over the other for a particular work are not supported by relevant documentation, and many can be discredited. The arguments also reflect a prejudice against the recorder that was common early in the revival of the instrument: "the recorder presented fewer problems to the player than the traverso"; Bach wrote for the recorder "not for preference, but simply because it was difficult to procure a competent player on the [traverso]"; the flute has "a more robust and personal tone" compared to the "ethereal, rather characterless tone of the recorder."

* Haynes, Bruce. "Johann Sebastian Bach's Pitch Standards: The Woodwind Perspective." Cited above as item **374**.

1204. Letteron, Claude. "Bach et la flûte à bec" [Bach and the recorder]. (Répertoire pour la flûte à bec; série compositeurs) *Flûte à bec* 1 (June 1981): 16–30.

A complete listing of Bach's music that includes recorders, both original works and arrangements, with modern editions.

1205. Letteron, Claude. "Des thèmes pour 1985" [On themes for 1985]. *Flûte à bec & instruments anciens* 13/14 (December 1984/March 1985): 16–23.

A thematic index of the recorder works by J.S. Bach and Handel (original and arranged) available in modern editions. Ignores the recent research by Best, Lasocki, et al. on the authenticity and classification of Handel's sonatas.

1206. Mann, Alfred. "The Use of the Recorder in the Works of Bach and His Contemporaries." Master's essay, Columbia University, 1950. 62 p.

A journeyman's piece by the noted musicologist. Written at a point in the revival of the recorder when interest had been centered on Renaissance instruments and repertory. Mann calls for a "turn to the scores of the late Baroque in which its use is specified and fully shown." Begins by describing the physical and practical characteristics of the Baroque recorder in comparison to both its Renaissance counterpart and the transverse flute. Then surveys national styles in Baroque recorder literature, discussing repertory by English, French, Italian, and German composers. Comparisons are made for the most part on the basis of instrumentation, range, and tessitura. Certain German composers of the 18th century, including Bach and Telemann, explored the upper limits of the recorder's range, where the instrument could hold its own alongside other solo instruments. Progressing chronologically through Bach's works, Mann sees a constant extension of the range of the recorder. Concludes that "In Telemann's works we find a summation of the entire literature for the instrument. . . . Nevertheless, Bach's more economic use of the instrument is more impressive. It is precisely the soloistic glory which weakens Telemann's use of the recorder compared [with] that of Bach."

1206.1. Ruëtz, Manfred. "Die Blockflöte bei Bach." *Zeitschrift für Hausmusik* 4, no. 1 (January–February 1935): 13–19; 4, no. 3 (May–June 1935): 75–82.

An important article in its day, setting out for the first time the extent of Bach's involvement with the recorder in "chamber music works" (i.e., concertos) and cantatas. Notes that Bach and his contemporaries clearly differentiated between the tonal properties of recorder and the flute. Recognizes the problems in the Bach Gesellschaft edition caused by some instruments being notated in *Chorton* and others in *Cammerton*. Briefly analyzes Bach's use of recorders in his concertos. (For Ruëtz's comments on Bach's cantatas, see item 1225.)

1207. Schmidt, Lloyd. "Bach and the Recorder." *The American Recorder* 5, no. 4 (November 1964): 30–36.

An informative examination of the topic and its related controversies, based exclusively on the studies of other scholars. The catalog of works that employ the recorder includes the following information: BWV number, title, place and date of composition, setting, sections including the recorder, range of recorder parts, location in the Bach Gesellschaft edition, and citations to secondary literature.

Brandenburg Concertos

1208. Higbee, Dale. "Alternate Instrumentation in Bach's Second Brandenburg Concerto." *The American Recorder* 18, no. 1 (May 1977): 11.

Proposes several solutions to the problems of balance between the recorder and trumpet parts. Traditional solutions include muting the trumpet, having the trumpet play down an octave, placing the recorder in an exposed position on the stage, and using a softer instrument for the trumpet part. Suggests possible alternatives to a trumpet, such as a horn, a soprano saxophone, or a modern flute (Higbee's preference).

1209. Marissen, Michael. *Scoring, Structure, and Signification in J.S. Bach's Brandenburg Concertos.* Ph.D. dissertation, Brandeis University, 1991. vii, 251 leaves. OCLC #25010846. UMI order no. 91-18708.

This magisterial dissertation on Johann Sebastian Bach's Brandenburg Concertos includes a long chapter on the fourth concerto that has already been updated and published as an article (see item 1218). Marissen sets himself the principal task of answering one of the traditional questions asked about the work: "Is this a solo concerto for violin with ripieno strings and woodwinds, or is it a concerto grosso for a concertino of violin and woodwinds with ripieno strings?" Before he can do so, he must answer the question "What instruments did Bach mean by the designation 'fiauti d'echo'?" He brings out a wide range of musicological artillery for Bach—instrumental terminology, range, clefs, technique (especially the appearance or avoidance of $f\sharp^1$ and $f\sharp^3$)—to show that the composer almost certainly intended plain alto recorders. Furthermore, the *f* and *p* markings probably did not represent a literal echo but merely an indication of the *tutti* and *solo* passages. Although it would be difficult to declare this question closed, Marissen has certainly discussed it more exhaustively and with more insight than any previous author.

Then returns to the central question, concluding that "the piece would appear essentially to be a triple concerto with tension-filled surface leanings towards the solo concerto." He sees the "general elevating of the recorder at the more than occasional expense of the violin" as a social allegory, "representing musically the breach between appearance and essence familiar from everyday social and religious experience." A tour de force.

1210. Taylor, Stanley. "Balancing the Brandenburgs." *The American Recorder* 2, no. 3 (Fall [i.e., Summer] 1961): 3–4.

Problems of balance in Brandenburg Concertos No. 2 and 4. Includes stage diagrams suggesting placement of instruments. Also discusses tempo, ornamentation, and phrasing. Taylor corrects an error in 3, no. 2 (May 1962): 23.

Brandenburg Concerto No. 4 and the fiauti d'echo controversy

Bach included the designation *fiauti d'echo* in the Brandenburg Concerto No. 4 (BWV 1049). Many scholars have speculated on the meaning of the term. The instrument is not mentioned in the dictionaries or tutors of the period, nor was it thought at first that it was found in any other 18th-century works. The articles are presented in chronological order.

1211. Dart, Thurston. "Bach's 'Fiauti d'Echo.'" *Music & Letters* 41, no. 4 (October 1960): 331–41.

Argues that Bach's *fiauti d'echo* are bird-flageolets in G sounding an octave higher than written. Dart's reasoning in support of the flageolet is tenuous and many of his conclusions are not convincing. He notes the numerous references in London newspapers between 1713 and 1718 to James Paisible's performances on an "echo flute." If performances on the "echo flute" were popular, Dart suggests that we might expect to find contemporary tutors for the instrument, but there are none. Possibly laymen referred to the "echo flute" by another name, just as they called the recorder a "flute" and the chalumeau a "mock trumpet." If so, Dart sees the French flageolet as the likely candidate for "echo flute" because of its popularity at the time. He then addresses the question of how Bach might have become familiar with the flageolet in Cöthen. Musical and political links existed between London and Berlin at the time.

Dart also presents musical reasons for using instruments sounding an octave higher than written: "[T]he inescapable fact remains that the gentle sounds of two treble recorders are quite inaudible during a considerable part of the work. . . . The only solution to all the problems encountered in the Branbenburg concerto is to assume that the *flauto d'echo* parts sounded an octave higher than written." This conclusion is supported by a letter in 42, no. 1 (January 1961): 101 by Peter F. Williams, who notes that certain 18th-century organs included stops with the designation "echo," which seems to have been an octave coupler. The fault with Dart's suggestion that the instruments were flageolets in G is hidden away in a footnote (p. 340): "the low F in bar 183 of the first movement is outside the compass of the instrument." Dale Higbee takes note of this problem with Dart's theory in 43, no. 2 (April 1962): 192–93 and argues that the intended instruments are altos in F. He suggests that Bach used the designation *echo* "because of the way they answer (or echo) and interchange with each other."

Dart's thoughts on the roles of the recorder and flageolet in the Baroque are also a part of his "Performance Practice in the 17th and 18th Centuries: Six Problems in Instrumental Music," in *International Musicological Society: Report of the Eighth Congress, New York 1961*, vol. 1: *Papers* (Kassel: Bärenreiter, 1961), 234–35.

1212. Krainis, Bernard. "Bach and the Recorder in G." *The American Recorder* 2, no. 4 (Fall 1961): 7.

Suggests the possibility that the "Flauto I" part of the Brandenburg Concerto No. 4 was written for recorder in G rather than F. Letter from Wesley M. Oler in 4, no. 3 (August 1963): 22 cites several references to Paisible's "echo flute" in English newspapers. Oler follows up in 4, no. 4 (November 1963): 21 by acknowledging Thurston Dart's earlier consideration of the Paisible echo flute (item **1211**), which had been brought to Oler's attention after writing the letter.

1213. "Bach's Brandenburgs and the Recorder." *The Recorder and Music Magazine* 1, no. 4 (February 1964): 113.

Summarizes the discussion of the *fiauti d'echo* controversy in Norman Carrell's *Bach's Brandenburg Concertos* (London: G. Allen & Unwin, 1963). For some time, it was thought that the term *d'echo* simply referred to the echo effects in the slow movement, but the discovery of references to an "echo flute" in London newpapers dating from 1713-18 suggests that perhaps Bach had a specific instrument in mind. Cites a number of problems with Thurston Dart's theory (see item 1211) that the intended instrument might have been a flageolet in G. Carrell supports the use of recorders. Internal evidence—and Bach's practice in other works—leads him to conclude that the appropriate instruments are a pair of altos: one in G and one in F. Beverly Smith argues in favor of two altos in F in a letter published in 1, no. 5 (May 1964): 154. More letters in 1, no. 6 (August 1964): 185.

1214. Montagu, Jeremy. "What was the flauto d'echo?" *FoMRHI Quarterly* 23 (April 1981): 20-21.

By comparing the Fourth Brandenburg Concerto with Bach's arrangement of it as the Concerto in F Major for Harpsichord, Two *Fiauti à bec*, and Strings (BWV 1057), Montagu comes to the conclusion that the *fiauti d'echo* were not plain recorders but capable of making a genuine echo. Considers "the only probability" that they had "some mechnical device such as an additional thumb or finger hole which would increase the area of open hole and thus sharpen the pitch just enough to compensate for the drop in air pressure of the *piano* passages."

1215. Higbee, Dale. "Bach's 'Fiauti d'echo.'" *The Galpin Society Journal* 39 (1986): 133.

Reconsiders the identity of the *fiauti d'echo*. Proposes that the "echo" is not a description of the instrument but rather the manner in which it was played—offstage, to provide a genuine soft answering effect. Bernard Krainis describes his theory that the instrument was an alto recorder fitted with a "whisper key" in *The American Recorder* 29, no. 2 (May 1988): 76.

1216. Martin, John. "Echoes From the Past." *The Recorder: Journal of the Victorian Recorder Guild* 9 (February 1989): 1-3.

Summarizes the views of various authors from Carl Dolmetsch (1941) to Dale Higbee (1986) on the identity of the *fiauti d'echo*. Concludes that they were probably altos in F, or altos in G and F; or else the term is a simple misprint. Continued by items 1217 and 1219.

1217. Morgan, Fred, John Martin, and Malcolm Tattersall. "Echoes Resounding." *The Recorder: Journal of the Victorian Recorder Guild* 10 (December 1989): 19–24.
    A series of letters to the editor continuing Martin's speculations on the identity of Bach's *fiauti d'echo* (see item **1216**). Morgan supports the idea that they were altos in G and F. Tattersall demolishes Dart's idea that they were flageolets. Martin cites historical evidence for his new belief that they consisted of two recorders fastened together to play loud and soft. Tattersall concludes that "the issue is ultimately unresolvable." Continued by item **1219**.

1218. Marissen, Michael. "Organological Questions and Their Significance in J.S. Bach's Fourth Brandenburg Concerto." *Journal of the American Musical Instrument Society* 17 (1991): 5–52.
    A slightly updated version of chapter 2 from item **1209**.

1219. Lasocki, David. "More on Echo Flutes." *The Recorder: Journal of the Victorian Recorder Guild* 13 (July 1991): 14–16.
    A follow-up to items **1216** and **1217**. Refutes John Martin's suggestion that Bach's term *fiauti d'echo* was a misprint. Then asserts that there are only two general avenues of approach to the identity of those instruments: Bach had in mind an instrument called an echo flute, or else the instruments were plain recorders and the appendage "d'echo" referred to an echo effect, either literal or figurative. Taking the first approach, shows that James Paisible's echo flutes were at least similar to ordinary recorders; adds two references to support John Martin's theory that they could have consisted of two recorders fastened together; and modifies Dart's belief that they could have found their way to Berlin and Bach. Taking the second approach, reports a reference to "flauti eco" in 1704, but opts for Michael Marissen's view (see items **1209** and **1218**) that Bach intended a figurative echo.

1220. Lasocki, David. "Paisible's Echo Flute, Bononcini's *Flauti Eco*, and Bach's *Fiauti d'Echo*." *The Galpin Society Journal* 45 (March 1992): 59–66.
    An extended version of the arguments presented in item **1219**.

Cantatas

1221. Bloodworth, Denis. "The Recorder Parts of the Bach Cantatas: A Practical Approach." *Recorder & Music* 6, no. 6 (June 1979): 162–65.

Repertory: Baroque and Classical 367

    Advice for players who must fit the recorder parts onto instruments in F and C. Each cantata is considered separately. Bloodworth bases his suggestions on the Heugel edition of the recorder parts (prepared by Michel Sanvoisin) rather than on a reliable critical edition, which leads Ralph Leavis to question a few of Bloodworth's recommendations and observations in 6, no. 7 (September 1979): 215. Bloodworth replies in 6, no. 8 (December 1979): 229. Eugene Reichenthal writes on the practicality of the key of E♭ major for Cantata 106 in *Recorder & Music* 6, no. 9 (March 1980): 276.

1222. Haynes, Bruce. "Questions of Tonality in Bach's Cantatas: The Woodwind Perspective." *Journal of the American Musical Instrument Society* 12 (1986): 40–67.

    Follows up his article on the pitches of woodwind instruments available to J.S. Bach (item 374) by furnishing practical solutions to the problems of performance posed by those early cantatas of Bach's—for recorder, nos. 18, 71, 106, 152, 161, and 182—in which the woodwind instruments (built at chamber pitch) were treated as transposing instruments in relation to the other instruments (sounding at the higher choir pitch).

1223. Higbee, Dale. "Recorders in Bach Cantata 161, *Komm, du süße Todesstunde.*" *Journal of the American Musical Instrument Society* 17 (1991): 83–84.

    Really only a "letter to the editor," following up on item 1222. Puts forward the opinion that the best modern solution for playing Cantata 161 is "to use an alto recorder in f' for Flauto I and a voice flute in d' for Flauto II, or use two voice flutes throughout except for movement five where Flauto I would use alto recorder."

1224. Höffer-von Winterfeld, Linde. "Die Blockflöte in den Kantaten J.S. Bachs." *Hausmusik* 17 (1953): 106–16.

    Covers the same territory as item 1225 in less detail.

1225. Ruëtz, Manfred. "Die Blockflöte in der Kirchenmusik Johann Sebastian Bachs." *Musik und Kirche* 7 (1935): 112–20, 170–86. Also published in *Collegium Musicum* 3 (1935): 13–19, 75–82.

    A pioneering article, outlining the extent of Bach's use of the recorder in his church cantatas for the first time. (The dating of the cantatas has been updated by later scholarship.) Recognizes the *Chorton/Cammerton* problem and proposes solutions for modern performances (at modern pitch).

1226. Sharp, Nan Ellen Orthmann. *The Use of Flutes and Recorders in the Church Cantatas of Johann Sebastian Bach*. D.M.A. dissertation, Eastman School of Music, University of Rochester, 1975. xxxiii, 406 leaves. OCLC #4651191. UMI order no. 75-20068.

Concentrates more on the flute than the recorder, partly because the author admits her "knowledge regarding technical matters of the recorder is far less than my experience with the flute." Chapter 1, on the recorder, describes all the cantatas with recorder parts, including musical motives symbolizing sleep, death, tears, the pastoral, and the supernatural (usually presented as fact not opinion, although ironically in her conclusions she recognizes that "[w]e must distinguish as precisely as possible between Bach's intentions and inferences made by others"). The information about the terminology and ranges of recorders other than the alto is confused. Chapter 6 briefly summarizes the differences between Bach's treatment of the recorder and the flute. Quotes heavily from other modern writers, the few original thoughts being drawn to our attention with asterisks! Perhaps useful as a compilation of opinion, if you can stand the appalling prose.

1227. Thalheimer, Peter. "Der flauto piccolo bei Johann Sebastian Bach" [The *flauto piccolo* in the works of J.S. Bach]. *Bach-Jahrbuch* 52 (1966): 138–46.

Begins by discussing the small sizes of the three types of "flute" used in the Baroque era: flutes, recorders, and flageolets. Then suggests what Bach meant by the term *flauto piccolo* in cantatas 96 (sopranino recorder) and 103 (sixth flute, using a narrow, strongly conically bored instrument to produce the large range of the part). In the absence of a sixth flute, believes that, because no other recorder has the necessary range, two players in tandem using soprano and sopranino recorders present the best solution.

Sonatas

1228. Marissen, Michael. "A Trio in C Major for Recorder, Violin and Continuo by J.S. Bach?" *Early Music* 13, no. 3 (August 1985): 384–90.

Suggests that Bach's Sonata for Flute and Harpsichord in A Major (BWV 1032) was originally written as a trio sonata in C major for alto recorder, violin, and basso continuo (the slow second movement remaining in A minor). The alto recorder would be suitable for the range of his reconstructed top part except for one note: the e^1 found in m. 6 of the slow movement, which Marissen believes could have been played by a virtuoso (covering the bottom of the instrument with the knee). Also discusses the completion of the excised middle section of the first movement. For criticism of Marissen's views, see item **1229** and Laurence Dreyfus, "J.S.

Repertory: Baroque and Classical

Bach and the Status of Genre: Problems of Style in the G-Minor Sonata BWV 1029," *Journal of Musicology* 5, no. 1 (Winter 1987): 55–78 (esp. 62–63).
On the Bach A-Major Flute Sonata, see also: Michael Marissen, "A Critical Reappraisal of J.S. Bach's A-Major Flute Sonata," *Journal of Musicology* 6, no. 3 (Summer 1988): 367–86; Marianne Betz, "Bearbeitung, Rekonstruktion, Ergänzung: Der erste Satz der Sonate A-Dur BWV 1032 für Flöte und obligates Cembalo von J.S. Bach" [Arrangement, reconstruction, completion: the first movement of the Sonata in A Major, BWV 1032, for Flute and Obbligato Harpsichord of J.S. Bach], *Tibia* 13, no. 3 (1988): 158–63; the letter from Erich Benedikt in *Tibia* 13, no. 4 (1988): 314, and the reply by Betz, p. 315.

1229. Kroesbergen, Willem, and Marijke Schouten. "Bachs triosonates gereconstrueerd" [Bach's trio sonatas reconstructed]. *Tijdschrift voor oude muziek* 1, no. 5 (15 November 1986): 115–18.

Rejects Marissen's suggestion (item 1228) that the A-Major Flute Sonata (BWV 1032) was originally a trio sonata for recorder, violin, and basso continuo, expressing skepticism about the suggested use of e^1 for the alto recorder and the key scheme (C major—A minor—C major). Also challenges his proposed reconstruction of the first movement. We await the publication of musicological support for their own theories.

BARSANTI, FRANCESCO (CA. 1690–1775)

1229.1. Bergmann, Walter. "Francesco Barsanti." *The Consort* 18 (1961): 67–77.

Gathers together all the biographical material about Barsanti known at that time. Also brief but cogent comments on Barsanti's music. The recorder sonatas "not only show unusual knowledge of the recorder, as one would expect from a master of that instrument, but also high musical imagination." Partly based on his article about Barsanti in *The Recorder News* 13 (Autumn 1955).

1230. Schneider, Michael. "Dekor oder Substanz?: Untersuchungen anhand der Sonate C-dur für Blockflöte und Bc von Francesco Barsanti" [Decoration or substance? Investigations into the Sonata in C Major for Recorder and Continuo by Francesco Barsanti]. *Musica* 40, no. 3 (May/June 1986): 239–44.

Discusses the first movement of Barsanti's C-Major Recorder Sonata, which is a rather rhapsodic written-out ornamentation. Shows that the ornamentation can be increasingly simplified until it becomes a melodic skeleton similar in appearance to some simple Baroque movements. Then analyzes the entire movement as written phrase by phrase, pointing up the surprising features of the melody, rhythm, and articulation. (Beware: some of the accidentals are incorrect or else supplied editorially without comment.) Encourages readers to experiment with their own ornamentation of the skeleton.

1231. Sharman, Ian G. "Francesco Barsanti: A Discography and Worklist." *Brio* 28, no. 1 (Spring/Summer 1991): 29-33.

Lists Barsanti's compositions, including modern editions and recordings. A complement to item **887**.

BIGAGLIA, DIOGENIO (CA. 1676–1745)

1232. Wind, Thiemo. "Bigaglia's Sonata in A Minor: A New Look at Its Originality." *The Recorder and Music Magazine* 8, no. 2 (June 1984): 49–54.

Argues, through extensive comparisons, that the version of the A-Minor Sonata edited by Hugo Ruf (Mainz: Schott, 1966) is not a work by Bigaglia but an anonymous reworking of the original, which had been published in Amsterdam by Le Cène in 1725. Similarly argues that the same arranger was responsible for the G-Minor Sonata edited by Ruf (Mainz: Schott, 1965). See also item **1233**.

1233. Wind, Thiemo. "New Facts Concerning Bigaglia's Sonata in A Minor." *The Recorder and Music Magazine* 8, no. 4 (December 1984): 106–8.

Shortly before item **1232** was published, Wind discovered yet another version of the sonata in a two-volume Walsh and Hare publication of arrangements by Pietro Chaboud dating from ca. 1723. This set, containing arrangements of the music of a number of composers, was reprinted by Le Cène ca. 1730. Wind discusses the history of the publications, the life of Chaboud, and the identity of the sonata's authentic version—which he continues to believe to be the 1725 Le Cène publication of Bigaglia's opus 1.

BOISMORTIER, JOSEPH BODIN DE (1689–1755)

1234. Peterman, Lewis Emanuel, Jr. *The Instrumental Chamber Music of Joseph Bodin de Boismortier with Special Emphasis on the Trio Sonatas for Two Treble Instruments and Basso Continuo*, 2 vols. Ph.D. dissertation, College-Conservatory of Music, University of Cincinnati, 1985. xx, 995 leaves. OCLC #13924601. UMI order no. 85-18112.

Part I, "The Background of French Music in the Baroque Era," surveys social history, the function of music, the Franco-Italian style, French ensemble music, performance practice, and the instruments (including the recorder) for which Boismortier composed. Part II summarizes Boismortier's life, then analyzes his instrumental chamber music in general and his trio sonatas in particular. Part III consists of complete modern editions of his opera 4, 12, 18, 28, 41, and 78 (none of which was primarily intended for recorders). The appendixes include lists of works (with locations of copies, if known) and of modern editions, both arranged by opus number. The thorough and stimulating analyses in this dissertation should prompt a reappraisal of a composer who is often dismissed as a money-grubbing scribbler.

CHARPENTIER, MARC-ANTOINE (1634–1704)

1235. Duron, Jean. "L'orchestre de Marc-Antoine Charpentier" [Marc-Antoine Charpentier's orchestra]. *Revue de musicologie* 72, no. 1 (1986): 23–65.

This otherwise excellent article suffers because Duron does not relate the instrumentation of Charpentier's orchestral pieces to actual ensembles used by the composer (such as that of Marie de Lorraine studied by Ranum [item 69]). Nevertheless, it is full of interesting material on the recorder. Charpentier's standard size of recorder was the alto; occasionally he asked for sopranino, soprano, tenor, and bass. The instrument represents birdsong, tender and calm love, evocation of the night, and peace.

CORELLI, ARCANGELO (1653–1713)

* Michel, Winfried. "Editionskunde—ein Stückchen Verbraucheraufklärung: Zur Bearbeitungspraxis von Instrumentalmusik des 18. Jahrhunderts" [The theory of making editions—a little consumer explanation: on the practice of arranging 18th-century instrumental music]. Cited above as item 1159.

DEMOIVRE, DANIEL (FL. 1687–1731)

1236. Stratford, Michael. "Daniel Demoivre (c.1675–c.1720) and his Music." *The Consort* 43 (1987): 13–16.

Discusses the three French-style collections of "aires" or "lessons" for alto recorder (1701, lost) and for alto recorder and basso continuo (1704 and ca. 1715) published by Daniel Demoivre. Stratford's contention that "virtually nothing" is known of Demoivre's life betrays ignorance of the recent research by Lasocki (item 72).

DIEUPART, CHARLES [FRANCIS] (CA. 1670–CA. 1740)

1237. Read, Robin. "Discovery of Six Sonatas by Dieupart." *The Recorder and Music Magazine* 1, no. 11 (November 1965): 332.

Brief report of a lecture by Walter Bergmann on the recorder compositions of Francis Dieupart, which consist of an arrangement of six harpsichord suites (1705) for recorder (some for fourth flute, others for voice flute) and continuo, and a set of six sonatas for alto recorder and continuo (1717).

THE DIVISION FLUTE

* Habert, Andreas. "Wege durch die *Division Flute*: Zur Variationspraxis in der englischen Kunst- und Volksmusik des 17. Jahrhunderts" [Ways through the *Division Flute*: on variation practice in English art and folk music of the 17th century]. Cited above as item 721.

* Hullfish, William R. "The Division Flute: An Introduction to Playing Upon a Ground." Cited above as item 722.

EYCK, JACOB VAN (CA. 1590–1657)

Jacob van Eyck's *Der fluyten lust-hof*, published in two volumes that went through five printings during the composer's lifetime, is the largest collection ever published of music for a solo wind instrument by a single composer. It consists primarily of variations on popular tunes and psalms.

* White, Beverly. "Frans Brueggen's Visit to Oberlin, 1973: A Recollection." Cited above as item 964.

1238. Baker, Christina. "The Psalm Variations in Jacob van Eyck's 'Der Fluyten Lust-hof.'" *Recorder & Music* 7, no. 8 (December 1982): 194–96.

Concerned with the sources for the psalm tunes used by van Eyck as the basis of sixteen sets of variations. Begins with a brief history of Dutch psalters and their dissemination during the last half of the 16th century. Notes general differences between van Eyck's versions of the tunes and the originals. Concludes with a table indexing the various tune sources.

1239. Griffioen, Ruth van Baak. "Some French Melodies in Jacob van Eyck's 'Der Fluyten Lust-Hof.'" *The Recorder and Music Magazine* 8, no. 11 (September 1986): 322-27. In Dutch as: "Iets over enkele 'bloempjes' in Jacob Van Eyck's 'Lust-hof.'" *Tijdschrift voor oude muziek* 1, no. 2 (1 May 1986): 42-44.

Nearly one quarter of the tunes van Eyck chose for the 144 sets of variations in *Der fluyten lust-hof* are probably of French origin. Griffioen discusses the history and texts of the six tunes that can be identified as part of the French *air de cour* repertory (songs performed and composed at French courts): "O Heiligh zaligh Bethlehem," "Courante Mars," "La Bergere," "Al hebben de Princen," "Repicavan," and "Aerdigh Martyntje." Includes versions of the tunes as they were published in French songbooks (some in facsimile).

1240. Wind, Thiemo. "Jacob van Eyck and his 'Euterpe oft Speel-goddinne.'" *The American Recorder* 27, no. 1 (February 1986): 9-15.

Describes the editions *Der fluyten lust-hof*, stressing the importance of the neglected first edition of volume 1 published under the title *Euterpe oft Speel-goddinne*, which included three pieces not found in later editions as well as many variant readings of other pieces. Also includes the first detailed information on van Eyck's life available in English (largely taken from van den Hul's dissertation [item 1456]).

1241. Wind, Thiemo. "Chain Variations in van Eyck's 'Der Fluyten Lust-Hof.'" *The American Recorder* 28, no. 4 (November 1987): 141-44. Adapted from: "Kettingvariaties in Der Fluyten Lust-hof van Jacob Van Eyck." *Tijdschrift voor oude muziek* 1, no. 2 (1 May 1986): 45-47.

Coins the term "chain variation" to describe van Eyck's use (in seventeen pieces) of variations in the pattern AA AA' A'A" ... ("variation chain" seems more appropriate). Shows how the recurrence of the phrases can be used to check for errors in the musical text of those phrases.

1242. Humphries, Nicholas. "A Translation of the Introduction to Jacob van Eyck's Der Fluyten Lust-Hof of 1649." *The*

Recorder: Journal of the Victorian Recorder Guild 8 (July 1988): 1–7.

English translation of the title page, dedicatory poem and preface, and the fingering instructions from the 1649 edition of the first part of van Eyck's collection (these instructions stem from the publisher, P[aulus] M[atthysz]).

1243. Griffioen, Ruth van Baak. *Jacob van Eyck's* Der Fluyten Lust-Hof *(1644–c1655)*. Ph.D. dissertation, Stanford University, 1988. xiv, 502 leaves. OCLC #20616800. UMI order no. 88-15005.

Studies the collection with the kind of exhaustive musicological approach usually reserved for the works of major composers; certainly one of the most impressive documents ever written about the recorder. First, spends thirty pages setting out the considerable amount that is now known about van Eyck's life (almost all of this was previously available only in Dutch).

Second, discusses *Der fluyten lust-hof* as a printed collection, including its complex bibliographic history, its publisher, its 17th-century audience, and its modern revival, ending with the astounding news that well over 100,000 copies of modern editions and facsimiles have now been sold.

Third, spends over 300 pages tracing each of van Eyck's melodies backwards and forwards in time, whenever possible printing the words (and English translations) of all the vocal melodies. Valuable for bringing to life what were popular and favorite tunes in van Eyck's day, as well as shedding light on the spread of music throughout Europe in the first half of the 17th century.

Fourth, briefly considers van Eyck's variation technique.

Finally, drawing on Griffioen's own study of the depiction of recorders in one hundred selected 17th-century Dutch paintings, discusses what instrument was used in van Eyck's day to play his music. Concludes that it was probably "a wooden one-piece recorder, with an inner design allowing for strong low notes and a responsive high range reaching to c^4 and even to d^4. No known surviving recorder matches this description, but analysis of known instruments and the continued accumulation of expertise by the world's recorder makers should lead to more fully satisfactory designs."

1244. Griffioen, Ruth van Baak. *Jacob van Eyck's* Der Fluyten Lust-hof *(1644–c1655)*. Utrecht: Vereniging voor Nederlandse Muziekgeschiednis, 1991. 467 p. ISBN 9063751516.

In its published form, the main strength of Griffioen's study (see item 1243) is still the detailed histories of the tunes used by van Eyck. For publication, she had to cut out all but the first stanza of each song; even so, this section still takes up two-thirds of the book. Shorter sections are devoted to van Eyck's life, *Der fluyten lust-hof* as a printed collection, the variations, and the instrument intended, and the appendixes list, among other things, recordings of van Eyck's pieces (brought up to date). Highly recommended. Reviewed by Judith Linsenberg in *American Recorder* 33, no. 4 (December 1992): 21-22. Scholarly reviews by Joan Rimmer, *Music & Letters* 74, no. 3 (August 1993): 428-31, and Thiemo Wind, *Tibia* 17, no. 4 (1992): 312-16. Wind, besides taking issue with some of Griffioen's premises and conclusions, warns of the large number of typographical errors in the musical examples. In his review (*Early Music* 20, no. 3 [August 1992]: 485-86), Jeremy Barlow laments that Griffioen did not include anything on ornaments, which would certainly have been added to van Eyck's tunes by 17th-century performers.

1245. Wind, Thiemo. "Die Psalm-Variationen Jacob van Eycks: Geschichte, Analyse, Interpretation" [Jacob van Eyck's psalm variations: history, analysis, interpretation]. *Tibia* 15, no. 1 (1990): 22-32.

Der fluyten lust-hof contains no fewer than fourteen psalms as well as the Our Father and the Magnificat, more than 10 percent of the collection, some of them located at strategic points, and "Psalmen" are named first on the title page among the types of pieces contained therein. Nowadays, however, these pieces are neglected today in favor of their more catchy secular counterparts. Considers the importance of psalms in van Eyck's time, including the fact that the Dutch would have heard them every day on their carillons, sometimes with divisions. Looks at the relationship between theme and variations (which retain it strictly as a cantus firmus), and uses the logic of their matching up to discover errors and missing accidentals. Discusses the tempo relations between theme and variations. Finally, classifies the psalm variations into three types (Th and V without rests; Th with rests, V without; Th and V with rests), then considers whether they were meant to be differentiated in performance, concluding that the notation of the second type is erroneous.

1246. Wind, Thiemo. "'Some Mistakes or Errors. . . .'" *The Recorder Magazine* 11, no. 3 (September 1991): 82-86.

Describes the various types of mistakes Wind encountered when preparing the New Vellekoop edition of *Der fluyten lust-hof* (Naarden: XYZ, 1986-88). Because van Eyck, owing to his blindness, could see neither the transcriptions of his musical compositions nor the printed results, errors inevitably crept into the 17th-century editions of *Lust-hof*. Wind believes that "we have to weigh the pros and cons of every note before deciding whether it is the right one or not." His work with *Lust-hof* also illustrates "how risky it is to rely gratuitously on original sources of early music. . . ." Some of the types of errors include notes printed upside down, omitted (or extra) notes, and misplaced barlines. Most of these become apparent through a comparison of the theme and its variations. Wind also includes a biography of van Eyck.

1247. Wind, Thiemo. "'Stemme Nova'—Eine neuentdeckte Komposition Jacob van Eycks" ["Stemme Nova"—a newly discovered composition of Jacob van Eyck's]. *Tibia* 18, no. 2 (1993): 466–69.

Argues convincingly that an anonymous "Stemme Nova" in *Der gooden fluyt-hemel* (1644) is actually the work of Jacob van Eyck, having been left over from *Euterpe*, the first edition of the first part of van Eyck's *Der fluyten lust-hof*. The argument is based on errors in the source (typical for the blind van Eyck), some publication considerations of *Der gooden fluyt-hemel* and *Der fluyten lust-hof*, and stylistic observations.

FINGER, GODFREY (CA. 1660–1730)

1248. Marshall, Arthur W. "The Chamber Music of Godfrey Finger." *The Consort* 26 (1970): 423–32.

An important article, drawing attention to the hitherto neglected chamber music (including a great deal for recorder) of a significant figure in the history of the instrument, possessed of a "genuine if modest inspiration." Analyzes his style, then surveys the output, pointing out works of merit or interest. Appendix 1 lists all the works with modern editions. A letter from Marshall in 31 (1975): 148 describes recent discoveries and makes corrections.

1249. Marshall, Arthur W. "The Recorder Music of Godfrey Finger." *Recorder & Music* 5, no. 11 (September 1977): 350–52.

Begins with a summary of how Finger's recorder compositions have come down to us; the author considered many to have been lost until they were discovered in the Library of Congress during the early 1970s. Lists the known compositions and offers stylistic analyses of a handful of the works. Concludes with an essay on Finger's compositional style.

FISCHER, JOHANN (1646–1716 OR 17)

1250. Delius, Nikolaus. "Johann Fischer: Allemande für Flöte und Generalbaß" [John Fischer: Allemande for flute and continuo]. (Die gelbe Seite) *Tibia* 17, no. 3 (1992): XIII–XIX.

A thorough study of the performance of Fischer's allemande (from his *Vier Suiten für Blockflöte*, ed. Waldemar Woehl, Hortus Musicus 59 [Kassel:

Bärenreiter, 1932], Suite 3, No. 9). Covers: the composer, the history of the allemande, phrasing, melody/motives, articulation, structure, ornaments.

FONTANA, GIOVANNI BATTISTA (D. 1630)

1251. Nitz, Martin. "G.B. Fontana: '6 Sonaten für Violine (Sopranblockflöte) und B.c.' Ueberlegungen zu den Temporelationen ihrer 2er- und 3er-Taktabschnitte" [G.B. Fontana, *Six Sonatas for Violin (Soprano Recorder) and Continuo*: reflections on the tempo relations of its duple- and triple-meter sections]. *Tibia* 15, no. 3 (1990): 205-8.

Fontana's sonatas are now available in three modern editions. Drawing on the work of Mirjam Nastasi ("Zur Tempofrage bei Frescobaldi," *Tibia* 4, no. 1 [1979]: 217-21) and Karin Paulsmeier ("Temporelationen bei Frescobaldi," in *Alte Musik, Praxis und Reflection: Sonderband der Reihe "Basler Jahrbuch für historische Musikpraxis" zum 50. Jubiläum der Schola Cantorum Basiliensis*, edited by Peter Reidemeister and Veronika Gutmann, 187-203 [Winterthur: Amadeus, 1983]), Nitz suggests solutions to the problems of the duple/triple tempo relations based on theory and experience.

FUX, JOHANN JOSEPH (1660-1741)

1252. Kubitschek, Ernst. "Block- und Querflöte im Umkreis von Johann Joseph Fux—Versuch einer Übersicht" [Recorder and flute in Johann Joseph Fux's circle: an attempt at a synopsis]. In *Johann Joseph Fux und die Barocke Bläsertradition*, herausgegeben von Bernhard Habla, 99-119. (Alta musica, Band 9) Tutzing: Hans Schneider, 1987. ISBN 3795204941.

A highly important article, bringing to light a great deal of information on an almost unknown subject. Begins with the use of *flauti* in the Austro-Hungarian empire of the late 17th century. Continues with the court, including Giovanni Battista Bononcini's employment of "2 Flauti Eco." Makes an aside on the transition from Renaissance to Baroque recorders. Concludes with Fux himself.

The recorder parts would have been played by the court oboists (see the companion article, Herbert Heyde, "Blasinstrumente und Bläser der Dresdner Hofkapelle in der Zeit des Fux-Schülers Johann Dismas Zelenka (1710-1745)" [Wind instruments and instrumentalists of the Dresden court chapel in the time of the Fux student Johann Dismas Zelenka (1710-1745)], 39-65).

See also the other companion articles: Herbert Seifert, "Die Bläser der Kaiserlichen Hofkapelle zur Zeit von J.J. Fux" [The winds of the royal court chapel during the time of J.J. Fux], 9-23, and Gunther Joppig, "Die hohen

Holzblasinstrumente (Chalumeau und Oboe) im Schaffen von Johann Joseph Fux" [The high woodwind instruments (chalumeau and oboe) in the production of Johann Joseph Fux], 67–71.

1253. Suppan, Wolfgang. "The Use of Wind Instruments (Excluding Chalumeau) in Fux's Music." In *Johann Joseph Fux and the Music of the Austro-Italian Baroque*, edited by Harry White, 95–108. Aldershot: Scolar Press, 1992. ISBN 0859678326. In German as: "Blasinstrumente (ohne Chalumeau) im musikalischen Schaffen von Johann Joseph Fux." *Das Musikinstrument* 39, no. 11 (November 1990): 68–74.

Mentions a few arias with parts for "Flöte," unfortunately not distinguishing between the recorder and transverse flute, and simply drawing on the work of Kubitschek (see item 1252).

GRAUN

* Hofmann, Klaus. "Gesucht: ein Graunsches Trio mit obligater Bassblockflöte. Ein Ermittlungsbericht—mit Seitenblicken auf ein Trio Carl Philipp Emanuel Bachs" [Sought: a trio by Graun with obbligato basso recorder—a research report, with side-glances at a trio by Carl Philipp Emanuel Bach]. Cited above as item 1198.

HANDEL, GEORGE FRIDERIC (1685–1759)

* Welch, Christopher. *Six Lectures on the Recorder and Other Flutes in Relation to Literature.* Cited above as item 18.

1254. Hillemann, Willi. "Auftreten und Verwendung der Blockflöte in den Werken George Friedrich Händels" [Occurrence and use of the recorder in the works of George Frideric Handel]. *Die Musikforschung* 8, no. 2 (1955): 157–69.

An early overview of the subject, touching briefly on terminology, range, keys, technique, articulation, and ornaments. The repertory is listed, then discussed.

* Newman, Joel. "A Commentary on the *Directions for Playing the Flute* (c. 1731)." Cited above as item 627.

1255. Newman, Joel. "Handel's Use of the Recorder." *The American Recorder* 5, no. 4 (November 1964): 4–9. Revision of an article in *ARS Newsletter* 22, 24, and 26.

Documents Handel's use of the recorder in vocal, orchestral, and chamber works, with an emphasis on the vocal. Through a perusal of the old Handel complete edition, Newman identifies twenty-five operas, ten oratorios, five Italian cantatas, and three serenatas and pastorals that use the instrument. Each entry in the listing includes title, date of composition, aria name, role and voice, tempo, meter, key, instrumentation, range of recorder part, and general remarks. Newman notes that Handel favors flat keys and rarely uses pitches higher than $e\flat^3$. The information on the chamber works is outdated. Discusses the "flauto piccolo" problem in Handel—similar to the one in Vivaldi's music.

* McGrady, Richard. "Corelli's Violin Sonatas and the Ornamentation of Handel's Recorder Sonatas." Cited above as item 742.

1256. Savage, Alan A. "On Performing the Handel Recorder Sonatas, Opus One." *Recorder & Music* 6, no. 1 (March 1978): 9–11.

Describes the author's experience as an amateur preparing for a performance of the four opus 1 recorder sonatas. Offers personal observations on the appropriate tempo, articulation, and ornamentation for each movement.

1257. Best, Terence. "Handel's Solo Sonatas." *Music & Letters* 58, no. 4 (October 1977): 430–38.

The first full survey of the manuscript and printed sources. Includes discussion of the sonatas attributed to Handel that are either spurious or of doubtful authenticity. A concluding table provides a concordance of contemporary prints, autographs, and locations of the sonatas in the *Hallische-Händel-Ausgabe*.

1258. Lasocki, David. "A New Look at Handel's Recorder Sonatas: I. Ornamentation in the First Movement of the F major Sonata." *Recorder & Music* 6, no. 1 (March 1978): 2–9, 19.

Suggests how a player might arrive at suitable ornamentation of the movement. The qualities of good ornamentation, being dependent on the judgement of the interpreter, are a matter of taste, but some guidance can be found by first analyzing the melodic and motivic content of the music and considering what historical sources have to say about the purpose of ornamentation. Although skillful ornamentation can resurrect a monotonous work, ill-considered ornamentation can just as easily ruin a piece. As an example of the latter, Lasocki cites the contemporary ornamentation of the sonata movement found on an 18th-century barrel organ, which David Munrow used as the basis for his recording of the work. (Lasocki includes a transcription.) Lasocki then proceeds through the movement and describes what appropriate ornamentation might be, given the content of the music and what ornamentation should and should not accomplish. Finally, as an example of a "musical, sensitive and convincing" performance, Lasocki offers a transcription of Frans Brüggen's second recording of the movement.

1259. Lasocki, David. "A New Look at Handel's Recorder Sonatas: II. The Autograph Manuscripts." *Recorder & Music* 6, no. 3 (September 1978): 71–79.

   Reviews the history of the manuscript sources and early editions. Compares the autographs, contemporaneous copies, and editions, then offers examples of variants among them. Suggests probable chronologies for the sources.

1260. Lasocki, David. "A New Look at Handel's Recorder Sonatas: III. The Roger and Walsh Prints: A New View." *Recorder & Music* 6, no. 5 (March 1979): 130–32.

   Reports Lasocki's revised theory on the circumstances surrounding the publication of the "Jeanne Roger" and Walsh prints of the Handel opus 1 sonatas (see item 1259 for his original thoughts).

1261. Lasocki, David. "New Light on Handel's Woodwind Sonatas." *The American Recorder* 21, no. 4 (February 1981): 163–70. In German as: "Händels Sonaten für Holzbläser in neuem Licht." *Tibia* 5, no. 3 (1980): 166–76.

   Summarizes recent research by Lasocki and Best (items 1257, 1259, and 1260), whose studies of early prints and newly discovered manuscripts have radically altered the accepted ideas about instrumentation and authenticity for certain sonatas. Speculates on the circumstances that might have led John Walsh to publish the first edition of the sonatas under the name of Jeanne Roger of Amsterdam. See also items 1265 and 1266.

1262. Hofmann, Klaus. "Zu Händels Fitzwilliam-Sonate in G-dur: Eine Replik" [On Handel's Fitzwilliam Sonata in G major: a reply]. *Tibia* 6, no. 3 (1981): 391–96.

   A long reply to David Lasocki's brief argument (see item 1261) that Handel's G-Major Sonata (HWV 358)—unattributed in the autograph manuscript found in the Fitzwilliam Museum, Cambridge—was intended for the violin, although Hofmann had claimed it for the alto recorder (in his edition published by Hänssler-Verlag in 1974). Points out that he suggested the recorder as a "provisional and more practical solution to the problem" of attribution. Discusses in detail the passage in the final movement containing four very high notes (b^3-e^4), concluding that they were erroneously notated by Handel, and suggesting two possible readings (e^3-a^3 or a^3-d^4). Rejects Lasocki's statement that these readings are "unplayable or unthinkable" on the alto recorders of the day: the first would have been possible on a Continental recorder, the second on an alto in G (still used by Bismantova in 1677) Also rejects Lasocki's argument that the impossibility of taking a breath in the sixteenth-note passages of the first movement points away from the recorder, remarking that the same could be said about the (clearly genuine) A-Minor Sonata. Concludes that the question of attribution is not closed. The sonata could have been written for a non-standard instrument or size of instrument. Of the standard instruments of the beginning of the 18th century, only the recorder comes into consideration.

Handel's G-Major Sonata has been accepted as a violin sonata by Handel scholars. Yet the fact that the sonata does not reach lower than g^1 (with an isolated $f\sharp^1$) does indeed strongly suggest that the question of attribution is still open.

1263. Levin, Lia Starer. *The Recorder in the Music of Purcell and Handel*. Ph.D. dissertation, International College, Los Angeles, 1981. xiv, 404 p. OCLC #8966035.

An extremely detailed study of these composers' use of the recorder (and the flute in the case of Handel), looking piece by piece at instrumental and vocal combinations, tempo and expression marks, keys, time signatures, the range of the recorder/flute part, and the texts (for verbal associations of the instruments). The final chapter sums up the results of the investigation. Begins with a brief history of the recorder, already considerably outdated.

1264. Solomon, Jon. "Polyphemus's Whistle in Handel's 'Acis and Galatea.'" *Music & Letters* 64, no. 1–2 (January–April 1983): 37–43.

Seeks an explanation for why Handel scored for recorder in Polyphemus's aria "I rage, I burn." Suggests it is only because John Gay's libretto, based on John Dryden's translation of Ovid, mentions a "whistle," although that is far from Ovid's original meaning (a panpipe with 100 pipes), and the recorder obbligato has "little of particular artistic importance."

* Letteron, Claude. "Des thèmes pour 1985." Cited above as item **1205**.

1265. Lasocki, David. "A New Dating for Handel's Recorder Sonatas." *The Recorder and Music Magazine* 8, no. 6 (June 1985): 170-71.

Updates information presented in items 1259-61. Surveys the surviving sources for the works. On the basis of recent research by Handel scholars, the autographs of the six sonatas can be assigned the date "probably 1725-26."

1266. Best, Terence. "Handel's Chamber Music: Sources, Chronology and Authenticity." *Early Music* 13, no. 4 (November 1985): 476-99.

An extremely useful review of the recent research on Handel's solo and trio sonatas, summarizing research on the solo sonatas dealt with in other articles (including items 1257, 1259-61, and 1265), and furnishing new information on the trio sonatas, one of which is definitely, and two of which are possibly, for recorder.

1267. Beeks, Graydon. "Handel and Music for the Earl of Carnarvon." In *Bach, Handel, Scarlatti: Tercentenary Essays*, edited by Peter Williams, 1-20. Cambridge: Cambridge University Press, 1985. ISBN 0521252172.

Draws together what is known about the music that Handel wrote for James Brydges, Earl of Carnarvon (later Duke of Chandos), at Cannons, 1714-19, and about the musicians who played it. The music involving recorders included *Acis and Galatea* and the Tenth Chandos Anthem.

1268. Lasocki, David, and Eva Legêne. "Learning to Ornament Handel's Sonatas Through the Composer's Ears." *The American Recorder* 30, no. 1 (February 1989): 9-14; 30, no. 3 (August 1989): 102-6; 30, no. 4 (November 1989): 137-41.

Starting from the premise of item 738 that ornamentation is "a type of composition, or rather, *re*composition," Lasocki and Legêne demonstrate how the study of various aspects of Handel's compositional style can enable players to ornament sensibly and effectively. Part I covers three of Handel's techniques: rhetoric, variation technique, and reworkings. Part II discusses essential graces and free ornamentation. Part III concludes the overview of free ornamentation and examines contemporaneous examples (barrel-organ ornamentations and William Babell's ornamented slow movements) that have—the authors believe inappropriately—been held up as models by modern performers.

1269. Möller, Dirk. *Besetzung und Instrumentation in den Opern Georg Friedrich Händels* [Scoring and instrumentation in Georg Frideric Handel's operas]. (Europäische Hochschul-schriften. Reihe 36: Musikwissenschaft, v. 38) Frankfurt am Main: P. Lang, 1989. ix, 231 p. ISBN 363140784X.
Handel's use of the recorder in his operas is surveyed on pp. 44-50.

1270. Cornsweet, Amy. *Handel's Use of Flute and Recorder in Opera and Oratorio*. M.M. thesis, The University of Arizona, 1990. 147 p.
A largely statistical study of the 125 "pieces" involving flutes or recorders found in Handel's operas and oratorios. Discusses keys, affections, and the doubling of musical lines. Lots of charts. Apparently done in ignorance of the work of Levin (item 1263). The musical examples are taken from the Chrysander edition. Makes no attempt to relate the instrumentation to the musicians of the time (as reported in item 72).

1271. Braun, Gerhard. "Von 'mäßiger Lustigkeit': Einige interpretatorische Anmerkungen zu den Menuetten von G.F. Händel für Sopranblockflöte und Klavier" [Of 'moderate gaiety': some interpretatory remarks on Handel's minuets for soprano recorder and piano]. (Die gelbe Seite) *Tibia* 17, no. 1 (1992): V-VIII.
The minuets in question are from a Walsh edition of 1762 (ed. Martin Heidecker). Sketches the background of the minuet in the 18th century: form, affection, and tempo, leading to advice on accentuation and articulation. Useful but leaves us asking for more. (The tag "mäßiger Lustigkeit," incidentally, is Johann Mattheson's.)

HAYDN, JOSEPH (1732-1809)

1272. Sahlin, Eva. "Blockflöte als Lirenersatz?" [The recorder as a substitute for the lira?]. *Tibia* 4, no. 1 (1979): 244-46.
The piano reduction of Joseph Haydn's concerto for two *lire organizzate* [organized hurdy-gurdies] published by Doblinger (ed. Karl Trotzmüller) replaces the solo instruments with alto recorders. Sahlin asks questions about the context and associations of the *lira organizzata* in the late 18th century, and the consequences for the substitution of recorders in Haydn's composition, admitting that the questions cannot be definitively answered. The instrument, a combination of hurdy-gurdy and bellows-driven organ, could therefore produce string timbre, wind timbre, or both together. It was characterized by a piercing tone, a drone (never notated), a limited

range of keys, and pastoral associations. Trotzmüller plumped for the recorder because it would have been similar to the organ part of the instrument. Sahlin argues that, on the other hand, using recorders misses the string and string/wind timbres, the instruments are an octave too low, their tone is too soft, they lack a drone, and they had no pastoral associations at Haydn's time. Prefers the solution that Haydn himself adopted for his Notturni written for the same instrumentation: flute and oboe on the solo parts. Ends with an editorial note that a German maker, Kurt Reichmann, is now making *lire organizzate*. Letters from Erich Benedikt and Diether Steppuhn in 4, no. 2 (1979): 363–65.

HEINICHEN, JOHANN DAVID (1683–1729)

1273. Kubitschek, Ernst. "Die Verwendung der Flöte im Schaffen von Johann David Heinichen und seinen Dresdner Kollegen" [The use of the recorder and flute in the works of Johann David Heinichen and his Dresden colleagues]. In *Musikzentren: Persönlichkeiten und Ensembles: Konferenzbericht der XV. wissenschaftlichen Arbeitstagung, Blankenburg/Harz, 19. bis 21. June 1987*, 34–45. (Studien zur Aufführungspraxis und Interpretation der Musik des 18. Jahrhunderts, 35) Michaelstein bei Blankenburg: Kultur- und Forschungsstätte Michaelstein bei Blankenburg/Harz, 1988. OCLC #9802675.

Recorders are found in several large-scale vocal works of Heinichen's: a trio of alto recorders in an aria about death and a bird aria for soprano with recorder obbligato in *Mario* (Venice, 1713); three recorders and bass recorder in *Zeffiro e Clori* (Venice, 1714); recorders in unison with "violini piano" in *Flavio* (Dresden, 1719/20); flute, recorder, and "violini sempre piano" in *Serenata fatta su l'Elba* (ditto); three recorders in the oratorio *La pace di Kamberga* (Dresden); and flutes and recorders together in the "Et in spiritum sanctum" and "Agnus Dei" from the Missa in D (Dresden, 1729). On the whole, Heinichen "distinguishes carefully between flute and recorder. The flute has obbligato parts in the orchestra; the recorder is only inserted as extra sound color in unison passages." Still, during the course of his life, Heinichen changed the manner in which he employed the two instruments, and even the range he favored. The recorder parts in Dresden were always played by the oboists in the orchestra.

HOTTETERRE, JACQUES (1674–1763)

1274. Bloodworth, Denis. "Performing Jacques Hotteterre's 'Echos.'" *Recorder & Music* 5, no. 12 (December 1977): 387–88.

    A brief article concerning the selection of a suitable instrument, articulation, and the fingering of ornaments.

* House, Delpha LeAnn. *Jacques Hotteterre "le Romain": A Study of his Life and Compositional Style.* Cited above as item **891**.

LOEILLET FAMILY

* Priestman, Brian. "An Introduction to the Loeillets." Cited above as item **892**.

1275. Skempton, Alec. "The Instrumental Sonatas of the Loeillets." *Music & Letters* 43, no. 3 (July 1962): 206–17.

    Contains a useful descriptive catalog of the original published sources for the sonatas of the three Loeillets. Also summarizes evidence supporting the conclusion that John Loeillet and Jean Baptiste Loeillet de Gant were two different people. Includes the text of John Loeillet's will.

1276. Deane, Morag. "Compositions by Members of the Loeillet Family." *Recorder & Music* 6, no. 11 (September 1980): 318–23.

    A catalog of historical and modern editions. Includes complete transcriptions of title pages and dedications from the early editions as well as information on library locations and contemporary advertisements. Three title pages are reproduced in facsimile.

1277. Reyne, Hugo. "Les oeuvres des trois Loeillet et leurs editions" [The works of the three Loeillets and editions of them]. *Flûte à bec* 5 (December 1982): 10–12.

    A listing of works and editions, intended to complement Janzen's article (item **896**).

LULLY, JEAN-BAPTISTE (1632–1687)

1278. Eppelsheim, Jürgen. *Das Orchester in den Werken Jean-Baptiste Lullys* [The orchestra in the works of Jean-Baptiste Lully]. (Münchner Veröffentlichungen zur Musikgeschichte, Band 7) Tutzing: Hans Schneider, 1961. 251 p. OCLC #22355493.

Section "Flöten" (pp. 64–98) discusses the apportioning of Lully's "flute" parts among flutes and recorders on the basis of nomenclature in sources, clefs, range, and contemporaneous usage (of which it provides many fascinating details, some otherwise unpublished). Section "Die instrumentale Besetzung . . . Flöten" (pp. 205–9) considers the types of stage situations in which Lully employed flutes and recorders (love; the pastoral; the Muses; peace, security, and tranquility; grief, lamentation, and supplications to the gods to free from torment; certain mythological situations). Glossary (*Anhang*, pp. 15–17) defines (with sources) the names for various sizes of flutes and recorders of the 16th-18th centuries. An essential book. Reviewed by Anthony Baines in *The Galpin Society Journal* 16 (May 1963): 110–11.

MANCINI, FRANCESCO (1672–1737)

1279. Kubitschek, Ernst. "Eine Sonatensatz von Francesco Mancini. Gedanken zu seiner Interpretation aus dem Blickwinkel der Komposition" [A sonata movement by Francesco Mancini: thoughts on its interpretation from the visual angle of the composition]. (Die gelbe Seite) *Tibia* 18, no. 2 (1993): XXIX–XXXII.

Analyses the second movement (Allegro) of the first sonata, in D minor, from Francesco Mancini's *XII Solos for a Flute or Violin with a Thorough Bass* (London, 1724). Since the movement is a fugue, also looks at some contemporaneous commentary on the character of fugues. Finally, discusses how the modern player could use this analysis and historical information to gain insights into how to perform the movement. A footnote: Kubitscheck suggests that a phrase was brought down by an octave to avoid f^3 because the oboes and flutes of the day were uncomfortable with that note; the same could be said, however, of English alto recorders.

Marcello, Benedetto (1686–1739)

1280. Clark, Paul. "Sonata in F: Marcello." (Playing) *The Recorder and Music Magazine* 1, no. 6 (August 1964): 170–71.

    Suggestions for interpreting the work, based on the Oxford University Press edition edited by Joseph Slater. Includes a brief biography.

* Kneihs, Hans Maria. "Musical Structure and Interpretation with Reference to Marcello's Sonata in D Minor." Cited above as item 765.

Mozart, Wolfgang Amadeus (1756–1791)

1281. Hunt, Edgar. "Mozart and the Recorder." *The Recorder Magazine* 10, no. 4 (December 1990): 109–10.

    It is now well known that the recorder survived to the end of the 18th century, so we might reasonably suppose that at least some of the *flauto piccolo* parts in Classical works were written for soprano or sopranino recorders. Yet there also existed various sizes of flageolets, and the true piccolo—a small flute in d^2—is heard of as early as ca. 1739 (Michel Corrette's flute method), so researchers need to display caution. Unfortunately, Hunt throws caution to the winds, declaring quite erroneously that "[t]he transverse piccolo seems not to have been used in the orchestra until the time of Beethoven" and claiming virtually all Mozart's *flauto piccolo* parts for the recorder. For a more realistic approach, see item 1471.

Purcell, Daniel (1660?–1717)

1282. [Newman, Joel]. "In Honor of Daniel Purcell (c. 1660–1717)." (Flauto Piccolo's Corner) *The American Recorder* 2, no. 1 (Winter 1961): 5.

    Discusses his music for recorders and lists modern editions (now quite out of date).

Purcell, Henry (1659–1695)

1283. Bergmann, Walter. "Henry Purcell's Use of the Recorder." In *Music Libraries and Instruments*, 227–233. (Hinrichsen's 11th Music Book) London: Hinrichsen Edition, 1961. Reprinted in *The Recorder & Music Magazine* 7, no.

12 (December 1983): 310-13. Also reprinted with slight revisions in *The Recorder and Music Magazine* 1, no. 11 (November 1965): 333-35.

A paper read at the Joint Congress of the International Association of Music Libraries and the Galpin Society at Cambridge, 1959. Begins by explaining the change in nomenclature from "recorder" to "flute" during the 17th century and the concurrent advent of the Baroque recorder, which, according to contemporaneous accounts, was treated as if it were a new instrument. Purcell called for recorders only in his secular works, and he used only altos—nearly always in pairs—which were usually played by the oboists of the orchestra. (Bergmann discounts the appearance of the bass recorder in the *Ode for St. Cecilia's Day* [1692] as a later addition.) Recorders most often accompany or introduce arias and duets and appear in the usual contexts: to establish a mood of tranquility, to evoke the supernatural, to paint text, to accompany a pastoral scene, to imitate birdsong, and to represent amorous love. The only chamber work for recorders is the fantasia "3 Parts upon a Ground" for three altos and continuo. (Another independent instrumental piece is the chaconne from *Dioclesian* for two altos and continuo.) Bergmann believes that Purcell must have been fond of the instrument, since several composers chose to use it in odes on his death (this use, however, could be attributable to the funereal associations of the recorder), and it appears in Edwaert Collier's portrait of the composer. Includes a list of compositions employing the recorder. Letter from Layton Ring in 8, no. 1 (March 1984): 26-27.

* Bergmann, Walter. "Three Pieces of Music on Henry Purcell's Death." Cited above as item **1189**.

* Levin, Lia Starer. *The Recorder in the Music of Purcell and Handel*. Cited above as item **1263**.

QUANTZ, JOHANN JOACHIM (1697-1773)

1284. Reilly, Edward R. "Quantz and the Recorder." *The American Recorder* 7, no. 4 (Fall 1966): 7-9.

Describes three trio sonatas, one flute trio, and a set of six flute duets intended by Quantz for possible performance on recorders. Offers a general description of Quantz's flute treatise and its importance to the study of performance practice.

SAMMARTINI, GIUSEPPE (1695–1750)

1285. McGowan, Richard A. "The Recorder Sonatas of Giuseppe Sammartini." *The American Recorder* 17, no. 2 (August 1976): 51–55.

Briefly surveys the extant flute and recorder sonatas. Includes an edition of two movements selected from two sonatas that are a part of a manuscript collection housed in the Sibley Library of the Eastman School of Music.

SCARLATTI, ALESSANDRO (1660–1725)

1286. Alton, Edwin H. "The Recorder Music of Alessandro Scarlatti (1660–1725)." *Recorder and Music Magazine* 4, no. 6 (June 1973): 199–200. In Italian as: "La musica per flauto dolce di Alessandro Scarlatti." *Il flauto dolce* 4 (July–December 1973): 7–9.

A brief biography followed by simple descriptions of chamber works either written for or suitable for recorder: Suites for Flute and Continuo in F Major and G Major (1699); Sonata for Flute, Two Violins, and Continuo in F Major; Sonata for Three Flutes and Continuo in F Major; Sonata for Two Flutes, Two Violins, and Continuo in A Major; Seven Sonatas for Flute, Strings, and Continuo (1725); and Sonata for Flute, Two Violins, and Continuo in D Major. Includes a bibliography of modern editions.

1287. Bettarini, Luciano. "Appunti critici sulle 'Sette sonate' per flauto e archi di Alessandro Scarlatti" [Critical notes on the seven sonatas for recorder and strings by Alessandro Scarlatti]. *Chigiana* 25 (nuova serie 5) (1968): 239–46.

Concerns the Seven Sonatas for Flute *[flauto]*, Strings, and Continuo (1725; copyists' manuscript score and parts in the Biblioteca del Conservatorio Musicale "S. Pietro a Majella," Naples), taking it for granted that the solo instrument in question is the transverse flute, although the name and range of the instrument indicate the alto. Considers that the attribution to Scarlatti is correct on stylistic grounds. Offers a descriptive analysis of each sonata.

1288. Müller-Busch, Franz. "Alessandro Scarlattis Kantaten mit obligaten Blockflöten" [Alessandro Scarlatti's cantatas with obbligato recorders]. *Tibia* 16, no. 1 (1991): 337–46.

Seeks to inform "recorder players, and not only them" about a neglected part of the repertory: Scarlatti's cantatas. Divided into:

introduction; an overview of the Italian *cantata da camera;* a brief biography of Scarlatti; a catalog of the eleven cantatas containing recorder parts; a discussion of the authenticity of the sources, dating, and texts (generally on the themes winds, waves, and birds); sizes of recorder (alto, or in two or three cases tenor); and conclusions. In a review of Müller-Busch's edition of the cantata "Clori mia, Clori bella" (p. 402 of the same issue), Thiemo Wind points out the existence of a further source in which the obbligato instrument is named as the oboe.

On Scarlatti's cantatas, see also Edwin Hanley, *Alessandro Scarlatti's "Cantate da camera": A Bibliographical Study* (Ph.D. dissertation, Yale University, 1963), and Cecilia Kathryn van de Kamp Freund, *Alessandro Scarlatti's Duet Cantatas and Solo Cantatas with Obbligato Instruments* (Ph.D. dissertation, Northwestern University, 1979).

SCHICKHARDT, JOHANN CHRISTIAN (CA. 1680-1762)

* Lasocki, David. "Johann Christian Schickhardt (ca. 1682-1762): Woodwind Composer, Performer and Teacher." Cited above as item 899.

* Lasocki, David. "Johann Christian Schickhardt (ca. 1682-1762): A Contribution to his Biography and a Catalogue of his Works." Cited above as item 901.

SCHÜTZ, HEINRICH (1585-1672)

1289. McCulloch, Derek. "Instrumentation and the Recorder in the Works of Heinrich Schütz." *Recorder & Music Magazine* 2, no. 7 (November 1967): 204-6.

Suggests that, although only four works in the *Schütz-Werke-Verzeichnis* specifically call for recorders, a number of his vocal works include parts for unspecified obbligato instruments or for violins "or the like" that can easily be performed on recorders.

TELEMANN, GEORG PHILIPP (1681-1767)

1290. Loonan, Martin. "The Published Recorder Music of Telemann." *The American Recorder* 5, no. 2 (May 1964): 11-12.

An outdated listing of limited use. Works are classified by instrumentation and described briefly. Includes information on modern editions.

1291. Silbiger, Alexander. "The Trio-Sonatas of Georg Philipp Telemann." *The American Recorder* 5, no. 1 (February 1964): 3–6.

Covers only the trio sonatas including recorder. Written for the performer interested in instrumentation possibilities and ornamentation. The discussion of the music itself is generalized.

1292. Anderson, Loren H. "Telemann's Music for Recorder." *The American Recorder* 8, no. 1 (Winter 1967): 3–6.

Proposes that Telemann's popularity among performers can be attributed to the "idiomatic suitability" of his music. Offers several examples of how Telemann's knowledge of the recorder is reflected in his writing for the instrument. Contrasts Telemann's facility to the awkwardness of Bach, who "did not compose as idiomatically for the instrument, either because of unfamiliarity with, or an equally relative lack of interest in, the recorder." Also enters the debate over the instrumentation of Brandenburg Concerto No. 4; Anderson believes the work was intended for two altos.

1293. Thaler, Alan. "Der Getreue Music-Meister: A 'Forgotten' Periodical." *The Consort* 24 (1967): 280–93.

Describes the publication and the works it contained, including several important ones for the recorder. Includes short biographies of the composers represented (except for Telemann). Appendix A is a complete table of contents; appendix B, an index; and appendix C, concordances with the Hortus Musicus edition (Bärenreiter).

1294. Metcalfe, William C. "The Recorder Cantatas of Telemann's *Harmonischer Gottesdienst*." *The American Recorder* 8, no. 4 (Fall 1967): 113–18.

Devotes a major part of the article to a summary of Telemann's *Vorbericht* [Preface], which contains important information on the history of *Der harmonischer Gottes-Dienst*, its instrumentation, performance considerations, and tempo markings. Includes Telemann's example of how appoggiaturas are added to the vocal line of recitatives. Metcalfe describes the form (aria—recitative—aria), tempo, key structure, and part ranges of a typical cantata and notes deviations from this model in certain cantatas. A table provides the following information for the thirteen recorder cantatas: numbering within the set, title, key, and position in the church calendar.

1295. Scheck, Gustav. "The Recorder Sonatas of Georg Philipp Telemann." *Recorder & Music Magazine* 2, no. 8 (February 1968): 236–38.

Flowery analyses of the two sonatas from *Essercizii musici* and the four from *Der getreue Musik-Meister.* Letter from Eric Gillett in 2, no. 9 (May 1968): 285.

1296. Mosser, Thomas R. *The Recorder Idiom in the Instrumental Music of George Philipp Telemann.* Ph.D. dissertation, West Virginia University, 1975. iv, 433 leaves. OCLC #4841229. UMI order no. 76-11776.

After an introduction giving some relevant biography and background material, has chapters on the history and technical aspects of the recorder. A chapter on the repertory mostly concerns sources. The main chapter, "The Idiom," analyzes the repertory in terms of key, range, tessitura, type of passagework, dynamics, and technical difficulty. Appendix 2 (pp. 182-342) is a complete thematic catalog, which will eventually be superseded by *Georg Philipp Telemann: Systematisches Verzeichnis seiner Werke: Telemann-Werkverzeichnis (TWV), Instrumentalwerke* (2 vols. to date, ed. Martin Ruhnke; Kassel: Bärenreiter, 1984, 1992). Appendix 3 consists of a "tessitura analysis" of all the recorder parts.

1297. Hunt, Edgar. "Telemann's *Der harmonische Gottesdienst* and the Recorder." *Recorder & Music* 7, no. 2 (June 1981): 40-42.

A brief history of the series of seventy-two solo cantatas published by Telemann in 1725, with a cursory survey of the thirteen that feature recorder obbligato.

1298. Hunt, Edgar. "Telemann's Essercizii Musici." *Recorder & Music* 7, no. 3 (September 1981): 65-66.

Describes the contents of *Essercizii musici,* a set of twelve solo sonatas (two for recorder) and twelve trio sonatas (four including recorder) published by Telemann during 1739-40. Includes a table showing the distribution of the parts among the three original partbooks, which were of equal pagination.

1299. Hunt, Edgar. "The Recorder in Telemann's Der getreue Music-Meister." *Recorder & Music* 7, no. 4 (December 1981): 90-91.

Der getreue Music-Meister was a biweekly publication produced by Telemann 1728-29; a total of twenty-five numbers appeared during its short life. Hunt surveys the seven works in the set that involve the recorder (three solo sonatas; a trio sonata; and three duets for two recorders, recorder and viola da gamba, and recorder and violin), with information on modern editions.

1300. Du Bois, Elizabeth Ann. *A Comparison of Georg Philipp Telemann's Use of the Recorder and the Transverse Flute as Seen in His Chamber Works*. (The Emporia State Research Studies, 30, no. 3 [Winter 1982]). 72 p. OCLC #9325841.

This poorly written book fails to live up to its promise. It begins with two long sections covering Telemann's life and the history of the recorder and flute up to his day. Only thirty pages, in fact, are devoted to "Telemann's Use of the Recorder and the Transverse Flute," and even they boil down to a largely descriptive analysis of three works: TWV 42:F7, 42:a7, and 43:d1. From such slim evidence Du Bois concludes that Telemann differentiates the two instruments by his choice of key, range, intervals (the flute may have wider ones than the recorder), and virtuosity (the recorder may be treated more virtuosically than the flute). The most useful part of the book may be the appendixes, which list Telemann's recorder and flute works by instrumentation, type, and key. The study "originated as a thesis for the degree Master of Music (Musicology) . . . in the Department of Music at Emporia State University."

* Coomber, David. "Rhetoric and Affect in Baroque Music." Cited above as item 690.

1301. Swack, Jeanne Roberta. *The Solo Sonatas of Georg Philipp Telemann: A Study of the Sources and Musical Style*. Ph.D. dissertation, Yale University, 1988. 2, xi, 322 leaves. OCLC #22744704. UMI order no. 90-09474.

Divides Telemann's solo sonatas into four main groups: Frankfurt, 1715–18; early Hamburg, 1728–32; later Hamburg, 1733–40; and manuscript sources. Group 1 includes, among other sonatas, the *Kleine Cammer-Musik*; group 2, *Der getreue Musik-Meister* and the *Neue Sonatinen*; group 3, the *Essercizii musici*; and group 4, the F-Minor Sonata (TWV 41:f2). For each group, presents background information, then detailed style analysis. Shows how in group 2 Telemann developed what Swack dubs "permutation technique," based on the setting out and subsequent reordering of short musical fragments (e.g., in the first movements of the F-Major Recorder Sonata and the F-Minor Bassoon/Recorder Sonata from *GMM*), and "partitioning technique," in which a motive is dissected into an array of submotives (e.g., in the third movement of the F-Minor Bassoon/Recorder Sonata). Cites the second movement of the F-Minor Bassoon/Recorder sonata as an example of a movement based on the *da capo* aria. Names the first movement of the C-Major Recorder Sonata from *EM* as a development of the capriccio movement, alternating lyrical slow sections with fast sections over pedal points, and now also including passages with an active bass part. Shows that the manuscript F-Minor Sonata includes "awkward melodic writing and an overall melodic repetitiveness that Telemann avoided in his published sonatas," concluding that "If the piece is authentic, it is not one of Telemann's better efforts."

Swack's general conclusion is that "Telemann's solos are highly original works, in which the composer experimented with the traditional concept of the sonata by introducing formal and stylistic procedures drawn from other genres, such as the operatic aria and the concerto, and by exploiting various manifestations of the new 'mixed taste' in a multitude of imaginative ways." A thorough and intelligent dissertation, with special insight into the compositional style. Essential reading for those playing Telemann's sonatas.

1302. Schwarting, Heino. "Zwei Altflötenstimmen suchen ihren verlorenen Baß—haben sie ihn gefunden? Zu zwei Rekonstruktionen eines Basso continuo für zwei Sonaten Telemanns" [Two alto recorder parts are looking for their lost bass—have they found it? On two reconstructions of a basso continuo part for two Telemann sonatas]. *Tibia* 14, no. 2 (1989): 412-18.

Only the recorder part of Telemann's *Neue Sonatinen* for alto recorder and continuo (TWV 41:c2 and 41:a4) has survived. Two editors have attempted to write a bass part: "Claus E. Maynfrank" [apparently a pseudonym for Klaus E. Hoffmann] (London: Musica Rara, 1978) and Winfried Michel (Winterthur: Amadeus, 1986). Schwarting makes the general comment that Michel's "reconstruction" is more daring, Maynfrank's more solid. Then analyzes in detail the first movements of the first and second sonatinas in both editions. He concludes that neither of the two new basses is optimal. "But they have achieved something worthwhile . . . so [the sonatinas] gain life and perhaps even currency; and perhaps through a third editor, or a team of editors, a version will be found that comes closer to an authentic model." Reply by Maynfrank in 15, no. 3 (1990): 253-54.

1303. Teske-Spellerberg, Ulrike. "Der unbekannte Telemann: Obligate Blockflötenpartien in seinen unveröffenlichten Kantaten" [The unknown Telemann: obbligato recorder parts in his unpublished cantatas]. *Tibia* 16, no. 4 (1991): 599-610.

Begins with overviews of Telemann and his reputation—then, now, and in between—as well as his production of cantatas (over 2,300 of them over a working life of 70 years). Telemann employed the recorder in no fewer than 93 cantatas and vocal serenades written between 1716 and 1762, but concentrated primarily in the years 1720-31. Few of them are published; most of the manuscripts are in Frankfurt am Main. Telemann generally called for the alto recorder, occasionally for the *flauto piccolo,* "Oktavflöte," and "Quartflöte." Looks at the scoring, then analyzes the textual situations in which the recorder is called for (humility, tranquility, idyll, sadness, lamentation, love, the imitation of natural sounds, and pastoral motives), giving several interesting musical examples. An important article.

1304. Swack, Jeanne R. "On the Origins of the *Sonate auf Concertenart.*" *Journal of the American Musicological Society* 46, no. 3 (Fall 1993): 369–414.

Shows that the "sonata in the style of the concerto" (as Johann Adolph Scheibe dubbed it) was more common than we have supposed, examples having survived not only by J.S. Bach but also by Telemann, Quantz, Zelenka, Bodinus, Heinichen, J.G. Graun, Förster, and others. At least one movement in such a sonata exhibits features of ritornello form. It also has much in common with the Vivaldian chamber concerto. Shows in passing that several of Telemann's recorder works fit into this category: the Quartet for Recorder, Violin, Viola, and Continuo in G Minor (TWV 43:g4); the Concerto à 3 for Horn, Recorder, and Continuo in F Major (TWV 42:F14); the Quartet for Recorder, Two Flutes, and Continuo in D Minor from *Musique de table* (TWV 43:d1); and the Quartet for Recorder, Oboe, Violin, and Continuo in G Major (TWV 43:G6). Well written and cogently argued.

VIVALDI, ANTONIO (1678–1741)

1305. Higbee, Dale. "Michel Corrette on the Piccolo and Speculations Regarding Vivaldi's 'Flautino.'" *The Galpin Society Journal* 17 (1964): 115–16.

Higbee argues that Vivaldi wrote the *flautino* concertos for a piccolo: "Some passages of these concerti are impossible on the recorder or flageolet—but possible, though very difficult, on the one-key (octave) transverse flute." Lasocki counters this argument (item **1307**).

In 1960, several years before this article was published, a review by Higbee of an edition of the C-major *flautino* concerto for "piccolo or flute or soprano recorder" (*The American Recorder* 1, no. 3 [Summer 1960]: 8) sparked a series of correspondence on the "*flautino* problem," one of the controversial topics in recorder literature. Higbee argued that the pieces were probably composed for piccolo and are not practical on soprano recorder. The editor of the edition under review, Josef Marx, made an unsubstantiated rebuttal following the review. Shelley Gruskin, in 1, no. 4 (Fall 1960): 22–23, supported performance on the sopranino recorder based on his own experience performing the works on both piccolo and recorder. Higbee reconfirmed his belief that the music was intended for "octave traverso or fife" in 2, no. 2 (Spring 1961): 22.

1306. Metcalfe, William C. "Dolce or Traverso? The Flauto Problem in Vivaldi's Instrumental Music." *The American Recorder* 6, no. 3 (Summer 1965): 3–6.

Vivaldi composed over fifty works for *flauto*, which, in earlier times, many scholars had assumed to be the transverse flute. More recent scholarship has shown that many of the *flauto* works were intended for recorder, but Vivaldi clouds the issue by using similar keys, tessituras, and ranges for both instruments. Since he used the term indiscriminately to mean either recorder or flute, Metcalfe considers all of the *flauto* works candidates for performance on the recorder and classifies them into three groups (he includes only the forty-seven works in print in 1965): eighteen recorder works, twenty-two flute works possible on recorder, and seven flute works not suitable for recorder. The tables include the following for each of the works: thematic-catalog number, key, instrumentation, range of the *flauto* part, and other comments.

1307. Lasocki, David. "Vivaldi and the Recorder." *The American Recorder* 9, no. 4 (Fall 1968): 103–7. Reprinted in *Recorder & Music Magazine* 3, no. 1 (March 1969): 22–27.

    A survey of Vivaldi's works including recorder. Cites twelve works definitely composed for recorder and three works for *flautino* published in the Ricordi collected edition. Disagrees with Higbee's belief (item 1305) that the *flautino* was a one-keyed piccolo and offers evidence in support of performance on the sopranino recorder. Traces the frequently misunderstood history of the opus 10 flute concertos, concluding that Vivaldi intended the entire set to be playable on both flute and recorder, even though all of the concertos were not originally written for recorder. Includes tables that list keys, instrumentation, thematic-catalog numbers, modern performing editions, and recordings. William Metcalfe corrects a few errors in *The American Recorder* 10, no. 2 (Spring 1969): 69, and Lasocki responds in 10, no. 4 (Fall 1969): 129. Letter from W.A. Ayre in *Recorder & Music Magazine* 3, no. 2 (June 1969): 66–67.

1308. Ohmura, Noriko. "I 'concerti senza orchestra' di Antonio Vivaldi" [The "concertos without orchestra" of Antonio Vivaldi]. *Nuova rivista musicale italiana* 13, no. 1 (January/March 1979): 119–49. Originally in English in *Ongakugaku* 17 (1972).

    Classifies Vivaldi's chamber concertos into four groups, depending on how many instruments there are and how many of them play the solos: (a) three/one, (b) three/several, (c) four or more/one, and (d) four or more/several. Looks at the structure of the movements with and without ritornellos, the character of the themes and the motivic work, the key schemes, and the use of instruments (marred by failing to distinguish between flute and recorder). This analysis is useful as far as it goes, although it would have taken a lot more space to do justice to the subject. Ironically, the article is billed as a synthesis of part of a master's thesis from Kunitachi Music School, Tokyo, 1971.

* Reyne, Hugo. "Interview de Jean-Claude Veilhan: 'autour des Quatre Saisons de Vivaldi'" [Interview with Jean-Claude Veilhan: concerning the Four Seasons of Vivaldi]. Cited above as item 1114.

1309. Heller, Karl. "Italienische Kammermusik in variabler Besetzung: Antonio Vivaldis Concerto für Kammerensemble" [Italian chamber music in variable settings: Antonio Vivaldi's chamber concertos]. In *Der Einfluß der italienischen Musik in der ersten Hälfte des 18. Jahrhunderts: Konferenzbericht der XV. Wissenschaftlichen Arbeitstagung Blankenburg/Harz, 19. bis 21. Juni 1987,* 35–44. (Studien zur Aufführungspraxis und Interpretation der Musik des 18. Jahrhunderts, Heft 34) Michaelstein/Blankenburg, 1988. OCLC #21374724.
A relatively brief overview of Vivaldi's chamber concertos, mentioning some obvious formal points, then analyzing some aspects of some of the individual concertos, including four that include the recorder: RV 92, 94, 103, and 105.

1310. Demoulin, Jean-Pierre. "A propos de Vivaldi, quelques réflexions sur l'interpretation actuelle de la musique ancienne et baroque" [About Vivaldi: reflections on the present-day interpretation of early and Baroque music]. In *Nuovi studi vivaldiani: edizione e cronologica critica delle opere,* edited by Antonio Fanna and Giovanni Morelli, 703–11. Florence: Leo S. Olschki, 1988. ISBN 8822236254.
Asks whether "the mature works [Vivaldi] composed after 1725 and designated by the word "flauto" are not destined for the flute" rather than the recorder. These works include the Concerto in C Minor (RV 441); the Sonata for Flute *[flauto]*, Bassoon, and Continuo in A Minor (RV 86); and the Concerto in C Major of 1740 (RV 558). Demoulin's argument, however, has many holes in it (for full details, see item 10).

1311. Talbot, Michael. "Vivaldi and Rome: Observations and Hypotheses." *Journal of the Royal Musical Association* 113, no. 1 (1988): 28–46.
Vivaldi scholars are now putting considerable effort into working out the chronology of his compositions. Michael Talbot makes some plausible hypotheses about which compositions Vivaldi wrote for Rome in the 1720s. Among them are the chamber concertos *Il gardellino* (RV 90) and *La pastorella* (RV 95), the *Concerto per la Solennità di S. Lorenzo* (RV 556), two

settings of *Laudate pueri* (RV 601 and 602a), and a *Salve regina* (RV 616)—all of which include recorder parts. They would have been performed by members of Cardinal Pietro Ottoboni's orchestra.

1312. Lescat, Philippe. "'Il pastor fido,' une oeuvre de Nicolas Chédeville" [*Il pastor fido*: a work by Nicolas Chédeville]. *Informazioni e studi Vivaldiani* 11 (1990): 5–10.

Lescat reports that he has discovered a notarized declaration by Jean-Noël Marchand, the publisher of Vivaldi's *Il pastor fido*, op. 13 (1737), that it was in fact the musette player Nicolas Chédeville who composed the work in 1736–37, partly using themes by Vivaldi and other composers. Then, "wanting to publish this work, and having particular reasons why it should not appear under his name," Chédeville persuaded Marchand to obtain the necessary publication *privilège* and gave him money for both that and the engraving costs. Curiously, Chédeville obtained his own *privilège* two years later entitling him to issue musette and vielle transcriptions of all Vivaldi's published works. Lescat has promised to return to the obvious questions: why Chédeville attributed *Il pastor fido* to Vivaldi and why he wanted Marchand to publish it. See also Peter Ryom's preface, "An Authentic Case of Falsification," to the facsimile of *Il pastor fido* published by C.D. Facsimilés, Le Vaud, Switzerland, 1991.

1313. Hünteler, Konrad. "Blockflöte und Querflöte bei Vivaldi" [The recorder and flute in Vivaldi]. *Zeitschrift SAJM* 20, no. 3 (May 1992): 3–8.

An up-to-date and intelligent overview of the problems of Vivaldi's flute and recorder pieces. Begins with the difficulties of getting to know them: the multiplicity of thematic catalogs, the poor quality of the complete edition (the practical editions published by Musica Rara are singled out for praise), the different versions of the opus 10 concertos, and the curious range and keys of some of the pieces. Considers the circumstances in which Vivaldi would have used the instruments, emphasizing the lack of technical difficulty in the earliest flute parts. Discusses the versions of the opus 10 concertos. Reasons that the solo recorder and *flautino* concertos as well as the Trio Sonata for Recorder, Bassoon, and Continuo seem to have been composed for Mantua rather than Venice, and that Vivaldi probably did not write for the flute before about 1728.

1314. Lescat, Philippe. "'Il pastor fido,' une oeuvre de Nicolas Chédeville" [*Il pastor fido*: a work by Nicolas Chédeville]. In *Vivaldi vero e falso: problemi di attribuzione*, edited by Antonio Fanna and Michael Talbot, 109–25. (Studi di musica veneta, Quaderni vivaldiani, 7) Florence: Leo S. Olschki, 1992.

Although it bears the same title as item **1312**, this is a completely different article. Lescat confesses that he has not come up with the answers to the questions raised in that article. Instead, summarizes the lives of Jean-Noël Marchand and Nicolas Chédeville (who were cousins), considers the publication of *Il pastor fido*, then looks at both French and Italian compositional elements in the collection as well as Chédeville's other arrangements. Ironically, Chédeville had more success with works published under his own name than those under Vivaldi's.

1315. Hermes-Neumann, Andrea. *Die Flötenkonzerte von Antonio Vivaldi* [The flute concertos of Antonio Vivaldi]. (Deutsche Hochschulschriften, 469) Egelsbach: Hänsel-Hohenhausen, 1993. 104 p. ISBN 3893494693. [Master's thesis, Johann Wolfgang Goethe-Universität, Frankfurt am Main].

"Flute" is used here to mean both transverse flute and recorder. Begins with a survey of Vivaldi's life in relation to the concertos, looks at the sources of the concertos, considers Vivaldi's terminology (*flauto, flautino, flauto traverso*), then comments on some idiosyncrasies of Vivaldi's notation. Then follow chapters on the opus 10 concertos (including their original versions), the manuscript flute concertos, the recorder concertos, and the *flautino* concertos, in each case briefly analyzing the form and commenting on questions of instrumentation. Ends with a conclusion and bibliography (the author acknowledges that she came across item **1307** too late to consider in her research and she was apparently unaware of items **1306** and **1310**).

See also Luca della Libera, "L'idioma vivaldiano nel repertorio per flauto traverso," *Nuova rivista musicale italiana* 26, no. 3-4 (July-December 1992): 469-81.

WOODCOCK, ROBERT (FL. 1722-1730)

"The twelve woodwind concertos of Robert Woodcock—three for sixth flute (soprano recorder in D), three for two sixth flutes, three for transverse flute, and three for oboe—were published in London around 1727. They are of historical importance as the first flute concertos and second recorder concertos ever published, and the first oboe concertos published by an English composer." (item **905**, p. 92) The authorship of the concertos has been debated since the 1950s, when Brian Priestman (item **892**) argued that at least two of them were composed by Jacques Loeillet.

* Lasocki, David, and Helen Neate. "The Life and Works of Robert Woodcock, 1690-1728." Cited above as item **905**.

1316. MacMillan, Douglas. "'A New Concerto, Compos'd by Mr. Woodcock.'" *The Recorder and Music Magazine* 8, no. 6 (June 1985): 180-81.

    Tackles the often raised question: did Robert Woodcock really compose the twelve concertos (three for sixth flute, three for two sixth flutes, three for transverse flute, and three for oboe) attributed to him in the Walsh print of 1727? Priestman (item **892**) noted that two of these concertos were identical to works attributed to a member of the Loeillet family (in manuscripts in Rostock; copy in Brussels). Having obtained one of the Rostock manuscripts, MacMillan points out that the slow movement of the D-major "Loeillet" concerto is different from that in the corresponding Woodcock concerto. For this reason and (apparently) on stylistic grounds, he concludes that "the manuscripts probably represented pirated copies of the Walsh edition," which was the work of Woodcock. Also some biographical information on Woodcock. For a later, more comprehensive survey, see item **905**.

29

Repertory: Modern

This chapter looks at the 20th-century repertory of the recorder. It begins with general sources, then deals with the music of individual composers (including biographical material on their work with the recorder).

1317. Dolmetsch, Carl. "An Introduction to the Recorder in Modern British Music." *The Consort* 17 (July 1960): 47–56.

    Recounts the circumstances of performance and gives brief descriptions of almost forty works, many of which were commissioned and first performed by the author.

1318. Vetter, Michael. "New Recorder Music from Holland = Neue Musik für Blockflöte aus Holland." *Sonorum Speculum* 31 (Spring 1967): 19–25. (English reprinted in *Recorder & Music Magazine* 2, no. 8 [February 1968]: 260 and *The American Recorder* 9, no. 2 [Spring 1968]: 47–49.)

    Parallel columns in English and German. Describes early 1960s works by Dutch composers that explore the unconventional sound possibilities of the recorder. Works discussed include: *Spiel und Zwischenspiel, Pastorale VII,* and *Ricercare* by Rob du Bois; *Paintings* by Louis Andriessen; and *Wonderen zijn schaars* by Will Eisma. The *RMM* version contains only the sections on the Andriessen and Eisma.

1319. Dolmetsch, Carl. "The Recorder's 20th Century Repertoire." *Recorder & Music Magazine* 2, no. 8 (February 1968): 247–49.

    An incomplete survey that dwells on compositions the author has performed. Descriptions of the music are quoted from newspaper reviews of performances. No bibliography of cited works.

1320. Horner, Keith. "Frans Brueggen on Contemporary Music for the Recorder." *Recorder & Music* 4, no. 10 (June 1974): 352–54.

Brüggen discusses the current state of avant-garde composition for the recorder. Covers: the origin of avant-garde recorder music with Michael Vetter in the late 1950s; the composers Brüggen hopes will write works for the recorder; *Gesti* and why Berio chose to compose it for recorder rather than for flute; Brüggen's own work as a composer and his performances with Sour Cream; his aversion to conservative contemporary music. (The source of the interview is presumably a BBC Radio 3 broadcast, similar to item 953.)

1321. Hunt, Edgar. "The Recorder and the Avant Garde." *Recorder & Music* 5, no. 6 (June 1976): 195–96, 198, 202.

Describes the extended techniques employed in avant-garde recorder music and surveys the principal works in the genre composed during the period 1960–75.

1322. Braun, Gerhard. "Blockflöte und Avantgarde: Versuch einer Typologie der zeitgenössischen Blockflötenmusik" [The recorder and the avant garde: an attempt at a typology of contemporary recorder music]. *Tibia* 1, no. 1 (1976): 19–25.

A pre-publication version of chapter 2 from Braun's book *Neue Klangwelt auf der Blockflöte* (item 823). Classifies avant-garde recorder music into the following: serial compositions, post-serial period, tone color and tone alteration, open form, other media (tape recorder, contact microphone and synthesizer, etc.), graphic notation, musical theater.

1323. O'Loughlin, Niall. "The Recorder in 20th-Century Music." *Early Music* 10, no. 1 (January 1982): 36–37.

An intelligent "short and selective" survey of the 20th-century repertory for recorder up through the early 1970s, with an emphasis on post-1945 compositions.

1324. Rolin, Étienne. "Un répertoire pour demain" [A repertory for tomorrow]. *Flûte à bec* 3 (June 1982): 36–37.

Brief remarks on the state of composing for the recorder in France, followed by the music of his one-page "pedagogical piece for alto recorder," *Phénix*.

1325. Linde, Hans-Martin. "Neue Musik für alte Instrumente" [New music for old instruments]. In *Alte Musik: Praxis und Reflexion. Sonderband der Reihe "Basler Jahrbuch für Historische Musikpraxis" zum 50. Jubiläum der Schola Cantorum Basiliensis,* edited by Peter Reidemeister and Veronika Gutmann, 395–404. Winterthur: Amadeus, 1983.

A quick overview of 20th-century music for the recorder, harpsichord, viola da gamba, viola d'amore, and ensemble pieces by Rudolf Komorous and Mauricio Kagel. Sees the recorder music in three phases: (1) that written under the influence of the German Jugendmusikbewegung [youth music movement] in the 1920s and 30s, (2) the post-World War II interest in the specific sound of early instruments, although the recorder was treated somewhat like the flute, (3) the avant-garde music of the 1960s onwards. Concludes with a two-page selected bibliography of compositions.

1326. Braun, Gerhard. "Ludus juvenalis: Moderne Blockflötenmusik für den Anfang" [Child's play: modern recorder music for beginners]. *Tibia* 9, no. 1 (1984): 8–12.

Considers it a mistake to conclude that "beginners" (or rather, inexperienced performers) should avoid all new music. Improvisation and graphically notated music spring to mind as being suitable means of getting started, leading on naturally to music in "duration notation." (The duration of a note is indicated by the length of a horizontal line at the pitch of the note, or by its positioning across the space between barlines set at regular [time] intervals.) Two of Braun's own compositions use a soprano recorder without the footjoint, an easy way to make unusual pitches. At Braun's request Erhard Karkoschka wrote a moderately easy piece, *Pointen* for recorder and two-channel tape recorder, incorporating simple avant-garde techniques. Such a piece leads on to little musical scenarios, such as Klaus Hashagen's *Gardinenpredigt eines Blockflötenspielers* [A recorder player's telling off from the wife]. Braun has also incorporated speech elements, e.g., in *Monologe III* for tenor recorder. Certain pieces make good studies for focusing on individual techniques. Ends with the hope that, by following such a schema, "soon the music of our time will be played as self-evidently as now the sonatas of Marcello, Boismortier, or Telemann are." Bibliography of relevant compositions and books.

* O'Kelly, Eve Elizabeth. *The Recorder in Twentieth-Century Music.* Cited above as item 819.

The catalog is arranged by medium (pieces for one recorder, then those for two recorders, etc.). Each entry gives the (O'Kelly) catalog number of the work, composer's name and dates, the title and publication date, the publisher, commercial recordings (if any), and the exact instrumentation. There is a composer index and a list of publishers (address given as city and country only).

1327. Martin, John. "Playing the Recorder Tongue-in-Cheek." *The Recorder: Journal of the Victorian Recorder Guild* 5 (November 1986): 12–15.

"Actually about tongue-in-cheek recorder music." First, describes how doing the unexpected with the music, instruments, or surroundings can produce tongue-in-cheekery. Then reviews a selection of such music (dance music, blues, fusion, etc.).

* O'Kelly, Eve Elizabeth. *The Recorder Today*. Cited above as item **820**.

Contains a catalog based on the one in item **819**. Unfortunately, the catalog has been cut down considerably, so that instead of "comprising as full a listing as possible of modern recorder compositions," it now "contains some 400 works out of about 800 known to me," the selection having been made on the basis of suitability for professional or semi-professional performance, current availability, and "sufficient musical merit."

1328. Kerwin, Michael. "Musica Nova: 20th Century Music for Historical Instruments." *Continuo* 12, no. 1 (February 1988): 5–10.

Sets 20th-century recorder music in the context of new repertory for all historical instruments. Attributes the enormous size of such repertory to the preoccupation of 20th-century composers with new and original sonorities, citing David Loeb to the effect that "nothing was more natural than for composers to seek out 'instruments left unused for so long that they seemed as fresh and tantalizingly unfamiliar as if they had been newly invented.'" Mentions the well-known recorder works by Hindemith, Britten, Baur, Berio, Andriessen, Staeps, and Kagel, as well as Harry Somers's *Twelve Miniatures* and Kazimierz Pyzik's *Symphonic Triptych Part 2: Action 2*.

1329. Davis, Alan. "Commissioned Works for the Recorder." *The Recorder and Music Magazine* 9, no. 10 (June 1989): 278–81.

Discusses six compositions commissioned by Davis: *Nightes Blacke Bird* by Philip Wilby, *Thymehaze* by John Casken, *Aubade* by Colin Hand, *Constellations* by Edwin Roxburgh, *The Hour Hand* by John Joubert, *Breakdance* by Philip Wilby, *Dancing Day* by Colin Hand, and *Antifonia* by Colin Touchin.

1330. McCutcheon, Mary. "Recorder in the Lives of Four Montreal Composers." *American Recorder* 31, no. 4 (December 1990): 10–16.

Profiles of Daniel Pilon, Walter Sheper, Michelle Boudreau, and Wolfgang Bottenberg. Includes reproductions of excerpts from the composers' manuscripts. Letter from Kennan Garvey in 32, no. 1 (March 1991): 35 concerns the comment made by one of the composers that amateurs should not play in public.

* Rose, Pete. "On the Cutting Edge." Cited above as item 907.

1331. Rose, Pete. "Avant-Garde Recorder Music: An Evolutionary View." *American Recorder* 33, no. 3 (September 1992): 19–22.

    A chart covering developments in avant-garde recorder music 1950–89. Divides the forty-year period into eight five-year segments and notes significant events and trends in the United States, Europe, and "elsewhere" for each.

1332. Rose, Pete. "Zum Stand der modernen amerikanischen Blockflötenmusik: Eine subjektive Betrachtung" [On the state of modern American recorder music: a subjective view]. *Tibia* 17, no. 2 (1992): 90–95.

    The Americas have tended to produce conservative and technically undemanding recorder compositions. Surveys the most interesting of them, classified as solos (some with tape), duets, trios, works for four or more recorders, recorder with keyboard, and recorder with other instruments. For each piece, gives background information and a few comments on special features.

1333. Rose, Pete. "What Pieces Would I Recommend to Someone Who Wanted to Begin Playing the Modern Repertoire?" *American Recorder* 34, no. 2 (June 1993): 18. Reprinted from *Early Music Newsletter,* November 1992.

    Suggests over two dozen compositions, mostly for solo recorder. Pieces are grouped by playing ability into six categories ranging from beginner to professional. Letter from Madeline M. Hunter, on the availability of a few of the titles, in 34, no. 3 (September 1993): 29.

Individual Composers

Bandt, Ros

1334. Bandt, Ros. "Original Wind: Ros Bandt, Composer-Performer, Artist in Sound." *The Recorder: Journal of the Victorian Recorder Guild* 1 (1984): 8–11.

Bandt says that "pipes, breath and sound have been the major preoccupations in my work since the early seventies." Describes four of her pieces involving recorders and other pipes: *Wind Instruments in the Environment (Tank Pieces, Silo Pieces, Car Park Pieces)*, *Disjointed Quartet*, *Soft and Fragile: Music in Glass and Clay*, and *Loops*.

Baur, Jürg (b. 1918)

1335. Vetter, Michael. "Recorder Works by Jürg Baur." *Recorder & Music Magazine* 2, no. 7 (November 1967): 226–27.

Concerns *Incontri* (1960) for recorder and piano, *Mutazoni* (1960) for alto recorder, and *Pezzi uccelli* (1964) for recorder solo.

Berio, Luciano (b. 1925)

1336. Brüggen, Frans. "Berio's 'Gesti.'" *Recorder and Music Magazine* 2, no. 3 (November 1966): 66.

Background and analysis. In a letter to Brüggen accompanying the manuscript of the work, Berio wrote: "As you can see I tried to celebrate a divorce between your fingers and your mouth." Brüggen commissioned the work and gave its British premiere soon after the publication of this article, on 7 December 1966.

Bois, Rob du (b. 1934)

1337. Arran, Roderick. "Muziek voor Altblokfluit—Rob du Bois." *Recorder & Music* 7, no. 4 (December 1981): 91–94.

A description of extended techniques and compositional devices employed in the work. Includes a reproduction of the entire score, complete with Arran's analytical notations.

* Vetter, Michael. "New Recorder Music from Holland." Cited above as item **1318**.

BORNEFELD, HELMUT (1906–1990)

1338. Bornefeld, Helmut. "Ein Leben mit Bläsern und Orgel" [A life with winds and organ]. (Das Porträt) *Tibia* 2, no. 2 (1977): 289–93.

Works for wind instruments and for organ occupied a central place in the output of Helmut Bornefeld. Here he traces his involvement with these instruments throughout his life, many of his compositions being based on folksong or sacred songs and hymns. Complete list of works.

1339. Braun, Gerhard. "Das andere Arkadien: Gedanken zur Flötenmusik von Helmut Bornefeld" [The other Arcadia: Thoughts on the flute music of Helmut Bornefeld]. *Tibia* 12, no. 2 (1987): 401–5. Reprinted from *Württembergische Blätter für Kirchenmusik*, 6/86.

Discusses the style and circumstances of composition of Bornefeld's works for both recorder and flute.

BRAUN, GERHARD (B. 1932)

1340. Devroop, Chatradari. "Monologe eines Blockflötenspielers: Anmerkungen zu den Kompositionen für Blockflöte solo von Gerhard Braun—Zum 60. Geburtstag des Komponisten" [Monolog of a recorder player: remarks on the compositions for one recorder by Gerhard Braun—on the composer's 60th birthday]. *Tibia* 17, no. 2 (1992): 85–90.

A complement to Braun's own comments on introducing recorder players to modern music (see item **1326**). Mentions three such pieces of Braun's, then goes on to describe other works of his that incorporate speech and graphical elements, notably the *Monologe I–IV*. The bibliography is restricted to those recorder compositions of Braun's published by Moeck, the publishers of *Tibia* (ironically, not including the *Monologe I–IV*). The article celebrates Braun's 60th birthday, praising his role as both recorder player and composer.

BRIDGE, J.C. (1853–1929)

* Kinsell, David. "J.C. Bridge and the Recorder." Cited above as item **96**.

BRITTEN, BENJAMIN (1913–1976)

1341. Strode, Rosamund. "Benjamin Britten and the Recorder." *The Recorder and Music Magazine* 1, no. 9 (May 1965): 262–63.

   Concerns five works either for or including recorders: *Scherzo* (1955), *Alpine Suite* (1955), *Noye's Fludd* (1958), *A Midsummer Night's Dream* (1960), and *Psalm 150* (1962). Describes the use of the recorder in each and, for the first two works, the circumstances of their composition.

1342. Winters, Leslie. "Benjamin Britten: Scherzo." (Playing) *The Recorder and Music Magazine* 1, no. 4 (February 1964): 106–7.

   Advice on rehearsing and interpreting the work.

BROADSTOCK, BRENTON

1343. Broadstock, Brenton. "Aureole 3—A Musical Drama." (Writing for the Recorder) *The Recorder: Journal of the Victorian Recorder Guild* 2 (March 1985): 16–18.

   Composer's commentary on his *Aureole 3* (1984) for recorder and harpsichord.

1344. Martin, John. "Preparing Aureole 3 for Performance." *The Recorder: Journal of the Victorian Recorder Guild* 3 (November 1985): 31–32.

   Briefly describes the work and the practical aspects of learning to play it.

BUCKLEY, JOHN

1345. Hamel, Peter Michael. "Zwischen Keltentum und Avantgarde: Der irische Komponist John Buckley" [Between Celticity and avant garde: The Irish composer John Buckley]. *Musik Texte: Zeitschrift für neue Musik* 20 (July–August 1987): 19–25.

   Lists three works Buckley has written for recorder, one of which, Fantasia No. 2 (1987) for alto recorder, is reproduced with the article.

BURROWS, BENJAMIN (1891–1966)

1346. "Benjamin Burrows, 1891–1966." *The Recorder Magazine* 11, no. 4 (December 1991): 99–100.

In response to a query about Burrows in 11, no. 3 (September 1991): 90, Ralph Hall, Gwilym Beechey, Bernard Barrell, and Paul Clark contribute short pieces on Burrows and his works, particularly the Suite for Soprano Recorder and Piano (1955). Clark offers an analysis and assessment of the work.

CHALLULAU, PATRICE

1347. Duhot, Jean-Joël. "Un jeune compositeur écrit pour la flûte à bec. Patrice Challulau entretien avec Jean-Joël Duhot" [A young composer writes for the recorder. Patrice Challulau interviewed by Jean-Joël Duhot]. *Flûte à bec & instruments anciens* 28 (July 1989): 4-5.

Briefly covers: his training, his influences, micro-intervals, being a composer today, earning "a lot less than a cleaning woman," his composition prizes, and his writing for recorder.

CLINGAN, JUDITH (B. 1945)

1348. Clingan, Judith. "The Seven Deadly Sins." *The Recorder: Journal of the Victorian Recorder Guild* 12 (December 1990): 26–27.

Describes her composition of that title (commissioned for the Recorder '90 festival in Canberra, Australia in October 1990) and its first performance there.

COATES, GLORIA (B. 1938)

1349. Coates, Gloria. "A Cockatoo Will Do." *American Recorder* 31, no. 4 (December 1990): 17–19.

The story behind Coates's *Breaking Through*, a composition for alto recorder commissioned and first performed by Dörte Nienstedt for an international contest sponsored by GEDOK (a German organization for women artists). The work is based on the songs of a cockatoo. Letter from Joanna Neroda in 32, no. 1 (March 1991): 36.

COOKE, ARNOLD (B. 1906)

1350. Whiting, B.C. "The Recorder Music of Arnold Cooke." *Recorder & Music* 5, no. 10 (June 1977): 318-22; 5, no. 11 (September 1977): 355-58.

Substantial analyses of the nine recorder compositions by Cooke published by 1977. The descriptions focus on theoretical matters but also include assessments of the difficulty of the recorder parts.

GAL, HANS (1890-1987)

1351. Thorne, J.O. "Hans Gal: A Seventy-fifth Birthday Tribute." *The Recorder and Music Magazine* 1, no. 10 (August 1965): 303.

A biographical sketch and survey of his compositions for recorder.

1352. "Dr Hans Gal OBE." *Recorder & Music* 6, no. 11 (September 1980): 325.

Profile in honor of Gal's 90th birthday. Covers: his musical activity in Austria; his immigration in 1938 to Great Britain and subsequent work at Edinburgh University; his activity as a composer.

1353. H[unt], E[dgar]. "Obituary: Dr Hans Gál OBE." *The Recorder and Music Magazine* 9, no. 4 (December 1987): 102.

Mentions his compositions for recorder and his contributions to the Society of Recorder Players.

HAND, COLIN

1354. Hand, Colin. "The Composer Writes: PLAINT for Tenor Recorder and Harpsichord (or Piano)." *Recorder & Music* 5, no. 3 (September 1975): 89.

Offers background to the piece and suggestions for performance.

HEIDEN, BERNHARD (B. 1910)

1355. Lasocki, David. "The Third Recorder Age of Bernhard Heiden." *The American Recorder* 30, no. 3 (August 1989): 109-12.

Written on the occasion of Heiden's having composed a recorder concerto (1987) for Eva Legêne and the Minneapolis Chamber Symphony, who premiered the work in August 1988. Opens with a biographical sketch. Heiden was introduced to the recorder as a composition student of Paul Hindemith's in Berlin from 1929-33. Sometime late in this period, Heiden joined Hindemith and, he believes, Harald Genzmer in the first broadcast performance of the trio from *Plöner Musiktag*. Heiden later conducted recorder players at summer camps in Lake Placid and organized the Indiana University Collegium Musicum. The idea of a recorder concerto came to him when the conductor of the Minneapolis Chamber Symphony "asked him to write something for orchestra at about the same time that Legêne approached him about a recorder piece for her." The remainder of the article describes in some detail the structure and musical content of the concerto as well as adjustments made by both Heiden and Legêne during rehearsals.

HEIDER, WERNER (B. 1930)

1356. Clausing, Susette. "Werner Heider." (Das Porträt) *Tibia* 10, no. 3 (1985): 421-24.

   A brief summary of the life, philosophy, and woodwind works of this avant-garde German composer.

1357. Kelber, Sebastian. "Werner Heiders *Katalog für einen Blockflötenspieler*: Eine Analyse" [Werner Heider's *Katalog für einen Blockflötenspieler* (Catalog for a recorder player): an analysis]. *Tibia* 1, no. 3 (1976): 145-48.

   Begins with the revelation that *Katalog* "owes its origin to a herring." Sitting with friends at a beer table under the trees, Heider was joined by Kelber, who started cutting a smoked herring. Slightly disgusted, especially by the sight of the "milk" of the herring, Heider said finally: "When you have eaten it all up, I'll write you a piece."

   Goes on to describe *Katalog*, the first solo piece to use several recorders played by one player. Heider wanted to explore the possibilities of the recorder: range, dynamics, articulation, ornaments, tone formation, and special effects. Shows the symmetry of the piece in a diagram. Then analyses the serial technique (twelve rows, each consisting of from one to twelve notes), based on information supplied by the composer.

HESPOS, HANS-JOACHIM (B. 1938)

1358. Braun, Gerhard. "'—schattenhaft ruhig—grob gekant—': Anmerkungen zu den Flötenkompositionen von Hans-Joachim Hespos" ['ghostly quiet—coarsely chewed':

remarks on the flute and recorder compositions of Hans-Joachim Hespos]. *Tibia* 8, no. 3 (1983): 418–21.

Based partly on radio commentaries by Reinhard Oelschlägel and Hans-Klaus Jungheinrich. Describes two recorder pieces by Hespos: *pico* for sopranino, and *ilomba* for three basses (bass, contrabass, sub-bass). See also David Smeyers, "Exploding Silence(s)—An Introduction to Hans-Joachim Hespos and his Music," *The Clarinet* 14, no. 4 (Summer 1987): 16–20.

1359. Kumpf, Hans. "Hans-Joachim Hespos." (Das Porträt) *Tibia* 9, no. 1 (1984): 33–35.

Covers: how he came to write for the recorder; reconciling his "aggressive" style with the sopranino recorder (in *pico*); comments on *ilomba*; dynamic markings in his compositions; provoking the public; his switch from school teaching to full-time composing; young people and his music; having his own publishing company; his opposition to minimalism; his compositional philosophy.

HINDEMITH, PAUL (1895–1963)

1360. Higbee, Dale. "Notes on Hindemith's 'Trio for Recorders.'" *The American Recorder* 10, no. 2 (Spring 1969): 39.

Reprints a letter from Hans Ulrich Staeps confirming Higbee's suspicion that Hindemith intended the "Fugato" as the middle movement of the trio when performed outside its context in *Plöner Musiktag*. Also includes suggestions for alternate instrumentation. See also item 1361.

1361. Bergmann, Walter. "Further Notes on Hindemith's Recorder Trio." *The American Recorder* 13, no. 1 (February 1972): 17.

A response to item 1360. When Bergmann submitted his edition of the trio (Schott 10094, RMS 474) to Hindemith for approval, he asked the composer to clear up several questions about the work. According to Hindemith, the second alto part may be played on a tenor, and the last two movements may be reversed. Nonetheless, Bergmann still favors retaining the original fast—fast—slow ordering of the movements.

1362. Neumeyer, David. "Hindemith's Recorder Trio: Sketches and Autograph." *The American Recorder* 17, no. 2 (August 1976): 61–68. In German as: "Hindemiths Blockflötentrio—Skizzen und Autograph." *Tibia* 6, no. 1 (1981): 262–67.

Describes the sketches and autograph score of the trio and the revisions that Hindemith made while preparing the autograph. Explores these revisions as they relate to the theoretical workings of the piece by providing a detailed musical analysis. Includes a reproduction of a page from the sketches.

1363. Chandelier, Christian. "A propos du trio de Hindemith" [Concerning Hindemith's trio]. *Flûte à bec et instruments anciens* 26 (November 1988): 18-19.

Background on Hindemith and his musical style, followed by detailed comments on the form and harmonic structure of his recorder trio, "without doubt the only important work of the first part of the 20th century written for recorder."

KAGEL, MAURICIO (B. 1931)

1364. Schmidt, Dörte. "Über Möglichkeiten—Zu Mauricio Kagel's Musik für Renaissanceinstrumente" [About possibilities: on Mauricio Kagel's *Musik für Renaissanceinstrumente* (Music for Renaissance instruments)]. *Tibia* 15, no. 3 (1990): 186-94.

Philosophical ruminations on, and analysis of, Kagel's 1968 work for Renaissance instruments (including recorders), probably the earliest ensemble work for recorders that included modern playing techniques and somewhat free notation.

KARKOSCHKA, ERHARD (B. 1923)

1365. Braun, Gerhard. "*mit/gegen sich selbst* und andere Schwierigkeiten: Zur Interpretation szenischer Blockflötenmusik am Beispiel einer Komposition von Erhard Karkoschka" [*mit/gegen sich selbst* (with/against oneself) and other difficulties: on the interpretation of staged recorder music as exemplified in a composition by Erhard Karkoschka]. *Tibia* 3, no. 3 (1978): 162-66.

An expanded version of a chapter in item **823**. Simply describes Karkoschka's piece, then comments briefly on the recorder in modern musical theater.

LECHNER, KONRAD (1911-1990)

1366. Lechner, Konrad. "Konrad Lechner über sich selbst" [Konrad Lechner on himself]. (Das Porträt) *Tibia* 1, no. 2 (1976): 89-93.

Describes his career as a composer, performer, and teacher, mentioning his involvement with the recorder in passing. Bibliography of his flute and recorder music.

1367. "Epitaph: zum Tode von Konrad Lechner" [Epitaph: on the death of Konrad Lechner]. *Tibia* 15, no. 2 (1990): 134-36.
   Tributes by Gerhard Braun, Peter Reidemeister, Hans-Martin Linde, Hans Darmstadt, Werner Heider, and Hans Leygraf.

LINDE, HANS-MARTIN (B. 1930)

1368. Prior, Susan. "Notes on Hans-Martin Linde's *Modern Exercises for Treble Recorder*." *Continuo* 2, no. 6 (March 1979): 4-8.
   Based on remarks made by the composer during a course (1975).

1369. Fairhall, Helen. "Music for the Bird—and for the Adventurous." *The Recorder: Journal of the Victorian Recorder Guild* 11 (June 1990): 10-12.
   Some general notes on performing modern music followed by a disappointingly brief discussion of performance problems in Linde's *Music for a Bird*.

MARX, KARL (1897-1985)

* Marx, Karl. "Begegnungen mit der Blockflöte" [Encounters with the recorder]. Cited above as item 1060.

MÜLLER-HARTMANN, R. (1884-1950)

1370. Grant, Dinah. "R. Müller-Hartmann: Suite." (Playing) *The Recorder and Music Magazine* 1, no. 5 (May 1964): 157-58.
   Suggestions for rehearsal and interpretation.

RAWSTHORNE, ALAN (1905-1971)

1371. Turner, John. "Rawsthorne's Recorder Suite." *The Recorder Magazine* 13, no. 1 (March 1993): 13-14.

Documents the discovery of a recorder composition by Alan Rawsthorne that had long been assumed lost. Rawsthorne, in order to fill a commission from a player of the viola d'amore, had taken the unpublished and unperformed composition for alto recorder and piano and revised it. Neither version was ever published. Turner was able to identify the revisions and fairly accurately reconstruct the original, which he premiered in July 1993.

ROOSENDAEL, JAN ROKUS VAN

1372. Hauwe, Walter van. "Jan Rokus van Roosendael's *Rotations*." *Key Notes* 25 (1988–89): 45–47.

Takes the view that modern recorder compositions have reached the point where they are "undeniably well written for the [instrument]" and "one could scarcely imagine [them] being played by any other instrument." Considers *Rotations* to be "an admirable example of this type of composition." Gives a little background information, then briefly describes the piece. Note that van Hauwe prefers the term "blockflute" to recorder, partly to differentiate it from tape and cassette recorders, and partly on (mistaken) historical grounds.

The same issue of *Key Notes* also contains "A Forum Discussion" on modern recorder music involving participants in the International Week of Twentieth-Century Recorder Music, Amsterdam, October 1988 (pp. 42–44) and a report on the festival by Eve O'Kelly (pp. 39–41).

RUBBRA, EDMUND (1901–1986)

1373. Hunt, Edgar. "The Recorder Music of Edmund Rubbra." *The Recorder and Music Magazine* 8, no. 10 (June 1986): 296–97.

Brief analyses of, and comments on, Rubbra's seven major works involving the recorder.

1374. [Hunt, Edgar?]. "Obituary: Dr. Edmund Rubbra." *The Recorder and Music Magazine* 8, no. 9 (March 1986): 277–79.

Includes a brief description of the genesis of the *Meditazioni*, op. 67, and Rubbra's interpretation of the work when he served as an accompanist to Hunt.

SAUX, GASTON

1375. Hunt, Edgar. "Gaston Saux: Quartet in F." *Recorder & Music Magazine* 3, no. 6 (June 1970): 201.

Suggestions for rehearsal and interpretation. The quartet, composed in 1959, was the "first sizeable work of its kind to achieve publication and acceptance among recorder players."

SCIORTINO, PATRICE

1376. Scharapan, Gérard. "*Salicionaux* de Patrice Sciortino (édition A. Zurfluh, 1973)" [*Salicionaux* by Patrice Sciortino (Paris: Zurfluh, 1973)]. (Musique d'ensemble: Présentation d'une oeuvre) *Flûte à bec & instruments anciens* 12 (September 1984): 11–12.

An abortive attempt to start a series of articles about ensemble works for the recorder. Consists of "a succinct analysis which, we hope, gives to prospective interpreters some working ideas and which will also help listeners"—or in other words, background and brief descriptive notes.

SEROCKI, KAZIMIERZ (1922–1981)

1377. Zielinski, Tadeusz A. "'Concerto alla Cadenza' by Kazimierz Serocki." *Recorder & Music* 6, no. 3 (September 1978): 68–71.

Covers the following topics: Serocki's musical aesthetic and his interest in tone color; the instrumentation of the *Concerto alla Cadenza* (1974) and the special techniques required of the soloist; a synopsis of the plan of the work; and Serocki's notational devices (including examples).

1378. Zielinski, Tadeusz A. "Anmerkungen zu 'Arrangements' für 1 bis 4 Blockflöten von Kazimierz Serocki" [Observations on *Arrangements* for 1 to 4 recorders by Kazimierz Serocki]. *Tibia* 5, no. 1 (1980): 23–28.

Describes Serocki as "one of the most interesting 'colorists' in contemporary music" and "one of the best in contemporary Polish music." *Arrangements* (1976) consists of seventeen segments, notated on separate sheets, which can be played in any order or in one of the fifteen specified orders, not to mention by from one to four recorders. Such a "large number of setting and performance possibilities is possible because the composer has employed tone colors as basic composition material"—some forty different tone colors "which are created through unconventional styles of playing on the whole instrument or only only the removed head joint." Goes on to briefly describe these tone colors and their combinations.

STAEPS, HANS ULRICH (1909-1988)

* H[unt], E[dgar] H. "Prof. Hans-Ulrich Staeps." Cited above as item **1105**.

* Primus, Constance M. "Memories of Hans Ulrich Staeps, 1909-1988." Cited above as item **1106**.

1379. Staeps, Hans Ulrich. "Saratoga Suite." *The American Recorder* 7, no. 4 (Fall 1966): 5-6.
   The composer discusses the genesis of his recorder trio *Saratoga Suite* and offers suggestions for performance.

STOCKHAUSEN, KARLHEINZ (B. 1928)

1380. Geddert, Geesche. "'In Freundschaft' von Karlheinz Stockhausen jetzt auch für Blockflöte" [Karlheinz Stockhausen's "In Freundschaft" now also for recorder]. *Tibia* 10, no. 3 (1985): 416-19.
   In Freundschaft was written in 1977 for clarinet alone and subsequently adapted for several other melody instruments (alto recorder, basset horn or bass clarinet, bassoon, flute, horn, oboe, saxophone, trombone, violin, violoncello). Geddert, who worked with the composer to produce the version for recorder, discusses why she believes the work to be important, analyzes it, comments on the recorder version, and gives help with its interpretation. See also the discussion and analysis of the clarinet version by Beate Zelinsky and David Smeyers, "Karlheinz Stockhausens 'In Freundschaft': Eine Herausforderung für Interpreten und Publikum," *Tibia* 10, no. 3 (1985): 412-16.

TIPPETT, MICHAEL (B. 1905)

1381. Bergmann, Walter. "Michael Tippett: His Recorder Works." *The Recorder and Music Magazine* 1, no. 8 (February 1965): 229-31.
   Concerns three compositions: *Four Inventions* (SA duet), *Bonny at Morn* (chorus and recorders), and *Crown of the Year* (girls' chorus with chamber orchestra). Offers background on the composition of the works and assesses the difficulty of the recorder parts. The section on *Four Inventions*

includes suggestions for performance and corrects an error in the published parts.

1382. Kenworthy, C. "Michael Tippett: An Appreciation." *The Recorder and Music Magazine* 1, no. 8 (February 1965): 229.
Concerns the role of Morley College in the promotion of early music in London during the 1940s and 1950s. Tippett served as Director of Music at the college.

WORRALL, DAVID

* Worrall, David. "Composing for a Large Recorder Ensemble." Cited above as item 839.

1383. Omitted.

30

Miscellaneous Fipple Flutes

During the course of compiling this book, without making a concerted effort to do so, we came across a number of sources on fipple flutes other than the recorder, including the czakan, flageolet, *flauto harmonico, flûte pastorelle*, folk instruments, gemshorn, ocarina, *Ruszpfeif*, and tabor pipe. We present these sources here in the hope that they will be useful to readers, although clearly more could be said about fipple flutes, particularly in folk music.

1384. Bosmans, Wim. "De russpfeif, schwegel en gemshorn van Virdung in het Brussels Instrumentenmuseum" [The Russpfeif, tabor pipe, and gemshorn of Virdung in the Brussels Instrument Museum]. *Musica Antiqua* 3, no. 2 (May 1986): 40–41.
    Identifies three types of recorder-like instruments in the writings of Virdung, Agricola, and Praetorius. Then gives measurements and background on the Brussels instruments of these types. Part of a projected study of all the instruments of the flute family in the folk music of the Low Countries.

* Galpin, Francis W. *Old English Instruments of Music: Their History and Character.* Cited above as item **71.1**.
    Discusses the flageolet and tabor pipe.

1385. Marvin, Bob. "A Double Recorder." *FoMRHI Quarterly* 31 (April 1983): 42–43 (Communication No. 453).
    Attempts to come up with measurements for "the double recorder of Oxford" (otherwise unidentified but apparently from a 14th-century work of art), the pipes of which seem to be a fifth apart.

* Meierott, Lenz. *Die geschichtliche Entwicklung der kleinen Flötentypen und ihre Verwendung in der Musik des 17. und 18. Jahrhunderts* [The historical development of the small members of the flute family and their use in the music of the 17th and 18th centuries]. Cited above as item 124.

1386. Moeck, Hermann. "Spazierstockinstrumente: Eine kurze Vorstudie zu folgendem Aufsatz" [Walking stick instruments: a short preliminary study to the following article]; "Czakane, Englische und Wiener Flageolette" [Czakans, and English and Viennese flagolets]. In *Festschrift to Ernst Emsheimer on the Occasion of his 70th Birthday January 15th 1974*, 149–51, 152–62, 279–80. (Studia instrumentorum musicae popularis, no. 3) Stockholm: Musikhistoriska Museet, 1974.

> The first article gives some documentation for walking-stick recorders. The second article gives a good overview of czakans and 19th-century flageolets, including composers, performers, methods, surviving instruments, makers, and repertory. Reviewed by Philip Bate in *Early Music* 3, no. 2 (April 1975): 155–56 and Edgar Hunt in *Recorder & Music* 5, no. 1 (March 1975): 21.

Czakan

1387. Betz, Marianne. *Der Csakan und seine Musik: Wiener Musikleben im frühen 19. Jahrhunder, dargestellt am Beispiel einer Spazierstockblockflöte* [The czakan and its music: Viennese musical life in the early 19th century, presented by the example of a cane recorder]. Tutzing: Hans Schneider, 1992. Inaugural-Dissertation der Philosophisch-Historischen Fakultät der Ruprecht-Karls-Universität Heidelberg. xii, 294 p. ISBN 3795207304.

> The first large-scale study of the czakan, the cane recorder that had a surprising vogue in early 19th-century Vienna. Betz looks at its etymology, form, makers (especially Franz Schöllnast), sellers, music, composers and players (especially Anton Heberle, Wilhelm Klingenbrunner, Joseph Gebauer, and Ernst Krähmer), and social history. Amazingly, more than 400 pieces were published for the czakan between 1807 and 1849. Appendixes list surviving instruments, czakan music, and methods and fingering charts. Highly recommended.

1388. Reyne, Hugo. "La flûte à bec romantique existe: Je l'ai rencontrée" [The Romantic recorder exists: I have encountered it]. *Flûte à bec & instruments anciens* 15 (June 1985): 4–5. In German as: "Die romantische Blockflöte existiert—ich habe sie gefunden." *Zeitschrift SAJM* 20, no. 6 (November 1992): 3-6.
On the czakan, its extensive repertory, and evolution.

ETHNIC AND FOLK INSTRUMENTS

1389. Allen, W.S. "The Double-pipes of the Adriatic." *The Recorder and Music Magazine* 1, no. 4 (February 1964): 114–15.
Describes the Yugoslav *dvojnice* and its use. Includes a transcription of a dance from the island of Krk.

1390. Barrett, J.H. "A Fipple Flute or Pipe from the Site of Keynsham Abbey." *The Galpin Society Journal* 22 (1969): 47–50.
Describes a bone pipe found in 1964 by the Folk House Archaeological Club, Bristol, in the grounds of Abbotsford House, Keynsham, Somerset [now Avon].

1391. Mayers, Dan E. "Introducing the Shakuhachi." *Recorder & Music* 6, no. 5 (March 1979): 135–37.
A fine introduction to the instrument, its repertory, and its position in Japanese history and culture.

1392. Megaw, J.V.S. "An End-blown Flute from Medieval Canterbury." *Medieval Archaeology* 12 (1968): 149–50.
Describes a bird-bone pipe discovered in 1953 during excavation of the 12th-13th century levels of medieval Canterbury, Kent. The pipe has three finger holes and plays a pentatonic scale.

1393. Megaw, J.V.S. "An End-blown Flute or Flageolet from White Castle." *Medieval Archaeology* 5 (1961): 176–80.
A study of a cannon-bone pipe found in the moat of White Castle, Monmouthshire, along with pottery dating from the second half of the 13th century. The instrument has five—rather than six—finger holes and is decorated with carvings.

* Moeck, Hermann. *Typen europäischer Blockflöten in Vorzeit, Geschichte und Volksüberlieferung* [Types of European recorders in antiquity, history and folk tradition]. Cited above as item 55.

1394. Negre, Louis. "Une flûte à bec archéologique" [An archaeological fipple flute]. *Flûte à bec* 6 (March 1983): 23–25.

    Describes and discusses a prehistoric, four-holed, bone fipple flute discovered in Antibes in 1965.

1395. Peskin, Carolyn. "The Lost World of Pre-Columbian Flutes." *American Recorder* 33, no. 1 (March 1992): 9–14.

    Describes the types of instruments used in Peruvian and Mexican cultures and civilizations prior to Spanish conquest in the early 16th century. The predominant types of flutes used in Peru were notched flutes and panpipes. In Mexico, the prevalent flute was the fipple flute; notched flutes were unknown and panpipes uncommon. Includes some discussion of repertory. Concludes with a transcription of three Quechua melodies from the Peruvian Andes.

1396. Reviers, B. de. "Le fume onu: Flûte-à-bec maldivienne" [The "fume onu": Maldivian recorder]. *Flûte à bec & instruments anciens* 23 (1987): 2–3.

    Describes a bamboo fipple flute from the Maldive islands and a visit to one of its makers, Kuda Mureedhu. The name *fume onu* means "bamboo into which one blows." The instrument is similar to a recorder in that it has seven finger holes and a thumb hole.

1397. Stobart, Henry. "The Devil's Music." *The Recorder and Music Magazine* 9, no. 4 (December 1987): 90–92.

    Discusses the use of four sizes of *pinkillo* or *flauta* (a duct flute with six finger holes) by Bolivian peasants. These instruments are similar in length to, and are probably an imitation of, a Renaissance consort of recorders (soprano, alto, tenor, bass), which could have been introduced to the country by the Spaniards in early colonial times. The *pinkillo* is associated with the devil, death, the growth of crops, and courtship—corresponding closely to the associations of the recorder in Europe in the 17th century.

    See also his article "The Sirens of the Andes," *Musical Times* 1788 = 133, no. 2 (February 1992): 73. "When I played virtuosic pieces on the recorder to friends in the [Bolivian Andes] community, they treated them with indifference or comments such as 'Why don't you blow properly?' I was not achieving the kind of sound quality, rich in overtones, that they listen out for in their instruments. It also became apparent that virtuosity has an intimidating or alienating aspect, and partly for that reason it is not valued in traditional Andean culture."

FLAGEOLET

1398. Steinmann, Conrad. "The Flageolet." *The American Recorder* 17, no. 2 (August 1976): 57-59.
    An informative history of the instrument and its music.

1399. Hunt, Edgar. "The Double Flageolet." *Recorder & Music* 5, no. 10 (June 1977): 322-24.
    Briefly traces the history of double pipes, which extends back at least to ancient Greece and includes such instruments as the Yugoslavian *dvojnice* (see item **1389**) and the 18th-century French *flûte d'accord*. In the early 19th century, William Bainbridge invented the double flageolet, a more elaborate, keyed instrument. Hunt describes the fingering and offers an example of original music for the instrument.

1400. Lindley, David. "A 17th-Century Flageolet Tablature at Guildford." *The Galpin Society Journal* 31 (1978): 94-99.
    A description of a 168-page manuscript containing about forty tunes. Includes five transcribed excerpts.

1401. Reyne, Hugo. "Trois sortes de flûtes à bec à ne plus confondre" [Three types of fipple flute to confuse no longer]. *Flûte à bec & instruments anciens* 8 (September 1983): 35.
    Distinguishes among the tin whistle, the English flute (flageolet), and the true flageolet.

1402. Wells, Charles. "The Early Flageolet." *The Recorder Magazine* 13, no. 3 (December 1993): 72-74.
    A brief history, including facsimiles of historical fingering charts and tablatures.

FLAUTO HARMONICO

* Weber, Rainer. "Der Flauto Harmonico—Ein seltenes Instrument und sein Erbauer" [The *flauto harmonico*—a rare instrument and its inventor]. Cited above as item **227**.

FLÛTE PASTORELLE

1403. Benedikt, Erich. "La flûte pastorelle." *Tibia* 11, no. 3 (1986): 168–74.

    Discusses the surviving repertory for the *flûte pastorelle* (Hertel, Kunzen, Telemann) in the light of 18th-century writings. Concludes what Edgar Hunt had already surmised (see item 123): that the term was one of the names for the panpipes (pitched in D, E♭, or E).

GEMSHORN

1404. Fitzpatrick, Horace. "The Gemshorn: A Reconstruction." *Proceedings of the Royal Musical Association* 99 (1972–73): 1–14. Abridged version: "Notes on the Gemshorn: A Reconstruction." *Recorder and Music Magazine* 4, no. 1 (March 1972): 6–9.

    Fitzpatrick offers an excellent history of the instrument as an introduction to his own work constructing gemshorns. After failing to create an airtight seal between a couple of appropriate horns and carefully designed wooden fipples, he experimented with a variety of soft compounds, finally settling upon dental plaster. Several of the thirty-two instruments he made were a success. He found it impossible to predict the final pitch of an instrument, but discovered that pitch could be adjusted by placing a metal band around the head and sliding it partially over the windway, which leads him to speculate that similar "tuning bands" might have been used on recorders of the 14th–15th centuries. Concludes with a discussion of probable repertory.

1405. Gould, Ian. "The Gemshorn—the Poor Man's Ocarina." *Recorder & Music* 6, no. 4 (December 1978): 103–5.

    Written in response to item 1408. Includes instructions for constructing a gemshorn from a raw cow's horn and plaster (for the plug). Also explains how to voice and tune the instrument.

1406. Parkinson, Andrew. "Guesswork and the Gemshorn." *Early Music* 9, no. 1 (January 1981): 43–46.

    Comments that "With no reliable specimens to copy, [modern] makers have nevertheless produced some beautiful-sounding instruments, similar to recorders but with a limited range, and made of various types of horn." Only three useful early pictorial sources provide useful information: a Dance of Death woodcut, Virdung, and Dürer's *Prayerbook*, the latter two showing only three fingerholes. Describes his making of such an instrument (also with a thumbhole) based on the ocarina principle.

1407. Waechter, Wolfram. "Das Gemshorn—ein neues 'altes Originalinstrument'?" [The gemshorn—a new "old instrument"?]. *Tibia* 5, no. 2 (1980): 101-5.

Musical instruments made from animal horns were used in the Middle Ages and early Renaissance, as they are today in many folk cultures. Unfortunately, only one, unplayable gemshorn from earlier times has survived (Berlin). Despite a few pictorial representations, we know little about the range of types of gemshorn: were they played with one hand (as in Virdung's engraving) or both? All modern gemshorns are necessarily reconstructions rather than copies. Surveys the reconstruction work of Horace Fitzpatrick, Rainer Weber, Meinrad Ertel, and James Furner. Concludes with suggestions for musical uses of the gemshorn today.

OCARINA

1408. Middleton, James. "The Ocarina—the Poor Man's Gemshorn?" *Recorder & Music* 5, no. 9 (March 1977): 290-91.

See also item **1405**. General description of the instrument. Raises questions about its history and the reason for its decline.

PIPE AND TABOR

1409. Thorn, Chris. "The Pipe and Tabour." *Recorder & Music* 7, no. 9 (March 1983): 225-27.

Advice on sources for instruments, playing technique (including a table of fingerings), and repertory.

1410. Bosmans, Wim. *Eenhandsfluit en trom in de lage landen = The Pipe and Tabor in the Low Countries.* Peer, Belgium: Alamire, 1991. 96 p. ISBN 9068530607.

A significant study that makes a good introduction to the general history of this combination of instruments. The musician played the three-holed pipe with one hand while beating the drum slung around his neck with the other hand. Bosmans's book is in Dutch, but there is a nine-page English summary (pp. 69-78) and there are more than one hundred illustrations (in black and white only but very clearly reproduced). Covers: names, iconography, extant instruments, musical properties, playing position, and social history. The instrument began to be depicted in the 13th century, reached its zenith in the period 1450-1650, then seems to have died out until some isolated occurrences in the 19th century, followed by the 20th-century revival. Reviewed by Alyson Lewin in *The Recorder Magazine* 12, no. 2 (June 1992): 52-53.

RUSZPFEIF

1411. Hettrick, William E. "Identifying and Defining the *Ruszpfeif*: Some Observations and Etymological Theories." *Journal of the American Musical Instrument Society* 17 (1991): 53–68.

An exhaustive inquiry into the nature of the *Ruszpfeif* in Sebastian Virdung's *Musica getutscht* (1511) and the etymology of its name. Shows that it was a four-holed fipple flute (no thumbhole), the upper portion of which may have been square or rectangular in cross-section, the fingerholes being cut into one of the flat sides. The instrument is clearly to be distinguished from the *klein Flöt* (1529 edition) or *klein Flötlein* (1545 edition) in Martin Agricola's *Musica instrumentalis deudsch* which had three fingerholes and a thumbhole. The term *rusz* has been linked to the Middle Low German noun *rusch* (rush or reed), various forms of the verb *rauschen* (all concerned with making noise), the noun or adjective *Russe* (a Russian; wild and coarse), the noun *Rusz* (soot, black), or *Ruszbaum* (an early form of Rüster)—of which Hettrick prefers the last.

31

Recorder, Early Music, and Musical Instrument Periodicals

This chapter is devoted to those periodicals (magazines and journals) that contain articles cited in this book as well as the other most important recorder, early music, and musical-instrument periodicals of more than local interest. (The first two items represent previous attempts at the same task.)

Periodicals are notoriously capricious: they come into being from nowhere and die away without notice; they change titles and subtitles, merge with other periodicals, then split off again; they alter their numbering schemes and frequencies; they change publishers and distributors. Our chapter will doubtless be out of date long before you read it. Still, we have thought it worthwhile to list what we could find out as of April 1994, including the most current subscription address and prices: it is a place to start. The ISSNs (and, in their absence, the OCLC numbers) will aid you in obtaining articles from these periodicals on interlibrary loan.

BIBLIOGRAPHIES OF PERIODICALS

1412. Reyne, Hugo. "Revue des revues" [Review of periodicals]. *Flûte à bec & instruments anciens* 13/14 (December 1984/March 1985): 51–54.
    Annotated bibliography of recorder and early music periodicals in the U.S.A., Canada, England, the Netherlands, Belgium, West Germany, Italy, and France.

1413. Baratz, Lewis R. "International Directory of Current Early-Music Periodicals." *Historical Performance* 1, no. 2 (Fall 1988): 110–14.

Annotated bibliography of early music periodicals in Canada, the U.S.A., Belgium, France, Germany, Italy, the Netherlands, Spain, Sweden, Switzerland, the U.K., and New Zealand.

INDIVIDUAL TITLES

1414. *Alte Musik Aktuell* [Early music news]. Monthly (July/August issue combined). 1985– . ISSN 0942-9034. In German. Postfach 10 08 30, D-93008 Regensburg, Germany. DM 42 (Germany), DM 52 (rest of Europe), DM 66 (overseas).

Includes reviews of recordings; masterclass, summer-course, and festival information; brief interviews and artist profiles.

1415. *The American Recorder*. Quarterly; bimonthly (five times per year) beginning with v. 35 (1994). 1960– . ISSN 0003-0724. The American Recorder Society, Inc., PO Box 631, Littleton CO 80160. Membership $30 (includes journal and newsletter). Back issues available from University Microfilms International.

The most widely circulated recorder journal in the English language, *AR* has maintained a generally high standard of writing for more than thirty years and today is stronger than ever. Scholarly and popular articles on a broad variety of topics of interest to recorder players; reviews of books, music, and recordings; as well as news, reports, and a lively correspondence column. Split off from *The American Recorder Society Newsletter* (item 1416). Edited by Martha Bixler, Winter 1960–Summer 1960; Ralph Taylor, Fall 1960–Fall 1961; Donna Hill, February 1962–August 1963; Elloyd Hanson, November 1963–Fall 1968; John Koch, Winter 1969–May 1974; Daniel Shapiro, August 1974–November 1976; Sigrid Nagle, February 1977–November 1989; Benjamin S. Dunham, March 1990– . Name changed to *American Recorder* (dropping the initial article) in March 1990. The present bibliography does not index all articles in *AR*; for a complete listing see Waddy Thompson and Jean Seiler, comps. and eds, *Indices to Volumes I through XXV of The American Recorder* (New York: *The American Recorder*, 1985), which offers access by author and broad subject category.

1416. *American Recorder Society Newsletter*. Quarterly (irregular); 1994– . Published five times per year with *American Recorder*. 1950– .

Edited by Bernard Krainis, 1950-53; LaNoue Davenport, June 1953-April 1959; Martha Bixler, the remainder of 1959 and continuing into 1960, when the *Newsletter* was expanded into *The American Recorder* (item 1415). The newsletter continued after 1960, but in a diminished role. See "The ARS *Newsletter* Revisited," *The American Recorder* 5, no. 4 (November 1964): 4-22, an anthology of articles, reviews, and letters selected from the newsletter, including items 783, 815, 1005, 1164, and 1255.

1417. *Basler Jahrbuch für historische Musikpraxis: Eine Veröffentlichung der Schola Cantorum Basiliensis, Lehr- und Forschungsinstitut für alte Musik an der Musik-Akademie der Stadt Basel* [Basel yearbook for historical performance practice: a publication of the Schola Cantorum Basiliensis, teaching and research institute for early music at the music academy of the city of Basel]. Annual. 1977- . Each issue has an individual ISBN. OCLC #4818899. Amadeus-Verlag, Am Iberghang 16, CH-8405 Winterthur, Switzerland. In German (occasionally in English).

Extensive scholarly articles on performance practice and other musicological topics of special interest to performers of medieval, Renaissance, and Baroque music. Bibliographies of recent writings on "historical performance practice" (really "early music").

1418. *Concerto: Das Magazin für Alte Musik* [Concerto: the magazine for early music]. Monthly (July/August and December/January issues combined); formerly six issues per year. 1983- . ISSN 0177-5944. In German. Postfach 42 01 57, D-50895 Köln, Germany. DM 64.

Scholarly and popular articles; reviews of books and recordings; concert, festival, and course listings; interviews.

1419. *The Consort*. Annual (since 1948; suspended 1938-48; irregular before 1938). Haslemere, Surrey: Dolmetsch Foundation, 1929- . ISSN 0268-9111. Mrs Elaine Land, Hindhead Grove, Hill Road, Hindhead, Surrey GU26 6QN, England. £12. Back issues available from University Microfilms International.

Scholarly and popular articles, reviews of books and music, and news of Dolmetsch Foundation affairs. Has largely degenerated into a repository for unwanted articles. We therefore hope that the newly appointed editor, Julie Anne Sadie, can improve its standard. For a selective listing of articles concerning the recorder published in nos. 1-19 (1929-62), see Dale Higbee,

"The Dolmetsch Foundation, *The Consort*, and the Recorder," *The American Recorder* 3, no. 3 (August 1962): 21.

1420. *Continuo: The Magazine of Old Music*. Irregular (now six issues per year). 1977– . Former ISSN 0706-6656. OCLC #4097094 or #17555823. PO Box 327, Hammondsport NY 14840. $30.

Minimally edited, popular research and technical articles; reviews of books, music, and recordings; course listings; and concert calendar. Began publication in Toronto with focus on early music in Canada, then moved to New York state and broadened coverage to North America. Penelope Mathiesen's news and research column on early woodwinds, "Winds of Yore," appeared April 1989–February 1994. Circulation has declined so much in recent years that the editor, Matthew James Redsell, has made a plea for a part-owner to put money into the magazine (February 1994 issue). First six issues (1977–March 1978) bore the title *Early Music Directory*.

1421. *Crescendo: Le magazine de la musique ancienne* [Crescendo: the magazine of early music]. Six issues per year. Nos. 32–38. Paris: SEPRA France, 1990–91. ISSN 1146-1764. In French. Continued *Flûte à bec & instruments anciens* (item 1425).

Briefly continued the broadened scope of *Flûte à bec et instruments anciens*: popular articles, news, and reviews.

1422. *Early Music*. Quarterly. 1973– . ISSN 0306-1078. Subscriptions and back issues: Oxford University Press, Walton Street, Oxford OX2 6DP, England. £35 (Europe), $68 (USA and rest of world).

A remarkably successful blend of scholarly and popular articles, addressed to both amateurs and professionals. Noted for its generous illustrations and abundant advertisements. Also extensive reviews of books, music, and recordings, as well as news items and auction reports. Of particular interest is 10, no. 1 (January 1982), an issue entitled "The Recorder: Past and Present," which includes items 73 (first part only), 81, 111, 450, and 452. Founded by J.M. Thomson.

1423. *Early Music New Zealand*. Quarterly. Wellington, New Zealand, 1985–87. ISSN 0112-5532.

Popular articles, interviews, and news. An editorial in the December 1987 issue announced the magazine's intention to become a yearbook in 1988 (not seen).

Periodicals 431

1424. *Il flauto dolce: Revista semestrale per lo studio e la pratica della musica antica* [The recorder: twice yearly review for the study and practice of early music]. Twice per year. Rome: Società Italiana del Flauto Dolce, 1971–88. OCLC #10047157. In Italian (abstracts of articles in English). Continued by *Recercare* (item 1437).
   Scholarly and popular articles as well as reviews of books, music, and recordings.

1425. *Flûte à bec & instruments anciens* [Recorder and early instruments]. Quarterly. Nos. 6–31. Saint Malo, France: Association Française pour la Flûte à Bec (later Association pour l'Édition Artistique), 1983–1990. ISSN 0753-9916. Continued *Flûte à bec*. Nos. 1–5. 1981–82. ISSN 0291-0624. In French. Continued by *Crescendo* (item 1421).
   Began as a recorder magazine, then broadened scope to cover other early instruments. Popular articles on repertoire, technique, performance practices, instruments, and instrument making, as well as reviews of books, music, and recordings, interviews, course information, and extensive European concert calendar.

1426. *FoMRHI Quarterly*. Quarterly. 1978– . OCLC #5158452. Memberships and back issues: Fellowship of Makers and Researchers of Historical Instruments, Jeremy Montagu, Hon. Secretary, c/o Faculty of Music, St Aldate's, Oxford OX1 1DB, England. Membership £10.50 (U.K. and surface mail elsewhere), £12 (airmail to Europe), £13.50 (airmail rest of world). Continues *Bulletin and Communications—Fellowship of Makers and Restorers of Historical Instruments*. Quarterly. October 1975–April 1978. OCLC #5158490.
   See appendix 2 for description of the aims of the magazine as well as a listing of relevant articles.

1427. *The Galpin Society Journal*. Annual. 1948– . ISSN 0072-0127. Pauline Holden, Secretary, The Galpin Society, 38 Eastfield Road, Western Park, Leicester LE3 6FE, England. Membership £15 (U.K.), £20 (overseas). Back issues available from University Microfilms International.
   Scholarly articles on musical instruments as well as shorter "Notes and Queries" and book reviews. For bibliographies of articles related to the recorder, see Dale Higbee, "The Galpin Society, its Journal and the

Recorder," *The American Recorder* 6, no. 4 (Fall 1965): 9-10 (covers nos. 1-16 [1948-63]), and "The Recorder and *The Galpin Society Journal*," *The American Recorder* 14, no. 2 (May 1973): 50-51 (covers nos. 17-25 [1964-72]).

1428. *Les goûts réunis*. In French.

Not seen. According to *RILM Abstracts* 1979-01540-bp, *Les goûts réunis* 4 (1978) "is a special issue entirely devoted to the recorder. Contains brief articles by Michelle Tellier, Kees Boeke, Robin Troman, and Jean-Claude Veilhan on diverse aspects of the modern instrument: fingering, breathing, pedagogy, and manufacture. A bibliographic essay by Tellier is included."

1429. *Historical Performance: The Journal of Early Music America*. Twice per year. 1988- . ISSN 0898-8587. Early Music America, Inc., 11421½ Bellflower Road, Cleveland OH 44016. Membership $35 (U.S.A.), $50 (overseas).

The journal of Early Music America, an organization devoted to the promotion of early music performance in North America. Mostly newsworthy and performance-practice articles as well as news and reviews.

1430. *Journal de musique ancienne* [Journal of early music]. Quarterly. 1987- . ISSN 0838-9349. Mostly in French. Studio de Musique Ancienne de Montréal, 3575, boulevard Saint Laurent, bureau 422, Montréal H2X 2T7, Canada. Continues *Le tic-toc choc* (item **1443**).

Scholarly and popular articles, reviews, course information, and Canadian concert calendar.

1431. *Journal of the American Musical Instrument Society*. Annual. 1975- . ISSN 0362-3300. The American Musical Instrument Society, c/o The Shrine to Music Museum, 414 E Clark Street, Vermillion SD 57069-2390.

Scholarly articles, book reviews, and bibliographical materials relating to organology. The quarterly *Newsletter*, also included with membership, contains society news and reports on special courses and museum acquisitions.

1432. *Leading Notes: Journal of the National Early Music Association*. Twice yearly. 1991- . ISSN 0960-6927. £13. Continues *NEMA Journal* (item **1435**).

Popular articles and reviews.

1433. *Musica Antiqua: Actuelle informatie over oude muziek* [Musica Antiqua: current information on early music]. Quarterly.

1983– . ISSN 0771-7016. In Dutch (Flemish). Vlaams Dienstencentrum voor Muziek, Postbus 45, B-3990 Peer, Belgium. BF 700 (Belgium), BF 800 (abroad), BF 900 (airmail).
Scholarly articles, particularly on music history in the Low Countries; artist interviews and profiles; reviews of books, music, and recordings; and news.

1434. *Musica Antiqua*. Monthly (ten issues per year). 1986– . In Spanish. Cardenal González, 38, 14003 Córdoba, Spain.
Scholarly and popular articles (often translated from other languages), discographies, bibliographies, interviews, and reviews of books and recordings.

1435. *NEMA Journal*. London: National Early Music Association, 1983–90. ISSN 0951-6573. Continued by *Leading Notes* (item **1432**).
Popular articles, reviews, and reports.

1436. *Performance Practice Review*. Twice per year. 1988– . ISSN 1044-1638. Music Department, The Claremont Graduate School, 139 E 7th Street, Claremont CA 91711-4405. $18.
Brief, light scholarly articles; reviews of books and recordings. Annual annotated performance-practice bibliography.

1437. *Recercare: Rivista per lo studio e la pratica della musica antica. Organo della Società italiana del flauto dolce* [Recercare: review for the study and practice of early music; organ of the Italian recorder society]. Annual. 1989– . ISSN 1120-5741. In Italian. Libreria Musicale Italiana Editrice, PO Box 198, I-55100 Lucca, Italy. Continues *Il flauto dolce* (item **1424**).
Still oriented towards early instruments but more scholarly.

1438. *The Recorder: Australia's Journal of Recorder and Early Music*. Approximately twice per year. 1985– . ISSN 0816-152X. Subscriptions and back issues: Victorian Recorder Guild, PO Box 85, Fairfield Park, VIC 3078, Australia. A$6.00 per issue.
A lively magazine, imaginatively edited by Jan Epstein (Nos. 1–9) and Malcolm Tattersall (Nos. 10–17). Popular articles, interviews, reviews, and news of the VRG. Good photographs and design. Amazingly, it is

sponsored by a state, not a national, recorder society. This has now left the magazine vulnerable. In issue 17 (September 1993) Tattersall announced his resignation and the president of the VRG predicted a cut-back to publication once a year because of "rising costs and lower membership." Original title (Nos. 1–14): *The Recorder: Journal of the Victorian Recorder Guild*.

1439. *The Recorder Magazine*. Quarterly. 1963– . ISSN 0961-3544. Ruth and Jeremy Burbidge, Scout Bottom Farm, Mytholroyd, Hebden Bridge, West Yorkshire HX7 5JS, England. £2 per issue. Formerly published by Schott, London; for back issues, write to Magnamusic Distributors, Inc., Route 41, Sharon CT 06069.

Succeeded *The Recorder News*. Edited by C. Kenworthy, May 1963–May 1964; Ronald E. Corcoran, August 1964–March 1966; J.M. Thomson, July 1966–May 1967; Ronald E. Corcoran, August 1967–March 1971; J.M. Thomson, June 1971–September 1974; Edgar Hunt, December 1974–December 1990; Eve O'Kelly, March 1991–March 1993; Andrew Mayes, September 1993– . See item **1441**.

The journal has undergone several name changes, and at certain points in its history a single issue has borne conflicting titles on its cover and title page, making the dating of the changes a matter of opinion. Citations to issues of *The Recorder Magazine* in the present bibliography use the form of the title appearing on the masthead.

According to an explanation in 3, no. 5 (March 1970): 179, "Music" was included in the original title (*The Recorder and Music Magazine*, ISSN 0034-1665) to avoid confusion with the many newspapers called *The Recorder* and periodicals on the topic of tape recorders. Beginning with the second volume, the initial "The" was dropped (*Recorder and Music Magazine*). With v. 2, no. 6 (August 1967), the "and" was replaced by an ampersand (*Recorder & Music Magazine*), but it returned with v. 3, no. 12 (December 1971).

In the early 1970s, editor J.M. Thomson attempted to broaden the scope of the magazine (see item **1441**). He planned to cease publication under the title *Recorder & Music Magazine* with the 3, no. 12 (December 1971) issue (the table of contents begins: "In this final issue") and bring out a revamped version of the journal under the title *Fanfare*. Readers (and the SRP) were against the change, and as Thomson later wrote in 4, no. 1 (March 1972), "The opposition proved so strong that the publishers felt they must reverse their decision," so the title remained and the content was essentially unchanged. Soon after the decision was overturned, Thomson founded *Early Music* (item **1422**) and the next year he resigned as editor of *RMM*.

In late 1973, the title was shortened to *Recorder & Music* (ISSN 0306-4409), although the copyright statement continued to read "©Recorder and Music Magazine." In December 1983, the original title (*The Recorder and Music Magazine*) was restored. The "and Music" was finally dropped from the title in March 1990, leaving it *The Recorder Magazine* (ISSN 0961-3544). Hunt explains the change in an Editorial in 9, no. 12 (December 1989): "It was hoped that those two words ["and Music"] might prevent confusion with the world of gramophones and hi-fi; but they have not, and the editorial waste-paper basket is filled with advertisements for all kinds of electronic gadgetry. So we go for the simpler title." With the change of editor in 1991 also came a change in format (from 7" x 9½" to A4), volume frequency (from twelve issues per volume to four), and design. (See the "Publishers' Announcement" in 10, no. 4 [December 1990]: 111 for details.) With the March 1993 issue, Schott abandoned publication of the magazine because of low circulation. Ruth and Jeremy Burbidge bought the magazine soon afterwards and publication was back on schedule in September 1993, missing only a June 1993 issue.

1440. *The Recorder News.* New Malden, 1937/38–1940/41 (4 issues), 1947 (1 issue); London, 1950–March 1963 (generally three times per year; 38 issues). OCLC #28228425. Succeeded by *The Recorder and Music Magazine* (see item 1439).

Edgar Hunt in *Recorder & Music* 4, no. 12 (December 1974) recounts the history of the *News:* "I shared the editing of the first four issues of *The Recorder News* (covering 1937–41) with Carl Dolmetsch, and was responsible for the first post-war issue (no. 5). Then followed a series of News-letters until Mr Kenworthy launched *The Recorder News, New Series* in February 1950, which was eventually incorporated, in May 1963, in the new *Recorder and Music Magazine* under his editorship." A more detailed account appears in item 1441.

1441. Hunt, Edgar. "The Background to The Recorder News and The Recorder and Music Magazine." *The Recorder and Music Magazine* 8, no. 1 (March 1984): 38–39.

Offers details on: the history of the two publications, the succession of editors throughout their runs, and J.M. Thomson's unsuccessful attempt to change the name of *RMM* to *Fanfare*. Letter by C. Kenworthy in 8, no. 2 (June 1984): 72 concerns the frequency of *The Recorder News,* New Series.

1442. *Tibia: Magazin für Holzbläser* [Tibia: magazine for woodwinds]. Three issues per year (1976–86); quarterly (1987–). ISSN 0176-6511. In German (article summaries in English). Hermann Moeck Verlag, Postfach 3131, D-29 231 Celle, Germany. DM 33 (Germany), DM 37 (abroad).

The leading woodwind journal in the world. State-of-the-art articles by top researchers on organology, repertory, performance practice, acoustics, and social history, together with profiles of players of historical and modern woodwinds, as well as reviews of books, music, and recordings, and listings of new publications (including theses and dissertations). Original title: *Tibia: Magazin für Freunde alter und neuer Bläsermusik* [Tibia: magazine for friends of old and new wind music]. A reader questionnaire discussed in 14, no. 2 (1989): 444–48 revealed that no fewer than 78% of the journal's readers play the recorder (6% more than in 1982). Since 1993 the official journal of the European Recorder Teachers Association (ERTA), German Section.

1443. *Le Tic-toc-choc: Journal du Studio de musique ancienne de Montréal* [Le tic-toc-choc: journal of the Montreal early music studio]. Three (later four) issues per year. 1979–1987. ISSN 0227-4299. In French. Continued by *Journal de musique ancienne* (item 1430).

Popular articles, reviews, and news. Volume 4, no. 4 (May 1983) was devoted to the recorder. "Le Tic-toc-choc" is the title of a harpsichord piece by François Couperin.

1444. *Tijdschrift voor oude muziek* [Journal for early music]. Five (later four) times per year. 1986– . ISSN 0920-6649. In Dutch. Stichting Organisatie Oude Muziek (STIMU), Postbus 734, 3500 AS Utrecht, The Netherlands. f35.

Largely a news magazine for the Dutch early music scene. Light articles, interviews, news items, reviews, and summaries of recent early music journals. Regular bibliography of writings about early music (interpreted broadly).

1445. *Woodwind Quarterly.* Quarterly. 1993– . Scott Hirsch, Editor, 1513 Old CC Road, Colville WA 99114-9526. $36 ($46 foreign).

Announced as a "reader-written magazine" that publishes submissions without any editing. Not surprisingly, the first issues were reportedly riddled with typographical errors. Although the title does not make it clear, the magazine seems to be aimed primarily at woodwind makers.

32

Societies

This chapter discusses articles about the history or philosophy of the recorder societies in three English-speaking countries (Australia, Great Britain, and the United States). It excludes news items about the activities of these societies (which are of course frequently found in their respective recorder magazines).

1446. Wyatt, Theo. "Is the Grass Greener on the Other Side?" *The Recorder and Music Magazine* 8, no. 7 (September 1985): 212–13.

   Compares the The American Recorder Society with the Society of Recorder Players (SRP), largely on the basis of financial resources and costs to members. Since members of SRP often donate their services to the society, costs are low compared to their sister society in "that affluent land." Similar arguments appear in a letter from Wyatt in *The American Recorder* 26, no. 4 (November 1985): 183.

AMERICAN RECORDER SOCIETY

The interviews cited below include discussion of the American Recorder Society and its history.

* * Bixler, Martha, and Ken Wollitz. "An Interview with Suzanne Bloch." Cited above as item 937.

* * Davenport, LaNoue. "Erich Katz: A Profile." Cited above as item 1035.

1447. [Krainis, Bernard]. "Amateurs, Professionals, and the ARS." *The American Recorder* 30, no. 4 (November 1989): 151–53.

Discusses the relationship between amateurs and professionals in the American Recorder Society. Argues that both groups are essential to the Society: "a healthy recorder movement is possible only if those who play for pleasure and those who perform and teach for a living can find some mutually beneficial way of coming together." Also speaks out against "recreational noodling" and urges amateurs to work at acquiring the skills necessary to enjoy music making. Finally, calls for the Society to develop a "program that would stimulate and challenge the vast number of potential players out there . . . ." Letters by Frank Plachte and William F. Long in 31, no. 1 (March 1990): 29 and David Keenleyside in 31, no. 2 (June 1990): 33.

* Nagle, Sigrid, with Marcia Blue. "An Interview with Bernard Krainis." Cited above as item **1042**.

1448. "Reflections on the Early Music Scene on the Occasion of AR's Twenty-fifth Anniversary." *The American Recorder* 26, no. 1 (February 1985): 4–11.

Contributions by LaNoue Davenport, Marvin Rosenberg, Suzanne Bloch, Dale Higbee, Colin Sterne, Shelley Gruskin, Susan Brailove, Friedrich von Huene, Bernard Krainis, Martha Bixler, Alexander Silbiger, and Thomas Binkley (all of whom were contributors to the first volume of *The American Recorder*). Mostly short, chatty pieces blending reminiscence with pleasure at present achievements. Three sections stand out: Krainis's criticism of the direction taken by the ARS; and Silbiger's and Binkley's comments on authenticity and the involvement of the recorder in the early music movement.

* Seibert, Peter, and Martha Bixler. "Remembrances of Erich Katz: Interviews with Winifred Jaeger and Hannah Katz." Cited above as item **1038**.

* Wollitz, Ken, and Marcia Blue. "An Interview with LaNoue Davenport." Cited above as item **984**.

SOCIETY OF RECORDER PLAYERS

1449. Hunt, Edgar. "The Society of Recorder Players: How It Began and What It Has Achieved." *Recorder and Music Magazine* 2, no. 1 (March 1966): 23–24; 2, no. 4 (February 1967): 127–28.

Recounts the activities and achievements of the Society, focusing on the period 1937–48.

1450. Wyatt, Theo. "Pioneering Days." *Recorder & Music* 5, no. 11 (September 1977): 353–54.

   Reminiscences of the early days of the Society of Recorder Players, inspired by Wyatt's acquisition of C. Kenworthy's stock of back issues of *The Recorder News* (1946–63).

VICTORIAN RECORDER GUILD

*   Norman, Janet. "I Just Wanted Someone to Play With." Cited above as item **1092**.

1451. Rodgers, Gwen. "Rewards and Challenges: The History of the Victorian Recorder Guild." *The Recorder: Journal of the Victorian Recorder Guild* 14 (December 1991): 25–34.

   An account of the VRG, not to mention the development of the recorder in Victoria and other parts of Australia, over the previous twenty years, interspersed with quotations from the Guild's newsletters. And did they have fun? Too right, mate.

33

The Future of Research on the Recorder

by David Lasocki[1]

Four things have struck me forcibly as we have been working on our guide to writings about the recorder. First, that many people who having been writing about the recorder are woefully ignorant of some other work being done in the field. What would we think of a scientist in England or America who did not read the major German journals? Or, conversely, a German scientist who was unaware of British articles or American dissertations? But recent parallel examples in the recorder world could readily be cited (items **715** and **1184/1185**). Look at the list of foreign subscribers to what we believe to be the leading recorder magazine in the world, *American Recorder*, and you may be surprised at how small that list is, including two in Belgium, one in France, nine in Germany, two in Italy, three in the Netherlands, three in Spain, and so on. Also, few researchers outside Australia seem to have been aware of *The Recorder: Australia's Journal of Recorder and Early Music* before I drew attention to it in my reviews of recent research on the instrument. Unfortunately, that imaginative magazine is now threatened with extinction for lack of readers. I sincerely hope that the present book will both demonstrate what research has been done and encourage researchers to keep up with the field.

The second thing that has struck me about research on the recorder is that we lack overview of the field. Edgar Hunt's *The Recorder and Its Music* (item **12**) and Hans-Martin Linde's *Handbuch des Blockflötenspiels* (item **13**) served something like that function when they were first published in 1962, but neither author has brought his work up to date adequately in subsequent editions, and even the second edition of Linde's book is overdependent on German sources. We desperately need a real history of the recorder. But before one can be written, I suggest, we need a series of good histories of portions of the recorder's history. Eve O'Kelly's *The Recorder Today* (item 819/820) goes some way towards constituting a history of the recorder in the 20th century, although that was not her primary intent. Laurence Pottier's dissertation, *La répertoire de la flûte à bec en France a l'époque baroque (musique profane)* (item 1193), does fulfill its intent of shedding light on a previously almost unknown corner of recorder history: the instrument's role in France in the Baroque era.

I have attempted a similar task myself. In my doctoral dissertation, *Professional Recorder Players in England, 1540-1740* (item 72), I looked at a portion of the history of the recorder in England from the unfamiliar primary viewpoint of recorder players. Who played the recorder, where, when, for whom, and even why? What instruments did they use? What music did they perform? What were the relationships among players, instrument makers, composers, patrons, and publishers? The approach of combining archival and musical research yielded insights into the size and nature of the repertory; the dependence of the publishers on music written by and for professionals; the changes in musical style, instrumentation, and performance practices that came to a country with the many foreign composers who made their living primarily as performers; and the attractions and limitations of the recorder itself. I mention this study not only because I am the most familiar with it but because I would like to suggest it as a model for one type of research. I hasten to add that I do not take credit for thinking of the approach. In the late 1970s, Frans Brüggen decided he wanted to make a movie—technically, I suppose, a documentary—about recorder players of the past. Realizing that we know little about those players, he commissioned researchers in several European countries to undertake research on the players in their own countries. Unfortunately, mine was the only study completed. I therefore encourage researchers to go and prepare similar studies for other countries—Germany, Italy, the Netherlands, Spain, etc.

The third thing that has struck me about research on the recorder is that its quality has vastly improved over the last decade or so. One has only to look at the work of such people as Rob van Acht, Maurice Byrne, Tula Giannini, Ruth van Baak Griffioen, Bruce Haynes, Michael Marissen, John Martin, Eve O'Kelly, Laurence Pottier, Patricia Ranum, Jeanne Swack, William Waterhouse, Thiemo Wind, and Phillip Young, who have truly advanced our knowledge and also point the way for the future. Among the most important characteristics of their studies are:

- Extreme thoroughness
- A mastery of archives
- Bibliographic control—that is, knowledge of all the important relevant sources in several languages
- A deep knowledge of the period and of the individual countries in question
- Imagination
- Open-mindedness

Some but not all of this work was done for academic theses or dissertations. This is not surprising, as such documents give researchers built-in advice, a chance to work on a large study, and an incentive to finish it. Academic training is helpful but not essential for good research; a great deal can be picked up through experience. Access to good libraries, however, is essential, both for original sources such as scores and archival records, and for secondary materials such as books, theses, and journals. To come back to an earlier point, let us not imagine any longer than good research on the recorder can be done without American dissertations or subscriptions to *Tibia*. For secondary sources, American music libraries still have a considerable edge over European ones.

The fourth thing that has struck me about research on the recorder is that, in this day and age, some people are still uncomfortable with the very idea of it. For a start, musicologists are discouraged from doing such research because it could be viewed as a fringe subject, not serious, not something that looks good on your résumé when you are trying to land a job. Ruth van Baak Griffioen has given me permission to say that she was discouraged from pursuing her work on Jacob van Eyck for a Ph.D. in musicology, and I know of several other such examples. In addition, some recorder publications are uncomfortable with the trappings of scholarship. For example, in 1990 under its new editor, Benjamin Dunham, *The American Recorder* abandoned the use of footnotes/endnotes, which, I am told, the Board of The American Recorder Society believed to scare off readers. The final straw was apparently an article co-written by me (item 905) which had a block of almost three pages of endnotes. Instead, *AR* now offers selected bibliographies. (One recent article with an extensive list of sources, however, has forced a capitulation to footnotes—or rather, sidenotes; see item 715.) I hope we can experiment with better ways to present scholarly research to a general public.

Let me now suggest research that needs to be done on various aspects of the recorder. First, the recorder's repertory, about the lack of which one always hears complaints. Yes, perhaps there are not enough stunning solo works to satisfy the voracious appetites of the enormous numbers of recorder virtuosi today. But it is abundantly clear that the recorder featured in a great many early compositions, especially vocal ones, that have not yet been cataloged or made available to the public. Two recent catalogs show what can be discovered by specialists in a particular part of the repertory: that by Diane Parr Walker and Paul Walker of German sacred polyphonic vocal music between Schütz and Bach[2] and that of Ingo Gronefeld on flute concertos (item 1143). Unknown compositions can even be found among the works of well-known composers such as Telemann (see item 1303). Since the recorder has not yet attracted a Frans Vester[3] or a Bruce Haynes[4] to catalog its entire (or early) repertory even adequately, let us at least begin with parts of the repertory. Would-be bibliographers, please note: a good bibliography, whether of writings or of music, can be done well only when the items in question are examined; cobbling together publishers' catalogs is a dangerous waste of everyone's time.

Once we have identified more of the repertory, we need more first-class analyses of it or commentary on it. Swack on Telemann sonatas (item 1301), Roderick Arran on *Muziek voor*

Altblokfluit by Rob du Bois (item **1337**), and Christian Chandelier and David Neumeyer on Hindemith's trio (items **1363** and **1362**) have been rare exceptions.

Second, the recorder players. We need more studies of historical performers (both professional and amateur) in a number of countries in their context of performing groups and situations. Who did play the recorder, when, where, why, and for whom?

Third, the recorder makers. We need more biographical studies of them, in particular pointing up how they fit in with the players, or in other words, the market for their work.

Fourth, the instruments. We need to make sure we have completely identified the surviving historical recorders, then we need to measure them and classify them—by maker, type, and size. We need thorough studies of the recorder in works of art. Then we need to relate the iconographic information to the physical, in the way that Jane Bowers did in her study of the Baroque flute.[5] Eventually we may be able to write a detailed history of the development of recorder construction. Iconographic research should also shed more light on the origins and early history of the recorder—still rather mysterious.

Fifth, performance practices. This is an area in which we would dearly like to know more, but probably never will know much, unless more treatises turn up. Professional musicians did not like to give away their trade secrets to the layman. Yet Patricia Ranum has been able to shed new light on tired old information about the French articulation syllables (see item **713**), and a study-in-progress by Marianne Mezger promises to do the same for English ornaments.[6] Above all else in recorder research, we need more revolutionaries like Ranum—and Manfred Brach—to shake us out of our complacency. The "authenticity debate" initiated by another revolutionary, Richard Taruskin, promises to modify our attitudes about performance practice and to inspire imaginative performances combining styles both historical and modern, serious and popular (Hesperus's "Crossover" music has made a good start along these lines).

Sixth, the symbolism of the recorder. Abundant evidence has survived about the way people saw the recorder in works of art, vocal music, and theater music in various countries. It would not take much work to tie it together.

Seventh, the acoustics of the recorder. For his dissertation (item 411, soon to be a book) John Martin both summarized past research and performed original research of his own. Let it be an inspiration for experimental research into the recorder.

In short, there is much work to be done. Let's do it.

NOTES

1. This chapter is based on my essay "Gaps in Our Knowledge of the Recorder in the 17th Century and How We Could Fill Them" (in item 63).

2. *German Sacred Polyphonic Vocal Music Between Schütz and Bach: Sources and Critical Editions*, Detroit Studies in Music Bibliography, 67 (Warren, MI: Harmonie Park Press, 1992). This book has many references to the recorder, under its own name or masquerading as a flute.

3. *Flute Repertoire Catalogue: 10,000 Titles* (London: Musica Rara, 1967); *Flute Music of the 18th Century: An Annotated Bibliography* (Monteux, France: Musica Rara, 1985).

4. *Music for Oboe, 1650-1800: A Bibliography*, 2nd ed., rev. & expanded (Berkeley, CA: Fallen Leaf Press, 1992).

5. "New Light on the Development of the Transverse Flute Between About 1650 and About 1770," *Journal of the American Musical Instrument Society* 3 (1979): 5-56.

6. For a preliminary report, see her article "Performance Practice for Recorder Players," *Leading Notes: Journal of the National Early Music Association* 7 (Spring 1994): 13-16, which came out too late for inclusion in the body of this book.

Appendix 1

Theses, Dissertations, and Similar Works Not Consulted

Foreign dissertations are difficult to obtain in the United States, and for that reason the following were left unexamined and unannotated and have been relegated to an appendix.

1452. Beyaert, Thérèse. *Etude analytique et descriptive de la collection de flûtes à bec conservée au Musée Instrumental du Conservatoire Royal de Musique de Bruxelles.* Mémoire de licence, Université Catholique de Louvain-la-Neuve, 1964.

1453. Bourguignon, Jacqueline. *Jacques Hotteterre le Romain (1680–1761), flûtiste de la Chambre du Roi.* Mémoire de licence, Université Catholique de Louvain-la-Neuve, 1973.

1454. Davis, Alan. *The Recorder in the Baroque Orchestra.* Ph.D. dissertation, Birmingham.

1455. Delvigne, Isabelle. *Le renouveau de la flûte à bec au XXe siècle. Un acteur de ce renouveau: Hans-Martin Linde.* Mémoire de licence, Université Catholique de Louvain-la-Neuve, 1984.

1456. Den Hul, Dick van. *Klokkenkunst te Utrecht tot 1700: Met bijzondere aandacht voor het aandeel hierin van Jhr. Jacob van Eyck.* Ph.D. dissertation, Rijksuniversiteit Utrecht, 1982.

Appendix 1: Theses and Dissertations Not Consulted

1457. Denis, Sandra. *De Blokfluit in de twingste eeuw.* Licentiaatsverhandeling, Katholieke Universiteit Leuven, 1985.

1458. Ehrlich, Robert. *An Ethnomusicological Study of a Modern Performing Tradition in Western Art Music: The "Dutch School" of Recorder Playing. Recorder Tuition in Dutch Conservatories: Transcription and Analysis of Three Performances of "English Nightingale."* Two M.Phil. theses, King's College, Cambridge University, 1989.

1459. Fahrnberger, Elisabeth. *Die Verwendung der Blöckflöte bei Georg Friedrich Händel* [Georg Friedrich Händel's use of the recorder]. M.A. dissertation, Performance practice, Hochschule für Musik und darstellende Kunst, Wien, 1982. 68 p.

1460. Feldhaus, Hannelore. *Über den Instrumentenbauer Robert Wijne und seine zuletzt aufgefundene Sopran-Blockflöte.* Hausarbeit für Staatliche Musiklehrer (Prüfungsamt beim Regierungspräsidenten in Münster), 1977.

1461. Fussenegger, Gernot. *Holzflöten und ihr Bau am Beispiel einer Blockflöte.* Maschinenschriftliche Hausarbeit im Rahmen des Lehramtstudiums, Wien, 1973.

1462. Göring, Lieselotte. *Die Stellung der Blockflöte im Musikleben des 20. Jahrhunderts.* Ph.D. dissertation, University of Halle, 1974.

1463. Greenberg, Susan Gloria. *The Treatment of the Flutes and Recorders in the Bach Cantatas.* Master's thesis, University of California at Los Angeles, 1970.

1464. Hübner, Eckart. *Die Blockflöte in der deutschen Jugendsmusikbewegung* [The recorder in the German youth music movement]. Diploma, Musicology, Hochschule für Musik und Theater, Hannover, 1983.

1465. Jenkins, David. *Woodwind Instruments in France 1690–1750—Their Makers, Theoreticians, and Music*. Ph.D. dissertation, Edinburgh University, 1973. 2 vols.

1466. Koch, Hans Oskar. *Die Spezialtypen der Blas-instrumente in der 1. Hälfte des 18. Jahrhunderts im deutschen Sprachraum*. Staatsexamensarbeit, Hochschule für Musik und Theater, Mannheim, Germany, 1979.

1467. Landkammer, Ulrike. *Zur Aufführungspraxis der französischen Musik für Bläser im beginnenden 18. Jahrhundert*. Wien: Hochschule für Musik und darstellende Kunst, maschinenschriftliche Hausarbeit im Fach Instrumentalmusikerziehung, 1979.

1468. Omitted.

1469. Loose, Ghislaine. *Fluitsonates van J.B. Loeillet*. Licentiaatsverhandling, Ryksuniversiteit Gent, 1970.

1470. Maass, Ulrike. *Die Flötensammlung des Oberösterreichischen Landesmuseums. Verzeichnis und entwicklungsgeschichtliche Untersuchungen*. Salzburg: Hochschule "Mozarteum," Abteilung Musikpädagogik, Hausarbeit, 1977.

1471. Meierott, Lenz. *Die geschichtliche Entwicklung der kleinen Flötentypen und ihre Verwendung in der Musik des 17. und 18. Jahrhunderts*. [The historical development of small flutes and their employment in the music of the 17th and 18th centuries]. Ph.D. dissertation (Musicology), University of Wurzburg, 1973.

1472. Moeck, Hermann. *Ursprung und Tradition der Kernspaltflöten des Europaischen Volkstums und das Herkommen der musikgeschichtlichen Kernspaltflötentype*. Dissertation, Göttingen, 1951.

1473. Pottier, Laurence. *La flûte à bec en Italie au XVIe siècle*. Maîtrise d'education musicale, Université de Paris IV-Sorbonne, 1986. 186 p. + catalog of iconography.

Appendix 1: Theses and Dissertations Not Consulted 449

1474. Robert, Cécile. *La redécouverte de la flûte à bec en France au XXe siècle*. Maîtrise d'education musicale, Université de Paris IV-Sorbonne, n.d. 154 p.

1475. Roos, Frédéric de. *Quelques aspects du répertoire de la flûte à bec au XVIIIe siècle*. Mémoire de licence, Université Libre de Bruxelles, 1980.

1476. Rummel, Luise. *Zur Wiederbelebung der Blockflöte im 20. Jahrhundert: Die Anfänge des Blockflötenbaus in Markneukirchen und Umgebung*. Diplomarbeit, Leipzig, 1977.

1477. Schwarz, Roswitha. *Die Renaissance der Blockflöte im 19. und 20. Jahrhundert* [The revival of the recorder in the 19th and 20th centuries]. M.A. dissertation (Music education), Hochschule für Musik und darstellende Kunst, Graz, 1982. 42 p.

1478. Shanahan, Ian. [master's thesis on recorder multiphonics]

1479. Shanahan, Ian. [undergraduate thesis on recorder articulation, vibrato, etc.]

1480. Stratford, Michael D. *A Critical Survey of the Recorder and its Music in England, c.1675–c.1790*. M.Phil. thesis, Hull University, 1984.

1481. Strong, Deborah. *A Review of Recorder Music by Australian Composers*. Thesis, Queensland University, 1980.

1482. Woodhill, Yollande Vanessa. *An Historical and Analytical Study of Renaissance Music for the Recorder and its Influence on Later Repertoire*. M.A. thesis, University of Wollongong (Australia), 1986.

Appendix 2

Articles in *FoMRHI Quarterly*

"FoMRHI" at first stood for Fellowship of Makers and Restorers of Historical Instruments; later "Restorers" was replaced by "Researchers." The intention of the *Bulletin*, later the *Quarterly*, was explained by Jeremy Montagu in the first issue. The circulation to FoMRHI members of the Communications (as the articles are called) "will not constitute formal publication and the authors are welcome to publish them properly elsewhere in due course. . . . The idea behind [them] is (a) to fly 'kites' so that authors may receive comments from other members on their ideas . . . (b) to pass information to other members; (c) to make information known quickly and informally in advance of proper publication" (p. 2). The Communications are reproduced from authors' typescripts with no editing for content, style, spelling, writing, or typographical errors.

As these Communications are not formally published, then, we have relegated almost all of them to this appendix. In a few cases in which the important subject matter of a Communication has not been published elsewhere, we have cited it as an item in the main part of the book (see items **191–92, 332, 351, 362, 376, 459,** and **1385**). Where the author has published the subject matter elsewhere, we have included a note on the relevant Communication in the citation for the item (see items **382** and **383**).

1483. Bigio, Robert. "Making Woodwind Keys." *FoMRHI Quarterly* 18 (January 1980): 40–44 (Communication No. 254). In Dutch as: "Doe het zelf kleppen voor houten blaasinstrumenten." *FoMRHI Quarterly* 22 (September 1980): 14–21.

Appendix 2: Articles in FoMRHI Quarterly

1483.1 Bouterse, Jan. "The Descriptions of the Dutch Recorders in the Collection of the Haags Gemeentemuseum." *FoMRHI Quarterly* 63 (April 1991): 51–54 (Communication no. 1037).

1483.2 Bouterse, Jan. "The Dutch Recorders and Traverse Flutes of the 17th and 18th Century: List of Instruments July 1991." *FoMRHI Quarterly* 64 (July 1991): 33–37 (Communication no. 1052).

1483.3 Bouterse, Jan. "Summary: 'De blokfluit: handleiding voor aanschaf, onderhoud, bijstemmen en kleine reparaties' 1990." *FoMRHI Quarterly* 63 (April 1991): 55 (Communication no. 1038). English summary of item 485.

1484. Cameron, Rod. "Drilling Deep Holes Accurately in Wood." *FoMRHI Quarterly* 15 (April 1979): 49–54 (Communication No. 197).

1485. Cameron, Rod. "Profile Turning of Reamer Blanks for Use in Woodwinds." *FoMRHI Quarterly* 8 (July 1977): 38–44 (Communication No. 70).

1486. Cronin, Robert H. "More Thoughts on Woodwind Bore Measurement." *FoMRHI Quarterly* 49 (October 1987): 24 (Communication No. 828).

1487. Desforges, A.N. "Artificial Ivory Rings for Woodwind Instruments." *FoMRHI Quarterly* 46 (January 1987): 51 (Communication No. 780).

1488. Drake, Julian. "A Temporary Debarockant Mock-Renaissance Cuneiform Recorder Windway Modifactory Acoustic Device." *FoMRHI Quarterly* 23 (April 1981): 37 (Communication No. 331).

1489. Esteves Pereira, L.A. "Artificial Ivory Made From Milk." *FoMRHI Quarterly* 15 (April 1979): 59 (Communication No. 201).

1490. Folkers, Catherine. "More on Dead Elephants." *FoMRHI Quarterly* 59 (April 1990): 38–39 (Communication No. 975).

1491. Hachez, R. "An Ivory Substitute." *FoMRHI Quarterly* 5 (October 1976): 25 (Communication No. 35).

1491.1 Haynes, Bruce. "Appeal for Pitches of Original Traversos and Recorders." *FoMRHI Quarterly* 63 (April 1991): 56-60 (Communication no. 1039).

1492. Haynes, Bruce. " . . . In Death I Sing." *FoMRHI Quarterly* 53 (October 1988): 25–26 (Communication No. 889). See also the response by Jonathan Swayne in 55 (April 1989): 22 (Communication No. 908).

1493. Haynes, Bruce, and Ardal Powell. "Urgent Communication No. on Ivory." *FoMRHI Quarterly* 54 (January 1989): 64–65 (Communication No. 903). See also 56 (July 1989): 40 (Communication No. 928) and 57 (October 1989): 12 (Communication No. 940).

1494. Heide, Geert Jan van der. "Effects Associated with Tuning Instruments Having a Conical Bore and Rules of Thumb Concerning the Intonation of Historical Wind Instruments." *FoMRHI Quarterly* 31 (April 1983): 48–50 (Communication No. 457). Untitled reply by Bob Marvin in 33 (October 1983): 34–35 (Communication No. 492).

1495. Jenkins, Simon. "Welcome Back the Hunter—Income from the Ivory Trade is the Best Assurance for the Survival of Elephants." *FoMRHI Quarterly* 72 (July 1993): 17-18 (Communication No. 1173).

1496. Karp, Cary. "Accuracy of Measurement of Woodwinds and the 'Exact Copy.'" *FoMRHI Quarterly* 9 (October 1977): 47–48 (Communication No. 84).

1497. Karp, Cary. "Devices for Measuring the Undercutting of Woodwind Toneholes." 23 (April 1981): 39–46 (Communication No. 333). In Dutch as: "Methoden voor het meten van ondersneden vingergaten bij houtblaasinstrumenten." *FoMRHI Quarterly* 27 (November 1982): 13–16.

1498. Karp, Cary. "Woodwind Bore Measuring Tools." *FoMRHI Quarterly* 45 (October 1986): 50–54 (Communication No. 762).

1499. Karp, Cary. "Woodwind Bore Oil." *FoMRHI Quarterly* 27 (April 1982): 20–24 (Communication No. 406). Anonymous reply in 35 (April 1984): 50 (Communication No. 533).

1500. Lewin, Greg. "A Proposed Device for Woodwind Bore Measurement and Analysis." *FoMRHI Quarterly* 27 (April 1982): 17–18 (Communication No. 404).

1500.1 Loretto, Alec V. "How Recorders Can Improve with Time." *FoMRHI Quarterly* 62 (January 1991): 18 (Communication no. 1019).

1501. Marvin, Bob. "The Fornication of Recorder Windways." *FoMRHI Quarterly* 35 (April 1984): 48–49 (Communication No. 532).

1502. Marvin, Bob. "Making Reamers on a Shoestring." *FoMRHI Quarterly* 14 (January 1979): 37–38 (Communication No. 180).

1503. Marvin, Bob. "Nuts, Bolts, and Plugs." *FoMRHI Quarterly* 12 (July 1978): 42 (Communication No. 146).

1504. Marvin, Bob. "Reamer-Saving Counterbores." *FoMRHI Quarterly* 41 (October 1985): 20 (Communication No. 648).

1505. Marvin, Bob. "Tuning Recorders." *FoMRHI Quarterly* 41 (October 1985): 23–24 (Communication No. 652).

1506. Miller, Theo. "Restoration of a Recorder Edge." *FoMRHI Quarterly* 24 (July 1981): 18–19 (Communication No. 353).

1507. Montagu, Jeremy. "Don't Go Overboard About Ivory." *FoMRHI Quarterly* 57 (October 1989): 13–14 (Communication No. 941).

1508. Montagu, Jeremy. "What Should Measuring Tools be Made of?" *FoMRHI Quarterly* 44 (July 1986): 33–36 (Communication No. 733).

1509. Powell, Ardal. "Ivory." *FoMRHI Quarterly* 54 (January 1989): 58–63 (Communication No. 902).

1510. Powell, Ardal. "Plastic, Ivory, Gold and South Africa." *FoMRHI Quarterly* 55 (April 1989): 23–24 (Communication No. 909).

1511. Powell, Ardal. "Throwing Ivory Overboard." *FoMRHI Quarterly* 59 (April 1990): 31–37 (Communication No. 974).

1512. Ransley, Michael. "Authentic Methods of Making Woodwinds." *FoMRHI Quarterly* 73 (October 1993): 47–49 (Communication No. 1199).

1513. Raudonikas, F. "Method of Woodwind Frequency Measurement Data Treatment." *FoMRHI Quarterly* 12 (July 1978): 38–41 (Communication No. 145).

1514. Schultze, Bernhard. "A Contact-Free Woodwind Bore Measurement Tool." *FoMRHI Quarterly* 59 (April 1990): 26–27 (Communication No. 970).

1515. Segerman, Ephraim. "Early 18th Century English Pitches, Especially 'Consort Flute Pitch' and 'Church Pitch of f.'" *FoMRHI Quarterly* 67 (April 1992): 54–56 (Communication No. 1100).

1516. Segerman, E. "Wood Contraction and Instrument Bores." *FoMRHI Quarterly* 31 (April 1983): 54–55 (Communication No. 460).

Appendix 2: Articles in FoMRHI Quarterly 455

1517. Stevens, W.R. "GPS Agencies Artificial Ivory." *FoMRHI Quarterly* 55 (April 1989): 24 (Communication No. 910).

1518. Stroom, Charles. "Some Measurement Techniques for Recorders." *FoMRHI Quarterly* 40 (July 1985): 73 (Communication No. 639). Includes answers to comments by Jeremy Montagu.

1519. Stroom, Charles. Untitled communication on measuring recorders. *FoMRHI Quarterly* 45 (October 1986): 55–57 (Communication No. 763).

1520. Swayne, Jon. "Another Reamer-Saving Counterbore." *FoMRHI Quarterly* 42 (January 1986): 30–31 (Communication No. 675).

1521. Swayne, J. "Teaching Woods to Sing." *FoMRHI Quarterly* 66 (January 1992): 27 (Communication No. 1077).

1522. Taggart, Stephen. "A Substitute for Ivory." *FoMRHI Quarterly* 4 (July 1976): 18 (Communication No. 24).

1523. Whinray, Paul. "A Shaper for Recorder Block Blanks." *FoMRHI Quarterly* 11 (April 1978): 51–52 (Communication No. 122).

1524. Whinray, Paul. "Woodwind Measurements." *FoMRHI Quarterly* 11 (April 1978): 49–50 (Communication No. 121).

1525. Willetts, Carl. "Moisture Blocking of Fipple Flutes." *FoMRHI Quarterly* 32 (July 1983): 29 (Communication No. 470).

1526. Willetts, Carl. "Woodwind Bore Oil." *FoMRHI Quarterly* 32 (July 1983): 39 (Communication No. 475).

1527. Williams, Ken. "Bore Gauging—Some Ideas and Suggestions." *FoMRHI Quarterly* 45 (October 1986): 48–49 (Communication No. 761).

Appendix 3

Articles in *Bouwbrief*

Bouwbrief is a newsletter in Dutch for instrument makers, originally published by Werkgroep Bouwerskontakt van de Vereniging voor Huismuziek, Utrecht. It is now published by Werkgroep Bouwerskontakt van Huismuziek, Vereniging voor muziek en instrumentenbouw, Keizerstraat 3, 3512 EA Utrecht; phone 030-302301; fax 030-300280. Editor, Arnold Riesthuis.

A "manifesto" in issue no. 1 (early 1975) proposed the following coverage: "algemeen, literatuur, leveranciers, ervaringen, bewerkingsmethoden, materialen, cursussen, werkgroepen, adressen tekeningen, adressen bouwpakketten, beoordelingen bouwpakketten, inkoop materiaal/gereedschap, rietenboek, bouwervaring per instrument, excursies, vragen en antwoorden" [general, literature, suppliers, experiences, methods of working materials, materials, workshops, study groups, addresses for drawings, addresses for building kits, reviews of building kits, purchase of materials/tools, reeds, building experience by instrument, trips, questions and answers].

1528. Acht, Rob van. "De bouw van houten blaasinstrumenten in Nederland in de periode 1670 tot 1820" [Woodwind instrument making in the Netherlands, 1670–1820]. 49 (May 1988): 3–13; 50 (August 1988): 3–10. [See also item 183.]

1529. Assendelft, Leen van. "Het korrigeren van te lage blokfluiten" [The correction of recorders that are too flat]. 15 (December 1979): 16.

Appendix 3: Articles in Bouwbrief

1530. Bigio, Robert. "Doe het zelf; kleppen voor houten blaasinstrumenten." 22 (September 1980): 14–21 [translation of "Making Woodwind Keys," *FoMRHI Quarterly* 18 (January 1980): 40–44 (Communication No. 254)].

1531. Boelens, Ben. "Ervaring met het korrigeren van te lage blokfluiten volgens Leen van Assendelft" [Experience with the correction of recorders that are too flat, according to Leen van Assendelft]. 17 (May 1980): 29.

1532. Bouterse, Jan. "De gulden snede in de fluitenbouw" [The golden section in recorder making]. 18 (August 1980): 18–19.

1533. Bouterse, Jan. "Korrekties op bestaande blokfluit- en traverso-tekeningen" [Corrections to existing recorder and traverso drawings]. 19 (November 1980): 5.

1534. Bouterse, Jan. "Gereedschap voor de blokfluitbouw: een goede kernspleetvijl" [Tools for recorder making: a good windway file]. 23 (December 1981): 13–14.

1535. Bouterse, Jan. "Maten van een barok-altblokfluit in moderne stemming" [Measurements of a Baroque alto recorder at modern pitch]. 55 (November 1989): 12–13.

1536. Bouterse, Jan. "Inventarisatie muziekinstrumenten in Nederlandse musea" [Inventory of musical instruments in Netherlands museums]. 62 (August 1991): 20.

1537. Bouterse, Jan. "Drie Baroksopraanblokfluiten van Richard Haka: Tips voor het maken van een copie" [Three Baroque soprano recorders by Richard Haka: tips for making a copy]. 70 (August 1993): 8–14.

1538. Bouterse, Jan. "Meetgegevens fluiten / Enkele hulpmiddelen voor het maken van blokfluiten" [Measuring data of flutes / a few expedients for the making of recorders]. 10 (April 1978): 19–21.

1539. Bouterse, Jan. "Nederlandse houtblaasinstrumenten in Amerikaanse collecties" [Netherlands woodwind instruments in American collections]. 67 (November 1992): 3–10.

1540. Bouterse, Jan. "Blokfluitbouw: mijn belangrijkste fouten en de korrekties" [Recorder making: my most important mistakes and their correction]. 23 (December 1981): 14–16.

1541. Bouterse, Jan. "Enkele hulpmiddelen voor het maken van blokfluiten / Meetgegevens fluiten" [A few expedients for the making of recorders / Measuring data of flutes]. 11 (August 1978): 11–12.

1542. Brach, Manfred. "Abraham van Aardenberg's Zeichenmethode" [Abraham van Aardenberg's drawing method]. 68 (February 1993): 3–5.

1543. Deerenberg, Baldrick. "Blokfluitbouw volgens 18e eeuwse principes" [Recorder making according to 18th-century principles]. 46 (August 1987): 30–31.

1544. Eijken, Eugène. "Stemmingen en klankbeïnvloeding bij de blokfluit" [Pitches and what has an influence on the sound of the recorder]. 46 (August 1987): 29.

1545. Hamoen, Dirk Jacob. "Blokfluittechnologie uit de 18e eeuw: Verslag van de cursus gegeven door Sverre Kolberg van 31 maart–3 april j.l." [Recorder technology from the 18th century: report of the workshop given by Sverre Kolberg, 31 March–3 April this year]. 43 (November–December 1986): 28–29.

1546. Heide, Geert Jan van der. "De kleppen van blaasinstrumenten, een overzicht" [The keys of wind instruments: an overview]. 61 (May 1991): 3–5.

1547. Heide, Geert Jan v.d. "Houtsoorten—gebruikt en bruikbaar voor blaasinstrumenten" [Kinds of wood—used and useable for wind instruments]. 7/8 (September 1977), Bijlage III (6 p.).

1548. Hendriks, Jan. "Het labium van de blokfluit—enkele opmerkingen" [The labium of the recorder: a few remarks]. 15 (December 1979): 20-21.

1549. Karp, Cary. "Methoden voor het meten van ondersneden vingergaten bij houtblaasinstrumenten." 27 (November 1982): 13-16 [translation of "Devices for Measuring the Undercutting of Woodwind Toneholes," *FoMRHI Quarterly* 23 (April 1981): 39-46 (Communication No. 333)].

1550. Kolberg, Sverre. "Figurazione I: Een inleiding in de kunst van het smeden" [Figurations I: an introduction to the art of welding]. 49 (May 1988): 14-18. "Figurazione delle cose invisibili II" [Figurations of invisible things II]. 50 (August 1988): 20-26. Reactions by Jan Bouterse and Leen van Assendelft, 30-32; reply by Kolberg in 51 (November 1988): 22.

1551. Kolberg, Sverre. "Alternatieve blokfluitbouw" [Alternative recorder making]. 40 (February 1986): 12-13.

1552. Lankhof, G.F. "Het bouwen van een basblokfluit" [The making of a bass recorder]. 69 (May 1993): 3-4.

1553. Loretto, Alec. "Op zoek naar een blokfluit met meer uitdrukkingsmogelijkheden." 19 (November 1980): 14-15; 20 (February 1981): 15-19; 21 (May 1981): 24-28 [translation of "Recorder Modifications: In Search of the Expressive Recorder," *Early Music* 1, no. 2 (April 1973): 107-9; 1, no. 3 (July 1973): 147-51; 1, no. 4 (October 1973): 229-31].

1554. Loretto, Alec V. "Where Have All the Ganassi Recorders Gone?" [interview with him in English by Ed van Weerd]. 59 (November 1990): 7-10.

1555. Moonen, Toon. "Bouwbeschrijving van het franse flageoletfluitje" [Making description of the small French flageolet]. 13 (May 1979): 29–33.

1556. Moonen, Toon. "Tekening + beschrijving French flageolet" [Drawing + description of French flageolet]. 12 (January 1979): 7–8.

1557. Moonen, Toon. "Voorbereidingen voor de blokfluitbouwkursus" [Preparations for the recorder making course]. 19 (November 1980): 20–22.

1558. Moonen, Toon. "Spitten en graven in de blokfluitbouw" ['Digging deep' in recorder making]. 16 (February 1980): 14–16.

1559. Moonen, Toon. "Het omrekenen van houtblaasinstrumenten" [The scaling of woodwind instruments]. 51 (November 1988): 19–20. German translation, "Das Umrechnen von Holzblasinstrumenten," *Tibia* 14, no. 1 (1989): 347–49 (see item 451).

1560. Nieuwhof, Ben. "Ervaringen met het omrekenen van mensuren van blokfluiten en traversos" [Experiences with the measuring of recorders and traversos]. 69 (May 1993): 5–6; some corrections in 71 (November 1993): 15.

1561. Nieuwhof, Ben. "Hoe gebruik ik een PC om blok- of andere fluiten te stemmen?" [How do I use a PC to tune recorders and other flutes?]. 64 (February 1992): 3–5.

1562. Ruyten, Hans. "Blokfluit-technologie" [Recorder technology]. 44 (February 1987): 12–13.

1563. Simons, J.A., and Paul Beekhuizen. "Reactie op: Spitten en graven in de blokfluitbouw door Ton Moonen" [Reactions to: 'Digging deep' in recorder making by Toon Moonen]. 17 (May 1980): 6–7.

Appendix 3: Articles in Bouwbrief

1564. Stroom, Charles. "Een Terton-blokfluit van het Haags Gemeentemuseum" [A Terton recorder in the Gemeentemuseum, The Hague]. 63 (October 1991): 7–8.

1565. Weber, Rainer. "Overdenkingen bij de restauratie van houten blaasinstrumenten" [Reflections while restoring woodwind instruments]. 40 (February 1986): 3–4; 41 (May–June 1986): 3–6; 42 (August–September 1986): 3–7; 43 (November–December 1986): 3–9.

1566. Weber, Rainer. "Hoe betrouwbar zijn de meetgegevens van houtenblaasinstrumenten?" [How reliable are the found measurements of woodwind instruments?]. 46 (August 1987): 3–7; 47 (November 1987): 3–6; 48 (February 1988): 3–5.
The original German text can be ordered from Huismuziek.

1567. Willoughby, Andrew. "Het intoneren van blokfluiten—antwoorden op mijn vragen." 37 (May 1985): 11–16. [Translated from "Recorder Voicing—Answers to my Questions." *FoMRHI Quarterly* 34 (January 1984): 57–69 (Communication No. 514), including the untitled reply by Angelo Zaniol in 35 (April 1984): 41–43 (Communication No. 529) and another comment by Bob Marvin].

Appendix 4

Conservatory Master's Theses

1568. "Hochschulschriften" [Conservatory master's theses]. *Tibia* 19, no. 1 (1994): 56.

   A useful section of *Tibia* that we hope will be continued. Lists the following relevant term papers, as well as others on the recorder in music education (housed at the libraries of the conservatories in question):

HOCHSCHULE FÜR MUSIK FREIBURG (Schwarzwaldstraße 14, 79102 Freiburg, Germany)

1569. Daeublin, Anette. "Jürg Baur: Concerto da camera" (1990).

1570. Kahl, Anne-Elisabeth. "Die Shakuhachi und ihr Einfluß auf moderne japanische Blockflötenkompositionen" [The shakuhachi and its influence on modern Japanese recorder compositions] (1989).

1571. Weidel, Evelyn. "Blockflöte und Traversflöte in der französischen Kantate des 18. Jhs." [Recorder and flute in the 18th-Century French cantata] (1989).

FOLKWANG-HOCHSCHULE ESSEN (Abt. Duisburg, Düsseldorfer Straße 19, 47051 Duisburg, Germany)

1572. Gamm, Norbert. "Des Klanges Süßigkeit—Idiom und Klischee in der Blockflötenmusik" [The sweetness of the sound: idiom and cliché in recorder music] (1989).

1573. Machan, Katja. "Das Pastorale in der Instrumentalmusik des Barock unter Berücksichtigung der Blockflöten-

Appendix 4: Conservatory Master's Theses 463

literatur" [The pastoral in Baroque instrumental music with special consideration of the recorder literature] (1990).

1574. Rosseborg, Theres. "Barocke Stimmungen unter Berücksichtigung der besonderen Problematik des Zusammenspiels von Blockflöte und Cembalo" [Baroque pitches with special consideration of the unusual problems of playing the recorder and harpsichord together] (1988).

1575. Scholl, Jürgen. "Der Einsatz von Videotechnik im Blockflötenunterricht" [The entry of video technique into recorder teaching] (1989).

MUSIKAKADEMIE KASSEL (Credéstraße 28, 34134 Kassel, Germany)

1576. Simko, Alex. "Die 'Verdrängung' der Blockflöte durch die Traversflöte im 18. Jahrhundert" [The displacement of the recorder by the flute in the 18th century] (1989).

STAATLICHE HOCHSCHULE FÜR MUSIK UND DARSTELLENDE KUNST (Urbanplatz 2, 70182 Stuttgart, Germany)

1577. Schiemer, Veronika. "Blockflötenbau heute—Kriterien zur Beurteilung neuer Blockflöten" [Recorder making today—criteria for the evaluation of new recorders] (1991).

1578. Vogel, Veronika. "Die Blockflöte im englischen Barock" [The recorder in the English Baroque] (1991).

Index

The index includes entries for authors, titles, and subjects. Authors' surnames appear in small capitals, titles in italics, and subjects in boldface type. Item numbers for articles and books by a particular author are in roman type; those for reviews, letters, less significant contributions, and incidental references are in italics. Title entries have been supplied for books, dissertations, theses, and periodicals but not for articles. Subject entries have not been included for citations in the appendixes, except for a few dissertations in appendix 1, the topics of which were apparent from their titles.

Aardenberg, Abraham van
   recorders by, 184, 261
Abbotsford House (Keynsham), 1390
Abreu, Aldo, 910–11
Accademia del Flauto Dolce, 110
Accademia Filarmonica (Bologna)
   recorders in, 257
Accademia Filarmonica (Verona)
   recorders in, 258, 375
   restoration of, 259
ACHT, Rob van, 183, 240, 261, 1528, *p. 442*
Acoustics, 17, 326, 403–4, 407–8, 411–13, 415–16
   beats and difference tones, 417–18
   harmonics, 409, 414
   historical studies, 396–97
   introduction to, 398–400
   of blown pipes, 402, 406
   of early woodwinds, 335
   relation of size and shape of mouth to pitch, 419
   and voicing, 405

Adams, Piers, *912*
ADORNO, Theodor W., 82, 89, 92, 161
Affections, 680, 690
AGRICOLA, Martin, 556–59
Agricola, Martin: *Musica instrumentalis deudsch,* 140, 560–61, 1384, 1411
AKAR, Etienne, 463
ALCALA, R.J., *1017*
ALEXANDER, Ellen, *1026*
ALIZON, Jean-François, 61
ALKER, Hugo, 1–3, 19, 132
All About the Recorder (Dantimo), 20
ALLAIN-DUPRÉ, Philippe, 371
ALLEN, W.S., 1389
Alte Musik Aktuell, 1414
ALTON, Edwin, 110, 991, 1286
Alton, Edwin, 913–14
Alto recorder. *See also specific topics (e.g.,* Acoustics; Construction and design; etc.*)*
   acoustical characteristics, 404
   plastic, reviews of, 477
Amateur players, 83–84, 87, 94, 104

The Amateur Wind Instrument Maker (Robinson), 456
American Musical Instrument Society, *Journal of the*, 1431
The American Recorder, 1415, *1416*
The American Recorder, 1010, 1415, 1448, p. 440, 443
American Recorder Society, 16, 20, 937, 984, 1035, 1038, 1042–43, 1074, 1446–48
  Education Program, 865
The American Recorder Society Newsletter, 1415–16
American Society of Recorder Players, 1119
Amis, Kingsley: *Lucky Jim*, 49
Ammann
  recorders by, 267
The Amorous Flute (Manifold), 23
Amplification, 523
Amsterdam Loeki Stardust Quartet, 915–16, 946
Amsterdam Recorder Ensemble, 1078
ANDERSON, Loren H., 1292
Anderson, Natasha, 917
ANDERSON, Wayne J., 210
ANDO, Yoshinori, 431
ANDRESEN, Ken, 803
Andriessen, Louis, 911, 1318, 1328
ANGERHÖFER, Günter, *183*
An Annotated Bibliography of Woodwind Instruction Books, 1600–1830 (Warner), 535
Antibes
  bone fipple flute discovered in, 1394
Antichi strumenti Veneziani 1500–1800 (Toffolo), 180
Antioch Consort, 1090
ANTONICEK, Susanne, 247
Antonicek, Theophil, 247
Apollo's Cabinet, 633
Arne, Thomas, 47
ARNO, Michael, *691*
Arno, Michael, 918–19
ARRAN, Roderick, 1337, p. 443

Arrangement. *See* Transcription and arrangement
Art, recorder in. *See* Iconography
L'art de preluder (Hotteterre), 655–57
The Art of Playing the Recorder (Waitzman), 758
The Art of Preluding, 1700–1830 (Mather & Lasocki), 749
ARTHUR, Bradford, 704.1
Articulation, 704.1–715, 771–73
  "cantabile" style, 712
  historical, 705–6, 708, 711–12, 714, 720
  French, 704.1, 710, 713
  slurring, 715, 772–73
  tonguing syllables, modern, 709
Ashbury, John, 167
ASHTON, Don, 356, *357*, 359
ASHWORTH, Jack, *1017*
ASSENDELFT, Leen van, 1529
Association Française pour la Flûte à Bec, *1425*
Attaingnant, Pierre, 142, 1171
ATWATER, Betty Ransom, 1034
Aulos recorders, 317, 478
AUSTIN, Louise, *756*
Australia, 104, 1040, 1451
  recorder in jazz in, 105
  recorder music from, 1144–45, 1481
  Victoria, history of recorder in, 103, 1451
Austria
  Hofkapelle (Vienna), 67, 247
  recorders in:
    Linz, Oberösterreichisches Landesmuseum, 1470
    Schlägl monastery, 244–45
    Schloß Sigmaringen, 246
    Vienna, Kunsthistorisches Museum C 8522 ("Ganassi" recorder), 4, 460, 462
Authenticity, 695–98, 947, 1044
Avant-garde repertory. *See* Repertory, 20th century, avant-garde
Avant-garde techniques. *See* Technique, avant-garde
AYRE, W.A., *1307*

Index

Baak Griffioen, Ruth van. *See* Griffioen, Ruth van Baak
Babell, William, 1268
BABITZ, Sol, 750
Bach, Carl Philipp Emanuel
    Trio for Viola, Bass Recorder, and Harpsichord (Helm 588), 136, 140, 1198
Bach, Johann Sebastian, 27, 1199–1229
    bibliography, 1204–5
    Brandenburg Concertos, 1209–10, 1213
        No. 2, 37, 1208
        No. 4, *fiauti d'echo* in, 394, 1209, 1211–20, 1292; key of recorders in, 1212
    cantatas, 37, 1221, 1223–25, 1226, 1463
    flauto piccolo in music of, 1227
    keyboard music, arranging for recorders, 1202
    Partita No. 2 for Violin in D Minor (BWV 1004), 1201
    pitch of instruments in music of, 374, 1206.1, 1200, 1222, 1225
    Sonata in A Major for Flute and Harpsichord (BWV 1032), as trio sonata, 1228–29
    Sonata in B Minor for Flute and Harpsichord (BWV 1030), 127
    transposition problems in recorder parts, 1200
Bach Aria Group, 1118
BACON, Francis, 396
Bacon, Francis, 413, p. 131
    reference to "wetting one's whistle," 512
Baghuis, Elly, 920
Bainbridge, William, 1386, 1399
BAINES, Anthony, 12, 15, 615, 702, 739, 1278
BAK, Niels, 419–21
BAKER, Christina, 1238
BALL, Christopher, 464
Ball, Christopher, 921
BALLESTER I GIBERT, Jordi, 143

Bamboo flutes
    from Maldive islands, 1396
BAMFORTH, Dennis A., 846
BANDT, Ros, 1334
Bandt, Ros, 1334
BANISTER, John, 603
Banister, John: *The Most Pleasant Companion*, 606
BÄR, Frank P., 246
Barab, Seymour, 835
BARATA, Antonio, 840
BARATZ, Lewis Reece, 730–31, 1413
Barbireau, Jacobus, 1169
Bärenreiter (instrument manufacturer), 464
Bariaux, Daniel, 272
Barker, Michael, 911, 936
BARNES, Julie, 1123
BARON, Samuel, 1199
BARRELL, Bernard, 1346
BARRETT, J.H., 1390
Barsanti, Francesco, 888–87, 1194, 1229.1, 1230–31
BARTHEL, Rudolf, 25, 847
Barthel, Rudolf, 922
BARTLETT, Clifford, 17
Baschenis, Evaristo, 227
Basler Jahrbuch für historische Musikpraxis, 1417, p. 222
Bassano, Giovanni, 192, 1168
Bassano, Jacomo, 179
Bassano, Santo, 180–81
Bassano family, 72, 186–191
The Bassanos: Venetian Musicians and Instrument Makers in England, 1531–1665 (Lasocki), 190
Bass recorder, 134–42
    Renaissance, 139
    Baroque, 41, 136
    20th century, 137
    clefs for, 815
    construction and design, 340–42
    historical instruments, 178, 193, 230, 269
BATE, Philip, 162, 1386
BAUR, Jürg, 822
Baur, Jürg, 91, 822, 1117, 1328, 1335
Beats (acoustics), 417–18

BEAUDIN, Jean-François, 249
Beaudin, Jean François, 240, 273
BEECHEY, Gwilym, 1346
BEEKS, Graydon, 1267
Beijer, Erik, 923
Belgium, 106
  recorders in:
    Antwerp, Vleeshuis, 139
    Brussels, Musée Instrumental du Conservatoire Royal de Musique, 1384, 1452
Bellinzani, Paolo Benedetto, 1194
Bell-keyed recorder, 356, 364-67, 758, 788, 791, 1030, 1118
BENADE, Arthur, p. 134
BENEDIKT, Erich, 119-21, 125, 434, 1228, 1272, 1403
BENN, Nicholas, 435
BENNETT, Rodney M., 993
Bense, Rotraud, 924
BERANEK, Leo, 409
BERGMANN, Walter, 2, 12, 45, 115, 154, 203, 372, 757, 777, 796, 815, 920, 922, 924, 990, 1081, 1096, 1127, 1161, 1183, 1189, 1229.1, 1283, 1361, 1381
Bergmann, Walter, 197, 908, 925-31, 1237
Bergner, Joseph, 155
Bergstrom, Ture, 333
Berio, Luciano, 1328
  Gesti, 823, 952, 961, 1320, 1336
Berkeley, Lennox, 697
Berlin, Johann Daniel: *Musicaliske Elementer*, 670
Berlioz, Hector, 99
BERNARDINI, Alfredo, 211-17
Besetzung und Instrumentation in den Opern Georg Friedrich Händels (Möller), 1269
Besivillibald, Giorgio Giacomo, 1211
BEST, Terence, 1257, 1266
BETTARINI, Luciano, 1287
BETZ, Marianne, 735, 1228, 1387
Beukers, Willem
  recorders by, 184, 261
BEYAERT, Thérèse, 1452

Bibliography, 1-3, 17, 40. For bibliographies of music, see Repertory, bibliography
  articles in *The American Recorder*, 1415
  essays on research published from 1985-92, 4-11
  articles in *The Galpin Society Journal*, 1427
Biblioteca Comunale (Assisi)
  bass recorder in, 178
BICKHARDT, Klaus, 352
Bigaglia, Diogenio: Sonata in A Minor for Recorder and Continuo, 1232-33
BIGIO, Robert, 1483, 1530
Bigio, Robert, 274
BINKLEY, Thomas, 566, 1448
Biographies. See Recorder players; Makers and manufacturers; *and under individual names*
The Bird Fancyer's Delight, 47
Birds, association of the recorder with, 47
BISMANTOVA, Bartolomeo, 597-98
Bismantova, Bartolomeo: *Compendio musicale*, 599-601
Bismarck, Otto von, 380
BITTERS, David L., 286
BIXLER, Martha, 14, 398, 732, 757, 937, 1017, 1026, 1038, 1047-48, 1084, 1115, 1415-16, 1448
Bixler, Martha, 934-35
Bizey
  recorders by, 270
BLAKER, Frances, 41, 478, 717
Blaker, Frances, 936
BLANCHFIELD, David, 233
BLANKENBURG, Gerbrant Quirijnszoon van, 593-95
Blankenburg, Gerbrant Quirijnszoon van: *Onderwyzinge hoemen . . .* , 536, 596, 752-53
BLOCH, Suzanne, 15, 1448
Bloch, Suzanne, 937, 1042
Block, 41, 502, 525
Die Blockflöte in der deutschen Jugendsmusikbewegung (Hübner), 1464

Index

Die Blockflöte in der zeitgenössischen Musik (Rechberger), 827
Die Blockflöte in Kantate, Oratorium und Oper des 17. Jahrhunderts (Thieme), 1185
Die Blockflöte: Instrumentenkunde, Geschichte, Musizierpraxis (Alker), 19
Die Blockflöte: Tips für Anschaffung und Pflege, Stimmkorrekturen, Reparaturen (Bouterse), 485
Blockflöten-Bibliographie (Alker), 1–3
De blokfluit, handleiding voor aanschaf, onderhoud, bijstemmen en kleine reparaties (Bouterse), 485
De blokfluit in de twingste eeuw (Denis), 1457
BLOOD, Brian, 517
BLOODWORTH, Denis, 340, 724, 1221, 1274
Blow, John: *Ode on the Death of Mr. Henry Purcell*, 1189
BLUE, Marcia, 984, 1042
BLUMENFELD, Harold, 582
Bobbin, Tim, 889
Boeckman, Vicki, 938
Boehm, Johann Michael, 886
BOEKE, Kees, 81, *1428*
Boeke, Kees, 939, 952, 1120
Boekhout, Thomas
  recorders by, 184, 261, 267
BOELENS, Ben, 1531
BOENAU, Marilyn, 478
Bogenhausen Kunstkapelle, 97, 99, 1060
Bois, Rob du, 1117, 1318, 1337
Boismortier, Joseph Bodin de, 1234
Bolhuis, Michiel van, 237
Bolivia
  duct flutes from, 1397
BOLTON, Philippe, 63, 325, 350, 384, 437, 525
Bononcini, Giovanni Battista
  use of "echo flute," 1220, 1252
BONSOR, Brian, *1032*
Bonsor, Brian, 940
BORAGNO, Pierre, 1018
BORNEFELD, Helmut, 1338

Bornefeld, Helmut, 941, 1338–39
BORNSTEIN, Andrea, 57
BOSMANS, Wim, 1384, 1410
Bottenberg, Wolfgang, 1330
Boudreau, Jean-Luc, 275–76
Boudreau, Michelle, 1330
BOULLET, Jean-Pierre, 106
BOURGUIGNON, Jacqueline, 1453
Bousted, Donald: *Four Pieces,* 907
BOUTERSE, Jan, 63, 184, 234, 261, 485, 1483.1-3, 1532–41
Bouterse, M.C.J. *See* Bouterse, Jan
BOWEN, Meirion, *1070*
BOWERS, Jane M., 68, 214, p. 444
BOWMAN, James, *1070*
BOXALL, Maria, 71, *508*, 718, *739*
Boxwood, 169, 388
BOYDELL, Barra, 193
BOYER, Margareth Anne, 658
BRACH, Manfred, 351, 1542, p. 444
Bradbury, Joseph, 167
  recorders by, 267
Bradford, Margaret, 937
BRAILOVE, Susan, 1448
BRAN-RICCI, Josiane, 250
Brauer, Emil, 942
BRAUN, Gerhard, 82, 823, 866, 943, 1013, 1039, 1051, 1058–59, 1079, 1271, 1322, 1326, 1339, 1358, 1365, *1367*
Braun, Gerhard, 107, 943
  recorder music by, 823, 907, 1326, 1340
Breathing, 776, 1047
  circular, 41, 775
Breath pressure
  effect on intonation, 407, 419–29
Breath support, 761, 774
BREED, Alexander, 837
BRELSFORD, Edmund, 947
Bressan, Peter, 167, 193–202, 231
  recorders by, 97, 201–2, 248, 250, 262, 270
  bass recorders, 193, 199
  Chester recorders (*see* Chester recorders)
  drawings of, 328
  left-handed, 200

Bressan, Peter (continued)
  recorders by (continued)
    measurements of, 351, 615
BREWER, Roy, 508
BRIDGE, J.C., 53
Bridge, J.C., 96, 1122
BRINDLEY, Giles, 430
British Broadcasting Corporation
  project to record the Chester
    recorders, 197
Britten, Benjamin, 1328, 1341–42
BROADSTOCK, Brenton, 1343
Broadstock, Brenton: *Aureole 3*, 1343–44
BROCK, John Earl, 1136
BRODIE, Gary, 309
BROOKES, Oliver, 1070
BROOKS, David R., 385
BROWN, Adrian, 486–87
BROWN, Howard Mayer, 7, 144
Brown, Howard Mayer, 944–45
BRUCKNER, Hans, 172
Brüggen, Daniel, 946
BRÜGGEN, Frans, 1032, 1336
Brüggen, Frans, 908, 947–65
  aesthetics of his playing, 952
  effect of historical copies on his playing style, 298
  interest in recorder players of the past, p. 441
  interviews with, 947, 951, 953–54, 956–60, 965, 1320
  Ricardo Kanji's study with, 1033
  work with Hans-Martin Linde, 1053, 1056
  master class in Rome (1973), 689
  on performance practice, 964
  ornamentation of the F major Handel sonata, 1258
  participation in 1965 BBC project, 197
  recorder collection of, 234, 260
  Steve Rosenberg's thoughts on, 1093
  teaching methods, as described by van Hauwe, 1018
Brunette, 1191

Brydges, James, Earl of Carnarvon, 1267
Buckley, John, 1345
BULLARD, Beth, 549–50
Bulletin and Communications (FoMRHI), 1426
BURAKOFF, Gerald, 317, 1147
BURBIDGE, Ruth and Jeremy, 1439
Burckart, J.V., 1182
BURFORD, Freda, 508
Burgess, Chris, 966
Burney, Charles, 53
Burrows, Benjamin, 1346
Butt, Valerie, 967
Buttress fingering, 572, 584, 667, 729
Byrd, William, 691
BYRNE, Maurice, 194–96, 228, 1014, p. 442

Cadenzas, 694
Caix d'Hervelois, Louis de: Suite in G Major, 691
The Cambridge Companion to the Recorder (Thomson), 17
CAMERON, Rod, 1484–85
CAMPBELL, Margaret, 992
Canada
  degree programs in early music, 877
Canessière, Philippe de la. *See* La Canessière, Philippe de
"Cantabile" style, 712
Cantata
  17th-century, 1184–85
Cardan, Jerome. *See* Cardano, Girolamo
CARDANO, Girolamo, 569–70
Cardano, Girolamo: *De musica,* 571
CARDUELIS, Susan, 804. *See also* Prior, Susan
Carl, Georg Franz, 176
CARLSON, Marilyn, 797
CARR, Robert, 604
Carrell, Norman, 1213
CARSE, Adam, 725
Carse Collection (London)
  recorder by Heitz in, 212

Index

CARTER, Stewart, 751
Cartoons, 159
Carved instruments, 343–44
Casa, Girolamo dalla, 1168
Case, carrying
  construction of, 506–7
Casken, John: *Thymehaze*, 767, 1329
CASTELLANI, Marcello, 601, 705
Castellani, Marcello, 968
CASTELLENGO, Michèle, 402–3
Castello, Dario, 1168
Catalogue général: musique pour flûte à bec 1989 (Letteron), 1129
CATRICE, Jean-Noël, 477, 479
CAVALIER-SMITH, Mary, *1032*
CAVICCHI, Adriano, 599
CAWLEY, Margaret E., 315
Cedar, 387
Céline, Louis-Ferdinand, 949
The Center for Old Music (New York City), 100
Chaboud, Pietro, 1233
Challulau, Patrice, 1347
CHANDELIER, Christian, 1363, p. 444
CHAPMAN, Roger E., *588*
Charpentier, Marc Antoine, 69, 1182, 1235
Checklist of Technical Drawings of Musical Instruments in Public Collections of the World (van Acht), 240
Chédeville, Nicolas, 1312, 1314
Chester recorders, 16, 53, 96, 197, 199–200, 203–4, 355
CHILTON, Charles, 197
Choirs, recorder, 856, 861. *See also* Ensembles
Christmas music, 1156
CHURCH, R.W., *360*
Cincinnati Art Museum
  Schuchart recorder in, 224
Circular breathing, 775
Clarion Concerts Orchestra, 1118
CLARK, Marcel, 64
CLARK, Paul, 126, 345, *756*, 759–61, 780–82, 843, 848, *1032*, 1138, 1162, 1280, *1346*
Clark, Paul, 969–70

Clarke, Jeremiah: *On Henry Purcell's Death*, 1189
CLARKE, Zana, 917
The Classical Woodwind Cadenza (Lasocki & Mather), 694
CLAUSING, Susette, 1356
Clefs, 813–15, 817
CLEMENCIC, René, 824
Clemencic, René, 908, 971–72
Clemencic Consort, 971
CLINE, Gilbert D., 805
CLINGAN, Judith, 1348
Clingan, Judith, 973, 1348
COATES, Gloria, 1349
Coates, Gloria: *Breaking Through*, 1349
Coconut, 394
COHEN, Albert, 610
COHEN, Joel, 948
Collections, p. 84–93. *See also under specific country or museum name*
Colleges and universities, 90, 875–77
Collier, Edwaert, 63, 145, 1283
Collin
  recorders by, 267
COLLINS, Lee, *300*
COLTMAN, John, p. 134
Colyer, Edwaert. *See* Collier, Edwaert
Combination tones, 851
Compendio musicale (Bismantova), 597
The Compleat Flute-Master, 616
The Compleat Flute-Master, 617
Compleat Instructions for the Common Flute, 640
The Compleat Instructor to the Flute, 618
The Compleat Musick-Master, 621
The Compleat Tutor for the Common Flute, 638
The Compleat Tutor for the Flute, 630–31, 634–35, 639
The Compleat Tutor for ye Flute (Rutherford), 637
The Compleat Tutor for ye Flute (Wright), 629
The Complete Flute Master, 632, 636

Composers. *See under individual names*
  biographical dictionaries, 885
Composing for recorder, 50, 832, 834–39, 1324
COMSTOCK, George W., 116
Concerto (periodical), 1418
Concertos, 1143
Condensation, 41, 508–12
CONKLIN, William T., *348*
CONN, Richard, *1026*
CONRAD, Ferdinand, 736
Conrad, Ferdinand, 908, 974–78
  Michala Petri's study with, 1081, 1083
The Conservation and Technology of Musical Instruments (Karp), p. 169
Conservatoire National Supérieur de Musique (Paris). *See* Paris Conservatoire
The Consort (periodical), 1419
Consorts, 60, 74, p. 350. *See also* Ensembles
Construction and design, 34, 325–95, 403. *See also* Maintenance and repair; Making; Measuring; One-handed recorders; Woods
  medieval, 338–39, 457
  Renaissance, 56, 192, 329, 339, 449
  Baroque, 327–28, 332
  for the music of van Eyck, 333
  bass recorder, 340–42
  carved instruments, 343–44
  fingerholes, 331, 438
  historical instruments, 63, 351
  historical vs. modern, 298, 328, 354
  history of, 334
  keywork, 356–57, 359, 361, 363
  modernization, 64, 354–63 (*see also* Bell-keyed recorder)
  effect on tone quality, 336
  windway, 383
Continuo (periodical), 1420
Continuo realization, 717–18

Contrabass recorder
  by Paetzold, 342
Contribution à l'étude éxperimentale des tuyaux à bouche (Castellengo), 402
COOK, S. Ronald, Jr., 1147
Cooke, Arnold, 1117, 1350
Coolen, Saskia, 923
Coolsma, Hans, 277, 357, 464
COOMBER, David, 690
Coomber, David, 979
Copyright law, 1147
CORCORAN, Ronald E., *1439*
Corelli, Arcangelo, 697, 735, 742, 1159
Cornetto, 59, 805
The Cornetto (Cline), 805
CORNSWEET, Amy, 1270
Corrette, Michael, 1305
Cotte, Roger, 980
Courteville, Raphael, 1182
Courtly Music Unlimited, 1020–21
Courvoiser, Walter, 1110
COUSEN, John, 435
Cousen, John, 464
Cramer-Chemin-Petit, Jeannette, 981
Cranmore, Tim, 278
CRAVEN, John, 745
Crescendo (periodical), 1421, 1425
CRISPIN, Brian, *64*
A Critical Survey of the Recorder and its Music in England, c.1675–c.1790 (Stratford), 1480
CRONIN, Robert H., 1486
CROOKES, David Z., *583*
CROSS, Lucy, *1017*
CULBERTSON, Dawn, 1146
CURRIE, John, *1070*
Czakan, 1386–88
Czech Republic
  recorders in:
    Prague, Nationalmuseum, 248

DAEUBLIN, Anette, 1569
DAHNK-BAROFFIO, Emilia, *567*
Dalla Casa, Girolamo. *See* Casa, Girolamo dalla

Index

DALLIN, Lynn, 1119
DANBURY, Graham, 1032
Danican-Philidor, Anne, 697
DANTIMO, Stanley, 20
D'Ariel Trio, 1118
DARMSTADT, Hans, *1367*
DART, Thurston, *71.1*, 198, 596, 607, 1174, *1175*, 1211
DAVENPORT, LaNoue, 783, 1035, *1416*, 1448
Davenport, LaNoue, 908, 982–84
  Martha Bixler's work with, 934–35
DAVENPORT, Mark, 373
DAVEY, A.J., *368*
DAVIDSON, Martin, *41*, 385, 422, 465
DAVIES, Malcolm, 608
DAVIES, Peter, 1109
DAVIS, Alan, *204*, 700, 726, 771, 784, 818, 1200, 1329, 1454
Dayton C. Miller Flute Collection (Washington, D.C.), 212, 314
Deafness, senile, 465
DEANE, Morag, 894–95, 1276
DEERENBERG, Baldrick, 1543
Deerenberg, Baldrick, 985
DEGEN, Dietz, 21
DEGGELLER, Kurt, *114*
DE GREGORIO, Vincenzo, 177
de Laborde, Jean Benjamin. *See* Laborde, M. de (Jean Benjamin)
DELAHOUSSE, D., 466
Delavigne, Philibert, 697, 703
The Delightful Companion (Carr), 604
DELIUS, Nikolaus, 585, 968, 1097, 1250
Delius, Nikolaus, 986
Del portar della lingua negli instrumenti di fiato (Castellani & Durante), 705
DELUSSE, Charles, *652*
DELVIGNE, Isabelle, 1455
Demoivre, Daniel, 890, 898, 1236
DEMOULIN, Jean-Pierre, 1310
De Musica (Cardano), 569
DEN HUL, Dick van, 1456
Den singende Knochen (Grasshoff & Moeck), 156

DENIS, Sandra, 1457
Denmark
  recorders in:
    Copenhagen, Musikhistorisk Museum, 207
Denner, Jacob, 205–6
  recorders by, 207, 246, 256, 266
Denner, Johann Christoph, 206
  recorders by, 208, 250, 254, 256, 262, 269
  drawings of altos, 328
Denner family, 175–76
  recorders by, 97, 208–9, 248, 266
A Descriptive Catalogue of Recorder Music (Hosoda), 1128
DESFORGES, A.N., 1487
DESSY, Lee, 326
DESSY, Raymond, 326
Detroit Public Library manuscript, 1190
DETTMAN, Carl E., *510*
DEVESON, Richard, *13*
DEVROOP, Chatradari, 113, 1340
DEWEY, Monica, 1071
DICKEY, Bruce, 600, 752
DIDEROT, Denis, 684–85
Diderot, Denis, 686, 949
Dieupart, Charles (or Francis), 1237
Difference tones, 417–18, 802, 851, 859
Dijk, Jan van: *Musique à trois,* 1188
DIKMANS, Greg, 1168
DINN, Freda, 691, 806, 1141
Dinn, Freda, 987–88
Di Pasquale, Marco. *See* Pasquale, Marco di
Directions for Playing on the Flute, 624, 628
Directions for Playing the Flute, 627
Discography, 1146
Discography of the Recorder (Paterson & Lasocki), 1146
Dissertatio physica de sono (Euler), 397
Dit is een seer schoon boecxken, 544
The Division Flute, 721–22
  "Faronell's ground," 723
Divisions, 720–23
DIXON, Kay, 973

Dolci, Amico, 110, 989-90
DOLCI, Danilo, 913
Dolci, Danilo, 991
DOLMERGUE, Sylvie, 1201
Dolmetsch, Arnold, 26, 279-80, 992, 1101, 1113
DOLMETSCH, Carl, 26, 54, 62, 64, 96, 204, 345, 355, 377, 386, 762, 788, 994, 1028, 1032, 1317, 1319, 1440
Dolmetsch, Carl, 204, 279, 281, 908, 937, 993-99
Dolmetsch family, 280-81
Dolmetsch Foundation, 16, 1419
Arnold Dolmetsch, Ltd., 357, 464, 993
J. & M. Dolmetsch, Ltd., 280, 993
Dolmetsch: The Man and His Work (Campbell), 992
DONINGTON, Robert, 27, 1070
Donizetti, Gaetano, 99
Dordrecht recorder, 185, 440, 457
Double pipes, 1385, 1389, 1399
DOUGLAS, Lorna M., 406
DOUGLAS, Paul Marshall, 653
DOUWES, Claas, 642-43
DRAKE, Julian, 1488
Drawings, of instruments, 240, 249, 260-61
DRILLON, Jacques, 949
DRISCOLL, Daniel A., 64, 404, 432, 497
Drumbleby, Samuel, 167
DU BOIS, Elizabeth Ann, 1300
Du Bois, Rob. *See* Bois, Rob du
DUCKLES, Vincent H., p. 84
Duct flutes, 1396-97
DUGGAN, Peter T., 438
DUHOT, Jean-Joël, 166, 314, 488-89, 1347
DULLAT, Günter, 439
DUNHAM, Benjamin, 41, 462, 486, 714, 910, 1415, p. 443
DUNN, John, 423
Dupuis
  copies of recorders by, 392, 394
DURANTE, Elio, 705
Dürer, Albrecht, 1406

DURON, Jean, 1235
Dürrenmatt, Friedrich: *Die Physiker*, 49
Dutch Recorders of the 18th Century (van Acht), 261
Dvojnice, 1389, 1399
DWIGHT, Frances, 1026
Dynamics, 777-79, 1047
Die dynamische Blockflöte (Fischer), 778

Early music
  in the United States, reflections on, 1448
  role of recorder in revival of, 81
Early Music (periodical), 1422
Early Music (periodical), 1111
Early Music America, 1429
Early Music Consort of London, 1068
Early Music Directory, 1420
Early Music for Recorders (Dinn), 691
Early Music Network, 1111
Early Music New Zealand, 1423
EASTMAN, Richard, 849
Eccles, John, 140
Eccles, Lance, 1002
Echo flute. *See* Bach, Johann Sebastian, Brandenburg Concertos, No. 4, *fiauti d'echo* in; Flauti eco; Paisible, James, and the "echo flute"
Editing music, 17, 1157-60
EDLER-BUSCH, Elli, 711, 774
EDRIDGE, Tom, 1202
EDWARDS, J.W., 4
Eenhandsfluit en Trom in de Lage Landen (Bosmans), 1410
Eggl, Johann (or Joseph), 172
Ehrhardt, Susanne, 1000
EHRLICH, Robert, 13, 83-84, 697, 756, 950, 1029, 1458
Ehrlich, Robert, 1001
Eichentopf
  recorders by, 256, 262
EICHHORN, Edgar L., 364
EIJKEN, Eugène, 1544
EISEL, Johann Philipp, 668-69

Index

Eisma, Will: *Wonderen zijn schaars*, 1318
ELDER, Samuel A., 405, p. 134
Electronic recorder, 348
Elements of Musick Display'd (Tans'ur), 672
Embouchure, 774
EMERSON, David, 499
Encores, 1152
Encyclopédie, ou dictionnaire raisonné des sciences, des arts et des métiers (Diderot), 684
ENDE, Vincent van den, 261
Endler, Johann Samuel: *Pièces*, 1188
ENFIELD, Patrick, 834
England, 32, 63, 71-77, 1480. See also Great Britain
  recorders in:
    Chester, Grosvenor Museum, 53, 96, 199-200, 203-4
    London: Carse Collection, 212; Horniman Museum, 280; Royal College of Music, 207, 216; Victoria and Albert Museum, 199
    Norwich, St. Peter Hungate, 199
English Harpsichord Magazine, 1030
Ensembles, 14, 23, 847-64. See also Consorts
  bass recorder in, 142
  choosing instruments, 471
  "golden rules" of, 154
  intonation and tuning, 851, 855, 862
  learning to read clefs, 817
  ornamentation, 733
  performing with one player, 852
  recorder choirs and orchestras, 846, 856, 861
  repertory, 848, 855
  technique, 855, 858-59, 863
Epitome musical (Jambe de Fer), 572
EPPELSHEIM, Jürgen, 1278
EPSTEIN, Jan, 273, 282, 939, 944, 951, 1040, 1049, 1064, 1080, *1438*
Erich Katz Foundation, 1003
ERIG, Richard, 720
Ertel, Meinrad, 1407

Essai d'une méthode pour apprendre à jouer de la flute traversiere (Quantz), 678
Essai-méthode de flûte traversière (Quantz), 679
ESTEVES PEREIRA, L.A., 1489
An Ethnomusicological Study of a Modern Performing Tradition in Western Art Music (Ehrlich), 1458
ETTLIN, Alex, 284
Etude analytique et descriptive de la collection de flûtes à bec conservée au Musée Instrumental du Conservatoire Royal de Musique de Bruxelles (Beyaert), 1452
Etymology of "recorder," 12, 42-45, 53, 1122
EULER, Leonhard, 397, p. 132
Evelyn, John, 53
Examinations
  in England, 1030
  Trinity College of Music, 878-80
Eyck, Jacob van, 964, 1238-49, 1456
Euterpe oft Speel-goddinne, 1240
Der fluyten lust-hof, 63, 596, 689, 1238-46
  depicted in a Vanitas by Edwaert Collier, 145
  "Engels Nachtegaeltje," 47
  methods associated with, 592-93
  composition in *Der gooden fluythemel* by, 1247
  recorder for the music of, 166, 333
EYRE, Chris, *1032*

Faber, Johann Christoph: *Parties sur les fleut dous*, 1150
Facsimile editions, 17, 1149
FADER, Bruce, 513, 522
FAHRNBERGER, Elisabeth, 1459
FAIRHALL, Helen, 1369
FAJARDO, Raoul J., 497-98, 522-23
The Falling Leaves (musical group), 101
Fanfare (periodical), 1441
FARLEIGH, John, 279

Fasch, Johann Friedrich, 136, 1180, 1186–87
Fehr, Hans Conrad, 357, 464, 1008, 1053
FELDER, Denise, 85
FELDHAUS, Hanne, 234, 1460
FELDMAN, Anna, 867
Fellowship of Makers and Researchers of Historical Instruments, 1426
FERGUSON, Suzanne, 812, 1026, 1030
Ferguson, Suzanne, 1003
FERRIS, Jill, 966
Fiauti d'echo. See Bach, Johann Sebastian, Brandenburg Concertos, No. 4, *fiauti d'echo* in
FIEDLER, JÖRG, 1191
The Fifth Book of the New Flute Master, 620
Fifth flute
  in 18th century, 128–29
FILIATRAULT, François, 275
Finch, Edward, 1190
Finger, Godfrey, 903, 1178, 1182, 1190, 1248–49
Fingerholes
  angled, 331
Fingering (technique), 14, 756–58, 780–82, 784–85, 817
  leaks, problems with, 786
  use of thumb, 792
Fingerings and fingering systems, 15, 724–29, 756–58, 787–91
  acoustical studies, 430
  alternate, 41, 756, 783, 785, 787, 791, 800
  avant-garde, 821, 826–27
  multiphonics, 841–42
  buttress, 572, 584, 667, 729
  German, 20, 99, 108, 303, 317, 345–47
  historical, 15, 438, 572, 609, 724–29
  high notes, 584, 727, 758, 790 f♯^{3}, 788–91
  humorous description of, 157
  trills, 756, 795
FINLAY, Ian F., 152

Fipple flute, 51, 55, 1390
Firth, Pond & Co.
  capped fipple flute by, 210
Fische
  recorders by, 266
Fischer, Johann: *Vier Suiten für Blockflöte*, 1250
FISCHER, Johannes, 775, 778
Fischer, Johannes, 107, 907
FISCHER, Pieter, 145
Fischer family, 172
Fistulatores et Tubicinatores Varsovienses, 112
FITZGIBBON, H.M., 28
FITZPATRICK, Horace, 440, 1404
Fitzpatrick, Horace, 1407
Flageolet, 1386, 1398–1402
Flauta (Bolivia), 1397
Flauti eco
  used by G.B. Bononcini, 1252
Flautino, 124. See also Vivaldi, Antonio, "flauto" and "flautino" problem
"Flauto curvo," 238
Flauto d'echo. See Bach, Johann Sebastian, Brandenburg Concertos, No. 4, *fiauti d'echo* in
Il flauto dolce (periodical), 1424
Il flauto dolce ed acerbo (Vetter), 821
Flauto harmonico, 227
Flauto piccolo, 124
  in music of J.S. Bach, 1227
Flauto Piccolo (pseudonym). See Newman, Joel
FLETCHER, Neville H., 399, 406, p. 134
Flexibility, 311, 502
Die Flötensammlung des Oberösterreichischen Landesmuseums (Maass), 1470
Fluitsonates van J.B. Loeillet (Loose), 1469
Flute, fipple. See Fipple flute
Flute, Recorder, and Oboe Before 1800: A Selected Bibliography (Rawski), 537
Flute, transverse
  history, 54, 62

Index

Flute, transverse (continued)
  repertory
    recorder literature suitable for, 1153
    with recorder, 1186-88
  Flûte à bec (periodical), 1425
  La flûte à bec en Italie au XVIe siècle (Pottier), 1473
  Flûte à bec et instruments anciens (periodical), 1425
  Flûte d'accord, 1399
  The Flute-Master Compleat Improved, 619
  Flûte pastorelle, 123, 1403
Folger Consort, 1090
Folk House Archaeological Club, 1390
FOLKERS, Catherine, 1490
FoMRHI Quarterly, 1426
Fontana, Giovanni Battista
  sonatas for violin and continuo, 697, 1251
For Four Recorder Quartet, 1004
Fornari, Andrea, 180-81, 211
FORTUNE, Nigel, *1070*
4900 Historical Woodwind Instruments (Young), 243
Four and Twenty Fiddlers: The Violin at the English Court 1540-1690 (Holman), 71, p. 350
Fourth flute
  in 18th century, 128-29
FOX, C.W., 1169
FRACCARO, Inga Kristina, *990*
France
  history, 68, 1465, 1474
  instrument making in, 168-71
  recorders in:
    Paris, Conservatoire, 250-53
    recorder instruction in, 881-82
FRANCIS, John, 1203
Free Ornamentation for Woodwind Instruments, 1700-1775 (Mather & Lasocki), 739
FREEMAN, Willa Fowler, 381
FREILLON-PONCEIN, Jean-Pierre, 644-48

Freillon-Poncein, Jean-Pierre: *La veritable maniere*, 536, 647-49, 701, 710
FREUND, Cecilia Kathryn van de Kamp, 1288
Freunde alter Musik in Basel
  concert programs of, 114
Fridrich
  recorder by, 248
FRINGS, Gabriele, 146
Fume onu, 1396
Furner, James, 1407
FUSSENEGGER, Gernot, 1461
Fux, Johann Joseph, 67, 1252-53

GAGNON, Robert, 275
Gahn, Johann Benedikt, 176
  recorders by, 244, 246, 250, 256, 267
Gal, Hans, 1351-53
GALPIN, Francis W., 71.1
Galpin, Francis W., 1005
Galpin Society, 1030
The Galpin Society Journal, 1427
Galway, James, 1083
GAMM, Norbert, 1572
GANASSI, Silvestro, 562-67
Ganassi, Silvestro, 964
  Opera intitulata Fontegara, 139, 568, p. 177
  attempts at making a "Ganassi recorder," 4, 459-62
GANNON, Lee, 825
Gannon, Lee, 825
GANTY, Henri, 122, 1148
GARDEN, Greer, 251
Garklein recorder, 125
Garrick, David
  portrait of, with recorder, 148
GARRIDO, Gabriel, 704
Garrido, Gabriel, 1006
GÄRTNER, Jochen, 1098
GARVEY, Kennan, *1330*
Gebauer, Joseph, 1387
GEDDERT, Geesche, 1380
Gedney, Caleb, 228-29
GEIGER, Georg, 490
Geiger, Georg, 282

GEISSMANN, Annemarie, 324
Gemeentemuseum (The Hague)
  18th-century Dutch recorders in, 261
  collection of drawings, 240
GEMMACH, Hans, 155
Gemshorn, 1404–7
The Genteel Companion (Salter), 605
GENTILI, Augusto, *146*
Gerhard Huber Recorder Factory, 284
GERHARDT, Russell, 210
GERHOLD, Hartmut, 986
Gerlach, Gottlieb, 97
German fingering, 20, 99, 108, 303, 317, 345–47
Germanisches Nationalmuseum (Nuremberg)
  recorders in, 174, 256
Germany, 21, 107–8
  Middle ages, 70
  primary education, 872, 883
  recorder making in:
    Berchtesgaden, 172
    Nuremberg, 63, 173–76
  recorders in:
    Munich, Musikinstrumentenmuseum, 254
    Nuremberg, Germanisches Nationalmuseum, 174, 256
    Würzburg, 185
  youth music movement, 1464
Germany, East (former), 1000
Die geschichtliche Entwicklung der kleinen Flötentypen (Meierott), 124, 1471
Gheier
  recorder by, 248
GIANNINI, Tula, 168, 215, p. 442
Gibbons, Orlando
  "The Silver Swan," setting by Staeps, 1107
Gibert, Jordi Ballester i. *See* Ballester i Gibert, Jordi
Giesbert, Franz Julius, 1007–8
Gijsbrecht, 220
GILLESPIE, Wendy, *1017*
GILLETT, Eric, 1162–63, *1295*

Gilliam-Turner, Rob, 310
Girdler, Thomas, 77
Glanville-Hicks, Peggy, 1009
GLASSGOLD, A.C., 235, 499, 506, 793, 835
Glassgold, A.C., 1010
Glassgold, Cook. *See* Glassgold, A.C.
Glätzk family, 67
Gleich, Clemens von, 185
Glösch, Peter, 886
Godard, Jean-Luc, 949
Der gooden fluyt-hemel, 596, 1197, 1247
Godfroy family, 168
GODMAN, Stanley, *15*
GODWIN, Joscelyn, 507
GOEBELS, Franzpeter, 719
Goetz, Edward (pseudonym). *See* Thomson, J.M.
GOETZ, Freddy, 706
GOHIN, Henri, 441
"Golden rules" for ensemble playing, 154
GOODMAN, Jan, 1086
Goodyear, Stephen, 1011
Gooselink, 85
Gordon, Edgar, *726*, 795
GÖRING, Lieselotte, 1462
GOULD, Ian, 1405
Les goûts réunis (periodical), 1428
Grabbe, 85
GRANT, Dinah, 1370
GRASSHOFF, Fritz, 156
Graun: Trio for Bass Recorder, Viola, and Continuo, 1198
GRAWE, Ursula, 939, 944, 1040, 1063
GRAY, Arlen, 776
Grayson, Arnold, 1012
Great Britain. *See also* England
  degree programs in early music, 875
  20th-century repertory, 1317
Great Flute Makers of France (Giannini), 168
GREENBERG, Abraham, 707
GREENBERG, Susan Gloria, 1463
GREENE, Margaret Duncan, *984*

Index

GREENHUT, Gary, *428*, *1042*
Greenwich House Music School (New York City), 100
GRIFFIOEN, Ruth van Baak, 63, 1239, 1243–44, p. 442
GRIMMER, Donald, *137*
Griselini, Francesco, 181
Griti, Santo, 179
Grondig ondersoek van de toonen der musijk (Douwes), 642
GRONEFELD, Ingo, 1143, p. 443
Grosvenor Museum (Chester) Bressan recorders in, 16, 53, 96, 199–200, 203–4
Grund-richtiger . . . Unterricht der musicalischen Kunst (Speer), 641
GRUSKIN, Shelley, *1305*, 1448
Guidebook to Published Recorder Music (Loonan), 1130–31
GUIDECOQ, P., 169
Guise, Mademoiselle de, 69, 613
Guitar with recorder, 1138–39
Gümbel, Martin, 1013
GURLITT, Wilibald, *581*
GUTMANN, Veronika, 579, 720
Guzman, Rodolfo, 907

HABERT, Andreas, 721
HACHEZ, R., 1491
HADEN, James C., *13*
HADIDIAN, Eileen, *1032*
Hague Conservatory, 1033
Haka, Richard
  recorders by, 184, 246, 250
  Aulos plastic instrument based on, 317
HALBIG, Hermann, 349
HALFPENNY, Eric, 157–58, 167, 199, 229–30, 327
Halfpenny, Eric, 1014–15
Halilith, 109
Hall, Henry: *Peace of Musike upon the Death of Mr. H. Purcell*, 1189
HALL, Ralph, *1346*
HAMEL, Peter Michael, 1345
Hamlet (Shakespeare), 18, 52
HAMOEN, Dirk Jacob, 1545

Hanchet, John, 457
HAND, Colin, 1354
Hand, Colin, 1329, 1354
Handbuch der Blockflöten-Literatur (Höffer-von Winterfeld & Kunz), 1127
Handbuch des Blockflötenspiels (Linde), 13, p. 440
Handel, George Frideric, 18, 27, 53, 1254–71, 1459
  Acis and Galatea, 18, 1264, 1267
  bibliography, 1205
  "bird" music, 47
  chamber music, 1266
  Chandos Anthem No. 10, 1267
  "flauto piccolo" problem, 1255
  minuets, arranged for recorder and piano, 1271
  music for the Earl of Carnarvon, 1267
  opera airs in *Directions for Playing on the Flute*, 627
  opera, 1269–70
  oratorio, 1270
  solo sonatas, 689, 697, 1256–57, 1261, 1265
    in C major (HWV 365), 740
    in F major (HWV 369), 1258
    in G major (HWV 358), 1262
    in G minor (HWV 360), 691
  manuscripts and early editions, 1257, 1259–60
  ornamentation of, 742, 1268
  trio sonatas, 1178
Handel's Use of Flute and Recorder in Opera and Oratorio (Cornsweet), 1270
HANLEY, Edwin, 1288
HANSON, Elloyd, *1415*
Hargail Music, 1074
Harlan, Peter, 99, 303, 1008, 1016
Harmonics, 409, 414
Harmonie universelle (Mersenne), 586–88
Harpsichord, tuning of, 745
Hart, David, 1017
HART, Günter, 212

Hashagen, Klaus: *Gardinenpredigt eines Blockflötenspielers,* 1326
Haslemere Festival, 993, 998, 1030, 1113
Haslemere Musical Instruments, Ltd., 993
Hauteloche brothers, 78
HAUWE, Walter van, 86, 756, 763–64, 1372
Hauwe, Walter van, 939, 1001, 1018–19
Hawkins, John, 53
HAY, Laurent, *441*
Haynes, Bruce, *64,* 328, 354, *355,* 374, 746, 886, *950,* 1222, 1491.1–1493, p. 442, 443
Haynes, Bruce, 283
HAYNES, J.L., 341
Heberle, Anton, 1387
HEDLUND, H. Jean, 952, *964*
HEDRICK, Peter J., 995
HEEL, S.A.C. Dudok van, *183*
Heerde, Jan Jurrians van
  recorders by, 250, 262
HEIDE, Geert Jan van der, 1494, 1546–47
HEIDECKER, Martin, *31*
Heiden, Bernhard, 1355
HEIDER, Werner, *1367*
Heider, Werner, 823, 1356–57
Heinichen, Johann David, 1273
Heinrich (instrument maker), 464
Heitz, Johann, 213
  recorders by, 212, 254
  measurement of, 351
HELLER, Karl, 1309
HELLWIG, Hans Joachim, *651*
HELMER, Barrie, *1200*
HELSLOOT, Loes, 923
HENDRIKS, Jan, 1548
Henry IV, of England, 43
Henry VIII, of England, 16, 139–40
Henthorn, Elizabeth, 71
Henzler, Elaine, 1021
Henzler, Richard, 1020–21
Herbst family, 176
HERMAN, R., 407
HERMES-NEUMANN, Andrea, 1315

HERSCHEL, Sir John, p. 132
HERSOM, Herbert, 135, 147–48, 925, 987, *1032*
Hertel, Johann Wilhelm, 1403
Hesperus Baroque Ensemble, 1090, p. 444
Hespos, Hans-Joachim, 1358–59
HESS, Stanley, 343–44
HETTRICK, William E., *99,* 553, 560–61, *1106,* 1157, 1411
HEYDE, Herbert, *1252*
HEYGHEN, Peter van, 63
HEYMANN, Ulrike, 868
Heytz
  recorders by, 250
HIGBEE, Dale, 2, 12, 29, 44, *65,* 127, *162, 200,* 243, *653, 654,* 663, 727, 1005, 1122, *1208, 1211,* 1215, 1223, 1305, 1360, 1419, 1427, 1448
HILL, Donna, *1415*
HILLEMAN, W., 1254
Hindemith, Paul, 1328
  Trio from *Plöner Musiktag,* 1150, 1360–63
HINTEREGGER, Richard, 245
Hirose, Ryohei: *Meditation,* 1000
Historical and Analytical Study of Renaissance Music for the Recorder and its Influence on Later Repertoire (Woodhill), 1482
Historical Performance (periodical), 1429
Historische Blasinstrumente—selbst gebaut (Robinson), 456
History, 12, 15–16, 19–24, 28–33, 35, 37–40, 53–54
  Middle ages, 185, 338–39, 457
    in Germany, 70
  Renaissance, 17, 56–57, 59–60, 339, 1473
  Baroque, 61–64, 1206
    decline of recorder in, 64, 354, 361
    in instrumental music, 1182
    in orchestra, 1454
    in relation to transverse flute, 62
    in the Hofkapelle, Vienna, 67

Index

History (continued)
Baroque (continued)
recorder in C in, 128
in England, 32, 56, 63, 72-75, 1480
in France, 68-69, 1193
opera, 1192
in Italy, 1196
in Spain, 63, 78-79
in the United States, 80
late 18th century, 65
19th century, 65
recorders made in, 210, 233, 235, 238, 1386
20th century, 82-86, 88-92, 819-20, 1457, 1462
in France, 1474
in German youth music movement, 303, 1464
revival, 12, 17, 26, 29-30, 33, 95-100, 303, 994, 1119, 1477
Hochschwarzer, A.
recorder by, 246
HÖFFER-VON WINTERFELD, Linde, 785, 981, 1022, 1127, 1224
Höffer-von Winterfeld, Linde, 1022
HOFMANN, Klaus, 1198, 1262, *1302*
Hoffman, Klaus, 1302
Holborne, Anthony: *Pavanes, Galliards, Almains and Other Short Aeirs,* 142, 691, 1173
Holland. *See* Netherlands
Höller, Günther, 1023
Holliger, Heinz, 1083
HOLM, Anna Lena, 906
HOLMAN, Peter, 71, p. 350
HOLSCHNEIDER, Andreas, *1070*
Holst, Imogen, 1024
Holtslag, Peter, 1025
Holzblasinstrumentenbau: Entwicklungsstufen und Technologien (Dullat), 439
Der Holzblasinstrumentenbau in der Freien Reichsstadt Nürnberg (Nickel), 176
Holzflöten und ihr Bau am Beispiel einer Blockflöte (Fussenegger), 1461

HOMFRAY, Tim, 912
Hopf (instrument maker), 464
HOPKINS, Bernard J., 1156, 1170
Hopkins, Bernard J., 1026
HOPKINS, Dennis W., *1026*
HORNER, Keith, 953, 1320
Horniman Museum (London)
A. Dolmetsch's instrument collection in, 280
HOSODA, Tsutomu, 1128
HOTTETERRE, Jacques, 650-57
Hotteterre, Jacques, 891, 1453
music including recorder, 689, 1191-92, 1193, 1274
recorders by, 216, 250, 270
treatises by
in comparison with Freillon-Poncein, 649
performance practice indicated in, 63, 536, 654.1, 700-701, 704.1, 710
Hotteterre family, 169, 214-16
HOULE, George, 708
HOUSE, Delpha Leann, 891
House of Schreiber, 799
HUBBARD, Frank, 502
Huber, Gerhard, 284
HÜBNER, Eckart, 1464
HÜBNER-HINDERLING, Renate, 709
HUDGEBUT, John, 602
Hudgebut, John: *A Vade Mecum,* 606
Huene, Friedrich von. *See* von Huene, Friedrich
HUGHES, Geoff, 103
Hul, Dick van den. *See* Den Hul, Dick van
HULLFISH, William R., 722-23
Hulsens, Guido, 285
Humor, 155-58, 1327
cartoons, 159
"golden rules" for ensemble playing, 154
HUMPHRIES, Nicholas, 1242
HUND-DAVIES, Malcolm, 692
HUNGER, Madeline M., 1333
HUNT, Edgar, 2-3, 12, *13-14, 18,* 22, 30, 35, *108,* 123, 130, 132, 136-39, 149, *162,* 200-1, 216, 231,

HUNT, Edgar (continued)
244, 278, 280, 296–98, 306,
316, 323, 329, 357, *368*, 369–
70, 378–80, 442, *456*, 491,
512,*524*, 540, 574, *589*, *625*,
641, 654.1, 737, *758*, 789, 790,
813, 878, *905*, 926–27, 934,
942, 985, 987, *992*, 1007, 1067,
1105, 1149–51, 1171, 1178–80,
1186, 1281, 1297–99, 1321,
1353, 1373–75, *1386*, 1399,
1439–40, 1441, 1449, p. 440
Hunt, Edgar, 197, 345, 908, 1028–32
HUNT, Enid, *1032*
HUNT, Rosemary, 112
HÜNTELER, Konrad, 1313
Hünteler, Konrad, 1027
HUNTER, Hilda, 58
HUNTER, Madeline M., *1333*
HUYGENS, Christiaan, 609

ICHIRO, Tada, *317*
Iconography, 16, 63, 143–52, 220, 1049
Improvement. *See* Maintenance and repair
Improvisation
  Baroque preludes, 748–49
  on Renaissance tunes, 730–31
An Index of Musical Wind Instrument Makers (Langwill), 162
Indiana University, 876
Indications of Performance Practice in Woodwind Instruction Books of the 17th and 18th Centuries (Warner), 536
Indo-Jazz Fusions, 1108
Inequality, 750
The Instrumental Chamber Music of Joseph Bodin de Boismortier (Peterman), 1234
Instrumentation
  and authenticity, 696
International Recorder School (Saratoga), 947, 1042
International Week of Twentieth-Century Recorder Music (1988), 1372

Interpretation of French Music from 1675 to 1775 for Woodwind and Other Performers (Mather), 702
Intonation, 20, 524, 796–802. *See also* Tuning
  acoustical studies, 426–29
  adjusting through fingering, 782, 800–1
  breath pressure and, 407, 419–29
  Brüggen on, 962
  use of electronic tuners, 798
  in ensembles, 851
  effect of "pulling out," 530
  teaching, 796
Introductio gschriben uf pfifen, 541
Inventories, preparing, 241
Iribarren: *Cantada al Santísimo con dos flautas de pico*, 79
Israel, 109
Italian Baroque Solo Sonatas for the Recorder and the Flute (McGowan), 1194–95
Italienische Diminutionen (Erig), 720
Italy, 110
  16th century, 1473
  recorders in:
    Assisi, Biblioteca Comunale, 178
    Bologna
      Accademia Filarmonica, 257
      Museo Civico, 227
    Florence, Museo Stibbert, 218
    Foligno, 177
    Modena, Musei Civici, 125
    Verona, Accademia Filarmonica, 258–59
  recorder in schools
    work of Edwin Alton, 913
  Venice
    makers, 179–81
    musical instruments in 16th-century homes, 182

JACKSON, Alan D., *354*, *834*
JACKSON, Roland, p. 222
Jacob, Gordon: *Suite*, 767
Jacob van Eyck's Der Fluyten Lust-hof *(1644–c1655)* (Griffioen), 1243–44

Index

JACOBS, Guido, 492
JACOBS, Paul, 204
JACOBY, Richard, 797
Jacques Hotteterre "le Romain": A Study of his Life and Compositional Style (House), 891
Jacques Hotteterre le Romain (1680–1761), flûtiste de la Chambre du Roi (Bourguignon), 1453
Jacques Hotteterre's L'art de préluder: A Translation and Commentary (Boyer), 658
JAEGER, Winifred, *1026*
Jaeger, Winifred
  on Erich Katz, 1038
Jaillard, Pierre. *See* Bressan, Peter
JAMBE DE FER, Philibert, 572
Jambe de Fer, Philibert, 964
  Epitome musical, 573–74, 729
James, Clarence, 286–87
JAMES, Lionel H., *815*
Janssen, Guus: *Largo*, 907
JANZEN, Rose-Marie, 896
Japan, 111
Jeger, Frederik de
  recorders by, 261
JENKINS, David, 1465
JENKINS, Simon, 1495
JOHNSON, Arthur, *1070*
Joints, 41, 513–16
JOLIBERT, Bernard, 693, 1181
JOOF, Laura Beha, 518, 526
Joubert, John: *The Hour Hand*, 1329
Journal de musique ancienne, 1430
Journal of the American Musical Instrument Society, 1431
Journals, bibliography of, 1412–13
Jouve
  bass recorder possibly by, 266
JÜRISALU, Heino, 117, 270
JURITZ, J.W.F., 791

Kagel, Mauricio, 1325, 1328, 1364
KAHL, Anne-Elisabeth, 1570
Kammermusikkreis Ferdinand Conrad, 978
Kammermusikkreis Scheck-Wenzinger, 978, 1099

Kanji, Ricardo, 911, 1033
Karkoschka, Erhard, 823, 1326, 1365
KARP, Cary, 262, 351.1, 1496–99, 1549, p. 169
KATZ, Erich, *1–2*, 13, 19, 95, *626*, 815, *1130*, 1164
Katz, Erich, 984, 1003, 1034–38
Katz, Hannah
  on Erich Katz, 1038
KATZ, Helen, 1052
Katz recorder competition, 1003
KAYE, Martin, 59
KELBER, Sebastian, 1357
Kelber, Sebastian, 1039
Kelischek, George, 288
KELLER, Michael, p. 84
KELLER-LÖWY, Walter, 1121
KENWORTHY, C., *162*, 889, 1382, *1439–41*
Kenworthy, C.
  and early days of the SRP, 1450
KENYON, Dorothy, *1032*
KENYON, Nicholas, 954
KENYON DE PASCUAL, Beryl, 63, 78, 186
KERWIN, Michael, 1328
Ketting, Piet: *Fantasia*, 1188
Keyed recorder, 235, 356–57, 359, 361, 363. *See also* Bell-keyed recorder
Keynsham Abbey
  fipple flute from site of, 1390
Keys. *See also* Construction and design, keywork
  history of, 349
  reducing noise of, 517
KIENTZY, Martine, 841
KIMBLE, Isabel, *46*
KING, Alexander Hyatt, *626*
KING, Ronald, 159
Kinsecker, Hieronymus Franciskus, 175–76
  recorders by, 256, 267
KINSELL, David, 96
KIRK, Douglas, 276
KIRNBAUER, Martin, 63, 97, 173–74, 205, 213, 255–56
KITSON, Linda, 962

KLEMISCH, Guido, *1032*
Klemisch, Guido, 289
Klingenbrunner, Wilhelm, 1387
KLIPHUIS, Harry, 277
Klokkenkunst te Utrecht tot 1700: met bijzondere aandacht voor het aandeel hierin van Jhr. Jacob van Eyck (Den Hul), 1456
Klukowski, Jozef, 112
KMETEC, Emil, *510*
KNEIHS, Hans Maria, 765
Kneihs, Hans Maria, 1040–41
KOCH, Hans Oskar, 1466
KOCH, John, 290, 814, *1415*
KOCH, William, *364*
Koch, William, 290
KÖHLER, Wolfgang, 31, 589–90
KOHN, Harold, *510*
KOLBERG, Sverre, 1550–51
KOLDEWEIJ, Jos, 150
Komorous, Rudolf, 1325
KÖNEKE, Hans W., 975
KOTTICK, Edward Leon, 524
Krähmer, Ernst, 1387
KRAINIS, Bernard, *714*, 792, 815, *1127*, 1164, 1212, *1215, 1416*, 1447–48
Krainis, Bernard, 908, 1042–43, 1093, 1118
KRICKEBERG, Dieter, 174, 213, 255
KRIEHN, George, *1026*
Krk (Adriatic island), 1389
KROESBERGEN, Willem, 1229
Kruspe, Carl, 125
KUBITSCHEK, Ernst, 971, 1252, 1273, 1279
KUHWEIDE, Peter, 387–88
KUIJKEN, Barthold, 63, *674*
KUMPF, Hans, 1359
KÜNG, Andreas, 223
Küng, Franz, 291–92, 328, 357, 464
Kunsthistorisches Museum (Vienna)
  "Ganassi" recorder (C 8522), 4, 460, 462
KUNZ, Harald, 1127
Kunzen, Friedrich Ludwig Aemilius, 1403

Kynseker. *See* Kinsecker, Hieronymus Franciskus

LABARRE, Kenneth, 467
Laborde, M. de (Jean Benjamin): *Essai sur la musique ancienne,* 66
La Canessière, Philippe de, 170
LACORNERIE, Agnès, 1006
La Couture Boussey
  boxwood of, 169
LAMBE, Joan, 918
LANDKAMMER, Ulrike, 1467
LANGWILL, Lindesay G., 162–3
LANKHOF, G.F., 1552
La Noue, Mathurin de, 170
La Riche, François, 886
LARSON, André P., 269
Lasch, Christopher, 89
LASOCKI, David, 4–11, *17*, 41, 63, 72–75, 128, 187–90, 461, *462*, *535*, 617, 649, *654*, 661, 680, 683, 686, 694–95, *701*, 710, 715, 728, 738–39, 748–49, *821*, 888, 890, 897–902, 905, 928, 1001, 1045, 1053, 1090, 1099, 1146, 1158, 1188, 1190, 1219–20, 1258–61, 1265, 1268, *1305*, 1307, 1355, p. 178, 441
Lasocki, David, 1044–46
LAVAIL, Patricia, 1006
Lavigne, Philibert de. *See* Delavigne, Philibert
Lavista, Mario: *Ofrenda,* 907
Layton, Roxanne, 1004
Leading Notes (periodical), 1432
LEAVIS, Ralph, *129, 1221*
LEBER, Eric, 807
LECHNER, Konrad, 1366
Lechner, Konrad, 823, 1060, 1366–67
Lectures on the Recorder in Relation to Literature (Welch), 18
Leenhouts, Paul, 1047
LEGÊNE, Eva, 63, 219, 1268
Legêne, Eva, 333, 936, 1048–50
LEHMAN, Robert A., 241
Lehner family, 176
Lehrer, Irmgard, 100, 937
Leigh, Walter, 697

Index

LEMAÎTRE, Edmond, 1192
LEMPFRID, Wolfgang, 1054
LEONARDS, Petra G., 600, 711
Leonhardt, Gustav, 960, 965
LERCH, Tom, 165, *352*
LESCAT, Philippe, 1312, 1314
LESURE, François, 170, 573, *587*, 591
LETTERON, Claude, 87, 1129, 1139, 1204–5
LEVIN, Lia Starer, 1263
LEVIN, Philip, 41, 389, 514, 519, 527, 792
Levin, Philip, 293
Levine, Joel, 907
Lewin, Alyson, *1410*
LEWIN, Greg, *1154*, 1500
LEWIS, Anthony, *1070*
LEWIS, Edgar Jay, Jr., 1182
LEWIS, Mildred, 443
LEYGRAF, Hans, *1367*
LI VIRGHI, Francesco, 178
Liber Fridolini Sichery, 1171
LIBERA, Luca della, *1315*
LIBIN, Laurence, 46, 224, 267
Limberg, Gabriele. *See* Frings, Gabriele
LINDE, Hans-Martin, 13, 98, 712, 1187, 1325, *1367*, p. 440
Linde, Hans-Martin, 908, 947, 1051–56, 1455
Music for a Bird, 1369
Modern Exercises for Treble Recorder, 1368
Trio, 1186, 1188
LINDLEY, David, 1400
LINSENBERG, Judith, 41, 478, *1244*
Lira organizzate
recorder as substitute for, 1272
Literary references, 16, 18, 39, 53
Livre plaisant et tres utile . . . , 543
Livre plaisant et tres utile . . . , 1169
Lockwood, Albert, 340
Loeb, David, 1328
Loeillet, Jacob. *See* Loeillet, Jacques

Loeillet, Jacques, 254, 895
Sonata for 2 Flutes, 2 Voice Flutes, and Continuo in B minor, 1186–87
Loeillet, Jean Baptiste (de Gant), 697, 895, 1469
Loeillet, John, 893–94, 897, 1178, 1275
Loeillet de Gand, Jean Baptiste. *See* Loeillet, Jean Baptiste (de Gant)
Loeillet family, 892–97, 1275
music by, 1275–77
Woodcock concertos attributed to, 1316
Löhner family, 176
LOONAN, Martin, 1130–31, 1142, 1290
LOOSE, Ghislaine, 1469
Loré, Etienne, 170
LORETTO, Alec V., 4, *127, 326,* 331, 390, 444–47, 460, 462, 468, 500–2, 511, 528, 969–70, 1500.1, 1553–54
Loretto, Alec V., 295–300
Ganassi recorder by, 4, 461–62
Lorraine, Marie de, 69
Lot, Louis
recorders by, 235, 270
Lot family, 168
LOTTERMOSER, Werner, 408
Lotti, Antonio: Trio Sonata for Recorder, Viola da Gamba, and Continuo, 1178
LOUGHRY, B.W., *507*
LOULIÉ, Étienne, 610
Loulié, Étienne, 69, 613–14
Méthode pour apprendre à jouer de la flûte douce, 611–14
Lully, Jean-Baptiste, 1193, 1278
Lunbeck, Linda, 1004
LÜPKE, Arndt von, 409
LUSCINIUS, Othmar, 545
LÜTZEN, Ludolf, 976
LYNDON-JONES, Maggie, 191
Lynn, Michael, 1057
LYONS, Donald H., 410

MAARBJERG, Mary, 850
MAASS, Ulrike, 1470
MACHAN, Katja, 1573
MACMILLAN, Douglas, 65, 129, 131, 1316
Magnamusic, 1066
Maintenance and repair, 13–14, 16, 19, 22, 466, 485–97. *See also* Restoration
  block, 41, 502, 525
  breaking in, 41
  condensation, 41, 508–12
  flexibility, improvement of, 311, 502
  joints, 41, 513–16
  lips, adjustable, 500
  oiling, 490, 518–21
  thumb hole reinforcement, 498
  tuning, 526–33
  voicing, 382, 525–27
  windway, 41, 501
MAJER, JOSEPH FRIEDRICH BERNHARD CASPAR, 664–66
Majer, Joseph Friedrich Bernhard Caspar:
  Museum Musicum, 667
  fingerings in, third-octave, 727
Makers and manufacturers. *See also under names of individual makers*
  biographical dictionaries, 885
  historical, 12, 16, 21, 162–238
    16th-century, 236
    Baroque, 165
    France, 168–70, 1465
    Germany, Nuremberg, 63, 173–76
    England, 167
    Italy, Venice, 179–81
    The Netherlands, 183
  index of, 162–63
  inventories of instruments, 242–43
  modern, 271–324
    directories, 271
    Switzerland, 324
Makers' marks, 164
  Bassano family, 187–89, 191
  Nuremberg, 173
  Wijne, Robert, 234

Making, 24, 34, 434–35, 437–40, 442–46, 448–62. *See also* Maintenance and repair; Manufacturing; Woods
  in the Baroque, 165
  entering the profession, 446
  based on historical models, 63, 242, 435, 442, 444, 449, 451–54
  approaches taken by makers, 309, 443, 448, 455, 458
  instrument for the music of van Eyck, 333
  medieval recorders, 440, 457
  Renaissance recorders, 448
  trends of the 1960s, 357
  do-it-yourself, 434
  in contrast to manufacturing, 450
  plastic instruments, 445
Maldive islands
  duct flutes, 1396
MALINOWSKI, Stephen A., *836*
Mancini, Francesco: Sonata for Recorder and Continuo in D Minor, 1279
Manhattan Consort, 982
MANIFOLD, John, 23, 32, 42
MANN, Alfred, 1164, 1206
Mann, Alfred, 1042
Mann, Manfred: "Trouble and Tea," 102
Manufacturing, 436, 441, 447, 450
Marcello, Benedetto
  sonatas by, 765, 1194–95, 1280
Marchand, Jean-Noël
  and *Il pastor fido,* 1312, 1314
MARGOLIS, Bob, 836
Margolis, Bob, 907
MARISSEN, Michael, 1209, 1218, 1228, *1229,* p. 442
MARSHALL, Arthur W., 1248–49
MARTIN, Anne, 47, 883
MARTIN, John, 400, 411–13, 417, 529, 1216–17, 1327, 1344, p. 134, 442, 445
MARTIN, Mariano, 79
MARVIN, Bob, 41, 192, 242, 301, 332, 339, 362, 448–49, 459, 701, 714, 1385, 1501–5

Index

Marvin, Bob, 301
 Ganassi recorder by, 459, 462
MARVUGLIO, Matt, 348
MARVUGLIO, Tony, 348
MARX, Josef, *1305*
MARX, Karl, 1060
Marx, Karl, 1058–60
MASCHER, Ekkehardt, 977
MASSY, Jim, 530, 786
MATHER, Betty Bang, 694, 702, 739–41, 749
MATHIESEN, Aksel H., 352
Mathiesen, Aksel H., 166
MATHIESEN, Irmgard, 352
Mathiesen, Irmgard, 166
MATHIESEN, Penelope, 220, 1044, 1057, *1420*
MATTHYSZ, Paulus, 592
MATTRAN, Donald, 1135
MAYER, Christian, 551
MAYERS, Dan E., 1391
MAYES, Andrew, *1439*
Maynfrank, Claus E. *See* Hofmann, Klaus
Mazel family
 garklein recorder by, 125
MCALLISTER, Maureen, *1032*
MCCAULEY, Denis, 842
MCCHESNEY, Richard, 94
MCCULLOCH, Derek, 1289
MCCUTCHEON, Mary, 1330
MCGOWAN, Richard A., 1194–95, 1285
MCGRADY, Richard, 742
MCRAE, Lee, 283, *1026*
Measurements, 242, 327, 329, 351–52
 computerized collection of, 352
Measuring, 350–53
MEDFORTH, Martin, 904
MEDLEY, Daphne, 401
Meech, Michael: *Puppet Show*, 1150
MEER, John Henry van der, 172, 175, *180*, *208*, 209
MEGAW, J.V.S., 1392–93
MEIEROTT, Lenz, 124, 1471
Mellor, Robyn, 1061
Melville, Alison, 1062

Les ménestriers, 1093
Mercier, Louis Sébastien: *L'an 2440*, 160
MERGER, Carl E., 318
MERRYWEATHER, James, 77
MERSENNE, Marin, 586–88, p. 131
 Harmonie universelle, 140, 187, 589–90, 755
METCALFE, William C., 64, 1294, 1306, *1307*
Méthode pour apprendre à jouer de la flûte douce (Loulié), 610
Methods (tutors) and treatises
 historical, 534–688
 bibliography, 534–40
 selected facsimile editions, 1149
 modern, 868–69, 871
Metropolitan Museum of Art (New York City)
 woodwind instruments in, 267–68
METT, Silke, 851
Metzger, Heinz Klaus, 82
Mexico
 pre-Columbian flutes, 1395
MEYER, Jürgen, 426–27
Meytz, Johann. *See* Heitz, Johann
MEZGER, Marianne, p. 444
MICHATZ, Hans-Dieter, 766
Michatz, Hans-Dieter, 1063
MICHEL, Winfried, 1159
Michel, Winfried, 1302
MICHON, Claire, 884
MIDDLETON, James, 418, *953*, 1152, *1200*, 1408
MIDI wind controllers, 85, 348
Mielich, Hans, 254
Miessen, Marijke, 1064
Miles, Rebecca, 1065
MILLER, Clement A., 571
MILLER, Theo, 1506
Miller Flute Collection, Dayton C. *See* Dayton C. Miller Flute Collection
Milton, John, 18
MINGUET É IROL, Pablo, 681–82
Minguet é Irol, Pablo: *Reglas, y advertencias generales*, 683, 727
MITCHELL, David, 1173

MIX, Theodore, 377, 501
Mix, Theodore, 1066
Modern Music for Recorder (music series), 1095
Moderne Blockflötentechnik (van Hauwe), 756
The Modern Musick-Master (Prelleur), 624, 626, 752
The Modern Recorder Player (van Hauwe), 756
Modernization. *See* Construction and design
Modes, medieval
 influence on recorder design, 338
MOECK, Hermann Jr., 33, 55, 89, 99, *108*, 156, *302*, 319, *337, 345, 363, 377,* 391, *447*, 450, *501*, 520, 929, 955, 1386, 1472
Moeck, Hermann Jr., 303-4
Moeck, Hermann Sr., 302
Moeck Verlag (publisher and manufacturer), 232, 303, 305, 447, 464
MOENS-HAENEN, Greta, 753
Mollenhauer, 357, 464
MÖLLER, Dirk, 1269
Monin, Claude, 306-7, 392
MONK, Christopher, *1070*
Monsbourgh, Lazy Ade, 105
MONTAGU, Jeremy, 151, *162, 243, 261, 486, 505,* 696, 1214, 1507, 1508
Montéclair, Michel Pignolet de
 brunettes by, 1191, 1193
Montreal
 four composers living in, 1330
MOONEN, Toon, 63, 451, 1555-59
Moore, Timothy: Suite in G, 1150
MORENO, Emilio, 956
Morgan, Fred, 4, *17, 34,* 260, *333-34,* 452-53, *462,* 1217
Morgan, Fred, 103, 312
 Ganassi recorder by, 4, 461-62
Morley, Thomas: *Consort Lessons*, 1174-75
Morley College (London), 1382
Morley College Recorder Consort, 1095

MOSAND, John, 670
MOSSER, Thomas R., 1296
The Most Pleasant Companion (Banister), 603
MOTZKIN, Elhanan, *146*
Mouth cavity
 effects on pitch and tone, 420-21
Mozart, Wolfgang Amadeus, 1281
Muffat, Gottfried, 67
MÜHLE, Christoph, 414
MULGAN, Anthony, *1070*
MÜLLER-BUSCH, Franz, 1288
Müller-Hartmann, R.: *Suite*, 1150, 1370
Multiphonics, 840-43
Multiple recorder
 by Manfredo Settala, 226
MUNDHENKE, Heike, 767
MUNKACSI, Joan, 14
MUNROW, David, 358
Munrow, David, 908, 1067-70, 1093, 1258
Mureedhu, Kuda, 1396
Murray, A. Gregory, *1202*
MURRAY, Dom Gregory, 1160
Murray, Dom Gregory, 1071
MURRAY, Roy, *1032*
Murrill, Herbert, 697
Musée Instrumental du Conservatoire Royal de Musique (Brussels)
 recorders in, 1384, 1452
Musei Civici (Modena)
 recorders in, 125, 227
Museo Stibbert (Florence)
 Rippert alto recorder in, 218
Muses
 and the instrumentation of Morley's *Consort lessons*, 1175
The Muses Delight (Sadler), 633
Museum der Stadt Meran
 alto recorder in, 376
Museum musicum theoretico practicum (Majer), 664-65
Museum of Fine Arts (Boston)
 recorders in, 1005
Music. *See* Repertory
MUSIC, David W., 80

Index

Music for a While, 293
The Music in English Drama (Manifold), 42
Music Reference and Research Materials (Duckles & Keller), p. 84
Music therapy, 20
Musica Antiqua (Belgium), 1433
Musica Antiqua (Spain), 1434
Musica Antiqua (Vienna), 971-72
Musica Dolce, 1080
Musica enchiriadis
  influence of tetrachord system on recorder design, 338
Musica getutscht (Virdung), 542, 546-48, 550
Musica instrumentalis deudsch (Agricola), 556-58
Musical Instruments and Their Symbolism (Winternitz), p. 54
Musicus autodidaktos (Eisel), 668-69
Musikhistorisk Museum (Copenhagen)
  Denner recorders in, 207
Musikhistoriska Museet (Stockholm)
  Baroque woodwinds in, 262
Musikinstrumentenmuseum (Munich)
  recorders in, 254
MUSKETT, Michael, 512
Musurgia (Luscinius), 545
Muziekkring Obrecht, 1078
Muzijkaal Kunst-Woordenboek (Reynvaan), 687
MYERS, Herbert, 335, 606

Nägeli, 284
NAGLE, Sigrid, 268, 1042, 1093, 1111, 1118, *1415*
NALLEN, Evelyn, 1025
Nallen, Evelyn, 1072-73
Narcissim, 89
NASTASI, Mirjam, 957
National Early Music Association, *1432, 1435*
National Early Music Association, 1111

National Portrait Gallery (Yorkshire), 148
Nationalmuseum (Prague)
  woodwind instruments in, 248
Naudot, Jacques Christophe, 168
NEATE, Helen, 905
NEGRE, Louis, 1394
NEMA Early Music Yearbook, p. 94
NEMA Journal, 1435
NERODA, Joanna, *1349*
The Netherlands
  conservatory study in, 884
  makers, 17th-18th centuries, 183
  recorder music, 1318
  Dutch recorders in U.S. collections, 184
  recorders in:
    Dordrecht, medieval recorder discovered in, 185, 440
    Groningen, collection of Michiel van Bolhuis, 237
    The Hague, Gemeentemuseum, 240, 261
Netherlands Recorder Trio
  Sourcream (1971), 952
Neue Klangwelt auf der Blockflöte (Braun), 823
Neueroeffneter theoretsch- und praktischer Music-Saal (Majer), 664
NEUMEYER, David, 1362, p. 444
The Newest Method for Learners on the German Flute, 624
The New Flute Master for the Year 1729, 622
The New Grove Dictionary of Music and Musicians, 35
The New Grove Dictionary of Musical Instruments, 35
New London Consort, 1085
Newman, Harold, 1074
NEWMAN, Joel, 66, 469, 627, 667, 729, 816, *1101*, 1132-33, 1137, *1173*, 1255, 1282
NEWMAN, Morris, 1134
A New Musical Grammar (Tans'ur), 671
A New System of the Flute a'bec, (Stanesby Jr.), 662

New York Pro Musica, 982–83,
　1042–43
New Zealand, 295, 1111
Niagara Falls (N.Y.) High School
　Recorder Quartet, 116
NICKEL, Ekkehart, 176, 206
Niederländische Blockflöten des 18.
　Jahrhunderts (van Acht), 261
NIEMEYER, Gerhart, 947
NIEMÖLLER, Klaus Wolfgang, 548
Nienstedt, Dörte, 1349
NIEUWHOF, Ben, 1560–61
"The Nightingale," 80
NITKA, Arthur, 476
Nitka, Arthur, 1075
NITZ, Martin, 1251
NOBLE, Jeremy, 1070
NOBLE, Richard D.C., 12, 88, 101–2
NORMAN, Janet, 966, 1092
NOSEK, Margaret A., 56
Notation
　clefs, historical survey, 813
　20th-century, 844
Notation der neuen Blockflötenmusik
　(Schmidt), 844
Notes inégales. See Inequality
Noue, Mathurin de la. See La Noue,
　Mathurin de
NUCHELMANS, Jan, 958

Oberlender, Johann Wilhelm I
　recorders by, 97, 250, 254, 256,
　　262, 267
　transverse flute with whistle
　　mouthpiece by, 237
Oberlender family, 176
Oberlin Conservatory, 876, 1057
Oberösterreichisches Landes-
　museum
　flute collection, 1470
Obizzi collection (Catajo)
　bass recorders in, 139
Ocarina, 1408
OESTREICHER, Klaus, 140
OHANNESIAN, David, 261, 454
OHMURA, Noriko, 1308
Oiling, 490, 518–21

O'KELLY, Eve, 17, 261, 819–20, 946,
　997, 1372, 1439, p. 441, 442
O'Kelly, Eve, 1076
Oki, Irène, 489
Old English Instruments of Music
　(Galpin), 71.1
Oler, Virginia C., 263
OLER, Wesley M., 263, 288, 667,
　1212
Oler, Wesley M.
　recorder collection of, 263
O'LOUGHLIN, Niall, 1323
Onderwyzinge hoemen alle de toonen en
　halve toonen (Blankenburg),
　593–95
One-handed recorders, 368–70
ONGARO, Giulio, 179
On Playing the Flute (Quantz), 677
Opera
　17th-century, 1184–85
　French Baroque, 1192
Opera intitulata Fontegara (Ganassi),
　562–66
Oratorio
　17th-century, 1184–85
Das Orchester in den Werken Jean-
　Baptiste Lullys (Eppelsheim),
　1278
Orchestra, 17
　Baroque, 1454
Orchestra of the 18th Century, 950,
　954–56, 965
Orchestras, recorder, 846. See also
　Choirs, recorder
Orléans, Elizabeth d', 69
Ornamentation, 13–15, 56, 730–44
　Renaissance, 730–34
　Baroque, 607, 735–44
　　as described in English meth-
　　　ods, 608
　French
　　compared to Japanese flute
　　　music, 743
　Italian, 735
　sonatas of Handel (see Handel,
　　George Frideric, solo sonatas)
Ortiz, Diego, 732, 964
OSMOND, D.W.J., 424

Index

O'SULLIVAN, Patricia, 875, 879
OTTEN, Kees, *1032*
Otten, **Kees,** 908, 965, 1077–78
OTTENBOURGS, Stefaan, 63, 221
Ottoboni, Pietro, 1311
Oxford
    double recorder of, 1385

Paetzold, Joachim, 85, 308
    contrabass recorder by, 342
Paisible, James, 72, 697, 1182, 1190
    and the "echo flute," 1211–12, 1219–20
Palanca, Carlo, 217
PALME, Natalie, 1102
PALMER, Frederic, *714*
Panpipes, 1403
PAOLIS, Luca de, *565*
Parent, Michiel
    recorders by, 237, 270
Paris Conservatoire
    recorders in instrument collection of, 249–53
PARKINSON, Andrew, 1406
PARKINSON, Janice M., 930
PARROTT, Jasper, *1070*
Pascal, Blaise, 949
PASCUAL, Beryl Kenyon de, *187,* 225
PASQUALE, Marco di, 258
Pasquale, Marco di, 660
Passions. *See* Affections
Patavino, Francesco, 153
PATERSON, Scott, 1116, 1146
Pedagogy, 17, 20, 770, 865–74, 912.
    See also Colleges and universities
    American Recorder Society Education Program, 865
    bass recorder, 135
    intonation, 796
    methods, 868–69, 871
    in France, 881–82
    in Germany, 872, 883
    in Italy, 913
PEHRSSON, Clas, 90
Pehrsson, Clas, 282, 1079–80
Pepusch, Johann Christoph: *Six Concerts,* op. 8, 1188

Pepys, Samuel, 16, 53, 100, 1220
Performance practice, 13, 15, 689–755. *See also under specific topics (e.g.,* Articulation; Authenticity; Fingerings; Ornamentation; etc.)
    use of analysis to develop an interpretation, 765
    Brüggen, Frans, on, 953
    dance suites, Baroque, 693
    correcting "errors," 1183
    French music, 700–703, 1467
    as indicated in historical methods, 534, 536
    historical styles, 692
    Italian music, 704
    solo sonatas, 697
Performance Practice: A Bibliography (Vinquist & Zaslaw), p. 222
Performance Practice: Medieval to Contemporary, a Bibliographic Guide (Jackson), p. 222
Performance Practice Review, 1436, p. 222
Performing, 766
Periodicals, 1412–45
    bibliography of, 1412–13
Peru
    pre-Columbian flutes, 1395
PESKIN, Carolyn, 41, 1395
PETER, Hildemarie, 15, *566–67,* 568
PÉTERI, Judit, 959
PETERMAN, Lewis Emanuel, Jr., 1234
Petri, Michala, 1081–84
Pfegl
    recorders by, 262
PHILLIPS, Michael H., 852
The Physics of Musical Instruments (Fletcher & Rossing), 399
Piano with recorder, 767, 1140
Piccolo, Flauto. *See* Newman, Joel
PICHLER, Isfried Hermann, 245
Pickett, Philip, 1085
Piloṭ, Daniel, 1330
Pinkillo, 1397
PINSON, Jean-Pierre, 48
Pipe and tabor, 1409–10

Pitch, 371–81. *See also* Intonation; Tuning
  a^1 = 440 as a standard, 377–81
  Baroque
    Italian music, 376
    music of Bach, 374, 1222
  effect of breath pressure on, 407, 422–29
  inconsistency of, in historical instruments, 373
  modern vs. historical, 372
  of 16th-century recorders, 375
  of soprano and tenor recorders as B♭, 337
Piwkowski, Professor, 112
PLACHTE, Frank L., 1036, 1091
Plaikner, Albrecht (or Jakob), 172
PLAMQVIST, Jonas, 219
Plastic recorders, 445, 477–84, 522. *See also under makers' names*
Playing Recorder Sonatas (Rowland-Jones), 697
Poland
  Warsaw, 112
POLK, Keith, 70
Popular music, 101–2
POST, Nora, 320
POTTIER, Laurence, 63, 1193, 1473, p. 441, 442
POWELL, Ardal, 1493, 1509–11
Powell, Verne Q., 318
POWERS, Wendy, 264–65
The Practical Acoustics of Early Woodwinds (Myers), 335
A Practical and Historical Source-Book for the Recorder (Schmidt), 16
Practicing, 803–4, 806–8, 811
PRAETORIUS, Martin, 798
PRAETORIUS, Michael, 580–83
Praetorius, Michael
  examples of bass parts by, 142
  Syntagma musicum, 583, 1384
    bass recorder in, 139–40, 142
Praetorius Consort, 921
PRAETZ, Barbara, 940
PRATT, Bill, 303
Prattica de musica (Zacconi), 575–76
PRELLEUR, Peter, 624–26

Preluding, 748–49
Presbycusis
  and the recorder player, 465
PRESCOTT, Thomas, 455
Prescott, Thomas, 309–10, 455
PRIESTMAN, Brian, 892
PRIMUS, Constance M., 141–42, 1037, 1106
Principes de la flûte (Schickhardt), 659–60
Principes de la flute traversiere (Hotteterre), 650–52
Principles of the Flute, Recorder & Oboe (Hotteterre), 653–54
PRINGLE, Rosa, 100
PRIOR, Roger, 190
PRIOR, Susan, 381, 808–9, 1165, 1368. *See also* Carduelis, Susan
Prior, Susan, 1086
Pro Arte (recorder quartet), 1006
Probleme und Lesarten historischer Modelle zur Blockflötenliteratur des Spätbarock (Staeps), 1183
Problems and Readings of Historical Models (Staeps), 1183
Professional Recorder Players in England, 1540–1740 (Lasocki), 72, p. 441
Prowo, Pierre: *Sonata a 3*, 1188
PUGLISI, Filadelfio, 218, 226, 257
Pugnani, Gaetano, 697
PUKLICKÝ, Milan, 248
Purcell, Daniel, 1182, 1282
Purcell, Henry, 27, 1263, 1283
  imitation of birdsong, 47
  music on his death, 1189
  tunes printed in *The Compleat Flute-Master*, 617
Pyzik, Kazimierz: *Symphonic Triptych, part 2: Action 2*, 1328

QUANDT, Reinhold, 304, 916, 1083
QUANTZ, Johann Joachim, 673–79
Quantz, Johann Joachim, 1284
  Trio Sonata for Recorder, Flute, and Continuo in C Major (QV 2:2), 680, 1178, 1186–87

Index

Quantz, Johann Joachim (continued)
  Versuch einer Anweisung die Flöte traversiere zu spielen
    and the passions, 680
    tonguing syllables in, 710
    vibrato in, 754
  Quelques aspects du répertoire de la flûte à bec au XVIIIe siècle (Roos), 1475

Ralph Roister Doister, 49
Ran'doo, 393
RANSLEY, Michael, 1512
RANUM, Patricia M., 63, 69, 611, 613-14, 713, p. 442, 444
RASCH, Rudi A., 1197
RASMUSSEN, Mary, 152, 1135, p. 54
RAUDONIKAS, F., 425, 1513
RAWSKI, Conrad, 537
Rawsthorne, Alan: Suite for Recorder and Piano, 1371
READ, Robin, 336, 1237
Recercare (periodical), 1437
RECHBERGER, Herman, 826-27
Recondo, Ezequiel M., 1087
"Recorder," etymology of, 12, 43-45, 53, 1122
Recorder. *See also under specific topics (e.g.,* Bibliography; Construction and design; History; Maintenance and repair; Repertory, etc.)
  general introductions, 12-14, 19, 21-22, 24-25, 27, 29-30, 32, 34-36, 38
The Recorder: A Basic Workshop Manual (Brown), 486
The Recorder: A Handbook of Useful Information (Hunt), 22
The Recorder and Its Music (Hunt), 12, p. 440
Recorder & Music (periodical), 1439
Recorder & Music Magazine, 1111
Recorder and Music Magazine, 1439
The Recorder and Music Magazine, 1441

The Recorder: Australia's Journal of Recorder and Early Music, 1438, p. 440
The Recorder Book (Wollitz), 14
Recorder choirs, 856, 861
The Recorder Collection of Frans Brüggen, 260
Recorder Humour (King), 159
The Recorder Idiom in the Instrumental Music of Georg Philipp Telemann (Mosser), 1296
The Recorder in the Baroque Orchestra (Davis), 1454
The Recorder in the Music of Purcell and Handel (Levin), 1263
The Recorder in Twentieth-Century Music (O'Kelly), 819
The Recorder: Its Traditions and Its Tasks (Peter), 15
The Recorder: Journal of the Victorian Recorder Guild, 1438
The Recorder Magazine, 1439
Recorder music. *See* Repertory
The Recorder News, 1440
The Recorder News, 1441, 1450
Recorder orchestras, 846
Recorder players, 17, 24, 907-9. *See also under the names of individual players.*
  attitude toward the instrument, 94
  biographical dictionaries, 885
  18th-century, 61
  in England
    16th-18th centuries, 72-74
  in Germany,
    Middle Ages, 70
  in Spain
    18th century, 78
The Recorder Player's Handbook (Linde), 13
Recorder Profiles (Thomson), 908
Recorder Technique (Rowland-Jones), 757
The Recorder Today (O'Kelly), 820, p. 441
Recorder Tutors of the Seventeenth and Eighteenth Centuries (Vinquist), 534

RECORDERS (musical composition), 923
La redécouverte de la flûte à bec en France au XXe siècle (Robert), 1474
REDSELL, Matthew James, 310, 321, *1420*
REES, Helen, 1088
Rees, Helen, 1088–89
Register of Early Music in America, p. 94
Reglas, y advertencias generales (Minguet é Irol), 681–82
REICHENTHAL, Gene, 787, 800, *801, 1030,* 1107, *1221*
REIDEMEISTER, Peter, 114, *1367*
REILLY, Edward R., *667,* 1284
REINHARD, Bruno, 361, 466
Reinhard, Johnny, 907
REISS, Scott, 714, *738, 740,* 792, 801
Reiss, Scott, 1090
REITER, Andrea, 1020
The Reluctant Consort, 1002
Die Renaissance der Blockflöte im 19. und 20. Jahrhundert (Schwarz), 1477
Le renouveau de la flûte à bec au XXe siècle (Delvigne), 1455
Le répertoire de la flûte à bec en France à l'époque baroque (musique profane) (Pottier), 1193, p. 441
Répertoire international des sources musicales **(RISM),** 1155
Repertory, 12–17, 27, 30, 35, 119, 121, 123. *See also under the names of individual composers*
  "authentic," 1154
  bibliography, 1–3, 14, 1127–45
    20th-century, 819–20, 1333
    concertos, 1143
    dance music, 1132
    sonatas, 1142
    unaccompanied solos, 1136–37
    Walsh catalog, 1133
  Christmas, 1156
  continuo realization, 717–18
  in early printed editions, 1155
  editing, 17

Repertory (continued)
  editions, desired qualities in, 1157–58
  encores, 1152
  ensembles, 848, 855, 864
  facsimile editions, 17, 1149
  with flute, 1186–88
    as suitable for modern flute, 1153
  with guitar, 1138–39
  high school and college, teacher's guide, 1135
  humorous, 1327
  with piano, 767, 1140
  sonatas, 697
  with strings, 1141
  transcription and arrangement *(see* Transcription and arrangement)
  trios, 1150
  unaccompanied, 1148
  in vocal works, 1184–85
  Middle Ages
    Germany, 70
  Renaissance, 17, 57, 59, 1168–72, 1482
  Baroque, 17, 63, 1475
    correcting "errors" in, 1183
    canzona and sonata, 63
    dance suites, 693
    England, 1480
    France, 1193
    Italy, 1196
    The Netherlands, 1197
    quartets for three instruments and continuo, 1180
    sonatas, 20, 1181, 1194–95
      bibliography, 1142
    trio sonatas, 1178–79
  20th-century, 88, 819–20, 1317–33, 1323, 1325
    avant-garde, 17, 819–20, 1320–22, 1328, 1331, 1333
    juvenile, 1326
    notation, 844
    Australia, 1144–45, 1481
    Great Britain, 1317
    The Netherlands, 1318
    United States, 1332

Reprise: The Extraordinary Revival of Early Music (Cohen), 948
Restoration, 503-5
 bibliography, p. 169
 Soubeyran, Claire, work of, 314
 of specific instruments, 185, 259
Reutter, Georg, 67
REVIERS, Bruno de, 392-94, 1396
A Review of Recorder Music by Australian Composers (Strong), 1481
Revival of the recorder in the 20th century, 12, 17, 26, 29-30, 33, 95-100, 303, 994, 1119, 1477
REYNE, Hugo, 38, 236, 271, 480, 909, 980, 1114, 1277, 1388, 1401, 1412
REYNVAAN, Joos Verschuere, 687
Reynvaan, Joos Verschuere, 727
Rhetoric
 and Baroque music, 690
Rhythm
 and articulation symbols, 708
 inequality, 750
Riccio, Giovanni Battista, 697, 751
RICE, Albert R., 237
RICE, Michael, 354
Riche, François la. *See* La Riche, François
Richter, Johann Christian, 886
Rijkel
 recorder by, 246
RILEY, Maurice, 538
RING, Layton, 1283
Rippert, Jean-Jacques
 recorders by, 218, 250, 254, 393
RISM, 1155
RITCHIE, Jacqueline, 272, 285, 307, 322, 1003
RIVERS, Lynton, 1064
Robbins, Shirley, 1091
ROBERT, Cécile, 1474
Roberts, Don "Pixie," 105
ROBINSON, M.B., 962
ROBINSON, Trevor, 456
RODGERS, Gwen, 1073, 1451
Rodgers, Gwen, 1092
Roessler, Heinz, 311
Roger, Jeane, 1260

ROLIN, Étienne, 1324
Rolin, Étienne: *Phénix,* 1324
Rolling Stones: "Ruby Tuesday," 102
ROOS, Frédéric de, 1475
Roosen, I.
 recorders by, 261
Roosendael, Jan Rokus van: *Rotations,* 1372
ROSE, Pete, 41, 107, *778,* 907, 911, 936, 1021, 1050, 1089, 1331-33
ROSENBERG, Marvin, 853, 1448
ROSENBERG, Steve, 41
Rosenberg, Steve, 1093-94
 The Recorder Book, 870
Rosenborg recorders, 219-20, 333, 1048-49
ROSSEBORG, Theres, 1574
ROSSING, Thomas D., 399, p. 134
Rössler
 Oberlender model, 442
ROTH, Ruth C., 810
Rottenburgh
 recorders by, 63
Rottenburgh family, 221
ROWE, John, *491*
Rowland-Jones, Anthony, 17, 697, 703, 715, *726,* 755, 757, 768-69, 772, 787, 794-95, *801,* 1175
Roxburgh, Edwin: *Constellations,* 1329
Royal College of Music (London)
 recorders in, 207, 216
Royal Shakespeare Theatre Wind Band, 1068
Rubbra, Edmund, 1373-74
Rudiments of the Flute, Recorder, and Oboe (Hotteterre), 653
RUËTZ, Manfred, 1206.1, 1225
Ruëtz, Manfred, 1060
Ruf, Hugo, 1232
"Rules for Gracing on the Flute," 607-8
RUMMEL, Luise, 1476
Russia
 St. Petersburg
 instrument collection, flutes and recorders in, 270

Ruszpfeif, 1411
RUTHERFORD, David, 637
RUYTEN, Hans, 1562
Ryder, Dudley, 898
Ryder, James, 1004
Rykel
  recorders by, 262

SACKSTEDER, Richard, 293, 398, *945*
SAHLIN, Eva, 1272
St. Peter Hungate (Norwich)
  Bressan bass recorder in, 199
SALB, Michael, 36
Salkeld, Robert, 1095
SALTER, Humphrey, 605
Salter, Humphrey: *The Genteel Companion*, 606
SALVATORELLI, Franco, *689*
Sammartini, Giuseppe, 1194, 1285
SANDFORD, Gordon, 1176
SANDMAN, Susan G., *876*
SANDNER, Erich, 337
Sansom, Roy, 1004
SANVOISIN, Michel, *657*
Sattler
  recorders by, 262, 266
SAUNDERS, Gordon, 470, 493
SAUNDERS, Joanne, 312
Saux, Gaston: Quartet in F, 1375
SAVAGE, Alan A., *64*, 1256
Savoldo, Giovanni Girolamo: *Portrait of a Man with a Recorder*, 153
Saxby, Joseph, 993, 995
SAYERS, Keith, 108, 311, *1200*
Scaling, 352, 451
Scarlatti, Alessandro, 1180, 1182, 1286–88
SCHARAPAN, Gérard, 1376
SCHARENBERG, Sointu, 555
SCHECK, Gustav, 37, 1100, 1295
Scheck, Gustav, 908, 978, 1051, 1056, 1097, 1096, 1098, 1100
Schell, Johann, 176
  recorders by, 97, 256
Scherer family, 222
SCHERLIESS, Volker, 153

SCHICKHARDT, Johann Christian, 659–60
Schickhardt, Johann Christian, 697, 899–902
  Principes de la flûte, 661
Schickhardt, Johann-Jakob, 198
SCHIEMER, Veronika, 1577
SCHIMMEL, Hans, 261
Schlägl monastery
  ivory recorders in, 244–45
Schlegel, Christian, 223
Schlegel, Jeremias, 223
  recorders by, 250
Schloß Sigmaringen
  musical instruments in, 246
Schmelzer, Johann: *Sonata a 7 flaut*, 1182
SCHMID, Manfred Hermann, 254
SCHMIDT, Dörte, 1364
SCHMIDT, Lloyd, 16, 1207
SCHMIDT, Susanne, 308
SCHMIDT, Ursula, 844
SCHMITZ, Hans-Peter, *676*
SCHNEIDER, Michael, 1230
Schnitzer family, 176
SCHNOLL, David, 471
SCHNUR, Andreas, *426*
SCHOLL, Jürgen, 1575
Schöllnast, Franz, 1387
Schollum, Robert, 697
Schön, Ludwig, 67
Schott
  manufacture of Concert recorders, 436
SCHOUTEN, Marijke, 1229
SCHRADE, Leo, *546*
Schratt, Hans Rauch von
  recorders by, 250, 254
Schrattenbach
  recorders by, 256
Schuchart, Johann Just, 198, 224
Schuechbaur
  recorders by, 97
SCHULTZE, Bernhard, 1514
Schuster, Max, 315
Schütz, Heinrich, 1289
SCHWARTING, Heino, 1302
SCHWARZ, Roswitha, 1477

Index

Sciortino, Patrice: *Salicionaux*, 1376
Scopolamine, 510
Scoring, Structure, and Signification in J.S. Bach's Brandenburg Concertos (Marissen), 1209
SCOTT, A., *838*
Seckendorf, Paul, 315
The Second Book of the Flute Master Improv'd, 623
SEELY, Neil, *41*
SEGERMAN, Ephraim, 1515-16
SEIBERT, Peter, 733, 1038
SEIFERT, Herbert, 67, *1252*
SEILER, Jean, *99*, 877, 1415
Selecting an instrument, 13, 32, 34, 41, 463-84, 1151
  accommodating hearing loss, 465
  plastic, 477-84
  wooden instruments, 464, 466, 468, 470, 473
SELFRIDGE-FIELD, Eleanor, *73*, *190*, 1196
Selma, Bartolomé de, 225
SEMMENS, Richard, 611-12
Septalius, Manfredus. *See* Settala, Manfredo
Serocki, Kazimierz, 1377-78
"Serpent in the Midst," 158
Settala, Manfredo, 227
  multiple recorder by, 226
Seymour, Charles, Duke of Somerset, 903
Shakespeare, William, 100
  allusions to flutes and recorders, 18, 52-53
  "dark lady" of the Sonnets, 190
Shakuhachi, 1391
SHANAHAN, Ian, 1478-79
SHAPIRO, Daniel, 960, *1415*
SHARMAN, Ian G., 887, 1231
SHARP, Nan Ellen Orthmann, 1226
Shaw, Bernard, 1101
Shaw, Joseph, 77
Sheper, Walter, 1330
SHERMAN, Elna, 880
Sherman, Elna, 1102
SHIMA, Tatsuro, 431
SIEKMAN, Ella, 261

Sight-reading, 812
  alto clef, 814
SILBIGER, Alexander, *18*, 837, 1291, 1448
SILVERSTEIN, Steven, 41, *355*, *364*
Silverstein, Steven, 313
SIMKO, Alex, 1576
SIMMONS, Terry, 521
SIMONS, J.A., 1563
SIMPSON, Adrienne, *17*, 300, 539, 854, 969-70, 979
Simpson, Christopher, 964
  The Division-Violist, 722-23
SINKS, Alfred H., *210*
Six Lectures on the Recorder and Other Flutes in Relation to Literature (Welch), 18
Sixth flute, 127, 129
Sizes of recorders, 119-42, 466. *See also under specific sizes (e.g., Fourth flute; Tenor recorder; Voice flute; etc.)*
SKEMPTON, Alec, 1275
SKINS, Ron, 49, 855, 1140
SLIM, H. Colin, 153
Slurring, 715, 733, 772
Smeyers, David, *1358*, *1380*
Smith, Beverly, *1213*
Smith, Beverly, 197
SMITH, Catherine P., 646-48
SMITH, Fabienne, *64*
Smith, Fabienne, 364
Smith, William C., 1133
SNELLING, Virginia, 457
SOBCZAK, Alain, 466
SOBEL, Willa, *75*
Società Italiana del Flauto Dolce, *1424*, *1437*
Società Italiana del Flauto Dolce, 110
Society of Recorder Players, 16, 26, 1028, 1030-31, 1446, 1449-50
SOKOLL, Christa, 779
SOLOMON, Jon, 1264
The Solo Sonatas of Georg Philipp Telemann (Swack), 1301
Somer, Harry: *Twelve Miniatures*, 1328

Sonatas. *See* Repertory
Sonaten auf Concertenart, 1304
Les sons multiples aux flûtes à bec (Kientzy), 841
Sopranino recorder, 126
 18th-century instrument found in Foligno, 177
Soubeyran, Claire, 314, 488
Sour Cream (musical group), 964, 1320
Sources, historical. *See* Methods (tutors) and treatises
South Africa, 113
Souvé
 bass recorder by, 266
Soviet Union, 117
"Spagna" tune
 improvising on, 730
Spain, 78–79, 186
Sparr, Thea von, 1103–4
SPEER, Daniel, 641
Die Spezialtypen der Blas-instrumente in der 1. Hälfte des 18. Jahrhunderts im deutschen Sprachraum (Koch), 1466
SPRINGFELS, Mary, 1017
STAEHLEIN, Walter, 541
STAEPS, Hans Ulrich, 1183, *1360*, 1379
Staeps, Hans Ulrich, 947, 972, 1105–7, 1328, 1379
STANESBY, Thomas, Jr., 662
Stanesby, Thomas, Jr., 228–29, 663, 727
Stanesby, Thomas, Sr., 229
 recorders by, 230, 250, 351
Stanesby family, 167, 231
STANSFIELD, Norman, 743
Staub, Nikolaus, 176
 recorders by, 256, 262
Stearns Collection (Ann Arbor, Mich.)
 recorders in, 207, 266
Steenbergen, Jan, 232
 recorders by, 262
STEINKOPF, Otto, 415
STEINMANN, Conrad, 1398
Steinmann, Conrad, 1001

Die Stellung der Blockflöte im Musikleben des 20. Jahrhunderts (Göring), 1462
STERN, Claudio, 494
STERN, Nina, 94
STERNE, Colin C., 14, 754, 1448
STEVENS, W.R., 1517
Stieber, Ernst, 315–16
STOBART, Henry, 1397
Stockhausen, Karlheinz, 1117, 1380
STOCKMEIER, Wolfgang, 1023
STRADNER, Gerhard, 247, 554
STRATFORD, Michael, 1236, 1480
Strings with recorder, 1141
STRODE, Rosamund, 1341
STRONG, Deborah, 1481
STROOM, Charles, 1518–19, 1564
STRUCK, Annette, 1027
Gli strumenti musicali del Rinascimento (Bornstein), 57
Strungk, Nicolaus Adam, 1182
STUART, Charles, 281
Study of Acoustical Aspects of the Recorder . . . (Martin), 411
A Study of the Acoustical Properties of a Renaissance, Baroque, and Contemporary Fipple Flute (Recorder) (Turicchi), 416
Sturbois, Annie, 272
Styles, historical, 692
SUPPAN, Wolfgang, 1253
Susato, Tielman: *Danserye*, 1171, 1176–77
SWACK, Jeanne R., 1301, 1304, p. 442, 443
SWAINE, N., 688
SWAINSON, Dorothy, *566*
SWAYNE, Jon, 1520–21
Sweden
 Stockholm
  Musikhistoriska Museet, Baroque woodwinds in, 262
Switzerland
 makers, 324
Sylva sylvarum (Bacon), 396
Symbolism, 38, 46–51, 75, 81, 152, 1226, 1235, 1278, 1283, 1303

Index

Syntagma musicum (Praetorius), 580
Syntagma musicum (musical group), 1078
Synthetics of a Recorder Tone-color (Driscoll), 432

TADA, Ichiro, 111
TAGGART, Stephen, 1522
Talbot, James, 615, 903
TALBOT, Michael, 1311
TANGUAY, James, 41
Tansman, Alexandre: *Suite,* 1150
TANS'UR, William, 671-72
TARR, Edward H., 600
Taruskin, Richard, 695, 1012, p. 222, 444
TATTERSALL, Malcolm, 104, 773, 1002, 1009, 1046, 1061, 1144-45, 1217, *1438*
Taylor, Christine, 1110
Taylor, Christopher, 908, 1108, 1110
TAYLOR, Laurence, 1153
TAYLOR, Ralph, 1010, *1415*
Taylor, Richard, 1110
TAYLOR, Stanley, 1210
Taylor, Stanley, 1109-10
The Taylor Consort, 1110
A Teacher's Guide to the Literature of Woodwind Instruments (Rasmussen & Mattran), 1135
Teaching. See Pedagogy
Technique, 13-14, 697, 756-818. See also specific topics (*e.g.,* Articulation; Breathing; Fingering; Multiphonics; etc.)
avant-garde, 819-44
Telemann, Georg Philipp, 1206, 1290-1304, p. 443
bibliography, 1290
cantatas, unpublished, 1303
Concerto for Recorder and Flute in E Minor, 1186-87
Essercizii musici, 1298
flûte pastorelle, music for, 1403
Der getreue Music-Meister, 1293, 1299
Der harmonischer Gottes-Dienst, 1294, 1297

Telemann, Georg Philipp (continued)
Die kleine Cammer-Music, 886
quartet sonatas, 1180, 1186-87
Sonaten auf Concertenart, 1304
sonatas, 697, 1295, 1301
Sonata in D Minor (TWV 41:d4), 690, 801
Sonatinen (TWV 41:c2 & 41:a4), 1301-2
Tafelmusik, 965
trio sonatas, 1178, 1291
TELLIER, Michèle, 252-53, 882, *1428*
Temperament, 41, 371-2, 401, 745-47
Tenor recorder, 122, 132-34
plea for by Stanesby Jr., 663
Terton, Engelbert
recorders by, 184, 261
TESKE-SPELLERBERG, Ulrike, 1303
TEUTSCHER, Marieke, *183*
THALER, Alan, 1293
THALHEIMER, Peter, 125, 205, 941, 1227
Theater, English
16th-17th centuries, 42, 75
Thibault de Chambure, Geneviève, 250
THIEDE, Christiane, 1054
THIEM, Jon, 160
THIEME, Ulrich, 304, 943, 1055, 1184-85
THOMAS, Jean W., 869
THOMÉ, Gilles, 171
THOMPSON, Richard, 210
THOMPSON, Waddy, 1415
THOMSON, J.M., 17, 24, *162,* 893, 908, 919, 921, 931-32, 961-62, 972, 978, 982, 988, 998, 1031, 1033, 1043, 1056, 1068-69, 1078, 1087, 1095, 1101, 1108, 1110, 1117, 1125, *1422, 1439*
Thomson, J.M., 1111, 1441
THORBY, Philip, *1032*
Thorby, Philip, 1112
THORN, Benjamin, 698, 828
Thorn, Benjamin: *Pipistrelli gialli,* 907

THORN, Chris, 870, 1154, 1177, 1409
THORNE, J.O., 1351
Thornowitz, Henry: *Sonata da camera in F Major*, 691
Thumb hole
  reinforcement of, 498
Thumb rests, 499, 793, 1047
Tibia (periodical), 1442
Le tic-toc-choc, 1443
TIDHAR, Shlomo, 109
Tijdschrift voor oude muziek, 1444, p. 222
Tin whistle, 1401
TIPPETT, Michael, 932
Tippett, Michael, 931, 1381-82
Titian, 149
TOFFOLO, Stefano, 180-82
TOL, Han, 1155
Tol, Han, 1047
TOMALIN, Miles, 1113
Tomalin, Miles, 994, 1113
Tone and Intonation on the Recorder (Kottick), 524
Tone quality, 336, 522-24, 799
  acoustical studies, 431-32
  affect of carvings on, 344
  improving, 522-23
  in relation to type of wood, 41, 385
Tonguing. *See* Articulation
Tons de ma flute (Huygens), 609
Topham, William, 1182
Touchin, Colin: *Antifonia*, 1329
Townsend, John
  sixth flute by, 233
Toyama Musical Instrument Company, 317
Toyama, Nobuo, 317
Transcription and arrangement, 719, 1159-67
  Bach keyboard music, 1202
  choral music, 1166, 1170
  controversy over, 1161, 1164
  suitable repertory for, 1162-63, 65
TRANTOW, Rüdiger, 1104
Treatises. *See* Methods (tutors) and treatises

The Treatment of the Flutes and Recorders in the Bach Cantatas (Greenberg), 1463
Tremolo, 751
Trichet, Pierre: *Traité d'instruments*, 591
Trills, 41, 794-95
Trinity College of Music (London)
  recorder examinations, 878-80
Trio Il Flauto Dolce, 934-35
Trio sonatas, 1178-79
TROMAN, Robin, 43, 829-31, 1428
TSUKAMOTO, Takashi, 367-68
Tucker, Tui St. George, 907
Tuners, electronic, 798
Tuning, 474, 490, 526-33. *See also* Intonation; Temperament
TURICCHI, Thomas E., 416
TURNER, John, 50, 88, 758, 1070, 1371
Turner, John: *Four Diversions*, 907
TUSCHNER, Wolfram, 338
Tutors. *See* Methods (tutors) and treatises
Tutto il bisognevole, 584-85
Twaalfhoven, 85
Twenty-five Hundred Historical Woodwind Instruments (Young), 243
TYLER, James, 1070
Typen europäischer Blockflöten in Vorzeit, Geschichte und Volksüberlieferung (Moeck), 55
TYSON, John, 756
Tyson, John, 907

Über den Instrumentenbauer Robert Wijne und seine zuletzt aufgefundene Sopran-Blockflöte (Feldhaus), 1460
Uffenbach, Wilhelm von, 891
't Uitnement kabinet, 1197
United States, 115
  degree programs in early music, 877
  Niagara Falls High School recorder quartet, 116

Index

United States (continued)
  recorders in collections, 264–65
  Ann Arbor, Michigan, Stearns Collection, 207, 266
  Boston, Mass., Museum of Fine Arts, 1005
  Cincinnati, Ohio, Art Museum, 224
  New York City, Metropolitan Museum of Art, 267–68
  Vermillion, South Dakota, Shrine to Music Museum, 265, 269
  Washington, D.C., Dayton C. Miller Flute Collection, 212
  repertory, 20th-century, 1332
  17th–18th centuries, 80
Untersuchungen über die Resonanzeigenschaften der Blockflöte (Mühle), 414
Unton, Henry
  painting of wedding of, 1174–75
UNWIN, Robert, 903
UPDIKE, John, 161
Ursprung und Tradition der Kernspaltflöten des Europaischen Volkstums und das Herkommen der musikgeschichtlichen Kernspaltflötentype (Moeck), 1472
The Use of Flutes and Recorders in the Church Cantatas of Johann Sebastian Bach (Sharp), 1226
The Use of Wind Instruments in Seventeenth-Century Instrumental Music (Lewis), 1182
Uzbekhian oak, 155

A Vade Mecum (Hudgebut), 602
Valentine family, 904
VALLEAU, Douglas, 294, 313, 999
van Aardenberg, Abraham. *See* Aardenberg, Abraham van
van Acht, Rob. *See* Acht, Rob van
van Assendelft, Leen. *See* Assendelft, Leen van
van Baak Griffioen, Ruth. *See* Griffioen, Ruth van Baak

van den Ende, Vincent. *See* Ende, Vincent van den
van den Hul, Dick. *See* Den Hul, Dick van
van der Heide, Geert Jan. *See* Heide, Geert Jan van der
van der Meer, John Henry. *See* Meer, John Henry van der
van Dijk, Jan. *See* Dijk, Jan van
van Eyck, Jacob. *See* Eyck, Jacob van
van Hauwe, Walter. *See* Hauwe, Walter van
van Heel, S.A.C. Dudok. *See* Heel, S.A.C. Dudok van
van Heerde, Jan Jurriaens. *See* Heerde, Jan Jurriaens van
VARGAS, Eduardo, *714*
VAUCANSON, Jacques de, p. 131
VEILHAN, Jean-Claude, 38, 909, *1428*
Veilhan, Jean-Claude, 1114
VENTZKE, Karl, *439*, 871
Verbruggen, Marion, 936, 1115–16
La veritable maniere (Freillon-Poncein), 644–45
Vernon, Margaret
  recorder in coat of arms of, 58
Vernon, William, 58
Versuch einer Anweisung die Flöte traversiere zu spielen (Quantz), 673–75
Vertoninge en onderwyzinge op de hand-fluit (Matthysz), 592
Vertue, George, 905
Die Verwendung der Blöckflöte bei Georg Friedrich Händel (Fahrnberger) 1459
VESTER, Frans, p. 443
VETTER, Michael, 91, 821, 832–33, 1318, 1335
Vetter, Michael, 822, 907–8, 1117, 1320
Vibrato, 751–54, 818
Das Vibrato in der Musik des Barock (Moens-Haenen), 753
Victoria and Albert Museum (London)
  Bressan bass recorder in, 199
Victorian Recorder Guild, *1438*

Victorian Recorder Guild, 1092, 1451
VINQUIST, Mary, 534, p. 178, 222
VIO, Gastone, 182
VIRDUNG, Sebastian, 542–44, 546–48
Virdung, Sebastian
  Musica getutscht, 549–55
    bass recorder in, 139–40, 142
    fipple flutes in, 1384
    gemshorn in, 1406
    Ruszpfeif in, 1411
Virghi, Francesco Li. *See* Li Virghi, Francesco
VIRGILIANO, Aurelio, 577–78
Virgiliano, Aurelio: *Il dolcimelo,* 579
VITZ, Carol, 963
Vivaldi, Antonio, 1305–15
  bibliography, 1306–7
  chamber concertos, 1308–9
  concertos, 1315
    Il Cardellino, 47
    "flauto" and *"flautino"* problem, 1053, 1305–7, 1310, 1313, 1315
    The Four Seasons, 1114
    Il pastor fido, 1312, 1314
    sonatas, 1194
    trio sonatas, 1178
Vleeshuis (Antwerp)
  great bass recorder in, 139
VOGEL, Veronika, 1578
Voice flute, 41, 122, 127, 130–31
Voicing, 335, 382–83, 405, 490, 525–27
Volkhardt, Ulrike, 1001
von Gleich, Clemens. *See* Gleich, Clemens von
VON HUENE, Friedrich, 152, 164, 207, 261, 266, 328, 377, 380, 381, 472, 495, 497, 502, 1008, 1448, p. 54
von Huene, Friedrich, 303, 309, 318–22, 344, 357, 443, 464
VON HUENE, Ingeborg, *446*
von Huene, Ingeborg, 321
VON HUENE, Nikolaus, *41*

WAECHTER, Wolfram, 342, 872, 1407
Waits, of York, 77
WAITZMAN, Daniel, 64, 360, 364–66, 467, 758, *821,* 837
Waitzman, Daniel, 1118
Wakefield, J. Homer, 1119
Walch
  recorders by, 97
Walch family, 172
Waldbaur, Thekla, 924
WALDO, Andrew, 734
Waldo, Andrew, 907
WALKER, Diane Parr, p. 443
WALKER, Paul, p. 443
Walking-stick instruments, 1386
Walsh, John, 1133, 1233, 1271, 1316
  print of Handel op. 1 sonatas, 1260–61
Ward, Leslie, 279
WARD, Stuart, 838
WARNER, Robert Austin, 207, 266
WARNER, Thomas E., 535–36
WATERHOUSE, William, 163, 243, p. 442
WATERMAN, Rodney, 105, 1120
Waterman, Rodney, 1120
Weber, Carl Maria von, 99
WEBER, Rainer, 185, 227, 259, 353, 375, 503, 1565–66
Weber, Rainer, 125, 1407
WEBER, Rhoda, 935
WEIDEL, Evelyn, 1571
Weigel, 140
WEILENMANN, Matthias, 92–93, *756,* 873, 1019
Weilenmann, Matthias, 1121
WEINECK, Isolde Maria, 856
WELCH, Christopher, 18, 39, 52
Welch, Christopher, 1122
WELLS, Charles, 1402
WENNER, Martin, 238
Wenzinger, August, 1056, 1099
Westminster Abbey
  recorder in wall paintings, 151
Wetting one's whistle, 512
Whaley, Judith I., *863*
WHINRAY, Paul, 1523–24
WHITE, Beverly, 51, 133, 857, 964
White Castle (Monmouthshire)
  bird-bone pipe found in, 1393

Index

WHITING, B.C., 1350
WHITNEY, Maurice C., 1066, 1166
WHITNEY, Stephen T., *41*
WHITTINGTON, Mary K., *1026*
Wijne, Robert, 234, 1460
  recorders by, 261
Wilby, Philip, 1329
Wilkinson, Ruth, 1123
WILLAN, John, 1070
WILLET, William C., 1094
WILLETTS, Carl, 1525-26
WILLIAMS, Ken, 1527
WILLIAMS, Peter F., *1211*
Williams, William, 1182, 1190
  Sonata in Imitation of Birds, 47
Willman, John, 323
WILLOUGHBY, Andrew, 382, 1565
WIND, Thiemo, 63, 1232-33, 1240-41, 1245-47, *1288,* p. 442
Windway, 41, 447, 501
Wingerden, Jeanette van, 1124-25
WINTERNITZ, Emanuel, p. 54
WINTERS, Leslie, 858, 1342
Winters, Ross, 372, 699, *756,* 965
Winters, Ross, 1126
Witt, Christian Friedrich, 1180
Wittgenstein, Ludwig, 949
Woehl, Waldemar, 82
WOGRAM, Klaus, 426-27
WOLEDGE, Henry, 435
WOLLITZ, Kenneth, 14, 94, 744, 811, 817, 859, 937, 983-84, 1012, 1047-48, 1074, 1084, 1115
WOOD, Francis, 1108
WOOD, Gordon, *502*
Woodcock, Robert, 27, 905, 1316
WOODHILL, Yollande Vanessa, 1482
WOODS, Brian, 395
WOODS, Timothy, 383
Woods, 384-95
  boxwood, 388
  of La Couture Boussey, 169
  cedar, 387
  coconut, 394
  dictionary of, 395
  effect of direction of grain, 390
  used by Alec Loretto, 300
  from the Maldive islands, 392

Woods (continued)
  plywood, used for a contrabass recorder, 342
  effect on tone quality, 41, 336, 385-86, 391
  randoo, 393
Woodwind Instruments in France 1690-1750 (Jenkins), 1465
Woodwind Quarterly, 1445
WORRALL, David, 839
Worrall, David: *Silhouettes,* 839
WRIGHT, Daniel, 629
WRIGHT, Laurence, 45, 60, 552, 1172
WYATT, Theo, 134, 428-29, 473-75, 481-84, 496, *509,* 532-33, 747, 770, 860-64, *908,* 933, 962, *1032,* 1167, *1202,* 1446, 1450

Yamaha
  Rottenburgh alto, 478
YATES, Thomas, 914
"York Music": The Story of a City's Music from 1304 to 1896 (Merryweather), 77
York Waits, 77
The Young Musician, or the Science of Music (Swaine), 688
YOUNG, Phillip T., 208-9, 222, 243, p. 442
Your Book of the Recorder (Thomson), 24

ZACCONI, Lodovico, 575-76
ZANIOL, Angelo, 40, 339, 376, *382,* 395, 458, 504-5
ZASLAW, Neal, p. 222
Zeitschrift für Instrumentenbau
  editors' 1884 petition on pitch, 380
Zelenka, Johann Dismas, 1252
ZELINSKY, Beate, *1380*
Zellbell, Ferdinand, 906
Zen-On
  Bressan alto, 442, 478
  redrilling holes to match Baroque fingering, 438
ZETZMANN, Liz, 1000

Zick
  recorders by, 256
Zick family, 176
Ziegler, Johann
  keyed recorder by, 235
ZIELINSKI, Tadeusz A., 1377-78
ZIMMERMANN, Manfredo, 802
Zoffany, John, 148
Zukerman, Pinchas, 1083
Zur Akustik der Blasinstrumente
  (Steinkopf), 415
Zur Aufführungspraxis der
  französischen Musik für Bläser
  im beginnenden 18. Jahrhundert
  (Landkammer), 1467
Zur Geschichte der Blockflöte in den
  germanischen Ländern (Degen),
  21
Zur Wiederbelebung der Blockflöte im
  20. Jahrhundert (Rummel),
  1476